Psalms

BAKER COMMENTARY *on the* OLD TESTAMENT

WISDOM AND PSALMS

Tremper Longman III, EDITOR

Volumes now available

Psalms, vol. 1, John Goldingay
Proverbs, Tremper Longman III
Song of Songs, Richard S. Hess

Psalms

Volume 1
Psalms 1–41

John Goldingay

Baker Academic
Grand Rapids, Michigan

©2006 by John Goldingay

Published by Baker Academic
a division of Baker Publishing Group
P.O. Box 6287, Grand Rapids, MI 49516-6287
www.bakeracademic.com

Printed in the United States of America

All rights reserved. No part of this publication may be reproduced, stored in a retrieval system, or transmitted in any form or by any means—for example, electronic, photocopy, recording—without the prior written permission of the publisher. The only exception is brief quotations in printed reviews.

Library of Congress Cataloging-in-Publication Data

Goldingay, John.
    Psalms / John Goldingay.
        p.   cm. — (Baker commentary on the Old Testament wisdom and Psalms)
    "The first of a three-volume commentary on the book of Psalms"—ECIP data view.
    Includes bibliographical references and indexes.
    ISBN 10: 0-8010-2703-9 (pbk.)
    ISBN 978-0-8010-2703-1 (pbk.)
    1. Bible. O.T. Psalms—Commentaries. I. Title. II. Series.
BS1430.53.G65 2006
223'.2077—dc22
                                                2006009724

Contents

Series Preface   *7*
Author's Preface   *11*
Abbreviations   *15*

Introduction   *21*
Psalm 1: Promises to Keep in Mind (I)   *79*
Psalm 2: Promises to Keep in Mind (II)   *92*
Psalm 3: The Question of Deliverance   *107*
Psalm 4: Who Shows Us Good?   *116*
Psalm 5: Responding to Life-Threatening Falsehood (I)   *125*
Psalm 6: Responding to Life-Threatening Falsehood (II)   *134*
Psalm 7: On Trial, in Battle, Hunted   *142*
Psalm 8: Humanity's Position in Creation   *153*
Psalms 9–10: How to Pray against the Powerful   *162*
Psalm 11: Stay or Flit?   *187*
Psalm 12: Responding to Faithless Triviality   *195*
Psalm 13: How Long, How Long, How Long, How Long?   *203*
Psalm 14: The Scoundrel   *210*
Psalm 15: Qualifications for Staying with God   *218*
Psalm 16: Trust in God for Life   *226*
Psalm 17: Yhwh's Eyes, Lips, Right Hand, and Face   *235*
Psalm 18: God's Acts and David's Acts   *247*
Psalm 19: The Fiery Cosmos and the Encouraging Law   *282*
Psalm 20: A Blessing for the King   *300*
Psalm 21: The Implications of Someone Else's Deliverance   *310*
Psalm 22: Prayer That Honors Two Sets of Facts   *320*
Psalm 23: God as Our Shepherd and Host   *344*

Psalm 24: Yhwh's Ownership of the World, Conditions for Approaching Yhwh, Admitting Yhwh to the City   *355*
Psalm 25: The Bases of Prayer from A to Z   *366*
Psalm 26: Prayer and Moral Integrity   *379*
Psalm 27: Prayer Arising out of Testimony   *389*
Psalm 28: Praying for the Punishment of the Faithless   *402*
Psalm 29: The Power of Yhwh's Voice   *411*
Psalm 30: How to Give Your Testimony   *423*
Psalm 31: When a Prayer Needs to Be Prayed Twice   *434*
Psalm 32: When Suffering Issues from Sin   *451*
Psalm 33: The Creator and the Lord of History   *462*
Psalm 34: Deliverance by Yhwh and Reverence for Yhwh   *475*
Psalm 35: How to Respond to Attack   *487*
Psalm 36: Human Faithlessness and Divine Commitment   *505*
Psalm 37: The Weak Will Take Possession of the Land   *514*
Psalm 38: Suffering and Sin   *536*
Psalm 39: Living in Light of the Fact That We Will Die   *553*
Psalm 40: Testimony Warrants Plea   *566*
Psalm 41: The Good Fortune of the Person Who Thinks   *580*
Psalm 41:13: Coda to Psalms 1–41: Yes, Yes!   *590*

Glossary   *591*
Bibliography   *602*
Subject Index   *606*
Author Index   *616*
Index of Scripture and Other Ancient Writings   *621*

Series Preface

At the end of the book of Ecclesiastes, a wise father warns his son concerning the multiplication of books: "Furthermore, of these, my son, be warned. There is no end to the making of many books!" (12:12). The Targum to this biblical book characteristically expands the thought and takes it in a different, even contradictory, direction: "My son, take care to make many books of wisdom without end."

When applied to commentaries, both statements are true. The past twenty years have seen a significant increase in the number of commentaries available on each book of the Bible. On the other hand, for those interested in grappling seriously with the meaning of the text, such proliferation should be seen as a blessing rather than a curse. No single commentary can do it all. In the first place, commentaries reflect different theological and methodological perspectives. We can learn from others who have a different understanding of the origin and nature of the Bible, but we also want commentaries that share our fundamental beliefs about the biblical text. Second, commentaries are written with different audiences in mind. Some are addressed primarily to laypeople, others to clergy, and still others to fellow scholars. A third consideration, related to the previous two, is the subdisciplines the commentator chooses to draw from to shed light on the biblical text. The possibilities are numerous, including philology, textual criticism, genre/form criticism, redaction criticism, ancient Near Eastern background, literary conventions, and more. Finally, commentaries differ in how extensively they interact with secondary literature, that is, with what others have said about a given passage.

The Baker Commentary on the Old Testament Wisdom and Psalms has a definite audience in mind. We believe the primary users of commentaries are scholars, ministers, seminary students, and Bible study leaders. Of these groups, we have most in mind clergy and future clergy, namely, seminary students. We have tried to make the commentary accessible to nonscholars by putting most of the technical discussion and interaction with secondary literature in the footnotes. We do not mean to suggest that such information is unimportant. We simply concede that, given the present state of the church, it is the rare layperson who will read such technical material with interest and profit. We hope we are wrong in this assessment, and if we are not, that the future will see a reverse in this trend. A healthy church is a church that nourishes itself with constant attention to God's words in Scripture, in all their glorious detail.

Since not all commentaries are alike, what are the features that characterize this series? The message of the biblical book is the primary focus of each commentary, and the commentators have labored to expose God's message for his people in the books they discuss. This series also distinguishes itself by restricting its coverage to one major portion of the Hebrew Scriptures, namely, the Psalms and Wisdom books (Proverbs, Job, Ecclesiastes, and Song of Songs). These biblical books provide a distinctive contribution to the canon. Although we can no longer claim that they are neglected, their unique content makes them harder to fit into the development of redemptive history and requires more effort to hear their distinctive message.

The book of Psalms is the literary sanctuary. Like the physical sanctuary structures of the Old Testament, it offers a textual holy place where humans share their joys and struggles with brutal honesty in God's presence. The book of Proverbs describes wisdom, which on one level is skill for living, the ability to navigate life's actual and potential pitfalls; but on another level, this wisdom presents a pervasive and deeply theological message: "The fear of the LORD is the beginning of knowledge" (Prov. 1:7). Proverbs also raises a disturbing issue: the sages often motivate wise behavior by linking it to reward, but in reality, bad things happen to good people, the wise are not always rewarded as they expect. This raises the question of the justice of God. Both Job and Ecclesiastes struggle with the apparent disconnect between God's justice and our actual life experience. Finally, the Song of Songs is a passionate, sensuous love poem that reminds us that God is interested in more than just our brains and our spirits; he wants us to enjoy our bodies. It reminds us that we are not merely a soul encased in a body but whole persons made in God's image.

Limiting the series to the Psalms and Wisdom books has allowed us to tailor our work to the distinctive nature of this portion of the canon. With some few exceptions in Job and Ecclesiastes, for instance, the material in these biblical books is poetic and highly literary, and so the commentators have highlighted the significant poetic conventions employed in each book. After an introduction discussing important issues that affect the interpretation of the book (title, authorship, date, language, style, text, ancient Near Eastern background, genre, canonicity, theological message, connection to the New Testament, and structure), each commentary proceeds section by section through the biblical text. The authors provide their own translations, with explanatory notes when necessary, followed by a substantial interpretive section (titled "Interpretation") and concluding with a section titled "Theological Implications." In the interpretation section, the emphasis is on the meaning of the text in its original historical setting. In the theological implications section, connections with other parts of the canon, both Old and New Testament, are sketched out along with the continuing relevance of each passage for us today. The latter section is motivated by the recognition that, while it is important to understand the individual contribution and emphasis of each book, these books now find their place in a larger collection of writings, the canon as a whole, and it is within this broader context that the books must ultimately be interpreted.

No two commentators in this series see things in exactly the same way, though we all share similar convictions about the Bible as God's Word and the belief that it must be appreciated not only as ancient literature but also as God's Word for today. It is our hope and prayer that these volumes will inform readers and, more importantly, stimulate reflection on and passion for these valuable books.

It has long been observed that the book of Psalms is a "microcosm" of the message of the Old Testament. Athanasius, the fourth-century theologian, called the Psalms "an epitome of the whole Scriptures." Basil, bishop of Caesarea in the same time period, regarded the Psalms as a "compendium of all theology." Martin Luther said the book is "a little Bible, and the summary of the Old Testament." The book of Psalms is theologically rich, so the readers of this commentary are privileged to be guided by John Goldingay, one of the foremost experts on biblical theology today. Our prayer is that as you read the Psalms with this commentary, you will grow in your knowledge of the God who reveals himself through the prayers of his ancient people.

Tremper Longman III
Robert H. Gundry Professor of Biblical Studies
Westmont College

Author's Preface

I am grateful for the excuse to spend time writing on the Psalms; like teachers, authors are the people who gain most from their work. As usual, I wrote much of the volume sitting on our patio with my disabled wife, Ann. I am glad for her companionship and sometimes glad for the way the nature of our life together has driven me into the Psalms. I am also grateful for the resources of the Fuller Theological Seminary library and for the seminary's encouragement to faculty to write.

My starting point for the commentary is the Masoretic Text as it appears in the Leningrad Codex copied by Samuel ben Jacob in the eleventh century and published in NJPS and *BHS*. I have assumed that this is a broadly reliable guide to a textual tradition going back into the pre-Christian period. In the translation I have also included some alternative renderings based on the LXX or other versions where these seem to reflect different Hebrew traditions (though I have assumed that much versional variation over matters such as suffixes cannot be assumed to indicate a different Hebrew tradition). I have assumed that variants in post-MT Hebrew manuscripts constitute post-MT errors or "corrections" rather than preserving pre-MT readings, but I have occasionally referred to these on that understanding. I have noted some modern proposals for emending the text, though also rarely followed them, and I have also rarely followed modern proposals for understanding Hebrew words in light of Arabic or Ugaritic.[1]

I went about the commentary in the following way (I schematize a little since the process is more spiral and untidy than this account suggests). With each psalm, I first sat with MT and the lexica and made a

---

1. For the latter, see Dahood's classic work, *Psalms*, and for interaction with this, see esp. Craigie, *Psalms 1–50*.

preliminary translation, checking my version especially against NRSV, NJPS, and NIVI. Where I could not see how to make sense of the Hebrew, I took a first look at one or two commentaries to see whether they gave me plausible ideas, or whether MT might be faulty. Making this preliminary translation usually gave me some impression of the structure of the psalm, of questions it raises, and of its significance. I then worked through LXX, Jerome,[2] the Targum, and the other Greek versions, noting where they differed from my translation and asking whether they raised questions about exegesis or text. This again made me dip into commentaries, and also into the Vulgate and Syriac. I then wrote a first draft of an introduction and commentary on the psalm, section by section in light of my preliminary understanding of its structure. As it seemed necessary, I attempted to describe the way the sentences work, the meaning of individual words, the way the poetry works, the development of the argument, and the psalm's implications regarding spirituality and theology. In the process, I again sometimes referred to commentaries and to OT theological dictionaries. After I had completed a first draft, I looked through the references to the psalm in the Hebrew syntaxes, worked systematically through twenty or thirty commentaries and other works to check out my preliminary conclusions and to correct or amplify my treatment, and read articles on the psalm in periodicals and other works. Finally, I worked through the whole to produce a finished version and wrote the closing reflection section. I drafted the introduction to the volume when I had completed work on Pss. 1–35 and subsequently amplified and reworked it in light of my further study and of other works on the Psalms.

In translating the Psalms I have often let the Hebrew's gendered language stand where (e.g.) using a gender-inclusive plural would obscure the dynamic of the poetry, and in other respects I have aimed at a translation that sticks close to the dynamics of the Hebrew even if that sometimes means it is not as elegant as a translation for reading in church. I have represented the name of Israel's God by the unvocalized form Yhwh (traditionally vocalized as Jehovah but most likely pronounced Yahweh). All Bible translations are my own except where otherwise noted. References are to the versification in English Bibles; where the printed Hebrew Bible differs, its reference follows in square brackets (e.g., "Ps. 51:1 [3]")—except that I omit these in the case of cross-references to other verses within the psalm I am commenting on. References to parts of verses such as "v. 1a" and "v. 1b" generally denote the verses as subdivided by MT, but where verses comprise more than two cola (or

---

2. Strictly, his third translation, *Psalterium juxta Hebraeos*, which he made from the Hebrew rather than by revising the Old Latin version made from the LXX.

where I differ from MT in understanding verse divisions), I have often used references that correspond to the subdivisions in my translation. Thus I have referred (for instance) to "v. 1c" and "v. 1d" rather than to "v. 1bα" and "v. 1bβ."

I am grateful to Tremper Longman for his comments on my initial draft of the manuscript, to Benjamin Galan for checking biblical references and noticing other slips, and to David Stec for letting me see an advance copy of his translation of the *Targum of Psalms*.

Abbreviations

Bibliographic and General

*	indicates that the word appears in the glossary
abs.	absolute
acc.	accusative
AJSL	*American Journal of Semitic Languages and Literature*
ANET	*Ancient Near Eastern Texts Relating to the Old Testament*, ed. James B. Pritchard, 3rd ed. (Princeton: Princeton University Press, 1969)
Aq	Aquila's translation of the Psalms, as printed in Fridericus Field, *Origenis Hexaplorum quae supersunt,* vol. 2 (Oxford: Oxford University Press, 1874; repr., Hildesheim: Olms, 1964)
ASV	American Standard Version
BC	before Christ
BASOR	*Bulletin of the American Schools of Oriental Research*
BCP	*The Book of Common Prayer . . . Together with the Psalter or Psalms of David* [repr. from the Great Bible of 1539] (repr., London: Collins, n.d.)
BDB	Francis Brown, S. R. Driver, and Charles A. Briggs, *A Hebrew and English Lexicon of the Old Testament* (Oxford: Oxford University Press, 1907; repr., Oxford: Clarendon, n.d.)
BHS	*Biblia Hebraica Stuttgartensia,* ed. K. Elliger and W. Rudolph (Stuttgart: Württembergische Bibelgesellschaft, 1967–77)
Bib	*Biblica*
BibInt	*Biblical Interpretation*
BN	*Biblische Notizen*
BSac	*Bibliotheca sacra*
BT	*The Bible Translator*
BWANT	Beiträge zur Wissenschaft vom Alten und Neuen Testament
BZ	*Biblische Zeitschrift*

BZAW	Beihefte zur Zeitschrift für die alttestamentliche Wissenschaft
C	The Cairo MS of the Masoretic Text, as reported in *Biblia Hebraica Stuttgartensia*
CBQ	*Catholic Biblical Quarterly*
const.	construct
CP	James Barr, *Comparative Philology and the Text of the Old Testament* (Oxford: Oxford University Press, 1968)
CTJ	*Calvin Theological Journal*
CTM	*Concordia Theological Monthly*
DCH	*The Dictionary of Classical Hebrew*, ed. D. J. A. Clines (Sheffield: Sheffield Academic Press, 1993–)
DDD	*Dictionary of Deities and Demons in the Bible*, ed. Karel van der Toorn et al., 2nd ed. (Grand Rapids: Eerdmans, 1999)
DG	J. C. L. Gibson, *Davidson's Introductory Hebrew Grammar: Syntax*, 4th ed. (Edinburgh: T&T Clark, 1994)
dittog.	dittography
DTT	Marcus Jastrow, *A Dictionary of the Targumim, the Talmud Babli and Yerushalmi, and the Midrashic Literature* (repr., New York: Choreb, 1926)
esp.	especially
EstBib	*Estudios bíblicos*
et al.	and others
EvT	*Evangelische Theologie*
EVV	(Many) English versions
ExpTim	*Expository Times*
f.	feminine
GKC	*Gesenius' Hebrew Grammar*, edited and enlarged by E. Kautzsch, 2nd ed., rev. and trans. A. E. Cowley (Oxford: Clarendon, 1910; repr. with corrections, 1966)
HALOT	Ludwig Köhler, Walter Baumgartner, et al., *The Hebrew and Aramaic Lexicon of the Old Testament*, 2 vols. (Leiden: Brill, 2001)
hapax	hapax legomenon
HAR	*Hebrew Annual Review*
HBT	*Horizons in Biblical Theology*
HTR	*Harvard Theological Review*
HUCA	*Hebrew Union College Annual*
IBHS	Bruce K. Waltke and Michael O'Connor, *An Introduction to Biblical Hebrew Syntax* (Winona Lake, IN: Eisenbrauns, 1990)
impv.	imperative
inf.	infinitive
Int	*Interpretation*
JANESCU	*Journal of the Near Eastern Society of Columbia University*
JAOS	*Journal of the American Oriental Society*
JBL	*Journal of Biblical Literature*
JBT	*Jahrbuch für biblische Theologie*

Jerome	Jerome's Latin translation of the Psalms as printed in *Biblia sacra iuxta vulgatam versionem*, 3rd ed. (Stuttgart: Deutsche Bibelgesellschaft, 1983)
JETS	*Journal of the Evangelical Theological Society*
JM	Paul Joüon, *A Grammar of Biblical Hebrew*, trans. and rev. T. Muraoka, 2 vols. (Rome: Pontifical Biblical Institute, 1991)
JNES	*Journal of Near Eastern Studies*
JNSL	*Journal of Northwest Semitic Languages*
JQR	*Jewish Quarterly Review*
JSOT	*Journal for the Study of the Old Testament*
JSOTSup	Journal for the Study of the Old Testament: Supplement Series
JSS	*Journal of Semitic Studies*
JTS	*Journal of Theological Studies*
K	*Kethib*, the written (consonantal) Hebrew text; contrast Q
KJV	King James Version (Authorized Version)
L	Leningrad manuscript of the Masoretic Text, as printed in *Biblia Hebraica Stuttgartensia*
lit.	literally
LXX	Septuagint translation of the Psalms, as printed in *Psalmi cum Odis*, ed. Alfred Rahlfs (repr., Göttingen: Vandenhoeck & Ruprecht, 1979)
mg	margin
MS(S)	manuscript(s)
MT	Masoretic Text, as printed in *Biblia Hebraica Stuttgartensia*
NEB	New English Bible
NedTT	*Nederlands theologisch tijdschrift*
NIDOTTE	*New International Dictionary of Old Testament Theology and Exegesis*, ed. Willem A. VanGemeren, 5 vols. (Grand Rapids: Zondervan, 1996)
NIVI	New International Version: Inclusive Language Edition
NJB	New Jerusalem Bible
NJPS	*Tanakh: The Holy Scriptures; The New JPS Translation according to the Traditional Hebrew Text,* Hebrew-English version, 2nd ed. (Philadelphia: Jewish Publication Society, 1999)
NRSV	New Revised Standard Version
n.s.	new series
NT	New Testament
NTS	*New Testament Studies*
OBO	Orbis biblicus et orientalis
OT	Old Testament
OtSt	*Oudtestamentische Studiën*
PBH	Postbiblical Hebrew
pl.	plural
ptc.	participle
Q	*Qere*, the Hebrew text as read aloud (i.e., with the vowels); contrast K
RB	*Revue biblique*

repr.	reprint/reprinted	
ResQ	*Restoration Quarterly*	
SBLDS	Society of Biblical Literature Dissertation Series	
sg.	singular	
SJOT	*Scandinavian Journal of the Old Testament*	
SJT	*Scottish Journal of Theology*	
Sym	Symmachus's translation of the Psalms, as printed in Fridericus Field, *Origenis Hexaplorum quae supersunt*, vol. 2 (Oxford: Oxford University Press, 1874; repr., Hildesheim: Olms, 1964)	
Syr	Syriac translation of the Psalms, as printed in *The Old Testament in Syriac according to the Peshiṭta Version*, part II,3 (Leiden: Brill, 1980)	
TDOT	*Theological Dictionary of the Old Testament*, ed. G. Johannes Botterweck et al. (Grand Rapids: Eerdmans, 1974–)	
Tg	Targum to the Psalms, as printed in *Miqra'ot Gedolot*, vol. 10 (repr., New York: Pardes, 1951)	
Th	Theodotion's translation of the Psalms, as printed in Fridericus Field, *Origenis Hexaplorum quae supersunt*, vol. 2 (Oxford: Oxford University Press, 1874; repr., Hildesheim: Olms, 1964)	
ThTo	*Theology Today*	
TLOT	*Theological Lexicon of the Old Testament*, ed. Ernst Jenni and Claus Westermann, 3 vols. (Peabody, MA: Hendrickson, 1997)	
TTH	S. R. Driver, *A Treatise on the Use of the Tenses in Hebrew and Some Other Syntactical Questions*, 3rd ed. (London: Oxford University Press, 1892)	
TynBul	*Tyndale Bulletin*	
TZ	*Theologische Zeitschrift*	
UBS	United Bible Societies, *Preliminary and Interim Report on the Hebrew Old Testament Text Project*, vol. 3 (New York: United Bible Societies, 1979)	
UF	*Ugarit-Forschungen*	
v(v).	verse(s)	
Vg	Vulgate Latin translation of the Psalms, as printed in *Biblia sacra iuxta vulgatam versionem*, 3rd ed. (Stuttgart: Deutsche Bibelgesellschaft, 1983)	
Vrs	ancient versions (LXX, Aq, Sym, Th, Vg, Jerome, Syr, Tg) or most of them	
VT	*Vetus Testamentum*	
VTSup	Vetus Testamentum Supplements	
WBC	Word Biblical Commentary	
Yhwh	Yahweh, or LORD in English Bible versions	
ZAW	*Zeitschrift für die alttestamentliche Wissenschaft*	
ZTK	*Zeitschrift für Theologie und Kirche*	

Abbreviations

Old Testament

Gen.	Genesis	Song	Song of Songs
Exod.	Exodus	Isa.	Isaiah
Lev.	Leviticus	Jer.	Jeremiah
Num.	Numbers	Lam.	Lamentations
Deut.	Deuteronomy	Ezek.	Ezekiel
Josh.	Joshua	Dan.	Daniel
Judg.	Judges	Hosea	Hosea
Ruth	Ruth	Joel	Joel
1–2 Sam.	1–2 Samuel	Amos	Amos
1–2 Kings	1–2 Kings	Obad.	Obadiah
1–2 Chron.	1–2 Chronicles	Jon.	Jonah
Ezra	Ezra	Mic.	Micah
Neh.	Nehemiah	Nah.	Nahum
Esther	Esther	Hab.	Habakkuk
Job	Job	Zeph.	Zephaniah
Ps(s).	Psalm(s)	Hag.	Haggai
Prov.	Proverbs	Zech.	Zechariah
Eccles.	Ecclesiastes	Mal.	Malachi

New Testament

Matt.	Matthew	1–2 Thess.	1–2 Thessalonians
Mark	Mark	1–2 Tim.	1–2 Timothy
Luke	Luke	Titus	Titus
John	John	Philem.	Philemon
Acts	Acts	Heb.	Hebrews
Rom.	Romans	James	James
1–2 Cor.	1–2 Corinthians	1–2 Pet.	1–2 Peter
Gal.	Galatians	1–3 John	1–3 John
Eph.	Ephesians	Jude	Jude
Phil.	Philippians	Rev.	Revelation
Col.	Colossians		

Other Jewish and Christian Writings

$b.$	Babylonian Talmud
$m.$	Mishnah
1–4 Macc.	1–4 Maccabees
Sir.	Sirach
$t.$	Tosefta

Introduction

We do not know why (humanly speaking) the Psalter as a collection came to exist or why it came to appear within the Scriptures, though we may make one or two guesses. It would not be surprising if the leadership of the Jewish community centered in Jerusalem thought it a good idea to collect prayers and praises that were used and could be used in worship in the temple and elsewhere. Such a collection would both free and constrain the community—it would be a resource for praise and prayer and also set checks on what counted as proper praise and prayer. The Psalter seems not to have needed fixed boundaries in this connection, since the LXX Psalter and the Qumran Psalter included extra psalms, though they are similar to those that appear in MT. The nature, function, and significance of such an anthology of prayers and praises need not be greatly affected by whether it included 140, 150, or 160 examples of things the community can say to God.[1]

Whether or not I have guessed aright regarding the original functions of the Psalter, these guesses illuminate the role the Psalter might play within Christian faith.

> If you ask the Father anything, he will give it to you in my name. (John 16:23)

> Be filled with the Spirit, speaking to one another in psalms, hymns, and spiritual songs, singing and making music to the Lord in your heart, giving thanks to God the Father at all times for everything in the name of our Lord Jesus Christ. (Eph. 5:18–20)

---

1. Contrast Aquinas's concern (*Commentary on Psalms*, on Ps. 2) about the idea that we link Ps. 2 with Ps. 1, which would mean the Psalter had only 149 psalms.

> With every prayer and request, pray on every occasion in the Spirit. (Eph. 6:18)

> I urge first of all that requests, prayers, intercessions, and thanksgivings be made for all people, for kings and all those who are in a high position. (1 Tim. 2:1–2)

How is the church to go about making such requests, praises, intercessions, and thanksgivings? And how are individuals or small groups to do that? The Bible assumes that we do not know instinctively how to talk with God but rather need some help with knowing how to do so. The Psalter is the Bible's book of praise and prayer to provide the answer to those questions and meet that need. It is given to us so that we can "adapt and adjust our minds and feelings so that they are in accord with the sense of the psalms."[2] Eugene Peterson thus comments that the Psalms are where Christians have always learned to pray—till our age![3] My own impression is that on the whole neither the Christian church nor Christian individuals have accepted the invitation to learn from the Psalter's teaching, though occasionally groups or individuals have recovered (e.g.) the enthusiasm of the Psalms' praise, the witness of their thanksgiving, and the freedom of their protest. Thus, one of the great twentieth-century Psalms scholars, Claus Westermann, tells of the way the "present transitions and disasters," the "church struggle" in Germany in the 1930s when the church was "under severe trial," confronted the church with the question of the praise of God. It was this that drove Westermann to study the nature of praise as the Psalms undertake it.[4] The reality of the way the Psalms speak to God has proved powerful as *kerygma* as well as *didachē*, as evangelistic preaching as well as teaching. At the end of the Second World War, a teenage German soldier who eventually became one of the two greatest German systematic theologians of the last third of the twentieth century found himself in a British prisoner-of-war camp. He describes how some of his contemporaries lost the will to live. He was initially unimpressed by the gift of a New Testament with the Psalms from a well-meaning chaplain, but found himself captured by the Psalms and by the way they speak "out of the depths."[5] They brought him to God. The Psalms make it possible to say things that are otherwise unsayable. In church,

---

2. Luther, *Selected Psalms*, 3:310.
3. See *Working the Angles* (Grand Rapids: Eerdmans, 1993), 50–58; further, his *Answering God*, 1–7.
4. See *Praise and Lament*, 5.
5. See Jürgen Moltmann, *Experiences of God* (Philadelphia: Fortress, 1980), 6–9.

they have the capacity to free us to talk about things that we cannot talk about anywhere else.[6]

A hint that the Psalter is designed as a teaching manual for worship and prayer is the fact that it is divided into five books, like the Torah (see the introductions in EVV before Pss. 1; 42; 73; 90; and 107, and the blessings in the Hebrew text that follow Pss. 41; 72; 89; and 106, marking the endings of these books). In both cases the fivefold division is artificial. There are some plausible divisions into which the Pentateuch could have been broken up, but the familiar fivefold division does not correspond very well to the dynamic of its narrative. The division of the Psalter into five books is even more random, but that makes its symbolic significance the clearer. It comprises a work of teaching concerning proper response to God in worship and prayer. As such it correlates to the work of teaching that appears in the Torah concerning God's story with Israel and the response God looks for in terms of worship and everyday life. Psalm 1 is then a fitting introduction to this book of teaching, especially if it means to invite readers to treat the Psalter like Torah.[7] Likewise, "Ps. 150 understands the book which it closes as a primer in worship"; from this point on, "the way stands open for every conceivable variation in praise" as the world takes up its hallelujah.[8]

But the Psalter teaches not by telling us how to pray but by showing us how to pray. Jesus follows its example. He responds to a request for teaching on prayer by giving his disciples an actual prayer that they can pray, which also is a prayer they can use as a model and a canon for their prayer. The Psalms speak *from* God by showing us how to speak *to* God. To paraphrase the first great Christian work on the Psalms known to us, Athanasius's *Letter to Marcellinus*, "Most of Scripture speaks *to* us; the Psalms speak *for* us."[9]

Historically, I assume, the Psalms came into being as Israelites prayed and praised in these words. They do not document so much their seeking of God as their responding to God's seeking of them, though this response is a spluttering and awkward one.[10] Its incorporation in the Scriptures suggests the conviction that God accepted these prayers and praises, which could therefore provide God's people with 150 examples of things one can say to God. They become part of God's inspired Word,

---

6. I owe this formulation to a lecture by Walter Brueggemann; I have not found it in his published works.
7. See the commentary (below). Brevard S. Childs views this as an aspect of the "canonical shaping" of the Psalter. See his *Introduction to the Old Testament as Scripture* (Philadelphia: Fortress, 1979), 511–22.
8. Seybold, *Introducing the Psalms*, 15.
9. See B. Anderson, *Out of the Depths*, 9.
10. Cf. Peterson, *Answering God*, 5–6.

capable of being instructive far beyond the context for which they were written (2 Tim. 3:14–17).

The Psalms and History

Not long after we start reading the Psalter, it becomes clear that the Psalms relate closely to the history of the people of God, the history of its leaders, and the history of individuals.

Admittedly, the Psalter actually begins with that general statement about the great good fortune of people devoted to Yhwh's teaching and about the trouble that comes to the wicked. That statement arose in history and was designed to be tested in history, but it is framed as a generalization. Historical particularity is nearer the surface in Ps. 2, which pictures nations making a concrete declaration of independence from Yhwh and from Yhwh's anointed, and it urges them to desist. In Ps. 3, someone speaks out of a similar situation, under enemy attack, but declares ongoing trust in Yhwh and pleads for deliverance and for blessing for the people as a whole; Pss. 4 and 5 are similar. In Ps. 6, an individual again speaks but does so out of less confidence and more sense of fear and weariness. Psalm 7 is slightly different again in speaking more overtly about a suppliant's integrity, which seems to have been impugned. Psalm 8 returns to the atmosphere of Ps. 1. It must again have arisen out of history, and it is designed to be tested in history, but it takes the form of a universal statement about the majesty of Yhwh and the delegated authority of humanity. Psalms 9–10 are originally one psalm that has been subdivided; the first part is more a testimony to what Yhwh has done in delivering someone and in sending enemies to their downfall, the second more a prayer for God to do that again. Continuing to work through the Psalter as a whole in this way broadly confirms the impression we gather from the opening psalms. While a number comprise general statements of praise, promise, or challenge and do not allude to specific historical circumstances, many talk as if they arise out of concrete events. But even these do not tell us what these events were.

Many parts of the Bible imply that we need to know their historical background if we are to understand them. This is so with the Prophets, which make it clear in two ways. The content of their prophecies makes many references to specific nations, individuals, and events. And the actual books begin by drawing attention to their historical background, to the period in which God gave these messages to the prophets, as if to say, "You will understand these prophecies aright only if you see that they are not timeless truths. They do transcend their time, speaking beyond their original context, but to understand how they do so, you must understand their original context."

With the Psalms, the opposite is the case. They do not contain the specific historical references that appear in the Prophets, and it is much more obvious that they stand independent of their original context and are designed for people to use as the vehicles for praise and prayer throughout the story of God's people. Beginning at the beginning again reveals how this is so. Psalm 1 is that general statement about paying attention to Yhwh's teaching and resisting wrongdoing. Psalm 2 is a promise and a challenge about Yhwh's commitment to the king of Israel, but no king is named; it speaks of underlings rebelling against the king but names none and points to no concrete context in which specific enemies did so. Psalms 3–7 are appeals to Yhwh for protection and help, affirmations of trust, declarations of confidence that Yhwh has heard the appeal and is answering, and promises of praise when the answer has become reality, but they refer to no specific dangers or enemies. Psalm 8 is a hymn of praise to Yhwh as the sovereign God and an expression of wonder that this God should have given such significance to human beings as God's servants, but it refers to humanity in general and offers no pointers to a context. Psalms 9–10 offer no information on who experienced the deliverance they refer back to, on what occasion, or why this person now needs deliverance once more. Working through the Psalter as a whole again establishes that this continues to be a feature of it. There are occasional exceptions: e.g., 60:9 [11] refers to Edom; 137:1 refers to Babylon. But even those exceptions prove the rule, because these Psalms do not tell us what crisis in relations between Israel and Edom or what stage in the exile in Babylon they apply to (though the heading has something to say about the former).

David and the Psalms

The Psalms conceal their origins. It is thus an odd fact that study of the Psalms in both the premodern and modern periods paid considerable attention to their authorship and historical background.

As far as we can tell, biblical books originally had no titles; like other ancient Middle Eastern works, books such as Genesis were referred to by their opening words. The collection of hymns, testimonies, prayers, prophecies, and other material that we call the Psalms eventually came to be known in Hebrew as *tĕhillîm*, "Praises." In LXX, Vaticanus calls it *psalmoi*, "Songs Sung to a Stringed Instrument," while Alexandrinus calls it *psaltērion*, apparently a term for the instrument itself; these two words generate the English titles "Psalms" and "Psalter." None of these titles is very accurate,[11] but there is no title that really does justice to the varied contents of the work.

Tractate *b. Baba Batra* (14b–15a) says that "David wrote the Book of Praises" (admittedly in collaboration with ten elders, such as the Levitical music leader Asaph, and the Korahites), and through the premodern period David was treated as the author of the Psalms, individual psalms being commonly linked with episodes in his life. The NT makes a link between David and Pss. 110 (e.g., Mark 12:35–37; Acts 2:33–35); 69 and 109 (Acts 1:15–20; Rom. 11:9–10); 16 (Acts 2:25–32); 2 (Acts 4:24–28); 32 (Rom. 4:6–8); and 95 (Heb. 4:7). In Christian tradition the Psalter as a whole became "The Psalms of David," and in the Psalter itself the headings to many individual psalms refer to David, but these allusions are more ambiguous than they may seem. That is true of other aspects of these headings to Psalms, which Today's English Version (the Good News Bible) therefore transferred to the margin, while the NEB simply omitted them.[12] The NEB, at least, was also influenced by indications that the headings are later than the content of the Psalms (though they are just as much part of the text as anything and have verse numbers in printed Hebrew Bibles).[13] One such indication is that some headings look as if they reflect adaptations of the psalm to new circumstances: e.g., Pss. 120–34 are "Psalms of Ascents," suggesting they were used for pilgrimage or procession, but they do not look as if they were written for that. Further, the LXX and the Qumran Psalter have extra headings, suggesting that the headings were still developing at the end of the OT period. It is in the LXX that Ps. 95 becomes "of David," as it is referred to in Heb. 4:7. Likewise Acts 4 refers to Ps. 2 as Davidic though the psalm itself is not so identified.

But what does the expression "of David" imply? There are two aspects to that question. First, as well as referring to David ben Jesse, in the OT "David" can refer to a subsequent Davidic king or to a coming David

---

11. The Greek versions use the two Greek words more accurately to render the Hebrew word for *strings that appears in psalm headings. Cassiodorus defines a psalm as a melody played by the psaltery (*Psalms,* 1:31).

12. The Revised English Bible restored them.

13. This can cause confusion when books refer to Psalms, because they may be using the Hebrew numbers rather than the English numbers; thus, e.g., Ps. 53:1 EVV = Ps. 53:2 MT; Ps. 54:1 EVV = Ps. 54:3 MT. I noted in the preface that in this commentary I include the Hebrew reference after the English one where necessary—e.g., "Ps. 51:1 [3]." Confusion can be exacerbated by a variation in the numbering of whole psalms. LXX correctly makes Pss. 9 and 10 one psalm, so Ps. 11 MT then equals Ps. 10 LXX, etc., until we reach Ps. 147 EVV, which the LXX divides into two. The Latin Bible (both Vg and Jerome's version) follows this, and so do some Roman Catholic English translations. So Ps. 51 MT is Ps. 50 LXX and Latin. In addition, Pss. 114–15 MT are Ps. 113 LXX and Latin, but Ps. 116 MT is divided as Pss. 114 and 115 LXX and Latin.

(see Jer. 30:9; Ezek. 34:23–24; 37:24–25; Hosea 3:5). In the latter case, "of David" would almost mean "messianic." That latter possibility links with the second matter. In the Hebrew expression translated "Psalm of David" (*mizmôr lĕdāwid*), "of" is not a genitive (as it is in expressions such as "the words of Isaiah"). It is the preposition *lĕ*. While *lĕ* can mean "of," it has many other meanings, mostly more common than "of." BDB lists some of these meanings as "to," "belonging to," "for," "on behalf of," and "about." This variety in the meanings of the preposition is in fact reflected in translations of the headings. In an expression such as "To the choirmaster. Of David" (Pss. 11 and 14 RSV), "to" and "of" *both* represent *lĕ*, and it may seem arbitrary to translate it in these two different ways. In light of the wide range of meanings of *lĕ*, we can see that *mizmôr lĕdāwid* might be understood in a variety of ways:

"to" (this psalm is addressed or offered to David or the Davidic king, present or future)

"belonging to" (cf. "belonging to the Korahites," Ps. 42; this psalm belongs to a collection sponsored or authorized by David or the Davidic king—compare expressions such as "Sankey's *Sacred Songs and Solos*" or "Alexander's *New Gospel Hymns*," compiled respectively by Ira D. Sankey and Charles M. Alexander, but written by many authors and composers)

"for" (for David or the Davidic king, present or future, to use or learn from)[14]

"on behalf of" (prayed for David or the Davidic king)

"about" (about David or the present or future Davidic king)

"by" (authored by David or the Davidic king)

BDB rightly implies that the meaning of the expression likely changed over the centuries. It might originally have suggested that a particular psalm is for the present king, then have pointed to the future king, then later have been understood to denote authorship—though Hab. 3:1 is the only passage outside the Psalms where the preposition might suggest authorship.

There is a recurrent pattern within the Scriptures whereby books that were anonymous come to have authors associated with them (e.g., Matthew, Mark, and Hebrews). Once books have become accepted within the community, people want to associate them with someone they know of. One can see how the references to David in the headings, the emphasis

---

14. Goulder argues that "The Prayers of David," Pss. 51–72, were written for David in connection with Absalom's revolt (see *Prayers of David*).

on David as patron of the worship in the temple (see Chronicles), and his reputation as a musician and poet would have made him a natural candidate for identification as author of the Psalter as a whole. This may have encouraged or followed the development of a tradition of linking psalms with incidents in David's life. The long headings attached to some psalms that do that (Pss. 3; 7; 18; 34; 51; 52; 54; 56; 57; 59; 60; 63; 142) must be referring to David ben Jesse, but they still need not imply his authorship; they could be "to," "for," "on behalf of," or "about" him. In commenting on references to David in the headings, I will take up one or other of these possibilities with regard to different psalms, but in translating the psalms, I shall render *lĕdāwid* "David's," leaving the meaning of the expression open.

A major argument that influences Christians in assuming David wrote the Psalms is the impression that Jesus refers to them as David's. We have seen that in fact Jesus connects David with only one psalm. I take it that Jesus is actually speaking conventionally, as when he speaks as if the sun goes round the earth, or refers to the mustard seed being the smallest of seeds, or takes up the traditional story of the rich man and the poor man in his parable about Dives and Lazarus. In such cases he is not pronouncing on questions of cosmology, botany, eschatology, or authorship, but taking up the way people speak about these matters in his culture and making his point by means of these ways of speaking. And in each case his argument does not depend on his adoption of this conventional way of speaking; it works without that. So I do not think that Jesus's comment on Ps. 110 constitutes a dominical declaration on its authorship. But someone who thought that it did would have no reason to infer that Jesus had also thereby pronounced on the authorship of the other 149 psalms. And if we do not assume that David wrote the Psalms, we do not have the problem of understanding how he could have been a combination of Napoleon (great general), JFK (great leader and womanizer), and Henri Nouwen or Eugene Peterson (great teacher on spirituality).[15]

The "long headings" referring to specific incidents in David's life may have a further significance. With these, too, there is no presumption that a heading such as "David's, when he fled from his son Absalom" (Ps. 3) is originally a statement about authorship, though people have come to understand it thus. When we label a stained-glass window with a title that relates it to a biblical person or scene, we do not imply that the person or scene actually looked like that. We are rather seeking to help people

---

15. The Psalms' many references to the "house of God" might also seem to preclude Davidic authorship, since the Jerusalem temple was not built in his day. But the term "house of God" could have been used for whatever sanctuary did exist in his day, even one that was less solid than Solomon's temple.

use their imagination to enter into the reality of the scene or come to an understanding of the person in such a way as to see how he or she impacts their lives. The long headings do something similar.

A comparison of these long headings with the content of the psalms they introduce reveals a significant pattern. It is characteristic that one can see both points of contact and points of discontinuity.[16] This is famously so with the heading to Ps. 51: "The leader's. Composition. David's, when Nathan the prophet went in to him as he went in to Bathsheba." On one hand, the psalm is very appropriate for a king who needs not to have Yhwh's spirit withdrawn from him, and a man who has blood on his hands. On the other hand, David can hardly say to Yhwh, "Against you alone have I sinned," and it is surprising (though not impossible) to have him asking Yhwh to build up the walls of Jerusalem.[17] This suggests that the psalm was not written in the circumstances to which the heading refers; the heading was added later. The object of the headings was to link these psalms with incidents in David's life to which the OT story refers in such a way that they function a little like the collocation of passages in a lectionary. Such collocation implies not that two passages originally belong together but that they have enough overlap to make it profitable for readers to look at them alongside each other.[18] There is no external evidence that this approach to the long headings is right, but it does account for both features of them—both the way they fit their psalms and the fact that the fit is incomplete. It also coheres with the fact that other aspects of the psalm headings convey information about the use of the psalms rather than about their origin.

The nature of the headings then reflects the way David became a hero for Bible readers, as early as the writing of Chronicles (where his portrait is less equivocal than that in Samuel–Kings). The traditional Jewish midrash on Psalms thus tells us that "R. Yudan taught in the name of R. Judah: All that David said in his Book of Psalms applies to himself, to all Israel, and to all the ages."[19] His prayers are not just his one-off prayers, nor are they illuminating just (e.g.) for great kings, but they are for praying by everyone. It may be that the development of such an interest in David generated the headings. Linking psalms with incidents from David's life helped people to see more of the significance of both psalm and narrative. The process has continued as people have tried to link many other "David psalms" (and other psalms) with specific

---

16. Cf. James D. Nogalski, "Reading David in the Psalter," *HBT* 23 (2001): 168–91.

17. Kidner therefore sees vv. 18–19 [20–21] as a later addition to the psalm (*Psalms* 1:194).

18. Cf. Brevard S. Childs, "Psalm Titles and Midrashic Exegesis," *JSS* 16 (1971): 137–50.

19. *Midrash on Psalms*, 1:230, on 18:1.

incidents in David's life. Although this is not a piece of historical study, it may be a helpful exercise in imagination (or it may not—not everyone likes stained glass).

The Modern Quest

The essence of criticism is to question tradition. Historical criticism thus questioned the tradition that David wrote the Psalms and tried to discover their origin and date from within the psalms themselves. Unfortunately (or not), this has been a fruitless exercise, or an overfruitful one. More than a century of careful study has produced no agreed-upon answers to the question. Critical conclusions about the dating of Psalms vary over a millennium (from before the time of David himself to the time of the Hasmoneans). They thus do not even agree over whether psalms come from before or after the exile, the great watershed of the OT story. From time to time the world of scholarship comes to a broad consensus on some aspects of the question, but that consensus then collapses. This situation will never change. The world of scholarship will never come to a conclusion on these questions, because the very task that scholarship here sets for itself works against the nature of the psalms themselves. They proceed and work by not making reference to the particularities of their origin, so that such information does not distract people who use them and make them more difficult for worshippers to identify with.

One way or another, it thus seems best to proceed on the assumption that we do not know who wrote the Psalms but that this is an advantage, not a disadvantage. In this commentary I therefore make little reference to the dating of psalms. In every case the reader may assume that there have been many opinions about the matter and that there are no criteria for deciding the question. I have thus followed the principle enunciated by the great patristic exegete Theodoret of Cyrrhus in connection with Ps. 29 (whose historical origin is even more controverted today than it was in the fifth century), to be brief in commenting on historical matters but to speak at greater length about ways in which the psalm relates to us.[20]

This conclusion troubles the world of modern scholarship, which works on the basis of the conviction that understanding is dependent on knowing a text's historical background and that understanding texts' historical backgrounds is necessary for portraying the history of Israelite

---

20. *Psalms*, 1:181. Ironically, the historically inclined Theodoret then goes on to a typological exposition of the psalm, seeing it as portraying the ministry of the apostles.

religion.[21] I think the first conviction is mistaken; the reader will have to decide from the commentary whether my sidelining this question makes understanding impossible. I think the second conviction is correct, but this only proves that portraying the history of Israelite religion cannot be done (or at least that the Psalms are of no help in this connection).

The conclusion also troubles the world of the modern believing community. One reason is that as part of the modern world it shares the scholarly world's conviction about understanding texts in light of their historical context. Another is the conviction that the authority of the Scriptures is related to the identity of their human authors. While there may be material of which this is true (perhaps Paul's letters with their appeal to his personal authority, and some material in the Prophets), in general that conviction is also fallacious. The fact that most of Scripture is of anonymous authorship is again an indication of this. God does not especially work through people with big names, and people through whom God works may not be very interested in others knowing their names. The Psalms' power and authority derive not from their being written by someone important whose name we know but from their having been prayers and praises that God accepted. Like (e.g.) Genesis or Ruth, psalms came to be accepted in the believing community because it knew they had the ring of truth, even if they were anonymous (for Christians, Jesus's acceptance of these books then buttressed that recognition). Actually, the same is true of the prophecies of people whose names we do know; they came to be accepted because their hearers knew themselves convicted by God when they heard them, not because bearing the name of (e.g.) Jeremiah automatically gave them authority (his story shows this was not so). The community that recognized them then invites us to listen for God speaking to us through them—in the case of the Psalms, to make them our own prayers and praises. And doing that does not depend on knowing who wrote them and when, as is also the case with Christian prayers and hymns. Often their power and meaningfulness derive from their having been the expression of real people's personal turning to God. Charlotte Elliott's "Just as I Am" is an example. But even if we do not know precisely what that experience was, our experience resonates with that human experience and enables us to interpret it.

One other possible implication of the Psalms' anonymity is worth mentioning. Several of the named composers of psalm-like praise elsewhere in Scripture are women: see Exod. 15; Judg. 5; 1 Sam. 2. It

---

21. For a recent advocacy of a historical approach to the Psalms, illustrated from Pss. 100; 79; and 95, see W. M. Schniedewind, "'Are We His People or Not?'" *Bib* 76 (1995): 540–50.

therefore seems likely that many of the composers of psalms in the Psalter were women,[22] though one can imagine that female authorship might need to be concealed in a patriarchal context in Israel. It may therefore give us some insight into the origin of psalms to imagine them on the lips of women. For instance, Ps. 6 "might be the prayer of a woman who was raped," Ps. 11 "might be the prayer of an abused woman against her inner enemies," Ps. 16 "might be the prayer of a devout elderly widow," Ps. 54 "might be the prayer of a woman who was the victim of slander," and Ps. 69 "might be the prayer of a woman prophet and reformer."[23] Although Marchiene Vroon Rienstra intends these as observations about the use of the Psalms today, reflecting on the use of the Scriptures today has the potential to offer us insight on their use in Israel.[24]

Psalmody before the Psalms

As is the case with other forms of writing in the OT such as proverbs and laws, the nature of the Psalms overlaps with the praise and prayer of contemporary Middle Eastern peoples, and it is illuminating to compare the Psalms with these.[25] Although most of this Middle Eastern material is centuries older than the Psalms, it is probably inappropriate to think in terms of direct development from it. The similarities rather reflect a common humanity and a common culture. The comparison also highlights contrasts, often reflecting differences of theology. For instance, Egyptian praises and prayers (whose form does not especially resemble the Psalms) naturally presuppose a number of gods, assume that the planets and stars represent deities, and manifest an interest in the afterlife—specifically that of the king.[26] At the same time, the way they characterize a particular god and the way that god relates to the suppliant may significantly overlap with the Psalms. The Egyptian king Amenophis IV's Hymn to the Sun (Aton) bears comparing with Ps. 104,[27] while an Egyptian hymn from about the time of Moses describes Amon-Re in this way:

---

22. See Lisa W. Davison, "'My Soul Is Like the Weaned Child,'" *HBT* 23 (2001): 155–67; Julio Trebolle Barrera ("Salmos de mujeres," *EstBib* 57 [1999]: 665–82, arguing specifically that Pss. 16 and 131 were written by women. Contrast Gerstenberger's declaration that "the Psalms were composed by men and for men alone" (*Psalms*, 1:32).

23. Rienstra, *Swallow's Nest*, 44, 28, 10, 33, 210.

24. Cf. Brenner's comments in *Wisdom and Psalms*, 29–30, and the papers on Pss. 55 and 109 in that volume.

25. For further examples, see Seybold, *Introducing the Psalms*, 91–212.

26. See, e.g., *Hymns, Prayers, and Songs: An Anthology of Ancient Egyptian Lyric Poetry*, trans. John L. Foster, ed. Susan Tower Hollis (Atlanta: SBL, 1995).

27. See *ANET* 369–71.

He who dissolves evils and dispels ailments, a physician who heals the eye without having remedies, opening the eye and driving away the squint. . . . Rescuing whom he desires, even though this one be in the Underworld; who saves from fate as his heart directs. He has eyes and ears wherever he goes, for the benefit of the one he loves. Hearing the prayers of the one who calls him, coming from afar in a moment for the one who cries to him. He makes a life long, or shortens it. He gives more than was fated to the one he loves. . . . He is more effective than millions for the person who sets him in their heart. One is more valiant than a hundred thousands because of his name, the godly protector in truth.[28]

A Babylonian prayer to the goddess Ba'u likewise illustrates theological similarities and differences that arise from its polytheistic assumptions.[29]

[24]O Ba'u, mighty lady who dwells in the bright heavens,
[25]O merciful goddess, the bestower of . . .
[26]Whose regard is prosperity, whose word is peace!
[27]I beseech you, lady, stand and hearken to my cries!
[28]. . . give judgment, make a decision . . .
[29]I have turned to you, I have sought you, your *ulinnu*[30] have I grasped like the *ulinnu* of my god and goddess!
[30]Give my judgment, make my decisions, . . . my path,
[31]Since you know to protect, to benefit, to save,
[32]Since to raise to life, to give prosperity rests with you!
[33]Lady . . . tears have I given you, your name have I . . .
[34]. . . my ears, will you protect me and let me . . . your divinity!
[35]The raising of my hand accept and take away my sighing!
[36]Let me send you to my angry god, to my goddess who is angry,
[37]To Marduk, the god of my city who is incensed, whose heart is enraged [?] with me!
[38]In the dream and the vision that . . .
[39]In the evil of an eclipse of the moon which in such and such a month and such a day has taken place,
[40]In the evil of the powers, of the portents, evil and not good,
[41]That are in my palace and my land,
[42]I am afraid, I tremble, and I am cast down in fear!
[43]At the word of your exalted command that . . . in Ikur,
[44]And your sure mercy that does not change,
[45]May my wrathful god return, may my angry goddess . . . ,

---

28. See further ibid., 369.
29. Cf. Moshe Greenberg's comparison of "Hittite Royal Prayers and Biblical Petitionary Prayers" (in *Neue Wege*, ed. Seybold and Zenger, 15–27), in which he notes how Hittite prayers can ask one god for support against another.
30. Some form of garment.

⁴⁶May Marduk the god of my city who is enraged . . . ,
⁴⁷. . . O Ba'u, mighty lady, . . . mother!³¹

Like a psalm, the prayer comprises invocations of the deity, laments at the suppliant's present experience, and pleas for the deity to act so as to change that. The lines also divide into complementary parts in the manner of psalms.

The following is a Babylonian prayer for forgiveness.

¹⁹Marduk, Great Lord, Compassionate God,
²⁰Who takes the hand of the fallen,
²¹[Who frees] the fettered, Who enlivens the dead.
²²[Because] of my misdeed, known or unknown,
²³[I have been neglectful], have trespassed, slighted, and sinned;
²⁴[As against] my father, my begetter, against your great divinity,
²⁵[I have been neglectful], have trespassed, slighted, and sinned.
²⁶[I have brought] myself before your great divinity;
²⁷may [the waters of tran]quility meet you.
²⁸May your angry heart be quieted.
²⁹May your sweet benevolence, your great
³⁰forgiveness, your venerable
³¹pardon exist for me, so that . . .
³²The glory of your great divinity let me glo[rify!]

Subscription: A "hand-raising prayer" to Marduk. With either a ritual arrangement or with a censer. ³²

A Babylonian prayer for the king may be compared with Ps. 72.

May Anu and Antum in heaven bless him,
May Bel and Belit in E-kur determine his fate.
May Ea and Damkina, who dwell in the great depths, grant him life unto distant days.
May Makh, the ruler of the great countries, provide him with complete dominion(?).

---

31. Reprinted with some updating of the language from Leonard W. King, *Babylonian Magic and Sorcery* (London: Luzac, 1896), 27–28. Ellipses and square brackets in such texts indicate that the text is broken or unclear or that we do not understand the words. For another example, see S. David Sperling, "A šu-íl-lá to Ištar," *Die Welt des Orients* 12 (1981): 8–20. A *šu-íl-lá* is a "lifting of the hand," a gesture of prayer; cf. line 35 of the Ba'u prayer and the title of the prayer to Marduk that follows.

32. Quoted from Joel H. Hunt, "The Hymnic Introduction of Selected *suilla* Prayers Directed to Ea, Marduk, and Nabu" (diss., Brandeis University, 1995). For another example, see Tzvi Abusch, "The Form and Meaning of a Babylonian Prayer to Marduk," *JAOS* 103 (1983): 3–15.

> May Sin, the light of heaven, give him royal progeny unto distant days.
> May the hero Shamash, the lord of heaven and earth, make firm the throne of his kingdom unto distant days.
> May Ea, the possessor of the source, provide him with wisdom.
> May Marduk, who loves his rule, the lord of the sources, grant him blessing in fullness.[33]

The History behind the Psalter

When did the Psalter as we know it come into being? A psalm such as Ps. 137 presupposes the exile and suggests that this exile has lasted a while, which points to the earliest time this could have happened. The prologue to Sirach (about 200 BC) refers to "the Law and the Prophets and the others that followed them" (NRSV), which must have included a version of the Psalter. It is known in approximately the form we have it to the authors of the LXX (in Alexandria in the third or second century BC?) and to the Qumran community (a little later), and there are no indications of Greek influence on the Psalms. All this implies that the Psalter came into being in something like the form we know it some time in the Second Temple period, in Persian or early Greek times. From the beginning it was presumably among the authoritative resources of the Jewish community, and in this sense the time it came into being is also the time when it became canonical.

But that was the end of a process, and presumably the Psalter's earlier versions would have had similar authority for their communities. Although we cannot know when individual psalms were written, we can trace a little of that process whereby the Psalter itself came into being.

Within the Psalter are a number of subcollections of psalms that have similar headings or similar subject matter or similar usage. There are two opening collections of David psalms, 3–41 and 51–72.[34] The latter closes by telling us that "the prayers of David are concluded," which is true of this collection but not of the Psalter as a whole. There are two collections of Korahite psalms, 42–49 and 84–88 (the latter divided by one David psalm, Ps. 86). Psalms 73–83 are Asaph psalms (as is 50). Psalms 138–45 are further David psalms. Perhaps the same psalm could belong in different collections (like hymns in different hymnbooks), and this explains the way a psalm can be (for instance) both "the leader's" and "David's" (e.g., Pss. 11–15) or can be described as (for instance) both a

---

33. Quoted from Roland E. Murphy, *A Study of Psalm 72 (71)* (Washington, DC: Catholic University of America, 1948), 47.

34. Psalm 10 has no heading, but it seems to be linked to Ps. 9. Psalm 33 has no heading.

"song" and a "composition" (e.g., Pss. 65–68). This phenomenon would reflect the conflating of headings when the collections were brought together. Further, one can sometimes see a significance in the way one psalm follows another (see, e.g., the comments on Pss. 1 and 2; 3 and 4; 16 and 17; 30 and 31; 32 and 33). Or one can see patterns in the arrangement of the larger collections: for instance, Books I, III, IV, and V begin with teaching psalms,[35] while psalms about the king almost open Book I (Ps. 2) and close Books II and III.[36]

There are also groupings characterized by shared features. Psalms 42–83 generally prefer the ordinary word *'ĕlōhîm* for God to the name Yhwh, in a way that statistically stands out from the rest of the Psalter. Sometimes one can see how the name might have been replaced by the ordinary word (e.g., 43:4; 45:7 [8]; Ps. 53 compared with Ps. 14; and Ps. 68 compared with its parallel passages). Psalms 93 and 95–99 all celebrate Yhwh's kingship. Psalms 113–18 are the Egyptian Hallel, used at Passover (Pss. 113–14 before the meal, Pss. 115–18 after; see Mark 14:26). We have noted that Pss. 120–34 are the Psalms of Ascents, used on pilgrimage or in procession. Psalms 135–36 are the Great Hallel, also used at Passover, and Pss. 146–50 are further Hallel Psalms. As has sometimes happened with hymnbooks, often the compilers of the Psalter kept earlier groups of psalms together rather than (e.g.) grouping them by subject. One consequence is that psalms or portions of psalms recur, partly because they were in more than one collection (notably, Pss. 14 and 53 are variants on the same psalm).

The process of its development means that the Psalter as a whole does not have a structure that helps us get a handle on its contents, as the structure of (e.g.) Genesis or Isaiah helps us grasp the whole and the parts. In the late twentieth century the structure of the Psalter as a whole became a topic of scholarly interest. Thus J. Clinton McCann speaks of understanding it as "a coherent literary whole. . . . The purposeful placing of psalms within the collection seems to have given the final form of the whole Psalter a function and message greater than the sum of its parts."[37] I have been more influenced by observations in the midrash:

---

35. See the section on "Prophecy and Wisdom" below.

36. See Gerald H. Wilson, "The Use of Royal Psalms at the 'Seams' of the Hebrew Psalter," *JSOT* 35 (1986): 85–94. For further attempts to infer the process of the development of the Psalter as a whole, see (e.g.) Wilson, *The Editing of the Hebrew Psalter*, SBLDS 76 (Chico, CA: Scholars Press, 1985); Erich Zenger, "Zur redaktionsgeschichtlichen Bedeutung der Korachpsalmen," in *Neue Wege*, ed. Seybold and Zenger, 175–98; Roger T. Beckwith, "The Early History of the Psalter," *TynBul* 46 (1995): 1–27; Seybold, *Introducing the Psalms*, 14–28.

37. In McCann, ed., *The Shape and Shaping of the Psalter*, JSOTSup 159 (Sheffield: JSOT, 1993), 7. Cf. Gerald H. Wilson, "The Shape of the Book of Psalms," *Int* 46 (1992): 129–42.

"As to the exact order of David's Psalms, Scripture says elsewhere: *Man knoweth not the order thereof* (Job 28:13)." Understanding the order belongs to God alone: "'Who, as I, can read and declare it, and set it in order[?]' (Isa. 44:7)." So "when R. Joshua ben Levi sought to arrange the Psalms in their proper order, a heavenly voice came forth and commanded: 'Do not rouse that which slumbers!'"[38] The Psalter does not work like Genesis or Isaiah.[39]

Instead of looking for a structure in the Psalter, a more fruitful way of seeking a grasp of the Psalms as a whole is the more traditional critical approach of seeking to understand the types of psalm that recur, categorizing them into various ways of speaking to God and being addressed by God.[40] This suggests a structure to the Psalter's understanding of prayer and worship. And in its implicit understanding of the interrelationship of these forms of speech, the Psalter does suggest a structure of spirituality.[41]

The Psalms as Poetry

In older translations such as the KJV, the Psalms appear in the same way as (for instance) the prose prayers in Ezra and Nehemiah. On what basis do we term them poetry and print them differently?

Rhythm

In traditional English poetry, rhyme has been an important feature. Occasionally rhyme features in the Psalms (e.g., 5:1–2 [2–3]; 18:46 [47]; 26:11; 35:23; 44:5 [6]; 55:9 [10]; 71:8), as does paronomasia (a play on words, as in 6:10 [11]; 28:5; 37:2; 38:6 [7]; 40:3 [4]; 48:3–4 [4–5]; 55:2, 8 [3, 9]; 60:4 [6]; 62:3–4, 9–10 [4–5, 10–11]; 64:4–6 [5–7]). But either may well be accidental. More certainly the result of design are the alphabetical psalms, in which lines or groups of lines open with words beginning with successive letters of the alphabet (Pss. 9–10; 25;

---

38. See *Midrash on Psalms*, 1:49–50.
39. For examples of attempts to discover the structure of the Psalter as a book and the intentionality that underlies it, see (e.g.), J. Clinton McCann, ed., *Shape and Shaping of the Psalter*; Christoph Rösel, *Die messianische Redaktion des Psalters* (Stuttgart: Calwer, 1999); and for reflection on and critique of this venture, E. S. Gerstenberger, "Der Psalter als Buch und als Sammlung," in *Neue Wege*, ed. Seybold and Zenger, 3–13; Whybray, *Reading the Psalms*; H. P. Nasuti, *Defining the Sacred Songs*, JSOTSup 218 (Sheffield: Sheffield Academic Press, 1999), 163–220.
40. See the section on "Form" below.
41. See the section on "The Psalms and Spirituality" below.

34; 37; 111; 112; 145; and, most spectacularly, 119).[42] The same may be true of the frequent instances of stepped structures (chiasms)—that is, psalms, sections, and lines arranged (e.g.) $abcc'b'a'$ (e.g., Ps. 29 as a whole; also 1:6; 7:16 [17]; 29:5–9; 51:1–9 [3–11]; 59:1 [2]; 66:16–20), though chiasms tend to lie in the eye of the beholder. Occasionally psalms incorporate refrains (e.g., Pss. 42–43) or other repetitions that may be refrains (e.g., Pss. 46; 49; 57; 62), though these have less uniformity in their wording and location than refrains in Western poetry and hymns.[43]

As poetry, psalms differ in two main ways from prose prayers.[44] First, they differ in the outward form of their sentences and thus in the form of their communication, in ways that affect the process of interpreting them. Psalm 2:1–9 illustrates this:

> [1]Why have nations thronged,
>   do peoples recite emptiness,
> [2]Do earth's kings take their stand,
>   have leaders taken counsel together,
>   against Yhwh and against his anointed?
> [3]"We are going to break off their fetters,
>   throw their ropes off us."
> [4]The one who sits in the heavens is amused;
>   the Lord laughs at them.
> [5]Then he speaks to them in his anger,
>   he dismays them with his fury.
> [6]"But I myself installed my king
>   on Zion, my holy mountain!"
> [7]I shall tell of Yhwh's decree:
>   he said to me, "You are my son;
>   I myself beget you today.
> [8]Ask of me
>   and I will make nations your possession,
>   earth's ends your estate.
> [9]You can break them up with an iron bar,
>   smash them like a potter's vessel."

---

42. These are often called acrostics, but an acrostic is strictly a composition in which the initial letters of lines make a word.

43. See J. Goldingay, "Repetition and Variation in the Psalms," *JQR* 68 (1978): 146–57.

44. On the Psalms' poetic form, the classic work is Robert Lowth, *Lectures on the Sacred Poetry of the Hebrews* (1753; repr., Hildesheim, NY: Olms, 1969). Recent works include James L. Kugel, *The Idea of Biblical Poetry* (New Haven, CT: Yale University Press, 1981); Watson, *Classical Hebrew Poetry*; Alter, *Art of Biblical Poetry*; David L. Petersen and Kent Harold Richards, *Interpreting Biblical Poetry* (Minneapolis: Fortress, 1992). Marvin E. Tate reviews such studies of the nature of Hebrew poetry in his 2004 supplement to Craigie, *Psalms 1–50*, 371–414.

First, the division into verses recognizes that poetic sentences tend to be shorter than prose sentences. In vv. 3–5, for instance, each sentence comprises six words. It is also characteristic of Hebrew poetry that vv. 3–5 divide neatly into two halves, as do vv. 1, 6, and 9. In vv. 3–5 the second half restates the first half, as also happens in vv. 1 and 9—though not in v. 6, where the second half completes the first. Thus vv. 1a, 3a, 4a, 5a, and 9a could stand alone as a complete sentence, as could vv. 1b, 3b, 4b, 5b, and 9b.

These verses thus introduce us to some characteristic formal features of the poetry of the Psalms. First, a sentence—that is, a line of poetry—often contains about six words divided into two groups, usually with three words each. I refer to such a line as a bicolon, made up of two cola (a three-colon line such as vv. 2, 7, and 8 is then a tricolon). Occasionally the second half of the line simply repeats the first part in different words and thus underlines it, but usually it goes beyond it in some way, for instance to sharpen the point or take it further or give it precision or clarify its ambiguity or complete it. Verses 1 and 5 provide examples. The traditional term for the stereophonic complementariness of the two cola is "parallelism," though this risks understating the way in which the second colon characteristically goes beyond the first.[45] We could not dispense with the second colon and lose nothing. Verse 6, where there is no parallelism at all but where either colon would be incomplete without the other, is an extreme version of the complementariness that regularly characterizes these lines, but it also underlines the danger in seeing parallelism as essential to the poetic form of a bicolon. When the two cola follow the strict pattern whereby two pairs of three words are parallel, these may also come in parallel order ($abca'b'c'$) or in an apparently randomly variant order (e.g., $abcb'c'a'$) or as stepped structures ($abcc'b'a'$). In both cola in v. 4 the subject precedes the verb, giving the subject emphasis (in Ps. 23, which we consider below under "Language," the same thing happens in vv. 4c–d and 6, while prepositional phrases similarly precede the verbs in v. 2). Sometimes the word order thus helps to make the point.

The complementariness of the cola extends to allowing a word that occurs in one colon to apply also to the other: thus the verb in v. 8b applies also to v. 8c. That practice can apply to smaller parts of speech such as prepositions and suffixes. It also means that compound expressions can be divided between two cola. Thus Ps. 42:8 [9] denotes not that Yhwh would show commitment (only) by day and the suppliant would offer

---

45. Alter (*Art of Biblical Poetry*, 29–37) offers an analysis of the variety of forms of parallelism in Ps. 18 (synonymity, complementarity, intensification/specification, consequentiality).

praise for that (only) by night, but that day and night Yhwh would show commitment and the suppliant would respond with praise.

Although the bicolon is the default sentence unit in the Psalms, Ps. 2 illustrates the way sentences can extend beyond one line, and parallelism can operate between lines as well as between cola. In vv. 1–2 the first two cola in v. 2 stand in parallelism with v. 1 as well as in internal parallelism with each other, and the third colon in v. 2 then qualifies vv. 1–2 as a whole. Like parallelism within a verse, parallelism between lines may (e.g.) follow an *abb'a'* order. Psalm 2 is also a rare instance of a Psalm that divides into sections or strophes of consistent length (in this case, each section comprises three lines), but generally efforts so to understand Psalms seem to impose structures on them artificially.

A second feature of the Psalms' poetry is that the default rhythmic arrangement of the lines is 3-3—that is, there are three words in each colon. To be more accurate, there are three stresses, because where words are joined by a *maqqēph*, or hyphen, the first word loses its accent and rhythmically the pair of words counts as one. Thus in v. 1 "recite" is hyphenated into "emptiness," in v. 3 the object-marker is hyphenated into "their fetters," and in v. 4 "laughs" is hyphenated into "at them." In MT the rhythm of v. 1 is thus 3-2, not 3-3 as it might appear, v. 3 is 2-3, and v. 4 is another 3-2. The 3-2 rhythm is the second most common regular rhythm in the Psalms, used especially for more reflective or distraught prayers (e.g., the opening verses of Pss. 14 and 27; also 119:25–32). In that connection, its effect is to keep bringing readers up short as the line stops one word sooner than we expect; the verse thus reflects the way life brings us up short.

Here in Ps. 2 that hardly applies. In v. 1, at least, it is tempting to reckon that the Masoretes were mistaken in their punctuation and that the line should be read as 3-3. But that risks importing an alien regularity into the psalm's rhythm. It is clear that many lines in the Psalms are neither 3-3 nor 3-2 nor (e.g.) 4-4 nor any other regular rhythm. In Ps. 2, v. 5 is a six-word line but divided 4-2. Verse 2 has ten words but only six stresses, arranged 2-2-2; I have laid that out as a tricolon. Verse 6 has seven words but five stresses, 3-2. Verse 7 is a 4-4-3 tricolon and v. 8 a 2-3-2 tricolon. Psalm 2 thus illustrates how the poetry of the Psalms does not follow a regular meter or rhythm; it is more regular than that of the Prophets but less so than that of the Wisdom books. This variety means it is hazardous for us to revise the Masoretes' prosody on the basis of a mistaken assumption that the Psalms' poetry may be expected to manifest a regular rhythm.[46] While 3-3 is a common rhythmic arrangement, cola may have two, three, or four stresses—or even one or five.

---

46. This is also a problem with the proposal to understand the Psalms' prosody on the basis of syllable count: see, e.g., Fokkelman, *Major Poems*.

It has been customary to emend the actual text of the Psalms on the assumption that they must have had a fairly regular rhythm. While emendation for the sake of the meter is now less common, *BHS* still suggests that "against Yhwh and against his anointed" in v. 2 is a gloss (v. 2 can then become a 3-3 line). More definitively, it directs us to omit (e.g.) "Yhwh" in 4:8 [9] "m cs," (*metri causa*, for the sake of the meter), likewise the same word in 5:4, and perhaps the word "because of my attackers" in 9:13 [14] and the word "anymore" in 10:18. I assume that the fact that the rhythm of the Psalms is inherently irregular means that irregularity in the meter is never a basis for emendation, even though I have sometimes differed from MT in the division of the text into lines and cola.

It is worth noting when the rhythm of a line stands out, when a line is (e.g.) especially long or short or oddly constructed, and asking what might be the effect of that. For instance, sometimes a tricolon marks the end of a section or the end of a psalm, and occasionally a line comprises only one colon. A related consideration is that the psalmists like to repeat words in a way that to modern readers may seem stylistically jejune (e.g., 1:2, 6). This contrasts with the way they like to incorporate variation in refrains and repetitions rather than repeat exactly the same line (as in Pss. 42–43). At this point the textual critic has to resist the instinct to introduce variety into their repetitions or exactitude into their instinct for variation.

Although the headings and contents of the Psalms make clear that they were often sung, they were apparently sung in a way that did not require regular meter in the manner of modern hymnody. It may be that they were sung by means of something like traditional Anglican chant, which itself descended via plainsong from synagogue forms of psalm singing. These allow for a varying number of words to be sung on one note, the "tune" being confined to the beginning and/or ending of the colon. More anachronistically but perhaps more helpfully, we might consider the rhythmic nature of psalmody in light of the rhythmic nature of blues, rap, or modern worship songs, where the music has a regular rhythmic form but varying numbers of words can be fitted into a bar. Blues and rap depend on a regular rhythm but can allow for vast difference in the number of words in each bar or at each beat. Many modern Christian songs such as the setting of "I am the Bread of Life" work in the same way. Also analogous is the approach to singing the Psalms developed by Joseph Gelineau, which again uses (semi)regular rhythms but varies the number of words in each bar in accordance with the wording of the Psalms.[47] If the Israelites did not sing the Psalms by a method such as

---

47. See *The Psalms: A New Translation* (Philadelphia: Westminster, 1963).

that of rap or Father Gelineau, they should have done so. And if they said or sang the Psalms responsively, then the characteristic division of lines into two halves would imply doing so by half-verses, not by whole verses as Christians often do.

There are psalms that alternate between (e.g.) "I," "we," "you," and "they," and in some instances this may indicate that the psalm constitutes a liturgy involving different participants. Psalm 118 is a good example, where we may plausibly see different verses spoken or sung by priest(s), king, and people, though we cannot be certain how to allocate the parts. It seems that even within the OT period, eventually such psalms came to be used in worship or devotion without any awareness of the way they had once been used liturgically.

Language

Psalms and prose prayers also differ significantly in language. One aspect of this is that poetic language is more compact and dense; a six-word poetic line may say much more than a twelve-word prose sentence. One mechanical reason for this is that poetry is inclined to leave out words such as particles that provide the links in prose; in Hebrew, this applies to words such as the relative *'ăšer* and the object marker *'ēt* (though there are two instances of the latter in Ps. 2). That is a facet of the way poetic grammar and syntax differ from those of prose. This includes the use of the Hebrew verb forms qatal and yiqtol (perfect and imperfect). The nature of the Psalms' contents requires less use of the qatal as a narrative verb form referring to past events. On the other hand, the qatal is used to describe what is characteristically the case more often than happens in prose. Conversely, the yiqtol is used more often to refer to past events than happens in prose, and not only to events for which an English imperfect would be appropriate. There is probably a historical explanation for this: this poetic usage preserves a significance of the yiqtol that hardly appears in prose.[48] The combined effect of these differences is to make the use of qatal and yiqtol overlap more than they do in prose, and psalmists capitalize on that by pairing the two forms in parallel cola. This happens in Ps. 2:1–2, where there is little difference in meaning between the qatals in the first and fourth cola and the yiqtols in the second and third. Elsewhere (e.g., Ps. 18), the yiqtol seems to be simply used as a past tense equivalent to an aorist, where prose would use a qatal or wayyiqtol.

Prose language majors on clarity; poetic language majors on suggestiveness. Psalm 23 provides a notable example.

---

48. See, e.g., the discussion in *IBHS* 29.

> ¹My shepherd is Yhwh; I do not lack—
>   ²he makes me lie down in grassy pastures.
> He guides me by completely restful waters;
>   ³he restores my life.
> He leads me in right paths
>   for his name's sake.
> ⁴Even when I walk in the darkest canyon,
>   I do not fear trouble,
> Because you are with me; your rod and your staff—
>   they comfort me.
> ⁵You lay a table before me
>   in the presence of my enemies.
> You bathe my head with oil;
>   my cup amply satisfies.
> ⁶Good and commitment will certainly chase me
>   all the days of my life.
> I will return to/dwell in Yhwh's house
>   for long days.

Psalm 23 has been particularly cherished in Jewish and Christian spirituality, though it is most associated with funerals. Its preciousness derives in part from its lyricism and metaphor. One cannot tie down any aspect of some concrete situation that its author had in mind. Everything is imagery. The consequence is that readers can directly access the psalm through their own experience of (e.g.) lack, provision, darkness, fear, and trouble. This may be especially easy for people who (e.g.) have experience of shepherding or dark canyons, but it is also quite possible for people who have no such experience, because the metaphors themselves have a capacity to transcend cultural and experiential gaps. Interpreting a psalm such as this cannot focus on seeking to establish the specific experience out of which it came. It focuses on the metaphors the psalm uses, so as to enter as deeply as possible into their content and resonances.

The openness of metaphor means that the way readers read a psalm may reveal to them important things about themselves. As we read the Psalms, they read us. Psalm 139 is a notable example. It makes a long series of statements about the way God can know all about us and we can never be beyond God's reach. It does not indicate whether this is good news or not, but simply makes objective statements. It then leaves readers to decide whether God's knowing all about us and always having access to us is good news or bad news. The way we read the psalm then tells us something about ourselves and our relationship with God. The psalm works precisely by being ambiguous, allusive, and open.

Much of the power of poetry comes from its use of imagery. Images have affective appeal, telling us what ideas feel like, and they also extend our knowledge: they make it possible to see and say new things. They are especially important in making statements about God, because we cannot make direct statements about God except ones such as "God exists" and "God is holy." We need the kind of images of which (e.g.) Pss. 23; 139; 95; and 100 are full. The problems about images are then similar to the problems about parables. They become overfamiliar (e.g., talk in terms of salvation). They become concepts or doctrines (e.g., God as creator). They are more culture-relative than we think (e.g., talk of God as father). They become obscure (e.g., the references to bulls and openmouthed lions in Ps. 22).

We have to recall the Psalms' commitment to imagery as we wonder what literal events lie behind a psalm. Psalms 42–43, for instance, speak of inner longing, weeping, insults, geographical isolation, drowning, mourning, oppression, physical attack, injustice, and deceit. The suppliant may not have been the victim of all these. Psalms 42–43 also illustrate another aspect of the interpretation of imagery. The precise way in which the Psalms describe human experiences may seem unfamiliar to us, but behind their concrete images, they often describe what a situation felt like in terms not so different from ours: "Everything was against me, God was miles away, things got on top of me, I was devastated, it was overwhelming."[49]

Form

Whether we realize it or not, prayer and praise follow forms. These help us to articulate what we want to say and help other people say "Amen" to our praises and prayers. Poetry, too, traditionally follows some form, and there are certain features that recur in different types of psalm. The creative work in analyzing these was the achievement of Hermann Gunkel. To schematize it, he identified three main ways of speaking to God in the Psalms: praise, thanksgiving, and prayer—*těhillâ, tôdâ,* and *těpillâ*. Gunkel called these hymns, thanksgivings, and laments;[50] Claus Westermann prefers to speak of descriptive praise (describing who Yhwh is), declarative praise (declaring what Yhwh has done for the worshipper[s]), and laments.[51] Each of these forms of speech has recurrent features, though psalmists use their forms with creativity and individuality; indeed, we do not know whether they would have recognized themselves as either following a form or varying it. Further,

---

49. Keel's *Symbolism of the Biblical World* provides the Middle Eastern background to many images that may be obscure or unfamiliar.
50. See Gunkel, *Psalms; Introduction to Psalms; Psalmen.*
51. See his *Praise and Lament; Living Psalms.*

not all psalms fit the types, and it is a mistake to try to make them do so. I have mentioned Ps. 139, and it is also an example of a psalm that seems to have been written somewhat independently of the types. We will consider the specifics of the forms further in looking at "The Psalms and Worship" and "The Psalms and Spirituality."

Awareness of the characteristic features of praise, thanksgiving, and prayer helps us understand the regular features and thus the central dynamic of each of these ways of speaking to God. Then we can compare and contrast them with our own speech and thereby learn how to express ourselves in worship. It also helps us perceive the distinctiveness of particular examples of each form. A praise psalm, for instance, characteristically comprises an invitation to worship and reasons for worship; contrasting (e.g.) Ps. 95 with Ps. 100 helps us see how distinctive is the last section of Ps. 95, in which the psalm addresses the worshippers instead of the worshippers addressing God. Similarly, a prayer psalm characteristically looks back and/or forward to praise; contrasting (e.g.) Ps. 88 with other examples helps us see how distinctive is its unrelenting lament and protest. While this distinctiveness of Ps. 88 likely also points to a profound and far-reaching sense of abandonment, another implication of the fact that we are reading poetry is that we should be wary of seeking to come to a psychological interpretation of a psalm. The psalmist was probably not journaling about experiential feelings in the actual midst of going through pain and suffering.[52] John Eaton comments about Ps. 38, "It is hard to imagine that anyone in the appalling physical condition depicted in this psalm could either have composed or rendered it. It is a work of controlled artistry, as are all the psalms."[53] Poetry and hymnody reflect experience but are often written in light of reflection on an experience rather than in the midst of it, and we may reckon that the same is true of psalms. Indeed, like secular songs that tell a story, they may not be directly autobiographical at all.

We do not know whether worshippers typically would have formulated their prayers or praises orally. If so, the written form will have issued from their being written down later by the suppliant or by someone else. That might have been designed to provide a record of what the suppliant has said to God: hence, when a prayer was answered, the written evidence of the prayer would enhance the glorifying of God for the answer, or the written form would stand before God as an ongoing challenge. The written form of a thanksgiving would be evidence that one had fulfilled one's promise to give testimony to God's act and would constitute an ongoing glorifying of God. Or groups such as the Korahites

---

52. Contrast Weiser's interpretation of, e.g., Ps. 35 (*Psalms*, 300–304).
53. *Psalms*, 109.

might value having it in its written form as part of their repertoire and part of a collection of models of thanksgiving and prayer. But we can imagine that other psalms were composed in writing by people such as the Korahites themselves and then became part of the oral repertoire of choir and/or congregation.

The Psalms and Worship

As well as studying the characteristic constituents of a form, Gunkel was interested in the Psalms' social context (*Sitz im Leben*). This usefully sidestepped the question about the particular historical context in which individual psalms were written, a question that cannot be answered. It replaced this with a question about the recurrent social context in which psalms were written and used, which promised to be more illuminating for our understanding of them. Admittedly, while Gunkel saw this as the right question to ask, his approach to answering it was skewed because he emphasized the significance of "piety which has freed itself of all ceremonies" and is purely "a religion of the heart."[54] While the Psalms eventually do take a place in the context of individual spirituality and individual study, in origin many of them belong at least as intrinsically in the context of liturgical worship and priestly ministry, in the temple, in other sanctuaries, and later in the synagogue and other community settings for worship and ministry. As the vehicles of such corporate worship and piety, in principle they express just as profound a spirituality as the individual piety Gunkel emphasized. And even as the incorporation of compositions such as Pss. 1 and 119 marks the Psalter as relating to individual piety, the headings of many psalms suggest an opposite development. Psalm 30, an individual thanksgiving, becomes "a song for the dedication of the temple." Psalms 120–34 become pilgrimage or processional songs.

Praise

We have recognized that many psalm headings are difficult to interpret,[55] but we can tell that many refer to the use of the psalm in worship. Some refer to worship occasions (e.g., 30; 38; 70) or to temple ministers or choirs or the worship leader (e.g., 4; 6; 8). Some seem to refer to ways

---

54. *Psalms*, 26. By the time he wrote his *Introduction to Psalms*, completed by Joachim Begrich after his death in 1932, his view was more nuanced, though he was still concerned to distance his views from those of Sigmund Mowinckel, who emphasized the psalms' context in worship.

55. For a survey of interpretations, see Kraus, *Psalms*, 1:21–32.

of singing or tunes (e.g., 6; 9; 12) or to instruments (e.g., 4; 5; 6). In general, they parallel the headings to hymns and songs such as "common meter" or "capo on second fret," which are difficult to understand in a different culture, but it is significant that in general they point us to worship as the psalms' context.

Many references to psalms and psalm-like compositions elsewhere in the OT point in the same direction, though they also nuance the point. First, the OT story tells of the community or of individuals offering psalm-like worship on the occasion of great events such as the deliverance at the Red Sea, the victory over Jabin, the birth of Samuel, and a battle against Ammon and Moab (Exod. 15; Judg. 5; 1 Sam. 2; 2 Chron. 20). The first and last of these take place at the scene of the event itself, the third in a sanctuary, so all three presuppose the context of the community's worship (Judg. 5 is not specific about its setting). Chronicles also tells of the use of actual material from Psalms at the move of the covenant chest to Jerusalem and at the temple's dedication (1 Chron. 16; 2 Chron. 7), and Ezra 3 tells of similar use at the reestablishing of the altar after the exile.

Such indicators in the headings and elsewhere in the OT cohere with the contents of many actual psalms.

> Come, let us resound for Yhwh,
> > let us shout for our rock, our deliverer.
> Let us come before him with thanksgiving,
> > shout for him with music. . . .
> Come, let us bow down, let us kneel,
> > let us bend the knee before Yhwh our maker. (Ps. 95:1–2, 6)
>
> Shout for Yhwh, all the earth;
> > serve Yhwh with joy,
> > come before him with resounding. . . .
> Come into his gates with thanksgiving,
> > into his courts with praise;
> > confess him, worship his name. (Ps. 100:1–2, 4)

We cannot press all this language; the summons to "all the earth" is surely figurative. But it makes more sense to see that as a figurative summons to an actual act of worship in the temple (Yhwh's gates/courts) than to see the whole psalm as (for instance) worship offered by individuals in their hearts.

It was Sigmund Mowinckel who spotted that Gunkel's prejudices had led him astray and that the Psalms' setting is indeed the worship of the people of God—what Mowinckel calls the cult (he does not mean heretical cults).

> The cult is a general phenomenon appearing in all religions, even the most "anti-cultic" Protestant sects and groups. It is indeed an essential and constitutive feature of a religion, that in which the nature and spiritual structure of a religion is most clearly manifested. . . . Cult or ritual may be defined as the socially established and regulated holy acts and words in which the encounter and communion of the Deity with the congregation is established, developed, and brought to its ultimate goal. In other words: a relation in which a religion becomes a vitalizing function as a communion of God and congregation, and of the members of the congregation amongst themselves.[56]

Israel's worship is the context in which people give powerful heartfelt expression to their relationship with God; there they experience God reaching out to them to speak and act, and they have their own fellowship expressed and deepened. The nature of such worship is to use forms, as it is the nature of individual prayers and praises to use forms; we are familiar with the fact that even congregations who do not use formal liturgies develop set ways of arranging their worship. The Psalms reflect the forms of the worship offered in that context.

Psalms 95 and 100 are examples of Gunkel's "hymns" or Westermann's "descriptive praise," praise from the community's worship that celebrates who God is, what God did in creation, and what God has done for Israel over the centuries. Other psalms express thanksgiving to Yhwh for specific acts of compassion and power experienced by the present community or by individuals within it (e.g., Ps. 30). Such thanksgiving is part of public worship, even when it is an individual who is giving thanks. By its nature, thanksgiving is a public, communal exercise, an act of confession (the verb "confess" in Ps. 100:4, *yādâ* hiphil, is related to the word "thanksgiving," *tôdâ*). In thanksgiving we give public testimony to what God has done. Thus people's immediate thanksgiving might naturally take place in the everyday life context in which they have experienced Yhwh's act of restoration or deliverance. But that is incomplete without going on to express thanksgiving in a psalm spoken or sung in a worship setting in a local sanctuary, in the first or second temple, in a synagogue, or in some other such context.

Prayer in the sense of supplication or intercession might also belong in the context of corporate worship. That is so in different senses with (e.g.) Solomon's prayer in 1 Kings 8, Jehoshaphat's in 2 Chron. 20, and Ezra's in Ezra 9. There are occasions when whole communities need to mourn, protest, and pray, as happens when (e.g.) a disaster devastates

---

56. *Psalms in Israel's Worship*, 1:15.

a community, and the Psalms are the prayers the Israelite community used on such occasions.[57]

In the case of more individual prayers outside the Psalter, there is no reference to such a context for Nehemiah's first prayer (Neh. 1) or for Daniel's prayer (Dan. 9). On the other hand, an individual in need such as Hannah prays her prayer at a sanctuary (1 Sam. 1), and Job prays his prayers in the company of the friends who are there to join him in his suffering and to support him in his bringing it before God—even if they end up providing a negative example. Thus even the prayers, laments, and protests of the individual could belong in the context of a sanctuary, the temple, a synagogue, or some other (small group) corporate context.[58]

There are varying views on how historical are these various narratives about prayer, but this does not affect their significance for an understanding of the setting of Israelite psalmody; even a fictional story would be likely to reflect the way people actually worshipped in the writer's day. This evidence thus confirms that one important context for the use of the Psalms would be the community's corporate worship.

Invitation and Reasons

The quotations from Pss. 95 and 100 illustrate one of the two formal features of Israelite praise, that it characteristically begins with an invitation or a challenge to worship, in first-person form (Ps. 95) or second-person form (Ps. 100). In both psalms the invitation or challenge comes twice, at the beginning and then resumptively later. In this praise the emphasis lies on loud and animated sound, in music and shouting. English translations routinely introduce words such as "joy," but Ps. 95 does not use such words. It no doubt assumes the sound is an expression of joy (as Ps. 100:2 makes explicit), but its emphasis lies on the sound, not the attitude. The renewed self-invitation in Ps. 95:6 is parallel in constituting an invitation to bodily action; once more, every verb is a body-word (again, contrast EVV). But the nature of the action and its implicit significance is quite different as the worship moves from noise to prostration. Psalm 100 indicates a complementary shift between its two invitations. This time the first verse again envisages noise, the second verse movement from life outside to worship inside the temple.

---

57. Cf. Gerald A. Arbuckle, *Grieving for Change* (Sydney: St Paul Publications; London: Chapman, 1991), on the application of this to groups today.

58. See Miller, *Interpreting the Psalms*, 6–7, following Erhard Gerstenberger, *Der bittende Mensch* (Neukirchen-Vluyn: Neukirchener Verlag, 1980).

We may set the words in Pss. 95 and 100 in the broader context of the Psalms' terms that are translated by words for worship and praise in EVV. These include:

bārak = bow the knee (e.g., 16:7)
dāraš = have recourse to, consult, seek guidance and help from (e.g., 24:6)
hālal = make a lalalalala noise (e.g., 22:23 [24])
zākar = cause people to think about, commemorate (e.g., 20:7 [8])
zāmar = make music (e.g., 21:13 [14])
yādâ = confess (e.g., 30:9 [10])
yārē' = revere (e.g., 33:8)
kāra' = kneel (e.g., 95:6)
'ābad = serve (e.g., 100:2)
qādam = come near (e.g., 95:2)
rānan = make a n-n-n-n noise (e.g., 33:1)
rûa' = shout (e.g., 95:1)
šābaḥ = commend (e.g., 63:3 [4])
šāḥâ/ḥāwâ = bow prostrate (e.g., 5:7 [8])

These terms combine body words, sound words, attitude words, and words for the purpose expressed in the praise. They are notably short on references to feelings; the feelings come out in the actions. None imply that "worship" involves acknowledging God's "worth-ship," as the etymology of the English word suggests—though no doubt a psalmist would acknowledge that this was true. One word (*'ābad*) coheres with the idea that worship is something that involves the whole of life; most of the terms refer to the distinctive acts characteristic of worship in the narrow sense.

The second of the two formal features of Israelite praise is a statement of the reasons for the praise.

> ... For Yhwh is a great God,
>   a great king over all divine beings,
> One in whose hand are earth's depths
>   and to whom the mountain peaks belong,
> One to whom the sea belongs—he made it,
>   and the dry land—his hands fashioned it. ...
> For he is our God
>   and we are the people he pastures,
>   the flock in his hand. (Ps. 95:3-5, 7)

> . . . Acknowledge that Yhwh is God;
>   it is he that made us,
>   and we belong to him. . . .
> For Yhwh is good,
>   his commitment is permanent,
>   his truthfulness lasts forever. (Ps. 100:3, 5)

The reasons for praise are also the contents of praise. The reasons in these two psalms are typical: Yhwh's greatness and goodness, Yhwh's lordship over the world as its creator, and Yhwh's particular commitment to Israel. The reasons do not lie in specifics of what Yhwh has done just now for this people or for an individual; in that circumstance, one's praise takes the form of thanksgiving.

Further examples of praise psalms with these two features, the invitation to praise and the reasons for praise, are Pss. 33; 47; 48; 65; 95; 96; 97; 98; 99; 100; 104; 105; 111; 113; 117; 135; 145; 146; 147; 148; 149; and 150. Many of these follow this pattern with creative variation, while Pss. 8; 19; 29; 68; 78; 87; 93; 114; 122; and 134 are praise psalms that are even more independently minded. On the other hand, Ps. 147 goes through the pattern in Pss. 95 and 100 not just twice but three times.

The New Year Festival

During the twentieth century scholars tried to be more specific about the Psalms' worship context and suggested a number of hypotheses on the matter.

The outline of Israel's worship year appears in Lev. 23 and Deut. 16 (for other references to occasions in this calendar see, e.g., Exod. 12; Deut. 31; Esther 9; John 10:22). Major writers on the Psalms have assumed that many psalms would link with one of the key worship festivals, as many Christian hymns link with festivals such as Christmas and Easter. They usually assume the key occasion would be Sukkot (Tabernacles/Shelters/Booths), the harvest festival in September/October. This festival comes at the turning point of the agricultural year, when people are looking back over the year and looking forward to the coming of the rains that make it possible to begin the new farming year. Sukkot thus seems to have been *the* feast (cf. 1 Sam. 1). It was at this festival time that the temple was dedicated (1 Kings 8). But there is disagreement on the significance of this festival for the Psalms.

Sigmund Mowinckel saw it as a celebration of Yhwh's being king and reasserting kingly authority in the world.[59] Psalm 47 offers a starting point for appreciating this understanding (see also Pss. 93; 95–99).

---

59. See *Psalms in Israel's Worship*, 1:106–92.

> All you peoples, clap hands,
>> shout for God with a resounding voice,
> For Yhwh, the Most High, is to be revered
>> as the great king over all the earth.
> He subdued peoples beneath us,
>> nations under our feet.
> He chose out for us our possession,
>> the majesty of Jacob, that which he loved.
> God has gone up with a shout,
>> Yhwh with the sound of the trumpet.
>
> Make music for God, make music;
>> make music for our king, make music.
> For God is king of all the earth;
>> make music with instruction.
> God has become king over the nations;
>> God has sat on his holy throne.
> The leaders of the peoples have gathered
>> with the people of the God of Abraham.
> For with God are the shields of the earth;
>> he is highly exalted.

In Babylon, each New Year (in the spring in Babylon) the community celebrated the fact that at this moment the god indeed took up his throne again, and Mowinckel inferred that this would have been the key motif at the equivalent Israelite festival.

Artur Weiser started from the conviction that Mowinckel was right about the key importance of Sukkot as background to the Psalms but that in his understanding of this festival he was too influenced by the ethos of Babylonian worship, which he read into the OT. Weiser suggested that it was better to see the festival as a celebration of Yhwh's covenant with Israel.[60] Psalm 50 then illuminates Weiser's understanding.

> El, God, Yhwh has spoken
>> and summoned the earth from the rising of the sun to its setting.
> From Zion, the perfection of beauty, God has shone out;
>> our God comes and does not stay silent.
> Fire consumes before him,
>> around him it storms mightily.
> He calls to the heavens above,
>> and to the earth, to adjudicate for his people.
> "Gather to me my committed ones,
>> those who sealed a covenant with me with a sacrifice."

---

60. See Weiser, *Psalms*.

> The heavens proclaimed his faithfulness,
>   for God is one who makes decisions.
> "Listen, my people, and I will speak,
>   listen, Israel and I will arraign you. . . ."
>
> To the faithless person God has said,
> "What right do you have to recite my statutes,
>   to take my covenant on your lips,
> When you have spurned instruction,
>   cast my words behind you? . . ."

The collocation of reference to Zion, the covenant, and Yhwh's speaking, Weiser suggests, implies a background in the affirming of the Sinai covenant that would have taken place in the context of a reading of the Torah at Sukkot as required in Deut. 31 (though admittedly that refers to a reading only every seven years).

Like many psalms, Ps. 50 presupposes the conviction that Yhwh dwells on Mount Zion. Hans-Joachim Kraus reckoned that Jerusalem is actually more central to the Psalms than Weiser allowed, and he saw the New Year festival as a celebration of Yhwh's commitment to Zion and to David's line enthroned there.[61] Psalm 46 then makes a starting point for understanding Kraus's approach to the Psalms.

> God is for us a refuge and stronghold,
>   a help in trouble, very available.
> Therefore we would not be afraid when the earth changed
>   or when the mountains toppled into the heart of the sea,
> When its waters roar and foam,
>   when the mountains shudder at its swell.
>
> A river with its streams—they rejoice God's city,
>   the holiest dwelling of the Most High.
> God is in its midst, it will not topple;
>   God will help it before morning comes.
> Nations roar, kingdoms topple;
>   he gives voice, the earth dissolves.
> Yhwh Armies is with us;
>   Jacob's God is a refuge for us.
>
> Come and look at Yhwh's deeds,
>   the great desolation that he wrought on the earth,
> Stopping wars to earth's end,
>   breaking the bow and snapping the spear,
>   burning wagons in fire.

---

61. See *Psalms*, vols. 1–2.

> Stop, and acknowledge that I am Yhwh;
>   I will be lofty among the nations, I will be lofty in the earth.
> Yhwh Armies is with us,
>   Jacob's God is a refuge for us.

In Ps. 50, Zion is the place from which Yhwh speaks; here in Ps. 46 it is the place where Yhwh acts. It is Yhwh's city, the place where Yhwh had agreed to dwell when David leaned on Yhwh to do so (see 2 Sam. 6–7). That made Yhwh committed to the defense of this city; one defends one's home. The city's human inhabitants can therefore trust that the nations' assertiveness against this city will get them nowhere. Kraus infers that the celebration of Sukkot in Jerusalem during the monarchy would give Sukkot a new focus; he infers that such a celebration is the background to the psalms, with their interest in Zion and in David.

It is a plausible view that a number of psalms were associated with Sukkot and that this festival would have celebrated Yhwh's kingship, Yhwh's covenant at Sinai, and Yhwh's commitment to Zion and to David. Yet to reckon that there was one festival with which psalms should be especially linked seems without evidence and counterintuitive. It is surely likely that psalms would have been sung on many occasions, not least on Passover (with which Pss. 113–18 were later linked), but also (e.g.) on Pentecost, the Day of Atonement, and the Sabbath. Further, it is a hazardous assumption that a psalm referring to a theme of Israel's faith (e.g., the covenant) must connect with a festival that celebrated that theme. Among Christian hymns, "O Come, All Ye Faithful" with its telling of the Christmas story does connect with Christmas, but "When I Survey the Wondrous Cross" is sung at many different times of year and not just on Good Friday. Scholars are inclined to infer the nature of Israelite worship from the words of the Psalms,[62] but we cannot infer the nature of Christian worship from the words of Christian hymnody, and it is no more plausible to do so with Israelite worship.

In reaction to the stress on the temple and its festivals, Erhard Gerstenberger has worked out the conviction that the Psalms' background lies rather in the worship of the postexilic synagogue.[63] His commentary illumines the Psalms by seeing them against that different setting, but we more likely need to reckon that while the general idea is secure that the Psalms link with Israel's worship, we cannot be specific beyond that. The attempt to do so has been as much of a failure as the attempt to date them. In this commentary, therefore, I make little comment on the

---

62. See, e.g., Weiser's commentary on Ps. 20, *Psalms*, 205–10.
63. See his *Psalms*.

individual psalms' specific liturgical backgrounds or on their implications for an understanding of Israelite liturgy.

Thanksgiving or Testimony

In contrast to praise psalms, which focus on God's characteristic nature, God's work in creation, and great events such as the exodus, thanksgivings focus on what God has done for a particular individual, for a leader, or for the community in delivering them from need. Psalms 18; 21; 30; 32; 34; 41; 66; 73; 92; 103; 107; 116; 118; 120; 124; 136; and 138 are examples. We may call these thanksgiving psalms insofar as they address Yhwh and express people's gratitude for what Yhwh has done for them, or testimony psalms insofar as they both implicitly and explicitly address other people so as to glorify Yhwh in their eyes and build up their trust in Yhwh, or confessional psalms insofar as they acknowledge what God has done. Thanksgiving or testimony is a matter of extolling Yhwh before people because of what Yhwh has done. Its nature is to put more emphasis on the facts of what has happened than on the worshipper's feelings of gratitude. Such confession takes the form *"You* have done this" more than *"We* are so grateful." God even has the glory in the grammar.[64]

Psalm 30 is an example:

> I will exalt you, Yhwh, because you put me down
>   but did not let my enemies rejoice over me.
> Yhwh my God,
>   I cried out to you and you healed me.
> Yhwh, you brought me up from Sheol;
>   you kept me alive from going down to the Pit.
> Make music to Yhwh, people committed to him;
>   confess his holy remembrance.
> For there is an instant in his anger,
>   a life in his delight.
> In evening weeping takes up lodging,
>   but at morning there is resounding.
>
> I myself had said when I was doing well,
>   "I will never falter."
> Yhwh, in your delight
>   you had established strength for my mountain.
> You hid your face;
>   I became terrified.
> On you, Yhwh, I was calling;
>   to my Lord I was pleading for grace.

---

64. Cf. Westermann, *Praise and Lament*, 29–30.

> "What is the profit in my being killed,
>   in my going down to the Abyss?
> Can dirt confess you,
>   proclaim your truthfulness?
> Listen, Yhwh, be gracious to me;
>   Yhwh, become a helper to me."
> You turned my mourning into dancing for me;
>   you undid my sackcloth and girded me with joy,
> So that my heart may make music to you and not wail,
>   and, Yhwh my God, I may confess you forever.

Like Pss. 95 and 100, the testimony goes through its sequence of elements twice, in a large-scale equivalent to the parallelism within individual lines. Even where there is no development between the two parts, the doubling of the structure keeps the psalm moving, keeps the hearers involved, and enables the psalmist to have two runs at expressing adequately what needs to be expressed. From this instance we can see features that recur in thanksgiving/testimony psalms.

First, there is a commitment to praise, in this case expressed in the first-person singular. It is perhaps because it is a commitment to praise in the future that the thanksgivings characteristically use the yiqtol, though the cohortative might seem even more appropriate (the yiqtol, too, could have modal significance—or could refer to the present, as NJPS assumes in translating by a present tense such as "I exalt you"). Then the psalm moves on to its inherently distinctive feature, a recollection of the worshipper's recent experience. Three elements may recur in the recollection: the affliction the person went through, the way the person prayed, and the way God responded. That story in turn leads to a further commitment to praise and an invitation to the rest of the community to join in. Such a commitment and invitation may issue in offering the kind of praise that belongs in an actual praise psalm, the kind that affirms the ongoing nature of God that the worshipper's recent experience has once again proved to be true.

Prophecy and Wisdom

The nature of psalms is to be prayers and praises addressed primarily to God, though secondarily to other worshippers. But we have already considered Pss. 2 and 50, which reverse that natural dynamic and have God speaking rather than being addressed. There are other examples of whole psalms in which God speaks (e.g., 82 and 110) and yet others that quote words from God, such as these:

> "Because of the devastation of the weak, because of the groaning
>   of the needy,
>   now I will arise," Yhwh says;
> "I will take my stand as deliverance," he witnesses to him. (12:5 [6])

> God spoke by his holiness:
> "I will exultantly allocate Shechem,
>   and measure out the Vale of Sukkot.
> Gilead will be mine, Manasseh will be mine,
>   Ephraim will be my helmet,
>   Judah my staff,
> Moab will be my washbasin,
>   at Edom I will throw my shoe;
>   raise a shout against me, Philistia.
> Who will bring me to the fortified city,
>   who might lead me to Edom?" (60:6–9 [8–11])

From time to time the OT refers to the activity of prophets in the context of worship ("cultic prophets"—again, the word "cultic" does not imply that their beliefs are deviant, though prophets who were part of the institutional apparatus were always in danger of saying what people wanted to hear, as are pastors in the church). It is a plausible guess that words from God to congregations or to individuals that appear within the Psalms are words that God gave to prophets—who might be laypeople or priests.

In general, the role of prophets can be seen as involving foretelling and forthtelling. They foretell the future in the sense of declaring God's promises and commitments that are bound to find fulfillment in the people's life, such as the promises or declarations of intent in Pss. 12 and 60 just quoted (see also Pss. 2; 20; 45; 91; 110). They also tell forth God's expectations of people and God's warnings about the consequences of ignoring these words (see Pss. 14; 15; 24; 50; 53; 81; 82; 127). Sometimes such a statement of expectations masquerades as a promise (see Pss. 112; 128; 133). Sometimes people praying may have hoped for an affirmative prophetic word and received the opposite, as happens outside the Psalter (see Jer. 14–15; Hosea 6). Psalms 2 and 110 show how prophets had a particular role in relation to leaders such as the king, and Ps. 72 is at least a magnificent exhortation to the king masquerading as a prayer for him. One would like to think that kings, too, sometimes found prophets confronting them instead of affirming their prayers.

Other psalms manifest the language and insights of wisdom books such as Proverbs. The Psalter in fact begins with a promise of the kind that a wise teacher would offer (Ps. 1), which precedes the first prophetic word (Ps. 2). In the midst of the first half of the Psalter is a psalm that expounds in detail how that opening promise should work out (Ps. 37) and another dealing with attitudes for when it fails to do so (Ps. 49). The second half of the Psalter begins with another dealing with that problem (Ps. 73). Books IV and V also begin with teaching psalms (Pss. 90 and 107), and the second half of the Psalter is dominated by a gargantuan exposition of attitudes toward God's teaching (Ps. 119).[65]

The Psalms and Spirituality

Exploring the explicit teaching element in the Psalter provides us with a segue from the Psalms and worship to the Psalms and spirituality. Even if we cannot discern purposefulness in the detailed order of the Psalter, the presence and location of psalms such as the ones just listed point to the way the Psalms became more explicitly what they had always been implicitly, a manual for spirituality, for relationships with God. The references to music in the headings may indicate that they were sung devotionally in a way not so different from Christian usage.

In this respect the Psalms suggest a delicate balance between various antitheses. A relationship with God is both corporate and individual. It holds together praise and prayer. It is both bodily expressed and inwardly felt. Praise itself holds together the great permanent truths about Yhwh and Yhwh's acting in contemporary life, while prayer holds together trust and protest, hope and hopelessness. The Psalms also envisage a relationship with God that involves both withdrawal (into worship) and engagement (in a faithful life), and both speaking to God and listening to God. By their nature they do not seek to maintain a balance between these but put the stress on worship and prayer rather than on engagement, and on speaking rather than listening. There are other parts of the Scriptures that put the stress the other way, so that the Scriptures as a whole embody a balance between them. The importance of the Psalms is to remind the community that their prayer is important alongside their action and that their side of the conversation is important alongside God's.

Individual and Community

We have noted that the Psalms' social context is Israel's corporate worship. They refer much to Israel and to Zion, to "we" and "us." The

---

65. See James L. Mays, "The Place of the Torah-Psalms in the Psalter," *JBL* 106 (1987): 3–12; and on the development from Ps. 1 to Ps. 150 via Ps. 73, W. Brueggemann's suggestion that we treat the Psalter as a kind of journal recording a journey from obedience via questioning to praise (*Psalms and the Life of Faith*, 189–213).

corporate nature of their spirituality is especially pervasive in the praise of the Psalms. "We" rejoice in Yhwh's past acts in creation and in Israel's story, and "we" acknowledge that Yhwh is faithful and powerful, merciful and decisive. The corporate aspect to the Psalms' spirituality finds further natural expression in prayer, when the community gathers to protest Yhwh's abandonment and then to give thanks for Yhwh's return. A less self-evident corporate aspect to the Psalms' spirituality emerges when individuals give thanks for what God has done for them, because these individuals do that in the company of the community. It is unthinkable that expressing gratitude to God should be a private transaction between individuals and God. Thanksgiving is an inherently public act whereby one gives glory to God in the presence of the community for some act, and invites the community as a whole to have its faith built up. Hence the fact that thanksgiving is testimony. It is also less self-evident that individual prayer should have a corporate aspect, but this, too, is so. Individuals bringing their prayers and protests to God commonly do so at the sanctuary and/or in the presence of friends. At the same time, the Psalms also assume that spirituality is an individual matter. This is most evident with psalms of protest or trust, in many of which an "I" speaks.

The intrinsic link between corporate and individual spirituality is symbolized by the fact that it is harder than we might have thought to distinguish between psalms prayed by individuals and psalms prayed by the community. To complicate this question, a number of psalms seem to express the needs of a leader—a king or a figure such as Ezra or Nehemiah—or to give such a person's testimony after having had a prayer answered. The distinction between the prayers of an ordinary individual and those of a leader can be hard to make, but it might be made as follows:

Of an individual: Pss. 6; 22; 26; 31; 38; 39; 40; 42; 43; 54; 55; 56; 57; 58; 59; 64; 70; 71; 86; 88; 109; 141; 142
Of a leader: Pss. 3; 5; 7; 9–10; 13; 17; 25; 27; 28; 35; 63; 69; 89; 102; 140; 143
Of the congregation: Pss. 12; 44; 60; 67; 74; 79; 80; 83; 85; 90; 94; 106; 123; 126; 137; 144

To complicate this question further, the mere use of "I" or "we" may not tell us which prayers belong to an individual or a leader and which belong to a community. A story from Israel's journey to the land shows why this is so. To illustrate my point, I quote here from the (American) Revised Version of 1881–85, because it uses "thee" and "thou."[66]

> And Moses sent messengers from Kadesh unto the king of Edom, Thus saith thy brother Israel, Thou knowest all the travail that hath befallen us . . . : and, behold, we are in Kadesh, a city in the uttermost of thy border. Let us pass, I pray thee, through thy land; we will not pass through field or through vineyard . . . until we have passed thy border. And Edom said unto him, Thou shalt not pass through me, lest I come out with the sword against thee. And the children of Israel said unto him, We will go up by the highway: and if we drink of thy water, I and my cattle, then will I give the price thereof: let me only . . . pass through on my feet. And he said, Thou shalt not pass through. And Edom came out against him with much people. . . . Thus Edom refused to give Israel passage through his border: wherefore Israel turned away from him. (Num. 20:14–21)

The story moves easily between speaking in terms of "I" (because the community comprises a group of such individuals or because it is one entity, or because a leader speaks on its behalf) and speaking in terms of "we"—yet it is the same people who speak throughout.

In light of that, we can allow for the possibility that the "I" of a psalm may be an ordinary individual, or may be a leader, or may be a member of the congregation as a whole. And we can allow for the possibility that movement between (e.g.) "we" and "I" in a psalm may not mean that the speakers change, only that the way of speaking changes. A further implication is that this aspect of the Psalms becomes another aspect of their fruitful openness or ambiguity. One can imagine people using a particular psalm in all three ways. It is illuminating to read (e.g.) Ps. 51 or 91 or 139 as an individual's prayer, then as a leader's prayer, then as the community's prayer.

The number of prayer psalms in contrast to the number of thanksgiving psalms is striking. Perhaps it suggests that like us, the Israelites often prayed, but only less often saw answers.

Prayer

By their nature, prayer psalms involve expressing hurt and pleading for help, and often protesting at the way things are. They have a series of characteristic features. Psalm 22 illustrates many of them.

> My God, my God, why did you abandon me,
>   far from my deliverance, my bellowing words?

---

66. Cf. Johnson, *Cultic Prophet*, 335–36.

> My God, I call by day and you do not answer,
>> by night, and I have no quietness.
> But you sit as the holy one,
>> the great praise of Israel.
> In you our ancestors trusted,
>> trusted and you rescued them.
> They cried out to you and they escaped;
>> they trusted in you and were not ashamed.
> But I am a worm, not a human being,
>> the scorn of others, despised by people.
> All who see me mock me,
>> open their mouth wide, shake their head.
> "Commit it to Yhwh; he must rescue him,
>> he must save him, since he likes him."
> For you are the one who made me break out of the womb,
>> making me trust on my mother's breast.
> On you I was thrown from birth;
>> from my mother's womb you were my God.
> Do not be far away from me, because trouble is near,
>> because there is no one to help. . . .
>
> But you, Yhwh, do not be far away;
>> my strength, hasten to my help.
> Save my life from the sword,
>> my very self from the power of the dog.
> Deliver me from the mouth of the lion;
>> me in my weakness from the horns of the buffalo.
> I will tell of your name to my kindred,
>> in the midst of the congregation I will praise you.
> You who revere Yhwh, praise him;
>> all you offspring of Jacob, honor him;
>> be in awe of him, all you offspring of Israel.
> For he has not despised, nor has he loathed,
>> the lament of the weak.
> He has not turned his face from him,
>> but when he cried out, listened to him.
> From you will come my praise in the great congregation;
>> my vows I will pay before the people who revere him. . . .
> (Ps. 22:1–11 [2–12], 19–25 [20–26])

The psalm naturally begins by calling on God, though it may do so with some irony, since (in this case) the invocation of Yhwh as "my God" is the introduction to a protest that Yhwh is not behaving as "my God." It is characteristic of prayer psalms to give most space to expressions of pain and protest—hence the conventional title "laments" and the title

I rather prefer, "protests." These can be expressed in three directions.[67] The psalm uses first-person expressions such as "I am a worm, not a human being" to describe how the experience of abandonment felt to the supplicant. It uses third-person expressions such as "all who see me mock at me" to describe the actions and attitudes of other people. And it uses second-person expressions, illustrated by the opening of this psalm, "Why did you abandon me. . . . You do not answer"; one suspects that these would be the most painful of all. The Psalms give people the means of expressing the pain and anger they need to express, yet they are not merely gaining emotional release but addressing another person, someone who is responsible and in a position to do something. Praise psalms affirm the world as it is; in contrast, a protest psalm "legitimates and articulates imagination at the margin. . . . These poems are voices of marginality."[68]

A protest psalm often goes on to speak of the contrast between such present experience and the characteristic nature of God and the way God has acted in the past, as happens twice in the first half of the above illustration. Such recollections might be both painful and hopeful. They are painful because of the fact that God is not acting in this way now. They may also be hopeful because if that is the character of God and God has acted that way in the past, there is the possibility that God could act that way again. A declaration about God's character can thus function as an actual declaration of trust in God that persists despite current experience.

Eventually a prayer psalm will reach prayer in the sense of plea, though it does so with significant contrasts to the way Christians often pray. First, the weight of protest over plea is noteworthy. Protest psalms characteristically give rather little space to plea in the sense of requesting Yhwh to act. In a protest psalm, people tell God what they want in one or two lines. The balance between protest or expression of pain, and plea or request, is the reverse of that which characterizes Christian prayer. Christians are reticent about telling God things that God presumably knows, though they are then oddly unrestrained about itemizing what God should do even though they recognize that God could work this out. Prayer psalms suggest that the aim of prayer is to get God to decide to take action rather than persisting in inaction, and the object of expressing pain and protest is to achieve that. They imply that if God can be provoked to act, God can be left to work out precisely what to do. Thus pleas characteristically express themselves

---

67. Cf. Westermann, *Praise and Lament*, 53–54, 66–69.
68. Walter Brueggemann, *Interpretation and Obedience* (Minneapolis: Fortress, 1991), 192, 193.

in three rather general terms that correspond to the three directions of the protest.[69] They urge God to listen instead of ignoring or abandoning, to deliver the suppliant, and to act against the people who are causing the suppliant trouble, in order to put right a world that is out of kilter.

A further feature of many protest psalms is that within the psalm itself there comes a transition from protest, presupposing God's inactivity, to praise, implying that the suppliant knows God has listened to the prayer and responded (cf., e.g., Ps. 6). In Ps. 22, this praise comes to occupy the whole of the last third of the psalm. Evidently the suppliant has come to be sure that God has indeed heard and is committed to responding. The answer in the form of action will need to follow, but the suppliant knows that it will follow.

One can imagine a number of possible ways in which the suppliant might have reached this conviction; different ones might apply in different cases. In several OT narratives, a suppliant receives an answer from a priest or prophet who makes this transition possible (e.g., 1 Sam. 1). Such a word from a priest or prophet that comes between the protest and the praise might not appear in the psalm itself because the psalm is simply the suppliant's words. The prophet or priest has to listen for Yhwh's response, whether that is then expressed in conventional words of reassurance (as in 1 Sam. 1) or in a special word from Yhwh that cannot be scripted. Psalm 12 might be an exception to this rule: there a word from Yhwh appears.[70] On other occasions the suppliant might recall and claim a word that God has uttered on a previous occasion, as may happen in Ps. 60. Or the suppliant might become open to seeing some truth afresh, as happens in Ps. 73. Or the conviction that God has listened to the prayer might derive from hearing general declarations of Yhwh's acts and faithfulness. Or the very process of pouring oneself out to God might convey the reality of passing one's difficulties on to God and knowing that God has received them (e.g., Ps. 3). One might compare the move with that in Jon. 2, where Jonah gives thanks when he knows he is being delivered (he has not drowned) but is not yet on the shore.[71]

The psalms of pain and protest shock Christians who are not used to this way of talking to God. Yet they have an explicit place in the NT. Jesus uses the phraseology of Pss. 6 and/or 42 in Gethsemane, and on the cross utters the extraordinary cry that opens Ps. 22 (Mark 14:34; 15:34). Nor does Jesus pray these prayers so that we might not have

---

69. Again, cf. Westermann, *Praise and Lament*, 53–54, 66–69.
70. But see the commentary on this psalm.
71. Gerstenberger, *Psalms*, 1:113.

to do so, for a lament such as Ps. 44 appears on the lips of Paul (Rom. 8:36). In the NT, believers grieve and protest. To refuse to do so is often to refuse to face our pains and our losses. But "if we are to mirror God, . . . we have to be willing to enter our individual wounds and through them the wounds of the community, . . . not hide them by casuistry, not seal them up."[72]

Confession of Sin; Trust; Intercession

In the church's tradition, there are seven "Penitential Psalms": Pss. 6; 32; 38; 51; 102; 130; and 143. Psalms 38 and 51 indeed express penitence, but Ps. 32 is a thanksgiving for Yhwh's forgiveness or a testimony to that forgiveness, not a penitential psalm. Psalm 130 acknowledges sinfulness but focuses more on the results of forgiveness, Yhwh's restoration, than on forgiveness in itself. Psalm 143 likewise refers incidentally to the suppliant's sinfulness but focuses on prayer for deliverance. Psalms 6 and 102 both refer to the possibility or the actuality of Yhwh's anger with the suppliant, but they are not explicit that this presupposes that the suppliant has done wrong, and they do not express penitence. Further, there are other psalms that imply that the speaker is not in a situation of gross sin but ask Yhwh not be angry with them (e.g., 27:9; 88:7 [8]; 89:46 [47]). Indeed, it is more characteristic of prayer psalms to assert that one is not a faithless person; that is another element in the form of a protest psalm and another reason why God should answer the prayer. So it is likely that Pss. 6 and 102 are protest psalms like others, not penitential psalms—though a penitent could use them. Even on a conservative estimate, however, penitence and confession have a rather small place in the Psalms. This is not a guide to their place in the OT as a whole, and it might mean that better places to start in understanding confession in the OT would be Lamentations or the prayers in Ezra 9, Neh. 9, or Dan. 9. It does indicate that the spirituality of the Psalms is not dominated by sin in the way that Christian spirituality has been. Designating the seven psalms as the Penitential Psalms "helps to maintain community identity" for the church by "actualizing the epistle to the Romans (as seen in an Augustinian light) in the lives of the faithful."[73] Like Job, the Psalms themselves recognize that everyone is a sinner, but they focus more on the importance of the general orientation of one's life as involving commitment to God than on the peccadilloes that mar this. They assume that the people of God are basically committed to Yhwh. That is part of the basis for an appeal to Yhwh. If they are not so committed,

---

72. Maggie Ross, *Pillars of Flame* (London: SCM, [1988]), xvii.
73. Nasuti, *Defining the Sacred Songs*, 55.

then they had better not be praying at all but putting this right. Then they can praise and pray.

We have noted that another frequent feature of protest psalms is a profession of trust and hope in Yhwh despite the events that generate the protest. In a number of psalms this element is so prominent that they are more appropriately treated as trust psalms than as protest psalms. While the boundary between trust psalms and protest psalms is fuzzy, we might put in this trust category Pss. 4; 11; 16; 23; 36; 46; 52; 61; 62; 63; 75; 76; 77; 84; 101; 108; 115; 119; 121; 125; 129; 131; 132; and 139. These refer to a number of aspects of the content of trust: that Yhwh is watching (Ps. 11), that Yhwh keeps me safe (Ps. 23), and that Yhwh puts the wicked down (Pss. 62; 75). They refer to a number of bases for trust that lie in the suppliant's own experience. These include Yhwh's speaking to me on my own (Ps. 16), Yhwh's presence in the temple (Pss. 36; 84), Yhwh's keeping me safe in the past (Ps. 129), my own commitment to Yhwh (Pss. 101; 119), and my standing against wrongdoing (Ps. 139). They also refer to a number of bases for trust outside my own experience. These include Yhwh's power and love (Pss. 62; 115), Yhwh's creation of the world and sovereignty in it (Ps. 121), Yhwh's deliverance of the people at the Red Sea (Ps. 77), Yhwh's commitment to Jerusalem (Pss. 46; 76), Yhwh's commitment to David (Ps. 132), and Yhwh's specific promises (Pss. 108; 119).

Only one psalm is immediately recognizable as having the form of an intercession, the prayer for the king in Ps. 72, a telling and powerful expression of the way one might pray for the government. Yet since it so tests the rule that there is no special form for intercessions, one must ask why it is so exceptional. I have already hinted at the answer. Psalm 72 is a magnificent exhortation to the king masquerading as a prayer for him. There are also one or two blessings in the Psalter that one might see as having a function like that of an intercession (e.g., Pss. 20; 91), but these are addressed in God's name to a human being (the king again?) rather than to God in the person's name.

So when Israel interceded, how did it do so? Perhaps the answer lies in the consideration we have recognized, that people likely used prayer psalms in the company of others, such as a priest or a group of worshippers or one's family. Those people, then, involve themselves in intercession by standing with a person in need and praying with and for them.[74] Part of that support would be listening to God for them, listening for what response God might offer to their prayer. In a quite literal sense, interceding or intervening on someone's behalf involves putting oneself

---

74. On such use of the Psalms in pastoral work, see Donald Capps, *Biblical Approaches to Pastoral Counseling* (Philadelphia: Westminster, 1981).

in another person's place. It does not involve praying *for* someone so much as praying *with* them and even *as* them. For this reason there are no special forms for intercession. Intercession is simply praying in the first person, by taking on the persona of the one in need.

Anger

Over against regular Christian spirituality, a distinctive feature of the protest psalms is the expression of anger and of desire for one's enemies to be put down.

The OT implies that anger along with (e.g.) hatred is a proper aspect of being a person. It has a place in the full-orbed character of God and thus in that of the human person made in God's image. It is less central to the person than (e.g.) compassion, but it is just as intrinsic. Both divine and human anger are important to the fulfillment of God's purpose in the world. In the context of the Psalms, this means that anger has an essential place in prayer, often expressed as an urgent plea for terrible trouble to come on one's attackers. Psalm 69 provides an example:

> May their table become a trap before them
>   and a snare for their allies.
> May their eyes dim so that they cannot see;
>   make their loins tremble continually.
> Pour out your indignation on them;
>   may your angry burning overtake them.
> May their camp become a desolation,
>   in their tents may no one live. (Ps. 69:22–25 [23–26])

In light of Christ's command to love our enemies, this might seem a prayer no Christian could pray. Erich Zenger relates the reaction any OT lecturer who manifests a "theological sympathy" for the Psalms receives: "Do you really think that, *as Christians* (the question is never *as Jews* or *as human beings*, and certainly not *as victims of rape*) we can pray this way?"[75] Yet Peter and Paul both quote it (Acts 1:16, 20; Rom. 11:9–10). They adapt its interpretation to their need to comment on the departure of Judas and the failure of the Jewish people to recognize Jesus, but this does not change the malevolent nature of the text. It seems that the NT accepts the notion of praying against one's enemies as well as the notion of praying for them.

Analogous considerations apply to the most offensive line in the Psalter.

75. *A God of Vengeance?* 2.

> Lady Babylon, one to be devastated—
> The good fortune of the person who requites you
>   for the deed that you did to us.
> The good fortune of the person who grabs your babies
>   and dashes them on the rocks. (Ps. 137:8–9)

This psalm links not forward with the NT but back with the Prophets, for it asks not for a punishment that its sick imagination dreams up but simply for Yhwh to do what Yhwh has already promised to do (see Isa. 13:13–19).[76] In the NT we might compare it with Paul's declaration: "It is right in God's eyes to repay with affliction the people who afflict you, . . . at the appearing of the Lord Jesus from heaven with his mighty angels in flaming fire, bringing punishment on people who do not know God and do not obey the gospel of our Lord Jesus, people who will suffer the punishment of eternal destruction away from the Lord's face and his mighty splendor" (2 Thess. 1:6–9). Such promises are the background for the plea of the martyrs, "How long, holy and true master, before you judge and avenge our blood on the people who live on the earth," to which the response is that they will only have to wait a little longer (Rev. 6:9–11).

The attitude of the psalms and of the martyrs is that when people resist God and persist in oppressing other people, eventually God must punish them for their wrongdoing and free their victims. But such action lies in God's hands, not in ours. We trust God to take action; and "it is an act of profound faith to entrust one's most precious hatreds to God, knowing they will be taken seriously."[77] It may also be that expressing our anger to God is better than denying that it exists, and also is calculated to make it less likely that we will act in anger (perhaps on people other than those who have wronged us—even on ourselves). But this is not a point the Psalms make.

The Interrelationship of Praise and Prayer

The spirituality of the Psalms embraces praise, thanksgiving, protest, trust, and obedience. These are all mixed up in the Psalter—it does not give us (e.g.) the praise psalms, then the thanksgiving psalms, then the prayer psalms, and so on. The Psalter mirrors and affirms our disordered lives. "Since life does not come to us in neat categories, neither does prayer."[78] Yet we still can ask, What is the relationship between these forms of prayer?

---

76. If Isa. 13 is later than the psalm, then it constitutes a positive response to the prayer in the psalm; the point I make here is thus not affected.
77. Brueggemann, *Message of the Psalms*, 77.
78. Peterson, *Answering God*, 107.

Mowinckel suggested that the starting point for understanding psalmody is the praise psalm,[79] but he did not discuss the relationship of this to other forms. Bernhard W. Anderson similarly comments that "every psalm . . . is actually a song that extols and glorifies God."[80] Westermann sees a more dialectical relationship between praise and prayer: "There is no petition . . . that did not move at least one step . . . on the road to praise. But there is also no praise that was fully separated from the experience of God's wonderful intervention in time of need."[81] He contrasts the Egyptian psalms that mainly praise a god in general terms, not in relation to the god's doing anything, and the Babylonian psalms that mainly praise a god as a lead-in to prayer, not for the god's own sake.[82] Even if this contrast is not justified, the formulation illumines key aspects of the Psalms. Brueggemann adds, "The praise has power to transform the pain. But conversely the present pain also keeps the act of praise honest."[83]

In the "vital, tension-filled polarity of plea and praise," Westermann sees the center in declarative praise, which looks back to the event about which one protested and forward to an ongoing life of praise.[84] In contrast, Brueggemann sees the center in the lament. He builds on a formulation by Paul Ricoeur concerning the way faith develops from orientation (we know who God is and how life works) via disorientation (all this collapses because of something that happens to us) to a renewed orientation (when we can reconceptualize who God is and how life works in a way that takes account of what has happened). Brueggemann sees these three stages reflected in praise psalms, protest psalms, and thanksgiving psalms.[85]

Understanding life with God and the spirituality of the Psalms as a spiral makes it possible to combine these two understandings and to do justice to the linear element in our lives with God.

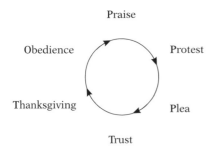

Because one can enter this spiral at any point, its course embraces both Westermann's and Brueggemann's understandings of the relationship between protest, thanksgiving, and praise. Understanding the movement as a spiral also recognizes that the next time a person sings a praise

---

79. *Psalms in Israel's Worship*, 1:81–105.
80. *Out of the Depths*, 39.
81. *Praise and Lament*, 154. Psalm 88 is perhaps an exception to his statement.
82. Ibid., 36–51.
83. *Israel's Praise*, 139.
84. *Praise and Lament*, 154.
85. See, e.g., *Psalms and the Life of Faith*, 3–32.

psalm, the words mean something different. Each time people go around the spiral, each element has more depth. The praise can be more nuanced. The protest can be more urgent. The trust can be deeper. The testimony can be more fervent.

The Psalms as Theology

Theologically, the Psalms are the densest material in the entire OT. There is a greater concentration of statements about God here than anywhere else. That reflects the fact that theology is the key both to worship and to pastoral care, and that worship and pastoral care generate theological insight.

Doxology and theology are closely related. Doxology requires theology; glorifying God involves making many a statement about God. Conversely, theology finds one of its natural forms in doxology. There is a role to be played by dispassionate analytical theological statements, though I cannot remember what it is, but the natural way to make statements that do justice to God's nature is to make them in the form of praise. Dispassionate analytical statements about God deconstruct.

Statements about God are also of key importance to pastoral care. First, the doxological statements to which I have just referred, the statements that are most at home in praise psalms, need to be the statements that shape Israel's worldview. Among other things, they may then issue in and support our living the right kind of life. Second, these are then the statements that Israel needs to keep in mind when trouble comes, when the temptation is to lose sight of or deliberately abandon the convictions about God that one affirmed when the going was not tough. A further significance of Ps. 22, observed above, is the magnificent way it insists on facing two sets of facts. It insists on being utterly real about the facts of abandonment. But it also insists on not losing sight of the facts about God that it also knows are true—who Yhwh is, how Yhwh has related to Israel in the past, and how Yhwh has been involved in the individual's life. When disaster strikes, the temptation is to deny one of the sets of facts. One may do this by refusing to face the reality of the abandonment and loss, or by abandoning the truths about God that one knew before. Psalm 22 insists on looking resolutely in the face both sets of facts.[86] Third, statements about God also have a prominent place in thanksgivings or testimonies, for one significance of these is both to confirm and to nuance affirmations about God to which Israel is committed.

---

86. I think this formulation is not my own, but I do not recall where it comes from.

God: Involved, Creator, Sovereign, at Home

In speaking of God, the Psalms' characteristic affirmation is that God is involved and active in Israel's corporate and individual life, in both its religious and its political aspects, and manifests a concern with both the material and the inward. God's dwelling is in the heavens, but from there God observes what happens on earth and comes to intervene (Ps. 18). God is thus a help and a shield, a deliverer and a rock, a shepherd and a host (Pss. 3; 23). Conversely, God is a threat and a destroyer for the wrongdoer (Ps. 52). The nature of God's involvement is sometimes continuous; it forms the background to the whole of life (Ps. 37). More characteristically, it is punctiliar, interventionist, and in the foreground. God is involved in this way on the basis of a committed relationship with Israel, though also on the basis of moral considerations. It is because Yhwh is a God who hates unfaithfulness, deceit, and violence (Ps. 5). Admittedly, this principle is often honored more in the breach than in the observance—that is, Yhwh is supposed to be involved in people's lives, but this is not working out (Ps. 13). Despite being the holy one and the praise of Israel as one who has acted to deliver in the past, and also being involved in the details of the life of the individual, Yhwh is also one who abandons (Ps. 22). But Yhwh can then reasonably and realistically be urged to return and act again. Then people can celebrate that Yhwh has indeed acted as king once more (Ps. 96).

Yhwh has been involved with Israel through its story, which relates to present worship in a number of ways. It is a basis for praise in the present (Pss. 78; 105), for protest and prayer that urges Yhwh to act now as in the past (Pss. 44; 80), for a challenge to commitment to Yhwh (Ps. 81), and for reflection that drives Israel to a wiser life (Pss. 106; 107).

> In the Psalms, prayer is political action. . . . That we have not collapsed into anarchy is due more to prayer than to the police. . . . The single most widespread American misunderstanding of prayer is that it is private. . . . The best school for prayer continues to be the Psalms. It also turns out to be an immersion in politics. . . . Prayer was [the Psalmists'] characteristic society-shaping and soul-nurturing act. . . . We often imagine (wrongly) that the psalms are private compositions. . . . All of them are corporate: all were prayed by and in the community. . . . We are made citizens of a kingdom, that is, a society. [God] teaches us the language of the kingdom by providing us the psalms, which turn out to be as concerned with rough-and-tumble politics as they are with quiet waters of piety.[87]

87. Peterson, *Where Your Treasure Is*, 6, 8.

Related in a number of ways to Yhwh's involvement in the world in both continuous and punctiliar ways is Yhwh's being the creator of the world. Psalm 104 suggests a number of models for understanding God's relationship with creation. God is like the clockmaker who started creation off and then leaves it to keep going. God is like the farmer who continues to look after creation, being personally involved with it on an ongoing basis. God is the energy or system of nature—including troublesome aspects such as volcanoes. God is the "God of the gaps," the explanation for the miraculous or disastrous things that happen. There are no other divine powers that can resist Yhwh's will. Many heavenly beings stand before Yhwh, but they are responsible to Yhwh for fulfilling their responsibilities in the world (Pss. 58; 82).

Yhwh's being the creator means that the powers of chaos cannot reassert themselves; the world is secure (Ps. 93). It means the cosmos continually declares God's glory (Ps. 19). It makes wondrous the fact that the mighty creator gets involved with mere human beings (Ps. 8). It means God provides for the people's needs each year (Ps. 65). It undergirds God's particular promises to Israel and to David (Ps. 89). As creator, God is the God of everyday life and of the everyday experience and needs of individuals. In the Psalms God is giver, healer, and deliverer more than lawgiver and judge, not merely God of the past (history) and God of the future (eschatology) but also God of the present—of worship and everyday life.

Being the creator means Yhwh is God of the whole world. The particularities of Yhwh's involvement with Israel are thus significant for the world as a whole (Ps. 22). God's reigning is good news for the whole world (Ps. 96). On the other hand, when the world resists Yhwh's reign and oppresses Yhwh's people, it finds Yhwh acting against it (Ps. 9). The fact that the world often does resist God's reign means that when God's people's praise declares that Yhwh does reign (e.g., Ps. 47), that worship is world-creating. It denies that the world the people of God experience outside worship is the ultimate world, declares that the real world is one where Yhwh reigns, and sends worshippers out into that world to live in that conviction.[88]

While in one sense Yhwh lives outside the cosmos and in another sense makes a home in the heavens, Yhwh also deigned to make a home on Zion, in the temple. It is Yhwh's house, Yhwh's place to settle permanently (Ps. 132). Or it is Yhwh's footrest (Yhwh's throne being above the cherubim), and thus a holy place, on a holy mountain (Ps. 99). The fact that this is Yhwh's house means that people who come to worship there have to live lives that match Yhwh's (Pss. 15; 24). In the absence of that, Zion becomes a place from which Yhwh speaks tough (Ps. 50).

---

88. See Brueggemann, *Israel's Praise*.

Jerusalem itself gains its significance from being the place where Yhwh lives—for this reason people are to pray for Jerusalem's well-being (Ps. 122), and for this reason Yhwh forcefully defends Jerusalem (Pss. 48; 76). City and temple are thus places that Israelites delight to visit, where they can imagine living their whole lives (Ps. 84), and from which they grieve to be exiled (Pss. 42–43).

King and Messiah

Yhwh's commitment to the king who reigns in Jerusalem is closely associated with a commitment to continue dwelling in Jerusalem (Ps. 132). From that sanctuary Yhwh acts to strengthen the king (Ps. 20). From there the king is to be a means of Yhwh's authority being exercised in the world (Pss. 2; 110). Sometimes the king is in a position to testify to that (Pss. 18; 118), though sometimes Yhwh's acts do not match the theory (Ps. 89). The king's challenge is to trust in the strength that comes from Yhwh (Ps. 21) and also (implicitly) to see that he has the right socio-moral priorities (Ps. 72).

The early Christian congregation saw (e.g.) the description in Ps. 2 of peoples gathering against Yhwh and against Yhwh's Anointed as applying to the people who had killed Jesus and were now attacking them (Acts 4:25–28), and Paul saw the statement "You are my son; I myself beget you today" as "fulfilled" in Jesus's resurrection (Acts 13:32–33). And the OT does contain messianic prophecies in the sense of promises that a descendant of David will eventually rule again in Israel (e.g., Isa. 11:1–9; Jer. 23:5–6). But psalms such as Ps. 2 are not such prophecies. They talk not about a coming king but about a present king. In applying them to Jesus under the inspiration of the Holy Spirit, then, the NT is using them to illumine the significance of Jesus, but using them in a way that sees new significance in them. It is not working with the meaning the Holy Spirit originally gave them, the meaning they had for their human authors and the people who first used them. The Psalms' picture of the king may go beyond anything that a king in Jerusalem was ever likely to realize, but this does not make them implicitly "messianic" or incipiently "eschatological." These psalms express Yhwh's commitment to the actual king and Yhwh's expectations of the actual king. Nor is there explicit indication in the Psalter that psalms originally applied to the actual king were now assumed to apply to a coming king.[89]

So what would they signify to people once there are no kings on the throne in Jerusalem? The OT suggests more than one answer to that

---

89. Against (e.g.) D. C. Mitchell, *The Message of the Psalter*, JSOTSup 252 (Sheffield: Sheffield Academic Press, 1997).

question. If one looks at them in light of actual messianic prophecies (as in Isa. 11; Jer. 23), one can imagine people applying them to a future king or in a more open way simply lamenting the fact that the psalms do not seem to be true. But other strands of the OT did not look for an individual coming king of whom these psalms would once again be true. Chronicles enthuses over David as the indispensable founder of the worship of Jerusalem but gives no indication that one day it expects there to be another David. Looked at in light of Chronicles, the kingship psalms become recollections of those vital deeds Yhwh did in the past. Isaiah 55 suggests yet another answer to the question. There Yhwh makes a promise:

> Bend your ear and come to me;
>   listen, so that you may truly live,
> And so that I may seal with you a lasting covenant,
>   the steadfast commitments to David.
> Now, I made him a witness to nations,
>   a leader and commander to peoples.
> Now, you will summon a nation you do not acknowledge,
>   and a nation that does not acknowledge you will run to you,
> For the sake of Yhwh your God, Israel's holy one,
>   because he has glorified you. (Isa. 55:3–5)

Yhwh's covenant with David seems to be suspended; there is no David on the throne. So what is to happen to Yhwh's commitment to David? Yhwh's answer is that it is fulfilled for the people as a whole. Theologically it was always subordinate to that—David existed for their sake, not they for his. The end of the monarchy makes possible a reversion to Yhwh's original intent, before Israel thought up the idea of kings and distanced itself from Yhwh. In the past, David had been the means of leading and witnessing to the world. Now the people themselves will take over that position. So they become participants in Yhwh's relationship with David. When the kingship psalms are read in light of Isa. 55, they become open to appropriation by the people as a whole in the present instead of having their fulfillment for an individual king postponed until the future. The NT's application of Ps. 2 to the believing congregation as well as to Jesus (see Rev. 2:26–28) coheres with this.

Life and Death

In isolation, the Psalms would give one the impression that human life is characterized by vulnerability and by wickedness, or that humanity is divided between the vulnerable and the people who take advantage of them. Both the vulnerable and the wicked are religious people, worshippers of Yhwh with sound theological views (the attackers of the vulnerable are people with the kind of sound views that are held by Job's friends). While the Psalms recognize the fact of universal sinfulness (Ps. 130), they focus on the deep sinfulness of believers, people who take advantage of the weak. The religious therefore need to open themselves to God's gaze to test the truth of their claim to commitment (Ps. 139). But the vulnerability of the weak to the wicked and the general precariousness of human life mean that death can seem ever to confront believers.

They then know that when one dies, the body becomes lifeless and incapable of action or movement. It is put into the family tomb (or in a communal grave pit, if one has no tomb). There it joins the remains of earlier members of the family and is left in darkness. They assume that what happens to the nonphysical aspect of a person needs to be understood along similar lines. One's "self" or "personality" ("soul" can be a misleading word) is also lifeless and unable to do anything. It also joins other lifeless personalities in a nonphysical equivalent of the grave, Sheol, or the Pit. You are then stuck there. There is nothing especially unpleasant about this experience of death; it is rather like being asleep.

The Psalms also assume that you may not wait until the end of your life to experience "death." They do not distinguish life and death as sharply as we do. People saw, or felt, experiences such as illness, depression, separation from God, oppression, and loneliness as a loss of fullness of life: it was as if death had seized them while the experience lasted (Ps. 88). The idea is a little like John's understanding of "eternal life" beginning now as fullness of life, while "eternal death" begins now as people fail to experience fullness of life. Indeed, we ourselves know that feeling abandoned by God and overwhelmed by troubles are deathly experiences. Thus the Psalms can speak of Yhwh's deliverance as a return from the grave (Pss. 18; 30).

When people die before the proper time, death is objectionable, but otherwise the OT accepts death as a natural end to life. The perspective contrasts with that of some other Middle Eastern religions. The Egyptians, for instance, believed in a fuller afterlife for important people such as kings, even though there was no evidence for this. The Canaanites believed that there was a god Death who was in charge of Sheol. The Psalms' perspective is more empirical: it does not require people to make a leap of faith about a positive afterlife. It is more egalitarian: it does not suggest that privilege in this life continues afterward. And it is monotheistic: it does not believe there is any realm in the charge of another deity, even the realm of death; if Yhwh does not act there, neither does any other deity. The Psalms' understanding fits well with the way the NT often speaks. There too believers are assumed to be in Hades, the Greek equivalent of Sheol. There too death is like sleep. The difference in the NT is the assumption that people will not stay in Sheol or asleep forever, because the coming of Jesus has made a difference. Now, people either will be raised to a new, transformed life or will be punished for their wrongdoing. But in the meantime, Sheol is still the place where the dead rest until resurrection day. That is all right because Jesus has been there and is there keeping an eye on us as we sleep until that day when we are all raised and judged together at the End (e.g., John 5:28–29; 1 Thess. 4:13–18; Rev. 20:11–15).[90]

One importance of the Sheol doctrine is that it tells the truth about the situation before and apart from Jesus's death and resurrection, which are what will eventually make our resurrection possible. The trouble is that once people believe in a positive afterlife, they can easily cease to take this life seriously, as Christians often have. So another importance of the Sheol doctrine is that it had the capacity to get Israel to take this life with the seriousness it deserves.

The Psalms and the New Testament

There are a number of aspects to the question of the relationship between the Psalms and the NT. One is a theological one. For instance, readers have often reckoned that the prominence of pained and angry protest in the Psalms, with their prayers for the punishment of the suppliants' attackers, are incompatible with the NT. Psalm 69 is a notable

90. There are two NT passages that are difficult to fit with these other passages. One is the parable of the rich man and Lazarus (Luke 16:19–31). Perhaps being in Abraham's bosom has similar significance to being gathered to join one's ancestors, implying that Sheol is (now) in some sense divided into a section for believers who are safe and on their way to resurrection, and a section for unbelievers who are on their way to judgment. That would fit with the idea that we go to be with Christ when we die. But it may be that we should simply hesitate to base a doctrine on the detail of a parable, particularly since Jesus is picking up a folktale (known from Egypt and from Jewish sources). His own point in taking up this story is that there will be a positive afterlife (contrary to Sadducean belief) and that one needs to take that into account in the way one lives one's life. The other passage is Jesus's promise, "Today you will be with me in Paradise" (Luke 23:43). "Paradise" is a term for the Garden of Eden and then for a future earthly paradise and for heaven. But it is odd to think of Jesus going to heaven on Good Friday (if anything, he was on his way to preach in Sheol, to tell God's people the good news that Sheol will not after all be the end; see 1 Pet. 4:6). It will be on Easter Day that he is ascending to his Father (John 20:17). Perhaps he means, "I say to you today, you will be with me in Paradise." Or perhaps "today" refers to the time of salvation that now dawns (cf. 2 Cor. 6:2; Heb. 3:7–4:10; cf. the "from now on" of Luke 22:69); what Jesus is doing today will open the gates of Sheol so that people will be able to leave for heaven at the resurrection. Or perhaps he means that the man is "in Christ" and therefore secure, "with Christ" (cf. Phil. 1:23), and is thus in effect in heaven, as we are "raised" to new life in Christ (e.g., Eph. 2:5–6) even though we are not yet raised to bodily resurrection life.

example of such prayers, and the commentary on that psalm considers this question in light of its several quotations in the NT. But we have already stated the key conclusion that the NT does not seem to be uneasy about questions that trouble modern Christian readers, and that we need to rethink our uneases. Psalm 2 suggests similar conclusions. Christian reading of that psalm looks for ways in which its violence can be sidestepped and recognizes the way its application to Jesus sets it in the context of someone who receives violence rather than showing it. The commentary reveals other aspects to the NT's use of the psalm that again suggest the NT is not uneasy about questions that trouble modern Christians. In general, what the OT and the NT do is fill out the nature of biblical faith for each other. It is not the case that theological insight develops through Scripture in such a way that the NT provides a kind of theological filter by which unacceptable aspects of the Psalms or other aspects of the OT can be strained out by being reinterpreted. The NT itself rather implies that the OT provides the broader context in which the NT needs to be understood.

A different set of questions is raised by the textual as opposed to the theological relationship between the Psalms and the NT. This has a broader as well as a narrower aspect. There is hardly a verse in the Revelation to John that would survive intact if one removed the allusions to the Psalms and other parts of the OT, but there is not a single actual quotation of the OT there. The use of the OT rather takes the form of allusion and the shaping of the book's linguistic world. This is the most spectacular example of a phenomenon that runs through the NT in its relationship with (e.g.) the Psalms. Jesus's blessings in Matt. 5:3–12, for instance, would be decimated if one removed the phrases that come from the Psalms and Isaiah. The declaration that the weak will take possession of the land in Ps. 37:11 reappears in Matt. 5:5. The pure of heart in Ps. 24:4 reappear in Matt. 5:8. Jesus's outline of a gospel spirituality is a new creation, but it comes into being and finds expression through the use of the Psalms and other Scriptures.

Actual quotations from the Psalms raise a different set of questions. As with quotations from Psalms in the Qumran documents (where the Psalms were also especially popular), it is typical of the NT to use the Psalms in a way that takes little account of their original meaning. For instance, in John 13:18 Jesus declares that his betrayal "fills" or "fulfills" or "fills out" (*plēroō*) Ps. 41:9. This does not take up the meaning of the verse in its context, the meaning it would have had for its writer or for believers who used it in OT Israel. The same is true of his quotation of Ps. 69:4 in John 15:25. I assume that these are examples of the way he "interpreted in all the scriptures the things relating to himself" (Luke 24:27). He used the Scriptures to enable his disciples to understand who he was. Paul in Rom. 3:1–20 similarly takes up a string of passages from Psalms (5:9 [10]; 10:7; 14:1–3; 36:1 [2]; 51:4 [6]; 130:3; 140:3 [4]; 143:2) to illustrate his thesis that the whole world, Jewish and Gentile, is under the power of sin. None of these makes the point that Paul wishes to make. For the NT, as for Qumran and for Philo, David is a prophet (Acts 2:30). He spoke by the Holy Spirit (Acts 1:16)—that is, he said things that speak with supernatural appropriateness to a context long after his own day. But they do so in a way that ignores those words' intrinsic meaning when the Holy Spirit first inspired them.

This premodern use of the OT is characteristic of the NT, as it has been characteristic of the use of Scripture by Jews, Christians, and unbelievers through the centuries. In the context of modernity it became a problem to Christians involved in scholarly study. The new cultural context caused objective exegesis of Scripture to become our ideal, and we found that we could make fresh discoveries about the Scriptures' meaning through pursuing that ideal. But it also meant that we had either to justify the NT's use of the OT by this ideal, or to seek to explain it on other bases, such as that the NT was using Jewish exegetical traditions or Jewish exegetical methods. That would mean we could understand NT interpretation of the OT even if we could not imitate it.[91]

The context of postmodernity gives us another way of approaching the question. Postmodernity can be simultaneously appreciative of modernity, suspicious of modernity's absolutist claims, and newly appreciative of the premodern, while also aware of the problems of premodernity that made modernity necessary. This makes it possible for us to look in another way at the use of the Psalms by Jesus and the NT writers. They were not trying to do exegesis. They were using forms of expression they found in the Psalms to help them understand themselves and formulate their beliefs. It will be important that their formulations do fit in with the inherent meaning of Scripture as a whole (and, for instance, it is indeed the case that Paul's claims in Rom. 3:1–20 fit OT convictions). But they do not need to fit the results of exegesis of the particular passage they quote. The Holy Spirit who inspired Scripture is inspiring the writers to see a new significance in the words that appear in Scripture.

Ephesians 4:8 provides a fine example. It quotes Ps. 68:18 [19] in a version that makes over the meaning of the psalm: it has Christ giving gifts to his people rather than receiving them. The rewriting of the text follows that in the Targum, which moreover in its parentheses applies the passage to Moses: "You went up on high (the prophet Moses), you

---

91. Cf. R. N. Longenecker, "Can We Reproduce the Exegesis of the New Testament?" *TynBul* 21 (1970): 3–38. Longenecker's article makes the point—we can follow it in the sense of understanding it if not in imitating it.

took captivity captive (you taught the words of the Torah), you gave gifts to human beings."[92] In Ephesians the quotation is introduced with the words "therefore it is said," which implies that the Holy Spirit was involved not only in the process whereby the original psalm was written but also in the process whereby Jewish tradition rewrote it so as to produce another text that had a quite different meaning from the original. Christ is now the new Moses, who through his cross and resurrection defeats the powers of evil that held the world captive and endows his people with the Holy Spirit and the Spirit's gifts. Psalm and epistle are not in tension with each other. Indeed, in the psalm itself God gives gifts as well as receiving them (Ps. 68:5–14 [6–15]). The gifts in the two texts complement each other. In Ephesians, Christ receives homage as well as giving gifts. Yhwh's victory over the nations and their acknowledgment of Yhwh by bringing their gifts, and Christ's victory over the powers of evil and his giving his people gifts—both are part of the same divine activity and purpose.

In the commentary that follows, I have often noted the way the NT quotes the Psalms, but in light of considerations just outlined, I do not attempt to show that this reworking corresponds to the Psalms' own meaning. Nor do I make the NT the filter or lens through which we read the Psalms. A modern aspect to the commentary is that I want the Psalms to speak their own message and to let them address Christian thinking, theology, and spirituality, rather than being silenced by a certain way of reading the NT that fits modern Christian preferences.

---

92. See Richard Rubinkiewicz, "Ps lxviii 19 (= Eph iv 8) Another Textual Tradition or Targum?" *Novum Testamentum* 17 (1975): 219–24; contrast Richard A. Taylor, "The Use of Psalm 68:18 in Ephesians 4:8 in Light of the Ancient Versions," *BSac* 148 (1991): 319–36.

Psalm 1
Promises to Keep in Mind (I)

Translation

> ¹The good fortune of the person who
>   has not lived[a] by the plans of the faithless
> Or stood in the path of failures
>   or sat in the seat of mockers!
> ²Rather, his pleasure lies in Yhwh's teaching:
>   he talks about his teaching day and night.
> ³He becomes[b] like a tree
>   planted by water channels,
> Which produces its fruit in season,
>   and its foliage does not wither—
>   he makes everything that he does thrive.[c]
> ⁴Not so the faithless;
>   rather, they are like the chaff that a wind blows away.
> ⁵Thus the faithless do not stand in the judgment,
>   nor the failures in the assembly of the faithful.
> ⁶Because Yhwh acknowledges the path of the faithful,
>   but the path of the faithless perishes.

  a. Gnomic qatal (v. 1) and habitual yiqtol or weqatal (vv. 2–6) are alternative ways of making general statements (see *IDIIS* 31.3c; also Max Rogland, *Alleged Non-past Uses of Qatal in Classical Hebrew* [Assen: Van Gorcum, 2003]).
  b. I take EVV "he is" as an under-translation of *wĕhāyâ*, given that the verb would be unnecessary.
  c. EVV generally imply "everything that they do thrives." The verb *ṣālaḥ* (hiphil) can be used intransitively with an impersonal subject (see Judg. 18:5) but the transitive usage is much more common (e.g., Ps. 37:7; Deut. 28:29; Josh. 1:8; Isa. 48:15); 2 Chron. 7:11 is esp. similar to this instance. NRSV likely presupposes this understanding (cf. its rendering at Ps. 37:7). While God can be the subject of this verb, neither those parallels nor the present context points in this direction.

Interpretation

Psalm 1 constitutes an unexpected beginning to a collection of songs and prayers, since it is not itself a song or prayer but a poem commenting on how life works, in such a way as to constitute a promise and an implicit exhortation. As a piece of teaching, it contrasts with the bulk of the Psalter, whereas within Prov. 1–9 it would not have seemed out of place. It does not look as if it was written especially to open the Psalter; perhaps it is a teacher's poem that has been secondarily utilized in this context.[1] Some of its syntax is that of prose (notably the three occurrences of *'ăšer*, "who/which/that"), but its poetic aspect shows itself substantially in its use of imagery and formally in its creative use of parallelism, repetition, and stepped structure.[2]

Specifically, this opening psalm commends attentiveness to Yhwh's teaching—the word *tôrâ* comes twice in v. 2. It is often translated "law" (e.g., LXX, NIVI). Elsewhere, "Yhwh's teaching" can refer to material in the Pentateuch (e.g., 2 Chron. 17:9), and that translation encourages the impression that the psalm refers to meditation on the teaching in Genesis–Deuteronomy, *the* Torah.[3] Psalm 1 would in fact have made a fine introduction to the Pentateuch or to the teaching that begins in Exodus, though "law" is a misleading term to describe those books as a whole, or even to describe the direct instruction about life that they contain. "Law" suggests requirements a society lays on its members. While Genesis–Deuteronomy includes requirements laid on Israelite society, they are laid by God, not by the society itself. Further, the books also comprise the story of what God has done and how God related

---

1. Cassiodorus sees its lack of a heading as appropriate to a psalm about Christ—nothing gets in his way (*Psalms*, 1:45), though Hilary of Poitiers had already argued strongly against a christological understanding (*Psalms*, 236–37).
2. See Sebastian Bullough, "The Question of Metre in Psalm i," *VT* 17 (1967): 42–49; J. Alberto Soggin, "Zum ersten Psalm," *TZ* 23 (1967): 81–96; O. Loretz, "Psalmenstudien," *UF* 3 (1971): 101–15, see 101–3; P. Auffret, "Essai sur la structure littéraire du psaume 1," *BZ*, n.s., 22 (1978): 27–45; idem, "Comme un arbre . . . ," *BZ* 45 (2001): 256–64; Rosario P. Merendino, "Sprachkunst in Psalm i," *VT* 29 (1979): 45–60; R. Lack, "Le psaume 1," *Bib* 57 (1976): 154–67; Walter Vogels, "A Structural Analysis of Ps 1," *Bib* 60 (1979): 410–16; Alter, *Art of Biblical Poetry*, 114–17; Yehoshua Gitay, "Psalm 1 and the Rhetoric of Religious Argumentation," in *Literary Structure and Rhetorical Strategies in the Hebrew Bible*, ed. L. J. de Regt, J. de Waard, and J. P. Fokkelman (Assen, Netherlands: Van Gorcum; [Winona Lake, IN]: Eisenbrauns, 1996), 232–40; and on grammatical features, Pierfelice Tagliacarne, "Grammatik und Poetik," in *Text, Methode und Grammatik* (Wolfgang Richter Festschrift), ed. Walter Gross et al. (St. Ottilien: EOS, 1991), 549–59.
3. Cf. Pancratius C. Beentjes, "The Function of Psalm 1 in a Text from the Genizah of Cairo," *EstBib* 52 (1994): 303–16. On the way Midrash Tehillim sees Ps. 1 as an introduction to the Psalter, see Thereses Hansberger, "'Mose segnete Israel mit *'sryk*, und David segnete Israel mit *'sry*,'" *BZ* 46 (2002): 25–47.

to Israel's first generations and their ancestors. They are not merely instruction on what people should do. To put it another way, "law" suggests something in antithesis to "grace," whereas Genesis–Deuteronomy does not oppose grace and *tôrâ*. The word itself does mean "teaching," not just "law," and it can thus include story as well as command. As a subject for meditation contrasting with and counteracting the folly of the mockers, this Torah importantly embraces the story of Yhwh's dealings with Israel as well as the collected instructions of Yhwh. The story shapes people into a community that walks in Yhwh's way as decisively as do the commands.

But Yhwh's teaching is not confined to Genesis–Deuteronomy. Indeed, that is more often termed *"Moses's* teaching." The expression "Yhwh's teaching" is more characteristic of the Psalms (esp. Ps. 119) and the prophets (e.g., Isa. 1:10; Jer. 8:8) and is not at all confined in its reference to material that now appears in Genesis–Deuteronomy. Against the background of the links with Proverbs in v. 1, "teaching" also recalls an emphasis of Proverbs (e.g., 3:1; 7:2; 28:4, 7, 9), though Proverbs never explicitly refers to *Yhwh's* teaching; the teaching there is that of father or mother or the scholars.

The fact that elsewhere in the OT *tôrâ* refers to the teaching of priests, prophets, or scholars again suggests that the psalm implicitly invites meditation on something broader than Yhwh's commands. The great Torah psalm, Ps. 119, emphasizes Yhwh's promises as well as Yhwh's commands, and the teaching about the faithless makes promises as well as offering exhortations (e.g., Prov. 1:8–19). Such teaching presupposes a whole worldview. The same is true of the teaching on which the faithful need to meditate. It comprises promises as well as exhortations, and an alternative whole worldview.

1:1–3. Declarations about the "good fortune" of someone appear frequently in the Psalter, though they generally form part of a poem involving praise or prayer, as one would expect in a book such as the Psalter (Pss. 127 and 128 are the exceptions). This beginning to the first "psalm" immediately establishes a resemblance to poems in Proverbs (e.g., 3:13; 8:32, 34). Indeed, if we allow for the difference in the books' lengths, the expression is as characteristic of Proverbs as of the Psalms.

> ¹The good fortune of the person who
>   has not lived by the plans of the faithless
> Or stood in the path of failures
>   or sat in the seat of mockers!

The expression "the *good fortune of" (*'ašrê*) recalls the verb *'āšar* ("go straight"), whether or not these are historically linked; *'ăšûr* means "step/walk" (e.g., 17:5). It thus immediately introduces the idea of the walk of life, with which the whole psalm works. The subject of this declaration is *hā'îš*, often a term for an individual person;[4] vv. 1–3 refer to such an individual over against a group of faithless. The individual has to stand against the pressure of this crowd, though vv. 5–6 will offer a reminder that this person does not actually stand alone—the explicit references to the "faithful" are plural. "Plans" (*'ēṣâ*) is another frequent word in Proverbs and in Job, which urges people to believe that God frustrates the plans of the faithless and not to support such plans (Job 5:13; 10:3; 21:16; 22:18; cf. Ps. 33:10–11).[5] The mockers appear almost exclusively in Proverbs, which often warns readers about their fate (e.g., 1:22; 13:1; 19:29).

The three parallel accounts of the life that will *not* lead to success progressively heighten the description. They again recall Proverbs, though they also overlap with Deut. 6:7.[6] Each description incorporates a noun prefixed by the preposition *bĕ* (by/in).

The basic form of wrongdoing involves simply action—"walking" by the advice of the faithless. Worse than that is "standing" (*'āmad*) in the path of moral failures, which implies more than simply taking that path but standing firm in it; the single action has become a way of life. Behind that is "sitting" in the "seat/session/company" of the mockers (cf. 107:32, where *môšāb* stands in parallelism with *qāhāl*, "congregation/assembly"). This implies not merely living their way but also taking part in their deliberations as they gather in a dark parody of the gathering of the elders at the city gate.[7] The analysis of the problem thus deepens through v. 1, though this need not imply a narrative progression—as if people first walk, then stand firm, and finally sit down.[8] The sitting might precede the walking and the standing firm.

---

4. Theodoret interestingly reassures readers that the reference to "man" does not exclude women (*Psalms*, 1:47), though we might not care for his argument to make the point.

5. EVV "counsel" could give the impression that *'ēṣâ* refers to "advice" the faithless give, but more likely it denotes intentions they formulate, into which they seek to draw other people (cf. Prov. 1:9–19). In PBH it can mean "council" (cf. *DTT*), but there is no need to hypothesize an occurrence of this meaning here (against Roland Bergmeier, "Zum Ausdruck *'ṣt rš'ym* in Ps 1.1, Hi 10.3, 21.16 und 22.18," ZAW 79 [1967]: 229–32). Syr transposes "plans" and "path," perhaps in light of the greater familiarity of the expression "live/walk in the path/way" (so Kraus, *Psalms*, 1:113).

6. Cf. André Gunnel, "'Walk,' 'Stand,' and 'Sit' in Psalm i 1–2," *VT* 32 (1982): 327. Stephen C. Reif ("Ibn Ezra on Psalm i 1–2," *VT* 34 [1984]: 232–36) notes that Ibn Ezra makes this point.

7. *Môšāb* usually means "home," so we could translate "lived [*yāšab*, the related verb] in the home," becoming acculturated to their attitude to life (Tg nicely has "sit at table"). But in the context this fits less well. Aquinas worryingly applies it to someone sitting in the chair of a teacher, teaching others to sin.

8. Cf. G. W. Anderson, "A Note on Psalm i 1," *VT* 24 (1974): 231–33.

In the threefold characterization of wrongdoers, the first term, *faithless, is a conventional yet significant one; the faithless are quite prominent in the Psalter and the Wisdom Books. As for the second term, although forms from the root *ḥāṭāʾ* are also prominent in both contexts, the noun *failures is less so (e.g., Pss. 25:8; 104:35; Prov. 1:10), so that gives some heightening. "Mockers" (*lēṣîm*) sharpens the point further. These are people who know what they think and do not want anyone telling them otherwise. Meditation on Yhwh's teaching, or on anything else, is not part of their way of life. "If not the most scandalous of sinners," they are "the farthest from repentance (Pr. 3:34)."[9] And dwelling or sitting in the company of such people risks becoming immersed in their worldview.

The final parallel sequence (plans, path, home) again turns the screw tighter and tighter. Listening to people formulating plans is one thing. Acting on them is another. Spending one's life in the company of such schemers is to walk into a marsh from which one is unlikely to emerge.

> ²Rather, his pleasure lies in Yhwh's teaching:
> he talks about his teaching day and night.

In these two parallel descriptions of the positive alternative the psalm commends, "teaching" appears in both cola, giving it significant emphasis. Both cola incorporate a noun prefixed by the preposition *bĕ* (in), like the clauses in v. 1, with the positives here contrasting with the negatives there.

Taking "pleasure" (*ḥēpeṣ*), delighting, in Yhwh's teaching is the "normal" stance for ordinary, faithful Israelites to take.[10] They thus contrast with mockers, who do not take pleasure in understanding (Prov. 18:2). Psalm 19 will in due course expand on the delightfulness of Yhwh's *tôrâ*, and there *tôrâ* will have more the connotation of direction and command (cf. the delighting of 112:1; 119:35). Insofar as Ps. 1 does have in mind such direction and command, this heightens the paradox of v. 2a. In Christian thinking, pleasure and direction/command do not belong together. Pleasure and teaching do not even belong together. Hans Frei has described a decisive development in modern thought in the following terms: Once, people read the scriptural story and sought to set their own story in its context. Since the eighteenth century we are more inclined to set Scripture's story in the context of ours. It is our story that provides the criteria for deciding whether the scriptural story

---

9. Kidner, *Psalms*, 1:48.
10. But see Uwe F. W. Bauer, "Anti-Jewish Interpretations of Psalm 1 in Luther and in Modern German Protestantism," *Journal of Hebrew Scriptures* (e-journal) 2 (1998): article 2.

is true or relevant. We measure Scripture's story by ours.[11] The attitude the psalm commends involves delighting in Yhwh's teaching—especially (we might add) when its story seems irrelevant or it takes a different stance from us. That is the moment when studying Scripture becomes interesting, significant, and important. We then delight in it. The way that delight expresses itself is by *talking about it day and night—in other words, ceaselessly.

In the present context, there is a further and more concrete referent for the word "teaching." While teaching about the moral life appears in the Psalms, it does not have a central place. The Psalter's central concern is to teach people to praise, pray, and testify. Perhaps the teaching on which it invites meditation is its own teaching on praise, prayer, and testimony. The faithless, failures, and mockers are people who do not believe in praise, testimony, and prayer. Inevitably, the lives of such people turn out to be unfruitful. The faithful, however, meet together as a congregation to praise, pray, and testify, and there they prove the truth of Ps. 1. Insofar as they spend their time in that way, they discover that they become people of good fortune.[12]

> [3]He becomes like a tree
>   planted by water channels,
> Which produces its fruit in season,
>   and its foliage does not wither—
> he makes everything that he does thrive.

To put it less prosaically, they find that their lives become fruitful. The image of a well-located tree, planted (perhaps transplanted) by water, is natural and familiar. In a Middle Eastern climate, the long dry season comes when a fruit tree most needs water as its fruit grows to maturity. It therefore needs to be planted near a water supply toward which its roots can reach. "Water channels" could then denote natural streams or irrigation ditches (cf. Prov. 21:1). The opening clause is exactly the same as the first clause in Jer. 17:8 except that the latter lacks the word "channels." The context in Jer. 17:5–8 spells out the simile, though it applies it to the results of trust in Yhwh rather than of godliness.[13] Ezekiel 17:1–10; 19:10–14 also work with the image, though applying it to the king as someone Yhwh planted. In its context, Jer. 17 may also have political implications.

---

11. See *The Eclipse of Biblical Narrative* (New Haven, CT: Yale University Press, 1974).
12. Reinhard G. Kratz ("Die Tora Davids," *ZTK* 93 [1996]: 1–34) thus suggests that Ps. 1 introduces the (fivefold) Psalter as "David's Torah."
13. On the relationship of Ps. 1 and Jer. 17 (and Amenemope), see E. Lipinski [*sic*], "Macarismes et psaumes de congratulation," *RB* 75 (1968): 321–67, see 330–39.

Over against these, Ps. 1 declares that its principle applies to everyone (cf. the opening *hā'îš*, the person), that it makes demands on their ordinary lives, and that its demands concern moral life. Though the "channels" are missing from Jer. 17, they are present in Ps. 46:4 [5]; 65:9 [10], and these links may suggest that the water channels refreshing the godly are ones Yhwh provides, specifically ones Yhwh makes flow to and around and from Zion—the channels of which Siloam is a symbol. But the psalm then suggests it is Yhwh's teaching that is the key to this.[14]

But how are the faithful like a well-located tree? The second line answers that question implied by the first—in the way such a tree keeps producing fruit and foliage. That raises suspense through the verse, because v. 3c–d develops the parable without interpreting it. These two cola are neatly parallel. A transitive verb and an intransitive one form a pair. Fruit and foliage balance each other: fruit is what the tree lives for, but without foliage there will be no fruit. At the center, the expression "in season" hints at the fact that the fruit-bearing season is also the one that brings the most pressure. The summer sun is both essential to the ripening of fruit and also threatening because it may make fruit and foliage wither.

The line thus smuggles in a threatening aspect to the psalm, which began by talking about good fortune but implicitly recognizes that the godly face the prospect of withering, not because they are ungodly but because they are godly. This assumption links with the nature of the psalms that will follow, which often presuppose an experience more like withering than flourishing. Psalm 1 promises that this is not how life will work and that those subsequent psalms reflect exceptional rather than regular circumstances.

What does this parable mean, then? The answer comes in an extra colon that makes v. 3c–e a tricolon, which is metrically unexpected but substantially necessary. MT divides the verse only after v. 3a–d, which reflects the way the final colon answers the question raised by v. 3a–d as a whole. The last colon also parallels the first (v. 3a), both being statements about the godly person rather than about the tree. Like good fortune, thriving has two aspects. It involves preservation from attack (Isa. 54:17; Ezek. 17:15) and positive achievement (Gen. 24:56; 1 Chron. 22:11; Jer. 22:30). In substance though not in words the "thriving" that closes v. 3 pairs with the "good fortune" that opens v. 1. The plaint "Why does the path of the faithless thrive" could have come in the Psalter, though it actually comes in Jeremiah (see Jer. 12:1). Each of Jeremiah's words appears in the psalm, and he goes on to lament the fact that it is the

---

14. Cf. Jerome F. D. Creach, "Like a Tree Planted by the Temple Stream," *CBQ* 61 (1999): 34–46.

faithless who produce fruit. His words and the psalm's words confront each other, as the psalm anticipates the laments that will follow in the Psalter.

The final colon has a feature of its word order in common with the two cola that precede. In all three, a noun expression unusually precedes the verb. This suggests: "Its fruit—it produces it in season. Its foliage—it does not wither. Everything they do—they make it thrive." The words take further a parallel with Yhwh's challenge to Joshua (Josh. 1:8), which has already urged him to keep reciting Moses's book of teaching. They also parallel the statement about Solomon in 2 Chron. 7:11. They thus once again promise that principles illustrated in the lives of great leaders and kings apply to ordinary individuals.

1:4–5. There follows a corresponding description of the ill fortune of the faithless. There is no description of the life of the faithless themselves, corresponding to the description of the life of the faithful—actually vv. 1–3 have already provided that. The focus lies on their fate.

> ⁴Not so the faithless;
> rather, they are like the chaff that a wind blows away.

The first colon is short and sharp; LXX achieves an alternative rhetorical effect by repeating the "Not so" at the end of the colon, and also expands on v. 4b by adding "from the face of the earth." Verse 4b then explains v. 4a, as happened within v. 3 as a whole and within v. 3a–d. How are the faithless not like the faithful? In the way things work out for them. But the difference in their destiny is matched by a change in the image used to describe it. Jeremiah and Ezekiel work out the implications of the tree image in two directions, according to whether the tree is planted by water or in the wilderness. One might thus have expected the psalm to say something like this: "Rather, they are like shrubs in the desert, withered by the hot desert wind." That alternative possibility hangs in the air, but the psalm itself abandons the tree image and takes up another. The image is secondary to the point the psalm wishes to make, and the change gives extra force to it. The new image is another that reflects the summer. When the grain has been harvested and threshed, the farmer makes a heap of it in a breezy place and throws it into the air forkful by forkful. The grains fall back to the ground, but the lighter husks blow away in the wind. Chaff is thus a standard image for something that is useless and therefore vulnerable, and it provides an image for the destiny of the faithless (cf. 35:5). It can be an image for punishment (e.g., Job 21:18; Isa. 17:13; 29:5; Zeph. 2:2), but it can simply suggest calamity (cf. Isa. 41:2). Once more the image drives the poem forward by raising the question "Exactly how are they like chaff?"

> ⁵Thus the faithless do not stand in the judgment,
> nor the failures in the assembly of the faithful.

Paralleling v. 3e is a literal account of what happens to the *faithless, *failures—the two terms are taken up from v. 1.[15] "Thus" (ʿal-kēn) is not itself an introduction to the pronouncement of judgment, like a prophet's "therefore" (lākēn); it makes a point about logic. The two cola are then parallel: "Thus . . . do not stand" applies to the second as well as the first colon, while "failures" parallels "faithless," and "in the assembly of the faithful" parallels "in the judgment." "Faithless" is the antonym of *faithful—the two words come in parallelism in v. 6.

When judgment comes, the faithless will not be able to take their stand or stand up confidently or survive or withstand. Verses 1 and 5 thus offer two alternatives.[16] Either one lives, stands, and sits with the faithless, the failures, the mockers; or one stands in the judgment, the assembly or company of the faithful. These are not two parallel actual assemblies into which the community is divided. The assembly of the faithful is the real assembly, the gathering of the mockers its dark shadow.

What is this judgment? If we read the psalm in light of Dan. 7 and later texts, judgment could refer to an event at the End. Thus LXX and Jerome speak of the faithless people not "rising again" at the judgment, and Tg of their not being acquitted on the Great Day—which would encourage the reader to refer the whole line to a judgment at the End. That fits the use of the verb qûm in Isa. 26:14, 19, where the subjects are dead. The "assembly of the faithful" would then be the assembly described in a passage such as Dan. 7. But elsewhere in the OT, "the judgment" or "the assembly of the faithful" would be a gathering assembled to make a decision on some dispute or issue or wrongdoing in the community.[17] It is the assembly of the faithful that makes the judicial decision to which the psalm refers.[18] This assembly contrasts with that dark counterpart in v. 1, a contrast underlined by the similarity between the words for "assembly" (ʿădat) and "plans" (ʿăṣat).[19] "The assembly of the faithful"

---

15. EVV move to a future tense, but the yiqtols continue from vv. 2–4, and more likely the verses continue to describe a pattern about ongoing life.

16. The verb for stand is here qûm and not ʿāmad, as in v. 1 (cf. 24:3; Josh. 7:12–13; Amos 7:2, 5; Nah. 1:6), but qûm can be used in parallelism with ʿāmad (Nah. 1:6; Job 8:15).

17. Cf. Theodoret, Psalms, 1:51, noting the renderings of Aq, Th, and Sym.

18. Paul Auvray ("Le Psaume 1," RB 53 [1946]: 365–71) argues against any eschatological interpretation of the psalm; contrast Edward P. Arbez, "A Study of Psalm 1," CBQ 7 (1945): 398–404. See also Loretz, Psalmstudien, 23–24.

19. Cf. D. L. Peterson and K. H. Richards, "Psalm 1," in Interpreting Hebrew Poetry (Minneapolis: Fortress, 1992), 89–97, see 96. LXX (though not Aq, Sym, Th) assimilates v. 5 to v. 1 here.

also recalls "the council of the upright, the assembly" (Ps. 111:1), the congregation in the temple.

The OT also often speaks of judicial proceedings between Yhwh and individuals or communities in the course of their ongoing life. Either side can initiate them (e.g., 143:2; Job 9:32; 14:3; 22:4; Isa. 3:14; Jer. 12:1). Jeremiah 4:11–12 interestingly links the ideas of Yhwh's judgment and the picture of winnowing. The relationship between God and people is thus pictured in light of those judicial proceedings at the city gate with which people would be familiar, though the use of the metaphor often presupposes the way these proceedings would work out in Jerusalem under the monarchy, when the king acts as judge (cf. 1 Kings 7:7; Prov. 20:8). The psalm, however, rather suggests the traditional picture of something more like a jury than a single judge. While Yhwh is involved in the process (v. 6), it is behind the scenes, as is the case in any court. We do not know what precise institution the psalm refers to, but Prov. 5:14 provides an analogous picture of the immoral person "in every kind of trouble in the midst of the congregation and assembly."

> [6]Because Yhwh acknowledges the path of the faithful,
> but the path of the faithless perishes.

1:6. What makes things work out the way v. 5 says? What grounds are there for reckoning they will do so? Yhwh's sudden appearance in the last line of the poem draws attention to the fact that there has been no such previous reference to God. In both respects this also matches the Proverbs-like ethos of the psalm. On the one hand, Proverbs often describes the way life works without referring to God (e.g., 1:8–19). It presupposes the conviction that life works out so that both moral and immoral living find their rewards, but it frequently implies that this happens by an immanent process built into how life works rather than by divine intervention. This does not mean God is not involved; elsewhere Proverbs often notes that God is so involved. But God works via that immanent process as well as by supranatural intervention (e.g., 3:31–36, on the topic that 1:8–19 treats). Proverbs' own introduction (1:1–7) in fact parallels the dynamic of this introduction to the Psalter, speaking wholly of insight and right-doing until its sudden reference to Yhwh in the last line (1:7). This further indication of a link with the ethos of Proverbs confirms that the court in v. 5 is a human one, rather than a heavenly one, behind which we can see God's activity.

Both Ps. 1 and Prov. 1 assume that practical insight, faithful living, and religious devotion go together and reinforce each other. None of these is in conflict with any of the others. Of course, their emphasizing the point reflects a recognition that life does not always work that way.

That is why it is an important conviction in light of which to consider everyday life (in Proverbs) or worship and prayer (in the Psalter).

The two cola of Ps. 1:6 are again parallel, and "path" occurs in both, like "teaching" in v. 2. The emphasis on this motif is increased by the fact that it is also taken up from v. 1. Likewise, the "faithful" and the "faithless" reappear from v. 5 but in the reverse order, symbolizing the contrast between their destinies. This also means that the "faithless" form a bracket around vv. 5–6, around vv. 4–6, and around the psalm as a whole. Verse 6 neatly sums up the psalm's delicate balance of emphasis on the faithful and the faithless. If its two cola had appeared in the opposite order, this would have tilted the psalm into an overall positive emphasis on the faithful, but as it is, the order contributes to the way the psalm resolutely lays two ways before its readers. The participle of a transitive verb and the yiqtol of an intransitive verb complement each other, as, more broadly, do a clause with the life of one group as its object and another with the life of the other group as its subject. The two forms of expression thus combine reference to God's involvement with further reference to the way things come to pass "naturally." The psalm notes God's personal involvement specifically in the positive, while picturing the negative simply working itself out. While Prov. 1–9 can also directly associate God with the negative (3:33), the passage is likewise more inclined to describe the negative as working itself out and to associate God with the positive (e.g., 3:5–6, 26), in keeping with the conviction elsewhere that love and compassion are nearer God's heart than wrath and punishment (e.g., Lam. 3:33).[20]

The two verbs are the two novel words in the line, and this gives them emphasis. On the one hand, the fact that Yhwh *acknowledges the path of the faithful explains the declaration in v. 3, or offers another level of explanation of the phenomena v. 3 refers to. The Psalter will soon be raising the question why the faithless prosper, but it begins with the question why the faithful prosper, and explains it in two ways. At one level this is just something about the way reality is. At another level, it comes about by the action of Yhwh acknowledging or recognizing the life of the faithful, like a king recognizing the work of his servants and seeing that it is rewarded.

On the other hand, talk of the path of the faithless "perishing" closes the psalm with a word that has not appeared before, and a frightening one. Elsewhere it is people who perish, or sometimes (e.g.) hopes or riches. The expression here involves an ellipse: "The path of the faith-

---

20. Contrast Fritz Goerling's declaration that "the psalm's central teaching is retribution" ("Psalm 1," *Notes on Translation* 14, no. 3 [2000]: 51–60, see 58); and with that contrast J. Clinton McCann, "Righteousness, Justice, and Peace," *HBT* 23 (2001): 111–31, see 113–14.

less [leads to destruction, so that they] perish." The psalm began with the misapprehension that the path of the faithless could lead to a good place. It closes by affirming that this path leads over a cliff and takes with it those who walk it (cf. Prov. 4:18–19; 14:12; Ps. 37 expounds this conviction at length).

Theological Implications

Psalm 1 constitutes a preemptive strike with regard to much that will follow in the Psalter. Prayers issuing from the experience of attack, shame, fear, isolation, divine abandonment, and divine anger will dominate the first half of the Psalter. These prayers could give the impression that such experiences are characteristic of the life of the godly. The Psalter begins by affirming that this is not so. Psalm 1 invites the godly to set such experiences in the context of its promise: "The words of the psalm are words of faith."[21] It thus functions a little like the ending to Ecclesiastes, which affirms the significance of that book's tough, hardheaded teaching but also warns the reader not to get it out of proportion, and brings the book to a close by reaffirming orthodox faith (12:9–14). Psalm 1 opens the Psalter in an analogous way. It would be nice if the reference to Ps. 2 as the first psalm in some readings of Acts 13:33 indicated that this witnessed to a tradition that saw Ps. 1 as a preamble to the Psalter rather than as the first psalm (L omits the number "1" at the beginning). But Ps. 2 is no more a psalm in the strict sense, and more likely it indicates that Pss. 1 and 2 were read as one chapter (cf. *b. Berakot* 9b).

"Fortunate those who hear the word of God and keep it!" (Luke 11:28). Interpreters have reckoned that the psalm had legalistic instincts,[22] but even Augustine recognized that "it is one thing to be in the law, another under the law."[23] Psalm 1 prepares the way for what follows also in its nature as implicit exhortation. From time to time the Psalter will remind readers that their access to Yhwh's presence and their claim on Yhwh's commitment depend on their living a moral and social life that meets with Yhwh's expectations (e.g., Pss. 15; 24; 50). Indeed, its teaching as a whole on the life of worship and prayer presupposes this life context. Psalm 1 hardly invites us to see the Psalter itself as teaching about right living. But the Psalter does give a prominent place to prayer that God will put down the faithless, the moral wanderers, and the mockers; it declares that God answers such prayer and also urges God to keep com-

---

21. Luther, *Selected Psalms*, 3:291.
22. See, e.g., Gunkel, *Psalmen*, 3.
23. *Psalms*, 1.

mitment with the faithful. In indirectly urging readers to godliness, Ps. 1 implies that in its absence their prayer cannot be expected to prevail. Before coming to praise Yhwh or seek help from Yhwh, they must see that they pay heed to Yhwh's teaching. Worship that lacks this feature may incur Yhwh's angry confrontation (e.g., Ps. 95). People come to Yhwh with their pleas for help on the basis that they have kept their side of the relationship of commitment between them and Yhwh (e.g., Pss. 44; 89). The moment of prayer will be too late to make sure that this is so; they have to do so before reading the Psalter and entering into its worship and prayer. In at least this sense, Ps. 1 is "the main entrance to the mansion of the Psalter."[24]

---

24. Jerome, *Homilies on the Psalms*, 3.

Psalm 2

Promises to Keep in Mind (II)

Translation

¹Why have nations thronged,
  do countries talk emptiness,[a]
²Do earth's kings take their stand,
  have leaders taken counsel[b] together,
  against Yhwh and against his anointed?
³"We are going to break off[c] their fetters,[d]
  throw their ropes off us."

⁴The one who sits in the heavens is amused;
  the Lord[e] laughs at them.
⁵Then he speaks to them in his anger,
  dismays[f] them with his fury.
⁶"But I myself[g] installed[h] my king
  on Zion, my holy mountain!"

  a. NRSV, NIVI, and BDB take *rîq* as adverbial, as if the form were *lārîq*, but this seems unnecessary. The word recurs in 4:2 [3].
  b. I take the verb as *sûd* (niphal), denominative from *sôd* (cf. NRSV), rather than as *yāsad* (niphal) (BDB), which means found or establish.
  c. Resultative piel.
  d. *Môsēr* from *'āsar*.
  e. C and some later MSS, also Tg, have the more predictable *yhwh* (cf. *BHS*).
  f. EVV have "terrify" for *bāhal*, but the word commonly appears in contexts where people are reacting with helpless despair to something that has happened rather than reacting with fear to something that might happen. Cf. LXX *taraxei*. J. VanderKam ("*Bhl* in Ps 2:5 and its Etymology," *CBQ* 39 [1977]: 245–50) suggests a different root, meaning "berate."
  g. *Wa'ănî*.
  h. *Nāsak* III. *IBHS* 489 sees this as a performative meaning "I hereby install," but the psalm seems to be recalling the event, not taking part in it. Contrast v. 7b. Revised Ver-

⁷I shall tell of[i] Yhwh's decree:[j]
he said to me, "You are my son;
I myself beget[k] you today.
⁸Ask of me and I will make
nations your possession,
earth's ends your estate.
⁹You can break them up [*or*, shepherd them] with an iron club,
smash them like a potter's vessel."[l]

¹⁰So now, kings, be sensible;
allow yourselves to be put right,[m] earth's leaders.
¹¹Serve Yhwh with reverence,
rejoice with trembling, ¹²submit sincerely,[n]

---

sion mg "anointed" requires the verb to be another *nāsak*, a variant for *sûk*, but this is used only for secular anointing (makeup). *DCH* sees this as a (unique) instance of *nāsak* I: "I poured a libation on [and thus consecrated]." Jeffrey H. Tigay ("The Divine Creation of the King in Psalms 2:6," *Eretz-Israel* 27 [2003]: 246*–51*) sees this verb as stretched to mean "create."

i. Oddly, the preposition *'el*—but the usage recurs in 69:26 [27]; see BDB 40.

j. I follow MT accents in construing v. 7a. NJPS construes "I shall tell of a decree: Yhwh said to me. . . ." Syr's "my decree" implies the same line division. This makes for two more-equal cola, but a reader would more likely take *ḥōq* as const. than take *yhwh* as subject placed before the verb.

k. The link with 2 Sam. 7:14 probably means that *yālad* here refers to fathering, but it usually refers rather to birthing, and "beget" preserves a little of the ambiguity.

l. Albert Kleber sees the background in the custom of smashing pots bearing an enemy's name as an acted prayer for their destruction ("Ps. 2:9 in the Light of an Ancient Oriental Ceremony," *CBQ* 5 [1943]: 63–67). For Mesopotamian parallels, see Bob Becking, "'Wie Töpfe sollst du sie zerschmeissen,'" *ZAW* 102 (1990): 59–79; "Noch einmal Psalm 2,9b," *ZAW* 105 (1993): 269–70. For the permissive understanding of the verbs, see J. A. Emerton, "The Translation of the Verbs in the Imperfect in Psalm ii.9," *JTS*, n.s., 29 (1978): 499–503.

m. Tolerative niphal of *yāsar* (BDB).

n. It is more coherent to take the opening exhortation in v. 12 with the exhortations in v. 11; this also means that vv. 10–12 form a sequence of 3-3 lines (plus an extra 3-stress monocolon at the end). For this opening clause in v. 12, NIVI's "Kiss the Son" presupposes the most common meaning of *nāšaq*. Kissing the king would be an expression of recognition and homage. But "son" is Aramaic *bar*, not Hebrew *bēn* (as in v. 7). Sym and Jerome have "kiss sincerely," more naturally taking this to be Hebrew *bar* used adverbially (cf. BDB 141). The expression as a whole is then odd, yet one of a number of puzzling occurrences of *nāšaq*. I take this to be *DCH*'s *nāšaq* III. LXX and Tg with "accept discipline/instruction" are then paraphrasing or guessing but have the same text (cf. Albert Pietersma, "Empire Re-affirmed: A Commentary on Greek Psalm 2," in *God's Word for Our World* [Simon J. De Vries Festschrift], ed. J. Harold Ellens et al., JSOTSup 389 [London: T&T Clark, 2004], 2:46–62 [see 60–61]). NRSV's "with trembling kiss his feet" involves the hypothesis that the second half of the word "his feet" (*běraglāyw*) became separated from the first half and the two resultant words were then read as "rejoice" and "the son" (*gîlû. . . bar*). Staffan Olofsson ("The Crux Interpretum in Ps 2,12," *SJOT* 9 [1995]: 185–99) argues on the basis of the meaning of Hebrew *bar* for "kiss the field," an expression that would signify an act of homage. For other emendations, see, e.g., Alfred Bertholet, "Eine crux

Lest he be angry and you perish° as regards the path,ᵖ
because his anger will soon blaze.ᑫ

The good fortune of all that rely on him!

Interpretation

Psalm 2 might seem a second false start for the Psalter, representing another form of speech we would not expect in a book called *těhillîm*. As Ps. 1 would be at home in Proverbs, so Ps. 2 would be at home in a prophetic book. In some cases the inclusion of a word from Yhwh in the Psalter may indicate that it was delivered in the context of worship. In this case its location at the beginning of the book points to a further reason for its inclusion. It constitutes another aspect of the theological context in which people are invited to use the Psalms. Thus "the introduction to the Psalter does not conclude with Ps. 1. It carries over to the second psalm."[1]

One Jewish tradition treated Pss. 1 and 2 as one psalm, and this reflects a number of points of connection between the two. Psalm 2 opens

---

interpretum," *ZAW* 28 (1908): 58–59; "Nochmals zu Ps 2 11f.," *ZAW* 28 (1908): 193; G. E. Closen, "Gedanken zur Textkritik von Ps 2, 11b + 12a," *Bib* 21 (1940): 288–309; R. Köbert, "Zur ursprünglichen Textform von Ps 2, 11.12a," *Bib* 21 (1940): 426–28; A. M. Dubarle, "*Draxasthe paideias*," *RB* 62 (1955): 511–12; Isaac Sonne, "The Second Psalm," *HUCA* 19 (1945–46): 43–55; Julian Morgenstern, "*Nšqw br*," *JQR* 32 (1941–42): 371–85; Andrew A. Macintosh, "A Consideration of the Problems Presented by Psalm II 11 and 12," *JTS*, n.s., 27 (1976): 1–14; A. Robinson, "Deliberate but Misguided Haplography Explains Psalm 2.11–12," *ZAW* 89 (1977): 421–22; William L. Holladay, "A New Proposal for the Crux in Psalm ii 12," *VT* 28 (1978): 110–12.

o. The form is weyiqtol, as if the "lest" were repeated.

p. *Derek*, acc. of respect, not (e.g.) of place (see GKC 118g, note 1).

q. EVV translate "kindle," but *bāʿar* usually (perhaps always) refers to coming to full blaze, not merely catching alight (see *DCH* in contrast to BDB). In the context this looks more like a particular warning to these leaders rather than a general statement ("his anger blazes quickly").

1. Miller, *Interpreting the Psalms*, 87. See further Gerald T. Sheppard, *Wisdom as a Hermeneutical Construct* (BZAW 151; Berlin: de Gruyter, 1980), 136–44; André Wénin, "Le psaume 1 et l'''encadrement' du livre des louanges," in *Ouvrir les Écritures* (P. Beauchamp Festschrift), ed. Pietro Bovati and Roland Meynet (Paris: Cerf, 1995), 151–76; Jesper Høgenhaven, "The Opening of the Psalter," *SJOT* 15 (2001): 169–80; Erich Zenger, "Der Psalter als Wegweiser und Wegbegleiter," in *Sie wandern von Kraft zu Kraft* (Reinhard Lettmann Festschrift), ed. Arnold Angenendt and Herbert Vorgrimler (Kevelaer: Butzon, 1993), 29–47; and for an alternative eschatological reading, Robert Cole, "An Integrated Reading of Psalms 1 and 2," *JSOT* 98 (2002): 75–88. The two hardly had a common origin, against William H. Brownlee, "Psalms 1–2 as a Coronation Liturgy," *Bib* 52 (1971): 321–36; see John T. Willis, "Psalm 1," *ZAW* 91 (1979): 381–401.

with an ironic link. Whereas people of insight *talk about* Yhwh's teaching (1:2), nations and peoples also *talk* something—emptiness (2:1). It closes with another link. Whereas Ps. 1 ends with the prospect of the *path* of the wicked *perishing*, 2:12 envisages nations *perishing* as regards the *path*. Whereas the opening of Ps. 1 comments on *the good fortune* of people who walk in the right way, Ps. 2 closes with a comment on *the good fortune* of everyone who relies on Yhwh. That declaration thus forms a bracket round the two psalms.

Verbal links between adjacent psalms are an occasional feature of the Psalter; they parallel links between adjacent sayings in Proverbs and links that the psalm headings make with stories from David's life (see on Ps. 3). These phenomena do not indicate that (e.g.) these two psalms were of common origin or were used together liturgically. Rather, they tell us something of the way the Psalter was compiled. In this case, they result in Ps. 2 joining Ps. 1 as an introduction to the Psalter. As Ps. 1 declares that it is not regularly the case that the faithless are like trees planted by water and the faithful are blown away like chaff, so Ps. 2 declares that it is not regularly the case that kings and nations terrify Yhwh's anointed with their fury and break him with their iron bar. As Ps. 1 conveys an implicit promise, Ps. 2 conveys an explicit one. Each provides people praying subsequent psalms with part of the encouragement that makes it possible to stand firm under pressure, and with part of the basis for pressing Yhwh to respond to their prayer.

The psalm presupposes some theological, religious, and historical background that is not made explicit in the OT narratives, but putting it alongside (e.g.) Pss. 18; 72; 89; Isa. 55; and the account of Yhwh's commitment to David in 2 Sam. 7 helps us reconstruct something of that background. God made a permanent commitment to David that his line would always reign. Yhwh would have a father-son relationship with him, defeat his enemies, make him the greatest king in the world, and thus make him a witness to Yhwh's might and purpose. This commitment represents a form of fulfillment of God's promise to Abraham that he would be blessed in such a way that people would covet the same blessing, while people who belittled him would be cursed (Gen. 12:1–3). As the family becomes a people, a nation, and a state, God's promise becomes more politicized. The nation is destined to rule the world on God's behalf. The introduction of the monarchy means God's undertaking comes to focus on the king. God promises the king victory over his enemies and submission from them; when he experiences attack from them, God gives him victory over them.

The psalm also reflects aspects of Israel's experience, such as the rebellion of subordinate peoples during the monarchic period, but it portrays them larger than life. While David and Solomon ruled an empire, we know of no time when Israel ruled the size of empire presupposed by the psalm, or one whose parts rebelled against their emperor at the beginning of his reign, as happened to the great empires. The psalm invites its hearers to *imagine* a situation like that. Perhaps they did so in their worship during the monarchy on the occasion of the king's accession or at (e.g.) an annual celebration of that accession. Or perhaps they did so on the basis of the fact that the Assyrians did look in this way at their own relationship with the world and with rebellious underlings.[2] The psalm deals with a hypothetical but destined sovereignty and then with a hypothetical situation, in such a way as to lead into a reaffirmation of Yhwh's commitment.

The psalm begins like a story, in the middle of things. We do not know who is the speaker or whom the speaker is addressing. A question asking why nations are threatening Israel could naturally be addressed to God, but it becomes clear that this is a rhetorical question. Only in the last section does the psalm directly address anyone—namely, the world's kings and rulers. But the fact that they are the subject of vv. 1–3 suggests that the psalm has another audience. When prophets address the nations (e.g., Isa. 13–23), generally the implicit real-life audience is Israel itself. When the psalm likewise addresses the nations, the audience overhears the psalmist indirectly encouraging it not to panic when nations threaten, and instead to join Yhwh in laughing. Perhaps the speaker is a prophet, but it is simpler to infer that the "I" who speaks in vv. 7–9, the king, is the speaker throughout.[3] The king's speechwriter might then be a prophet or might be a wisdom teacher speaking in the manner of a prophet, as Wisdom sometimes does in Prov. 1–9. Either way, the psalm is *lĕdāwid* ("for David" or "David's"), even though it does not say so.[4]

It divides into four equal sections. Verses 1–3 describe the nations' plans, vv. 4–6 the Lord's response to them, vv. 7–9 the king's own response, and vv. 10–12 the implications for the nations. The sections thus work *abb'a'*.[5] The poem includes many fairly regular bicola, but an extra colon brings vv. 1–2 to a climax, an isolated colon introduces vv. 7–9 as a whole,

---

2. Cf. Helmer Ringgren, "Psalm 2 and *Bēlit's* Oracle for Ashurbanipal," in *The Word of the Lord Shall Go Forth* (David Noel Freedman Festschrift), ed. Carol L. Meyers and M. O'Connor (Winona Lake, IN: Eisenbrauns, 1983), 91–95. The text also appears in *ANET*, 450–51.

3. LXX begins the king's first-person words in v. 6: "But I was installed as king on Zion, his holy mountain." J. Alberto Soggin (among others) follows: See "Zum zweiten Psalm," in *Wort–Gebot–Glaube* (Walther Eichrodt Festschrift), ed. Hans Joachim Stoebe (Zürich: Zwingli, 1970), 191–207, see 193–94.

4. John T. Willis ("A Cry of Defiance," *JSOT* 47 [1990]: 33–50) sees it as a king's cry of defiance before a battle.

5. Cf. Fokkelman, *Major Poems*, 2:55.

another introduces v. 8, one closes v. 11 (MT attaches it to v. 12), and one closes off the entire psalm.[6]

2:1–3. Verses 1–2 have an *abb'cc'd* structure, in substance rather than in prosody, as the opening "Why?" and the closing "against Yhwh and against his anointed" apply to the rest of vv. 1a–2b. These four cola comprise two parallel pairs, one about the peoples as a whole, one about their rulers. In each, there is one qatal and one yiqtol verb, themselves arranged in an *abb'a'* pattern. In each, the verbs and nouns are arranged *abb'a', abb'a'*. And in each, a more common noun (*gôyim, malkê*) is followed by a less common one (*lĕ'ummîm, rôzĕnîm*). Verse 3 then gives precision to and heightens the extraordinary stupidity of the talk reported by vv. 1–2.

> ¹Why have nations thronged,
>   do countries talk emptiness?

The verbs form an ironic pair. Neither thronging (*rāgaš*) nor *talking (*hāgâ*) is an activity one would expect of nations. Understood in light of the use of the noun "throng" (*rigšâ*) in 64:2 [3], the first verb suggests that the nations are making a disorderly ruckus like a gang of thieves. The second then suggests that they are also growling like a lion (Isa. 31:4) or muttering like a sorcerer (8:19) or plotting like thieves (Prov. 24:2).[7] On the other hand, a similar word for "throng" (*regeš*) denotes a religious procession with its holy disorder (Ps. 55:14 [15]), and this links well with the fact that the parallel verb "talk" recalls the behavior of people meditating out loud on God's word (cf. 1:2). So the verse almost suggests that the nations are behaving the way Ps. 1 encourages, but the "Why?" at the beginning, a noun at the center, and the phrase at the end undermines this understanding. They are talking "emptiness" (*rîq*). This could point to the moral emptiness of their intentions (cf. the "worthless men" of Judg. 9:4, *rêqîm*), but *rîq* more often refers to the practical emptiness of someone's deeds—they get nowhere (e.g., Isa. 49:4; 55:11). This fits the context (vv. 4–12): their thronging and talking give birth to nothing. R. Isaac suggestively assumes that vv. 1–3 are addressed to God, in the manner of a lament,[8] like the "Why?" question in (e.g.) Ps.

---

6. On the psalm's structure, see also Pierre Auffret, *The Literary Structure of Psalm 2* (JSOTSup 3; Sheffield: JSOT, 1977); "Étude structurelle du Psaume 2," *EstBib* 59 (2001): 307–23; Lucas Kunz, "Der 2. Psalm in neuer Sicht," *BZ*, n.s., 20 (1976): 238–42; Barnabas Lindars, "Is Psalm ii an Acrostic Poem," *VT* 17 (1967): 60–67; H. H. Rowley, "The Text and Structure of Psalm ii," *JTS* 42 (1941): 143–54; Marco Treves, "Two Acrostic Psalms," *VT* 15 (1965): 81–90.

7. Victor Sasson ("The Language of Rebellion in Psalm 2," *Andrews University Seminary Studies* 24 [1986]: 147–54) compares the language with that in Deir Alla texts.

8. See *Midrash on Psalms*, 1:36.

22, with the quotation from the enemies' words in (e.g.) Ps. 83, but the word "emptiness" points against that reading. The rhetorical question "Why?" can also be a statement of conviction, and so it is here. The whole psalm is a statement of confidence. Peoples weary themselves for the sake of emptiness (Hab. 2:13), but not Israel (Isa. 65:23).[9]

> ²[Why] do earth's kings take their stand,
>   have leaders taken counsel together,
>   against Yhwh and against his anointed?

Before we discover the implicit answer to how this is so, v. 2 begins by raising suspense. First, two further parallel cola make explicit that it is not the nations/peoples as a whole that are taking action, but their rulers. It is always the misfortune of the former to be implicated in the actions of the latter. The picture is superficially impressive. These are not just kings but "earth's kings"—kings from all over the world.[10] This is not an ordinary, small-scale rebellion but the whole world asserting itself. And the kings are working "together" (*yaḥad*). It is a serious threat—or they think it is. "Take their stand" (*yāṣab* hitpael) suggests another irony, because the verb often refers to people presenting themselves before Yhwh or standing still as Yhwh acts (e.g., Exod. 14:13; Deut. 31:14). They will be doing that, but it is not their original intention or expectation. They are getting ready for attack (cf. Jer. 46:4, 14). But their planning can get nowhere.

The reason is that they are taking this action against Yhwh and against his *anointed. This unexpected, isolated third colon (indeed, people could have understood the first two cola as a complete 3-3 line) brings vv. 1–2 to a climax. Psalm 2 will go on to offer "a comprehensive realization of the *māšîaḥ* concept."[11] How could the nations and kings possibly succeed, when one thinks about who Yhwh is and who his anointed therefore is? Hence the incredulous tone of the opening "Why?" The rhetorical question reflects the extraordinary, stupid nature of the action.

> ³"We are going to break off their fetters,
>   throw their ropes off us."

In two further parallel cola the kings declare how they think they are going to throw off these constraints and run wild again. Literal "fetters" are the ropes by which human beings constrain animals to get them to

---

9. Ibid.
10. Randy G. Haney (*Text and Concept Analysis in Royal Psalms* [New York: Lang, 2002], 87–89) argues this also from the use of the words "nations" and "peoples."
11. K. Seybold, *TDOT* 9:51.

serve them (e.g., Job 39:5), specifically the ropes linked to a yoke (e.g., Jer. 27:2).

2:4–6. The second section parallels and contrasts with the first. Once again two lines describe someone's stance and a third line brings it to a close by reporting the speaker's actual words, but this section reports the response to that earlier implausible declaration of intent.

> ⁴The one who sits in the heavens is amused;
>   the Lord laughs at them.

God is "the one who sits in the heavens" and is then the *Lord: the second expression makes clear that God sits in the heavens enthroned and sovereign, not just relaxing. "Sits in heaven" (EVV) could give the impression that Yhwh was some distance away, but the phrase rather locates God within the cosmos and easily able to look down to see what is going on (e.g., 11:4; 14:2; 33:13). God's reaction is merriment and scorn: the second verb makes clear that there is a serious side to Yhwh's smile. Prosaically put, "The one who sits in the heavens as Lord laughs in amusement at them." Yhwh does not take them with the seriousness with which they take themselves (e.g., 37:13; 59:8 [9]; Isa. 37:22).

> ⁵Then he speaks to them in his anger,
>   dismays them with his fury.

In a further parallel bicolon, God speaks, and dismays: the second expression specifies the effect of the first. The reason for the dismay is the awareness that they are on the receiving end of God's anger (cf. 6:2–3 [3–4]; 90:7). "Fury" (*ḥārôn*, from *ḥārâ*, "burn") usually appears along with the much more common word "anger" (*'ap*) in order to give it emphasis by suggesting blazing rage (e.g., 69:24 [25]; 78:49). Prosaically put, "Then he speaks in his blazing anger to dismay them." Verse 5 as a whole also pairs with v. 4 as a whole. Yhwh first laughs in amusement, then (*'āz*) speaks and dismays. It is not enough merely to be amused; the situation requires an emotion that will generate action. Typically, the psalm makes clear that Yhwh has the full emotional range of a person. Here, Yhwh has both the capacity to be amused and the capacity to become angry. The first enables a person to keep things in perspective and not to take bluster seriously. The second gives a person the energy to act toughly when tough action is required.[12]

---

12. Chrysostom comments (on 6:1 [2]) that of course God does not really feel anger and wrath; God is without passions (*Psalms*, 1:95–96). If so, it was risky of God to speak so consistently in the Psalms and elsewhere about having such passions (e.g., Isa. 10:6; Jer. 49:37; Ezek. 7:14; Zeph. 3:8).

> ⁶"But I myself installed my king
> on Zion, my holy mountain!"

Yhwh's words then confront the kings' words in v. 3. Once more the direct speech is unannounced and thus the more forceful: there is no prosaic "saying" (NRSV). "I installed *my* king": the first-person statement picks up the expression "*his* anointed." The second half of the line completes the first half, indicating where the king was installed rather than making any parallel statement. The reference to Zion is an isolated note in the psalm. Perhaps the promise would have been delivered there, and the psalms that follow would be sung there. It thus adds to the force of the statement for its hearers. The polarity between Yhwh sitting enthroned in the heavens and Zion being Yhwh's holy mountain forms a bracket around vv. 4–6. Zion is the place where the God who eternally dwells in heaven and who at creation established a dwelling in the heavens then established a further home on earth. It is thus "my holy mountain."

2:7–9. After a resumptive introduction by the king, the psalm continues Yhwh's words with three lines that all involve neat parallelism. They spell out the implications of v. 6 and thus further explain the incredulous stance of vv. 1–3.

> ⁷I shall tell of Yhwh's decree:
> he said to me, "You are my son;
> I myself beget you today."

Verse 7 makes clear that the speaker in this psalm is the king, who now gives more information on the way the declaration in v. 6 makes the nations' rebelliousness laughable. Yhwh as king made a decree (cf. 1 Sam. 30:25) concerning the king who rules from Zion. Perhaps this is something similar to the "declaration" (*ʿēdût*) that could be given to a king at his accession (2 Kings 11:12).[13] The king is Yhwh's son (cf. 2 Sam. 7:14), who rules his father's realm as his regent. The king implies that he heard Yhwh give this decree, so the occasion was hardly the day of his physical birth, but his designation or coronation. Yhwh did not bring him into being then but did enter into a fatherly commitment to him in adopting him as son. The words uttered on that occasion made him heir to his father's wealth and authority and are the undergirding of his position now. To judge from practice elsewhere in the Middle East, "You are my son" is a performative declaration of adoption; 89:26 [27] will

---

13. On the background of the idea of a "decree," see G. H. Jones, "The Decree of Yahweh," *VT* 15 (1965): 336–44.

then indicate the correlative response, and Hosea 1:9 the dark opposite.[14] The parallel colon explains how that works, in another performative, "I hereby beget you."[15]

> [8]"Ask of me and I will make
> nations your possession,
> earth's ends your estate."

"Ask of me and I will make" applies to both the phrases that follow, which come in *abb′a′* order in the Hebrew. The second phrase makes the promise more extravagant than the first. The undertaking concerning nations and earth's ends takes up the threat formulated by nations and earth's kings (vv. 1–2), while "ask of me and I will make" recalls Yhwh's words to Solomon, "Ask what I should give you" (1 Kings 3:5): the first verb form is the same and "make/give" is *'ettĕnâ/'ettēn*. The circumstances of Yhwh's commitment to David (2 Sam. 7) and Solomon warn us against assuming that the commitment referred to here must link with the king's actual accession.

> [9]"You can break them up [*or*, shepherd them] with an iron club,
> smash them like a potter's vessel."

Verse 9 also comes in *abb′a′* order ("You can break them with an iron club, like a potter's vessel smash them"). The two prepositional phrases apply to both cola, and the second verb goes beyond the first: "You can smash them to pieces with an iron bar as if they were a potter's vessel." But "break" (*rā'a'*)[16] is an Aramaism, and LXX, Syr, and Jerome rather link the verb with the more familiar *rā'â*, "shepherd" (the noun is *šēbeṭ*, the shepherd's "rod" in 23:4).[17] The line then lays alternative possibilities before the nations—either firm shepherding or devastating destruction. Verses 10–12 as a whole will certainly do that.

2:10–12. In the closing section "the poet directly takes on the powerful, by pelting them with commands."[18]

---

14. So Gerstenberger, *Psalms*, 1:46–47. Richard Press ("Jahwe und sein Gesalbter," *TZ* 13 [1957]: 321–34) argues for Egyptian influence here, though Ansgar Moenikes ("Psalm 2,7b und die Göttlichkeit des israelischen Königs," *ZAW* 111 [1999]: 619–21) suggests that the psalm is distinctive in seeing the king as adopted, not born, as son; cf. also Gerald Cooke, "The Israelite King as Son of God," *ZAW* 72 (1960): 202–25.

15. Cf. DG 61, 64.

16. The form is *tĕrō'ēm* from *rā'a'* II, instead of a form of *rāṣaṣ*.

17. This perhaps requires the repointing *tir'ēm*. Revelation 2:27; 12:5; 19:15 presuppose this reading, and Gerhard Wilhelmi ("Der Hirt mit dem eisernen Szepter," *VT* 27 [1977]: 196–204) argues that it is the original reading.

18. Fokkelman, *Major Poems*, 2:56.

> ¹⁰So now, kings, be sensible;
> allow yourselves to be put right, earth's leaders.

Another line comprises two parallel cola in *abb'a'* order, with the second colon giving the first more precision. How are the kings to be sensible? By accepting a warning. Behaving sensibly is a basic requirement of a nation's leaders, though one often not fulfilled (e.g., Jer. 3:15; 23:5); how much less do leaders welcome being confronted. In v. 3 they were throwing off the constraints that were designed to keep them on the right path (*môsĕrôt*); now they are urged to allow themselves to be put on the right path (*yāsar*). There is a condescending but realistic tone to v. 10, which in speaking of good sense and openness to correction addresses the kings like a parent addressing a child, like the teacher in Proverbs, where the nouns (*śēkel*, *mûsār*) are especially at home (e.g., Prov. 1:2–8; 16:22). But this is one king addressing other kings!

> ¹¹Serve Yhwh with reverence,
> rejoice with trembling, ¹²ᵃsubmit sincerely,

The next line explains its predecessor. How do they show good sense by letting themselves be put right? There are three parallel answers to the question.

First, they will serve Yhwh with reverence. It does not come naturally to *leaders* to *serve*—indeed, it is a contradiction. How can a leader be a servant? But leaders have to see themselves as standing in a chain of command in which they are not at the top. They serve God, and thus they lead with *reverence (it suits the context to assume the positive meaning of *yir'â*). Once more, this is an exhortation to act with wisdom (cf. Prov. 1:7).

Second, they will "rejoice with trembling." The combination of joy and awe recurs: see the twin exhortations in 95:1–2 and 6 and the twin descriptions of earth in 97:1, 4. Psalm 100:1–2 will similarly exhort "all the earth" to "serve Yhwh with gladness." Psalm 2 thus affirms both that service, reverence, joy, and trembling go together,[19] and that the *nations* are invited into this combination. The close of the psalm will fit with this: there they are implicitly invited to rely on Yhwh. And the double stance to the nations fits the promise to Abraham, noted in the introduction to this psalm above. If they belittle, they are cursed; but if they let themselves be attracted, they can find blessing.

---

19. Cf. Carsten Vang, "Ps 2,11–12," *SJOT* 9 (1995): 163–84, see 173–77. But see *DCH* for the possibility that another verb, *gîl*, means "worship."

Third, they will submit to Yhwh instead of rebelling, and do so with sincerity—with pure hearts, the inner attitude corresponding to the outward words (cf. *bar* in 24:4; 73:1; also Job 11:4).

The three answers link with each other in *abcb'a'd* fashion. "Serve" and "submit" form a pair, as do "reverence" and "trembling," each time a less-common word reinforcing the more-common one. The unexpected and generous positive invitation to rejoice stands out as the central word in the line, while the requirement of sincerity (no secret further plotting) reminds the hearers that the king has not gone soft.

> ¹²ᵇLest he be angry and you perish as regards the path,
>   because his anger will soon blaze.
>
> The good fortune of all that rely on him!

The subsequent two cola manifest that striking link with the close of Ps. 1: if you rebel, you will "perish" as regards your "path." There is indeed still an iron fist behind the preceding exhortation. The nations are being invited to choose whether they "perish" (*'ābad*) or "serve" (*'ābad*). In the context of the Psalter more broadly, they are being invited to choose between Ps. 48:4–7 and Pss. 95–100.

The midrash quotes Isa. 40:22–23 and comments that the nations resemble grasshoppers trapped in an urn, flinging themselves upward only to fall down.[20] The leaders would therefore be wise to take advantage of the alternative prospect in the closing colon—apparently a one-colon line standing in isolation at the close of the psalm and thus carrying some emphasis. The promise about *relying on Yhwh immediately applies to the Davidic king under pressure from his foes, the subject of the psalm as a whole (cf. 7:1 [2]; 11:1, when read in light of these psalms' headings), but the line generalizes the point with its "all," which will be taken up in 5:11 [12]. The message of the psalm is for the whole community. Indeed, the world leaders who have just been mentioned and given their exhortations could not be excluded from it. The psalm has told them how to find protection from Yhwh's violence. J. F. D. Creach suggests that this comment on finding protection or refuge with Yhwh, closing the two psalms that together open the Psalter, is a key to the message of the Psalter as a whole.[21]

Theological Implications

Eugene Peterson comments that in the Psalter "two psalms are carefully set as an introduction: Psalm 1 is a laser concentration on the person;

---

20. *Midrash on Psalms,* 1:35.
21. *Yahweh as Refuge and the Editing of the Hebrew Psalter* (JSOTSup 217; Sheffield: Sheffield Academic Press, 1996).

Psalm 2 is a wide-angle lens on politics. . . . We love Psalm 1 and ignore Psalm 2."[22] Psalm 2 denies the apparent meaninglessness of history. "At the centre of history is no longer the struggle of the great world powers for existence, but God, whose relationship with the earthly powers will determine their destiny."[23] But the psalm thus presupposes a relationship between Yhwh and the world based on force and violence. Yhwh insists on the nations' submission and is prepared to use violence to put down nations that seek their independence. Like Israel's own story, it illustrates the way God is prepared to be tough. Yhwh is God, who in the end is prepared to require recognition of that. It also thereby offers hope to peoples who are themselves under pressure. The Israelites who used this psalm were never a superpower; for most of their history they were a vassal state or a province under some imperial power. The psalm promises that this will not always be how things are. It also presupposes that Yhwh associates the Israelite king with this control of the world by force and violence.[24] Its stance thus corresponds to the attitude taken in (e.g.) the story of Yhwh and Pharaoh in Exodus, even when one makes allowance for the fact that Pharaoh was himself an oppressor (there is no indication in Ps. 2 that the nations had acted wrongly except in desiring their independence).

To whom does this psalm belong, with its warnings and promises, when there is no individual anointed king to speak it? One possibility is that it belongs to a future king such as one promised in passages like Isa. 9:2–7 [1–6]; 11:1–9. That coheres with one aspect of its reapplication to Jesus in the NT (Acts 4:25–26; 13:33; Heb. 1:5; 5:5; 2 Pet. 1:17; cf. Matt. 3:17; 17:5; Rev. 12:5; 19:15).[25] On the other hand, the risen Christ himself applies the promises in vv. 8–9 not to himself but to "everyone who conquers" (Rev. 2:26–27). He thus affirms the psalm's declaration regarding the violent stance in relation to the world that God takes, and associates the churches with it. Like Israel for much of its history, the readers of Revelation were the underlings of a great empire, and they are promised that this is not how things will always be.[26]

22. *Where Your Treasure Is*, 10.
23. Weiser, *Psalms*, 111.
24. See D. J. A. Clines, "Psalm 2 and the MLF (Moabite Liberation Front)," in *Interested Parties* (JSOTSup 205; Sheffield: Sheffield Academic Press, 1995), 244–75.
25. For a subsequent Christian appropriation, see Allan K. Jenkins, "Erasmus' Commentary on Psalm 2," *Journal of Hebrew Scriptures* (e-journal) 3 (2000): article 3; and on the psalm's theological significance, see also James W. Watts, "Psalm 2 in the Context of Biblical Theology," *HBT* 12 (1990): 73–91.
26. Thus Martin Luther's exposition of 1532, while presupposing a christological understanding of the psalm, combines it with a remarkable, sustained reading in light of the "raving of the world" against him (*Selected Psalms*, 1:3–93, see 5). Contrast his earlier exposition dedicated to the Duke of Saxony (*Selected Psalms*, 3:31–49).

That fits with other pointers in the OT, also taken up in the midrash. Yhwh's promises originally related to the people as a whole; promises to Israel's king were theologically subordinate to that. Working via a king was a temporary feature in Israel's life. Davidic kingship came to an end in 587 and was never reestablished. Instead, Yhwh made (or remade) the kind of covenant with the whole people that had once obtained with David.[27]

So Ps. 2 belongs to the Jewish people as the people of God. Over the centuries the nations have often plotted against the Jewish people, but the psalm promises that such plots will never succeed. They have a secure central place in God's purpose, and that is destined to be acknowledged. Psalm 2 belongs in particular to the State of Israel as a focal embodiment of the Jewish people. It is entitled to trust in such promises as it experiences the same pressures. (This is not to imply that God takes its side irrespective of the rights or wrongs of its own policies; any generation can forfeit God's promises by its life, as Israel did in the wilderness on the way from Sinai to the promised land, and the State of Israel could do that.) The psalm thus has a dangerous capacity to legitimate oppressive imperial violence. It illustrates the risk involved in Yhwh's agreeing to Israel's misguided request for a king like the nations. It is thus fortunate that in practice Yhwh never put Israel in a position to implement the program in Ps. 2, or fortunate that apparently an Israelite king never took up the invitation to "ask of me. . ." (v. 8).

Psalm 2 also belongs to the church as an expanded version of the people of God. Christian nations have been in a position to implement its program and have sought to do so. One might have thought that the positive stance sometimes expressed in the NT regarding the accepting of other people's violence might have had an influence on the Christian church, but more often the attitude expressed in the psalm has found an embodiment in the freedom Christian nations have felt to attack and oppress other peoples.[28]

The stance of vv. 1–9 and of Revelation constitutes a striking contrast with the attitude to the nations in (e.g.) the promise to Abraham (Gen. 12:1–3) or Christ's commission to his disciples (Matt. 28:16–20), though the latter also speaks of authority and submission. But the stance of Ps.

---

27. See the section on "King and Messiah" in the introduction to this commentary.

28. Mary R. Huie-Jolly sees Ps. 2 behind John 5 and comments that the version of the father/son relationship it suggests "re-creates its divine warrior mythic structure in social and ecclesial reality. It projects authoritarian, patriarchal, and exclusive structures" (see "Threats Answered by Enthronement," in *Early Christian Interpretation of the Scriptures of Israel* [ed. Craig A. Evans and James A. Sanders; Journal for the Study of the New Testament: Supplement Series 148; Sheffield: Sheffield Academic Press, 1997], 191–217; see 216–17).

2:10–12 also compares with these latter. The psalm invites kings and rulers to show some insight and to find a new attitude toward Yhwh that will involve reverence, submission, and joy; it closes with a blessing on all who rely on Yhwh—which can hardly exclude them. So the psalm indeed places two destinies before the nations. They choose one or the other. But negative consequences really do follow from the wrong choice. Yes, Yhwh is prepared to be tough.

The psalm implicitly forestalls ideological appropriation in another way. While the king is prominent in the middle of the psalm, he disappears in vv. 10–12. The nations are not bidden to serve him or submit to him, and the psalm does not speak of his getting angry and annihilating them. The king asks for submission to Yhwh, not directly to himself. Like David, the nations are in a position to choose to fall into the hands of God, whose compassion is great, rather than to fall into human hands (2 Sam. 24:14). Like Jesus's warnings about the prospects of rotting in hell, these warnings to the nations are designed to shake people to their senses (though this is not to say that the warnings have no teeth). Further, the close of the psalm shows that the people of God are invited to share Yhwh's concern that the nations may see sense, not to look forward to their punishment.

Living in a post-Christian era in the West means living in an era when the culture has thrown off the constraints of Christian faith, but the psalm promises that this will not be the end of the story.

Psalm 3
The Question of Deliverance

Translation

Composition. David's. When he fled from his son Absalom.

¹Yhwh, how many my adversaries have become,[a]
  [how] many people are rising against me.
²[How] many are saying to me personally,[b]
  "There is no deliverance[c] for him in God."[d] (Rise)

³But you, Yhwh, are a shield about me;
  you are my honor, one who lifts up my head.[e]
⁴I would call out[f] to Yhwh,
  and he answered me[g] from his holy mountain. (Rise)

a. Or simply "are" (JM 112a; DG 57a).
b. After a verb of saying the *lĕ* on *lĕnapšî* could mean either "to" or "of" (BDB 510, 514), but "to" is more common and more forceful here, and corresponds to the meaning of *lĕnapšî* in 11:1; 35:3. NRSV assumes that "to" requires a different text in v. 2b so that it refers to "you" rather than "him." But Hebrew poetry often changes perspective and thus changes prepositions between cola (cf. v. 8), and such a change of reference is possible with MT's text. Syr "for you" is assimilating to the sense.
c. *Yĕšûʿātâ*, an archaic long form used for rhythmic reasons (JM 93j) rather than merely for emphasis (GKC 90g) or as retaining acc. implication (GKC 152n).
d. LXX has "in his God," which would be a legitimate inference; Syr has "in your [f.] God," continuing its assimilation to the previous colon.
e. As usual, it is difficult to be sure how to construe the multiple noun clause. I assume that the "you [are]" holds for the second colon as well as the first. We could translate "You are Yhwh, a shield . . . ," or "You are Yhwh, you are a shield. . . ."
f. Lit., "[with] my voice I would call" (cf. GKC 144m). Such occurrences of *qôl* are hardly just a grammatically odd way of saying "My voice would call" (so JM 151c); they often draw attention to the out-loud-ness of the prayer or praise, and thus to its fervency (e.g., 5:2 [3]; 26:7).
g. For the wayyiqtol after the yiqtol, cf. 80:8 [9]; see *IBHS* 33.3.3 (though it takes this particular example as referring to the present).

⁵Even I lay down and slept;
   I woke up, because Yhwh would uphold me.
⁶I would not be afraid of a ten-thousand-strong people
   that took its stand against me all around.

⁷Arise, Yhwh;
   deliver me, my God,
Because you hit all my enemies on the jaw,ʰ
   you smashed the teeth of the faithless.
⁸Deliverance belongs to Yhwh;
   your blessing is on your people.ⁱ (Rise)

Interpretation

With Ps. 3 the Psalter begins to support the dictum quoted in the introduction above: "Most of Scripture speaks *to* us; the Psalms speak *for* us." The opening of this protest psalm still suggests it will hardly fit in with the Psalter's title, *tĕhillîm* (praises), because it starts with a lament (vv. 1–2)—contrast (e.g.) Pss. 4; 5; and 6, which start with an initial plea. But after that Ps. 3 immediately becomes a declaration of trust twice as long as the lament (vv. 3–6), and thus it provides an illustration of the dictum that there are no laments that do not take at least one step on the road to praise.¹ "In the language of poetry, perhaps the two perspectives of before (time of difficulty) and after (rescue), have been set side-by-side."² It then makes a transition to plea (v. 7a) before reverting to a declaration of trust (vv. 7b–8). Compared with other prayer psalms, then, its distinctive features are its beginning with lament but then its emphasis on recollection and trust, and the brevity of any actual plea.

Coming together near the beginning of the Psalter, Pss. 3 and 4 offer prayers for morning (3:5) and evening (4:8 [9]); there are other verbal links between the two psalms that could have encouraged their juxtaposition (see the comments on Ps. 4). They then function to shape the congregation's attitudes so that they know how to respond when they confront crises of the kind that the psalms describe.

Composition. David's. When he fled from his son Absalom.

---

h. On the construction, see GKC 117ll.
i. There is no verb in v. 8b. EVV take it as a wish, as in 129:8, but there the parallelism makes clear that this is so; other instances (see DG 154) also have imperatives in the context. Here the parallelism suggests that it is a statement.

1. Westermann, *Praise and Lament*, 154.
2. Robert C. Culley, "Psalm 3," in *Text, Methode und Grammatik* (Wolfgang Richter Festschrift), ed. Walter Gross et al. (St. Ottilien: EOS, 1991), 29–39, see 38.

Heading. See glossary. The heading, particularly the term *composition, already signals that at last we are nearer to reading something that belongs in a worship book. The psalm's "I" could be taken up by the king (David or the David of the day), especially its language that suggests military attack, or by a leader of the postmonarchic community under pressure from the communities around (e.g., Ezra 4:1; Neh. 4:11 [5]). In either case, one can imagine the psalm being used on occasions of community prayer. But the generality of its language would make it also usable by individuals within the community who were under attack from others (people in Job's position), on their own or with family and friends.

The words of the psalm and the story to which the heading refers enable us to see the nature of the psalm's link with this particular incident in David's life. The psalm begins by noting how adversaries have increased (*rabbû*) and how many are the suppliant's attackers (*qāmîm*). The context of 2 Sam. 15:14–17 describes how Absalom's group continued to increase (*rāb*; 15:12) and how a messenger expressed a wish concerning David's attackers (*qāmû*; 18:32). Other elements in the story fit the psalm more generally. Shimei (2 Sam. 16:5–8) might have nodded his head at v. 2. David's subsequent experience fits vv. 3–8. On the other hand, other elements in the story do not point to a link between this incident and the content of the psalm. The story does not describe David as having the confidence that vv. 3–6 implies, the psalm conveys no suggestion of flight, and the reference to Yhwh's people (v. 8) makes this look like a psalm for a national crisis, not a civil war. The links, the general suitability, and the tensions fit with the view that psalm and story are of separate origin but that someone who noticed the precise verbal links brought psalm and story into relationship with each other to aid people using the psalm by enabling them to imagine it being used in a specific context.

3:1–2. We have noted that Pss. 1–2 provide theological undergirding for the psalms that follow. The need for this now emerges in vv. 1–2. The attackers are many, many, many, but Yhwh/God has the first and last word in vv. 1–2.[3]

> ¹Yhwh, how many my adversaries have become,
> [how] many people are rising against me.

The two cola make parallel statements; a qatal verb and a participle pair with each other, while the "how" and the invocation "Yhwh" apply

---

3. Cf. McCann, "Psalms," 693.

to the second colon as well as the first. The second colon gives precision to the way the adversaries are acting.

> ²[How] many are saying to me personally,
> "There is no deliverance for him in God." (Rise)

The participle in the first colon then takes up from that in v. 1b and suggests that the "how" continues to apply there. The suppliant's experience is the converse of the prayer in 35:3. The second colon completes the statement begun in the first. While enemies might well have been declaring that God would not be delivering the suppliant, one may guess they are also the externalizing of the suppliant's fear (cf. the story in 2 Kings 18:30–35, though the verb there is *haṣṣîl*). Their words get to the suppliant's very *nepeš*, the self (*person). They may be implying that God is not involved in human life in such a way to deliver, as the Rabshakeh says to Hezekiah. We are on our own, they then say, and people should not fool themselves; it is human action that is decisive. But "for him" suggests that they are people who do believe in God's power but do not believe that God will act for this person. Why would they do that? On an occasion such as Absalom's rebellion or Sennacherib's invasion, this would suggest that they are confident they can defeat him. On an occasion such as Job's suffering or the conflicts in Ezra and Nehemiah, these attackers would not be the people responsible for the original predicament at all. The suppliant's problem is a different, consequent one, people's action that follows on whatever has happened. They dismiss the suppliant as someone cast off by God, who therefore has no prospects of deliverance and will not escape defeat or evade failure or find healing. On *Rise, see glossary.

3:3–6. A statement of trust confronts the enemies' taunts with the truth the suppliant is committed to and needs to reaffirm both to Yhwh and to the self.[4] The declaration is then characteristically backed up by lengthy recollection of Yhwh's past acts of deliverance. Here yiqtol and qatal verbs alternate, offering general statements about past experience and concrete recollections that illustrate the general statement.[5] I take it

---

4. Pierre Auffret ("Notes sur la structure littéraire du Psaume 3," *ZAW* 91 [1979]: 93–106) links v. 3 with what precedes rather than what follows; cf. John S. Kselman, "Psalm 3," *CBQ* 49 (1987): 572–80.

5. LXX translates both verbs in v. 4 as past, which makes little difference, and v. 5b as future. Tg translates both verbs in v. 4 with "imperfects," all the verbs in v. 5 with "perfects"; Jerome follows in translating both verbs in v. 4 as future and v. 5b as past. NRSV translates all the verbs in vv. 4–6a (and 7b) as present. NIVI translates vv. 4–5 as present, v. 6a as future. Such variations reflect the inherent ambiguity of the Hebrew verbal system, and some of the renderings have the advantage and disadvantage of making the psalm less specific. The regular use of the qatal to refer to past events fits with the inclination in the

that the psalm recalls three recurrent experiences—crying out to Yhwh, having Yhwh sustain and protect, and not being afraid of a huge army. Those experiences follow logically from each other. It also recalls three concrete experiences associated with those generalizations, specific occasions when Yhwh answered pleas, and when the suppliant thus lay down, slept, and woke rather than dying in bed, when an army took its stand around.

> ³But you, Yhwh, are a shield about me;
> you are my honor, one who lifts up my head.

The actual statement of trust expresses itself as a statement about Yhwh, not a statement about the suppliant's trust. It reaffirms three characteristics of Yhwh. *Shield can be accompanied by reference to Yhwh's being a help or a deliverance, as in v. 2 here, so that v. 3 directly confronts that jibe. "About me" strengthens the point. The expression is an unusual one, often used for shutting the door "on" someone, and elsewhere it usually has negative significance (e.g., Job 3:23). But it is positive in Job 1:10, as here. A regular handheld shield does not wholly enclose a person, but this shield has that effect. My *honor also comes in the company of such expressions in 21:5 [6]; 62:7 [8], but more immediately the question in 4:2 [3] stands in contrast with this statement of faith. The declaration that Yhwh is my honor goes beyond the declaration that Yhwh is a shield: Yhwh restores the honor as well as the person. "One who lifts up my head" then spells that out more concretely (cf. 27:6; 83:2 [3]; 110:7). It may be a legal expression, but in itself this hardly establishes that the suppliant is on trial. In defeat and dishonor we cannot lift up our heads (Job 10:15); in victory we hold our heads high.

> ⁴I would call out to Yhwh,
> and he answered me from his holy mountain. (Rise)

The account of Yhwh's past acts of deliverance begins with a recollection of the regular shouting out loud to get Yhwh's attention. Perhaps that presupposes that Yhwh is some way off, in the heavens, but is quite able to hear and act from there (2:4; cf. 20:6 [7]); 33:13–19; 80:14 [15]). But in this psalm Yhwh's answer comes not from the heavens but from the holy mountain, Mount Zion (2:6), where Yhwh also has a home (e.g., 43:3; 74:2[3]). If the king utters this plea, the reference

---

Psalms to recall what Yhwh has done before, and taking vv. 4–6 to refer to the past generates a more nuanced and dynamic understanding of the psalm as a whole. But readers could easily understand and use the psalm in one of those other ways.

to Yhwh's holy mountain will take up the fact that Yhwh did install him there (2:6).

> ⁵Even I lay down and slept;
> I woke up, because Yhwh would uphold me.

The grammatically unnecessary "I" corresponds to the "you" of v. 4.[6] If we may read vv. 4–6 narratively (however we translate the verbs), the fact that Yhwh answered prayer made it possible to sleep safely. When the psalms talk about Yhwh answering prayer, they mean this in the narrow sense. Yhwh has heard the prayer and uttered a response, though not yet acted to implement the undertaking expressed in the response; the answer is the words, not the action. But the words issue in action. Yhwh "upholds" (*sāmak*). The more common implication of this verb would be that Yhwh gives protection so that the suppliant survives the danger of the night, when enemies might attack while people sleep (e.g., 4:8 [9]; 37:17; 145:14). But readers might refer it to an inner upholding that makes it possible to sleep soundly without worrying (e.g., 2 Chron. 32:8).[7]

> ⁶I would not be afraid of a ten-thousand-strong people
> that took its stand against me all around.

In isolation, one could take this as a statement of the suppliant's subsequent, ongoing inner confidence (cf. LXX, Jerome, Tg), which could then form a bracket with v. 3 around vv. 4–5. But it again combines yiqtol and qatal verbs and more likely provides another declaration of ongoing past attitude and concrete experience. In substance, though not in words, v. 6b provides a nice inclusion with v. 3a: "I was not worried by the gathering of enemies around me, because I have Yhwh's shield about me."

3:7–8. Verses 3–6 no doubt function to build up the suppliant's own confidence in Yhwh, but as the three parallel bicola of vv. 7–8 bring the psalm to its climax, they suggest that vv. 3–6 function more directly to motivate Yhwh to act in accordance with the established character that those events reflected.

> ⁷Arise, Yhwh;
> deliver me, my God,

---

6. Cf. Kidner, *Psalms*, 1:54.
7. Christoph Schroeder ("Psalm 3," *Bib* 81 [2000]: 243–51) suggests that the psalmist has been awakened from sleep by Yhwh and given a promise of deliverance; the psalm is then praying for this to become reality.

> Because you hit all my enemies on the jaw,
> you smashed the teeth of the faithless.

The practical point of the psalm comes in the brisk, direct, punchy 2-2 first line. The plea takes up the words of the opening plaint, which addressed "Yhwh" about people "rising up" against the suppliant and reported what people were saying about the suppliant's "deliverance" and "God." Verse 7 once more addresses Yhwh and goes on to call on "my God."[8] The reminder that Yhwh is "*my* God" makes explicit for the first time the point that underlies the whole psalm and further underlines the basis on which the psalm presses Yhwh to intervene. Its description of God is thus actually quite different from that of the adversaries, who only talk about "God." In its verb, too, the second colon takes the point further. At the moment, Yhwh is sitting enthroned in the heavens. The suppliant wants Yhwh to get up, like the king getting off his throne and coming to investigate the shouts he hears from the city—indeed, to get up as the assailants have (v. 1). But the suppliant wants God to act as well as to get up and investigate, and specifically to act to deliver—the act that the assailants said would never come (v. 2). The imperative parallels the one Moses would utter when the covenant chest was to set out, which likewise spelled out its implications in terms of the scattering of foes (Num. 10:35–36). That urging goes on to refer to the "ten thousands of Israel." The phrase is enigmatic in context, but whatever its precise meaning, that further buttresses the conviction in v. 6.

The second line once again makes explicit that this plea bases itself on the way Yhwh has acted in the past. It thus takes vv. 3–6 further, as the previous line took vv. 1–2 further.[9] Those verses spoke only of protection and made no statement about trouble for the enemies. But in the real world, protection and deliverance mean the defeat of enemies, and this is not a pretty matter. While the language is different from that of 2:9, the reality and the realism are similar, though the language may be metaphorical. The second colon is literally "The teeth of the wicked you smashed," so that the line has a neat stepped structure, *abcc'b'a'*. The form thus mirrors the reversal the words describe, even as its neat poetic form contrasts with its horrifying content. The second colon goes beyond the first in unpleasant ways, as smashing teeth suggests a more

---

8. The parallel is even closer in LXX and Syr, which had "his God" or "your God" in v. 2.

9. *IBHS* 30.5.4cd argues that after the imperatives the qatal verbs in v. 7 are precative (cf. DG 60c; NIVI). But the contextual argument can work either way: a restatement of the basis for the prayer is quite appropriate and means the *kî* can have its regular meaning "because" rather than having to be purely emphatic (*IBHS* 39.3.4e). The *kî* also makes it hard to take the line as an anticipatory testimony to Yhwh's having answered the plea.

devastating assault than hitting someone on the jaw or makes explicit the implications of that. But hitting someone on the jaw or cheek is at least as much a gesture of shaming as of physical hurt, and the image of shattering teeth may also be a legal metaphor for disempowering.[10] At the same time, the move from "enemies" to "faithless" introduces a moral note into the psalm for the first time (there was none in Ps. 2 at all). The claim for deliverance cannot be based merely on the fact of having enemies.[11]

> [8]Deliverance belongs to Yhwh;
>   your blessing is on your people. (Rise)

"Deliverance" recurs once more; it is the key motif in the psalm. The line constitutes a final statement of trust. One might have expected this third reference to deliverance to close off the psalm, but the second colon goes beyond the first in setting the whole psalm in a broader horizon. The bulk of the psalm focuses on a crisis in the life of an individual. Yhwh is involved in that. But the suppliant also knows that the more fundamental matter is the ongoing fruitfulness of the whole people. In particular, the point about having a king or a leader is to serve the people, and the object of the leader's deliverance is to get the people's life back to its normal fruitfulness. Or, conversely, Yhwh's commitment to blessing the people is a final basis for trust that there can be blessing for the leader as a member of this people. There is thus a suggestive asymptotic relationship between "my God" (v. 7) and "your people" (v. 8).

Theological Implications

The suppliant and the suppliant's adversaries may have a shared theology and spirituality, a mutual agreement that "deliverance belongs to Yhwh" (v. 8)[12]—as Job and his friends had an agreed theology, particularly before calamity came to Job. Agreement on principles of theology and spirituality may not mean a great deal until these principles confront a context. Here, as often happens, people who agree on such principles dismiss each other. These adversaries declare, "There is no deliverance

---

10. So Nahum M. Sarna, "Legal Terminology in Psalm 3:8," in *Sha'arei Talmon: Studies in the Bible, Qumran, and the Ancient Near East Presented to Shemaryahu Talmon*, ed. Michael Fishbane and Emanuel Tov (Winona Lake, IN: Eisenbrauns, 1992), 175–81.

11. LXX adds another form of value judgment or motivation with its *mataiōs* ("without reason," or perhaps "in vain"). Perhaps it read *ḥinnām* for *leḥî*.

12. Spurgeon comments that v. 8 "contains the sum and substance of Calvinistic doctrine" (*Treasury of David*, 1:24).

for *him* in God." Perhaps they do not think that God is active in the world, but more likely (like Job's friends) they do believe that God is real but think they have reason to conclude that God will certainly not deliver the likes of this person. Against that, the suppliant sets "You are a shield about me, . . . one who lifts up my head," and thus makes the bare appeal, "Deliver me, my God." How can the suppliant know that this appeal will meet with Yhwh's response, that the adversaries are wrong? The answer lies in the way Yhwh has consistently acted in the past. But there is no way of proving whether the adversaries or the suppliant is right except by casting oneself on God.

Psalm 4
Who Shows Us Good?

Translation

The leader's. With strings. Composition. David's.

¹When I call, answer me,
   my faithful God.
In my[a] constraint give me room;
   be gracious to me, listen to my plea.

²You people,[b] how long is my honored one for shaming,
   how long will you dedicate yourselves to emptiness,
   have recourse to falsehood? (Rise)
³Acknowledge that Yhwh has set apart the committed person for himself;
   Yhwh himself listens when I call to him.
⁴Tremble,[c] do not fall short;
   say it[d] within yourselves on your beds and be silent.[e] (Rise)
⁵Offer true sacrifices;
   trust in Yhwh.

   a. Understanding the pronoun from the context, specifically from the second colon, "my plea."
   b. Lit., "sons of an individual"; over against the much more common "sons of humanity," the phrase may imply important people (cf. 49:2 [3]; 62:9 [10]), but used on its own this may not be so (cf. Lam. 3:33).
   c. LXX and Jerome translate "be angry" (cf. Eph. 4:26), but *rāgaz* never means that directly. It refers to physical perturbation; the cause has to be inferred from the context, which here suggests awe.
   d. There is no "it": cf. Exod. 19:25; Judg. 17:2.
   e. Tg understands this not as *dāmam* I but as *DCH*'s *dāmam* IV: "destroy" (cf. Stec, *Targum of Psalms*, 32). John S. Kselman ("A Note on Psalm 4,5," *Bib* 68 [1987]: 103–5) takes

⁶There are many people saying, "Who shows us good?—ᶠ
   the light of your face has fled from over us, Yhwh
   [or, lift the light of your face on us, Yhwh]."
⁷You put joy in my heart
   at the time when their grain and wine increase.
⁸In well-being I shall lie down and sleep at once,
   because you alone are Yhwh;
   you make me live in security.ᵍ

Interpretation

This prayer psalm has many verbal links with the psalm that precedes: call, answer me (v. 1; cf. 3:4 [5]); constraint/adversary (*ṣār, ṣārar*; v. 1, cf. 3:1 [2]); my honor (v. 3; cf. 3:4 [5]); many are saying (v. 6, cf. 3:2 [3]); increase (v. 7, cf. 3:1 [2], "become many"); lie down and sleep (v. 8; cf. 3:5 [6]). We noted in connection with Ps. 3 that the two psalms then form a pair in that they are open to being related to morning (3:5 [6]) and evening (4:8).

Another feature of the psalm is a series of ambiguities that make readers uncertain how to interpret it until we reach the closing two lines, which clarify the whole.[1] In that whole, in light of the experience of Yhwh answering prayer, delivering, and blessing, the suppliant voices a personal assurance about trusting God for the future and urges other people not to have recourse to inferior alternative resources. Outside the heading, there are no pointers to a specific suppliant for whom the prayer is designed or any specific context for its use.[2]

> The leader's. With strings. Composition. David's.

Heading. See glossary.

> ¹When I call, answer me,
>   my faithful God.

---

it as *dāmam* II, "weep," following Dahood, *Psalms*, 1:24–25; cf. Michael L. Barré, "Hearts, Beds, and Repentance in Psalm 4,5 and Hosea 7,14," *Bib* 76 (1995): 53–62.

f. Many EVV close the quotation marks here, but v. 6b follows from v. 6a, and the pl. subject continues. The change to sg. in v. 7 indicates that the end of the quotation comes at the end of v. 6.

g. LXX takes the second and third cola as one clause, "You, Yhwh, alone enable me to live in security," but "You [are] Yhwh" looks like a confession of faith, and more likely MT is right to take it as two clauses.

1. Mandolfo describes the psalm as "rhetorically complex" (*God in the Dock*, 33). On its structure, see Pierre Auffret, "Dieu ma justice," *BN* 118 (2003): 5–12, and his references.

2. L. Dürr ("Zur Datierung von Ps. 4," *Bib* 16 [1935]: 330–38) argues for a fifth-century date.

> In my constraint give me room;
>   be gracious to me, listen to my plea.

4:1. The psalm begins with its only lines of plea. As in 3:7 [8], the brisk opening 2-2 line conveys the urgency of the plea. It assumes that there is person-to-person communication between God and the person who prays, communication characterized by call and response. Chrysostom nicely comments that God listens *when* I call and not merely *after* I call—while we are still speaking, God hears and responds (cf. Isa. 58:9).[3] The second colon completes the first by naming the addressee in such a way as to issue a reminder of the basis for that conviction about God answering prayer: Yhwh is my *faithful or true God.[4]

On the traditional understanding of MT (see NRSV, NJPS), the third colon then expands on the basis for the plea by recalling what God has done in the past, giving specificity to the way Yhwh has been faithful in answering prayer, which is the basis for prayer in the present: "In my constraint you gave me room." The psalm thus opens with two lines in *abb′a′* format, the first and last cola being the suppliant's plea and the middle cola stating the basis for it. These encourage the suppliant and put the pressure on God.

But what then is the "plea" the psalm urges God to heed? There is no explicit plea in vv. 2–5, which rhetorically confront people with a bad attitude, though no doubt there is an implicit plea for God to change them. There is a plea in v. 6, though only in one version of the text; it is uttered by people the suppliant is quoting, not directly by the suppliant, and it may not be meant seriously. There is no plea in vv. 7–8, only a declaration of trust in Yhwh. Might the psalm use *tĕpillâ* in the way English can use the word "prayer," to refer to address to God that does not focus on asking for things? The verb *hitpallēl* is used thus (see 1 Sam. 2:1; Jon. 2:2), but there are no other definite examples of *tĕpillâ* used in this way. More likely, then, the psalm is indeed urging God to pay heed to a plea. So what is the plea?

NIVI thus plausibly understands the verb in v. 1b, *hirḥabtā*, as a precative, "Give me room," rather than a recollection of Yhwh's past act. It thereby makes the whole verse a plea. Preceded by an imperative and followed by two more, this proposed instance of precative qatal well satisfies the criterion that context should make it possible to rec-

---

3. *Psalms*, 1:45.
4. NRSV translates literally, "God of my right!" but a second noun in the genitive regularly functions as an adj. in Hebrew, with any personal pronoun applying to the whole phrase. Syr implies the repointing *'ĕlōhay ṣidqî* "my God, my right/faithfulness."

ognize precative qatal.⁵ Indeed, the absence of plea after v. 1 indicates that the broader as well as the narrower context of the psalm supports the precative understanding. Further, an isolated past reference in this colon would in any case be strange; the psalm gives no further indication of what this earlier giving of room might have been.⁶ If we take v. 1 as a whole to comprise a series of pleas, this makes more sense of its closing appeal to "be gracious and listen to my plea." It is the preceding clauses in the verse that comprise the plea the psalm asks God to listen to.

"Constraint" and "give me room" are antonyms. While *ṣar* commonly means "trouble" more generally, here the collocation with *rāḥab* (be broad) suggests an awareness of the more specific root meaning of *ṣar*. The psalm speaks of being constrained and confined, though it does not indicate the nature of this experience and of Yhwh's turning that into freedom.

The last colon incorporates two key urgings from pleas in the Psalms. "Be gracious" (*ḥānan*) is perhaps surprising, for *grace is the attitude a person shows to someone when there is no existent relationship or desert to appeal to. The psalm is thus appealing to something that lies further back than God's faithfulness or God's past acts, in God's fundamental nature. "Listen" comes last, again with some illogic: should this plea not have come first? But the psalms assume that if they can only get God's attention, everything else will follow. In the Psalter, *tĕpillâ* and *tĕhillâ* (*plea and *praise) are about equally common, suggesting the two sides to psalmody.

4:2–5. The psalm turns to address the suppliant's human troublemakers. There are other occasions when the psalms do that (6:8 [9]; 62:3 [4]), but the context and the length of this exhortation reflect a unique trust in Yhwh that issues in this attempt to get them to change their ways more for their own sake than for the suppliant's.⁷ At the same time it could function somewhat like a lament; the suppliant has something to lament about but diverts this into preaching. The psalm could then fulfill a role for people who are uneasy about complaining to God; they can protest at other people.

By a tour de force we could imagine the person who speaks being both in God's presence and in the presence of these addressees, such as

---

5. See *IBHS* 30.5.4; Buttenwieser, *Psalms*, 18–25. Contrast the comments on 3:7 [8] above. In the first colon, LXX implies *'ănanî* for *'ănēnî* and thus in contrast confines plea to the last colon, but this still raises the question "What plea?" See (e.g.) Gerstenberger, *Psalms*, 1:57, against (e.g.) Weiser, *Psalms*, 119.

6. Thus Kraus (*Psalms*, 1:145) comments that this clause "has a strange position, as if it were an interpolation."

7. Cf. Westermann, *Living Psalms*, 125.

in the temple, but this is probably too prosaic. It is enough to imagine someone praying somewhere and aware of the existence of these people: they are present to the imagination. Insofar as the purpose of the psalm is to challenge such people about their attitudes, they are present as the audience in the house, as opposed to the audience on the stage. They are present as people overhearing the psalm and realizing it confronts them.[8] In the four metrically distinctive lines, the first three are very long, conveying the impression of pouring out protests. Verse 5 then forms a punchy 2-2 conclusion.

> ²You people, how long is my honored one for shaming,
>   how long will you dedicate yourselves to emptiness,
>   have recourse to falsehood? (Rise)

*Honor and shame are another correlative pair. Whose honor and shame are referred to? The first colon reads more literally, "How long is my honor for shame?" which could suggest the suppliant is being treated as someone shameful, like Job, who exchanged honor (19:9; 29:20) for humiliation (16:10; 19:5). In the second colon, "emptiness" will then denote people's moral emptiness, and "falsehood" the lies they utter about the suppliant, in the manner of Job's friends (cf. Ps. 5:6 [7]). And/or the "emptiness" of their words could suggest their futility, the same emptiness as that of 2:1. It is then themselves that the friends are deceiving (cf. 62:9 [10]; Isa. 28:15, 17). By shaming the suppliant, they are behaving like faithless people, not servants of God. If they are acting in God's name, like Job's friends, this is a telling observation.

But subsequent lines will suggest that v. 2 refers to Yhwh's honor rather than the suppliant's. Yhwh is Israel's *kābôd* (106:20; Jer. 2:11) and thus the one the suppliant honors,[9] but people have changed this glorious one for something shameful that brings shame on Yhwh and will bring shame on them. The second colon spells out the point in two further parallel clauses. They have *dedicated themselves to something empty (*rîq*), something that cannot help them (cf. Isa. 30:7). How have they done that? "They have recourse to falsehood" recalls the use of this verb (*biqqēš*) in (e.g.) 27:4, 8; 105:4 and the use of "falsehood" to refer to other gods (40:4 [5]; Amos 2:4). The suppliant's addressees are not personal attackers but people who have recourse to other gods.

---

8. Mandolfo (*God in the Dock*, 30–35) sees vv. 2–3a, 4–5 as addressed to the suppliant by God, but this seems to introduce implausible unevennesses; v. 3b does not fit, and the suppliant's further words in vv. 7–9 do not really respond to Yhwh's admonition.

9. Cf. BDB 459.

> ³Acknowledge that Yhwh has set apart the committed person for himself;
> Yhwh himself listens when I call to him.

Against their stance, the psalm then puts the real facts from which they are hiding. Anyone who has recourse to falsehood in any of the senses that v. 2 allows is shown to be not the kind of *committed person with whom Yhwh identifies. In contrast (contrary to their lies), the suppliant *is* that kind of person; the singular *ḥāsîd* points to the suppliant as an individual. Their behavior shows that they do not belong to this company, and they need to face the fact. "Set apart" (*pālâ*) otherwise occurs only in connection with Yhwh's treatment of the Israelites in Egypt (Exod. 8:22 [18]; 9:4; 11:7; also 33:16).[10] The "friends" are not behaving like proper Israelites, and they risk Yhwh treating them like Egyptians rather than Israelites.

The second colon suggests a further significance of the suppliant's being a committed person whom Yhwh has set apart. It means "Yhwh listens when I call to him." "Yhwh" comes in emphatic position before the verb. Yhwh listens when no one else does, and Yhwh is the only God who really listens. The statement of faith is the one whose truth the psalm was claiming in v. 1. It is a bold one, not least because it seems to go against the evidence (cf. v. 6).

> ⁴Tremble, do not fall short;
> say it within yourselves on your beds and be silent. (Rise)

Verse 4 continues the urging of proper attitudes on the friends. At the end LXX and Syr read "and be silent on your beds," so that the line is a regular 2-2-2. MT gives the line a unique 2-3-1 configuration, putting great emphasis on the isolated, punchy final verb.

Trembling is an appropriate response of awed submission to Yhwh rather than having recourse to other resources (cf. 99:1). "Do not fall short" (*fail) thus restates that point. For the third verb, modern translations have "Ponder in your hearts" or "Search your hearts," but this reads too much into the ordinary expression "Say in your hearts." That is a common enough phrase, though with two contrasting possible significances. "Say within yourselves" could imply saying something inside that we do not say aloud (i.e., being dishonest), but in this context it

---

10. In 17:7; 139:14 *pālâ* "perform a wonder" is a different verb, a byform of *pālāʾ* (see *TDOT* on *pālāʾ*), which C and many later MSS read here (see *BHS*). Here Tg has "separate"; LXX and Jerome imply the byform: "Yhwh has done wonders for the person committed to him" (cf., e.g., Seybold, *Psalmen*, 37).

implies saying something (the acknowledgment about Yhwh) inside and not merely outwardly, saying it and really meaning it (cf. 10:13; 14:1). "On your beds" has similar implications, because the privacy of the bedroom is where people can think and say things they would not express publicly—specifically, negative intentions about someone else (36:4 [5]; Eccles. 10:20; Mic. 2:1) or thoughts about approaching other deities.[11] Even when you are on your beds, the psalm urges, you must acknowledge Yhwh, not entertain other secret thoughts. "Be silent" has similar implications; it is a sign of ceasing to speak wrongfully and of submitting oneself to Yhwh (Pss. 31:17–18 [18–19]; 37:7; 62:5 [6]).

> [5]Offer true sacrifices;
> trust in Yhwh.

The urging closes with another brisk 2-2 line paired with the one that opened the psalm. Turning to Yhwh expresses itself in the context of worship and *trust in everyday life. "True sacrifices" (*zibḥê ṣedeq*) will be liturgically proper ones, but in light of the description of Yhwh as "faithful God" (*'ĕlōhê ṣedeq*; cf. v. 1) they will also be ones that are true in a broader sense, ones where the offerers' worship and life cohere.[12] In a situation where sacrifices are impossible, Tg reinterprets to make the psalm look for what we might call the sacrifice of a disciplined life.[13]

4:6–8. The psalm turns back to address Yhwh, though this is not explicit until v. 7. Thus in the psalm as a whole the addressing of God in vv. 1 and 6–8 forms a bracket around the addressing of people in vv. 2–5. Address of God has the first and last word.

> [6]There are many people saying, "Who shows us good?—
> the light of your face has fled from over us, Yhwh
> [*or*, lift the light of your face on us, Yhwh]."

In this further long 4-4 line, the word order emphasizes the numerousness of the "many people." Who are they? If they are a group who have not been mentioned before, their sentiments make them look like people the suppliant might identify with, but the reversion to first-person singular in vv. 7–8 then looks odd. More likely these are the people who were rhetorically addressed in vv. 2–5. Their question is the one that lies behind the clash between them and the suppliant. They ask a question about whom one is to trust for *"good"—for blessings such as the fruitfulness of the harvest, mentioned in v. 7. Their question can be read in several ways. It

---

11. Or are the beds the setting for other religious rites (e.g., Hosea 7:14)?
12. Cf. Kraus, *Psalms*, 1:148–49.
13. Cf. Stec, *Targum of Psalms*, 32. So also Rashi.

might imply that they lack these good things and do not know whom to turn to. Or it could be a rhetorical question, though there are then several senses it could have. It might express a wish.[14] But more often such a rhetorical question expresses a statement, which would be equivalent to "No one shows us good" (cf. 12:5 [6]; 76:8 [9]). Or perhaps they do have those good things, and their words constitute another kind of rhetorical question. They know the one to whom they have been having recourse and who has given them these things—and it is not Yhwh.

In v. 6b, the text seems to combine two readings, one implying a plea, the other a complaint.[15] A plea would urge upon Yhwh the act needed in light of v. 6a. To ask for the shining of God's *face is to ask for Aaron's blessing to be implemented (Num. 6:24–26): the words "lift" and "face" recur, and *light comes from the verb $'ôr$, "shine."[16] On the part of these people, there would be a skeptical or ironic or hurt tone about the plea. In a complaint people would be speaking of the way they cannot see Yhwh's work in their midst—which would be the background to their having turned to other deities.

> [7]You put joy in my heart
>   at the time when their grain and wine increase.

Indeed, these people have proved that having recourse to Baal works, whereas for the suppliant recourse to Yhwh has not worked; hence the opening plea. The suppliant has had to settle for inner joy, which does not fill the stomach but does compensate for hunger. Indeed, a worshipper could easily take it to mean "more than the time. . . ."[17] The inner joy derives from the certainty the psalm will go on to express, that Yhwh will see that the suppliant comes to enjoy shalom.

> [8]In well-being I shall lie down and sleep at once,
>   because you alone are Yhwh;
>   you make me live in security.

---

14. So BDB here.

15. That is, $n^e s\bar{a}$ comprises the consonants of third person f. s. of $n\hat{u}s$ and the vowels of the impv. of $n\bar{a}\acute{s}\bar{a}'$. LXX "was signified" implies a form of a verb linked with $n\bar{e}s$. J. H. Eaton, "Psalm 4.6–7," *Theology* 67 (1964): 355–57, argues for reading the colon as a complaint.

16. Michael A. Fishbane calls Ps. 4 as a whole an "aggadic transformation" of Aaron's blessing (*Biblical Interpretation in Ancient Israel* [Oxford: Oxford University Press, 1985], 331).

17. "At the time when" understands this as the *min* that can come before the temporal expression but lose its force (BDB 581; cf. Jerome). "More than the time when" understands it as comparative *min* (BDB 582–83). LXX has "from the time" (cf. M. Mannati, "Sur le sens de *min* en Ps iv 8," *VT* 20 [1970]: 361–66).

The psalm closes with a statement of faith that Yhwh's involvement will not stop at the gift of inner joy. The line begins by speaking of *shalom*, which can mean safety from foes, and the broad context of the psalm means one could use these words to express an expectation of that. But Aaron's blessing spoke of shalom, *well-being of the whole person, and a worshipper could use these words to express an expectation of experiencing shalom in that broader sense. Either way, the suppliant intends to lose no sleep over whether there is food to eat or foes to face. "Living in security" (*beṭaḥ*) is a frequent description of God's ideal intention for Israel (e.g., Lev. 25:18–21; Deut. 33:28; 1 Kings 4:25 [5:5]; Ezek. 34:25–29), combining the idea of crops growing well and of being safe from human or animal attack. The psalm has referred to a plea that Yhwh should grant the people this, and it closes with a statement of confidence concerning a personal share in it.

The declaration "You alone are Yhwh" provides the basis for the actual statements of confidence on either side. Strictly, the declaration is a tautology, the effect being heightened if in light of the word order we translate as "You are Yhwh, you alone." But in such statements the implication is that being Yhwh means being the only God who counts. It is correlative to Yhwh's declaration "I am Yhwh and there is no other" (Isa. 45:5, 6, 18). There is only one answer to the question "Who will show us any good?"

Theological Implications

A distinctive feature of Ps. 4 is the series of ambiguities that run through it, which are resolved only when we come to the end of the psalm. It is then that we know how to read it. The psalm ends with a statement of conviction that Yhwh will provide well-being and security—the suppliant will not have to settle for only inner joy forever (valuable though that is). At the moment, it is other people who enjoy well-being, and they attribute that to the fact that they look to resources other than Yhwh, who is manifestly not providing for this person who is maintaining a commitment to Yhwh. So the psalm begins by pleading with Yhwh to put that right. Yet the problem of identifying the psalmist's plea points us to the fact that formally the psalm is more a declaration of trust than a request for help.[18] The suppliant needs Yhwh to deliver from constraint to roominess, but the psalm presupposes a degree of trust about that and focuses more on recruiting other people to share this reliance on Yhwh rather than looking to other resources.

18. So, e.g., A. Anderson, *Psalms*, 1:76.

Psalm 5

Responding to Life-Threatening Falsehood (I)

Translation

The leader's. To flutes. Composition. David's.

¹Do attend[a] to my words, Yhwh,
    consider my utterance,
²Give ear to the sound of my cry for help,
    my king and my God,
    because you are the one with whom I plead.

³Yhwh, in the morning you listen to my voice;
    in the morning I set it out[b] to you and watch.
⁴Because you are not a God who delights in faithlessness;
    an evil person[c] cannot stay with you.[d]
⁵Wild people[e] cannot take their stand before your eyes;
    you are against all who do harm.

    a. The imperatives in vv. 1–2 have the extra sufformative -â, affective and perhaps honorific (JM 49d), and making for rhyme or paronomasia.
    b. ʿĀruk, with ellipse of a noun (cf. Job 33:5); the implicit object may be the words/utterance/cry of vv. 1–2.
    c. As the subject of *gûr*, impersonal "evil" is less likely than the personal translation (cf. LXX, Jerome).
    d. Adverbial acc.: see *IBHS* 10.2.2.
    e. BDB's *hālal* II may combine two roots, one meaning "praise/exult," the other "be mad." EVV "boastful" links qal *hālal* with the former, but I follow *DCH* and *TDOT* in linking it with the latter. Tg has "mock"; LXX and Jerome paraphrase on the basis of the context, which suggests that the term is a general one for wicked people (cf. the other occurrences, 73:3; 75:4 [5]).

⁶You destroy those who speak falsehood;
  the person who seeks bloodshed by fraudulence^f Yhwh repudiates.
⁷But I, in the greatness of your commitment, can come^g to your house.
  I bow low to your holy palace in reverence for you.^h

⁸Yhwh, lead me in your faithfulness
  in view ofⁱ my watchful foes;
  direct^j your way before me.
⁹Because there is no truth^k in such a person's mouth;^l
  their heart is destruction.^m
Their throat is an open tomb;
  they are slippery with their tongue.

¹⁰Make them pay, God;
  may they fall because of their plans.
For the greatness of their rebellions, drive them out,
  because they have defied you.
¹¹But may all who rely on you rejoice,
  resound forever.
As you cover over them, may they exult in you,
  the people dedicated to your name,
¹²Because you yourself bless the faithful, Yhwh,
  you surround him with acceptance like a body shield.

---

f. Lit., "a person of bloodshed and fraudulence," two nouns depending on the one construct, tying the two words together (cf. GKC 128a; *IBHS* 9.3b).

g. Cf. *TTH* 37a.

h. The two long, five-word cola balance each other, in substance in *abcb′c′a′* order, and with some subtlety. Each has a first-person yiqtol verb; coming leads to prostration. Each has a *bĕ*-phrase leading into an abstract noun with a second-person suffix referring to Yhwh, but the first is subjective genitive (in the greatness of your commitment), the second objective genitive (in reverence for you).

i. *Lĕmaʿan* means something more subtle or less specific than "because of" (see BDB 775), though the context does not suggest "for the sake of."

j. Cf. Prov. 9:15; 15:21; the idea of removing obstacles seems less relevant here. K *hwšr* and Q *hayšar* are variant forms of the hiphil (GKC 70b).

k. The f. niphal ptc. from *kûn* used as an abstract noun (BDB 465; GKC 122q).

l. Lit., "in his mouth." LXX, Syr, Jerome, and Tg have "in their mouth," the reading one would expect. In MT sg. and pl. stand in parallelism as in v. 6 and in vv. 11–12. GKC 145m sees the sg. as distributive. W. A. Irwin sees the change to sg. as a sign that two psalms or parts of psalms have been combined ("Critical Notes on Five Psalms," *AJSL* 49 [1932–33]: 9–20, see 9–11).

m. *Hawwôt*; most occurrences are pl., suggesting this is an abstract noun (*IBHS* 7.4.2).

Interpretation

How is a person to react when maligned by people using deceit and fraud in a life-threatening way? This is an experience shared by Naboth, Jeremiah, Daniel, Job, Jesus, Stephen, and other martyrs. Psalm 5 suggests one way they might pray. Like Ps. 4, it begins with a plea (vv. 1–2) and then looks as if it is not going to come to its point; the confession of trust in God's faithfulness and God's punishment (vv. 3–7) takes the place of the confrontation in 4:2–5. But come to its point it does, with a plea for action corresponding to both aspects of the confession of trust (vv. 8–9 and 10–12). Each section backs up a plea or a confession with a "because"—two in the last section (vv. 2b, 4, 9, 10b, 12).[1] There are no pointers to any specific speaker for whom the prayer is designed or any specific context for its use, except for the suggestion in v. 3 that it is a morning psalm, so that (like Ps. 3) it might link with Ps. 4.

> The leader's. To flutes. Composition. David's.

Heading. See glossary. "Flutes" takes *hannĕḥîlôt* as from *ḥālal*, but it could come from (e.g.) *ḥālâ* and mean "sickness" or from *nāḥal* and mean "possessions,"[2] or it might denote a tune—but the preposition "to" (*'el* instead of *'al*)[3] would then be odd.

> ¹Do attend to my words, Yhwh,
>   consider my utterance,
> ²Give ear to the sound of my cry for help,
>   my king and my God,
>   because you are the one with whom I plead.

5:1–2. Verses 1–2 (3-2, 3-2-2) begin the psalm with parallel lines, each comprising two clauses and an address to God at the center: the psalmist surrounds God with petitions.[4] The second line is systematically longer than the first: in numbers of words, v. 1 is 2-1-2 (arranged *abcb'a'*), while v. 2 is 3-2-3.

The first three clauses are parallel and accumulate an emphasis on the audibility of the psalmist's plea—these are not merely written words but words that can be heard, and not merely inner meditation but spoken

---

1. On the psalm's structure, see Pierre Auffret, "'Conduis-moi dans ta justice!'" *JANESCU* 23 (1995): 1–28.
2. See *DCH*.
3. A few later MSS have *'al* (cf. *BHS*).
4. Cf. McCann, "Psalms," 700.

utterance (*hāgîg*, *talk). Indeed, some words from the root *hāgâ/hāgag* suggest groaning, and v. 2a points in that direction: the sound of a *cry for help can be heard. The two further cola then close the lines with a different kind of emphasis, because they do not repeat the plea another time but instead provide the basis for it. The one addressed, "Yhwh" the personal God of Israel (v. 1), is "my king," not just *the* king or the king of kings; "my God," not just God or God of gods. That is the basis for saying, "*You* are the one with whom I *plead." Declaring simply that Yhwh is king makes an objective affirmation about Yhwh's sovereignty; declaring that Yhwh is "my king" makes an affirmation about the application of that sovereignty on my behalf. It is correlative to my being Yhwh's servant, which implies a commitment on my part but also a commitment on Yhwh's part.

5:3–7. Verses 3–7 comprise a declaration of convictions about Yhwh that hint at the nature of the psalmist's situation, though this will not be explicit until vv. 8–12. The yiqtol verbs, continuing from v. 2b, denote habitual truths, which also provide the background to the pleas in vv. 1–2a and declare the conviction that those pleas do become answered.[5] The opening and closing lines express the suppliant's confidence. The further basis for it is Yhwh's attitude to people who do wrong, expressed in six parallel cola in vv. 4–6.

> ³Yhwh, in the morning you listen to my voice;
> in the morning I set it out to you and watch.

In a reverse of the natural order, Yhwh's listening comes before the psalmist's appealing and looking for an answer, but this thus suggests that Yhwh's listening is the basis for the daily appealing and expectant watching. These can therefore be done in confidence. It is a neat 3-3 line introduced by the resumptive opening invocation "Yhwh" standing outside these paired clauses and thus having some emphasis, like the invocations in vv. 1–2. In prose *babbōqer babbōqer* means "morning by morning"; here *bōqer . . . bōqer*, divided between the cola, has similar implications. Morning is a time for one of the daily sacrifices and therefore also for prayer. It is also a time of danger as a new day of pressure dawns, and thus (hopefully) a time when one experiences deliverance.

> ⁴Because you are not a God who delights in faithlessness;
> an evil person cannot stay with you.

---

5. NJPS takes the yiqtol as imperative in meaning, but here the transition from imperatives in vv. 1–2a to yiqtols throughout vv. 2b–7 is a transition from exhortation to statement.

> ⁵Wild people cannot take their stand before your eyes;
> you are against all who do harm.

Verses 4–5 recall 1:1–2 and affirm by their implicit exhortation that Yhwh lives. They suggest a series of vivid images representing what is *not* the case—no delighting (cf. 1:2), no finding hospitality (*gûr*; contrast 15:1), no taking a stand (cf. 2:2). An abstract noun (*faithlessness), a singular concrete noun (a *bad person), and a plural noun (wild people) complement each other. "Setting out [words]" (v. 3) and "taking a stand" come together in Job 33:5; thus v. 5a declares that "wild people" cannot approach God as the suppliant can. The parallel colon (v. 5b) makes a correlative positive confessional statement about God's being *against people who do *harm (contrast 4:2b [3b], which uses the antonym "dedicate yourself to"). In having God as the subject of the clause, this second colon pairs with v. 4a—so that vv. 4–5 as a whole work *abb'a'*.

> ⁶You destroy those who speak falsehood;
> the person who seeks bloodshed by fraudulence Yhwh repudiates.

How do the people do harm, and how does God stand against them? They do harm through their words, as in other psalms. Words can kill. These are people of murderous deceit (*bloodshed), who use false accusation to defraud others of their land and thus their livelihood and, potentially, their lives (see 1 Kings 21). People's judgmentalism can effectively banish persons from the community and destroy them (see Job). But Yhwh's being against them will mean destruction (cf. 1:6; 2:12) and rejection.[6]

> ⁷But I, in the greatness of your commitment, can come to your house.
> I bow low to your holy palace in reverence for you.

Verse 7 then pairs with v. 3, so that these two lines form a bracket around vv. 4–6 as statements of the psalmist's regular practice. The "greatness of Yhwh's *commitment" sums up the implications of vv. 1–6: Yhwh is my king and my God, one who listens to prayer every day, one who is against wrongdoers. Each colon refers to Yhwh's dwelling, but "your house" suggests Yhwh's abode on earth, while bowing low to "your holy *palace" suggests Yhwh's kingly abode in heaven. The psalmist comes to the earthly temple and bows to the heavenly one.[7] The use of "house"

---

6. EVV translate *tā'ab* as "loathe," but contexts indicate that like *śānē'* (be *against) it suggests an attitude issuing in action.
7. Cf. Johnson, *Cultic Prophet*, 256. Hauge (*Between Sheol and Temple*, 163–242) sees "the struggle to dwell in the temple" as the key motif of the psalm.

and "palace" points to the fact that the latter is more glorious than the former.

5:8–9. It is on the basis of the awareness that Yhwh listens to prayer (vv. 3, 7) and is against wrongdoers (vv. 4–6) that the psalm comes to its specific positive plea (v. 8) for one under attack from the kind of people Yhwh is against (v. 9).

> ⁸Yhwh, lead me in your faithfulness
>   in view of my watchful foes;
>   direct your way before me.

The transition to plea is marked by the renewed invocation: "Yhwh." "In view of my *watchful foes" stands at the center of v. 8. The parallel three-word clauses on either side of this central colon would themselves comprise a fine 3-3 line; the central phrase thus stands out and applies to both clauses. The psalm asks that Yhwh may lead like the shepherd who protects sheep from attackers (cf. Ps. 23),⁸ and spells out the implications of "lead me" in asking, "Direct your *way before me": be purposeful and focused about it. "In *faithfulness" thus also applies to both clauses. Prosaically put, "In view of the people who are my watchful foes, in your faithfulness lead me protectively and go straight for it."⁹

> ⁹Because there is no truth in such a person's mouth;
>   their heart is destruction.
> Their throat is an open tomb;
>   they are slippery with their tongue.

The statements in vv. 4–6 were generalizations; v. 9 now claims their relevance by spelling out the implications of the phrase "in view of my watchful foes." Each of the four cola contains an anatomical reference; they are arranged *abb'a'*. The attackers are evil through and through.¹⁰ The noun clause asserting the lack of truth in their words is explained by the verbal clause declaring that they are slippery tongued. In other contexts that might mean they speak insincere words designed to flatter, but here it more likely means they speak plausible untruths designed to get the suppliant into trouble. The inner two noun clauses spell out the effect of that: they are set on destruction, like an open tomb waiting

---

8. See *TDOT* on *nāḥâ*.

9. The psalmist might equally have prayed, "Direct/smooth *my* way before *you*"—so some LXX MSS. MT's own suffixes are again worked with some delicacy: a verb with a first-person suffix and an abstract noun with a second-person suffix is paralleled by a concrete noun with a second-person suffix and a prepositional expression with a first-person suffix.

10. McCann, "Psalms," 701.

to swallow people (like the Canaanite god Death, who does that).[11] The opening of a tomb is a little like an open mouth, and "heart" is *qereb* while "tomb" is *qeber*.

5:10–12. The closing lines form a matching pair of pleas, first for punishment and then for blessing, each comprising three jussives or imperatives, then a "because" clause. At each point the blessing plea is longer than the punishment plea. Thus v. 10 is 2-2 for the first pleas, 3-2 for the last plea and the "because" clause. Verses 11–12 are 3-2 for the first two pleas, 4-2 for the third, 4-3 for the "because" clause.

> [10]Make them pay, God;
>   may they fall because of their plans.
> For the greatness of their rebellions, drive them out,
>   because they have defied you.

In the first line, the second clause explains how the first should work out; a jussive pairs with an imperative, and both the invocation and the adverbial phrase belong with both verbs. Although the attackers are trying to make the suppliant fall, the plea is that things may work out the opposite way. "Make them pay" (*'āšam* hiphil) is linked to the noun "restitution offering" (*'āšām*), whereby one pays a penalty to compensate for an offense. Like "fall," "drive them out" is an open expression without specified implications (from the temple? from Yhwh's presence? from the land? from the earth?). In the second line the psalm's contention is that behavior of the kind described in vv. 3–9 is not just an attack on a human being or a contravention of moral standards or an imperiling of the community. It counts as a monumental *rebellion against Yhwh: the greatness of their rebellions contrasts with the greatness of Yhwh's commitment. The "because" clause then restates the adverbial phrase.

> [11]But may all who rely on you rejoice,
>   resound forever.
> As you cover over them, may they exult in you,
>   the people dedicated to your name,

The pleas in vv. 11–12 are not merely the converse of those in v. 10. They ask not for flourishing as opposed to losing, falling, and leaving, but for something that would issue from such flourishing—noisy rejoicing. *Resound "forever" takes the first colon further by asking for more than rejoicing at one act of deliverance. Verses 11–12 also broaden the horizon in another way. They ask this not just for the psalmist but for

---

11. See *DDD* 599.

all who *rely on Yhwh under pressure from people's attacks. The psalmist thus finds encouragement in the recollection of belonging to such a community. Individual experience of attack is not just some isolated event that might not engage Yhwh's attention but part of a pattern for which Yhwh has a policy.

The second line in v. 11 begins with two short clauses paralleling the first. The circumstantial clause[12] parallels the participial clause so that correlative to people's "relying" is Yhwh's "covering," like a bird covering chicks that hide under her wings (91:4). This suggests that the psalm does work with the idea of "taking refuge" that lies behind the idea of *relying. "Exulting" takes further "rejoicing" and "resounding." The closing description of the people who rely on Yhwh draws out the contrast between them and the attackers: they are not rebels against Yhwh but people *dedicated to Yhwh's *name—that is, to Yhwh's reputation (contrast 4:2 [3] for this verb).

> [12]Because you yourself bless the faithful, Yhwh,
> you surround him with acceptance like a body shield.

The closing "because" clause makes the same contrast and broadens the horizon in other ways. The psalm relates to a crisis from which the suppliant needs deliverance, but deliverance will then restore the psalmist to the life of blessing, which is Yhwh's ongoing intention for people. Blessing is the broad horizon of life with God, suggesting a life of creative fruitfulness. As v. 3 began with an emphatic extra-metrical invocation of Yhwh, so v. 12 contains one at its center. The people Yhwh blesses are those who are *faithful or true, like Yhwh (v. 8) and unlike the attackers. The narrow context (v. 10) suggests faithful and true in relation to Yhwh; the context of the psalm as a whole suggests faithful and true in human relationships. Yet another way v. 12 broadens the horizon is by being directly a statement about Yhwh, or rather a confession to Yhwh, rather than about the people. Indeed, it is already exulting in Yhwh in the way v. 11 prayed would come about. To add to the image of a bird covering its young, the last clause offers the image of a body shield, a shield large enough to cover the whole body. This is not the small, handheld shield of 3:3 [4] (*māgēn*)—though even that shield was enlarged so that it stretched all around—but the huge, cumbersome shield that protected the whole person and might even need to be carried by someone else (*ṣinnâ*; 1 Sam. 17:7). Yhwh's acceptance or welcome or delight (*rāṣôn*) surrounds and protects them thus (cf. 30:5 [6]), with what follows from that acceptance.

12. See GKC 156d.

Theological Implications

Under pressure, then, it is appropriate to turn to Yhwh, to recall Yhwh's commitment against evil, to ask for one's attackers to be put down, and to ask for deliverance and blessing for ourselves. Christian commentators contrast the psalm unfavorably with Jesus's prayer for his enemies' forgiveness (Luke 23:34). The psalm assumes it is acceptable to tell God what we want. Perhaps it implies that it is better for desires to be owned than repressed, not just for the sake of our psychological well-being but also for the sake of the assailants from whom we might otherwise seek our own vengeance (cf. 37:8–9?). We then leave it to God to decide what to do with our prayer.

Psalm 6

Responding to Life-Threatening Falsehood (II)

Translation

The leader's. With strings. On the eighth. Composition. David's.

¹Yhwh, do not in your anger rebuke me
 or in your fury chastise me.
²Be gracious to me, Yhwh,
 because I am faint.
Heal me, Yhwh,
 because my entire body shakes in dismay.
³My whole being shakes in great dismay—
 and you, Yhwh: How long?ª

⁴Turn, Yhwh, saveᵇ my life;ᶜ
 deliver me for the sake of your commitment.
⁵Because there is no celebrating of youᵈ in death;
 in Sheol who can confess you?

 a. Or perhaps "You are Yhwh. How long?"
 b. Placed asyndetically before another verb, one would usually take *šûb* as an auxiliary verb and translate "Save my life again," but in the context the more literal translation is more likely, and this is confirmed by v. 10. On the imperative form of the two verbs, see on 5:1 [2].
 c. My *nepeš*, again; *nepeš* (*person) can mean "soul," but "Deliver my soul" (KJV) gives a misleading impression.
 d. *Zikrekā*; LXX presupposes the pointing *zōkěrekā*, "Because no one mentions you."

> ⁶I have become weary with my moaning;
>   every night I make my bed swim,
>   I melt my couch, with my weeping.
> ⁷My eye has wasted away through aggression,
>   grown feeble, because of all my assailants.
>
> ⁸Get away from me, all you who do harm,
>   because Yhwh has listened to the sound of my weeping.
> ⁹Yhwh has listened to my prayer for grace;
>   Yhwh receives my plea.
> ¹⁰They will be shamed and will shake in dismay greatly, all my enemies;
>   they will turn and be shamed[e] instantly.

Interpretation

Once again attackers stand behind this prayer psalm, though they are a long time appearing at the front of the stage. The psalm begins from a new twofold starting point, Yhwh's anger and the suppliant's severe illness. Verses 1–3 constitute a first appeal to Yhwh, supported by reasons in terms of the suppliant's suffering. Verses 4–7 repeat such appeals and develop the reasons. Verses 8–10 then represent a sudden and radical change in atmosphere.[1]

> The leader's. With strings. On the eighth. Composition. David's.

Heading. See glossary. "The eighth" (cf. Ps. 12; 1 Chron. 15:21) perhaps refers to tuning to play in octaves or to an eight-stringed instrument.

6:1–3. The psalm begins with an appeal for the abating of Yhwh's anger. In Ps. 38 it is explicit that Yhwh's anger is a reaction to the suppliant's wrongdoing, and the church designated both psalms among the Seven Penitential Psalms used in Lent; David Qimchi, for instance, also makes this assumption.[2] But Ps. 6 expresses no awareness of sin or penitence. People who know that Yhwh has been angry with them for a long time (v. 3) because of their faithlessness could use its words to bid Yhwh

---

e. See the first translation note on v. 4. The compound verbal expression contains a paronomasia, *yāšubû yēbōšû*: the reversal of the letters mirrors the reversal the words describe.

1. On the psalm's literary nature, see Auffret, *La sagesse a bâti sa maison*, 183–94; J. Smit Sibinga, "Gedicht en getal," *NedTT* 42 (1988): 185–207. J. Coppens ("Les Psaumes 6 et 41 dépendent-ils au livre de Jérémie," *HUCA* 32 [1961]: 217–26) argues against a dependence of the psalm on Jeremiah. On its significance, see Elizabeth Achtemeier, "Overcoming the World," *Int* 28 (1974): 75–88.

2. So (e.g.) Soggin (*Old Testament and Oriental Studies*, 138); Robert Althann, "Atonement and Reconciliation in Psalms 3, 6 and 83," *JNSL* 25 (1999): 75–82, see 77–79.

determine that enough was enough, but more likely the suppliant is under God's wrath like Job (e.g., Job 9:13–15; 14:13; 16:9; 19:11).³ The proper expression of Yhwh's wrath is to punish wrongdoing, and Yhwh's acting in wrath against wrongdoing is grounds for confidence in prayer for victims of wrongdoing (e.g., 7:6). The suppliant is asking not to be treated as a wrongdoer but as a victim of others' wrongdoing.

> ¹Yhwh, do not in your anger rebuke me
>   or in your fury chastise me.

After the invocation come two exactly parallel clauses, "In your anger/fury do not rebuke/correct me." The verbs are rather mild, but they are preceded by the two adverbial phrases that put the stress on Yhwh's burning wrath. Separating the negative from the verb ("Do not in your anger rebuke . . .") is very unusual and adds to this emphasis. Is the suppliant asking Yhwh to stop doing something or to refrain from starting it? Verses 2b–3 will surely imply the former, and this is explicit when similar words recur in 38:1–3 [2–4]. The suppliant's severe illness is an indication that Yhwh is already angrily chastising.

> ²Be gracious to me, Yhwh,
>   because I am faint.
> Heal me, Yhwh,
>   because my entire body shakes in dismay.

In two further parallel lines, "Be gracious to me/heal me, Yhwh, because I/my entire body am faint/shakes in dismay," the two imperatives set forth the positive antithesis to the two in v. 1. The psalmist looks for *grace and healing rather than angry rebuke and furious chastisement. Although the psalm includes no acknowledgment of sin, the appeal for grace implies a recognition that we have no claim on God and seeks to motivate God in a context of need. When people and life are against us, we have nothing to turn to but God's generosity (e.g., 4:1 [2]; 26:11; 27:7).

The concrete expression of that grace is healing. Such prayers for healing are rarer in the Psalms than one might have expected (see 41:4 [5], in connection with illness that results from wrongdoing; 60:2 [4], metaphorically). The Psalms focus on the causes or consequences of illness in the form of attacks from people like Job's friends rather than on the illness itself.⁴ "I" is then spelled out as "my entire body" (liter-

---

3. Cf. Lindström's discussion, *Suffering and Sin*, 128–52.
4. Norbert Lohfink claims that this is central in NT allusions to the psalm (Matt. 7:23; Luke 13:27; John 12:27) ("Was wird anders bei kanonischer Schriftauslegung?" *JBT* 3 [1988]: 29–53).

ally, "my bones"), and "faintness" is spelled out as "shaking in dismay" (*bāhal*; see on 2:5), an inner panic as well as an outer trembling. The verb *'āmal*, from which comes the adjective "faint" (*'umlal*), is twice used of a woman who loses the capacity to have children (1 Sam. 2:5; Jer. 15:9). We can imagine it on the lips of a person such as Hannah (1 Sam. 1–2), who cannot have children and expresses the pain this brings in her relationship with herself, with other people, and with God.[5] Or we can see the psalm as a whole as "the prayer of a woman who was raped."[6] The psalm speaks to God as one who responds to such women.

> ³My whole being shakes in great dismay—
> and you, Yhwh: How long?

Repeating the verb (adding an adverb) but now making the subject "my *nepeš*" makes the consuming effect of the experience more explicit. "My *nepeš*" also suggests my entire being, but perhaps puts more focus on the inner person. Jesus takes up these words to express his feelings in Gethsemane (Mark 14:34). Although questions beginning "How long?" recur (e.g., Pss. 74:10; 80:4 [5]; 82:2; 94:3), and there are others where the phrase stands alone (90:13; Isa. 6:11; Jer. 23:26), in its disjointedness this is the starkest and most urgent.

6:4–7. As often happens, the second section of the psalm repeats the first, restating it in different words and thus underlining its concerns. Here there is just one line of plea but even more extensive reasoning in terms of the suppliant's affliction. The further element in v. 5, a future-oriented rhetorical question, parallels the one in v. 3b. Like the previous four lines, v. 4 uses the name "Yhwh" in its appeal. Surprisingly, it is the last such appeal. Verses 6–7 focus on the psalmist without reference to Yhwh, and vv. 8–10 address the attackers and refer to Yhwh three times in the third person. Appeal to Yhwh comes to an end with death (v. 5); reflecting that, the appeal comes to an end in the psalm here.[7]

> ⁴Turn, Yhwh, save my life;
> deliver me for the sake of your commitment.

"Save my life" (restore it to what it was before) restates the appeal for healing; "Deliver me" restates it once more before adding a new basis for the appeal. This basis is not merely the suppliant's need (vv. 2–3) but also

---

5. See Miller, *Interpreting the Psalms*, 56–57.
6. Rienstra, *Swallow's Nest*, 44; cf. Ulrike Bail, "Die Psalmen," in *Kompendium feministische Bibelauslegung* (ed. Luise Schottroff and Marie-Theres Wacker; Gütersloh: Kaiser, 1998), 180–91, see 180, 183.
7. Cf. Schaefer, *Psalms*, 20.

the *commitment Yhwh has made and cannot escape. Against Yhwh's furious anger, the psalm appeals to Yhwh's commitment.

> ⁵Because there is no celebrating of you in death;
>   in Sheol who can confess you?

From what does the suppliant need delivering? From death, because Yhwh has made a commitment to a relationship that will not continue in the realm of death. Verse 5 need not be merely an appeal to Yhwh's self-interest, for being incapable of celebration is a loss for human beings, especially for the people who would listen to the testimony of someone whom Yhwh had delivered and would thus have their faith built up. Nor does v. 5 imply that Yhwh has no power over the realm of death. There is no god Death who rules there, as the Canaanites believed, and who might stop Yhwh from intervening in Sheol (cf. 139:8). The problem is that once we are dead, we are incapable of relating to God, because that involves making mention of God's name, confessing who God is and what God has done, and we cannot do that when we are dead.[8] The verb *confess pushes the point further. The fact that people generally stay dead shows that in Sheol Yhwh chooses not to be active, so there is nothing to confess or give thanks for in Sheol. Yhwh's commitment (v. 4) has to be shown now; it does not apply then. It has to be shown now in order to be lauded now; it cannot be lauded then.

> ⁶I have become weary with my moaning;
>   every night I make my bed swim,
>   I melt my couch, with my weeping.

The first two clauses would make a fine bicolon; the third, more exactly parallel to the second, is thus a surprise and underlines the suppliant's distraught state. Weariness (cf. 69:3 [4]) is a common result of suffering and crying. The suppliant's suffering is expressed audibly (cf. 5:1–3 [2–4]), but only as a moan, like that of the people in Egypt or in Jerusalem after its fall, or the suffering of Job (Exod. 2:23; Lam. 1:4, 8, 11, 21; Job 3:24; 23:2; also Pss. 31:10 [11]; 38:9 [10]; 102:5 [6]). It is also expressed bodily, in weeping. Its extremity is expressed with hyperbole that seems laughable to us, but hardly to the people who used the psalm. In the parallelism between the second and third cola, the hiphil verbs and the nouns with first-person suffixes correspond, while "every night" and "with my weeping" apply to both cola.

---

8. On this motif, see Christof Hardmeier, "'Denn im Tod ist kein Gedenken an dich . . .' (Psalm 6,6)," *EvT* 48 (1988): 292–311; and see the introduction to this commentary.

> ⁷My eye has wasted away through aggression,
>   grown feeble, because of all my assailants.

The hyperbole continues. If it is the weeping that makes the eyes waste away,⁹ we might compare the English expression "I cried my eyes out." But the psalms more often refer to the eyes in connection with looking for God to act (e.g., 25:15; 141:8) and refer to problems with the eyes in connection with not being able to see that act (e.g., 69:3 [4]; 119:82, 123). It is the fact that the suppliant has been looking for this act for a long time that is causing the eyes to waste away. The adverbial phrases add a new note. The suppliant is tired because of *ka'as*. NRSV has "grief," but both verb and noun usually suggest rage (cf. LXX); these two can of course be related. In light of what precedes, we might have assumed that the psalm does refer to sorrow, but the parallel colon suggests that the word has its usual meaning. Perhaps the suppliant is raging because of people's attacks (see 5:8 [9]). Either they cause the suffering that the whole psalm refers to, or more likely (given their late appearance in the psalm) they add to it in the manner of Job's friends by treating the suppliant as one whose suffering must issue from wrongdoing. But the parallel colon suggests that the suppliant is tired because of the attackers' aggression. The two adverbial phrases pair an abstract and a concrete noun and two different prepositions.

6:8–10. After this double lament, protest, and plea, the psalm takes an extraordinary turn, declaring that God has responded to the lament, the protest, and the plea. The suppliant has not yet seen the answer but has heard it (vv. 8b–9; see on 3:4 [5]) and can on this basis utter the dismissal of v. 8a and the statements of confidence in v. 10. Being heard itself brings relief and release. But in the Psalms, Yhwh's listening to prayer implies accepting a commitment to action. The suppliant stands not between assurance of being heard and uncertainty whether this will result in anything but sympathy; instead, the stance is between assurance that Yhwh is committed to action and experience of the action itself.

> ⁸Get away from me, all you who do harm,
>   because Yhwh has listened to the sound of my weeping.

The first colon might not advertise the extraordinary turn: in the midst of abandonment by God, the suppliant could be summoning up the strength to tell people who do *harm to get lost, in the manner of 4:2–5 [3–6]. But the second declares that Yhwh has responded to the

---

9. For a comparison with a similar Ugaritic expression, see Loretz, *Psalmstudien*, 82–98.

plea. How does the suppliant know? Perhaps the simple fact of turning to Yhwh in the manner of vv. 1–7 led to an assurance of having been heard. Perhaps the qatal verbs are statements of confidence that speak of something that is still future as if it has already happened (we might then translate "Yhwh is listening").[10] But the sharpness of the transition suggests that something happened between vv. 7 and 8 (cf. Ps. 22). Perhaps vv. 8–10 are a subsequent postscript composed after the prayer has been answered—but there is no indication that the psalm was composed and used in two stages. The suppliant may have taken part in worship and heard declarations of Yhwh's acts and Yhwh's faithfulness, or Yhwh may have spoken a personal word to the suppliant via a prophet or priest (cf. Ps. 12).[11] Whatever the way the psalm was used, it invites people using the psalm to expect Yhwh to respond to their prayers.

> [9]Yhwh has listened to my prayer for grace;
> Yhwh receives my plea.

The repetition of "Yhwh has listened" suggests the powerful impression this made. Yhwh has heard both the pain (v. 8b) and the prayer that arose from it (v. 9a). The suppliant prayed for God to show grace (*ḥānan*; v. 2) and now knows that Yhwh has listened to this plea for *grace (*těḥinnâ*). In v. 9b the yiqtol verb complements the qatal, and "receiving" makes explicit the implication of listening: Yhwh does not listen and then ignore, but listens and accepts and then acts. The two verbs form the bracket around the parallel and rhyming expressions "Yhwh my prayer for grace" and "Yhwh my *plea," two complementary ways to describe the nature of prayer. The poetics thus explains the unusual word order in v. 9b, subject-object-verb.

> [10]They will be shamed and will shake in dismay greatly, all my enemies;
> they will turn and be shamed instantly.

If Yhwh has made a commitment to act in grace and intervene in the suppliant's life, v. 10 indeed follows. At the beginning and end of the line are parallel clauses, each comprising "be shamed," another verb, and an adverb. The subject of both clauses, "all my enemies," then stands at the center (cf. 5:8 [9], where the phrase at the center also refers to the enemies). Why will the enemies be shamed and dismayed? The fate of Job's friends may suggest the answer. They are exposed as people whose fundamental religious perspective is wrong. They thought they

---

10. Cf. *TTH* 14β.
11. Cf. Johnson, *Cultic Prophet*, 241.

knew how life and God work, that they could make this understanding the basis of their own lives with God, and that they could hold forth on other people's relationship with God on the basis of their understanding. Their entire position has imploded.

This heightens the possibility that the psalm's underlying concern in vv. 1–7 was not merely the illness itself but also the people who caused it or made it worse. If Yhwh disposes of them, the whole situation will be put right or will become bearable. Like Job's friends, at present people are shaming the suppliant, who is shaking in dismay (vv. 2b, 3a). That will be reversed as they and their community see that they were in the wrong. Their apparent honor will be turned back to dishonor. The double "shaming" follows on the double "listening," and their great shaking corresponds to the suppliant's double shaking. The "turn" of v. 10 corresponds to the "turn" of v. 4, and whereas v. 3 asked "How long?" now the suppliant knows the shaming will come about "instantly." Perhaps that means it will take only an instant when it happens, or more likely it will happen instantly because Yhwh has heard the suppliant's prayer, so there is nothing to stop it from happening.

Theological Implications

Most present to this suppliant's awareness is physical pain, inner pain, fear for the future, awareness of God's wrath, and a sense of being overwhelmed by death. It is a long time before the psalm refers to attackers, suggesting that they stand in the background for the suppliant. Yet their eventual appearance indicates on the edge of the suppliant's awareness a social dislocation issuing from people's attitude to the illness, which now comes into prominence. All this can be brought to God without expressing either a correlative awareness of sin that needs confessing or a conviction about personal commitment that makes it possible to make a statement that trouble is undeserved. And the close of the psalm indicates that Yhwh responds to such prayer and deals with the issues we raise. Martin Luther comments on this psalm, "No one who has not been profoundly terrified and forsaken prays profoundly."[12]

---

12. *Selected Psalms*, 3:141.

Psalm 7
On Trial, in Battle, Hunted

Translation

Lament. David's, which he sang for Yhwh about the words of Sudan; the Benjaminite.

¹Yhwh my God, I rely on you;
 deliver me from all my pursuers, save me.
²Or one will tear me apart like a lion,
 dismembering[a] me with no one to save.

³Yhwh my God, if I have done this,
 if there has been[b] meanness in my hands,
⁴If I have dealt calamity to my friend[c]
 but released[d] my watchful foe without reason,
⁵May an enemy pursue[e] me[f] and overtake me,
 trample my life to the ground,
 lay my honor in the dirt. (Rise)

a. *Pāraq* usually means "tear away," and we could perhaps understand the colon to mean "with no one to tear away and save," but "tear apart" (cf. Jerome) is established by 1 Kings 19:11 and fits the parallelism here.

b. Translations render as present, but *yēš* takes its time reference from the context.

c. A *šôlēm* could be a requiter rather than someone in a peaceful relationship (cf. LXX), in which case it refers to the person who now is the suppliant's attacker.

d. *Ḥālaṣ* never otherwise means "to plunder" (NRSV; cf. NIVI) in Biblical Hebrew (cf. BDB). Tg "oppressed" may imply *wā'elḥăṣâ* for *wā'ăhallĕṣâ* (cf. LXX?). The second colon then repeats the idea of the first, "my assailant" being the "ally" who has now become an attacker because of the action described in v. 4a.

e. *Yiraddōp* combines two readings, the qal and the piel forms of the verb.

f. Again "my *nepeš*" (*person); the noun is also the implicit object of the second verb.

⁶Rise, Yhwh, in your anger;
   lift yourself up at the outbursts of my assailants;
Awake, my God,ᵍ you must have ordered a decision;
   ⁷the assembly of the countries must gather around you.
Returnʰ to it on high;
   ⁸Yhwh must rule for the peoples.
Decide for me, Yhwh, in accordance with my faithfulness
   and with my integrity, which are over me.ⁱ
⁹The evil of the wicked really must come to an end;
   may you establish the faithful person—
The faithful God
   probes minds and hearts.ʲ

¹⁰God is my shield on high,ᵏ
   one who delivers the upright of heart.
¹¹God exercises authority for the faithful person;
   God expresses indignation always.ˡ
¹²If someone does not turn, heᵐ whets his sword;
   he has directedⁿ his bow and set it.
¹³He has prepared deadly weapons for himself;
   he makes his arrows into flames.
¹⁴So. He twists with harm, he is pregnant with troublemaking,
   he gives birth to falsehood.

   g. Taking *'ēlay* as pl. of majesty (cf. *'ĕlōhîm*, *'ădōnāy*; see GKC 124g–i) rather than as meaning "for me."

   h. NRSV "sit" repoints *šûbâ* as *šēbâ*, though it is possible that *šûbâ* can be understood to mean "sit" (so UBS). For other emendations in the psalm, see Jacob Leveen, "The Textual Problems of Psalm vii," *VT* 16 (1966): 439–45.

   i. Readers might take *'ālāy* as an invocation of Yhwh as "Most High."

   j. Lit., "hearts and kidneys." Both can be the locus of thought and emotion; in this combination (cf., e.g., 26:2), together they form a kind of hendiadys for thoughts and attitudes of the inner being.

   k. MT punctuates as "my shield is over/with God," taking *'al* (over) as a preposition. I take it as an adverb (cf. 2 Sam. 23:1). NIVI takes it as an abbreviated form of *'elyôn* (Most High); cf. v. 17.

   l. On the translation of v. 12, see A. A. Macintosh, "A Consideration of Psalm vii. 12f.," *JTS*, n.s., 33 (1982): 481–90 (esp. 481–82). On *běkol-yôm*, see BDB 400b. GKC 127b has "every time." Hardly "every day"/"all day"!

   m. NJB has "but," taking vv. 12–13 as a description of the wrongdoer (cf. NIVI). But the Hebrew has no "but," and the alternation of tenses in vv. 12–13 is easier to understand if it describes God's habitual action. "So" (*hinnēh*, v. 14) then marks the change of subject to the wrongdoer. Indeed, v. 12 might mean "Will he not again whet . . . ?" though this requires readers to spot the use of two idioms, the use of *'im-lō'* to introduce a strong assertion and the use of *šûb* to mean to do something again.

   n. *Dārak*, perhaps lit., "treads"—i.e., puts his foot on the bottom of the string; but not all bows were that big, so either this can be a dead figure of speech, or the verb has the meaning "direct."

>¹⁵He has dug a pit, dug it deep,
>   and fallen into the hole he was making.
>¹⁶His troublemaking falls back on his head;
>   onto his skull descends his violence.
>
>¹⁷I will confess Yhwh for his faithfulness,
>   and I shall make music to the name of Yhwh as the Most High.°

Interpretation

The psalm speaks for someone under attack, this time because wrongly accused and therefore in deadly danger, like Naboth. Perhaps it might be used on occasions such as those described in Num. 5:11–28; Deut. 8:7–20; 1 Kings 8:31–32. It comprises an opening plea (vv. 1–2), a declaration of innocence (vv. 3–5), a more urgent and extensive plea for action (vv. 6–9), an act of praise at who Yhwh is (vv. 10–16), and a promise of thanksgiving when deliverance has come (v. 17).

> Lament. David's, which he sang for Yhwh about the words of Sudan; the Benjaminite.

Heading. See glossary. I render *šiggāyôn* "lament" on the basis of Akkadian *šigû*. Rather than assuming that the heading then refers to some incident we do not know about, I take it to refer to the Sudanese[1] in 2 Sam. 18:20–32, and to Shimei and/or Sheba, both styled Benjaminites.[2] All three stories have verbal links with the psalm. The Sudanese person's words bring news that Yhwh has "decided for" David; whereas Absalom and his supporters "arose" against David, Yhwh has now "arisen" for David; whereas Yhwh had done no "evil" to Absalom, Absalom has done "evil" to David (2 Sam. 18:31–32; cf. Ps. 7:4, 6, 8). Shimei risks his "head" in laying David's honor in the "dirt" but eventually "falls" before David (cf. 2 Sam. 16; 19; cf. Ps. 7:5, 14, 15). David fears Sheba will "do evil" to him and sends people to "pursue" him, and one of Israel's "friends" delivers his "head" (2 Sam. 20; cf. Ps. 7:4, 5, 16). In general, psalm and story have in common the question about how one

---

o. While "Yhwh Most High" could be a combined name, that exact expression comes elsewhere only in 47:2 (3) (Tg replaces *yhwh* with "God"), and here "Most High" balances "in accordance with his faithfulness."

1. "Cush" is the area south of Egypt and thus corresponds most closely to modern Sudan (rather than Ethiopia).

2. Rodney R. Hutton ("Cush the Benjaminite and Psalm Midrash," *HAR* 10 [1986]: 123–37) sees the heading as designed to fill out the story in 2 Sam. 18–19. Slomovic rather notes links with 1 Sam. 24 ("Historical Titles," 360–61).

treats enemies or traitors—v. 4 recalls the criticism earned by David's wish that he had not caused the death of his rebel son. Once again, therefore, verbal links make it possible to juxtapose psalm and story, though broader differences indicate that the psalm was not written in connection with these events.

> ¹Yhwh my God, I rely on you;
>   deliver me from all my pursuers, save me,
> ²Or one will tear me apart like a lion,
>   dismembering me with no one to save.

7:1–2. The psalm also begins with a plea for Yhwh's deliverance. In terms of metaphor, v. 2 makes clear why this is necessary, though the psalm does not yet tell us more literally why the psalmist needs to seek such refuge.

The suppliant *relies on or takes refuge with Yhwh for safety and *deliverance; Ps. 2:12 has already provided the basis for such reliance. In v. 2 the psalm expounds the first of a number of vivid figures of speech in the psalm, the only one that is a simile. The two verbs are parallel, one yiqtol, one participle, and the other phrases apply in both cola, with "me" in v. 2a (*napšî*; *person) the implicit object of all three verbs. The link with v. 1 is emphasized by the recurrence of "save" as the closing word in each line, with the plural of v. 1 complemented by the singular in v. 2.

7:3–5. Beginning with another invocation of "Yhwh my God," vv. 3–5 indicate that the suppliant has had to turn to Yhwh because of being falsely accused of something, yet claiming to be innocent. This is not a claim to sinlessness but a denial of being the gross wrongdoer that the accusation implies. One might compare Job's claim, or later Paul's (e.g., 1 Cor. 4). The psalm assumes that people who belong to God *should* be able to claim that they have been living faithful lives. The world can be divided into the faithful and the faithless, and the suppliant claims to belong to the former group.[3]

> ³Yhwh my God, if I have done this,
>   if there has been meanness in my hands,

The second colon begins to make specific what "this" is. The suppliant's hands have not been involved in meanness (*'āwel*), an attitude toward other people involving deception or hostility, the opposite of faithfulness. They have not been involved in killing; they are not stained by blood (cf. Isa. 1:15; 59:3, 6).

---

3. See Gert Kwakkel, *According to My Righteousness*, OtSt 46 (Leiden: Brill, 2002).

> ⁴If I have dealt calamity to my friend
> but released my watchful foe without reason,

More concretely, the suppliant has apparently been accused by a friend or ally, a *šōlēm* (someone in a committed *šālôm* relationship),⁴ of acting in a way that goes against that relationship. But the matter continues to be expressed allusively, facilitating the use of the psalm in a variety of contexts. The second colon takes the point further by denying a form of capriciousness, as if disloyalty to allies were accompanied by unprincipled leniency to *watchful foes, like the leniency Saul showed to Agag (1 Sam. 15). Such an act (perhaps mentioned only as a theoretical possibility) would underscore the enormity of the act referred to in the previous colon.⁵

> ⁵May an enemy pursue me and overtake me,
> trample my life to the ground,
> lay my honor in the dirt. (Rise)

The climax of the claim to faithfulness is the prayer against oneself. The second colon would comprise a fine parallel to the first, but then it transpires that the second and third constitute much closer parallels, arranged *abcc′b′a′*. The verse's form as a tricolon gives it extra importance and signals that we come to the end of a section. *Honor is *kābôd*, which can sometimes refer to the liver or inner being and thus heart (usually *kābēd*) (e.g., 16:9); both connotations are appropriate here.⁶ The four verbs in the clauses tell a vivid story of pursuit, capture, and subjection, the end being humiliation. People who believe in prayer are acting quite seriously when they express a wish like this one (cf. Job 31), and the willingness to do so thus constitutes a significant evidence of a faithful life.

7:6–9. The wish that the suppliant does not expect to see fulfilled is succeeded by a plea and a series of wishes that the suppliant longs to see fulfilled. The versification in vv. 6–9 is subtle.⁷

> ⁶ᵃ⁻ᵇRise, Yhwh, in your anger;
> lift yourself up at the outbursts of my assailants;

---

4. Cf. Jeffrey H. Tigay, "Psalm 7:5 and Ancient Near Eastern Treaties," *JBL* 89 (1970): 178–86.

5. For the translation, see D. Winton Thomas, "A Further Note on Psalm 7:4," *BT* 25 (1974): 247–48; against Robert G. Bratcher, "A Translator's Note on Psalm 7:4b," *BT* 23 (1972): 241–42; also Christian Macholz, "Bemerkungen zu Ps 7.4–6," *ZAW* 91 (1979): 127–29.

6. John W. McKay ("My Glory—A Mantle of Praise," *SJT* 31 [1978]: 167–72) argues for the translation "glory" with the connotation "sense of personal worth."

7. I follow Fokkelman's understanding (*Major Poems*, 2:66).

Two parallel urgings seek to rouse Yhwh to action. They recall the exhortation in Num. 10:35–36 (cf. Ps. 3:7 [8]) but here relate to action in connection with a particular circumstance that deserves Yhwh's attention. Both refer to wrath, with the neat variation that the first refers to Yhwh's wrath, which is the suppliant's hope, and the second to the attackers' wrath, which is the suppliant's threat. The suppliant makes the Psalms' characteristic assumption that the aim of prayer is to rouse Yhwh to action. God generally leaves the world for human beings to control and does not make a habit of interfering in it. The object of prayer, then, is to prevail upon God to make this one of the occasions to give up inaction for action. The suppliant knows that Yhwh must be angry at what is going on, and uses this as motivation for getting Yhwh to intervene; v. 12a will point to Yhwh's reason for delaying.[8] The commands look for action now; they are not appealing for something to happen at a judgment at the End.

> 6cAwake, my God, you must have ordered a decision;
> 7athe assembly of the countries must gather around you.

The first colon begins with a further urging and another invocation, parallel to v. 6a. The subsequent qatal verb is surrounded by imperatives and jussives and is naturally understood as a precative, a kind of statement of faith: "You must have ordered a *decision" (*mišpāṭ*). If this suppliant is an ordinary individual, the conviction that it is possible to arouse Yhwh to act on an individual's behalf is striking.

> 7bReturn to it on high;
> 8aYhwh must rule for the peoples.

The line completes an *abb'a'* sequence with vv. 6b–7a, with a further paralleling of imperative and jussive. The assumption underlying the jussives is also striking. To take action on this individual's behalf, Yhwh is to summon all the nations of the earth. Evidently this is a meeting on earth, not a meeting of the heavenly court (e.g., 96:10; 98:9). But if the suppliant is a king troubled by foreign assailants, this is particularly appropriate.

> 8b–cDecide for me, Yhwh, in accordance with my faithfulness
> and with my integrity, which are over me.

The line explicitly asks for the decision-making power of the court to be applied to this individual. First, Yhwh must return to chair the

---

8. Kidner, *Psalms 1–72*, 64–65.

decision-taking council, which has not been acting (v. 6). *"Decide for" is *šāpaṭ*, parent verb to *mišpāṭ*, and a synonym of the rarer *dîn* (rule for). The basis for the suppliant's appeal is a life of faithfulness and integrity. *Faithfulness suggests the person's relationship with the community, *integrity the person's personal moral wholeness. These stand "over" the person almost as separate entities (cf. *'al* in Ezek. 18:20, with *ṣĕdāqâ*; Ps. 90:17b; Neh. 5:7).[9] They are aspects of the suppliant's own being manifest in relationships with God and with the community, and they are thus genuine objective realities.

> [9]The evil of the wicked really must come to an end;
>   may you establish the faithful person—
> The faithful God
>   probes minds and hearts.

These two lines then bring to a close the plea in the psalm and effect a transition to the statements of trust, praise, and confidence that will follow. They thus form the hinge of the psalm. The two cola in v. 9a balance each other in form and content. A second-person yiqtol follows a jussive, and the personal singular "faithful person" as the object follows the impersonal plural "evil of the faithless" as the subject. Both verbs take polite form: the jussive has the particle *nā'* attached, and the second-person verb is a yiqtol rather than an imperative. The two cola thus plead for the two aspects of what Yhwh needs to do, the negative and the positive.

The copula that opens v. 9b (usually not represented in translations—I have signified it by a dash) suggests that v. 9b gives the basis for the appeal in v. 9a, which in turn suggests that this is a clause, not a pair of invocations ("you who try minds and hearts, faithful God"). By implication, the suppliant is again giving evidence of having been honest in vv. 3–5. On that basis it is possible to be happy with the fact that God can investigate the inner person to see whether the plans and attitudes there match the outward words. That is part of what is involved in "integrity." The declaration suggests that God *can* look into the inner person whether one wishes that or not, but that God does not automatically know what is going on inside a person: God does have to look. This is the third successive line that speaks of *faithfulness: on the basis of human faithfulness (vv. 8, 9a), one can appeal to divine faithfulness (v. 9b).

7:10–16. Like the preceding psalm, Ps. 7 makes a transition to a statement of faith, this one being remarkable because of its length; it

---

9. See BDB 753b.

occupies virtually half the psalm. The transition is less abrupt and less in need of a word from God to explain it, but as a statement of faith in noun clauses and yiqtol clauses it corresponds to the response to a word from God in Ps. 12. The thanksgiving in v. 17 would be an appropriate further response to a word from God, or it might suggest that vv. 10–16 or 11–16 *are* a word from God.[10]

> [10]God is my shield on high,
> one who delivers the upright of heart.

It begins with two lines of noun clauses comprising four statements about God, each pair being parallel in meaning. This first such line describes God's nature as it affects the suppliant in the context of undeserved threat. Once again the suppliant claims to be a person of integrity, one in whom there is no gap between the outward words and the inner heart.

> [11]God exercises authority for the faithful person;
> God expresses indignation always.

The subsequent two such statements describe God's nature in itself, the characteristics that lie behind the affirmations in v. 10. By nature God makes decisions in a way that reflects commitments, and is always prepared to act in a tough way toward people who deserve it. "Indignation" (*zaʿam*) is another word that combines attitude and action, a sense of outrage and a denunciation or curse (cf. Prov. 24:24–25). LXX adds a "not" to reassure us that God does not express indignation every day, not perceiving that God's indignation is good news for the oppressed.

> [12]If someone does not turn, he whets his sword;
> he has directed his bow and set it.
> [13]He has prepared deadly weapons for himself;
> he makes his arrows into flames.

The psalm expresses that indignation concretely and vividly, though metaphorically. The verses start with the presupposition that people can always escape God's wrath. When people turn from wrongdoing in response to God's indignation, God and their victims heave a sigh of relief. Forgiveness is now possible, and there is no need to express indignation in more painful ways. But if they do not turn, wrath must

---

10. Mandolfo (*God in the Dock*, 35–41) calls them "instructional discourse" (cf. Carleen Mandolfo, "Finding Their Voices," *HBT* 24 [2002]: 27–52).

follow. In describing God's preparation of weapons, these first four cola alternate in *abb'a'* order in using habitual yiqtol and gnomic qatal/wayyiqtol, alternative ways of making general statements (see 1:1). Yhwh has a series of weapons of death—sword whetted, bow taut and aimed, arrows flaming so as to set on fire the persons or the homes they hit. In all four cola the objects, the weapons, have the prominence, through their coming before the verb; the exception that tests the rule is v. 13a, where the order is "for himself he prepares. . . ."

> ¹⁴So. He twists with harm, he is pregnant with troublemaking,
> he gives birth to falsehood.

A concrete and vivid portrayal of the wicked begins with three different metaphors, with further vivid picture-painting. The "so" introduces three two-word clauses describing the wrongdoer as a woman giving birth to a monster. NRSV has the clauses describing conception, pregnancy, and birthing, so that the line presents to the imagination a nine-month-long story in six words. But the first verb (*ḥābal*) elsewhere describes the pain and anxiety of actually giving birth (cf. LXX, Jerome). Further, there are several roots *ḥābal*,[11] and a common one denotes "act corruptly" or "destroy." The order is then rhetorical, not chronological: the first clause allusively suggests more than one possible idea. The second and third then make it more specific. *Harm and troublemaking often accompany each other as terms for wrongdoing toward other people. *Falsehood then gives precision to the way people wrong others (cf. 5:5–6 [6–7]), by lies that imperil their freedom, their livelihood, their place in the community, or their lives.

> ¹⁵He has dug a pit, dug it deep,
> and fallen into the hole he was making.

The metaphor changes, or another builds on it. In the household economy, a woman's effort goes especially into bearing children, while a man's job is to make sure that the home is properly equipped (e.g., with a water cistern or a well) or that the farm is protected from wild animals (by digging pits to catch them). So the wrongdoer is a man digging a superb deep cistern or well or pit and falling headlong into it. Begetting is like digging (Isa. 51:1–2), and pregnancy and digging even sound like each other (*hārâ* and *kārâ*), so perhaps throughout v. 15 digging is a metaphor for bringing to birth, which is a metaphor for acting wickedly. And again the first clause summarizes and the second gives

---

11. See *DCH*; *NIDOTTE*.

some detail and slows the action, before v. 15b relates the coup de grâce. The lion (v. 2) duly falls into the pit.

> ¹⁶His troublemaking falls back on his head;
> onto his skull descends his violence.

Once more the metaphor changes, or another builds on it (troublemaking appears again; cf. v. 14). Imagine instead that while the wife is preparing to give birth, the husband is remodeling the house, perhaps strengthening the roof or adding an extra story, and a beam falls on his head. Or imagine that the sides of the well fall in on him as he tumbles down it. "Falls back" is *yāšûb*, the same as "turns" (v. 12): turning back from wrongdoing or having your work fall back on your head are alternatives. The more specific meaning for *ḥāmās* (*violence) fits here, both because this wrongdoing involves harming others, and because the poetic justice that comes on the wrongdoer involves physical harm. The line works *abcc'b'a'*. The reverse thus mirrors the scene the words relate, and the stepped structure closes off the description on vv. 10–16.

> ¹⁷I will confess Yhwh for his faithfulness,
> and I shall make music to the name of Yhwh as the Most High.

7:17. All that is now required is testimony to the God who makes this happen, which comes in a final *abca'b'c'* line. We might take the first verb to describe what the suppliant does on an ongoing basis because of these facts regarding who Yhwh is; but the second, cohortative verb suggests that the suppliant is rather promising praise in the future, on seeing Yhwh's actual act and/or as a continuing feature of life. *Confess indicates the significance of the words the suppliant will offer, while the second verb refers to the *musical aspect without which praise would be incomplete. The first verb's object is simply "Yhwh," while the second's is Yhwh's *name, Yhwh's character as the suppliant knows it. The first clause again emphasizes Yhwh's faithfulness; the second puts alongside it the fact that Yhwh is the *Most High, as the earlier reference to Yhwh's being "on high" came between the two earlier references to Yhwh's faithfulness (vv. 9, 10, 11). The psalm's hope lies in the combination of Yhwh's faithfulness and power. One without the other would be insufficient; together they are the suppliant's assurance and confidence. Prosaically put, "I will make music to confess Yhwh, the one revealed as the faithful one and as the Most High."

Theological Implications

In this psalm, as often elsewhere, judicial procedures, war, and hunting are described in terms of each other.[12] A trial is often experienced as a battle and a hunt; it involves a potentially deathly confrontation of wills and the seeking of someone else's freedom or death by cunning and the setting of traps. People fighting a battle will often claim that they are fighting a just war for the sake of their own or someone else's rights, and then they will talk about ambushing their opponents or hunting them down. Hunting involves one creature seeking to confine or kill another by cunning or force, so it resembles war and judicial procedures. Thus in a psalm such as this one, legal opponents may be portrayed as enemies or as hunters or beasts of prey, or enemies may be portrayed as legal opponents or as hunters or beasts of prey. The psalm begins with the imagery of the hunt. The suppliant is in danger of being dragged off and torn apart as by a pursuing lion, without a rescuer, and needs to find a refuge (vv. 1–2). It then moves to the imagery of the court (vv. 3–5). The suppliant speaks as one on trial for wrongdoing, and specifically for action that has done wrong in a legal context. Verses 4–5 talk about a watchful foe and an enemy but then return to the imagery of the hunt rather than speaking in terms of battle. Verses 6–11 take further the imagery of the court, but battle imagery comes to the forefront in vv. 12–13 before v. 14 returns to court language. Finally, vv. 15–16 take us back to the hunt. The fact that battle and trial can each be used as an image for the other means we may not be able to determine which is the literal reality. To put it another way, either a suppliant who was literally on trial or one who was literally under physical attack could use the psalm.

There is another, more theological both-and in the psalm. It portrays events both as divine acts of a rather interventionist kind (e.g., vv. 10–13) and as the natural outworking of earlier events (vv. 15–16).[13] It thus asserts both that Yhwh is involved in the world in active ways, and that the world is a place into whose working a moral order is written—though one may sometimes need to urge Yhwh to make sure that this order does work itself out.

---

12. Cf. Pietro Bovati, *Re-establishing Justice*, JSOTSup 105 (Sheffield: JSOT, 1994), 292–96.

13. See Robert L. Hubbard, "Dynamistic and Legal Processes in Psalm 7," *ZAW* 94 (1982): 268–79.

Psalm 8

Humanity's Position in Creation

Translation

The leader's. On/concerning the Gittite. Composition. David's.

¹Yhwh, our Lord,
  how mighty is your name in all the earth,
One who put[a] your majesty above the heavens
  [or, you whose majesty was acclaimed above the heavens]
  ²at the word[b] of babies and sucklings.[c]
You founded a barricade in view of your assailants,
  to stop enemy and requiter.

a. MT *těnâ* looks like a composite form, the consonants of *tnh* (acclaim) and vowels to suggest *nātěnâ* (he gave/put; cf. GKC 66h). On possible emendations of vv. 1–2, see (e.g.) Petrus Sfair, "De genuine lectione Ps. 8,2," *Bib* 23 (1942): 318–22; Herbert Donner, "Ugaritism in der Psalmenforschung," *ZAW* 79 (1967): 322–50 (esp. 324–27); R. Tournay, "Le psaume viii et la doctrine biblique du nom," *RB* 78 (1971): 18–30; J. Alberto Soggin, "Textkritische Untersuchungen von Ps. viii vv. 2–3 und 6," *VT* 21 (1971): 565–71; Vinzenz Hamp, "Ps 8,2b.3," *BZ* 16 (1972): 115–20.

b. Lit., "from the mouth"; for this usage, see Jer. 36:4, 6, 17, 27. This thus involves less inference than the suggestion that *min* is comparative (so H. Kruse, "Two Hidden Comparatives," *JSS* 5 [1960]: 333–47). Barbara Pitkin ("Psalm 8:1–2," *Int* 55 [2001]: 177–80, esp. 177) notes how NRSV "out of the mouths . . . you have founded" gives more power to the children than RSV "chanted by the mouth. . . ."

c. Two nouns depending on one construct, as in 5:7 [8].

³When I look at your heavens, the work^d of your fingers,
   moon and stars that you established,
⁴What is a mortal that you should be mindful of him,
   a human being that you should attend to him?

⁵But^e you made him fall short of God by a little,
   yet crown him with honor and glory.
⁶You make him rule over the work of your hands,
   put all things under his feet,
⁷Sheep and oxen, all of them,
   but also wild beasts,
⁸Birds in the heavens, fish in the sea,
   what travels the paths in the sea.
⁹Yhwh, our Lord,
   how mighty is your name in all the earth.

Interpretation

We come to the Psalter's first actual praise song, though both its form and its subject are untypical. There is neither an invitation to praise (it is indeed the only praise psalm wholly addressed to God)¹ nor reasons for praise in a "because" clause. Verses 1–2 directly praise Yhwh as the powerful, majestic creator. Verses 3–4 wonder whether this God would be involved with mere human beings. Verses 5–9 marvel that actually Yhwh has bestowed glory and honor on them in giving them authority and dominion over the animate creation and close the psalm by repeating the opening praise.²

The leader's. On/concerning the Gittite. Composition. David's.

Heading. See glossary. The Gittite may be an instrument (Tg) or a melody. It might be named after the "winepress" (*gat*; cf. LXX), or it might be the feminine of the word for a person or thing from Gath. Ibn Ezra links it with Obed-edom the Gittite, a Levitical singer (see 1 Chron. 13:13–14; 16:4–5).

   d. *Ma'ăśê*; L and many later MSS, also Syr, have sg. *ma'ăśeh* (so also in v. 6) (see *BHS*).
   e. The antithetical *w*-consecutive follows loosely from the question that precedes (DG 142d).
   1. Cf. Marvin E. Tate, "An Exposition of Psalm 8," *Perspectives in Religious Studies* 28 (2001): 343–59, see 344.
   2. For a detailed study of the psalm's structure, see Pierre Auffret, "Essai sur la structure littéraire du Psaume viii," *VT* 34 (1984): 257–69; O. Loretz ("Die Psalmen 8 und 67," *UF* 8 [1976]: 117–21, see 117–20) suggests a staged process for the psalm's development, building on comments in his "Psalmenstudien," *UF* 3 (1971): 101–15, see 101–12.

8:1–2. Three sonorous lines praise Yhwh as mighty sovereign. Verse 1a–b might begin from a sense that creation as we see it gives testimony to Yhwh's majesty or that Yhwh's activity in history as we experience it does so. But vv. 1c–2 link either of these with the past act of creation that caused them to be so now, and perhaps actually the declaration in v. 1a–b is made by faith in light of that act. The difference in focus, first on the present and then on the past, suggests that v. 1a–b is a line in its own right. Verses 1c–2 then belong together as statements about that original act of creation (cf. NRSV, NIVI). This fits the recurrence of v. 1a–b alone as the last line of the psalm. Thus the two verses comprise three bicola rather than two tricola (cf. NJPS), which would be a very novel beginning to a psalm.

> ^{1a–b}Yhwh, our Lord,
>   how mighty is your name in all the earth,

Addressing Yhwh as "Lord" or sovereign is a much more unusual form of address than we might think as a result of translations' usual replacement of the name Yhwh by a word for "Lord." The invocation spells out the implications of Yhwh's being "Lord" in acknowledging that Yhwh's *name is 'addîr, splendid and majestic, "usually with the implication of mighty or powerful" (e.g., 76:4 [5]; 93:4; 136:18).[3] The response to might, then, is not merely wonder or admiration but deferent submission. That implication will be significant for all that follows. The psalm is about Yhwh's power and might as creator. Not only is there something splendid about creation that makes people wonder at God's glory. Against all the evidence that suggests Yhwh does not rule in the world, the psalm declares that Yhwh is a powerful sovereign here (e.g., Pss. 95–98).

> ^{1c}One who put your majesty above the heavens
>   [*or*, you whose majesty was acclaimed above the heavens]
>   ^{2a}at the word of babies and sucklings.

That is so because Yhwh asserted sovereignty at the Beginning over the entire cosmos. The line complements v. 1a–b with a testimony to Yhwh's "majesty" (*hôd*), again suggesting awesome power and authority (cf. 1 Chron. 29:11; Job 37:22; 39:20; Isa. 30:30; Hab. 3:3). Yhwh asserted this not merely on the earth but also in the heavens, and not merely "in

---

3. C. J. Collins, *NIDOTTE* 1:276. Walter Harrelson sees the psalm as especially glorying in the human capacity to name Yhwh, which distinguishes humanity from the rest of creation ("Psalm 8 on the Power and Mystery of Speech," in *Tehillah le-Moshe* [M. Greenberg Festschrift], ed. Mordecai Cogan et al. [Winona Lake, IN: Eisenbrauns, 1997], 69–72).

all" the earth but "over" the heavens (cf. 57:5, 11 [6, 12]; 108:4–5 [5–6]; 113:4; 148:13). The context suggests that this is more than a hyperbole. It indicates recognition that God is greater than all created reality and is in authority over it and over all other supernatural powers (see v. 2b–c). Yhwh's majestic might is a present reality because of a past assertion of it. It goes back to the way God created the world.

How were "babies and sucklings" involved? The OT mentions "babies" twenty times, usually as victims of oppression, war, and death (e.g., 137:9; Lam. 1:5; 2:11, 19, 20). "Sucklings" appear eleven times, often alongside "babies" and again usually as victims (e.g., Deut. 32:25; Lam. 2:11; 4:4).[4] In the OT, then, the mouths of babies and sucklings are not likely to be crying out for milk or in praise or as a sign of life,[5] but crying out in pain or for protection or justice, as the babies in Matt. 2:16–18 might have done.[6] The cry of children is a dominant note in history, and this reference to their cry suggests that in creating the world Yhwh was aware that this would be so and was taking action to ensure that the forces of violence could not always do as they wished to babies and sucklings. Yhwh's might and majesty were asserted and/or acknowledged at the Beginning in anticipatory recognition that this would be important for the vulnerable. Aware as we are of the way children are history's victims, we may be inclined to wonder whether that actually happened. It resembles other statements of faith in the psalms, like that in Ps. 1 (cf. also Ps. 91), statements of faith or promises that we are encouraged to believe despite much evidence to the contrary. Yet the suffering of children would be much greater if God were not protecting them in accord with this act at the Beginning.

> 2b–cYou founded a barricade in view of your assailants,
> to stop enemy and requiter.

The way Yhwh asserted might and majesty was by "founding a barricade." "Founding" is a frequent image for God's bringing the world into being, suggesting among other things that the cosmos is like a building securely established, with foundations going down into rock (e.g., 104:4). But bringing the world into being also involved gaining control of dynamic forces that could work against God's purpose to create a cosmos with

---

4. Cf. Øystein Lund, "From the Mouth of Babes and Infants You Have Established Strength," *SJOT* 11 (1997): 78–99, see 85.

5. So Wilhelm Rudolph, "'Aus dem Munde der jungen Kinder und Säuglinge...,'" in *Beiträge zur alttestamentlichen Theologie* (Walther Zimmerli Festschrift), ed. Herbert Donner et al. (Göttingen: Vandenhoeck & Ruprecht, 1977), 388–96.

6. Thomas L. Thompson looks at the babies' cry in the context of other cries such as that in Gen. 21:16–17 ("From the Mouth of Babes, Strength," *SJOT* 16 [2002]: 226–45, see 231).

order and stability, and setting bounds for them (e.g., Pss. 74; 89; 93).[7] "Founding a barricade," more literally "founding strength,"[8] is this psalm's way of picturing that. "Majesty" and "strength" belong together as royal divine attributes (cf. 96:6).[9] The succeeding reference to assailants makes more explicit that Yhwh's act of creation was not a simple, uncontested event.[10] The abusers of children are the powers that opposed Yhwh's creative purpose. "In view of your assailants" in the first colon is explained in the parallel colon, "to make enemy and requiter stop."[11] In other contexts we might go on to reckon that the "your" on the first noun applies also to the other nouns; but while Yhwh does have "assailants" (e.g., 74:23) and "enemies" (e.g., 37:20), it is odd to think of Yhwh having a would-be "requiter." Rather, the two cola complement each other in another way. The first refers to Yhwh's assailants, the second to the enemy of the babies and sucklings (*yōnĕqîm*), the one who takes requital on them (*nāqam*).[12] While Ps. 137 asks for requital for people who have slaughtered Judah's babies, Ps. 8 declares that Yhwh acted at the Beginning to stop requital being exacted on babies and sucklings. The link with Ps. 137 and with Lamentations may indicate that the psalm has specifically in mind the suffering that came to babies and sucklings (who may be a symbol for the people of Jerusalem as a whole) as a result of the Babylonian capture of Jerusalem.[13] The verb "stop" (*šābat*) appears frequently in connection with God's stopping work at the end of the week's activity involved in creating the world; it is therefore a nice touch to use the hiphil to refer to God's making others stop, in the course of the work of creation. The verb often refers to God's making objectionable things or people to cease (e.g., 46:9 [10]; 119:119).

---

7. See further J. Alberto Soggin, "Salmo 8,3," *Bib* 47 (1966): 420–24; Mary Tanner, "Psalm 8:1–2," *Theology* 69 (1966): 492–96; Mark S. Smith, "Psalm 8:2b–3," *CBQ* 59 (1997): 637–41.

8. *'Ōz* is often used as abstract for concrete to refer to a strong person (e.g., 28:7; 118:14) or strong thing (e.g., 46:1 [2]; Jer. 16:19). LXX reworks the colon in seeing the babies and sucklings as involved in praise. Perhaps it was puzzled by v. 2a but understood it in light of one of those verbs in v. 1c, *tnh* (acclaim). Jesus's inspired new use of the passage in Matt. 21:14–16, stimulated by something that happens in his own context, takes up this rewriting, and NIVI reads it back into the psalm itself.

9. Walter Beyerlin, "Psalm 8," *ZTK* 73 (1976): 1–22, see 11.

10. Cf. P. A. H. de Boer, "Jahu's Ordination of Heaven and Earth," *OtSt* 2 (1943): 171–93.

11. The infinitival clause complements the prepositional phrase, and the singular complements the plural.

12. See on 18:47 [48].

13. So Beyerlin, "Psalm 8," 15–17. Otto Kaiser takes them as a figure for the righteous and as a later addition ("Erwägungen zu Psalm 8," in *Gottes und der Menschen Weisheit*, BZAW 261 [Berlin: de Gruyter, 1998], 56–70).

All this threatens to deconstruct any sharp distinction between God's act at the Beginning and God's ongoing activity. The OT often assimilates these two (e.g., Ps. 93; Isa. 51:9–11). God's activity at the Beginning, God's activity at the exodus, and God's ongoing activity in Israel's life are all one. God's ongoing sovereignty in the world and God's ongoing defeat of powers that assert themselves are based on and are an outworking of an event at the Beginning, when God asserted sovereignty and put disorderly powers in their place.

8:3–4. The psalm takes a new turn as the *mâ* (what) of v. 4 takes up the *mâ* (how) of v. 1 and the speaker becomes "I" rather than "we."

> ³When I look at your heavens, the work of your fingers,
> moon and stars that you established,

The length of v. 3 (4-4) underlines the sense of awe that creation arouses. Reference to Yhwh's fingers underlines the hands-on nature of creation—God did not merely utter orders and leave someone else to do the work, but became personally involved in the most delicate and intricate way. The linking of "heavens" with "moon and stars" suggests that the former refers to the regular daytime sky, and the latter draws attention to the features of the sky at night. "Work" or making is likewise complemented by "establishing"—like "founding," a declaration that the elements of creation are firmly and securely in place (cf. 93:1; 96:10).

> ⁴What is a mortal that you should be mindful of him,
> a human being that you should attend to him?

But in light of that powerful majesty of Yhwh's embodied in the cosmos, how could one expect Yhwh to pay any attention to mere human beings? In v. 4 the second colon restates the first; at the center of the poem "semantic movement is slowed to allow for the strong, stately emphasis of virtual synonymity."[14] There is little difference between the implications of "mortal" and "human being" (*'ĕnôš, ben-'ādām*); both hint at human beings in their weakness.[15] But "attend to" (*pāqad*) takes further "be mindful of" (*zākar*). God first thinks, then acts. But could we expect God to bother with mere humanity? The question parallels those of Ecclesiastes (also Ps. 90), but more concretely Ps. 144:3 and more gloomily Job 7:17–18.[16]

---

14. Alter, *Art of Biblical Poetry*, 120.
15. Ludwig Köhler ("Psalm 8, 5," *TZ* 1 [1945]: 77–78) suggests the first denotes humanity, the second the individual human being.
16. But Raymond C. Van Leeuwen questions whether Job is parodying Ps. 8. See "Psalm 8.5 and Job 7.17–18," in *The World of the Aramaeans I* (P.-E. Dion Festschrift), ed. P. M. Michèle Daviau et al., JSOT 324 (Sheffield: Sheffield Academic Press, 2001), 205–15.

Perhaps, like a lament, the psalm functions to give people opportunity to articulate their uncertainties about their positions as human beings in the world, before drawing them into statements of faith.[17]

8:5–9. Notwithstanding the awesome facts of vv. 1–2 and the question they raise (vv. 3–4), the powerful sovereign delegated authority over the world to humanity. Whereas vv. 1–2 presuppose the kind of picture of creation that emerges from the Psalms and Job when they talk about conflict and victory, vv. 5–8 parallel the Gen. 1 story of God's making men and women godlike and giving them power over the rest of the animate world. In v. 5 the two cola link by contrast, and in v. 6 they are directly parallel, but the verbs in vv. 5–6 come in *abb'a'* sequence as wayyiqtol, yiqtol, yiqtol, qatal. The arrangement thus binds vv. 5–6 together. A reader might take the verbs as all referring to the past or as alternating reference to the past and the present in a way that brings out the present implications of the past act.

> [5]But you made him fall short of God by a little,
> yet crown him with honor and glory.

Human beings are thus little less than divine—perhaps little less than the gods, the other heavenly beings or angels (LXX, Tg, Syr), but more likely little less than God (Jerome, Aq, Sym, Th), because the psalm goes on like Genesis to note how they take up God's sovereignty in the world. As sovereigns, they are crowned. Their crown is a share in God's *honor and glory—different words from those used of God in v. 1 because humanity is not divine, but similar words to those, to signify that humanity is little less than divine. Like Gen. 1–2, the psalm reckons that human beings in general are kings, which puts kings in their place.

> [6]You make him rule over the work of your hands,
> put all things under his feet,

As sovereigns, human beings were commissioned to rule over the work of God's hands and thus to receive the obeisance of beings put under that authority. They are "between God and the world."[18]

> [7]Sheep and oxen, all of them,
> but also wild beasts,
> [8]Birds in the heavens, fish in the sea,
> what travels the paths in the sea.

---

17. Cf. Gerstenberger, *Psalms*, 1:67–72.
18. Werner H. Schmidt, "Gott und Mensch in Ps. 8," *TZ* 25 (1969): 1–15, see 13.

The itemizing of the handiwork that they rule moves us out of seeking to imagine how they were to rule (e.g.) the moon and the stars. But like Gen. 1 it still sets up a noteworthy vision, because they rule not only domestic animals but also wild animals, birds, fish, and other sea creatures (cf. Gen. 1:21). They rule *all* of them—the twofold "all" in vv. 6–7 corresponds to the twofold "all" in vv. 1 and 9. They so rule when they stop predators from damaging their crops and herds: the statements imply a promise that the life of the farmer can work. But the horizon is larger than that and recalls the OT's vision of the animate world living in harmony (Isa. 11). That suggests a larger commission. When the work of creation was finished, this did not mean it had already reached its destiny; humanity's calling was to take it there. How extraordinary that God should want to use humanity thus! Of course, humanity failed from the beginning, and the creation has to continue to look forward to reaching its destiny and groan for its redemption (Rom. 8:22), but how grievous that in our own time we despoil it instead!

> [9]Yhwh, our Lord,
>   how mighty is your name in all the earth.

The repetition of the opening praise underlines the positive wonder and ensures that the worshippers close their praise with thoughts of God, not of themselves. Paradoxically, praise psalms do not usually begin by addressing God, but address other human beings with a challenge, then give the reasons for the challenge. This praise song is unique for its focus on God, emphasized by this bracket around the psalm.

Theological Implications

The NT uses Ps. 8 to help it express aspects of the significance of Jesus (1 Cor. 15:27; Heb. 2:6–8).[19] It is therefore important for us to reflect on its inherent meaning and not simply read it through NT spectacles.[20] It

---

19. See Conrad Louis, *The Theology of Psalm VIII* (Washington, DC: CBA, 1946); Francis J. Moloney, "The Reinterpretation of Psalm 8 and the Son of Man Debate," *NTS* 27 (1980–81): 656–72; Felix Asensio, "El protagonismo del 'Hombre-Hijo del Hombre' del Salmo 8," *EstBib* 41 (1983): 17–51; Michael Goulder, "Psalm 8 and the Son of Man," *NTS* 48 (2002): 18–29.

20. Cf. Brevard S. Childs, "Psalm 8 in the Context of the Christian Canon," *Int* 23 (1969): 20–31, see 31; cf. J. Alberto Soggin, "Zum achten Psalm," *Annual of the Swedish Theological Institute* 8 (1970–71): 106–22; A. R. Hulst, "Ansatz zu einer Meditation über Psalm 8," in *Travels in the World of the Old Testament* (M. A. Beek Festschrift), ed. M. S. H. G. Heerma van Voss et al. (Assen: Van Gorcum, 1974), 102–7; Ute Neumann-Gorsolke, "'Mit Ehre und Hoheit hast Du ihn gekrönt' (Ps 8,6b)," *JBT* 15 (2000): 39–65; Gerhard Wallis, "Psalm 8 und

does not look forward to a new age: it has a vision that belongs to this age. It shows us what humanity is and specifically presupposes that "we can say 'human being' only after we have learned to say 'God.'"[21] It does not refer to the Messiah but places a responsibility on and makes a promise to humanity. Further, if Hebrews sees human beings as almost like gods only "for a little while" (so NRSV) rather than "by a little," that could imply that we were in that position only for the short period before disobedience caused us to lose our sovereignty in the world, as if the world "fell" because humanity "fell." In contrast, the psalm manifests an "unrestrained cultural optimism."[22] It implies that Gen. 1 was not devastatingly undone by that human failure. Human disobedience did not undo God's placing the animate world under humanity's authority any more than it eliminated the divine image from humanity (Gen. 5:1–3; 9:1–2, 6). The psalm does not have a hidden eschatological sense. It has an open sense for this age.[23] It links creation and present experience and promises that this link still holds. What God intended humanity to be, God still intends humanity to be. If we look one way, at the extraordinary nature of the cosmos as a whole, we can be overwhelmed by our insignificance. God bids us look the other way, at the earthly creation project that God still intends to complete, and in which we have a significant role. Our vocation is to work for the completing of God's creation project instead of its frustration by the spoiling of God's world, as nations in general (and not least Christian nations) do. We can give ourselves to this implausible project, knowing that we are working with the grain of God's creation purpose. We can do it knowing that the cry of suffering children came up to God and made God determined to set up strong barriers that stop opposition powers from overcoming that purpose. We say by faith that God still holds majestic power in all the earth. God is "More than an 11 a.m. Savior."[24]

---

die ethische Fragestellung der modernen Naturwissenschaft," *TZ* 34 (1978): 193–201; John Nordin, "Preaching Psalm 8," *Currents in Theology and Mission* 20 (1993): 259–64.

21. James L. Mays, "What Is a Human Being," *ThTo* 50 (1993–94): 511–20, see 519.
22. Gerstenberger, *Psalms*, 1:70.
23. Contrast Kraus, *Psalms*, 1:186.
24. Dusty Kenyon Fiedler, "'More Than an 11 A.M. Savior,'" in *God Who Creates* (W. S. Towner Festschrift), ed. William P. Brown and S. Dean McBride (Grand Rapids: Eerdmans, 2000), 104–6.

Psalms 9–10
How to Pray against the Powerful

Translation

> The leader's. The girls/Secrets/Eternities/On dying. The son's. Composition. David's.

['] **9:1**I will confess Yhwh with all my heart;
  I will tell of all your awesome deeds.
2I will rejoice and exult in you,
  I will make music to your name, Most High,
[*b*] **3**When my enemies turn back,
  stumble and perish before you,
4Because you have given decisive judgment for me,[a]
  you have sat on your throne as one who makes decisions faithfully.

[*g*] **5**You thundered at[b] nations,[c] you caused the faithless person to perish,
  you eliminated their name forever and ever.
6The enemy were finished, ruins without end;
  you uprooted cities, their memory perished—

---

a. Lit., "my decision [*mišpāṭ*] and my judgment [*dîn*]"; the second word is a synonym of the first.

b. *Gā'ar* is more than a "rebuke" (NRSV, NIVI): see *NIDOTTE*. NJPS has "blast."

c. Stanley N. Rosenbaum ("New Evidence for Reading *ge'im* in place of *goyim* in Pss. 9 and 10," *HUCA* 45 [1975]: 65–70) supports the view that the text originally read *gē'îm* ["the proud"], not *gôyim*. Cf. *ga'ăwâ* in 10:2.

[h] ⁷Them!ᵈ But Yhwh is seated forever,
    as one who establishes his throne for making decisions.
⁸He himself makes decisions for the world in faithfulness,
    exercises authority for the countries with uprightness,
[w] ⁹So that Yhwh may beᵉ a haven for the broken person,
    a haven for times of trouble,
¹⁰And people who acknowledge your name may trust in you,
    because you did not abandon those who sought help from you, Yhwh.

[z] ¹¹Make music to Yhwh who is seated on Zion,
    tell his assertive actionsᶠ among the peoples,
¹²Because one who seeks bloodshed was mindful of them;
    he did not ignore the cry of the weak.

[ḥ] ¹³Be gracious to me,ᵍ Yhwh;
    look at my weakness because of the people who are against me,
    you who can lift me from the gates of death,
¹⁴So that I may tell of all your praiseworthy acts,
    within the gates of Ms. Zionʰ
    be glad in your deliverance.
[ṭ] ¹⁵Nations plunged into the pit they made;
    in the net that they hid, their foot got caught.
¹⁶Yhwh caused himself to be acknowledged, he took decisive action,
    by the act of his hands knocking down the faithless person
    [*or*, by the act of his hands the faithless was snared].ⁱ (Recitation.ʲ Rise)

d. The superfluous *hēmmâ* takes up the pronominal suffix on "their memory" and emphasizes it (GKC 135f; *IBHS* 16.3.4). MT thus attaches it to the end of v. 6, but it seems to be present for the sake of making the alphabetical structure work. LXX *met' ēchous* suggests *hōmeh* "roaring," though roaring and sitting do not go well together, and nowhere else is Yhwh the subject of this verb. We would also have to omit the *w* ("but"). For an emendation to provide a *d* line, see Patrick W. Skehan, "A Broken Acrostic and Psalm 9," *CBQ* 27 (1965): 1–5.

e. Simple *w* plus jussive, continued in v. 10; cf. *TTH* 62.

f. *'Ălîlâ* usually refers to wanton or arbitrary deeds (BDB), and I assume that a positive form of such a meaning attaches to the word when it is used without such connotations. "Extraordinary" is another possible connotation.

g. MT combines the consonants of a qatal verb *ḥănānanî* and the vowels of an imperative; Aq and Jerome presuppose qatal pointing for this and the next verb, assimilating to the context. On the text of the verse, see Karl Marti, "Zu Psalm 9.14," *ZAW* 36 (1916): 245–46.

h. Lit., "daughter Zion"—not "daughter of Zion"; the genitive is explicative (see GKC 128k).

i. MT has the ptc. *nôqēš*. LXX, Aq, Syr, Tg, Jerome imply *nôqaš*, niphal qatal from *yāqaš*.

j. *Higgāyôn* from *hāgâ* (see 1:2). Cf. 19:15; 92:4; but we do not know what it implies here.

[y] ¹⁷Faithless people turn . . . to Sheol,
   all nations that ignore God,
[k] ¹⁸Because the needy person is not ignored without end;
   the hope of the weak ones does not[k] perish forever.

¹⁹Arise, Yhwh. A human being must not prevail;
   nations must have their decision made before you.
²⁰Appoint something fearful [or, a teacher][l] for them, Yhwh;
   nations must acknowledge they are human. (Rise)
[l] ¹⁰:¹Why do you stand far off, Yhwh,
   why do you hide in times of trouble?
²In his loftiness the faithless[m] hounds the weak person;
   they must be caught by the schemes that they have thought up.[n]

³Because the faithless gloried over the desire of his heart,
   the robber worshipped,[o]
[n] ⁴The faithless disdained Yhwh[p]
   in accordance with the exaltedness of his look:
"He does not seek for requital—there is no God";
   ⁵all his schemes—his ways are profane[q] all the time.
[m] Your decisions are on high,[r] away from him;
   all his assailants—he snorts at them.

k. The "not" in the first colon carries over into the second.

l. MT has a composite reading, the consonants of *môreh* (teacher; cf. LXX, Syr) and the vowels of *môrā'* ([object of] fear; cf. Aq, Th, Tg, Jerome). EVV have "put fear into them," but the context suggests reference to something objectively fearful, not to the subjective feeling of fear.

m. Lit., "In the loftiness of the faithless, he . . ."

n. LXX understands "They [the weak] are caught in the schemes that they [the faithless] have thought up," but this involves more complicated changes of subject.

o. Cf. LXX, Jerome. EVV take this as an instance of *bārak*, meaning "curse," which might then be a "scribal correction" (so UBS)—though it is not one of the "official" scribal corrections. But the usage otherwise comes only in direct speech in Job 1–2 and 1 Kings 21, and the parallelism here works against it (cf. G. J. Thierry, "Remarks on Various Passages of the Psalms," in *Studies on Psalms*, by B. Gemser et al., OtSt 13 [Leiden: Brill, 1963], 77–97 [esp. 83]; also Carmel McCarthy, *The Tiqqune Sopherim*, OBO 36 [Göttingen: Vandenhoeck & Ruprecht, 1981], 192). Further, this psalmist would hardly feel the need to hold back from saying that the faithless cursed Yhwh, as the next verb implies.

p. I follow LXX in making "disdained Yhwh" the beginning of v. 4; MT attaches the words to v. 3, but the asyndeton is hard.

q. *Yāḥîlû* is a form from *ḥûl*, which usually means "writhe," esp. in birthing (cf. Jerome). Tg *maṣlĕḥîn* perhaps links it with the noun *ḥayil*; BDB takes Job 20:21 as the only other instance of this verb meaning "prevail," and there is no other comment on the prevailing of the faithful in the context here. LXX "his ways are profane" more plausibly connects *yāḥîlû* with *ḥālal*, which perhaps had a byform *ḥûl*. I have linked "all his schemes" (apparently omitted by LXX) from the end of v. 5 with this line.

r. Lit., "are height."

⁶He said in his heart, "I will not fall down, ever."
"Not be in adversity," he swore.ˢ
[p] ⁷His mouth is full of both fraudulence and oppression;ᵗ
under his tongue are troublemaking and harm.
⁸He sits in a hiding place in the villages
so thatᵘ in secret he may slay someone innocent.
[ʹ] His eyes watchᵛ for the wretched person;ʷ
⁹he hides in a secret place like a lion in its lair.
He hides in order to catch the weak person,
catches the weak by dragging him into his net.
¹⁰Broken,ˣ he sinks down,
the wretchedʸ fall by his might.ᶻ
[or, The wretched are broken, sink down,
fall by his might.]
¹¹He said in his heart, "God ignored it,
he turned his face, he never looked."

[q] ¹²Arise, Yhwh;
God, lift your hand—
do not ignore the weak.
¹³Why has the faithless disdained God,
said in his heart, "You do not seek for requital"?
[r] ¹⁴You looked, because you yourself pay attention to troublemaking and
aggression,ᵃ
so as to recompense by your hand.

s. Linking *'ālâ* with what precedes rather than with v. 7 (so MT) generates better parallelism here and makes v. 7 begin with *p*. "Say" and "swear" stand in parallelism in Judg. 17:2. Perhaps the unusual word order then links with the unusual use of *'ăšer* before "Not be in trouble," to introduce the content of the words (BDB 83b). But there may well be some textual corruption in the line. See (e.g.) A. Leveen, "Psalm x: A Reconstruction," *JTS* 45 (1944): 16–21; "A Note on Psalm 10:17–18," *JBL* 67 (1948): 249–50.

t. Meaning "oppressive fraudulence." C lacks the first *w*, which may have been added through the linking of *'ālâ* to v. 7. "Fraudulence" (cf. 5:6 [7]) is here an abstract pl., and *tōk* occurs elsewhere only at 55:11 [12]; 72:14; Prov. 29:13, but "oppression" fits the contexts (see *NIDOTTE*) and fits PBH usage (see *DTT*).

u. The second verb implicitly signifies the aim of the first (cf. LXX, Jerome).

v. One of the occurrences of *ṣāpan* (hide) where it is a byform of *ṣāpâ* (cf. similar usage of the latter in 37:32; 66:7); cf. LXX, Syr.

w. See comments on v. 10.

x. Pointing K as *wĕdākeh* (ptc.); cf. Aq, Sym, Jerome. The second translation follows Q *yidkeh*.

y. It is the versions that imply the meaning "wretched" for *ḥēlkâ* (though the pointing is questionable: see BDB). Here alone is the word pl. Q points as *ḥēl kā'îm*, "the army of the disheartened" (it has a variant on this pointing for the sg. occurrences), trying to make sense of an unknown word, on which see W. G. Simpson, "Some Egyptian Light on a Translation Problem in Psalm x," *VT* 19 (1969): 128–31.

z. Not numerical pl. ("his mighty ones") but abstract pl.

a. *Ka'as* (see on 6:7 [8]).

> The wretched leaves it to you;
>   the orphan—you have been a helper.
> [*ś*] ¹⁵Break the strength of the faithless and evil person;
>   seek for his faithlessness until you find none.
>
> ¹⁶Yhwh is king forever and ever;
>   nations perished from his land—
>   ¹⁷you listened to the desire of the weak, Yhwh.
> [*t*] You establish their heart; you bend your ear,
>   ¹⁸to decide for orphan and broken person
>   so that a human being from the land may terrify no more.

Interpretation

LXX makes these one unit, and together they form an alphabetical psalm.[1] In addition, a number of significant words recur in both psalms (see the list below); Ps. 9 closes with "Rise" (which otherwise comes only in the midst of a psalm); and Ps. 10 has no heading, unlike most psalms in this part of the Psalter. I infer that LXX follows the original format and MT reflects a later division of the psalm in usage.[2]

The psalm begins with a commitment to praise and ends in praise, rejoicing in Yhwh's acts of deliverance (9:1–12; 10:16–18), but the long opening praise eventually leads into plea and lament, which dominate the body of the psalm. Three times the suppliant urges Yhwh to take action again (9:13–14; 9:19–10:2; 10:12–15). Thus the initial impression that this will be a testimony psalm turns out to be misleading. It is a prayer psalm, which like other prayer psalms incorporates recollection of Yhwh's great acts and also the prospect of returning to praise Yhwh for an act of deliverance. The combination of praise and prayer is common enough (e.g., Ps. 44), but in this instance the prospect of praising God for acting comes at the beginning rather than the end.[3] The effect

---

1. See the section on "Rhythm" in the introduction to this commentary.
2. Cf. (e.g.) George Buchanan Gray, "The Alphabetic Structure of Psalms ix. and x.," in *The Forms of Hebrew Poetry* (London: Hodder & Stoughton, 1915), 267–95; H. Junker, "Unité, composition et genre littéraire des psaumes ix et x," *RB* 60 (1953): 161–69; Robert Gordis, "Psalm 9–10," *JQR* 48 (1957): 104–22. Max Löhr ("Psalm 7 9 10," *ZAW* 36 [1916]: 225–37) sees Pss. 7; 9; and 10 as originally independent but brought together because of common themes (Ps. 8 then being inserted later). Rendsburg sees Pss. 9–10 as written in northern Israelite Hebrew, a fact that might also explain its above-average number of difficulties of interpretation (see *Linguistic Evidence*, 19–27).
3. Thus John Strugnell and Hanan Eshel (hypothesizing a different order for the alphabet) suggest that Ps. 10 originally preceded Ps. 9 ("Alphabetical Acrostics in Pre-Tannaitic Hebrew," *CBQ* 62 [2000]: 441–458, see 453–58; "It's Elementary," *Bible Review* 17 no. 3 [2001]: 41–44).

is to make the prayer more God-focused than (e.g.) a great prayer psalm such as Ps. 22. This instance is also jerkier than some other examples of the combination of prayer and praise. The jerkiness hardly issues from the constraints imposed by the alphabetic form, which in any case the psalm does not closely follow. Following the form does not require great skill, and the need to do so does not explain unexpected features such as the transition to plea at 9:19 and the transition to a statement of faith at 10:16. Indeed, in its repeated alternation between plea or lament and declarations concerning God's acts, it compares with Ps. 22. It is an example of the way psalms sometimes work hard to keep a focus on two sets of facts, both the grim facts about present experience and the encouraging facts about Yhwh's past and Yhwh's true nature. They do this by alternating in their focus on these.

The distinctive way the psalm interweaves praise and plea and its sharing the conventional practice of interweaving yiqtol verbs (9:3, 7–8, 17–18; 10:2, 4–10, 14, 17b–18) and qatal verbs (9:4–6, 10, 12, 15–16; 10:3, 11, 14, 16b–17a) mutually reinforce uncertainty in interpreting it. A more regular form would help interpret the verbs, or more certainty about the verbs would help interpret the form. Translations sometimes render some of the yiqtols as past or future and some of the qatals as present or precative, illustrating the way readers can work with varying understandings of the balance within the psalm. I have given weight to the fact that most of the qatal clauses refer to acts of God toward the nations, the faithless, and so on, which do not directly affect the suppliant or the community for which the psalm speaks. Only in 9:3–4 does the suppliant speak of God's acts toward "*my* enemies" (in the yiqtol) and of God's taking decisions for *me*. I infer that the psalm's qatal clauses generally refer to the way God has related to Israel in the past, not least in connection with the exodus and occupation of the land. Then 9:3–4 is the exception that proves the rule. I take its yiqtols to refer to the future act that the suppliant looks for, and its qatals as perfects dependent on those futures. In the rest of the psalm, the yiqtols are statements of ongoing truth, and the qatals support these by declaring how matters have turned out in the past. The psalm as a whole thus tells of what God has done in the past, grieves over how things are in the present, pleads with God to act again in keeping with those acts in the past, and expresses the conviction that God will do so. One might then outline its structure as follows:

>Statement of faith and praise for Yhwh's past acts (9:1–12)
>   Plea (9:13–14)
>Statement of faith and praise for Yhwh's past acts (9:15–18)
>   Plea (9:19–10:2)

Lament at the present (10:3–11)
Plea (10:12–15)
Statement of faith and praise for Yhwh's past acts (10:16–18)

As happens with any poetic form, the alphabetical structure helps give shape to the poem as a whole, while variants from the form also have an effect. In this case the form is incomplete and uneven (cf. Pss. 25; 34). The psalm lacks *d*, *s*, and *ṣ* lines. Further, the *m* and *n* lines are reversed, as are the ʿ and *p* lines, though such phenomena appear in other alphabetical psalms and may simply mean that the order of letters in the alphabet was not settled (cf. Lam. 2–4). Further, the number of lines allocated to each letter varies, and changes of letter do not always coincide with transitions in the content (e.g., 9:19). The incompleteness and unevenness is so extensive that it is hazardous to reckon that the alphabetical form must once have worked perfectly, and hazardous to attempt to "restore" it,[4] though I have redivided verses to produce the *h* and *n* lines. The incompleteness and unevenness, like the jerkiness of the psalm's structure, correspond to the nature of the experience the psalm expresses and thus add to its effect. The psalm looks as if it is affirming that life has the order of the alphabet but also acknowledges that this is not always so.

A related feature of the psalm is the recurrence of different words in different connections, sometimes with changing meaning. I look forward to *telling of* Yhwh's acts (9:1, 14) and to making music to your *name* as one who eliminated the *name* of the faithless (9:2, 5). Under pressure from my *enemies*, I recall Yhwh's putting down the *enemy* in the past (9:3, 6). I expect my enemies to *perish* in keeping with Yhwh's acts in the past, whereas Yhwh does not let the weak *perish* (9:3, 5, 6, 18; 10:16). I look forward to Yhwh's acting in *faithfulness* because that is Yhwh's habit (9:4, 8). Yhwh will *make authoritative decisions* for me and must do so because that is what Yhwh habitually does and actually has done (9:4, 7, 8, 16, 19; 10:5, 18). Yhwh *sits on a throne* and therefore does act and will act (9:4, 7). The faithless perish *forever*, but not the needy, whereas Yhwh sits enthroned as king *forever* (9:5, 7, 18; 10:16). The *faithless* and the *nations* did cause trouble and were put down; they do cause trouble and must be put down (9:5, 15, 16, 17, 19, 20; 10:2, 3, 4, 13, 15). The enemy perishes *without end*, but the needy are not ignored *without end* (9:6, 18). Yhwh *establishes* a throne and *establishes* the heart of the weak (9:7; 10:17). Yhwh is a refuge for *times under pressure* and must therefore behave as such (9:9; 10:1; also "time," 10:5). The *broken* are vulnerable, but Yhwh is their refuge and decides for them (9:9; 10:10, 18). Yhwh

---

4. For attempts, see (e.g.) Jesús Enciso, "El Salmo 9–10," *EstBib* 19 (1961): 201–12.

makes himself *known* for people who *acknowledge* him and nations who do not (9:10, 16, 20). People *seek for help from* Yhwh, but Yhwh *seeks for* requital and is urged to *seek for* faithlessness (9:10, 12; 10:4, 13, 15). *Zion* is the place for praise (9:11, 14). Yhwh *sits* on Zion, and therefore the faithless futilely *sits* in hiding (9:11; 10:8). Yhwh does not *ignore* the needy nor *ignore* wrongdoing, but people *ignore* Yhwh (9:12, 17, 18; 10:11, 12). The psalm speaks for the *weak*, for whom Yhwh does act (9:12, 13, 18; 10:2, 9b, 9c, 12, 17). Yhwh must *look*, did not *look*, did *look* (9:13; 10:11, 14). Yhwh rescues from death's *gates*, so there is praise in Zion's *gates* (9:13, 14). *Human beings* must acknowledge who they are and not pretend to be more (9:19, 20; 10:18). Yhwh must *arise* (9:19; 10:12). The faithless get caught by their own *schemes* (10:2, 5). The faithless have the desires of their *heart* and say things in their *heart*, but Yhwh strengthens the *heart* of the needy (10:3, 6, 11, 13, 17). The *desire* of the faithless and of the weak contrast (10:3, 17). The faithless *disdained* Yhwh (10:4, 13). The faithless *hide in secret* (10:8, 9). The *wretched* are vulnerable but leave it to Yhwh (10:8, 10, 14). Yhwh must act with his *hand* (10:12, 14; cf. 9:16). Yhwh acts for the *orphan* (10:14, 18). Nations perished from Yhwh's *land*; no one will terrify from the *land* (10:16, 18).

In describing the situation the psalm reflects, it talks in both plural and singular terms about both the assailants and their victims (and sometimes has plural verbs with singular subjects). It does the same in describing Yhwh's great acts in the past. This may simply indicate the application of a generic term in the singular to people of that kind;[5] it then does not tell us anything about the people being referred to. The psalm also uses terms that could suggest either an individual or a national crisis, though Ps. 9 speaks more in national terms, Ps. 10 more in individual terms, and this may be a reason for their being separated in use.[6] We might imagine the psalm being written for a leader such as Nehemiah, under personal strain because of pressure brought by other peoples and their leaders. But even then some of the description will have to be taken figuratively (see 10:8–10), and the whole may have no one kind of trouble in mind. The psalm might represent the piety of the Second Temple period, when the community knew of Yhwh's deeds in the past but was aware that its present experience did not correspond to that. It then provides a wide-ranging portrayal of personal and communal attacks that individuals and communities can utilize in different situations, interpreting different parts more or less literally as they need.

5. Cf. GKC 126m.
6. Cf. Paul-Richard Berger, "Zu den Strophen des 10. Psalms," *UF* 2 (1970): 7–17, see 7.

> The leader's. The girls/Secrets/Eternities/On dying. The son's. Composition. David's.

Heading. See glossary. For the second expression K implies *'ălāmôt*, "The girls" (cf. 46:1), or *'ălumôt*, "Secrets" (LXX); Sym "Eternal things" assumes the root is rather *'ālam* III. Q implies *'al mût* ("On dying"; the form is construct, so the compound expression implies "On the son's dying/death"); cf. C.[7] All these might refer to a melody or some other musical direction (cf. 1 Chron. 15:20), while "the son's" might designate the supplicant.

9:1–4. The psalm thus begins like a testimony or thanksgiving but soon complicates that impression. Actually, the supplicant is in need of God acting. In the meantime, the psalm signals that this is no regular testimony psalm by appending to the commitment to praise (vv. 1–2) an allusion to when this praise will begin (vv. 3–4).

> [ʾ] ⁹:¹I will confess Yhwh with all my heart;
>   I will tell of all your awesome deeds.
> ²I will rejoice and exult in you,
>   I will make music to your name, Most High,

In the opening first-person commitment to praise, all four cola begin with the letter *'ālep* (noted by the symbol ʾ in the translation). The initial verb might indeed suggest that this is the beginning to a testimony psalm (cf. 138:1); it is the declaration of intent to tell of "your awesome deeds" that complicates this. The phrase "awesome deeds" does not suggest acts of deliverance for an individual; they are normally, if not invariably, the great acts of God in creation and in Israel's history (e.g., 26:7; 78:4, 11, 32; 106:7, 22). A praise psalm that gives praise for such wonders can also begin with the commitment, "I will confess Yhwh with all my heart" (cf. 111:1; on the verb, see 6:5 [6]). It will transpire that this psalm's praise indeed relates to Yhwh's great acts of deliverance. The undertaking addressed to Yhwh (v. 1b) complements the testimony addressed to other people (v. 1a),[8] which issues from the person's inner being: "All your awesome deeds" finds its match in "all my heart."

The two verbs in v. 2a spell this out further. At the same time, the two verbs in vv. 1b and 2b spell out the complementary feature of praise, that it must be outwardly expressed. Praise involves "telling"; it has to be public, glorifying God before the congregation. Words and *music

---

7. And for several of these understandings, see *Midrash on Psalms*, 131–32.
8. LXX has "I will thank you, Yhwh," perhaps inferring a suffix from the second colon, and perhaps rightly.

are what make this into praise. All four cola thus stand in parallelism, with the references to Yhwh and to the *Most High acting as a bracket around them.

> [b] ³When my enemies turn back,
>   stumble and perish before you,
> ⁴Because you have given decisive judgment for me,
>   you have sat on your throne as one who makes decisions faithfully.

If this were a testimony psalm, one might then expect an account of God's deliverance from trouble in response to prayer. Reference to an act of Yhwh indeed follows in v. 3, but it takes the form of a "when" clause (which conveniently begins with *b*), dependent on v. 2; its finite verbs are yiqtol, not qatal.[9]

A "because" clause with qatal verbs, the kind of clause one might have expected, does then follow in v. 4. The question then is how it relates to the yiqtols in v. 3. Further, it is the last first-person praise clause in the whole of Ps. 9–10. The rest of the psalm will rather recall Yhwh's great acts in the people's history, and this will also be true of subsequent statements about Yhwh's acts (9:12, 15–16; 10:16). I therefore take vv. 3–4 to refer not to what Yhwh has already done (so NRSV) nor to what Yhwh habitually does (so NIVI), but to what the suppliant expects Yhwh to do (cf. LXX, Jerome, Tg); v. 4 looks back from the perspective of that future event (cf. 13:6b). The logic of this will soon emerge: the suppliant is not in a position to give testimony but is in need of Yhwh's acting. When Yhwh has acted, that testimony will be possible. The suppliant looks forward to giving Yhwh praise, confident that the enemies will retreat, stumble, and perish, because they will find themselves faced with God (lit., they will stumble and perish "to your *face"). And that will come about because Yhwh has exercised *authority in a way that was *faithful to Israel. The implication is not that justice will be on the suppliant's side, though the psalm will go on to imply that. It is that the faithful God will be on the suppliant's side. The psalm will go on to elaborate on the "disputatious framing of social reality and social power" already presupposed here. Only in Yhwh's court does the weak party receive a fair hearing against the strong. But it is important to keep in mind that "this odd court is convened *in the poem* and *only in the poem*." That is what makes the poem or prayer

---

9. LXX assumes that the stumbling and perishing follow on the turning (cf. NRSV); v. 3 is then a self-contained sentence. Jerome more plausibly takes the cola as parallel, with the yiqtol verbs in v. 3b continuing and complementing the infinitival expression in v. 3a (cf. NIVI?—though it omits the "when"); cf. GKC 114r.

so important.[10] If there is no prayer, there is no decision of the court and no action of God.

9:5–10. The suppliant thus stands between the reality of Yhwh delivering the people in the past and the need for deliverance in the present. The psalm begins to recall Yhwh's acts in Israel's history (vv. 5–6) with their implications for Yhwh's power (vv. 7–8) and for people's trust in Yhwh (vv. 9–10). The aim is to encourage Yhwh to act that way again and to build up the suppliant's trust that Yhwh will do so.

> [g] ⁵You thundered at nations, you caused the faithless person to perish,
>   you eliminated their name forever and ever.
> ⁶The enemy were finished, ruins without end;
>   you uprooted cities, their memory perished—

The psalm recollects the kind of story Exodus and Joshua tell. Yhwh "thundered" at the Red Sea (Ps. 106:9) and caused "the enemy" (Exod. 15:6, 9) to "perish" (Deut. 11:4) "forever" (Exod. 14:13). It was their "faithlessness" that justified Yhwh's dispossessing the "nations" (Deut. 9:4–5). Yhwh declared the intention to "eliminate" Amalek's memory (Exod. 17:14) so that among the "nations" Amalek perishes for "ever" (*ʿad*; Num. 24:20). Yhwh's actions increase in devastation through v. 5—thundering, death, elimination of the *name so that they are never remembered. Verse 6 has an equivalent powerful effect by superimposing or interweaving two aspects of this devastation, the elimination of a people and the destruction of their cities.[11] First the enemy is spoken of as if it were a city ("in ruins"). Then the cities are spoken of as if they were people ("their memory perished"). Meanwhile, "you uprooted cities" can suggest both "you utterly destroyed them," like the uprooting of a plant (cf. Jer. 31:40), and "you depopulated them," uprooting their people (cf. Jer. 12:14, 17). The line eventually ends at the same point as v. 5. The objects of this treatment are foreigners, enemies, and the faithless. The issue, this combination implies, was not merely ethnicity or conflict but failure to keep commitments. It is a fact that can rebound on Israel, for the language in vv. 5–6 (thunder, perish, eliminate the name, ruins, uprooting) can all be used against Israel when it turns faithless.

> [h] ⁷Them! But Yhwh is seated forever,
>   as one who establishes his throne for making decisions.

---

10. Brueggemann, *Psalms and the Life of Faith*, 220–21.
11. Cf. D. T. Tsumura, "'Inserted Bicolon,' the AXYB Pattern, in Amos i 5 and Psalm ix 7," *VT* 38 (1988): 234–36.

> ⁸He himself makes decisions for the world in faithfulness,
>   exercises authority for the countries with uprightness,

Yhwh's permanency (cf. Exod. 15:18) contrasts with the nations' vulnerability. Verses 7–8 recycle most of the words in v. 4 that spoke of a future exercise of sovereignty to make here a statement about the fact of Yhwh's sovereignty that undergirds the expectation. The first colon raises the question about what Yhwh is doing sitting down (nothing?), and the second answers the question, with another nod to the Red Sea event (see Exod. 15:17). Verse 8 nuances that answer. Verse 4 spoke only of decisions on the suppliant's behalf. Verse 8 jumps to another extreme: Yhwh is making decisions for the world. In repeating that, the second colon adds uprightness to *faithfulness as Yhwh's modus operandi. All this makes explicit the point we noted about the language in vv. 5–6. Yhwh's acts in the world cannot favor Israel in a way that ignores the rights or the destinies of other peoples. Yhwh's faithfulness and uprightness also apply to them. How could it be otherwise?

> [w] ⁹So that Yhwh may be a haven for the broken person,
>   a haven for times of trouble,
> ¹⁰And people who acknowledge your name may trust in you,
>   because you did not abandon those who sought help from you,
>   Yhwh.

To underscore that implication, Yhwh is a *haven for the person who collapses under the pressure of enemy attack. Such people are the broken (*dak*), the people in trouble (*ṣārâ*; see 4:1 [2]). That is the qualification for seeking refuge with Yhwh, and that is implicitly the suppliant's self-identification, but the designation is thus not (e.g.) inherently an ethnic one. The same applies to the designation that follows. People who *acknowledge Yhwh as such a resource should therefore *trust in this haven. "People who acknowledge [Yhwh's] *name" would be a good definition of what Israel was called to be, but Israel can give up doing that, and other peoples can take up this acknowledgment. Verses 9–10 close with a renewed declaration of the basis for this trust. Israel had proved that *seeking help from Yhwh worked. To say that Yhwh did not "abandon" Israel is to indicate that Yhwh fulfilled the promise made on the eve of Israel's entry into the land (Deut. 31:6, 8; Josh. 1:5); it is another way of saying that Yhwh indeed proved faithful (Ps. 9:4, 8). But Yhwh's not abandoning has also characterized Israel's subsequent story (e.g., 1 Chron. 28:20; Ezra 9:9; Neh. 9:17, 19, 31), and "seeking help from Yhwh" has continued to be key (e.g., 2 Chron. 17:3–4; 25:15; Ezra 6:21).

[z] **¹¹**Make music to Yhwh who is seated on Zion,
  tell his assertive actions among the peoples,
¹²Because one who seeks bloodshed was mindful of them;
  he did not ignore the cry of the weak.

9:11–12. The recollection of Yhwh's great acts with their implications leads into a challenge to give praise for these acts. The challenge again brings together a verb for making *music and one referring to words (cf. vv. 1–2). Yhwh is once more described as seated (cf. vv. 4, 7), but now on Zion, in the earthly equivalent of the heavenly palace where Yhwh sits enthroned (see 5:7 [8]). Perhaps one reason for referring to Zion is that this praise is to be offered there. But the second colon adds that the praise is to be offered among the peoples (cf. 57:9 [10]; 108:3 [4]). Why so? Verses 7–10 would fit with other psalms assuming that praise is public so that the peoples can join in (cf. 47:1 [2]; 66:8), because God is taking decisive action *for* them (cf. 67:3–5 [4–6]; 96). The psalm has spoken both of Yhwh's destroying nations and of Yhwh's acting decisively for the world (cf. Ps. 47) and apparently reckons there is no contradiction between these. Putting down faithless nations is good news for peoples who are prepared to acknowledge Yhwh.

Verse 12 speaks in a more concrete way about the past deed that incites this praise. "Be *mindful" is repeated in different words by means of the second, negatived verb "did not *ignore," but in other respects the first colon raises questions that the second answers. Why does Yhwh seek (the verb *dāraš* as in v. 10) for blood? Who were the people of whom Yhwh was mindful? The suffix "them" refers forward to "the *weak," who reappear in 9:18; 10:12.¹² Yhwh requires *bloodshed because the cry of the weak is a *cry like Abel's, the cry of blood shouting out from the ground for recompense.

9:13–18. The psalm might have come to an end with v. 12. To our surprise, not only does it continue, but it also turns into a prayer psalm. The praise now functions to persuade Yhwh to listen to this prayer in a way that is in keeping with that celebration of Yhwh's character and deeds, and to encourage the suppliant to believe that Yhwh will do so. The development within the psalm thus parallels that in (e.g.) Pss. 44 and 89, in which recognition of Yhwh's past acts is the lead-in to prayer.

---

12. The weak are the *'ănāwîm* (Q)/*'ănāyyim* (K); in 9:18 Q and K are reversed. Singular *'ānî* comes in 10:2, 9b, 9c, plural *'ănāwîm* also in 10:17 (the noun "weakness," *'onyî*, will shortly appear in 9:13). These data support the view that the two forms of the word have the same meaning.

> [*h*] ¹³Be gracious to me, Yhwh;
>   look at my weakness because of the people who are against me,
>   you who can lift me from the gates of death,
> ¹⁴So that I may tell of all your praiseworthy acts,
>   within the gates of Ms. Zion
>   be glad in your deliverance.

The implications of "be *gracious" are spelled out in the appeal to "look," because Yhwh will surely act in compassion when Yhwh sees the *weakness resulting from the acts of "people who are *against me." Verse 13c summarizes an implication of vv. 1–12: Yhwh is (lit.) "my lifter from the gates of death." "Lifting" is what is needed because these attacks put the suppliant on the verge of going through the gates leading into Death City, below. The participle could suggest the one who *has* "lifted me," or who *does* or *will* "lift me," but the context more likely suggests Yhwh is the one who *could* "lift me." The prayer seeks to move Yhwh to do that.

But the jump to the prospect of praise for Yhwh's deliverance suggests that the participial phrase does anticipate Yhwh's action: it is the only reference to an event that would constitute rescue. As the prayer looks for an act that reprises Yhwh's past great acts of which vv. 5–10 spoke, so it looks forward again to taking up the "telling" and the gladness of the testimony of which vv. 1–4 spoke. The telling and the gladness are here in parallelism, suggesting the words and the emotion, while "your praiseworthy acts"¹³ is spelled out as "your deliverance." At the center of the line and applying to both cola is the location of this joyful testimony, which the suppliant will offer "*in* the gates of *Ms. Zion*" after being rescued "*from* the gates of *death*." Perhaps there is an implication that over against Zion, death is the place where we cannot give testimony, both because Yhwh has ceased acting and because we have lost our voices (cf. 6:5 [6]). Conversely, over against death, Zion is the place of life, not least because it is the place of testimony. "Ms. Zion" occurs only here in the Psalms, though frequently elsewhere (e.g., Isa. 1:8; 52:2; Jer. 6:2; Lam. 1:6) as a personification of the city to which Yhwh is committed as father or lover.

> [*ṭ*] ¹⁵Nations plunged into the pit they made;
>   in the net that they hid, their foot got caught.
> ¹⁶Yhwh caused himself to be acknowledged, he took decisive action,
>   by the act of his hands knocking down the faithless person

13. *Tĕhillâ* (EVV "praise") can denote a quality or act that deserves praise (cf. 78:4; 79:13; see BDB 239–40).

[*or*, by the act of his hands the faithless was snared]. (Recitation. Rise)

Verses 15–16 return to recall the past events that are the basis for this prayer, offering complementary accounts of these. On the one hand, the events illustrate the way people's wrongful plans can turn back on them (cf. 7:15–16 [16–17]). Verse 15a leaves open how they came to fall into their own pit, and v. 15b indicates how. More literally, we might imagine an army running out of supplies through attempting to starve a city to death.

On the other hand, past events have also illustrated how Yhwh can act to bring an army to its end (e.g., 2 Kings 19:35), and vv. 4 and 8 have already spoken of Yhwh's decisive acts. Verse 16a makes explicit that by such acts Yhwh has been known; it provides a proof text for the idea of revelation in history, of Yhwh's being known in decisive acts. But the recurrence of "acknowledge" from v. 10 sets that idea in a broader context. This revelation reaches its goal only when it receives the response of acknowledgment. To put it the other way, the acknowledgment v. 10 refers to forms a response to Yhwh's making himself known in events. The first colon of v. 16 again leaves open *how* this happened, and v. 16b indicates how—though the text leaves us with some ambiguity about the matter. MT has Yhwh knocking down the faithless like someone bringing down a bird with a stick (BDB). LXX has the faithless being snared. In MT vv. 15–16 simply set alongside each other the two ways the faithless may get their comeuppance. These might be two ways of describing the same event or two different ways things work out on separate occasions. LXX implies that they are indeed two ways of describing the same event. When people devise a trap and it "accidentally" rebounds on them, it is Yhwh who makes that happen. Indeed, the directness of this is emphasized: it comes about "by the act of his hands." Grammatically, this might mean "by the hands of the faithless person"; that would underline the assumption that events can happen simultaneously by human will and by divine will. But the word order rather suggests that "his hands" refers to Yhwh.

[y] ¹⁷Faithless people turn . . . to Sheol,
  all nations that ignore God,
[k] ¹⁸Because the needy person is not ignored without end;
  the hope of the weak ones does not perish forever.

Once again acknowledgment of God's past acts leads to present statement of faith. Whereas the suppliant is at Sheol's gates, past occasions when the *faithless fell into their own traps give assurance that it is they who are really on their way there. "[Re]turning to Sheol" (cf. NIVI) does not mean (e.g.) they are returning whence they came (one cannot speak of returning to Sheol as one can of returning to the soil from which we came, because we did not come from Sheol). Rather, the expression involves an ellipse: they will turn to flee and perish (cf. v. 3) and will thus find themselves in Sheol. Everyone goes there in due course, but neither party would be due to go there yet. Nevertheless, the conflict means that either the attackers or their victims must. Alongside the further reference to death (cf. v. 13) is the further reference to *ignoring (cf. v. 12). Yhwh does not ignore the weak (v. 12); v. 18 will reaffirm the point. Their attackers are people who do ignore God, who put God out of mind. It is another way of saying that when Yhwh makes himself known, they do not respond by acknowledging Yhwh. The psalm assumes that "nations" can be expected to be faithful rather than faithless (see on vv. 5–6) and to be mindful of God rather than to ignore God.

The "because" that opens v. 18 makes explicit the link between the death of the faithless and the deliverance of the weak. There are circumstances in which the latter requires the former. Indeed, there is a sense in which the latter metaphysically always requires the former. If people have killed others or tried to do so, the mere deliverance of some intended victims does not restore balance in society. Society remains out of kilter. Both cola indicate how it can seem as if attacks are going on forever as Yhwh delays responding to prayer. *Hope thus stands over against "forever/finally." Deliverance will come. Verse 18a raises the question "Who are the *needy, and what will their not being ignored look like?" Verse 18b answers that the needy are the *weak, whom we know, and their not being ignored will mean that their hope does not finally perish. The nations will perish and their memory will perish (vv. 3, 6) before the *hope of the weak does.

9:19–10:2. The psalm returns to plea, which the four verses present in three or four ways. It is expressed as a direct imperative (vv. 19a, 20a), slightly less directly as a jussive (vv. 19a, 19b, 20, 2b), less directly again as a rhetorical question (v. 1a, 1b); and perhaps even v. 2a, the only colon that might be judged a statement, is also an indirect plea: You have to stop this person. The four lines are the most concentrated sequence of pleas in the psalm; they come at its very center. Reflecting the fact that this is the densest sequence of pleas, each of the first three lines includes an invocation of Yhwh, associated with each of the two imperatives and with the line of rhetorical questions. It is the densest sequence of references to Yhwh in the psalm, let alone of invocations of Yhwh. When we use someone's name in this way, it is an aspect of the attempt to get them to do as we ask in light of who we are and our relationship with them. The four lines also interweave talk in terms of an individual (vv. 19a, 2a) and of nations (vv. 19b, 20, 2b). While this movement may be merely rhetorical, one can imagine the psalm being used by a leader such as Nehemiah under pressure from people such as Sanballat, confronted by another individual but knowing that both stand for whole communities.

> ¹⁹Arise, Yhwh. A human being must not prevail;
> nations must have their decision made before you.
> ²⁰Appoint something fearful [or, a teacher] for them, Yhwh;
> nations must acknowledge they are human. (Rise)

Poetically, these two lines are particularly intricate. As usual, each develops in a self-contained way. In v. 19, Yhwh's arising will issue in making sure a human being does not prevail and that nations thus discover the *authoritative decision Yhwh has made for them (*šāpaṭ* niphal). For humanity to "prevail" (*'āzaz*, "be strong") would hardly be appropriate in light of Yhwh's founding a barricade (*'ōz*, "a strong thing") against attackers long ago (8:2 [3]). In one sense the psalm rejoices that Yhwh is seated, on a throne (9:4, 7, 11), but in another sense it wants Yhwh to get up to take action instead of letting things continue to unfold according to their own dynamic. If the nations are to fall into the pit they have made (cf. 7:15; 9:15; 10:2), they need to be pushed. In v. 20, Yhwh's appointing a fearful experience to be their teacher will force them to *acknowledge who they are.

At the same time, the two whole lines are parallel in comprising direct plea followed by a jussive or two. "Arising" will issue in "appointing" (these two verbs come in sequence in 12:5 [6] in a more pleasant context). The sequence between the jussives implies that discovering the decision Yhwh has made will lead to that acknowledgment. In addition, the clauses in vv. 19–20 come in *abb'a'* sequence after the opening imperative. Nations must have their decision made as Yhwh appoints something fearful for them; and that will mean that a human being does not prevail and that they acknowledge they are human and not divine. "A human being/human" (*'ĕnôš*) links the first and last cola.

> [*l*] ¹⁰:¹Why do you stand far off, Yhwh,
> why do you hide in times of trouble?
> ²In his loftiness the faithless hounds the weak person;
> they must be caught by the schemes that they have thought up.

The rhetorical questions are parallel, with the "Why?" in the first colon applying also to the second. The imagery changes again. Yhwh is standing, not seated, yet standing far off, looking and listening but not acting; or rather, hiding eyes and ears so as not to see or hear (cf. Isa.

1:15; Lam. 3:56)—because if Yhwh saw and heard, surely action would be bound to follow (cf. Ps. 4:1 [2]; 9:13). The psalm has declared that Yhwh is a refuge "for times of trouble" (9:9). This is not working out.

Verse 2 opens with that single indicative statement in 9:19–10:2. The people of *loftiness are those whose exalted position enables them to behave in a *faithless way toward the *weak. Their attacks are described as "hounding," a new and rare verb,[14] though one that takes up the imagery of 9:15–16. The second colon then takes it further. The faithless did not literally set traps but laid plots, like the ones that robbed Naboth of his land or tried to stop Nehemiah from building his wall. Justice requires that they be caught by their own traps/schemes, so that they stop being a threat to the weak.

10:3–11. The longest characterization of the faithless person opens and closes in the qatal (cf. also v. 6) but is dominated by the yiqtol. Here the weak characterize the strong, and it is the words of the weak that we have. "The wicked have *lost their control of the social conversation*," which they normally control. "Now, perhaps for the first time, the strong are at the mercy of the weak."[15]

> ³Because the faithless gloried over the desire of his heart,
>   the robber worshipped,
> [n] ⁴ᵃ⁻ᵇThe faithless disdained Yhwh
>   in accordance with the exaltedness of his look:

"Gloried" is *hillēl*. It is an inauspicious beginning for the career of this verb in the Psalter, but it will recover. Instead of glorying in/praising Yhwh, the faithless gloried over the thing his heart desired (heart is *nepeš*, *person)—the thing he gained by his scheming. "The robber *worshipped" repeats the point, using the verb *bārak*, another verb that deserves to be applied to Yhwh and often appears in parallelism with *hillēl* (e.g., 104:35; 135:21; 145:2). The clauses work *abb'a'*, and the intervening prepositional phrase applies to both.

The implication of the point is that in glorying and worshipping over the desire of his heart, the faithless has treated Yhwh with contempt—as implied by the very use of those verbs in that way. He has disdained Yhwh by behaving as if Yhwh were not involved in the world (cf. 74:10, 18). "Exaltedness" (*gōbah*) has similar implications to "loftiness." There is nothing inherently wrong with it, but it easily makes the exalted person react as if he were *the* exalted one. This is what the faithless has done.

---

14. I take this as *dālaq* II, a different root from *dālaq* meaning "burn" (7:13 [14]); see **DCH** but contrast **BDB**.
15. Brueggemann, *Psalms and the Life of Faith*, 226.

> ⁴ᶜ"He does not seek for requital—there is no God";
> ⁵all his schemes—his ways are profane all the time.
> [m] Your decisions are on high, away from him;
> all his assailants—he snorts at them.

"There is no God," says the faithless person. The evidence of this is that God "does not seek for requital" (cf. v. 13). In saying this the faithless person in effect says, "There is no God." For practical purposes God can be left out of account (cf. 14:1–3 in the same connection). God is not involved in the everyday world. To put it another way, all the schemes of the faithless person (cf. v. 2) manifest a profaneness. He is the kind of person who ignores covenant relationships and thus profanes them (e.g., 55:20 [21]). And that is so "all the time," all those "times" when Yhwh is supposed to protect but is not doing so (9:9; 10:1).

Verse 5b–c restates the assumption on which the faithless thus act. Yes, Yhwh makes *decisions (cf. 9:4, 7, 8, 16, 19), but they are on high, up there in heaven, far away; they do not affect life down here. The parallel colon works out the implications of that. People may resist or attack the faithless person, but he remains confident of success.

> ⁶He said in his heart, "I will not fall down, ever."
> "Not be in adversity," he swore.

He can be so because of the encouragement he gave himself (v. 6). The line takes *abb'a'* form: the two verbs of speaking open and close the line, with the content of the words coming between. He swears an oath to himself about the security of his own future. He will not *fall down or see adversity (*bad).

> [p] ⁷His mouth is full of both fraudulence and oppression;
> under his tongue are troublemaking and harm.

A description of his habitual acts runs through vv. 7–10, with a series of interlocking verbal links. Here, mouth and tongue complement each other, as do two words each for what mouth and tongue achieve (the four words come together again in 55:10–11 [11–12]). Although his mouth is "full" of oppressive fraudulence, the picture of *harm and troublemaking (cf. 7:14 [15]) being "under" his tongue reflects the fact that the words that are actually *on* his tongue are of course friendly ones: that is their deceitfulness.

> ⁸He sits in a hiding place in the villages
> so that in secret he may slay someone innocent.

> [ʾ] His eyes watch for the wretched person;
> ⁹he hides in a secret place like a lion in its lair.
> He hides in order to catch the weak person,
> catches the weak by dragging him into his net.

He is a hunter. The parallel cola in v. 8a–b each have a *b*-expression (one singular/concrete, one abstract/plural) and a yiqtol verb, though they describe sequential acts, the second being the aim of the first. The villages might be dangerous because they lack walls to keep out wild animals, and there is then nothing wrong with being a hunter. Such a person protects the community by hiding, keeping watch, and slaying. But this hunter is hiding in order to keep watch for vulnerable people and slay them.

In v. 8c–9a, the first colon summarizes the previous line, while the second adds a simile to underline the point. Instead of catching wild animals, this hunter resembles one; he is in hiding in order to catch the vulnerable. The "wretched" appear only in this psalm (cf. vv. 10, 14).

The first colon in v. 9b–c in turn repeats a verb from v. 9a, then the second colon repeats one from the first, while "hide" and "secret place" take up roots from v. 8a–b. The faithless person catches the weak like a hunter catching an animal, by drawing together the net into which his prey has wandered.

> ¹⁰Broken, he sinks down,
> the wretched fall by his might.
> [*or*, The wretched are broken, sink down,
> fall by his might.]
> ¹¹He said in his heart, "God ignored it,
> he turned his face, he never looked."

Two cola portray this catch in more detail, offering painfully repeated accounts of the event—the wretched keep falling into the net before our eyes. The power of the "hunter" is too much for them. Verses 8–10 have thus formed an overlapping linear sequence: v. 8 focuses on the plotting, v. 9 goes on from the plotting to the seizing, v. 10 focuses on the seizing. "Breaking" or "crushing" generates the metaphor of "oppressing" (*dākāʾ, dākâ, dākak*), which is common in the Psalms; "broken" is another term for "weak" or "wretched" (cf. 9:9; 10:18).

Verse 11 returns to the themes of vv. 4–6. His self-reassurance corresponds to v. 6, but though there he looked forward, here he looks backward with words that re-express the convictions of vv. 4–5.[16] He is doing some hiding (vv. 8–9), but he believes God is doing some, too

---

16. Graham S. Ogden ("Translating Psalm 10:11," *BT* 42 [1991]: 231–33) takes the victim as the subject, but in the preceding colon the victims were pl., the faithless person sg.

(his *face), so he is safe. To close off the section, the line comprises four two-stress clauses, the first introducing three parallel restatements of the same conviction that increase in intensity and confidence through the verse until they reach the "never" with which it closes.

10:12–15. Verse 11 was a provocation, like the Rabshakeh's in 2 Kings 18–19. It must meet with a response.

> [q] ¹²Arise, Yhwh;
>   God, lift your hand—
>   do not ignore the weak.
>   ¹³Why has the faithless disdained God,
>   said in his heart, "You do not seek for requital"?

The psalm once more reverts to plea. No doubt the words attributed to the faithless in v. 11 express the suppliant's own fears, and the psalm therefore urges Yhwh to prove that what the faithless says is not true. Again it urges Yhwh to arise (cf. 9:19). The implications of that are worked out in a new expression. Lifting the hand suggests taking firm action for or against someone; the same act often does both. "Do not *ignore the *weak," as the faithless said Yhwh did, suggests the focus here lies on deliverance, but that will involve putting down the faithless.

The parallel rhetorical questions then recycle words in vv. 3–4, 11 and sum up the burden of vv. 3–11. The second colon (to which the "Why?" carries over) explains how the faithless disdained God.

> [r] ¹⁴You looked, because you yourself pay attention to troublemaking and aggression,
>   so as to recompense by your hand.
>   The wretched leaves it to you;
>   the orphan—you have been a helper.
> [š] ¹⁵Break the strength of the faithless and evil person;
>   seek for his faithlessness until you find none.

The questions' common point is in turn explained: the conviction of the faithless that he can renounce God and get away with it has been disproved by Yhwh's acts in the past. "You looked" contradicts v. 11, and the succeeding clause links that with ongoing truth about Yhwh. When people do wrong to others, Yhwh does notice (*nābaṭ* hiphil). The verb recurs in pleas (e.g., 13:3 [4]; 80:14 [15]). It does not ask Yhwh to look and be sympathetic but to look and act, by "giving it to them"—giving recompense to the faithless[17] and/or to the wretched (so Tg). On the basis of that fact, the wretched can leave things with Yhwh, and the orphan

---

17. Cf. 28:4a, 4b; so Briggs, *Psalms*, 1:80.

can do the same. The second clause again explains the basis for this in terms of past experience of Yhwh's *help.

In light of that, the suppliant again pleads for Yhwh to take action, now making explicit the negative side to what is needed. If there is to be rescue, there has to be putting down. Literally, the plea is for Yhwh to break the arm of the faithless in order to stop his strong-arm tactics. The second colon suggests that "arm" is a figure for "strength" (cf. 71:18), though no doubt the suppliant will be happy to be taken literally if necessary. But the aim of the destructiveness will be the elimination of his faithless acts. Once more the psalm takes up the verb *dāraš*, suggesting *seeking something from someone.

> ¹⁶Yhwh is king forever and ever;
>   nations perished from his land—
>   ¹⁷you listened to the desire of the weak, Yhwh.
> [*t*] You establish their heart; you bend your ear,
>   ¹⁸to decide for orphan and broken person
>   so that a human being from the land may terrify no more.

10:16–18. A series of further statements of faith, forming a double tricolon, brings the psalm to its close. In each, the opening line makes a timeless statement—one a noun clause, the other a double yiqtol clause. The first is supported by two qatal clauses that again support the statement of faith. The second leads into two purpose clauses that again indicate the positive aim of Yhwh's acts. In another psalm these might be once-for-all closing expressions of confidence that the prayer has been answered, and here they may be that, but they are also part of the pattern running through the psalm, the interweaving of plea, statement of faith, and statement about God's acts.

The psalm has referred to Yhwh as sitting enthroned; here for the first time in the Psalms Yhwh is "the king" (in 5:2 [3] Yhwh was "my king," which makes a different point), and that "forever"—linking with the past declaration that nations perished from Yhwh's land. This link recalls the OT's first declaration that "Yhwh reigns" (LXX assimilates to that) "forever and ever" (Exod. 15:18), when the Israelites rejoiced in Yhwh's victory over enemies and saw this as a guarantee that Yhwh would complete the task of bringing them into possession of "Yhwh's mountain." Here the psalm looks back to the fulfillment of that expectation. Nations indeed "perished" (cf. 9:3, 6, 18) from Yhwh's land. Yhwh had "listened" to Israel's pleas in its "weakness" (cf. Exod. 3:7) and responded to their cry again at the Red Sea: here again (Ps. 10:17a), talk of the "desire" of the *weak takes up a word used earlier (v. 3) and applies it in a new direction. The longing of the faithless and the longing of the weak were diametrically opposed, and Yhwh long ago demonstrated a commitment to the latter.

Verses 17b–18 return one more time to the implications for ongoing life. When the people's heart fails as it did in Egypt and at the Red Sea, and more explicitly at Kadesh (Deut. 1:28), Yhwh establishes it, giving them the resolve to keep going. Yhwh's listening (v. 17a) is not just in the past. Yhwh continues to listen (cf. 4:3 [4]; 5:3 [4]; 6:8–9 [9–10]), in keeping with another standard plea in a psalm (e.g., 4:1 [2]). Yhwh habitually "bends an ear" to them, inclining a head from the heavens so as to be able to hear exactly what is going on and to hear the cries that are being uttered down on the earth. The result is indeed the kind of action that a king (cf. v. 16a) is committed to (v. 18). The king of a city is the one who has the power to do something about wrongdoing there, and the one who is morally obliged to do something about it. The orphan and the broken appear again (9:9; 10:10, 14), and so does Yhwh's making the *decisions on behalf of such people. The weak always have Yhwh as their potential deliverer. Given that nations perished from Yhwh's land (v. 16b), it is appropriate that Yhwh should not allow mortals from the nations (cf. 9:19–20) to "terrify" those in that land now. The verb is one associated with the Israelites' conquest of the land (Deut. 1:29; 7:21; 31:6; Josh. 1:9), supporting the impression that the psalm is asking that the great acts of the past be repeated. These links suggest that *hā'āreṣ* is here the land, not the earth (so EVV).

Theological Implications

This is the longest psalm in the Psalter so far, and it has the most comprehensive theology. Indeed, Patrick D. Miller argues that "no other psalm so fully joins the basic themes of the Psalter—the rule of God, the representative role of the king, the plea for help in time of trouble, the ways of the wicked and the righteous, and the justice of God on behalf of the weak and the poor."[18] It speaks especially solemnly to powerful nations and especially encouragingly to weak ones. Most readers of this commentary therefore have to see themselves as the people who are being prayed against.

1. Yhwh is one who has acted in numerous amazing ways in Israel's story, delivering them from nations that attacked them and never abandoning them when they sought Yhwh's help. Yhwh thus acted in decisive

---

18. "The Ruler in Zion and the Hope of the Poor," in *David and Zion* (J. J. M. Roberts Festschrift), ed. Bernard F. Batto and Kathryn L. Roberts (Winona Lake, IN: Eisenbrauns, 2004), 187–97, see 188–89.

and violent ways toward nations that behaved faithlessly, eliminating the nations themselves and their civilization from Yhwh's land. This often involved making their own destructiveness rebound on the nations, by a "natural" process that was also one behind which Yhwh was active.

2. These acts reflect the fact that Yhwh is the Most High God, who sits enthroned as king and is established there permanently as one who exercises authority over the world and its peoples. Yhwh sits enthroned in Zion, Yhwh's capital city, the focus of Yhwh's reign. Yhwh thus continues to act decisively, faithfully, and uprightly, in ways that also affect the life of the individual, bringing deliverance. So Yhwh is a refuge available to the broken in times of pressure. When the weak cry out because people are killing them, Yhwh responds to that cry and acts to punish the killers. Yhwh does not allow people from the land to terrify anymore. Yhwh can send the faithless to their death and can lift up the needy when they are at death's door. Yhwh strengthens their heart and listens for their prayer. The psalm does not suggest an "eschatological orientation"[19] but describes God as involved now.

3. But the very fact that people have to cry out shows that Yhwh sometimes just sits there or stands far off or hides, and needs to be aroused to action. It can thus seem that the hope of the weak is lost and that Yhwh has ignored their cry, but this is not finally so.

4. The nations continue to be characterized by faithlessness. They ignore and disdain Yhwh. They are aware of their own lofty and exalted position, know they rule the world, and see Yhwh as far away and not really involved in the world. God ignores the world and does not look to see what goes on there. In effect, there is no God. The ways of the nations are thus consistently profane. They scoff at opposition and are absolutely confident they will never fall from power. They do not see themselves as merely human.

5. They are also faithless in their relationship with the rest of humanity, specifically with the weak, whom they take advantage of. They are robbers who treat their inner desires as if these were God. They work by combining fraud and oppression, using legal but underhanded means to achieve oppressive ends, bringing death to the vulnerable.

6. The people for whom Yhwh is concerned are the people who acknowledge Yhwh's name, have to put their trust in Yhwh, and cry out to Yhwh because they are weak and needy, broken and wretched, and thus vulnerable to people who are rich in power and resources. Their relationship with Yhwh involves acknowledging Yhwh's name: recognizing who Yhwh is and living appropriately by that. It involves appealing on the basis of their weakness for Yhwh to act in grace.

---

19. So McCann, "Psalms," 719.

7. This relationship embraces the people corporately and the individual "I." It expresses itself in acknowledging who Yhwh is, and doing so by acknowledging what Yhwh has done in Israel's story. It involves joy in the inner being and in the audible voice. It involves telling of Yhwh's deeds in Zion and among the peoples.

8. It involves the conviction that God does notice when nations act aggressively, and the expectation that Yhwh will act similarly in their lives in delivering them from attack. It is a relationship of trust that can leave things to Yhwh.

9. It involves asking God to act decisively in the affairs of the nations and not to ignore the plight of the vulnerable. It thus involves urging Yhwh to bring calamity on attackers and to make their schemes rebound on them, so that they come to acknowledge that they are human. It involves asking Yhwh to break the power of the faithless, to seek out their faithlessness until it is all gone. It thus combines concern for God's honor, for what is right, and for what is in their interests.

In the psalm as a whole, the name of Yhwh is regularly on the lips of the speaker but absent from the speech of the wicked, "who want to eliminate Yahweh politically and theologically." But "the intrusion of Yahweh into social relationships decisively transforms the prospect of both the wicked and the poor." The psalm itself is thus "a practice of alternative politics."[20]

---

20. Brueggemann, *Psalms and the Life of Faith*, 231.

Psalm 11
Stay or Flit?

Translation

The leader's. David's.

¹On Yhwh do I rely;
   how can you say to me,
   "Flit to your mountain, birds,
   [*or*, "Flit to a mountain like a bird,]ᵃ
²Because there are the faithless,
   who bend the bow;
They have fitted their arrow on the string
   to shoot in the darkness at the upright of heart."

³When the foundations are destroyed,
   the faithful—what could he have done?

⁴Yhwh in his holy palace,
   Yhwh whose throne is in the heavensᵇ—

---

a. The first version follows K, *nwdw hrkm ṣpr*. "Flit" and "your" are pl., and *ṣippôr* is presumably collective (BDB)—though we could render K itself ". . .[like] birds" (so *DCH*; GKC 118r). The second version presupposes (e.g.) *nûdî har kĕmô ṣippôr* (cf. LXX). Q has a composite reading, sg. *nûdî* but pl. "your mountains," while Tg has "flit [pl.] to the mountain like the birds." For the verb, EVV have "flee," but while there is some cross-influence between *nādad* and *nûd* (cf. English "flight"), the latter often means simply "fly off" (cf. LXX, Jerome, Tg), and flying is here part of the bird image. There is no preposition "to," and Rashi understands "from your mountain," meaning from the land.

b. I follow Pierre Auffret ("Essai sur la structure littéraire du Psaume 11," *ZAW* 93 [1981]: 401–18, esp. 403) in taking the first line in v. 4 as *casus pendens*.

His eyes behold,
   his gaze examines, human beings.
⁵Yhwh—he examines faithful and faithless;
   with all his being he is against[c] the person dedicated to violence.
⁶He rains/must rain snares on the faithless,
   fire and sulfur,
[or, He rains/must rain on the faithless
   blazing coal and sulfur,][d]
A scorching wind
   as the share[e] in their cup.[f]
⁷Because Yhwh is faithful—
   he is dedicated to faithful acts;
   his face beholds the upright person.[g]

Interpretation

Psalm 11 is a statement of trust, very radically so, for it contains no direct plea at all except the possible jussive in v. 6 (contrast Ps. 4). It is rhetorically addressed to people who are warning the speaker to flee from the dangerous attacks of other members of the community, and it encourages them to stand as firm as the speaker does, when necessary. These addressees can presumably be identified with the faithful/upright who appear in the psalm. But its actual audience could be any of the characters it mentions. That could thus be Yhwh—the psalm could be a covert declaration to Yhwh and a challenge to Yhwh to justify the trust it declares (an overt challenge, perhaps, in v. 6). Or it could be the attackers—it could indirectly be designed to warn them that they will not frighten the object of their attacks into fleeing and/or to warn them to change.[1] Or it could be the speaker's own self, the words being designed to bolster the very boldness and trust they express.

Verses 1–2 relate the warnings of those other members of the community, and vv. 4–7 constitute the statement of faith. Verse 3 could belong with either grouping.

c. Lit., "his *nepeš* [*person] is against."
d. MT has Yhwh raining bird snares (*paḥîm*), which is odd, though there would be poetic justice in doing so. Sym implies *peḥam* (coal, which can be collective).
e. *Měnāt*, a variant for *mānâ*.
f. EVV take this line as a separate noun clause, but LXX and Jerome more plausibly see "and a scorching wind" as continuing the description of Yhwh's means of bringing calamity.
g. EVV "the upright behold his face" requires *yāšār* to be collective, which it never is elsewhere, but the implications are similar. The form of suffix on *pānêmô* would usually be pl., but there is no antecedent for a pl., and the form is sometimes sg. (see GKC 103f; JM 94i). The long suffix gives the psalm a more solid ending.
1. Cf. M. Mannati, "Le Psaume xi," *VT* 29 (1979): 222–28.

The leader's. David's.

Heading. See glossary.

11:1–2. Like Ps. 7, this statement of trust starts in the middle of things. We will shortly learn of the pressure on the speaker that raises the question of trust, but we will learn this only from the words of worried friends.[2] For the speaker, it is Yhwh who counts.

> ¹On Yhwh do I rely;
>   how can you say to me,
>   "Flit to your mountain, birds, [*or*, "Flit to a mountain like a bird,]

The point is made punchily in the two-word opening colon, "On Yhwh do I rely." Subsequently Yhwh will be the direct or indirect subject of every line in vv. 4–7 and will actually be named four times, the name coming in emphatic position at the beginning of the clause three times in vv. 4–5. That is a rhetorical reflection of the place Yhwh has in the speaker's life. The friends never mention Yhwh, a rhetorical reflection of the place Yhwh has in their thinking about life.

A declaration about relying on Yhwh commonly comes at the very beginning of a psalm (e.g., Pss. 7; 16; 31; 57; 71), usually as the basis for appeal to Yhwh for protection. Here, uniquely, it is the basis for a response to those well-meaning friends whose statement raises the question of trust and the need for a safe place. Both MT and LXX picture the speaker as a bird, either in a metaphor (MT) or in a simile (LXX). MT's plural fits with the eventual plural "upright of heart" and implies that the advisers are making a generalization about danger affecting a number of people, which the speaker refuses to have applied personally.[3] LXX's singular has them addressing their warning simply to the speaker, who is in particular danger for some reason. The image of flitting to the mountains suggests that the psalm's opening words about relying on Yhwh already had this exhortation in mind, because "*relying on Yhwh" suggests more literally "sheltering in/with Yhwh." A user of the psalm might be literally "taking refuge" in the temple (cf. 1 Kings 1:50).[4] Metaphorically, the speaker is certainly doing so.

---

2. Gerstenberger (*Psalms*, 1:77) takes v. 1b as the words of the attackers, whom the psalmist then describes in v. 2, but it seems odd for attackers to bid the speaker to flee for safety. Isaiah Sonne ("Psalm Eleven," *JBL* 68 [1949]: 241–45) emends to eliminate the bidding; so does Julius Morgenstern ("Psalm 11," *JBL* 69 [1950]: 221–31) in interpreting the psalm in connection with magical practices.

3. "To me" is *lĕnapšî* (*person).

4. W. H. Bellinger ("The Interpretation of Psalm 11," *Evangelical Quarterly* 56 [1984]: 95–101) takes the psalm originally to have related to seeking asylum, but then to have been reinterpreted more metaphorically.

Mountains are places of refuge, high up, inaccessible, covered in trees, dotted by caves, and offering many places to hide, but there is no tradition of human beings hiding there, and a speaker in Jerusalem or most other likely places is already in the mountains; that is where the danger lies, not the security. (Gen. 19:17 and 1 Macc. 2:28 prove the rule, because Sodom is in the Jordan Valley and Modin near the coastal plain.) Human beings take refuge in the wilderness, not in the mountains (e.g., 1 Sam. 24; 26). But birds can fly to a mountain crag effortlessly and find a ledge on which to perch in safety, or they can take refuge in the trees that covered many of the mountains. This suggests that the whole colon is a metaphor. The advisers urge the speaker to behave like a bird taking refuge on its favorite mountain ledge or in its favorite mountain tree. Where the speaker would literally go is an open question.

> ²Because there are the faithless,
>   who bend the bow;
> They have fitted their arrow on the string
>   to shoot in the darkness at the upright of heart."

Why should the speaker flit? The bird imagery continues: the faithless are like hunters preparing to shoot a bird, bending their bow.[5] That is why the bird needs to flit. But why should they be hunting in this way? Initially, the second line in v. 2 doubly raises suspense. First, it does not answer that question. Second, it turns from yiqtol to qatal, thus doing more than merely describing how hunters regularly act. We see the actual placing of the arrow on the string. That precedes the bending of the bow. It has already happened. They have cocked their gun and are about to shoot. So why are they doing that? The second colon explains. They are shooting in the darkness, not in the sense that their target is in the dark (which would be a protection), but in the sense that they are hiding in the dark, operating deceptively like other attackers the psalms mention (e.g., Ps. 5). And their target is the upright of heart. Though the imagery is different, the words contrast attackers operating in the dark with people of integrity whose inner and outer life cohere. They are the target. Anyone who belongs to that company must flee.

> ³When the foundations are destroyed,
>   the faithful—what could he have done?

11:3. The advisers' words may continue here (so EVV), or this may be the psalmist's reflection, though if so, v. 1 suggests the verse hardly

---

5. See on 7:12 [13].

indicates despair. The word for "foundations" (*šātôt*) comes only here;[6] the OT's metaphorical use of more familiar Hebrew words for foundations (from *yāsad*) to refer to the foundations of society (e.g., 82:5) then supports the idea that the foundations in Ps. 11 are the metaphorical bases on which social life rests. When it has become customary for people to attack the upright for no reason other than (e.g.) their personal gain, those bases are gone. The colon thus draws an inference from the observations in v. 2. The rule of violence has replaced the rule of law.

The obvious literal translation of the second colon is "The faithful one—what has he done?" (cf. LXX). The faithful one might be Yhwh, which would fit with v. 7 but requires considerable inference at this point; the faithful person reappears in v. 5 and is more likely a human being. Alternatively, v. 3b could be a critique of faithful people for doing nothing or a defense of them for doing nothing wrong, but it is again rather an isolated comment, whereas a reflection on the fact that nothing could have been done follows on well from v. 3b.[7] The faithful could have done nothing to stop the collapse and/or could have done nothing once the collapse had happened. As the advisers' words, they imply that the speaker has every excuse to get out of here.

11:4–7. The psalm does not deny that human beings can do nothing to fix the situation, but against that justified hopelessness it sets a series of affirmations about Yhwh that occupy the bulk of the psalm. The psalm gives no grounds for these affirmations. They are simply facts it knows are true.

> [4]Yhwh in his holy palace,
>   Yhwh whose throne is in the heavens—
> His eyes behold,
>   his gaze examines, human beings.

First, Yhwh is in a position of sovereignty within the cosmos. Verse 4a–b might begin by referring to the earthly temple (cf. 79:1) and then complement that with a reference to Yhwh's throne in heaven, as in 5:7 [8]. But there Yhwh's holy *palace was the dwelling that was in heaven, and more likely that is also so here. So v. 4a raises the question, Where is Yhwh's holy palace with its throne? and v. 4b answers that it is in the heavens. It is not merely a building on earth, but it is within creation, not in some far-off ethereal realm.

---

6. The translation follows Sym and less directly LXX and Jerome, who are following clues from related words in PBH; see *DTT* 1637–41.

7. For the qatal in an incredulous question, cf. 39:7 [8]; 60:9 [11]; 73:11; 80:4 [5] (see *TTH* 19; DG 59; cf. GKC 106p).

Yet for Yhwh to be in his palace in the heavens might convey no good news: people need Yhwh to pay attention to what is happening on earth. Verse 4c–d declares that Yhwh does so. From the palace Yhwh sees what is going on. But to what end? What kind of seeing is this? The unusual verb "behold" (*ḥāzâ*) already hints that this may not be just ordinary looking. The parallel clause makes clear that the seeing has a purpose. Yhwh's "gaze" is literally Yhwh's "eyelids," perhaps suggesting that Yhwh's eyes never close. Yhwh thus "examines" or tests (*bāḥan*) people, looking at them carefully to discover the real truth about them (cf. 17:3; 26:2; 95:9; 139:23). As in 7:9 [10] the psalm assumes that Yhwh is not "automatically" omniscient but can choose to discover what is going on in people's inner beings.

> ⁵Yhwh—he examines faithful and faithless;
> with all his being he is against the person dedicated to violence.

After the two six-word lines comes a long 4-4 line. The examination means Yhwh can look behind people's words to see the real truth about them and thus distinguish among "human beings" between *faithful and *faithless (NRSV obscures the point slightly by translating *bāḥan* in a different way in this line). The word order helps to make the point: literally, "Yhwh faithful examines and faithless." Yhwh's examining divides faithless from faithful. Once more, the second colon takes the logic onward. After the examination Yhwh does not just conclude that this was an interesting piece of research: Yhwh takes action. The second clause brings together two further antonyms, *dedicate oneself and be *against. Yhwh acts with energy (once more, *nepeš*, *person) against those who themselves act with energy to "destroy the foundations" by their lawless *violence.

> ⁶He rains/must rain snares on the faithless,
> fire and sulfur,
> [or, He rains/must rain on the faithless
> blazing coal and sulfur,]
> A scorching wind
> as the share in their cup.

So what does that action look like? Verse 6 explains this in the longest line in the psalm, almost impossible to construe poetically as it heaps up expressions for devastation.⁸ The experience of the faithless will re-

---

8. The verb is *yamṭēr*; such jussive forms can also be used as yiqtols (GKC 109k) but need not be (cf. *TTH* 58, 172; Gerstenberger, *Psalms*, 1:78), so a reader could interpret this as a statement or as a wish.

peat that of Sodom and Gomorrah, on which Yhwh rained sulfur and fire (i.e., burning sulfur; Gen. 19:24), or the experience threatened for Edom (Isa. 34:9–12) and for Israel itself (Deut. 29:23 [22]). This raining from Yhwh's palace in the heavens with its storehouses of storm and lightning is much more devastating than the mere individual arrows that the faithless shoot.[9] Yhwh's bow is equipped with devastating flaming arrows (7:13 [14]; 18:12–14 [13–15]). This rain's effect is not merely (or at all) to kill the people but to make their land utterly sterile, incapable of growing anything.

The "scorching wind" is not a different form of chastisement but another aspect of that rain or another way of describing it. The scorching wind is the fiery, sulfurous breath issuing from Yhwh's mouth (cf. Isa. 30:33). And that is their allocation, the drink in their cup. The psalm combines two images. Someone's "share" should be something rather nice, like the tasty parts of a sacrificial animal that went to the priests (e.g., Exod. 29:26). So it is when Yhwh allocates people's share (Ps. 16:5). But this share is not nice (cf. Jer. 13:25). In turn, behind the image of a cup is the cup of wine that could suggest blessing (see Ps. 16:5 again; also 23:5; 116:13). But a cup can also be filled with poison, and it is such a cup that goes to Yhwh's enemies—which can again include Israel (e.g., 75:8 [9]; Isa. 51:17–23). There is no way of knowing what v. 6 might literally refer to. The psalm uses familiar images to express the significance and terror of the act whereby Yhwh delivers.

> [7]Because Yhwh is faithful—
>   he is dedicated to faithful acts;
>   his face beholds the upright person.

The bringing of devastating calamity on the faithless is an expression of Yhwh's faithfulness to the upright, who are thereby rescued from the former's schemes. The tricolon closing the psalm reuses a series of words spread through earlier lines. We know that Yhwh takes the side of the faithful; now we are reminded that this is because *faithfulness is one of Yhwh's character traits. The implication of that declaration is that Yhwh is *dedicated to faithful acts. It is not merely an inner personality characteristic but also a feature of Yhwh's deeds, and Yhwh's dedication to faithful deeds thus contrasts with the dedication of the faithless (v. 5). Yhwh's beholding (v. 4) reappears as simply a beholding of the upright, which therefore has a different significance. The upright were the victims of the faithless in v. 2, but Yhwh's *face beholds them, implying that Yhwh takes action for them, and that is what the upright

---

9. Schaefer, *Psalms*, 28–29.

need. Reliance on Yhwh (v. 1) and being the object of Yhwh's beneficent look (v. 7) form a bracket enfolding and surrounding the faithless and their activity.[10]

Theological Implications

When the foundations collapse, you can (e.g.) flit (like Elijah), seek to rebuild them (like the Deuteronomists), preach (like Amos), tell stories to build faith (like Genesis), promise a better future (like Isaiah), or feel overwhelmed (like Ecclesiastes). Or you can just stand tall and look for Yhwh to act, like this psalmist. The verbs through vv. 4–7 are yiqtol, and it seems both arbitrary to move from present to future for vv. 6–7 and potentially misleading because it could imply that Yhwh's acts of faithfulness and deliverance lie in some (eschatological?) future. The psalms know that Yhwh is involved in life now, and they often testify to that involvement; Psalm 11 is declaring a conviction about this. If Yhwh's activity belonged only in the future, the scornful response to the advisers (vv. 1–2) would hardly make sense. That involvement does not belong only to communities of the distant past (Gen. 18–19) or to a day at the End (Isa. 34:9). It also belongs to ordinary individuals in the present.

---

10. Ibid., 28–30.

Psalm 12
Responding to Faithless Triviality

Translation

The leader's. On the eighth. Composition. David's.

¹Do deliver, Yhwh, because the committed have come to an end,
   because the true people have vanished from among humanity.
²People speak emptiness, each to his neighbor;
   with smooth lip by a double mind[a] they speak.

³Yhwh must cut down all smooth lips,
   the tongue that speaks big things,
⁴People who have said, "With our tongue we will prevail;[b]
   our lips will be our blade[c]—
   who will be our lord?"

⁵"Because of the devastation of the weak, because of the groaning of
      the needy,
   now I will arise," Yhwh says,
   "I will take my stand[d] as deliverance,"[e] he witnesses to him.[f]

a. Lit, "a lip of smooth things with a mind and a mind."
b. The hiphil of *gābar* used with a similar sense to the qal (see *DCH*, against **BDB**).
c. Translations have "our lips are with us," which is allusive. I take this as an occurrence of the noun *'ēt* (see **BDB** 88; *DCH*), which fits the imagery in the context.
d. EVV have "I will set," but the verb has no object and the subsequent *běyēšaʻ* ("in deliverance") is unique and odd. I take the verb rather as in (e.g.) 3:6, which fits the parallelism.
e. Cf. "arise as [*qûm bě*] my help" in 35:2. That implies "my helper" (so 118:7) as here "deliverance" implies "deliverer" (as 27:1).
f. NIVI and NRSV derive *yāpîaḥ* from *pûaḥ* I, "breathe," but NJPS more plausibly derives it from *pûaḥ* II, "witness" (cf. Tg; see *HALOT*; Paul-Richard Berger, "Zu den

⁶Yhwh's words are pure words,
   silver refined in the furnaceᵍ on the ground,ʰ
   purged seven times.

⁷May you yourself keep them, Yhwh,
   protect him from the generation that lasts forever.ⁱ
⁸All around, the faithless walk about,
   as triviality stands high for humanity.ʲ

Interpretation

The content of Ps. 12 shows that it has its background in the destruction of the foundations of life in society, like Ps. 11, and it manifests the same confidence in Yhwh as appears there. Yet here it is the triumph of the faithless over the committed that embraces the psalm (see vv. 1, 8). At the same time the psalm adds a focus on prayer (v. 1), a longing for things to be different (v. 3), and the sharing of a word from Yhwh (v. 5). It is this word that generates the psalm's eventual confidence (v. 7). Comparison with Hab. 1 suggests it might reflect a conversation between a prophet and Yhwh, which then came to be used by the community in general,¹ though this may be a literalistic reading of a rhetorical device to introduce Yhwh on the scene.² It is the reverse of laments from Yhwh to the people such as appear in Isa. 57; Jer. 5; Hosea 4 and 7; Mic. 7; see also Isa. 33:7–12. Initially the psalmist is fulfilling the other aspect to the prophetic calling, speaking to Yhwh for people as well as speaking

---

Strophen des 10. Psalms," *UF* 2 [1970]: 7–17 [see 10–17]; Patrick D. Miller, "*Yāpîaḥ* in Psalm xii 6," *VT* 29 [1979]: 495–501; J. G. Janzen, "Another Look at Psalm xii 6," *VT* 54 [2004]: 157–64).

   g. *ʾĂlîl* comes only here; "furnace" follows Tg.
   h. I take *lāʾāreṣ* to mean that the refined silver is flowing on the ground. "Earthen" (cf. KJV) is unlikely, esp. when the word is *ʾereṣ* rather than *ʾădāmâ*. NEB emends to *ḥārûṣ*, "gold," but it is difficult to see how such a natural word could have been corrupted to this difficult reading. *Midrash on Psalms*, 1:173, suggests "before the world."
   i. Translations have "from this generation forever," but "this" (*zû*) has no article and thus is more likely a relative (see *IBHS* 19.5d; *DCH*; and comments on misunderstanding of *zeh* in BDB 261b; contrast GKC 126y; UBS).
   j. W. E. March ("A Note on the Text of Psalm xii 9," *VT* 21 [1971]: 610–12) redivides and repoints the line to produce a reference to "the constellations" (*mazzālôt*), objects of worship in 2 Kings 23:5. P. Wernberg-Møller ("Two Difficult Passages in the Old Testament," *ZAW* 69 [1957]: 69–73 [see 69–71]) emends to *krm gzlt*, "[in] the vineyard [with] spoils." Eugene Zolli ("*Kerum* in Ps. 12:9," *CBQ* 12 [1950]: 7–9) sees *krm* as a word for worm, suggesting the translation "despicable worms to men."

   1. Cf. Kraus, *Psalms*, 1:207.
   2. So Gert T. M. Prinsloo, "Man's Word–God's Word," *ZAW* 110 (1998): 390–402, see 398.

to the people for Yhwh. But like Habakkuk, the psalmist is also in a position to share Yhwh's response.

So vv. 1–2 combine direct plea and lament at the life of the community. Verses 3–4 combine wish (jussive declarations) and lament at the life of the community. Verses 5–6 bring Yhwh's word in light of the life of the community, and respond to that word. Verses 7–8 declare confidence in Yhwh, but close with further reference to the depraved life of the community.[3]

> The leader's. On the eighth. Composition. David's.

Heading. See glossary, and commentary on the Ps. 6 heading.

> [1]Do deliver, Yhwh, because the committed have come to an end,
>   because the true people have vanished from among humanity.

12:1–2. It is rather impolite to begin with the bald imperative "deliver" (Ps. 69 is the only parallel), though the baldness is tempered by the -*â* sufformative (hence the "Do" in the translation). But Yhwh evidently finds it acceptable for the psalmist to come with such heartfelt urgency. As Anne Lamott says, "Here are the two best prayers I know: 'Help me, help me, help me,' and 'Thank you, thank you, thank you.'"[4] The psalm's imperative even lacks an object,[5] unlike the imperative that opens Ps. 69, but this fits with the fact that it does not relate to the speaker's own needs. Its background is the state of community life, described in the rest of the two long lines that make up vv. 1–2. There is not a single *committed person left in this community. Presumably, "humanity" means "humanity as the suppliant experiences it," though the point might apply in other communities, too. The second colon re-expresses the point in less familiar terms. *True (*'ĕmûnîm*) is a rare form of a common root to refer to people who steadfastly keep their commitments. Then, while "come to an end" (*gāmar*) is itself an unusual word, "vanish" (*pāsas*) occurs only here, but the meaning is clear enough from the context.

> [2]People speak emptiness, each to his neighbor;
>   with smooth lip by a double mind they speak.

---

3. Watson (*Classical Hebrew Poetry*, 247–48) and Rolf A. Jacobson (*"Many Are Saying,"* JSOTSup 397 [London: T&T Clark, 2004], 30) see it as a stepped structure, but they have two different understandings of this structure.

4. *Traveling Mercies* (New York: Pantheon, 1999), 82. She is agreeing with Spurgeon (see *Treasury of David*, 1:141).

5. LXX "deliver me" provides an object.

Verse 2 expresses more concretely what this looks like. People speak *emptiness to their neighbors, to other people in the community. There is no content to what they say. Why does that matter? Talking emptiness does not mean they only talk about football. The second colon explains where lies the emptiness of their words. Their words are smooth—they are nice, bringing good news, gliding easily down the throats of their recipients, who are glad to receive them (see comments on 5:9 [10]). But the speakers are double-minded—a paradoxical way of saying that they seem and purport to think and intend one thing, but in their *minds they think and intend something quite different. They are not people of one heart and one way (Jer. 32:39), whose inner and outer life cohere.

12:3–4. The psalm reverts to declarations that things must change, but moves from imperative to jussive, almost as if appealing to some obligation bigger than Yhwh. Again these are long lines, with *abb'a'* references to lips-tongue-tongue-lips. The *aa'* lines pair "cut down" with "blade," the *bb'* lines pair "big things" with "prevail."

> ³Yhwh must cut down all smooth lips,
>   the tongue that speaks big things.

"All smooth lips" takes up the words from v. 2, though it extends the point in expressing the wish or demand that Yhwh should cut down lips and tongues. The second colon adds a new point about people, that they talk big. The frightening nature of the psalm's demand ("cut down") corresponds to the strangely devastating power of these apparently harmless organs (cf. James 3). But the "[people] who" that opens v. 4 confirms that the wish involves a synecdoche: cutting down lying lips and tongues means cutting down the people to whom they are attached (e.g., 37:9, 22, 28, 34, 38). These people want to cut down others by means of the blade of their lying words, and the psalm urges Yhwh to reverse this process.

> ⁴People who have said, "With our tongue we will prevail;
>   our lips will be our blade—
>   who will be our lord?"

What are those "big things"? As well as the mismatch between their words and intentions, there is the magnitude of what they think they can achieve through those smooth words of theirs. They think they can talk their way to success. The second colon restates the point. Their lips seem smooth but are devastatingly sharp, not in being emotionally hurtful, but in having the capacity to kill. No one will be able to defeat them. The line would be quite complete at the end of v. 4a–b, but the third colon adds a frightful coup de grâce whose implication is similar to that of (e.g.) 10:4. They are saying that there is no *lord (*ʾādôn*) but them, thus implicitly denying God's existence.[6]

12:5–6. Yhwh answers with a stately, thundering 4-4-4 tricolon; the prophet in turn responds with another tricolon. In many psalms (e.g., Ps. 6) one might suspect that an answer from Yhwh makes possible a transition from prayer to praise, though Yhwh's words do not appear in them, perhaps because by its nature the psalm represents the human side of the conversation. This exception proves the rule if the psalm represents a conversation between a prophet and Yhwh like that in Hab. 1.

> [5] "Because of the devastation of the weak, because of the groaning of the needy,
> now I will arise," Yhwh says,
> "I will take my stand as deliverance," he witnesses to him.

The answer starts from another aspect of people's behavior that the psalm has not yet made clear. So far it might have been speaking about dishonesty among the well-to-do, but actually this dishonesty primarily affects the weak and needy (see on 9:12, 18 [13, 19]), and that is the aspect that drives Yhwh to act (perhaps Yhwh might not care so much what the wealthy do to each other). The first colon tells of two things that motivate Yhwh to intervene. We might have expected them to include a sense of affront at the implicit denial of God's existence in v. 4, but Yhwh's motivation comes from elsewhere. First, there is the devastation of the *weak and *needy. No doubt this involved their being treated as spoils (cf. NRSV), but what the destroyers gain is not in focus. What moves Yhwh is the oppression and devastation that their actions bring to the weak. Second, there is their groaning. The psalm does not suggest that they were groaning to anyone. Their groan is not necessarily a prayer (though the word is used for prayer in Mal. 2:13). It may just be a cry of pain. But Yhwh hears it (cf. 102:20 [21]). Yhwh's words are an anticipatory answer to the plea in 79:11. They also repeat the dynamic of the exodus story (Exod. 2:24; 6:5). In the middle colon, "now" (*ʿattâ*) is not primarily a chronological note but a logical one. "But/and now" often introduces a prophet's declaration that Yhwh is acting in light of facts the prophet has described. Yhwh has not been explicitly 'bidden to "arise" (as in 3:7 [8]; 7:6 [7]; 9:19 [20]; 10:12), but undertakes to do so. The third colon sums up the point. Psalm 3:6–7 [7–8] spoke of people "taking their stand" against the suppliant and appealed to Yhwh to "arise" and "deliver." The words recur here. In parallel to Yhwh's first declara-

---

6. Cf. Tg; also *Midrash on Psalms*, 1:171.

tion, "I will arise," is the less usual expression "I will take my stand," and the implication is worked out in terms of Yhwh's being *deliverance, in keeping with the appeal in v. 1. Then the phrase "Yhwh says" is taken further in the words "Yhwh witnesses": Yhwh solemnly avers that this will indeed happen.

> ⁶Yhwh's words are pure words,
>   silver refined in the furnace on the ground,
>   purged seven times.

The first colon raises the question how Yhwh's words[7] come to be pure, and the second explains that this is because they have been refined, like silver. In case that does not sound enough, it adds a third colon with a less-familiar word for refining, and the declaration that the process involves a thorough testing. Yhwh's promises are not made lightly, said without reflection as the expression of the first thing that comes into Yhwh's head. The purity of Yhwh's words consists in their being promises that have been tested and proved before being uttered (cf. 18:30 [31]; 119:140; Prov. 30:5). They have been discussed carefully in Yhwh's council, with the accuser looking carefully for flaws in Yhwh's proposals (see Job 1–2; Zech. 3). There is a testing of Yhwh's words that comes after they are uttered, but the psalm knows they are bound to pass that test because of the rigorous quality-control testing (seven times, meaning completely) they have already undergone. Human words have been tested and fail (vv. 1–4). Yhwh's words have been tested and pass.

12:7–8. The grim background to the psalm is that "the generation of the lie"[8] seems destined to last forever. It is this that imperils the foundations of society, for society depends on words being trustworthy.

> ⁷May you yourself keep them, Yhwh,
>   protect him from the generation that lasts forever.

Initially one could understand this as a statement of confidence about the outworking of Yhwh's promise, in light of the general fact of the reliability of Yhwh's word (so most EVV), and then read v. 8 as a statement of defiance: "Let them walk about! [I am not worried!]."[9] But that is a rather subtle reading. An equally plausible response to a promise from Yhwh is a plea for Yhwh to do what it says, and in this psalm the earlier

---

7. NRSV "promises" interprets "words" correctly, but the Hebrew is simply "words" (*'imărôt*).

8. M. Buber, *Right and Wrong* (London: SCM, 1952), 11 = *Good and Evil* (New York: Scribner's, 1952), 7.

9. Cf. *TTH* 38a.

prominence of plea makes that a natural way to read the verb. Plea thus takes the form of an imperative (v. 1), a jussive (v. 3), and a yiqtol (v. 7). This inference will be confirmed by v. 8, which is naturally explicable as a support for a plea but less natural if v. 7 is a statement of confidence. The suffixes on the verbs refer to the people first as "them" and then individually as "him," as singular and plural alternated in vv. 1 and 5.

> ⁸All around, the faithless walk about,
> as triviality stands high for humanity.

Verse 8 begins as jerkily as the whole psalm did and underlines the moral disorder that continues to appall the suppliant. It is "all around," wherever one looks. The faithless "walk about" (*hālak* hitpael), bold and confident because they are quite accepted within the community (NRSV "prowl" obscures the point). The second colon puts the point more sharply. Their faithlessness can be characterized by a less-familiar word as "triviality" or worthlessness (*zullût*). They turn things upside down, treating the insubstantial as if it counted, the worthless as if it were valuable, and the despicable as if it were honorable (cf. the antitheses in Jer. 15:19; Lam. 1:8). And as they do so they are able to walk about, head held high, because their inversion of standards is accepted within the community as a whole. The opening line laments the disappearance of trustworthy people from humanity; the closing colon laments the converse. The abstract complements the concrete, but the implication is that trivial people stand high among humanity (cf. KJV). It is also another indication of godlessness (v. 4), given that Yhwh is the one who rightly stands high (*rûm*; e.g., 18:46 [47]; 21:13 [14]; 46:10 [11]; 66:7).

Theological Implications

The psalm thus gives the last word to the grimness of the social and moral situation, as it gave the first word to impolite urging. It thereby illustrates how speech to Yhwh does not have to observe proper social, liturgical, or theological convention. The suppliant knows that Yhwh has made a promise and that Yhwh's promises can be relied on, but still stands affronted by the way things are in the community. Specifically, falseness of speech destroys the human community.[10] As is the case in our own experience, false speakers affect the community of faith with their scandalous life, not just the "secular" community. In both commu-

---

10. Cf. Robert A. Coughenour, "The Generation of the Lie," in *Soli Deo Gloria: Festschrift for John H. Gerstner*, ed. R. C. Sproul ([Nutley, NJ:] Presbyterian & Reformed, 1976), 103–17.

nities, at their best there is emptiness alongside truthfulness. Whether one looks on a national or a global scale, the weak and needy in both communities are characterized by devastation and groaning. In both, "triviality" rules. In themselves Yhwh's promises do not make that seem all right. They do not turn the suppliant into someone who relaxes into trust in Yhwh's promises (unlike the author of Ps. 11), and the suppliant does not need to pretend that this is so when it is not. As is the case in our own world, there are no signs of the reign of God arriving, and believing that it will come is a matter of sheer trust in Yhwh's word. It issues in urgent pressure on God to bring it about, and not to wait till the End to do so. Thus "the word of God does not provoke the violence of the victims against their executioners; the vicious circle of violence is broken here by remembrance of YHWH as the rescuer and protector of the poor."[11]

---

11. Zenger, *A God of Vengeance?* 28.

Psalm 13

How Long, How Long, How Long, How Long?

Translation

The leader's. Composition. David's.

¹How long, Yhwh? Are you to ignore me forever—
  how long are you to hide your face from me?
²How long am I to lay up plans[a] in my spirit,
  lay up sorrow in my heart through the day[b]—
how long is my enemy to stand high over me?

³Give attention, answer me, Yhwh my God;
  brighten my eyes so that I may not sleep in death,[c]
⁴So that my enemy may not say, "I have put an end to him,"[d]
  nor my adversaries rejoice because I fall down.[e]

    a. In isolation *'ēṣôt* is odd, and translations here introduce a note of pain, but that comes from the parallelism; the second and third cola explain what sort of plans are referred to.

    b. *Yômām* elsewhere means "by day" as opposed to "by night," but that "yields a lame sense" here (BDB). Some LXX MSS add the expected "and by night," which also turns the line into another neat 4-4. "Daily" is another possibility.

    c. GKC 117i and DG 93b assume that *hammāwet* is used pregnantly for *šĕnat hammāwet*, "the sleep of death," which is then an instance of a cognate noun used after a verb as an "internal object." It is simpler to take *hammāwet* as acc. of place (cf. LXX; GKC 118g; *IBHS* 10.2.2).

    d. Translations take *yĕkoltîw* as a form from *yākôl*, "prevail," but that is an intransitive verb. I derive it from a byform of *kālâ*, which also gives a better sense in the context.

    e. The "so that . . . not" (*pen*) applies to both cola, "say" is complemented and taken further by "rejoice," singular "enemy" is complemented by plural "adversaries," direct speech is complemented by a "because" clause, and transitive verb is complemented by intransitive.

⁵But I—I have put my trust in your commitment;
   my heart will rejoice^f in your deliverance.^g
⁶I will sing to Yhwh,^h
   because he has acted fully^i for me.

Interpretation

Faced with the faithless and their attacks, if Ps. 11 manifests cool confidence and Ps. 12 a wrestling for confidence in Yhwh's word, Ps. 13 arises out of deep sense of abandonment, even though it ends in confidence. The supplicant, under attack by enemies, does not say why or whether anything else is wrong (e.g., illness).

Hermann Gunkel called Ps. 13 a model prayer psalm.[1] Verses 1–2 comprise its plaint about "How long," vv. 3–4 its plea, and v. 5–6 its declaration of confidence and commitment to praise. The sections become steadily shorter as the supplicant climbs step by step through questions and laments via fears and pleas to expressions of trust and praise:[2] vv. 1–2 comprise five cola, 4-4-4-3-4, vv. 3–4 four, 4-4-3-4, vv. 5–6 four, 3-3-2-3.[3] Perhaps the attention given to the plaint makes it possible for the plea to be briefer and the expression of trust to be quite short. Or perhaps the attention given to the plaint indicates that this continues to be where the real energy of the prayer lies. A worshipper might use it either way. The development in the way the psalm speaks of and to Yhwh tells a parallel story. In vv. 1–2 it is an aggressive, confrontational "Yhwh." That perhaps frees the supplicant to pray "Yhwh, my God" (vv. 3–4). And that in turn makes possible the commitment "I will sing to Yhwh" (vv. 5–6).[4]

   f. *Yāgēl* is jussive in form, but future meaning makes better sense in the context (see on 11:6).
   g. The cola complement each other, though the order is *abcc'a'b'*. "My heart" follows on "I," yiqtol "rejoice" follows on qatal "trust," "in your deliverance" follows on "in your commitment." The first colon refers more to the present, the second to the future, the two moments that the eye-brightening of v. 3 refers to.
   h. Or "for Yhwh" or "about Yhwh"; see P. A. H. de Boer, "Cantate Domino," in *Remembering All the Way*, by B. Albrektson et al., OtSt 21 (Leiden: Brill, 1981), 55–67. These possibilities apply through the Psalter.
   i. Translations have "acted bountifully" for *gāmal*, but the verb means to do all that should be done; it is the context that decides whether the action is positive or negative. See *NIDOTTE*; *TDOT*; *TLOT*.
   1. *Psalmen*, 46.
   2. Cf. Seybold, *Psalmen*, 64.
   3. LXX gives more body to the end by repeating 7:17b [18b]. On the psalm's structure, see further Pierre Auffret, *La sagesse a bâti sa maison*, 195–206.
   4. Clearly a "speech-act"; on speech-act theory applied to Ps. 13, see Hubert Irsigler, "Psalm-Rede als Handlungs-, Wirk- und Aussageprozess," in *Neue Wege*, ed. Seybold and Zenger, 63–104.

The leader's. Composition. David's.

Heading. See glossary.

> ¹How long, Yhwh? Are you to ignore me forever—
> how long are you to hide your face from me?

13:1–2. The plaint introduces us to the question "How long?" that recurs in prayer psalms in Israel and elsewhere.⁵ The fourfold expression of it makes this the OT's classic articulation of the question, and a uniquely "impertinent" one.⁶ "Here, time itself becomes a destructive force, wearing down a man's ability to hold out and intensifying the suffering to an inhuman level."⁷ The precise expression (*ʿad-ʾānâ*) occurs only once more in the Psalms (62:3 [4], addressed to other people; also Hab. 1:2), but an alternative formulation (*ʿad-mātay*) appears elsewhere (e.g., 74:10; 80:4 [5]; 94:3). Yhwh's own pressing of this question (e.g., Exod. 16:28; Num. 14:11, 27) shows that it is a rhetorical one, not a request for information. It implies: "This is intolerable and needs to stop now" (cf. Jer. 47:6). The midrash links the psalm's fourfold "How long?" with Yhwh's fourfold "How long?" in Exod. 16 and Num. 14 and also with Yhwh's declaration in Zech. 7:13. It imagines Israel asking these questions in the context of oppression by Babylon, Persia, Greece, and Rome, assuming that in these contexts Israel is experiencing the consequences of its own ignoring of Yhwh.⁸ Although the equally rhetorical question "Why?" (e.g., Pss. 10:1; 22:1 [2]) presupposes that it is not the people's faithlessness that has caused Yhwh to abandon them, the question "How long?" leaves this an open question. The psalm would allow for Yhwh's turning away to have been a response to Israel's, but it does not make that explicit. The temporal expression "How long?" pairs and contrasts with the "forever" with which the first colon closes, and with the subsequent "through the day," all day long. The coupling of "How long?" with "forever" suggests taking the opening colon as two questions. The first is then a pregnant one (cf. 6:3 [4]; 90:13), which introduces the whole of vv. 1–2. It raises the question "How long what?" and vv. 1–2 give a series of answers.⁹

---

5. See (e.g.) the prayer to Ishtar in *ANET* 383–85. On the Middle Eastern background to the form of a prayer psalm as illustrated by Ps. 13, see Loretz, *Psalmstudien*, 131–70.
6. Gerstenberger, *Psalms*, 1:84.
7. Westermann, *Living Psalms*, 71.
8. *Midrash on Psalms*, 1:176.
9. Jerome takes the colon as one clause and renders *neṣaḥ* as "utterly." That may be a possible meaning of *neṣaḥ* (see *DCH*), but the word is usually a temporal expression, not

Verses 1–2 also introduce us to the full form of the classic three-directional plaint of a prayer psalm, instinctively holding together the religious, the psychological, and the sociological.[10] Verse 1 asks its question about "you," Yhwh. Yhwh is *ignoring the supplicant. Yhwh's *face is hidden. The second colon thus pictures Yhwh's neglect "more personally and concretely—in a way more terribly."[11] It might seem that there is at least some paradox about addressing Yhwh when one believes that Yhwh has turned away, but talk of ignoring or hiding the face is a matter of action, not mere awareness. Of course Yhwh knows and hears. Yhwh cannot be ignorant of what is happening. But Yhwh is not acting on that knowledge. Once again the supplicant is not experiencing the blessing that comes when Yhwh's face shines (Num. 6:24–26). On the other hand, the good news is that at least Yhwh is not actively attacking the supplicant, as sometimes happens. The problem is simply one of neglect.

> ²How long am I to lay up plans in my spirit,
>   lay up sorrow in my heart through the day—
> how long is my enemy to stand high over me?

Verse 2 then moves from the religious to the psychological and asks in terms of "I," in terms of the effect of Yhwh's (in)action on the suppliant; its last colon adds the third-person, sociological reference ("my enemy") to the first and second. The first two cola are neatly and subtly parallel, with the verb applying to both. "In my mind" repeats "in my spirit" (*nepeš*, *person). The closing "through the day" balances the opening "How long?" The second noun then helps us understand the first. What are these plans that the supplicant is laying up? They are sorrowful plans. What can that mean? The second colon also thus teases us. Out of context, laying up plans in one's spirit or heart would suggest making plans of one's own (cf. Prov. 26:24). But one does not (intentionally) lay up in one's heart plans that bring trouble and sorrow; other people do that (cf. again Prov. 26:24). The last colon clarifies what the first colon refers to. It is impossible for the supplicant to avoid thinking about the trouble-bringing plans formulated by this enemy, who "stands high" over the supplicant like the faithless in 12:8. What kind of a person is this enemy? The term can apply to another member of the community (e.g., Exod. 23:4) or a political enemy (1 Sam. 18:29) or a national enemy (e.g., Exod. 15:6, 9). The midrash suggests Haman as an example (see Esther

---

least in association with being mindful or ignoring and/or in parallelism with another temporal expression (e.g., 9:18 [19]; 10:11)—as here.

10. Cf. Westermann, *Living Psalms*, 69–70.
11. Alter, *Art of Biblical Poetry*, 65.

3:1, though the verbs are different).[12] But the term may be a collective (e.g., Exod. 15:6, 9), and in the Psalms the singular term often appears in parallelism with a plural, as in v. 4. There are passages where the enemy might be Death (e.g., 61:3 [4]), which receives a mention in the next line, but this is never explicit. The regularity with which the singular alternates with the plural makes it unlikely that this is the psalm's meaning, though no doubt readers might apply it that way.

> ³Give attention, answer me, Yhwh my God;
>   brighten my eyes so that I may not sleep in death.

13:3–4. Plaint now yields to plea. The second verb directly follows the first without "and," conveying a sense of urgency that ignores politeness, like the opening of Ps. 12. The invocation "Yhwh my God" increases the pressure on Yhwh. There is a relationship between the suppliant and God, a commitment of the suppliant to God. God should respond. The Psalms often look for two forms of response: attention and action. That expectation is expressed in a distinctive way: there are three aspects to what the suppliant looks for. First, Yhwh must give attention instead of ignoring and looking the other way. Second, Yhwh must answer instead of staying silent. Verse 3b then puts matters in a fresh way. After the reference to Yhwh's face being hidden (v. 1), we would not have been surprised if the psalm had urged, "Shine your face" (e.g., 31:16 [17]; cf. Num. 6:25). The second colon indeed begins with that verb (*'ôr* hiphil), but unexpectedly its object is different; the plea is "brighten my eyes." The phrase suggests encouragement (cf. Ps. 19:8 [9]; 118:27; Ezra 9:8), the encouragement that comes from knowing that Yhwh has paid attention and answered (cf. the change in Hannah, 1 Sam. 1:21–22). But that change in the face can come about only on the basis of the fact that Yhwh's answer is not merely words but also action. The brightening is an anticipatory reflection of a change in circumstances. Yhwh's brightening will come about because Yhwh is acting so that the trouble the enemy is bringing does not issue in that long sleep we call death. Death is sleeplike because it is restful, though occasionally disturbed by people coming into the room, but it permits no activity or worship and is ultimately boring and pointless because it is not a refreshment that restores us for a new day.

> ⁴So that my enemy may not say "I have put an end to him,"
>   nor my adversaries rejoice because I fall down.

---

12. *Midrash on Psalms,* 1:178.

The continuation of the "so that . . . not" clauses shows that the suppliant grieves not merely the prospect of death but also the fact that death would actually not be the end of sorrow and of the enemy's standing high—rather, the opposite. The moment of death would give the enemy the further satisfaction of knowing they brought this about. And the world will continue to be out of kilter—indeed, will be even more so. Translations render the final verb *'emmôṭ*, "I am shaken," but the verb refers to dying (*mwṭ* and *mwt* are here related); it suggests *falling down to the ground and not getting up again, not merely shaking or stumbling so as to rise again.

13:5–6. Commentators observe a sharp change in attitude compared with vv. 1–4, but the wording also indicates links.

> ⁵But I—I have put my trust in your commitment;
>   my heart will rejoice in your deliverance.

The "but" suggests continuity as well as discontinuity, and the presence of the pronoun "I" adds to that effect. The adversaries might be thinking that they will triumph and may be looking forward to congratulating themselves, "but I" know there is another way to look at things. They think they will be rejoicing (v. 4), but I know "my heart" will be doing so. The heart that is currently preoccupied with their threatening plans (v. 2) will not always be so. Typically, the basis for the suppliant's act of trust is Yhwh's *commitment, and the object of hope is Yhwh's *deliverance. The links and contrasts with what precedes suggest that we do not need to hypothesize that the suppliant received a word from God to make the transition possible. In this case, at least, the statement of faith is simply a statement of faith. Psalms 42–43 explicitly record an internal argument between lament and hope, and Ps. 13 implies such an argument. The suppliant lives with a tension between the questioning of vv. 1–2, the pleading of vv. 3–4, and the expectation of vv. 5–6. The psalm suggests "the state in which hope despairs, and yet despair hopes."[13] Or perhaps we should infer that the very questions of vv. 1–2 and the pleas of vv. 3–4 were acts of trust. They were that, whether or not the suppliant means to imply it.

The psalm comes near its close in the way Ps. 11 began, with a declaration of trust—though the verb is now *bāṭaḥ*. Although that can be a stative verb (so that a present-tense translation of the qatal is possible),[14] *trusting is a deliberate act, and the use of the qatal rather than participle or yiqtol suggests that the psalm refers to the act of

---

13. So Luther, according to James L. Mays, "Psalm 13," *Int* 34 (1980): 279–83, see 281.
14. Cf. DG 57, remark 1.

trust, which happened in the past but continues to be effective in the present.[15]

> ⁶I will sing to Yhwh,
>   because he has acted fully for me.

The cola in the closing verse complement each other in a different way as the second answers the "Why?" question raised in the first by referring to the deed that is still future but will be actual when the praise is offered.[16] The closing ʿālāy (for me) contrasts with the one in v. 2 (over me).

The midrash again comments that under Babylon we said, "I trust in your commitment"; under Persia we said, "My heart will rejoice in your deliverance"; under Greece we said, "I will sing to Yhwh"; and under Rome we will say, "Because he has acted fully for me."[17]

Theological Implications

There is a sense in which trust implies a quiet, relaxed resting in God (Isa. 30:15). It excludes efforts to fix things ourselves, which the situation in Ps. 11 implies we should attempt. Psalm 13 shows that trust does issue in insistent questioning of God that asks why God is ignoring us in our need, and in urgent pressing of God to give us attention and brighten our eyes with the promise of action. As before, this action does not belong just in the great past and the eschatological future. It belongs now.

---

15. See *TLOT*.
16. Cf. Hans Jänicke's discussion, "Futurum exactum," *EvT* 11 (1951–52): 471–78.
17. *Midrash on Psalms*, 1:179.

Psalm 14
The Scoundrel

Translation

The leader's. David's.

¹A scoundrel has said in his heart,
 "God is not here."
People have made their doings corrupt, loathsome;^a
 there is no one doing good.
²Yhwh has looked out from heaven
 at human beings
To see if there is anyone showing insight,
 seeking help from God.

³Everyone^b has turned aside;
 altogether they have become foul.
There is no one doing good,
 there is not even one.
⁴Have they not acknowledged,^c
 all those who cause harm?

    a. EVV "They are corrupt" presupposes that the first verb is a declarative hiphil, but the asyndeton makes it more likely that the first verb qualifies the second: "By making their doings corrupt, they have made them loathsome." Cf. BDB and contrast Deut. 4:25, as well as Ps. 53:1 [2]. The asyndeton conveys a breathless and thus appalled impression.
    b. *Hakkōl* usually means "the whole," but see (e.g.) Gen. 16:12.
    c. Stuart A. Irvine ("A Note on Psalm 14:4," *JBL* 114 [1995]: 463–66) proposes a reinterpretation of v. 4 on the basis of the claim that *hălō'* must expect the answer yes, but there are other examples with *yāda'* where the answer should be yes but is effectively no (e.g., Gen. 44:15; Judg. 15:11; Isa. 40:28).

>   Those who eat my people
>   have eaten bread.
>   They have not called on Yhwh—
>   ⁵there, they have been seized by terror,ᵈ
>   because Yhwh is among the faithful company.ᵉ
>
>   ⁶By the plan of the weak may you be put to shameᶠ
>   because Yhwh is their refuge.
>   ⁷O thatᵍ Israel's deliverance
>   would come from Zion;
>   When Yhwh brings a restoration of his people,
>   Jacob shall rejoice, Israel be glad.

Interpretation

The psalm is complex in form and ethos and open to being used in several ways. Initially its form resembles that of teaching rather than prayer, and the talk in terms of the scoundrel and of showing insight, with the associated moral comments, recalls a teaching psalm such as Ps. 1. But it constitutes more a kind of statement of faith encouraging people to believe that scoundrels will not win out than a direct attempt to encourage them to be people of insight rather than scoundrels. Further, in the description of the wrongdoers there is the sense of offense that appears in prophecy and in prayers, and the rhythm is mostly 3-2 or shorter, like that of a lament. Indeed, the description does constitute a protest, which eventually in v. 6 directly (if still rhetorically) addresses the faithless. The psalm does not overtly address God and it contains no plea, though it closes with a wish; if it is designed to be used in worship, it might presuppose that God is listening. It will reappear in slightly different form as Ps. 53.[1]

  d. In isolation, v. 5 might be instantaneous qatal (so Kraus, *Psalms*, 1:222–23), but there is no hint of a change in meaning from the qatals in vv. 1–4.
  e. Cf. Frank J. Neuberg, "An Unrecognized Meaning of Hebrew *dôr*," *JNES* 9 (1950): 215–17; Kraus (*Psalms*, 1:219) takes it to mean simply "class of people."
  f. Cf. Robert A. Bennett, "Wisdom Motifs in Psalm 14 = 53," *BASOR* 220 (1975): 15–21, esp. 20, though I have translated the verb modally, since "You will be put to shame" seems rather strong in light of the wish that follows in v. 7 (*TTH* 38a takes v. 6a as permissive or concessive). EVV have "You shame the plan of the weak," but then have difficulty with the *kî* in v. 6b, and the word order hints that this is not a straightforward verb-object clause. Kraus renders "plans against the weak" (cf. *Psalms*, 1:218), but the objective genitive is unparalleled.
  g. *Mî yittēn*, lit., "who will give," but idiomatically this often means simply "O that" (see GKC 151a–b; JM 163d).
  1. For attempts to define the original of the two versions, see C. C. Torrey, "The Archetype of Psalms 14 and 53," *JBL* 46 (1927): 186–92; Karl Budde, "Psalm 14 und 53," *JBL* 47 (1928): 160–83; Goulder, *Prayers of David*, 91–92.

Heading	Psalm 14

In isolation vv. 1–3 could be taken as a statement about universal wickedness, but vv. 4–6 indicate that the psalm concerns the particularities of experience affecting "my people." Likewise, in isolation vv. 4–6 might imply that the psalm reflects conflict within the community in which "everyone" refers to people in power. But "my people" (v. 4) more often denotes the community as a whole, and v. 7 confirms that "my people," "the faithful company," and "the weak" are terms to describe Jacob-Israel as a people. We might imagine this as the sixth-century community feeling assailed by the peoples around, or the Second Temple community feeling assailed by surrounding provinces.

I divide the psalm into three parts. The prophet comments on the words and deeds of scoundrels (v. 1), people who have turned aside (vv. 3–4), and "you" (v. 6), and sets each of these in the context of Yhwh's look (v. 2), Yhwh's presence with the faithful (v. 5), and Yhwh's act of restoration (v. 7). Throughout vv. 1–5 the finite verbs are gnomic qatal; in vv. 6–7 they are yiqtol.

> The leader's. David's.

Heading. See glossary. In the context of David's life, the scoundrel, *nābāl*, might be Nabal (see on v. 1a).

14:1–2. The scoundrel starts from the conviction that God is not interested in what is happening on earth, and then behaves accordingly. Three of the four lines have the halting 3-2 rhythm (MT understands v. 2a as 3-1, but it too might be read as 3-2).

> ¹A scoundrel has said in his heart,
>   "God is not here."
> People have made their doings corrupt, loathsome;
>   there is no one doing good.

The scoundrel is a *nābāl*, a fool (LXX) who has no insight (cf. v. 2), but also a villain, the opposite of the noble or honorable person (Isa. 32:5), the kind of person who rapes his half sister (2 Sam. 13:13) or scoffs at God (Ps. 74:18, 22). Here the psalm starts from the last kind of villainy. It is "a sustained comment on the *nābāl*."[2] Sometimes such scoffing in the heart might contrast with outward words that profess commitment to Yhwh. Even an intellectual might not dare openly to deny God's reality[3]—not a hesitation that survives into the modern world. But this psalm may have in mind a life and heart that match. The scoffing is not a superficial discounting of God. It takes place not merely on the lips but

---

2. Bennett, "Wisdom Motifs," 18.
3. Cf. Augustine, *Psalms*, 46.

in the heart: it deeply characterizes the person. Either way, saying "God is not here" (EVV "There is no God") is not merely a statement of theoretical atheist conviction but a declaration that God can be discounted from everyday life (see on 10:4). It is the attitude explicitly expressed by the Rabshakeh to Hezekiah (2 Kings 18:29–30)[4] and implicit in the action of Nebuchadnezzar (cf. Isa. 14:14).[5] Thus Tg's paraphrase "said in his heart, 'There is no rule of God in the land/earth'" may express the point, even if it is designed reverentially to hold back from expressing the conviction "God is not [here]" even on a scoundrel's lips.[6]

The singular scoundrel with his words is then balanced by plural wrongdoers who make their way of life corrupt and loathsome ($tā\'ab$).[7] So the psalm does not have in mind an individual or isolated wrongdoer; the scoundrel is a generic, the kind of person who characterizes the society. The corrupt state of the world corresponds to Yhwh's assessment of it in its lawless violence before the flood (Gen. 6:11–12). Things seem just as bad in the psalmist's day. As a moral category loathsomeness is especially characteristic of Proverbs, where (e.g.) pride, lying, murder, perjury, and dishonesty are loathsome to Yhwh (Prov. 6:16–19; 11:1). "There is no one doing good" brings the verse to a close by repeating "There is no" ($\'ên$) and reverting to the singular: the missing person doing *good matches the scoundrel. The last clause presumably implies a hyperbole[8]—to start with, the suppliant presumably excludes himself or herself.

> ²Yhwh has looked out from heaven
>   at human beings
> To see if there is anyone showing insight,
>   seeking help from God.

The psalm controverts the scoundrel's view. The noun comes first in the sentence, forcefully confronting the statement "There is no God." The verb is not the usual one for Yhwh's looking down from the heavens but one that suggests leaning through a window (e.g., Judg. 5:28). Yhwh is looking to see if there is anyone with insight ($śākal$), which is the opposite of being a $nābāl$; it suggests moral and religious good sense. The second colon clarifies what insight consists in—*seeking help from God,

---

4. Theodoret, *Psalms*, 1:106–7.
5. Cf. Rashi's comments on the passage.
6. So Stec, *Targum of Psalms*, 44.
7. Frank Crüsemann takes $\'ĕlōhîm$ as the subject of this pl. line (for the point then cf. Ps. 82) ("Gottes Ort," in *Gott an den Rändern*, ed. Ulrike Bail and Renate Jost [Gütersloh: Kaiser, 1996], 32–41, see 33–36), but this seems forced, though grammatically elegant.
8. So Watson, *Classical Hebrew Poetry*, 320.

or seeking instruction from God (Tg). Scoundrels assume they must take responsibility for their own destiny and welfare and that they can do what they like to make sure they do all right. People of insight know that they must live morally wholesome lives, not corrupt ones, and that they can afford to do that because they can look to God.

14:3–5. The psalm continues with four even shorter, 2-2, lines in vv. 3–4d. Within v. 4a–d, the middle two cola are participial expressions, giving the cola an *abb'a'* shape. At the same time, the repetition of "eat" binds together the *a'b'* line in v. 4c–d. All this serves to set off the three-word colon comprising v. 4e, which I have taken with the further 3-3 cola in v. 5, bringing reversal to the situation lamented.

> ³Everyone has turned aside;
>   altogether they have become foul.
> There is no one doing good,
>   there is not even one.

Verse 3 repeats v. 1, putting even more emphasis on the universality of corruption as the psalmist looks out at the society: "Everyone . . . altogether . . . there is no one . . . not even one." In v. 3a–b, singular and plural verbs complement each other in the two cola. If we are to press the word, "everyone" must refer to those outside "my people" and "the faithful company," later called "the weak" and Jacob-Israel. It would therefore denote foreign people. But this may involve literalism with the poetic language, and the words may suggest that all around in Israel the psalmist sees people who act wrongly toward their fellows. "Turning aside" (*sûr*) is another way of speaking of a life that says there is no God; it commonly involves religious unfaithfulness, departing from a way that properly acknowledges Yhwh (e.g., Deut. 9:12, 16; 11:16, 28). That nuance will be taken further in v. 4: they do not acknowledge or call on Yhwh. In turn, words from v. 2 ("People make their doings corrupt, loathsome") are restated in much less familiar terms as "they are foul" (*'ālaḥ*). The verb comes only here and in Job 15:16; in Arabic it refers to milk going sour (BDB). "There is no one doing good" then exactly repeats v. 1, and "There is not even one" underlines the point. So the verse achieves its rhetorical effect partly by novelty and partly by repetition.

> 4a–dHave they not acknowledged,
>   all those who cause harm?
> Those who eat my people
>   have eaten bread.

EVV take the question in v. 4a–b to refer to knowledge, but more likely this is a typical instance of *yāda'* meaning *acknowledge, and the implicit object is Yhwh (v. 4e). The combination of "seeking help from God" (v. 2) and "acknowledging God" recurs from 9:10. The wrongdoers are then identified by means of the familiar expression for people who do *harm, which may refer to false accusations or curses. Novel expressions again complement familiar ones. The troublemakers "eat my people" (cf. Mic. 3:1–3). "My" might denote Yhwh's people or the psalmist's people, but either way v. 7 will make explicit that the expression refers to Jacob-Israel. In addition, they "eat bread." The collocation is allusive but suggestive. LXX assumes that they devour people as easily as they eat food, but this is not explicit. Perhaps they can move easily from eating people to eating a good meal, like a contract killer going out to dinner; the repetition of the verb underlines the incongruity of the movement. Or perhaps it is *by* devouring the people that they eat bread. They live on the basis of making life hard for others.

> ⁴ᵉThey have not called on Yhwh—
> ⁵there, they have been seized by terror,
>   because Yhwh is among the faithful company.

In isolation, the further move to "they have not called on Yhwh" could suggest another incongruity. They eat bread and ought to be grateful for the fact, but they fail to call on Yhwh as the one who provides their bread. In the context, however, it more likely restates the point in vv. 1–2. Instead of calling on Yhwh for what they need, they oppress others in order to make sure that their needs are met.

With v. 5 comes a move from a lament at the way things are to a description of Yhwh's reaction, paralleling the move from v. 1 to v. 2. Terror seizes the people who are so laid back in their acts of oppression and are confident that they will be all right, because they think they can safely leave God out of account. More literally, "They fear [with] fear" or "panic [with] panic": the verb *pāḥad* is strengthened by the addition of its cognate noun as a kind of internal object or adverbial accusative. They are overcome by fear "there," in the midst of their acts of oppression.[9] Why is that? The explanation comes in the parallel colon. "My people" whom they are consuming are the "faithful company" in whose midst Yhwh dwells. It is therefore dangerous to mess with them.

14:6–7. Thus far the psalm has had no explicit addressee. It has spoken of God in the third person and may have implicitly addressed fellow Israelites, or it may have constituted reflection formulated for the psalmist's own benefit, to build up conviction when experience threatens such conviction. Verse 6 hardly changes that, though rhetorically things

---

9. LXX glosses "where there was no terror" from Ps. 53.

change as the psalm formally addresses the kind of people vv. 1 and 4 have described. It moves from qatal to yiqtol, suggesting a move from general statements to a statement that more explicitly relates to the present and future. It thus sharpens the psalm's point. It is not a mere theoretical reflection on human sinfulness but a lament that issues from the attacks of other people. But the attitude to God stays the same.

> ⁶By the plan of the weak may you be put to shame
> because Yhwh is their refuge.

The weak are people who have no alternative but to make Yhwh their refuge, and this is their "plan" for coping with life's pressures. A refuge (*maḥseh*) is a shelter where vulnerable animals or vulnerable human beings hide from attack or storm or sun (61:3 [4]; 104:18)—poverty may mean a human being has no such shelter (Job 24:8). It thus comes to be a figure for Yhwh's relationship with vulnerable people (Pss. 46:1 [2]; 62:7–8 [8–9]).[10] The addressees are people who discount God (vv. 1, 4) and therefore scorn this way of coping with life. They have no hesitation about attacking people who make Yhwh their refuge, because they "know" that God is not involved in the world and that taking such shelter is therefore a pointless ploy.

> ⁷O that Israel's deliverance
> would come from Zion;
> When Yhwh brings a restoration of his people,
> Jacob shall rejoice, Israel be glad.

Verse 7 then expresses the point in another way, though still as a kind of wish for God to act rather than a plea addressed to God. Here the indications become stronger that the scoundrels are not people within the community but people attacking the community. The psalmist longs for God to act to deliver and restore. Reference to deliverance coming from Zion implies the conviction that Yhwh resides there: Yhwh is "among the faithful company," the community that worships there. This idea complements the picture of Yhwh residing in the heavens (v. 2). The midrash notes that out of Zion come the Torah, strength, shining, greatness, and blessing (Isa. 2:3; Pss. 20:2 [3]; 50:2; 99:2; 128:5; 134:3).[11] "Brings a restoration" (*šûb šĕbût*) usually refers to the restoration of the community after the exile: indeed, LXX, Jerome, and Tg render the phrase "brings back the captivity." This presupposes the natural assumption that *šĕbût*

---

10. On its importance in the Psalms, see J. F. D. Creach, *Yahweh as Refuge and the Editing of the Hebrew Psalter*, JSOTSup 217 (Sheffield: Sheffield Academic Press, 1996).
11. *Midrash on Psalms*, 1:185–86.

comes from the verb *šābâ*, "take captive" (cf. BDB). But this does not fit all occurrences of the phrase (esp. Ezek. 16:53; Job 42:10); more likely *šĕbût* comes from *šûb* itself, so that the phrase means "turn a turning" (cf. *HALOT*). This fits with the prospect of joy on the part of "Jacob" and "Israel,"[12] as reference to Jacob-Israel is prominent in the context of the exile in Isa. 40–49 (e.g., 40:27; 42:24; 43:1). Joy is the opposite of shame, because it implies vindication rather than confounding.

Theological Implications

As a whole the psalm suggests that a wise and good life involves recognizing that God is involved in the world, doing good, and looking to God for help. Throughout, it holds together a religious question and a moral one. The scoundrels ignore Yhwh and ignore right and wrong. Perhaps they decide that Yhwh is not involved in the world and therefore they may as well do what they like, or perhaps they decide to do what they like and therefore come to discount God. But it is a stupid life that discounts God's activity in the world, perverting one's way of life and thus making it loathsome to God. When people behave as if God is not involved in the world, that is a threat to the weak; but they are challenged to continue living by the conviction that God is active in their midst and to look for the confounding of scoundrels and for their own restoration. That in turn implies a theology. God's "place" in the world is defined as among the faithful company when it is weak and under pressure from the strong who seek to put it down.[13]

Paul quotes from vv. 1–3 in Rom. 3:10–12 (LXX then adds Rom. 3:13–18 to the psalm) to make the point that the whole of humanity can be described in terms of vv. 1–3. The psalm's own point is that sometimes communities can degenerate to that point and be a fearful threat to their victims. Paul thus encourages us to be realistically hopeless about humanity and then grateful for what God has done in Christ. The psalm's own aim is to give us a way of thinking in God's presence if we live in a time when the communities that threaten us are especially degenerate.

---

12. The verbs are jussive in form; *TTH* 50a takes them as permissive.
13. See Crüsemann, "Gottes Ort."

Psalm 15
Qualifications for Staying with God

Translation

Composition. David's.

¹Yhwh, who may stay in your tent,
 who may dwell on your holy mountain?ᵃ

²One who walks with integrityᵇ
 and does faithfulness
 and speaks truthfulness in his heart.
³He has not gone about talking—
 he has not caused calamity for his fellow
 or taken up abuse against his neighbor.
⁴In his eyes a contemptible person is despised,ᶜ
 and he honors people who revere Yhwh;
 he has sworn to bring calamityᵈ and does not change it;
⁵He has not put out his money at interest
 nor taken a bribe against the innocent—
 one who does these things, never faltering.ᵉ

 a. The yiqtols are permissive (*IBHS* 31.4d).
 b. Lit., "walks whole"; it seems unnecessary take this to mean "[in] a whole [way]" (so BDB).
 c. Tg may imply that he is despised in his own eyes as contemptible (cf. Qimchi), but this fits the context less well since the psalm is concerned with relationships with other people.
 d. For the understanding of *lĕhāraʿ* as "to bring calamity," cf. *Midrash on Psalms* 1:191 and the note. Jerome has "to bring calamity to himself": he swears an oath that would damage himself. But this requires considerable inference. LXX *tō plēsion autou* implies *lĕhārēaʿ*, "to his neighbor," but this does not follow well from the rest of v. 4.
 e. For the ptc. followed by yiqtol in apposition, see (e.g.) 147:14–16; the change to a finite verb is necessary when the second verb is negatived (cf. vv. 2–3; see DG 112e, though not giving this example).

Interpretation

Once again the psalm is not praise, prayer, or thanksgiving. Initially it is addressed to Yhwh, though in the form of a rhetorical question. The psalmist knows the answer to this question, and he asks it and answers it not for Yhwh's sake nor for the sake of personal reflection but for the sake of hidden listeners—the kind of people who want to spend time in Yhwh's tent on Yhwh's holy mountain. The question may have a background in a liturgical context (cf. 24:3), when a worshipper might make an inquiry of a minister. But the OT parallels to such questioning that are routinely cited (2 Sam. 21; Hag. 2; Zech. 7; see also Jer. 7; Mic. 6:6–8) are not very similar in content, and we can hardly assume that Ps. 15 is simply a transcript of what went on at the temple gates.[1] It also parallels Wisdom thinking,[2] though this need not imply that it was composed in the circles of the "Wise." It is a teaching psalm like Ps. 1, lightly disguised as a request to Yhwh for guidance, and it may thus be based on a liturgical form, formulating its teaching by using a question-and-answer form used in the temple—a question in v. 1 and an answer in vv. 2–5. The talk of "dwelling" raises the question whether the minister is not only the person who asks the question, but the one who has to answer it, since it is ministers who regularly dwell in the temple courts (cf. 65:4 [5]).

The lines grow steadily longer as the psalm opens up. In MT they have 6, then 7, then 8, then 10, then 11 stresses.[3] We know nothing of the psalm's authorship or date.

> Composition. David's.

Heading. See glossary. Read in connection with David himself, and given the crisis of integrity, faithfulness, and truthfulness to which he

---

1. See John T. Willis, "Ethics in a Cultic Setting," in *Essays in Old Testament Ethics* (J. Philip Hyatt Memorial), ed. James L. Crenshaw and John T. Willis (New York: Ktav, 1974), 145–70; R. E. Clements, "Worship and Ethics," in *Worship and the Hebrew Bible* (John T. Willis Festschrift), ed. M. Patrick Graham et al., JSOTSup 284 (Sheffield: Sheffield Academic Press, 1999), 78–94, against (e.g.) Gunkel, *Psalmen*, 47–50, Keel, *Symbolism of the Biblical World*, 126–27; J. L. Koole ("Psalm xv—eine königliche Einzugsliturgie?" in *Studies on Psalms*, by B. Gemser et al., OtSt 13 [Leiden: Brill, 1963], 98–111], who sees it as specifically an entrance liturgy for a king.

2. See (e.g.) Walter Beyerlin, *Weisheitlich-kultische Heilsordnung* (Neukirchen-Vluyn: Neukirchener Verlag, 1985).

3. Michael Barré ("Recovering the Literary Structure of Psalm xv," *VT* 34 [1984]: 207–11) sees the psalm as having a stepped structure. See also Pierre Auffret, "Essai sur la structure littéraire du Psaume xv," *VT* 31 (1981): 385–99; idem, "YHWH, qui séjournera en ta tente?" *VT* 50 (2000): 143–51.

arrives in the middle of his life, the psalm comes to abound in irony. Is this the standard that judges him at that point, or the challenge he now needs to face?

> ¹Yhwh, who may stay in your tent,
> who may dwell on your holy mountain?

15:1. The psalm opens with a neat 3-3 balancing line. Yhwh's holy mountain is presumably the hill on which the temple stands (Pss. 2:6; 43:3; 48:1–2 [2–3]; 99:9; cf. 24:3). Most commonly "tent" refers to the portable wilderness sanctuary described in Exod. 25–40, but David also pitched a tent for the ark, which apparently continued as part of the temple complex (2 Sam. 6:17; 1 Kings 2:28–30; 8:4); the part would then stand for the whole. But "tent" seems open to being a poetic term for the temple as a whole as Yhwh's earthly home (Pss. 27:5–6; 61:4 [5]), just as it can be a poetic term for the permanent homes of human beings (e.g., Ps. 91:10). The poetic expression might also facilitate the psalm's use with reference to staying in God's presence in a figurative sense.[4]

Why might someone want to stay or dwell there? In a literal sense visitors no doubt sometimes stayed near the temple, such as at festival times, and this might suggest the image.[5] The metaphorical talk of "staying" with Yhwh (*gûr*), like a resident alien (*gēr*), is unusual. A resident alien is dependent on the goodwill of the community for protection and sustenance, and the context in Pss. 39:12 [13]; 61:4 [5] confirms that this is the resonance here. The metaphorical talk of "dwelling" (*šākan*) is also uncommon, and perhaps it too suggests security and provision (cf. 65:4 [5]), though it also recalls the fact that the OT usually talks in terms of *God's* dwelling in the wilderness tent or in the temple or on Zion (e.g., 74:2; Isa. 8:18). With some adventurousness, the questioner is asking about dwelling where Yhwh dwells. "Dwell" may imply something more permanent than "stay," yet both suggest something less permanent than "living." That is realistic, for one cannot actually live in Yhwh's house: there is work to do (contrast Pss. 23:6; 27:4, though these passages confirm that the object of staying with Yhwh is that this is a place of safety and provision). But the uncertainty about whether dwelling is less permanent than living suggests that the more basic question concerns who may *remain* in God's presence—for a moment, a night, or a lifetime.

15:2–5. The description of the person Yhwh welcomes covers four areas in the four tricola. These are the general integrity of the person in

---

4. But it is hard to imagine that Yhwh's "tent" and "holy mountain" refer to the land as a whole (against Johnson, *Cultic Prophet*, 92–105).

5. So Weiser, *Psalms*, 168.

relation to other people in the community, the equivalent lack of wrong actions toward others, the response to people's stance in relation to Yhwh, and the right attitude toward money. Verse 2 thus comprises the generalizations whose implications vv. 3–5b spell out, with v. 5c reverting to generalization.

> ²One who walks with integrity
> and does faithfulness
> and speaks truthfulness in his heart.

First, v. 2 holds together walking, doing, and speaking, and *integrity, *faithfulness and *truthfulness. Verse 2b adds inner attitude to outward walk: both are important. It is possible for there to be a disparity between what people do and what they say in their heart. They might be planning deception when apparently behaving honorably. Yhwh does not countenance that.

> ³He has not gone about talking—
> he has not caused calamity for his fellow
> or taken up abuse against his neighbor.

To complement the point thus made generally, comprehensively, and positively, v. 3 moves to qatal verbs to make the point more concretely, illustratively, and negatively. The former is incomplete without the latter. Again three clauses refer to walk, action, and words. The person Yhwh welcomes does not (literally) "go about on his tongue." The verb (*rāgal*) is a denominative from the word for "foot," and it thus provides a good parallel for "walk," though the clause does not make clear for what purpose the person is going about using their tongue. Elsewhere the verb denotes going about as a spy, the subjects usually being the people plotting to take the land from the Canaanites, and the two subsequent clauses will confirm that the verb here implies something such as going about plotting.[6] Tg infers that it denotes making false accusations. Parallel to doing faithfulness is not causing calamity (*ra'*, something *bad) to a fellow member of the community (a *rēa'*—the similarity of the words emphasizes the scandal of the idea). Not taking up abuse (*ḥerpâ*) against a neighbor parallels speaking truthfulness from the heart and implies much more than casual insults. It suggests making accusations against other members of the community and thus seeking to defraud them or even threaten their life.

---

6. *HALOT* defends the translation of *rāgal* as "slander," but it is doubtful that the verb ever means this, at least in the qal, even in Sir. 4:29; 5:14 (see, e.g., NJB); perhaps not even in the piel in 2 Sam. 19:27 [28], where it might as easily suggest plotting.

> ⁴In his eyes a contemptible person is despised,
> and he honors people who revere Yhwh;
> he has sworn to bring calamity and does not change it;

Attitudes toward other people's wrongdoing and right-doing are another area foundational for community life. Whereas vv. 2–3 contrast with each other, v. 4a contains its own antithesis. Weiser faults the psalm for suggesting that we should despise the contemptible (he infers that the psalm operates with an understanding of retribution like that of Job's friends).[7] The psalm's view is that the person Yhwh welcomes takes the appropriate negative attitude toward the irreligious/immoral as well as the appropriate positive attitude toward the religious/moral. That will discourage the immoral, encourage morality in the community, and encourage the person who does the despising to make sure they are not this kind of person.

What makes a person contemptible? The only other occurrence of the word (*mā'as* niphal participle) describes silver that has been tested and rejected (Jer. 6:30), and the verb is often used for Yhwh's rejection based on disobedience, rebellion, and unfaithfulness (e.g., Jer. 7:29). This fits the parallelism here. Conversely, the people who are properly honored are people who *revere Yhwh. This can be a term for all Israelite worshippers, but here it denotes members of the community who actually do revere Yhwh, keeping faithful to the Torah in their worship and behavior. Despising and honoring (*bāzâ*, *kābēd*) also form a contrasting pair, the parallelism being further nuanced by the combination of qatal niphal and yiqtol piel.

The last colon then takes further the duty of a responsible member of the community to see that people do not get away with wrongdoing. It would be tempting (e.g.) to deal softly with one's friends, but the person Yhwh welcomes is one who vows to bring trouble and does so. W. A. Irwin calls this "astonishing nonsense,"[8] but the psalm assumes that just as it is wrong to bring about calamity for someone who does not deserve it (v. 3), so it is wrong to act with unilateral leniency when someone does not deserve it (cf. 7:4 [5]).

> ⁵He has not put out his money at interest
> nor taken a bribe against the innocent—
> one who does these things, never faltering.

Fourth, v. 5 turns to attitudes toward money. This may underlie the answers presented in vv. 2–4. In monetary matters it is especially tempt-

---

7. *Psalms*, 170.
8. "Critical Notes on Five Psalms," *AJSL* 49 (1932–33): 9–20, see 17.

ing not to be truthful (v. 2), to seek to wrong other people (v. 3), and to suspend moral standards in relation to other people (v. 4). Verse 5a–b comprises further negatives, like v. 3, itemizing monetary temptations to be resisted. The first temptation is to lend money on interest (etymologically, "with a bite"). The presupposition of the Torah's attitude to lending is that it is a means of helping the needy fellow Israelite, not a means of the rich increasing their wealth (e.g., Exod. 22:25–27 [24–26]); Lev. 25:35–38), and it may also presuppose high rates of interest. It does not have in mind what we might call commercial loans (which may be what Deut. 23:20 refers to). To lend at interest is to take advantage of the needy. The second temptation is to pervert justice by taking a bribe. The psalm has in mind a senior member of the community taking part in the administration of justice at the city gate, who could easily be bribed by a wealthy person.

LXX takes the last colon as a promise that the person who lives by vv. 2–5b will never be caused to fall down. This corresponds to a common usage of the verb *môṭ* (e.g., 55:22 [23]; 94:18). The line then forms an inclusion with v. 1. But neither the form nor the content of the line suggests such an inclusion. This reference to not *falling down or faltering works within a different framework from that of being welcome in Yhwh's presence, and the reversion to a participle to describe the person who does right rather suggests an inclusion with v. 2, while the negatived verb in the parallel colon in turn echoes v. 3.[9] The last line rather emphasizes the need to stand firm in doing "these things"; for this meaning of *môṭ*, cf. 17:5. Since it completes yet another tricolon, it presumably links especially with v. 5 and thus particularly urges persistence in the attitude to money urged by v. 5a. But its "these things" could extend to the rest of vv. 2–4, so that it also underlines the need for persistence with regard to all the prescriptions in vv. 2–5.

Theological Implications

There are eleven verbs in vv. 2–5a, and the midrash comments that the psalm thus sums up the 613 commands in the Torah in eleven expectations.[10] One might hold together the first two verbs and reckon that the psalm expounds a decalogue,[11] though it is not a systematic account of Yhwh's expectations, and it moves between the general and the illustrative—like *the* Decalogue. But it does not include any of the topics in *the*

---

9. Cf. Patrick D. Miller, "Poetic Ambiguity and Balance in Psalm xv," *VT* 29 (1979): 416–24, see 424.
10. See *Midrash on Psalms*, 1:227.
11. Cf. Cassiodorus, *Psalms*, 1:155–60.

Decalogue (contrast, e.g., Jer. 7). "The psalmist is not so much giving rules as painting a portrait of the kind of man who can remain in God's presence."[12] Indeed, it confronts people who might reckon that they have kept the Decalogue's requirements, except perhaps the tenth—though we could even see it as spelling out the implications of the tenth.

If the psalm has a background in questions that worshippers might ask of a minister in the temple, these questions might have in mind an answer in terms of formal requirements. One must be appropriately dressed or cleansed (cf. 2 Chron. 23:19), or one must have gone through the appropriate sacrament (e.g., baptism) or the appropriate experience (e.g., baptism in the Spirit or speaking in tongues). The psalm subverts such assumptions. The lack of such qualifications does not debar a person, and the possession of them does not make a person welcome. The qualifications God looks for belong in a different realm. Isaiah 33:14–16 uses the same form to make the point less subtly, and it may be an adaptation of the psalm. The psalm thus makes the same point as the Torah, the Prophets, and the Wisdom books, that sacramental observance is not enough without the moral, as the moral is not enough without the sacramental.

The prescriptions in vv. 2–5 make clear that the question in v. 1 does not relate to ordinary people. The psalm's challenge addresses people who have the power to cause calamity to others when they deserve it and when they do not, people with money to lend and money to use for bribes. In any society people with power and money are subject to particular temptations, and this psalm reminds them that they need to resist them if they want to spend time in Yhwh's presence. Happy the person who is not subject to such temptations.

Taken in isolation the psalm could give several misleading impressions. It could suggest that the initiative in a relationship with Yhwh comes from human beings, as if it is their doing right that makes it possible to approach Yhwh—to be anachronistic, it could be affirming that salvation comes by works of a moral kind. Or it could be suggesting that God expects perfection of us and makes no allowance for our needing the help of God's grace and for God's accepting us despite our failures, not on the basis of our perfect obedience.[13] Or it could suggest that Yhwh is interested in right behavior toward other people in the community and not in right performance of worship—to be anachronistic, it could be denying that salvation comes by works of a religious kind such as Sabbath-keeping or circumcision. In the context of OT faith as a whole, it indicates that people need to be living lives committed to Yhwh as part

---

12. Rogerson and McKay, *Psalms*, 1:64.
13. Cf. Weiser, *Psalms*, 171.

of their response to Yhwh's taking the initiative in relation to them. It implies that they can be doing that, suggesting concrete expectations that spell out the nature of wholeness, faithfulness, and truthfulness in a way that is not so horrendously demanding. And it indicates that people need to have lives that are morally correct as well as religiously correct if they are to come into Yhwh's presence.

Psalm 16
Trust in God for Life

Translation

Inscription. David's.

¹Watch over me, God,
  because I rely on you.
²I have said[a] to Yhwh: "You are my Lord,
  my good, none besides you."[b]
³To the holy people who are in the land[c]
  and the leaders in whom is my entire delight.[d]

    a. *'Āmart*: see GKC 44i.
    b. If *bal* can have a positive meaning (see *DCH* and *HALOT*), we might translate "my good is indeed with you."
    c. For the use of the retrospective pronominal subject *hēmmâ*, see JM 158g. *TTH* 198 links *hēmmâ* with what follows, "*They* are the leaders . . ." (cf. NRSV and NIVI), but the *w* on the next word makes that difficult.
    d. On the const. expression, see GKC 130d. Many emendations have been proposed for v. 3 (see, e.g., *BHS*), but none has carried conviction. LXX has "For the holy ones who are in his land he magnified all his delights in them." For MT *wĕ'addîrê*, "and the leaders of," LXX implies a form from *'ādar* hiphil. The form *ya'dîr*, which appears in Isa. 42:21, would fit; it is the only occurrence of the verb except for the niphal ptc. in Exod. 15:6, 11. Isa. 42:21 also begins with the verb *ḥāpēṣ* (delight). All this suggests that to make sense of a line it found difficult, LXX has assimilated it to Isa. 42:21; the third-person pronouns would follow from that. For modern emendations of the line, see (e.g.) G. Behler, "Une conjecture critique sur *Ps.* xvi, 3–4a," *RB* 49 (1940): 240–43; Sigmund Mowinckel, "Zu Psalm 16, 2–4," *Theologische Literaturzeitung* 82 (1957): 649–54; Claus Schedl, "'Die Heiligen' und die 'Herrlichen' in Psalm 16.1–4," *ZAW* 76 (1964): 171–75; M. Mannati, "Remarques sur Ps. xvi 1–3," *VT* 22 (1972): 359–61; Johannes Lindblom, "Erwägungen zu Psalm xvi," *VT* 24 (1974): 187–95; Franz D. Hubmann, "Textgraphik und Psalm xvi 2–3," *VT* 33 (1983): 101–6.

⁴"Their pains will be many, those who[e] serve[f] another.
  I will not pour their blood libations
  or take up their[g] names on my lips."

⁵Yhwh, my apportioned share and my cup—
  you hold on to[h] my lot.
⁶The measuring ropes fell for me in loveliness;[i]
  yes, the possession[j] is perfect to me.
⁷I will worship Yhwh, who has guided me;
  yes, by night[k] my spirit instructs me.
⁸I have set Yhwh before me continually;
  because he is at my right hand, I shall not falter.
⁹Therefore my heart rejoices, my soul is glad;[l]
  yes, my flesh will dwell in confidence.
¹⁰For you will not abandon me to Sheol;
  you will not let someone committed to you[m] see the Abyss.
¹¹You will make known to me the way to life;
  joyful abundance[n] will be with your face,
  lovely things in your right hand always.

Interpretation

The psalm begins with a plea, but it is the only plea in the psalm, whose nature is more an expression of trust in Yhwh. The content of

e. For the asyndetic relative clause (lacking *'ăšer*), see JM 158a.

f. LXX assumes *māhārû* comes from *māhar*, "hasten," but this gives poor sense, and elsewhere the verb is piel. BDB derives from *māhar*, "pay a dowry," but this seems forced. DCH notes a possible homonym meaning "serve"; alternatively, *māhar* might be a byform of *hārar*, "desire" (on which see *DCH*). ASV "exchange" takes *māhar* as a byform of *mûr* (cf. 106:20; Jer. 2:11) or requires emendation to *hēmîrû* and also has to assume the omission of a preposition and two nouns (change [Yhwh for] another [god]). NRSV "choose" emends to *bāḥārû*.

g. The suffix presumably refers to the other gods, despite the formal mismatch with the sg. "another" in v. 4a.

h. One would expect yiqtol *titmōk* or ptc. *tōmēk* (cf. LXX), not *tômîk*, which looks like hiphil from a byform *yāmak* (cf. GKC 50e).

i. Taking the pl. as abstract (cf. DG 18a).

j. The form *naḥălāt* is odd, though see *IBHS* 6.3.2b; LXX, Jerome, and Syr "my inheritance" might imply *naḥălātî*.

k. Pl. *lêlôt* perhaps suggests the different parts of the night (JM 136b).

l. *Wayyāgel* takes its present-tense significance from the stative *śāmaḥ*. The yiqtol in v. 9b then complements the qatal/wayyiqtol forms.

m. *Ḥāsîdkā*; perhaps "someone to whom you are committed."

n. Lit., "abundance of joys," with the pl. *śĕmāḥôt* further intensifying the expression; cf. also pl. "lovely things." EVV "abundance of joys" gives the impression that it is the joy that is abundant, but the const. indicates that it is the abundance that is joyful.

the psalm suggests two pressures on this trust. The first part speaks of the pressure of people who worship other gods; the second speaks of the threat of death. These are presumably related. People who worship other gods assert that this is the key to well-being (v. 2), the flourishing of crops, flocks, and herds, so that reliance on Yhwh imperils the things on which life depends. One need hardly think of the suppliant as in mortal danger at the moment.[1] Psalms 15 and 16 both concern not faltering or falling down (15:5; 16:8) in respect to faithfulness, the one in relation to the community, the other in relation to Yhwh. The psalm alternates between address to God, asking for protection and declaring trust (vv. 1, 5–6, 9–11), and address to people who might be tempted to worship other gods as they seek such protection and provision (vv. 2–4, 7–8). In its way, the address to other people is also an indirect statement of trust, and the address to Yhwh is an indirect challenge to other people, as well as an implicit act of self-encouragement to the suppliant.

After the opening 2-2 line the psalm is characterized by long cola and lines—in MT 2-2, 4-2, 3-2, 4-3-3, 3-3, 3-3, 4-3, 4-3, 5-3, 4-4, 3-3-3. The first tricolon brings a section of the psalm to a close as the declaration of the suppliant's commitment comes to an end, and the second tricolon brings the entire psalm to a close. The psalm may belong to the Persian period (see on vv. 5–6).[2]

Inscription. David's.

Heading. "Inscription" is the meaning LXX and Tg ascribe to *miktām* in the headings of Pss. 16; 56–60. It might indicate that the psalm was inscribed in clay in the manner of Babylonian psalms; Keel suggests that such a psalm was inscribed on a stele as a way of giving permanent expression to the prayer before God.[3] This fits its application to Hezekiah's prayer in Isa. 38:9–20.

16:1–4. The psalm begins with a plea, a testimony, and an implicit exhortation.

> ¹Watch over me, God,
>   because I rely on you.

---

1. Against Kraus, *Psalms*, 1:235.
2. But Rendsburg sees it as having features suggesting a northern Israelite origin (see *Linguistic Evidence*, 29–33).
3. *Symbolism of the Biblical World*, 329. Raymond Tournay suggests "secret prayer" ("Sur quelques rubriques des Psaumes," in *Mélanges bibliques* [A. Robert Festschrift; Paris: Bloud & Gay, 1957], 197–204). See further Craigie, *Psalms 1–50*, 154; Tate, *Psalms 51–100*, 66.

> ²I have said to Yhwh: "You are my Lord,
>   my good, none besides you."

"Watch over me" presupposes some insecurity (cf. 17:8–9; 25:20; 86:2; 140:4 [5]; 141:9), and the parallel reference to *relying on Yhwh confirms this.

Verse 2 details it further. On one hand, Yhwh is the suppliant's sovereign *Lord, not only *the* Lord but *my* Lord—a confession of commitment then implying that Yhwh's servants have a right to expect their Lord's support and provision. And the suppliant is wholly dependent on Yhwh for *good—in effect, Yhwh *is* the suppliant's good. The nature of this good will be spelled out in vv. 5, 6, and 11. The preposition in "besides you" (*ʿāleykā*) is difficult, but it parallels the one in "besides my face" in the first commandment (Exod. 20:3), which is also enigmatic. The significance of the commitment, then, is as a declaration about being the kind of person the Decalogue has in mind, one who indeed recognizes Yhwh alone as Lord.

> ³To the holy people who are in the land
>   and the leaders in whom is my entire delight.

I take v. 3 as also dependent on the "I have said" of v. 2—the psalm has things to say to people as well as things to say to God, things with essentially the same significance.[4] NIVI mg assumes that the holy people/leaders are the devotees of these other gods,[5] but there are no other occurrences of "holy people" or "leaders" with that meaning. More likely these are a group with whom the suppliant identifies (or wishes to identify), and they are set over against people who have turned to other gods and are urged not to join them (so NIVI text and other EVV). While "the holy people" are sometimes heavenly beings (see 89:5, 7 [6, 8]), they can be Israel as a whole (cf. 34:9 [10]). The parallelism might suggest that "holy people" is given more precision by "leaders" (*ʾaddîrîm*) and vice versa, so that the expressions refer to priests (cf. the expressions in 1 Chron. 24:5). I rather take the two cola to refer to the people as a whole and their leaders (cf. Neh. 10:29 [30]), whom there is no reason to limit to priests.

> ⁴"Their pains will be many, those who serve another.

4. We might render the *lĕ* "as for" and take v. 3 as a lead-in to v. 4, but the usage is unusual and the link of thought is rather subtle, though the implication is still that v. 4 is a warning to the holy people/leaders not to join the worshippers of other gods.

5. Cf. Hendrik G. L. Peels, "Sanctorum communio vel idolorum repudatio," *ZAW* 112 (2000): 239–51. Eugenio Zolli ("Die 'Heiligen' in Psalm 16," *TZ* 6 [1950]: 149–50) identifies them as the powerful dead.

> I will not pour their blood libations
> or take up their names on my lips."

On these people the psalm wants to urge a commitment to Yhwh that contrasts with that of people who turn to another god (again cf. Exod. 20:3). Those who do so presumably believe that this is the key to ensuring well-being, but actually it will mean "their pains will be many." There are two verbs *ʿāṣab*, respectively meaning "hurt" and "shape," with associated nouns meaning "pain" and "image." This lays each open to suggesting the resonances of the other. The many pains issue from their many images.[6] The supplicant is committed not to be involved in their worship, by action or by word, and implicitly urges that commitment upon others.

There need be no implication that the supplicant physically pours the libation and must therefore be a priest.[7] Blood libations (i.e., pouring out blood as an offering) are not otherwise explicitly mentioned in the OT, but wine libations and the offering of blood were part of sacrificial practice (see, e.g., the reference to "sacrificing my sacrificial blood" in Exod. 23:18; cf. Lev. 7:33). There need thus be no implication that blood libations were inherently abhorrent: what is objectionable is making them to other gods.

Undertaking not to take up the *name of other deities is presumably a way of undertaking not to call on them (e.g., as witnesses to oaths or to ask for their blessings). Once again the unusual expression links with the Decalogue, since it comes otherwise only in the further enigmatic requirement that people not "take up Yhwh's name with regard to emptiness" (Exod. 20:7; though for other ways of making the same point, see Exod. 23:13; Hosea 2:17 [19]). The psalm's commitment complements this: "Not only will I not disobey that command with regard to Yhwh's name; I also will not take up the name of other gods at all." These undertakings are the negative equivalents to the positive statements in vv. 1–2.

16:5–11. There is perhaps a heightening through the psalm as we move from reliance on Yhwh (v. 1) to worshipping Yhwh (v. 7) to joy and gladness (v. 9).

> ⁵Yhwh, my apportioned share and my cup—
> you hold on to my lot.

"Share" and "portion" (*mānâ*, *ḥēleq*) are both terms used of the allocation of the parts of a sacrificial animal (e.g., Lev. 6:17 [10]; 7:33),

---

6. Tg, Th, Jerome have "their images will be multiplied"—perhaps rightly.
7. Raymond Tournay argues that the psalmist is a postexilic Levite ("À propos de Psaume 16,1–4," *RB* 108 [2001]: 21–25).

though Israel can then be described as Yhwh's portion (Deut. 32:9), and Yhwh as the individual Israelite's portion (Pss. 73:26; 119:57; 142:5 [6]; Lam. 3:24). It would thus be possible for v. 5a to declare that Yhwh *is* the suppliant's apportioned share. The devotee, while knowing that one does not have an exclusive claim on Yhwh, also knows that one can be so confident of Yhwh's entire attention that it is as if one were the only person to whom Yhwh had to give it. For the further image of the "cup" that contains one's share, see on 11:6.

But v. 5b suggests we should read v. 5a in a different way. "My lot" (usually a term for the allocation of the land to different clans and families) is now a further parallel expression to "my apportioned share" and "my cup," which implies that all these expressions are objects of the verb "hold on to." The suppliant is aware of having a designated share, portion, cup, or lot, and knows that Yhwh upholds this and thus protects the person to whom it belongs. The psalm does not make specific what the "share" refers to. The prophets make clear that there would be situations when people's allocation of land was in danger from fraud or the toughness of creditors, but the expression could be open to more metaphorical reference.

> ⁶The measuring ropes fell for me in loveliness;
> yes, the possession is perfect to me.

Verse 6 indicates why it is worth holding on to and confirms the understanding of v. 5. The "lines" are the cords by which allocations of land were measured out, and by metonymy the allocation itself (e.g., 78:55; 105:11). The suppliant has received a lovely allocation. Perhaps it is lovely simply by virtue of being in the land; perhaps it is a particularly delightful tract of land. Verse 6b then restates the point. These comments may imply a return from exile and a rejoicing in the land the speaker has "returned" to; the people in the land (v. 3) are then people here as opposed to being in exile, and the adherents of other deities are the members of other communities in Judah and neighboring Persian provinces.[8]

> ⁷I will worship Yhwh, who has guided me;
> yes, by night my spirit instructs me.

The verb *worship can be at home near the beginning of a psalm (e.g., 34:1 [2]; 63:4 [5]; 145:1–2) or near the end (e.g., 26:12; 115:18; 145:21). In v. 7 it marks a transition to overt praise in light of the conviction that Yhwh will answer the suppliant's plea (v. 1). Yhwh's guidance (*yāʿaṣ*)

---

8. So Briggs, *Psalms*, 1:117–20.

presumably relates to what we have read thus far and thus to an urging to stay faithful to Yhwh (cf. 73:24, using the related noun *ʿēṣâ*).

The second colon spells out the way God guides, the yiqtol complementing the qatal. Yhwh's guidance comes from within the suppliant.⁹ That the inner person has such a teaching role is unusual (cf. Prov. 16:23 for the "heart" teaching). It presupposes that Yhwh's teaching is written into the "heart" (cf., e.g., Deut. 30:14).

> ⁸I have set Yhwh before me continually;
> because he is at my right hand, I shall not falter.

Night is often a time when God may speak (e.g., Gen. 46:2; Job 4:13; 33:15; and cf. Ps. 17:3), but when v. 8a in turn restates v. 7b and takes it further, it may complement its "by night" with "continually" (as "right hand" is sometimes complemented by "hand"). The way the heart instructs is by causing the person to put Yhwh before the eyes at all times.¹⁰ "To set God before us is nothing else than to keep all our senses bound and captive, that they may not run out and go astray after any other object."¹¹ That has the effect of encouraging reliance on Yhwh (v. 1) and discouraging recourse to other deities.

As v. 8b once more takes the argument further, we may infer that faltering or *falling down again refers to wavering in commitment (cf. 15:5). Yhwh's being at the suppliant's right hand is a complementary image to that in v. 8a. The right hand is the position of support, and Yhwh's being there encourages the suppliant to stay faithful (cf. 73:23; 109:31; 110:5; 121:5).

> ⁹Therefore my heart rejoices, my soul is glad;
> yes, my flesh will dwell in confidence.

This provides a basis for a joyful confidence for the future that embraces the whole person. Once more the "yes" clause likely reiterates what has preceded (cf. vv. 6, 7), so that *beṭaḥ* in v. 9b refers to a sense of confidence that parallels the rejoicing of v. 9a, rather than to an objective security, though it presupposes that. Flesh (*bāśār*) likewise parallels heart and soul (lit., liver).¹² Each term refers to a part of the human person but stands for the whole person viewed from a particular aspect.

---

9. Literally, this instruction comes from the kidneys (cf. 7:9 [10]), but I have avoided the translation "heart" here because of the reference to the "heart" in v. 9; NJPS has "conscience").
10. For the use of the rare verb *šāwâ* piel, cf. 119:30 with Yhwh's decisions as object.
11. Calvin, *Psalms*, 1:228; cf. Kraus, *Psalms*, 1:239.
12. *Kābôd*; see on 7:5 [6].

> ¹⁰For you will not abandon me to Sheol;
> you will not let someone committed to you see the Abyss.

The basis for joyful confidence comes in two further parallel cola; here my *nepeš* ("me") appears as yet another term for the human *person or self as a whole. We noted that the psalm's opening reference to keeping and reliance implied a sense of pressure, and this is now more overt. The suppliant is aware of some vulnerability, presumably because of the possibility that the harvest may fail in fulfillment of the warnings of people who chide those who rely on Yhwh rather than on Baal. The psalm expresses a confidence that a person committed to Yhwh will not be abandoned to death and thus to the Abyss (cf. 30:9 [10]). LXX and Jerome translate *šaḥat* with words such as "corruption," as if it came from *šāḥat*, which would be plausible if there were not the ordinary noun *šaḥat*, meaning "pit," from *šûaḥ*. Its use for the home of the dead presumably derives from the fact that people were sometimes buried in a grave pit rather than a rock-hewn tomb. But the fact that burial does lead to dissolution of the body might mean that the connotations of *šāḥat* carry over to *šaḥat* when used in connection with death.

> ¹¹You will make known to me the way to life;
> joyful abundance will be with your face,
> lovely things in your right hand always.

On the contrary, Yhwh will open up a way that leads to life rather than ending in premature death.[13] A further tricolon brings the psalm to a triumphant climax. When Yhwh's *face shines on people, they experience great joy through Yhwh's abundant provision for their needs. "Abundance" (*śōbaʿ*) signifies rich material provision (e.g., 78:25; Exod. 16:3). Throughout their lives they will experience Yhwh's right hand full of lovely things to bestow on them. Again, these lovely things (cf. v. 6, though the word there was masculine) will be pleasant material provision such as good things to eat (cf. Prov. 24:4). The "holy people" (v. 3) will not just survive, but also enjoy life.

Theological Implications

There are several reinterpretations of Ps. 16. These begin in a reading that sees the psalm as promising that people who belong to Yhwh will

---

13. Cf. Klaus Seybold, "Der Weg des Lebens," *TZ* 40 (1984): 121–29.

not be abandoned to Sheol but will enjoy resurrection. The NT takes up this reading in using vv. 8–11 to help interpret the death and resurrection of Jesus (see Acts 2:25–31; 13:35), whom God did not leave in the grave or Sheol long enough for his body to see corruption. Reapplication continues in a reading of the psalm that sees God as believers' religious or "spiritual" resource in this life, so that they enjoy eternal life now.[14]

While these are all inspired and edifying reinterpretations of the psalm, we need to recognize the importance of the psalm's original meaning rather than lose its distinctive testimony. Its promise is that people who seek God's reign and God's righteousness will find that all the other things they need such as food, drink, and clothing will also be theirs (cf. Matt. 6:32–33). Gentiles and people who worship other gods have other ways of seeking to ensure that these needs are met and are inclined to scorn believers' trust in God for them. In the context of modernity, Christians are also inclined to distance God's involvement from the provision of everyday needs, because we can seem more in control of our environment and able to take provisions for granted. Psalm 16 knows that Yhwh is the God of this life and not just of the future life nor just of religious life, and provides for this life in abundance. It is one of the reasons why people should stay faithful to Yhwh. The psalm thus refuses us the right to confine God to the realm of Christology, eschatology, or religious experience and dissociate questions of our relationship with God from questions about land and food. Psalm 16 belongs not just to Christ or to the future or to religious life but also to material life now. The psalm does not treasure a relationship with God more than the gifts of life, but it assumes that the one is key to the other.[15]

---

14. See (e.g.) H. W. Boers, "Psalm 16 and the Historical Origin of the Christian Faith," *Zeitschrift für die neutestamentliche Wissenschaft* 60 (1969): 105–10; Armin Schmitt, "Ps. 16,8–11 als Zeugnis der Auferstehung in der Apg," *BZ* 17 (1973): 229–48; Walter C. Kaiser, "The Promise to David in Psalm 16," *JETS* 23 (1980): 219–29; J. J. Kilgallen, "The Use of Psalm 16:8–11 in Peter's Pentecost Speech," *ExpTim* 113 (2001–2): 47–50; Wolfgang Fenske, "Aspekte biblischer Theologie dargestellt an der Verwendung von Ps 16 in Apostelgeschichte 2 und 13," *Bib* 83 (2002): 54–70; Gregory V. Trull, "Views on Peter's Use of Psalm 16:8–11 in Acts 2:25–32," and "An Exegesis of Psalm 16:10," in *BSac* 161 (2004): 194–204 and 304–21.

15. Against Kraus, *Psalms*, 1:236.

Psalm 17

Yhwh's Eyes, Lips, Right Hand, and Face

Translation

Plea. David's.

¹Do listen in faithfulness, Yhwh;
  do attend to my voice.
Do give ear to my plea
  from lips without deceit.
²My decision must come from your presence;
  your eyes must see what is righteous.

³Did you try my heart, visit by night,
  test me, you would not find anything;
I determined my mouth would not pass over ⁴human deeds
  according to the word of your lips.
I did watch[a] for the ways of the robber,
  ⁵my steps holding on[b] to your tracks;
  my feet would not falter.[c] [MT]

    a. The translation reflects the inclusion of the unnecessary pronoun *'ănî* before the verb.

    b. LXX, Jerome, and Tg take *tāmōk* as an example of the common use of the inf. abs. as an impv., but the context suggests rather that it functions as a finite verb. *IBHS* 35.5.2a sees it as emphatic, but there is no suggestion of emphasis in the context, and more likely it has no significant force (cf. DG 103a, but not giving this example) yet is rather used for rhetorical variation along with the preceding qatal and the following yiqtol.

    c. Once again *môṭ* refers to faltering in faithfulness; cf. 15:5; 16:8.

[or, ³Did you try my heart, visit me by night,
   test me, you would not find my determinations;
My mouth will not pass over ⁴human deeds
   according to the word of your lips.
I did watch for the ways of the robber,
   ⁵my steps holding on to your tracks;
   my feet would not falter.ᵈ (Jerome, Aq, Sym)]

⁶I myself call on you,ᵉ for you answer me, God;
   extend your ear to me, listen to my word.
⁷Show your wondrous actsᶠ of commitment,
   you who deliver by your right handᵍ those who rely on you,ʰ
   from people who raise themselves.
⁸Watch over me as the apple of your eye;ⁱ
   may you hide me in the shade of your wingsʲ
⁹From the face of the faithless who have assaulted me,
   my enemies who surround me with longing.

¹⁰They have closed their midriff;
   with their mouth they have spoken grandiosely.
¹¹Our tracksᵏ—now they have surrounded me/us [K/Q];
   their eyes they set to extend over the land.
¹²His appearanceˡ is like a lion that is eager to tear,
   like a young lion lying in ambush.

¹³Rise, Yhwh,
   go to meet him face to face,ᵐ put him down.
Rescue my life from the faithless by your sword,
   ¹⁴from mortals by your hand, Yhwh,

d. In MT *zammōtî* opens v. 3c as a verb, "I determined" (cf. GKC 67ee, and on the construction, *IBHS* 38.8b). In Jerome, Aq, and Sym the word is taken as a noun, "my determinations" (presumably *zimmōtay*), closing v. 3b; the noun would have pejorative connotations (cf. LXX *adikia*, Syr *'wl'*; EVV often translate "devices"). Tg has a double translation.

e. Taking the verb as performative qatal (see DG 60b).

f. *Pālâ* is here a byform of *pālā'* (which C has).

g. "By your right hand" comes at the end of the line. "Against your right hand" (Vg, Jerome) fits the word order, but there are no parallels for that expression.

h. The pronominal suffix can be inferred from those in the phrases on either side.

i. Again, the suffix can be inferred from the clauses on either side.

j. Assuming with Jerome that the yiqtol functions as a polite impv. (JM 113m).

k. NIVI "They have tracked me down" involves repointing the noun *'aššurênû* as a verb, *'iššěrûnî* (cf. Sym). For further text-critical observations, see M. Cohen, "*'aššūrēnû 'attâ sĕbābûnî* (Q. *sĕbābûnû*)," *VT* 41 (1991): 137–44.

l. For the noun *dimyōnô* LXX implies the verb *dimmûnî* (They are like), but the *kě* (like) is then odd.

m. Lit., "meet his face."

> From mortals—in their lifetime[n] will you fill[o] their belly
> with their share in life, with what you have stored up.[p]
> Their[q] children are to be replete,
> they are to leave what they have left to their offspring.
> [15] I myself will see your face in faithfulness;
> when I wake, may I be replete with your form.

Interpretation

The heading "plea" is apposite, because plea is unusually central to the psalm; the space given to lament and to plea is the reverse of the usual. I structure the psalm as follows.

> Plea to Yhwh to pay attention (vv. 1–2)
> Declaration of faithfulness (vv. 3–5)
> Plea to Yhwh to pay attention and act (vv. 6–9)
> Lament (vv. 10–12)
> Plea to Yhwh to act (vv. 13–15)[1]

From each plea to the next there is a development (just for attention, then for attention and action, then just for action). There is also a development from each of the first two pleas to the material that directly follows it. The first plea asserts the suppliant's honesty and uprightness, and the declaration of faithfulness develops from that. The second plea refers to the people from whom the suppliant needs deliverance, and the lament develops from that. The third plea provides an inclusion through its reference to faithfulness. The five sections also hold together through the running references to parts of the body—the suppliant's, the enemies', and Yhwh's. They refer to lips (v. 1), face and eyes (v. 2), heart and mouth (v. 3), lips (v. 4), feet (v. 5), ear (v. 6), right hand (v. 7), eye (v. 8), face and appetite (*nepeš*, v. 9), midriff and mouth (v. 10), eyes (v. 11), face and self (*nepeš*, v. 13), hand and belly (v. 14), and face (v. 15).

n. LXX takes the rare word *ḥeled* (I assume the suffix from the next word) to mean "world," as in 49:1 [2] (cf. NRSV, NIVI), but in its other occurrences (39:5 [6]; 89.47 [48], Job 11:17) it means lifetime, which fits better here.

o. LXX and Tg imply niphal *timmālēʾ*.

p. K has the noun *ṣāpîn* (something stored up), Q the ptc. *ṣĕpûnĕkā*—the meaning is similar. The verb means "to hide" and thus "protect." This line as a whole (and the rest of v. 14) is very difficult. The line reads more literally: "From mortals from [their] lifetime [with] their share in life and what is stored up by you will you fill their belly."

q. The suffix in the preceding clause carries over to this word (DG 3).

1. For a detailed study of the structure, see Pierre Auffret, "'Je serai rassasié de ton image,'" *ZAW* 106 (1994): 446–58.

Heading

The psalm could be used by a person accused of wrongdoing, though it is hazardous to attempt to infer the process of a trial from the poetry. The psalm is placed after Ps. 16 because of verbal links: see (e.g.) v. 3 (cf. 16:7, night); v. 4 (cf. 16:11, way); v. 4 (cf. 16:1, watch); v. 5 (cf. 16:5, hold on to); v. 5 (cf. 16:8, falter); v. 6 (cf. 16:1, *ʾēl*); v. 7 (cf. 16:1, rely); v. 7 (cf. 16:10, committed/commitment); v. 8 (cf. 16:1, watch over me); v. 14 (cf. 16:5, share); v. 15 (cf. 16:11, abundance/replete). The two psalms thus represent overlapping reactions to overlapping circumstances. Psalm 17 concerns personal attack rather than the challenge to stay faithful to Yhwh, and implies more sense of pressure.

> Plea. David's.

Heading. See glossary and introduction (pp. 25–30). The title "plea" (cf. v. 1) is also applied to Pss. 86; 90; 102; and 142 (also Hab. 3), though they are no more *pleas or prayers than many other psalms (cf. Ps. 72:20).

17:1–2. So the psalm begins with appeals for Yhwh to hear and respond, appeals based on who Yhwh is and who the suppliant is.

> ¹Do listen in faithfulness, Yhwh;
>   do attend to my voice.
> Do give ear to my plea
>   from lips without deceit.

The characteristic opening plea for Yhwh to give attention is expressed in three parallel imperatives, all made slightly more deferential or appealing by their *-â* ending, occupying a pair of lines (3-2 and 2-3) in *abb'a'* order. The middle two, short cola are exactly parallel and simply make appeal to Yhwh, while the two outside, longer cola both offer grounds for this appeal. In the first, the basis for the appeal is not the suppliant's faithfulness but Yhwh's (cf. 65:5 [6]; *ṣĕdāqâ* in 31:1 [2]; 71:2; 143:1; and cf. Sym and Th, "Lord of my righteousness").[2] The object of the imperatives is then the suppliant's voice, suggesting the sound of the prayer (*resounding), and the suppliant's *plea, suggesting its content. Grounds in terms of the suppliant's person do come in the last colon, complementing the first. No doubt the suppliant might assert that there is no untruthfulness in the actual prayer, with its declaration of reliance on Yhwh and its account of the enemies, but usually "deceit" refers to untruthfulness in words designed to deceive other people (e.g., 5:6 [7];

---

2. Cf. Theodoret, *Psalms*, 1:119. EVV follow Jerome in taking *ṣedeq* (faithfulness) as the object of the verb but then have to paraphrase, e.g., as "a righteous plea," and there are no parallels for this usage. On the other hand, there are instances of the adverbial use of the noun (9:4 [5]; Jer. 11:20; Prov. 31:9).

10:7; 34:13 [14]; though 24:4 may be an exception). The suppliant claims a truthfulness in relation to other people that contrasts with that of (some) other people's words (v. 10).

> ²My decision must come from your presence;
>   your eyes must see what is righteous.

Verse 2 then moves from polite imperatives to even more polite jussives, to take the plea further. The quasi-judicial content of the appeal is developed in the talk in terms of a *decision that needs to issue from the presence (*face) of the one who presides over the heavenly court. As the outside cola in v. 1 undergird its claim, the second colon in v. 2 supports the first colon with a further claim to integrity such as is intrinsic to any expectation that Yhwh will hear one's pleas. The suppliant needs Yhwh not only to listen there but also to look here, so as to be able to confirm that this plea comes from a person of righteousness, or straightness (*mêšārîm*), and therefore must be granted.³

17:3–5. Developing v. 2, the claim to integrity now comes into exclusive focus. The psalms commonly assume that a person who prays needs to be able to say they are doing so from a life lived God's way (cf. 1 John 3:18–22).⁴ In psalms such as this, there is a particular reason for the claim to integrity: it is this integrity that is under question, and this questioning is then the basis for people's attacks.

> ³Did you try my heart, visit by night,
>   test me, you would not find anything;
> I determined my mouth would not pass over ⁴human deeds
>   according to the word of your lips. [MT]
>
> [or, ³Did you try my heart, visit me by night,
>   test me, you would not find my determinations;
> My mouth will not pass over ⁴human deeds
>   according to the word of your lips. (Jerome, Aq, Sym)]

The opening line once more pictures Yhwh not "automatically" knowing what is inside people but able at any point to choose to look inside them and discover what they are thinking (cf. 44:21 [22]). The suppliant acknowledges this and does not fear such an investigation.⁵ But the language of trying, testing, and visiting suggests that the suppliant

---

3. LXX has "*My* eyes must see what is righteous," i.e., see right prevail.
4. Kidner, *Psalms*, 1:87. See the comments on 7:1–5 [2–6] above.
5. LXX and Jerome take v. 3 as stating that Yhwh *has* tested the psalmist, but there is no indication of how that had taken place, and the sequence of four asyndetic verbs, three qatal and one yiqtol, is striking and unusual. With NRSV and NIVI, I rather take them as

invites not merely investigation but also pressure—the kind of trying, testing, and visitation of which Job had a horrific experience (see Job 7:18; 23:10; 34:36). Such testing establishes whether apparent gold is real gold. Night is the time for Yhwh to catch people out in their lack of integrity, because their thinking as they lie in bed reflects and reveals their real attitudes (cf. 4:4; 36:4 [5]).

I take the two cola referring to speech (vv. 3c–4a) as one line, pairing reference to the suppliant's mouth and Yhwh's lips. Otherwise it is enigmatic. I have reckoned that the use of the verb "pass over" (*'ābar*, followed by *lĕ*) follows that in Amos 7:8; 8:2 and refers to a willingness to ignore wrongdoing. Yhwh's word forbids one to hold back one's own word when confronted by the kind of human deeds that v. 4b will refer to. In the context, this refusal to hold back will also imply a commitment not to follow the ways of wrongdoers.[6]

> ⁴ᵇI did watch for the ways of the robber,
> ⁵my steps holding on to your tracks;
> my feet would not falter. [MT]
> [or, ⁴ᵇI did watch for the ways of the robber,
> ⁵my steps holding on to your tracks;
> my feet would not falter. (Jerome, Aq, Sym)]

The point is explicit in these three cola referring to ways/tracks/feet and forming a tricolon that closes off the section. In keeping with Yhwh's word, the suppliant has been wary of the ways of the robber (*pārîṣ*)—etymologically, someone who breaks in or breaks out (e.g., Ezek. 7:22; 18:10). The violence the psalm is concerned with is violence that robs other people of (e.g.) their food or their land (not so much their stereo), presumably the kind of violence the suppliant is accused of. The two parallel cola in v. 5 then put the point positively. The suppliant walks in the tracks that have been made by Yhwh's feet and thus avoids wavering in this walk and wandering into those other ways.

17:6–9. The psalm moves from the declaration of faithfulness to a second plea, which initially reprises that in vv. 1–2.

> ⁶I myself call on you, for you answer me, God;
> extend your ear to me, listen to my word.

---

a conditional clause (cf. Job 19:4; 23:10—which is also about a hypothetical "trying"). Cf. GKC 159h, though not giving this as an example.

6. We might alternatively render it, "I will not transgress as regards human deeds" (cf. A. Anderson, *Psalms*, 1:149). Similar implications then follow, but there are no parallels for this intransitive usage.

In the first colon, the opening *'ănî* parallels that which opens vv. 4b–5: "I did watch . . . I do call." The former is part of the grounds of appeal in the latter. I have taken the reference to Yhwh's answering as a declaration of ongoing conviction, but one might render it "for you will answer" and take it as a statement applying to this particular circumstance. The two imperatival clauses in the second colon are internally parallel. The further reference to the suppliant's word (*'imrâ*) takes up this motif from vv. 3c–4a. The suppliant can appeal to Yhwh to listen to this word because of the integrity of that other word and on the basis of having listened to Yhwh's own words: Yhwh must thus also listen to the suppliant's.

> [7]Show your wondrous acts of commitment,
>   you who deliver by your right hand those who rely on you,
>   from people who raise themselves.

The suppliant makes a transition to a plea for action and not merely for a hearing. The line comprises six "highly-charged" Hebrew words.[7] "Do a wonder," "commitment," "raise themselves," and "your right hand" parallel Exod. 15:7, 11–13, while "deliver" is also a word with Red Sea resonance (14:30; and cf. "deliverer" in Isa. 63:8). The suppliant prays as an individual whose position in relation to Israel is imperiled by people's attacks and who needs Yhwh to act as Yhwh had acted for Israel, needs to be treated as a member of Israel. The psalm asks that Israel's story become the suppliant's story, asks for a personal exodus deliverance as someone who *relies on Yhwh.[8]

> [8]Watch over me as the apple of your eye;
>   may you hide me in the shade of your wings

The plea for action continues in the two parallel urgings in v. 8. Both also continue the plea for a personal reprise of Yhwh's acts at the beginning of Israel's story (cf. Deut. 32:10–11).[9] Both comprise an imperative with a first-person suffix and a prepositional phrase that utilizes a common figure. The simile in the first takes up from the idea that in the eye one can see a tiny image of oneself (cf. Prov. 7:2). The metaphor in the second again suggests that the psalm is aware of the idea of taking refuge that lies behind that of *relying.

> [9]From the face of the faithless who have assaulted me,
>   my enemies who surround me with longing.

---

7. Cf. Kidner, *Psalms*, 1:87.
8. Cf. Craigie, *Psalms 1–50*, 163.
9. Ibid.

Verse 9 then continues syntactically from v. 8 with two further parallel cola. This time both begin with a prepositional phrase (the preposition carrying over from the first colon to the second), and both go on to a relative clause (the relative carrying on from the first to the second). Face and longing, or appetite (*nepeš*), also stand in parallelism, the former suggesting a hostile look, the latter a desire for the person and the person's possessions (for the use of *nepeš*, cf. 27:12; 35:25; 41:2 [3]; 107:9).[10]

17:10–12. As the claim to integrity follows from the first plea, so this notably brief lament follows from the second plea, expanding on v. 9.

> [10]They have closed their midriff;
> with their mouth they have spoken grandiosely.

Initially the lament also takes up the earlier talk about the suppliant's use of the mouth and about the inner being (e.g., vv. 3–4a). There is a contrast between the way the suppliant and the enemies use their inner being and mouth. The midriff (*ḥēleb*, lit., "fat") suggests the part of the body where the heart is located. Closing the midriff implies being unwilling to rethink their attitudes and their lives. The parallel complaint is that they also give full rein to their mouths to declare ambitious plans for causing trouble to the suppliant.

> [11]Our tracks—now they have surrounded me/us [K/Q];
> their eyes they set to extend over the land.

Verse 11 in turn first picks up the subsequent talk in vv. 4b–5 about a commitment regarding ways, tracks, and feet. These tracks are imperiled. The parallel colon speaks about the attackers' eyes, taking up earlier references to Yhwh's eyes (v. 2), which must look at what the attackers' eyes are doing; Yhwh must indeed treat the suppliant as the apple of Yhwh's eye (v. 8). The psalm has asked for the extending (*nāṭâ*, v. 6) of Yhwh's ear, a common request in the Psalms. Here it is unusually set in contrast with some extending of the eyes that is already going on. Extending is often a hostile act, whether of the hand, the arm, or the sword; the extending of the eyes links with the talk of longing in v. 9. It suggests a greedy and ambitious look.

> [12]His appearance is like a lion that is eager to tear,
> like a young lion lying in ambush.

---

10. LXX takes this to refer to the psalmist's *nepeš*, but it is hard to parallel such an allusive expression.

A familiar simile underlines the danger the suppliant senses. The parallel cola offer complementary aspects to the picture, the second going beyond the first. The attacker (the psalm moves to the singular for vv. 12–13) is like a lion with its appetite. Worse, he is like a young lion (*kĕpîr*)—not a whelp but the equivalent of a teenager, full of energy. Further, as well as thinking about how nice it would be to have some meat (v. 12a), this creature is actively (but invisibly) involved in making sure it will soon have some.

17:13–15. Once more the psalm reverts to plea. This time there is no appeal for attention, only an appeal for action. It has the dual aspect characteristic of the plea for action in a psalm, a plea against one's foes and for one's own rescue and restoration. In v. 13 the psalm reverts to the more deferential imperatives with -*â* endings. Verse 14 has one yiqtol request and two jussives. Verse 15 has a first-person yiqtol and a cohortative. Verse 14 is difficult and much emended, with much variation in the ancient versions,[11] but none of the proposed emendations has carried conviction. I have reckoned that one problem is the line division and have redivided the lines as bicola, which issues in more regular lines and makes the repetition (of "from mortals") the resumptive opening of a new line.

> [13]Rise, Yhwh,
>   go to meet him face to face, put him down.
> Rescue my life from the faithless by your sword,
>   [14a]from mortals by your hand, Yhwh,

The first three imperatives form a logical sequence—rise, go, put down. The first ("rise") urges an act equivalent to that of the enemies (v. 7). The second line then comprises parallel cola expressing the object of that sequence. The act of putting them down is the act of rescuing me (*napšî*, *person). "Mortals" is *mětîm*, a word that could simply mean "human beings" but likely suggests their wretchedness (cf. Isa. 41:14)—it will, after all, recall the word for "dead people," *mētîm* (cf. Tg). It hints that it should not be too much for Yhwh to rescue me from them.

> [14b]From mortals—in their lifetime will you fill their belly
>   with their share in life, with what you have stored up.
> Their children are to be replete,
>   they are to leave what they have left to their offspring.

---

11. See (e.g.) Jacob Leveen, "The Textual Problems of Psalm xvii," *VT* 11 (1961): 48–54; J. van der Ploeg, "Le psaume xvii et ses problèmes," in *Kāp hê: 1940–1965*, ed. P. A. H. de Boer et al., OtSt 14 (Leiden: Brill, 1965), 273–95.

Two lines go on to itemize in frightening terms the action against the enemies that the suppliant longs for, perhaps including the plea that the human beings from whom the suppliant looks for rescue should die an early death, the fate they seek to impose on the suppliant. The effect of the garbled phrases in the first line as we have it conveys the suppliant's incoherent spluttering, anxious fear, and bitter resentment. NIVI makes a move within the verse to positive hopes for people the suppliant identifies with, but there is no overt indication of such a move before v. 15, and the language rather parallels other passages that refer to Yhwh's bringing on people the punishment "stored up" for them (see esp. Job 21:17–19).[12] Reference to someone's "share" sometimes alludes to their deserved fate (20:29; 27:13; Isa. 17:14).[13]

Verse 14d–e comprises a coherent but chillingly understated continuation of the plea against the enemies in the form of a request that their children share in their fate—as children do, and as the Decalogue thus warns. The plea recognizes the way a family or community forms a whole, so that merely disposing of an oppressive individual does not solve the problem of oppression (cf. Ps. 109). Further, as usual, the psalm thus allows for the expression of the violent feelings and desires that occupy the human heart under pressure rather than declaring that they should not be expressed because they should not be there. Again the passage compares with Job 21:17–19, where Job urges God to impose punishment on the wicked themselves and not to delay it so that only their children experience it.

> [15]I myself will see your face in faithfulness;
> when I wake, may I be replete with your form.

The first verb is a straightforward yiqtol, which might suggest yet another transition from plea like those after vv. 1–2 and 6–9, this time to a statement of confidence and hope for the future. But the reference to Yhwh's faithfulness means the psalm is closing as it began (v. 1), and that reference stood within a plea. The parallel colon links more immediately with what precedes in vv. 13–14 in its talk of being replete, and the cohortative form of the verb "May I be replete" (*'eśběʻâ*)[14] makes explicit that v. 15 is a plea, the positive counterpart to the previous two lines in v. 14. At the moment, the suppliant is imperiled by the look on his enemies' face, and he wants instead to see Yhwh's face in its active faithfulness. Whereas modern readers are scandalized by v. 14, LXX senses something scandalous about this talk of seeing Yhwh's face (con-

---

12. Dario Gualandi, "Salmo 17(16), 13–14," *Bib* 37 (1956): 199–208, see 205.
13. See Briggs, *Psalms*, 1:136.
14. Cf. *TTH* 49β; JM 114c.

trast, e.g., Exod. 33:20) and renders: "But I will appear in righteousness before your face; I will be satisfied when your glory appears." But the talk of seeing Yhwh's face has a different significance from that assumed by LXX. Yhwh's *face looking our way is what brings vindication and deliverance. In the context of the psalm, that is the point about seeing this face. It is thus hardly the case that the assurance of seeing Yhwh's face makes the answer to the prayer in vv. 1–2 unnecessary.[15] Seeing Yhwh's face brings the answer.

Likewise, LXX has reason to be astonished at the idea of seeing Yhwh's form (*těmûnâ*). At Sinai Israel saw no form, while Yhwh's form was uniquely visible to Moses as one who was more than a prophet (Num. 12:8; Deut. 4:12, 15). But in this context, the reference to Yhwh's form follows naturally from the psalm's references to Yhwh's eyes, lips, ears, right hand, hand, and face. If Yhwh has all these, it is logical enough to envisage Yhwh's having a form. And having appealed for each of these body parts to be utilized in deliverance, it is logical enough finally to ask for the involvement of Yhwh's whole person to this end. The suppliant will indeed be replete on seeing the involvement of Yhwh's whole person in this way. Having invited Yhwh's testing by night (v. 3), the suppliant is sure of surviving that testing and sure of waking in the morning before Yhwh's face, not cast out by Yhwh. "Waking" can suggest being resuscitated or resurrected (Isa. 26:19; Dan. 12:2), but such a reference hardly makes sense here. The appeal for Yhwh to be involved in rescuing in this life would be undermined by allusion to fulfillment in an afterlife. The psalm's affirmation is that believers do not have to wait until the next life to see God act. God acts now.

Theological Implications

The effect of the running references to different parts of the body in Ps. 17 is to underline the concrete personal reality of suppliant, enemies, and Yhwh, and the nature of Yhwh's real involvement with humanity. Human lives are physical lives, not just spiritual ones, and the troubles that come to them affect the body and not just the spirit and psyche. Likewise, Yhwh is concerned not just about spiritual or psychological matters but also about the physical. Further, Yhwh can express that concern as a result of having analogous features to those of human beings (or rather, Yhwh has the originals, and human beings have equivalents through being made in God's image). Yhwh has a form. Unlike gods who have only the appearance of bodily features (e.g., Ps. 115), Yhwh has

---

15. So McCann, "Psalms," 742.

eyes that can actually see human beings, lips that can speak to them, ears that can hear them, a right hand that can protect them, a hand that can act for them, and a face to shine on them. Yhwh is as real a person as the suppliant and as the enemies. That is the basis for the suppliant's encouragement when under pressure.

Psalm 18
God's Acts and David's Acts

Translation

The leader's. Yhwh's servant's. David's, who spoke the words of this song to Yhwh on the day Yhwh rescued him from the clutch[a] of all his enemies and from the hand of Saul. He said:

¹I dedicate myself to you, Yhwh, my strength;[b]
  ²Yhwh is my cliff, my fastness, the one who enables me to escape.[c]
My God[d] is my crag on which I take refuge,
  my shield, my peak[e] that delivers, my haven.[f]

³As one to be praised,[g] I called on Yhwh,
  and I was delivered from my enemies.

a. 2 Sam. 22:1 repeats "clutch" (*kap*).
b. 2 Sam. 22:2 lacks this colon.
c. 2 Sam. 22:2 has *lî* (for me).
d. *ʾĒlî*; 2 Sam. 22:3 has *ʾĕlōhê*.
e. *Qeren* usually means "horn," but there are no parallels for describing Yhwh as a horn. The word denotes a hill in Isa. 5:1, and the context suggests that this will be the meaning here (cf. *NIDOTTE*). "The horn of my salvation" for *qeren-yišʿî* (EVV) also does not make clear the role of the construct.
f. 2 Sam. 22:3 also has "my refuge, my deliverer, you who deliver me from violence."
g. Syr links with v. 2. With "I will dedicate myself to you" it then provides an inclusion around vv. 1–2.

⁴Death's ropes[h] have encompassed me,
    Belial's torrents overwhelmed me.
⁵Sheol's ropes have encircled me,
    death's snares have confronted me.
⁶In my trouble I called on Yhwh,
    to my God I cried for help.[i]
From his palace he heard my voice;
    my cry for help before him came to his ears.[j]

⁷And the earth has shaken and rocked;
    the mountains'[k] foundations quaked.
They have shaken about because he has raged;
    ⁸smoke has gone up in his anger.
Fire from his mouth consumed;
    coals have blazed from him.
⁹He has spread the heavens and come down,
    thundercloud beneath his feet.
¹⁰He has mounted a cherub and flown,
    swooped[l] on the winds' wings.
¹¹He has made darkness his screen,[m]
    [made] his shelter around him
    rain cloud,[n] masses of mist.
¹²Out of the brightness before him, there have come through his masses
    hail and burning coals.[o]
¹³Yhwh has thundered in the heavens;
    the Most High gave forth his voice.
Hail and burning coals[p]—
    ¹⁴he has sent his arrows and scattered them;
    he has shot[q] lightnings and driven them.
¹⁵Streams of water[r] have appeared;
    the world's foundations have come into sight

h. 2 Sam. 22:5 begins *kî*, "for," and has *mišběrê*, "breakers," for "ropes." With Jerome I take *heblê* as a form of *hebel*, from *ḥābal* IV (in *DCH*'s enumeration). LXX and Tg take it as a form of *ḥēbel*, "pain," from *ḥābal* III, implying that when the word recurs in v. 5, the psalm is using a homonym.

i. 2 Sam. 22:7 repeats "called" in place of "cried for help."

j. 2 Sam. 22:7 lacks "before him came."

k. 2 Sam. 22:8 has "the heavens'."

l. 2 Sam. 22:11 has "appeared" (*wayyērā'* for *wayyēde'*).

m. 2 Sam. 22:12 lacks "his screen."

n. 2 Sam. 22:12 has "mass" (?) (*ḥašrat*) for "cloud" (*ḥeškat*, lit., "darkness").

o. 2 Sam. 22:13 lacks "his masses" and "hail and" and has "blazed" (*bāʿărû*) for "come through" (*ʿābĕrû*).

p. 2 Sam. 22:14 (and LXX) lacks this colon.

q. LXX takes *rāb* as from *rābab* I, "be many." I take it as from *rābab* II. 2 Sam. 22:15 lacks this verb.

r. 2 Sam. 22:16 has "sea" (*yām*) for "water" (*mayim*).

> At your roar, Yhwh,
>> at the blast of the breath of your anger.
>
> ¹⁶He reached from on high, took me,
>> drew me out of great waters.
> ¹⁷He rescued me from my strong enemy
>> and from people who were against me, because they were too strong for me.
> ¹⁸They confronted me on the day of my calamity,
>> but Yhwh has become my support.
> ¹⁹He has brought me out into roominess;
>> he has saved me because he has delighted in me.
> ²⁰Yhwh has dealt with me in accordance with my faithfulness;
>> in accordance with the purity of my hands he has recompensed me.
> ²¹For I have kept Yhwh's ways
>> and not been faithless in leaving my God.
> ²²For all his decisions have been before me,
>> and I have not put away his statutes from me.ˢ
> ²³I have been a person of integrity with him
>> and have kept myself from waywardness I might have done.ᵗ
> ²⁴So Yhwh has recompensed me according to my faithfulness,
>> according to the purity of my handsᵘ before his eyes.
> ²⁵With the committed you showed commitment,
>> with the personᵛ of integrity you showed integrity,
> ²⁶With the pure you showed purity,
>> but with the crooked you showed refractoriness.
> ²⁷For you are one who delivered a weak people,
>> but lofty eyes you humbled.ʷ
> ²⁸For it is you who kept my lamp alight, Yhwh;
>> my God illumined my darkness.
> ²⁹For through you I rushed a barricade;
>> through my God I leaped a wall.
>
> ³⁰God—his way has integrity,
>> Yhwh's word is proven;
>> he is a shield for all who take refuge in him.
> ³¹For who is Godˣ except Yhwh,
>> and who is a crag apart from our God?—

s. 2 Sam. 22:23 has "I have not turned away from his statutes."

t. Lit., "my wrongdoing." First-person suffixes are very prominent in vv. 16–29; the reference to "my [possible] wrongdoing" makes for a particular contrast with "my [actual] faithfulness" in v. 20, which is about to be repeated in the next colon (v. 24a).

u. 2 Sam. 22:25 has "according to my purity."

v. 2 Sam. 22:26 has *gibbôr*, "warrior," for *gĕbar* (the Aramaic form for *geber*).

w. 2 Sam. 22:28 has "You lowered your eyes on the lofty."

x. *'Ĕlôah*; 2 Sam. 22:32 has *'ēl*.

³²The God who has girded me^y with strength
    and made^z my way whole,
³³Who has made my legs like deer
    and stood me on my high places,^a
³⁴Who has trained my hands for battle
    so that my arms could bend^b a bronze bow.

³⁵You have given me your shield that delivered me;
    your right hand sustained me,^c
    your response^d made me great.
³⁶You have given my steps room beneath me;
    my ankles have not given way.
³⁷I pursued my attackers and overtook them;^e
    I did not turn before eliminating them.
³⁸I struck them down and they were not able to rise;^f
    they fell beneath my feet.
³⁹You have girded me with strength for battle,
    brought down my adversaries under my feet.
⁴⁰You have made my enemies turn tail for me,
    and I have wiped out the people who were against me.
⁴¹They have cried for help^g but there was no one to deliver—
    [cried] about Yhwh, but no one has responded to them.
⁴²I have ground them like dust on the wind,^h
    like mud in the streets—I made them empty.^i
⁴³You rescued me from the attacks of people;^j
    you made^k me head of nations.
People I did not know served me;
    ⁴⁴on hearing with their ear, they obeyed me.

y. 2 Sam. 22:33 has *mā'ûzzî*, "my refuge," for *hamĕ'azzĕrēnî*, "who has girded me."

z. 2 Sam. 22:33 has the difficult reading *wayyattēr* for *wayyittēn*.

a. Cf. the "myself" in v. 23; first-person suffixes run through vv. 32–34, and this one adds to the effect.

b. On the f. verb, see GKC 145k.

c. Or, "with your right hand you sustained me." 2 Sam. 22:36 does not have this colon.

d. LXX ("discipline") and Jerome ("gentleness") assume that *'ănāwâ* links with *'ānâ* III, but LXX's translation makes poor sense, and Jerome gives the word a unique meaning. Sym points to its being a homonym linked with *'ānâ* I, which comes in v. 41 along with contrasting further reference to Yhwh's deliverance (cf. v. 35a).

e. 2 Sam. 22:38 has *wā'ašmîdēm*, "and destroyed them."

f. 2 Sam. 22:39 has "I have consumed them and struck them down and they did not rise."

g. 2 Sam. 22:42 has "They have looked."

h. 2 Sam. 22:43 has "like the dust of the earth."

i. 2 Sam. 22:43 has "I stamped them, crushed them."

j. 2 Sam. 22:44 has "my people," suggesting reference to the internal conflicts after Saul's death and/or to Absalom's rebellion.

k. 2 Sam. 22:44 has "kept."

Foreigners withered[l] before me;
⁴⁵foreigners wilted
and came trembling[m] out of their strongholds.[n]

⁴⁶Yhwh is alive—my crag is to be worshipped;[o]
God[p] my deliverance shall be on high,
⁴⁷God who has given me complete requital[q]
and subdued[r] peoples under me,
⁴⁸Who has saved me[s] from my enemies;
yes, you put me on high above my adversaries,
you rescued me from a violent man.

⁴⁹For this I will confess you among the nations, Yhwh,
and make music to your name,
⁵⁰One who gives great acts of deliverance[t] to his king,
keeps commitment to his anointed,
to David and his offspring forever.

Interpretation

This gargantuan testimony to the way Yhwh has delivered from attack and turned danger into triumph, peril into victory, is much the longest of such testimony or thanksgiving psalms. Indeed, of all the Psalms, only 78 and 119 are longer, though for all its length "its energy [is] unflagging."[1] I take it as resolutely backward-looking, though it incorporates many yiqtols, which one would usually take to refer to what will, might, or does happen rather than to what has happened. But EVV recognize that a number of the yiqtols in the psalm (e.g., v. 6) must refer to past

l. EVV "cower"; but the next colon confirms John H. Eaton's suggestion regarding the nuance of *kāḥaš* ("Some Questions of Philology and Exegesis in the Psalms," *JTS*, n.s., 19 [1968]: 603–9 [esp. 603–4]; and cf. BDB).

m. 2 Sam. 22:46 has *wĕyaḥgĕrû*, "limped," for *wĕyaḥrĕgû*.

n. *HALOT* translates *misgĕrôtêhem* as "prisons," which makes good sense etymologically but not contextually here or in Mic. 7:17, its other occurrence with this general meaning.

o. GKC 116e says that the qal passive ptc. cannot have gerundive force, but this seems to be required in 137:8 (JM 121i also cites 111:2), and it is a natural understanding for *bārûk* here and elsewhere (cf. BDB), where the meaning seems similar to the pual in v. 3.

p. 2 Sam. 22:47 has "God the rock."

q. "Complete requital" represents the pl. *nĕqāmôt*.

r. 2 Sam. 22:48 has another ptc., *ûmôrîd*, instead of the unusual *wayyadbēr* (a different root from *dbr*, "speak"—see *HALOT*, *DCH*).

s. 2 Sam. 22:49 has "who brought me out" and lacks the subsequent "Yes."

t. 2 Sam. 22:51 has "a tower of deliverance."

1. Kidner, *Psalms*, 1:90.

events[2] and thus use an English aorist or perfect to translate them. On the other hand there are other yiqtols that require a present or future translation (e.g., vv. 1–2). There is then some uncertainty about some of the yiqtols, and some that EVV translate as present I have taken to refer to the past in light of the general narrative nature of the psalm (e.g., vv. 3, 25–30). To make the alternation of tenses clear in the translation, I have used an English perfect tense for qatals and wayyiqtols, and a simple past tense for those yiqtols that I take to refer to the past.

Verses 1–2 and 49–50 form the framework for the testimony, within which the main body comprises a first-person quasi-narrative. Broadly, it relates how mortal danger assailed the speaker and how the speaker prayed (vv. 3–6), how Yhwh responded (v. 7–15) and delivered (vv. 16–29), and how the situation thus reversed (vv. 30–48). Admittedly, the testimony is slightly less tidy than that, since deliverance is anticipated at the beginning (v. 3b), and ongoing truths about Yhwh are affirmed in the midst (vv. 30–31, 46). The psalm's rhythm is much more consistent than usual; many lines are 3-3. With this psalm it is thus particularly tempting to rework MT's understanding of the rhythm by adding or removing a *maqqēph*, where MT understands lines as (e.g.) 4-3 or 2-3.

The antithesis of heights and depths runs through the psalm.[3] Yhwh is a crag, fastness, and high haven (v. 2). Yhwh came down from the heavens to the earth, acting in such a way as to disturb the lowest depths (vv. 7–15). Yhwh reached down and drew me up (v. 16). The enemies are people that rose up (vv. 39, 48), but Yhwh humbled lofty eyes (v. 27), and they will not be able to rise up again (v. 38). Yhwh stood me on high places (v. 33). I struck down and Yhwh struck down my enemies beneath my feet (vv. 38–39, 47). Yhwh made me head of nations/on high above my adversaries (vv. 43, 48). Nine times the psalm talks about enemies and adversaries and attackers, eleven times about Yhwh's delivering or rescuing or saving.[4] One party thus goes from height to depths, the other from depths to height. And the key to these moves is God, who is described by means of a number of metaphors (see esp. vv. 1–2) and a number of names or literal descriptors. God is *Yhwh* (e.g., vv. 1, 2), *hā'ēl* (v. 30, 32, 47), *'ēl* (v. 2, with personal suffix), *'ĕlōhîm* (v. 46; also vv. 6, 21, 28, 29, 31, with personal suffix), *'elyôn* (v. 13), *'ĕlôah* (v. 31).[5] The main

---

2. See the discussion in (e.g.) DG 62; *IBHS* 31.1.1.

3. Cf. Donald K. Berry, *The Psalms and Their Readers*, JSOTSup 153 (Sheffield: Sheffield Academic Press, 1993), 98–99.

4. Cf. Schaefer, *Psalms*, 41, though his computation is different.

5. David Noel Freedman studies the terms for God in the psalm as pointers to a tenth-century date, in "Divine Names and Titles in Early Hebrew Poetry," in *Magnalia Dei: The Mighty Acts of God* (G. Ernest Wright Memorial), ed. Frank Moore Cross et al. (Garden City, NY: Doubleday, 1976), 55–102.

point the psalm makes by means of these variations is that the speaker's God (Yhwh, my God) is the powerful, actual, only real God.

The speaker has been delivered from peril brought by human enemies, and for most of the psalm this could imply the kind of intra-community conflict presupposed by many preceding psalms. The opening might be the praise of an ordinary individual. But vv. 30–48 imply a military leader, and vv. 49–50 refer to Yhwh's commitment to David, which suggests that the psalm is one for the king to pray after a deliverance and victory. The specific reference to David does not actually require that David be the person envisaged as praying the psalm, but it points in that direction, as does the content of the psalm. And the heading fits with that, as does the appearance of a variant on the psalm in 2 Sam. 22 in the context of a retrospective on David's life.

I have noted differences between these two variants in the notes to the translation (except matters of spelling and small divergences such as the presence of *w* or of suffixes, and the use of different prepositions). They are recensions of a common original, but I do not seek to establish what that original was.[6] It is inappropriate to assimilate the two to each other; there are simply two versions. In some ways, the language of Ps. 18 is less idiosyncratic than that in 2 Sam. 22; it would not be surprising if a version for general use has been accommodated to more regular usage. Psalm 18 also includes some Aramaisms not present in the 2 Samuel version, at least in vv. 1 and 25.[7] The psalm might have been compiled from already existent units.[8] Parallels of phrasing with other passages in the OT may indicate its being alluded to in those other places or may indicate that these are sources other than the David story that the psalmist used, as in v. 30 (Prov. 30:5) and v. 34 (Ps. 144:1). I handle the question of authorship in discussing the psalm's heading.

> The leader's. Yhwh's servant's. David's, who spoke the words of this song to Yhwh on the day Yhwh rescued him from the clutch of all his enemies and from the hand of Saul. He said:

---

6. On their interrelationship, see Frank Moore Cross and David Noel Freedman, "A Royal Song of Thanksgiving," *JBL* 72 (1953): 15–34; Georg Schmuttermayr, *Psalm 18 und 2 Samuel 22* (Munich: Kösel, 1971); Douglas K. Stuart, *Studies in Early Hebrew Meter* (Missoula, MT: Scholars Press, 1976), 171–86; Klaus-Peter Adam, *Der königliche Held* (Neukirchen-Vluyn: Neukirchener Verlag, 2001), 191–203. Adam also offers a hypothesis concerning the psalm's redactional history; cf also Jean-Marie Auwers, "La rédaction du Psaume 18 dans le cadre du premier livre des Psaumes," *Ephemerides theologicae lovanienses* 72 (1996): 23–40.

7. Cf. Briggs, *Psalms*, 1:139. His further examples (*ḥārag*, v. 45; *dābar*, v. 47) are more dubious.

8. So (e.g.) Terrien, *Psalms*, 204.

Heading. See glossary. Yhwh's servant is presumably the king; the title is frequently applied to David (e.g., 78:70; 132:10) but could be applied to other kings (e.g., 2 Chron. 32:16). There is another *lĕ* before "David," so it is more natural to see "Yhwh's servant's" as an independent phrase (against NRSV); cf. the heading to Ps. 36. As is the case with Ps. 7, the form of the subsequent phraseology does not correspond to that of other headings that make links with David's life (e.g., Ps. 51), which involve a *bĕ*-clause ("When he . . ."). In addition, other headings simply make a link with one incident, whereas this heading refers to his deliverance from "all" his enemies as well as to his escape(s) from Saul. This fits the content of the psalm, which refers both to "my enemy" and to "my enemies." The dual context suggested by the heading suggests that we should not seek to limit the reference of the psalm to one moment in David's life. The odd "he said" at the end corresponds to the version in 2 Sam. 22 and may indicate that the main part of the heading comes from there.[9]

There are a number of views on the psalm's origin.

1. The traditional view is that it is David's personal testimony, but there is no direct evidence for it, and general considerations do not point in this direction. Neither the heading nor the reference in 2 Sam. 22 would require that David personally wrote the psalm, any more than the president of the United States writes his own speeches. He needs to affirm them but usually does not draft them. Further, the picture we receive of David from his story is that he was a great killer, a great politician, and something of a womanizer, but a failure in personal relationships. Even though he was also an accomplished musician, this does not look like the personality profile of a great composer of prayers and worship songs. Yet further, although the psalm's nature as a testimony suggests a link with a specific context, and the account of Yhwh's coming in vv. 6b–15 suggests a specific event, the heading with its double reference to Saul and to other enemies suggests more a review of David's leadership as a whole. This also fits with its location in 2 Sam. 22 as David looks back on his life. The general nature of the heading and the location in 2 Samuel makes it artificial to suggest that the heading relates only to an earlier stage in David's life, such as a time before the crisis related in 2 Sam. 11–12. Yet further, the actual account of Yhwh's intervention with its unusual transcendent portrayal of Yhwh's act suggests something larger than life. It seems hyperbolic as a personal description of his deliverance from Saul or the Philistines or Absalom. And given his wickedness, it is hardly proper for David himself to speak of his integrity in such unequivocal terms.

9. So Gunkel, *Psalmen*, 68.

2. A more plausible view is that it was written for David in his lifetime, or perhaps soon afterward, possibly in connection with the writing of an account of David's reign such as appears in 2 Samuel. This fits with the thesis that its language is archaic. It also fits with the tone of the description of David. While David might hardly speak thus of his integrity, other people might properly do so in focusing on the positive aspects to his significance, including his respect for Saul's life and monarchy. In 2 Sam. 22 there might still seem to be massive irony in setting vv. 20–26 on David's lips after the huge moral and personal failures of the time when he was king. But outside 2 Samuel David is regularly described in positive terms; priority is perhaps given to his resolute commitment to Yhwh rather than to other gods, which contrasts with that of his successors.

3. It might have been written for the Davidic king during the preexilic period, perhaps by the music "leader." This view emerges from the general conviction that the main background of the Psalms is the worship of the temple, which suggests that this psalm was written for occasions when the king had won a great victory, or for regular celebrations of Yhwh's commitment to the king. This might fit with the exalted metaphorical description of Yhwh's coming in vv. 7–15 and with the hyperbolic description of the king's victories. The heading would then need to be seen as a later adaptation of the psalm to give it a particular association with David. The weakness of this view is that it depends strongly on that theory about the Psalms' liturgical background for which we have little direct evidence.

4. It might have been written in honor of David in the Persian period. We know from Chronicles that the postexilic community attached great importance both to the figure of David and also to the extraordinary military deliverances and victories of the Davidic kings. Composing a psalm that embodied such experiences on David's part would fit this interest. The psalm's archaic language would then mean that the author had adopted a style in keeping with the subject.

5. It might have been written in the Persian period as an anticipatory testimony for the Messiah. This view emerges from the general consideration that, in the absence of actual kings, the Persian period saw increased emphasis in some circles on the hope of a king to come, and from the conviction that in this context the psalm is part of an "eschatological reading" of the Psalter. Again, the weakness of this view is that it depends strongly on a theory about an eschatological reading of the Psalms that is not explicit in the texts. Within the psalm itself the only indication is its hyperbolic, universalistic, cosmic language and imagery,[10]

---

10. McCann, "Psalms," 746–47; cf. Gerstenberger, *Psalms*, 1:99.

but there is no need for these to imply an eschatological understanding. It seems more natural to associate the psalm with a non-eschatological understanding of David's significance such as appears in Chronicles. We have noted in the introduction that there did develop an eschatological reading of the Psalms, but it involves a reinterpretation of them not worked into the text itself.

Of these five views, 3 and 5 seem most hazardous as statements about the psalm's original significance insofar as they have the least basis in the psalm or in the OT. View 4 seems most plausible, though what views 1, 2, and 4 have in common is more important than where they differ. All assume that the psalm is about David. The psalm is a testimony by David or put on David's lips that honors Yhwh in David's name and also honors David himself. It testifies to Yhwh's involvement in David's life as a whole and reflects the awareness that Yhwh acted in extraordinary and decisive ways in his life, granting him escapes and achievements that are hard to parallel, not for his own sake but also for the sake of Israel, in whose story his reign has a decisive place.[11] But the last verse also indicates that the psalm was open to being claimed by subsequent kings and implies a permanent commitment to David's line on Yhwh's part, justifying both a use by subsequent kings (view 3) and an eschatological reading (view 5). Several times the midrash suggests how the psalm applies to Babylon, Medo-Persia, Greece—and Edom, meaning Rome, the overlord of the present.[12] Whatever its origin, its presence in the Psalter and not merely in 2 Samuel invites such appropriation.

> [1]I dedicate myself to you, Yhwh, my strength;
>   [2]Yhwh is my cliff, my fastness, the one who enables me to escape.
> My God is my crag on which I take refuge,
>   my shield, my peak that delivers, my haven.

18:1–2. The psalm begins with an act of commitment. The first two lines[13] open with a first-person yiqtol verb and invocation of Yhwh, like the testimony in Ps. 30, though the verb (*rāḥam*) raises eyebrows. In the piel it means "have compassion"; the qal appears only here.[14] Psalm 116:1 makes similar use of the verb *'āhēb* (love, dedicate oneself), and

---

11. See Jean-Luc Vesco, "Le Psaume 18, lecture davidique," *RB* 94 (1987): 5–62.
12. E.g., *Midrash on Psalms*, 1:239.
13. Perhaps v. 2a, the only four-word colon, is a conflate text and originally had only three words.
14. Ibn Ezra renders, "Beg compassion from you."

the cognates of *rāḥam* have this meaning.[15] The term does not suggest intimacy so much as commitment.

The opening act of dedication leads into nine descriptions of Yhwh, all having similar implications. They thus pile up affirmation of the point by repetition. Jerome sees the descriptions as a series of noun phrases addressed to Yhwh, but the repetition of "Yhwh" and the subsequent occurrence of "my God" suggests rather that LXX is right in seeing v. 2 as noun clauses.

All but the first are concrete expressions, which makes one wonder whether the first, the hapax *ḥēzeq*, rather means "strong one." Strength regularly implies the ability to defend, rescue, or defeat (e.g., 35:10), but it is not a common idea in the Psalms. It is especially associated with Yhwh's action in bringing the people out of Egypt, though usually with reference to Yhwh's strong hand (e.g., 136:12; Exod. 6:1; 13:3, 9, 14, 16). So the suppliant is hinting at Yhwh's proving to be the exodus God. There will be other such hints.

The concrete imagery of cliff, fastness, *crag, place of refuge, peak, and *haven in v. 2 is much more characteristic of the Psalms (e.g., 31:3–4 [4–5]; 42:9 [10]; 61:2–3 [3–4]; 62:2 [3]; 71:2–3; 91:2, 4, 9; 94:22; 144:1–2). All the terms refer to places of natural security, not to humanly made strongholds or fortresses. They are a remote and inaccessible place in the mountains or the wilderness such as provide safe refuge for a bird or a small creature or a man on the run (104:18; 1 Sam. 24:2, 22 [3, 23]; Job 39:28). They are thus places of "deliverance" that "enable me to escape" (*pālaṭ* piel). A number of the terms occur elsewhere in contexts that do not draw attention to their original significance. "My cliff" can be an isolated title for Yhwh, "enable me to escape" can become simply "deliver," and "take refuge" can become simply "rely." But here, in this combination, the images keep their concrete connotations. David's seeking refuge from Saul and finding deliverance in mountain wilderness areas (1 Sam. 22–24) is one resonance of the language. The implication would be that while at one level it was natural fastnesses and rocks that enabled David to escape, at another level Yhwh was the only one who did so. Or conversely, while it was Yhwh who enabled David to escape from Saul, Yhwh did so via natural resources that mirrored Yhwh's own nature.

The term "my shield" belongs in a different symbol system but has similar implications (and thus also appears in 144:1–2). A shield protects from attack as a rock does, and in real-life terms the image is nearer

---

15. See the comments in *Midrash on Psalms*, 1:235, on Aramaic usage, including Lev. 19:18 Tg; *TLOT*; Georg Schmuttermayr, "*Rḥm*—eine lexikalische Studie," *Bib* 51 (1970): 499–525.

literal reality for the speaker (cf. vv. 30, 35). A fighter knows the literal indispensability of a shield if he is to survive.

18:3–6. This typical stanza for a thanksgiving psalm summarizes the life-threatening peril that assailed the speaker, the plea this person uttered, and the way Yhwh responded in hearing and acting. It is also typical that the psalm first offers a summary of the whole "story," then goes back to the beginning to give us the details. In this the effect is to make vv. 3 and 6 the envelope around vv. 4–5. Verse 3 summarizes the cry and the deliverance, vv. 4–5 detail the danger the supplicant was in, and v. 6 gives a longer account of the cry and of Yhwh's response. In keeping with the fact that this is not the end of the psalm, however, the second account in v. 6 describes only Yhwh's hearing and stops short of describing Yhwh's deed. Appropriately, then, vv. 3–6 do not quite achieve closure.

> ³As one to be praised, I called on Yhwh,
>   and I was delivered from my enemies.

LXX understandably takes the yiqtol verbs in v. 3 as futures, continuing vv. 1–2. But in a testimony, one does not expect reference to an expectation of future deliverance before we have heard about the past deliverance (e.g., Pss. 30; 34; 116). In the next verse, moreover, the yiqtol verb has past reference, and the yiqtol verb in v. 3a recurs in v. 6 with past meaning; many subsequent yiqtols in the psalm have past meaning. All this suggests that while v. 3 might be a generalizing statement (cf. NIVI), more likely it is the beginning of the psalm's testimony about the past (cf. NJPS). Indeed, with its reference to praise, prayer, and deliverance, it summarizes vv. 4–50.

> ⁴Death's ropes have encompassed me,
>   Belial's torrents overwhelmed me.
> ⁵Sheol's ropes have encircled me,
>   death's snares have confronted me.

Verses 4–5 then recall the trouble from which the speaker was rescued. Deep trouble it evidently was, described in four overlapping ways: "I was one, two, three, four times lost."[16] Psalms 6; 9; and 16 have spoken of Sheol as a future threat. Here, vv. 4–5 speak of Sheol as having already overwhelmed in the present. Instead of its gates being unable to hold on to people who belong to God (Matt. 16:18), it was extending its grip beyond its gates and putting its clutches around someone still alive. To put it prosaically, the speaker was in mortal danger and there seemed no way of escape. The impossibility of escape is suggested by the repeti-

---

16. Berry, *The Psalms and Their Readers*, 113.

tious way the psalm describes the situation in the parallel cola, in terms of being surrounded by death's pains, overwhelmed by Belial's torrents, encircled by Sheol's ropes, and confronted by death's snares. The two verses interweave verbs and construct phrases in *abb'a'*, *baa'b'* order.

The talk of Belial's torrents makes the point in a particularly pressing way. Death is not merely a threatening or confronting future reality, and its potential victim is not merely standing before a sea that threatens to overwhelm. The sea is already overwhelming, its victim already drowning and gasping for air. Some might understand *bĕlîyaʿal* as combining *bĕlî* and *yaʿal*, so that it means "worthlessness" (cf. BDB); this fits most OT occurrences of the word (e.g., 101:3). But the picture of Belial's overwhelming torrents carries other resonances. Others might see the word as combining *bĕlî* and *ʿālâ* and thus as suggesting "without ascending"; Sheol is the place from which no one comes up. They could also link the word with *bālaʿ*, "swallow," for death's torrents do swallow people (e.g., 69:15 [16]). This would also connect with the personification of Death in Canaanite theology and the way Belial becomes a name for Satan.[17]

> ⁶In my trouble I called on Yhwh,
> > to my God I cried for help.
> From his palace he heard my voice;
> > my cry for help before him came to his ears.

"Trouble" that indeed is. Verse 6a duly repeats "I called on Yhwh" and parallels it with the reminder that the one addressed is "my God" and with the less common verb *cry for help.

Verse 6b[18] describes Yhwh's response in familiar terms and in *abcc'b'a'* order. As v. 6a forms a lengthier equivalent to v. 3a, this line forms a lengthier equivalent to v. 3b. In the heavenly *palace Yhwh heard the suppliant's voice (cf. 6:8–9 [9–10]); the *cry for help (the noun related to the verb in v. 6a) reached Yhwh's ears (cf. 17:6). The language also recalls the exodus, when Yhwh heard Israel's cry for help and this cry came to Yhwh (Exod. 2:23–24; 3:7). Psalm 17 asked for a personal exodus experience; Ps. 18 testifies to one.

18:7–15. Verses 7–15 take Yhwh's response further with distinctive extravagance, though its terms are also conventional (e.g., 144:5–6); MT treats vv. 7–8 as two tricola, but they form three satisfactory bicola. Verse 7 speaks in a way that recalls an earthquake, and earthquakes were known in Palestine (cf. Amos 1:1; Zech. 14:5), but they were

---

17. See *DDD*; *TDOT*.

18. If the line was originally 3-3, "before him/to his ears" may be a composite reading.

rare, and few people would ever experience one; they did not wait anxiously for "the big one." The imagery more likely suggests the shuddering of the ground in a storm, or the mudslides or landslides that can result from a storm. Similarly, v. 8 could be describing a volcano, but volcanoes were not known in this region, and similar language applies to lightning in vv. 12–14. Other terms in vv. 9–15 also suggest a thunderstorm.

There might be several reasons why the psalm should describe the deliverance and victory in terms of such physical phenomena. Perhaps there was a victory that involved extraordinary weather phenomena. But elsewhere in the Scriptures the point of such phenomena is to express Yhwh's involvement in events (e.g., Exod. 14–15; 19; Judg. 4–5), and this language thus portrays David as a figure in whose life Yhwh acted as Yhwh had for Moses, at the Red Sea and at Sinai. The language follows tradition rather than having a background in a liturgical event (a "theophany," whatever that would mean).[19] It signifies that the psalmist saw Yhwh's activity in this deliverance and victory.

The story of Deborah and Barak's victory (Judg. 4–5) is particularly instructive. There the prose account celebrates Yhwh's involvement in events but pictures Yhwh working via human processes, while the poetic account speaks more figuratively about the stars fighting from heaven and a torrent sweeping Sisera's forces away. Here, then, talk of land shuddering, cloud, mist, lightning, and thunder are symbolic ways of referring to the fact that the deliverance and victory described in vv. 16–48 involved extraordinary supernatural action on Yhwh's part. The experience of a thunderstorm with its awesome and frightening power provides a way of describing Yhwh's coming, perhaps mediated by the way earlier Middle Eastern thinking had already used the thunderstorm as a way of picturing the coming of a deity such as Baal.[20] (OT thinking would assume that Yhwh and not Baal is the *real* deity who rides on the clouds, though the context does not suggest that the description is intentionally polemical here.) At the same time, there is a marked objectivity about the account, in the sense that whereas vv. 1–6 were full of first-person verbs and suffixes, in vv. 7–15 there is not one of either.[21]

Verses 7–15 describe this supernatural action of Yhwh several times, working not in linear fashion but by repeating different versions of the

---

19. Links with Mesopotamian forms of expression may also point in this direction (so Frank Schnutenhaus, "Das Kommen und Erscheinen Gottes im Alten Testament," *ZAW* 76 [1964]: 1–22).

20. So Keel, *Symbolism of the Biblical World*, 210–17; Craigie, *Psalms 1–50*, 173–74.

21. Cf. J. Kenneth Kuntz, "Psalm 18," *JSOT* 26 (1983): 3–31, see 10.

same fundamental drama. The elements in the picture appear in the following configuration:

land shuddering	7			15a
Yhwh's anger	7b–8a			15b
lightning	8		12	13b–14
Yhwh's descent		9a, 10		
cloud shield		9b, 11		
thunder			13a	15b

The order in which the elements appear is hardly the order in which they might occur (if they can be put in such an order). The verses describe Yhwh's coming, but like Ezekiel's throne vision, they never quite describe Yhwh; like that vision, the more they go on, the more unimaginable Yhwh becomes.

> ⁷ᵃ⁻ᵇAnd the earth has shaken and rocked;
> the mountains' foundations quaked.

The events were indeed earthshaking. "Shake," "rock," and "quake" are very similar words (*gāʿaš, rāʿaš, rāgaz*)—the first a rare verb, the second and third more familiar ones. The qatal and yiqtol verbs in the two cola also complement each other. To say that the mountains' "foundations" shook further suggests that these events threaten the earth's stability; those foundations are part of the security of the world that goes back to creation (Prov. 8:29; Isa. 40:21). They guarantee the stability of the world below, as the sky dome guarantees its protection from overwhelming floods (Isa. 24:18). Yhwh's rocking these foundations imperils them; Yhwh takes such a risk for the sake of an act of deliverance that actually undergirds the world's security.

> ⁷ᶜThey have shaken about because he has raged;
> ⁸ᵃsmoke has gone up in his anger.

The verb "shake" recurs (though now hitpael), but the line then adds the reason for this shaking. "He has raged." The parallel colon expands on that with a more vivid picture of Yhwh's nostrils smoking, like Leviathan (Job 41:20 [12]). While smoke could come from the earth and be part of earthquake imagery (cf. Exod. 19:18 and the related verb in Pss. 104:32; 144:5), it can also be a description of anger (cf. the related verb in 74:1; 80:4 [5]), which fits the parallelism here. It is Yhwh's raging that caused earth to shudder.[22]

---

22. But there is no need to render *běʾappô* as "from his nostrils," which requires an odd meaning for *bě*, though one known in Ugaritic.

> ⁸ᵇFire from his mouth consumed;
> coals have blazed from him.

Two more cola pair yiqtol and qatal and likewise refer to fire coming from Yhwh rather than fire coming from the earth, volcano-like. The first colon raises the question what form this fire takes. The parallel colon begins to suggest an answer with its reference to blazing coals, since as well as being another Leviathan feature (Job 41:21 [13]) these will turn out to be a way of referring to lightning (vv. 12–14; cf. Ezek. 1:13–14).

> ⁹He has spread the heavens and come down,
> thundercloud beneath his feet.

Verse 9 starts the description again. Yhwh is still located in the heavens, where the suppliant's cry had been heard. But Yhwh now moves, first spreading the heavens (*nāṭâ*; cf. 144:5). LXX has "bows heaven," but it is not obvious what this would mean in a pre-Einsteinian universe or what would be the point of it.²³ I take the verb to denote parting the heavens (cf. Isa. 64:1; Mark 1:10) in order to break through them. "Coming down" might raise the question how one can talk about Yhwh coming down to earth, because this would inevitably consume anyone Yhwh came near. The parallel colon offers reassurance: a mass of dark thundercloud (*'ărāpel*) stands beneath Yhwh's feet for the world's protection, as this dark cloud surrounded Yhwh at Sinai (Exod. 20:18–21; Deut. 4:11; 5:22 [19]; cf. 1 Kings 8:12; Ps. 97:2). In imagination, then, Yhwh hides atop the dark thundercloud that presages a storm, and this protects the earth from actually seeing Yhwh. As the revealed God, Yhwh remains the hidden God.²⁴

> ¹⁰He has mounted a cherub and flown,
> swooped on the winds' wings.

The two lines that follow spell out the implications of each colon. Verse 9a might also raise the question *how* Yhwh came down. Yhwh and other heavenly beings do not have wings and do not fly.²⁵ While some heavenly beings walk up and down a staircase or ramp (Gen. 28:12),

---

23. Keel (*Symbolism of the Biblical World*, 24) links it with the Egyptian view that the sky slopes from east to west; but if the sky already slopes, why does Yhwh need to bend it?
24. Cf. Kuntz, "Psalm 18," 17.
25. Metaphorically, Yhwh has wings, but for protecting or carrying young birds (e.g., 17:8; Exod. 19:4; Deut. 32:11), not for flying; Yhwh is human-shaped (cf. Ps. 17) and thus walks (e.g., Gen. 3:8).

that would hardly do for the sovereign Yhwh, who rides on cherubim (v. 10, with 3–2 rhythm).[26] Ezekiel 9–10 identifies its cherubim with the living creatures of Ezek. 1–3 and thus indicates that for Ezekiel, at least, they are winged beings of partly animal and partly human appearance that carry the throne on which Yhwh sits.[27] Other passages suggest that the throne would sit in or on a limousine that the cherubim carry (cf. 1 Chron. 28:18), or (on the contrary) that the cherubim's wings constitute the throne, so that Yhwh directly rides on them.[28] Because of their connection with Yhwh's presence, the cherubim can suggest the presence of the invisible Yhwh, and they are represented in the wilderness sanctuary and the temple in this connection (e.g., Ps. 80:1 [2]; 99:1). They are in turn carried about by the wind, soaring on it as a bird does. While v. 10b could imply that the cherub is identified with the wind, there is no parallel for that assumption, and it is as natural to see the second colon as going beyond the first and indicating how the cherubim bearing Yhwh flew. The winds themselves are like wings in carrying the cherubim and their cargo through the air.

> ¹¹He has made darkness his screen,
>   [made] his shelter around him
>   rain cloud, masses of mist.

In turn, v. 11 returns to the cloud that shields Yhwh from people and shields people from Yhwh (v. 9b).[29] With "masses of mist," the line as a whole puts extraordinary emphasis on the cloud shield that protectively screens the holy God. It is like the shelter (*sukkâ*) that protects an animal or provides a human being with temporary protection from the elements (cf. 31:20 [21]; Job 27:18; 38:40; Isa. 1:8; Jon. 4:5). It comprises dark thunderclouds full of water, huge cloud masses.

> ¹²Out of the brightness before him, there have come through his masses
>   hail and burning coals.

---

26. I take the psalm's sg. "cherub" as collective (cf. LXX), since elsewhere cherubim work in pairs or groups.

27. Ezek. 9:3; 10:2, 4 also has sg. "cherub."

28. Cf. Keel, *Symbolism of the Biblical World*, 167–71. But see Sigmund Mowinckel, "Drive and/or Ride in the O.T.," *VT* 12 (1962): 278–99, see 296–99.

29. The tricolon as a whole works *abcc′b′*. A regular colon describes Yhwh making darkness a screen behind which to hide. Its verb then carries over into the second colon, which reaches its length by making the *c′* element ("his shelter around him") twice as long as its exemplar. The third colon then does the same with the *b′* element—indeed, it is twice as long again. Without "masses of mist," the line would make a regular 3-3, which might mean it is a conflate line.

> ^{13a–b}Yhwh has thundered in the heavens;
> the Most High gave forth his voice.

Verse 12 starts the description again, and vv. 12–15 parallel vv. 9–11 in offering a brief description (vv. 12–13a) that will then be expanded (vv. 13b–15). As vv. 9–11 did this for Yhwh's descent and the cloud shield, vv. 12–15 do it for the lightning and thunder. At the same time, by returning to the lightning (cf. v. 8) and eventually to the earth shuddering (cf. v. 7) and to Yhwh's anger (cf. vv. 7b–8a), they also take us back to the beginning of the section and round it off with an inclusion.

Job 22:13–14 notes that the cloud screen protecting the world from Yhwh could also hide it from Yhwh, rendering Yhwh ignorant of what happens on earth. Verse 12 in the psalm makes clear that Yhwh can penetrate the cloud, sending fiery missives (hail and lightning bolts) from the fiery divine presence. The first colon reads *mngh ngdw 'byw 'brw*, the use of assonance here complementing the use of a long line in v. 11 to convey the impressive nature of what happens. Yhwh's own presence is brightness, not cloud (a brightness that would be blinding were it not for the cloud shield), and it is from that fiery brightness that the fiery lightning comes. Hail usually appears in the OT as a fiercely destructive phenomenon that devastates all that it touches (e.g., 78:47–48; Isa. 28:2, 17).

Verse 13a–b then moves to talk briefly of the thunder that the *Most High causes.

> ^{13c}Hail and burning coals—
> ¹⁴he has sent his arrows and scattered them;
> he has shot lightnings and driven them.

Verses 13c–15 reprise and expand on the account of lightning and thunder in vv. 12–13b. I thus take v. 13c, which repeats v. 12b and may be an expansion, as the opening of this subsection and the opening of a tricolon.[30] The language of v. 14 recurs in 144:6, and in both passages EVV assume that it is the suppliant's foes that are scattered. In isolation, that makes good sense, but there is no antecedent for the suffixes with this meaning since v. 3 (cf. the addition in NIVI). More likely it is the arrows that God scatters (cf. Job 37:11; 38:24; 40:11; and BDB), in their zigzag pattern,[31] and thus the lightning that God drives or agitates (*hāmam*).[32]

---

30. Verse 14 works *abcb'a'c'*, with v. 13c an anticipatory further *b* element.
31. Cf. Keel, *Symbolism of the Biblical World*, 215.
32. Cf. *TDOT* 3:420. NEB seems to link with *hāmâ* and translates "sent them echoing," but echoing is an odd thing for lightning to do.

> ¹⁵Streams of water have appeared;
>   the world's foundations have come into sight
> At your roar, Yhwh,
>   at the blast of the breath of your anger.

It is not immediately obvious that the first line begins a reprise of v. 13a, but the link will become clear in the next line. "Streams" (*'āpîq*) always denote watercourses in the world rather than the waters above the sky (e.g., 42:1 [2]; 126:4). Here the idea is that the effect of the meteorological phenomena (vv. 7–14) was to drive the seas apart and expose the subterranean waters. The parallel colon complements that with a picture of the exposure of the pillars that are sunk into these waters to keep the earth secure. The whole line thus takes up v. 7, which already referred to the "mountains' foundations."

This came about because Yhwh roared. The thunder is that roar (cf. 104:7; Job 26:11), Yhwh's snort of anger. This aspect of the section's close thus also takes us back to its beginning (vv. 7–8). EVV again render *'ap* as "nostrils," as in v. 7, but this obscures the fact that reference to the nostrils as usual suggests an angry snort. Yhwh's anger is good news for people with whom Yhwh identifies. It means that the energy of anger is being applied to their deliverance from their attackers.

18:16–29. The psalmist moves to a different imagery, though still portraying Yhwh operating from on high to a realm below. This facilitates a transition to a more down-to-earth account of events, one that relates more explicitly to the worshipper's experience (first-person suffixes reappear). But it continues to be a thoroughly theological (and moral) one, not giving much information about exactly what happened. The section follows an *abcb'a'* stepped pattern:

> *a* Yhwh delivered me (no reference to the reason; vv. 16–18)
>   *b* Yhwh delivered me because of my faithfulness (vv. 19–20)
>   *c* How I had been faithful (no reference to the deliverance; vv. 21–23)
>   *b'* Yhwh delivered me because of my faithfulness (vv. 24–27)
> *a'* Yhwh delivered me (no reference to the reason; vv. 28–29)

The effect is to underline the fact of Yhwh's deliverance, the fact of the worshipper's faithfulness, and the link between these; it puts the focus on the former in the prominent *a* and *a'* subsections and on the latter in the prominent central subsection, and interrelates them in the bridging *b* and *b'* subsections.

> ¹⁶He reached from on high, took me,
> drew me out of great waters.

The resumed account of Yhwh's act of deliverance could in fact have continued directly from v. 6. Yhwh is still in heaven, not journeying to earth, and Yhwh's listening there leads to Yhwh's acting. From there Yhwh stretched out a hand[33] and lifted the suppliant out of the "great waters" that threatened drowning. "Great waters" takes up the idea of deathly powers imperiling people (vv. 4–5; and cf. 32:6; 69:1–2, 14–15 [2–3, 15–16]; 124:4–5; 144:7), though with its background in Canaanite thinking it also suggests tumultuous powers asserting themselves against Yhwh (e.g., 29:3; 93:4).[34] Yhwh thus reached from the heights of heaven right down to the depths of Sheol that were threatening the suppliant. The verb (*māšâ*) is the one used to describe Moses as one "lifted" out of the waters (Exod. 2:10). This is its only other occurrence, so once again David is established as a figure the equal of Moses. Water was potentially Moses's route to death but became his route to deliverance. In line with the common symbolism of water, eventually it meant death for Israel's oppressors (Exod. 15:10), and here it is the suppliant's metaphorical peril.

> ¹⁷He rescued me from my strong enemy
> and from people who were against me, because they were too strong for me.
> ¹⁸They confronted me on the day of my calamity,
> but Yhwh has become my support.

Verses 17–18 put the point more literally; the powers of death are embodied in human attackers. In v. 17, plural "people who were *against me" complements the singular "enemy" and suggests reference to David's various foes as well as to Saul in particular (see the heading); cf. v. 48. The qatal verb complements the yiqtol. Then in v. 18 the tenses are reversed as the worshipper looks back to the day that threatened calamity.[35] In that context, Yhwh was a "support" (*miš'ān*), like a staff that one could lean on and would not let one down. "Enemy" (*'ōyēb*) and "people who were against me" (*śōnē'*) reappear together in v. 40 (though the latter is piel there); "enemy" comes separately in vv. 3, 37,

---

33. For the omission of *yad* after *šālak*, cf. 2 Sam. 6:6.
34. Cf. *tĕhôm rabbâ*, "the great deep" (e.g., Isa. 51:10); *mayim rabbîm* can mean "much water" (e.g., Num. 20:11; 24:7), but that seems prosaic here, esp. in light of those other occurrences of the phrase.
35. For the pregnant construct, cf. Job 30:12.

48a. A third participle, "adversary" (*qām*, someone who rises up), appears in vv. 39, 48b.

> ¹⁹He has brought me out into roominess;
> he has saved me because he has delighted in me.

Was there any reason for Yhwh's acting in this way, beyond the suppliant's plea? Verse 19 continues to speak of Yhwh's act of deliverance but begins to explain the reasoning behind it.

A negative event is often experienced as one of constraint and confinement, like imprisonment. Etymologically, that is the meaning of the word *ṣar* (trouble) in a passage such as 4:1 [2]. There the verb *rāḥab*, "be roomy," also comes as, conversely, the suppliant now experiences Yhwh's deliverance as a release into "roominess" (*merḥāb*), openness and freedom, spaciousness and airiness.

The reason for Yhwh's act of release was that "he was pleased with me." Why was that? It might simply be a delight that emerges from Yhwh's own person and has little or no basis in its object, like Yhwh's commitment to David the shepherd boy. But the Psalms' sole previous reference to Yhwh's delight assumes it has a moral basis (see 5:4 [5]). Here, as vv. 16–18 raise the question why Yhwh acted, the preliminary answer in v. 19 raises the question "So why did Yhwh take this delight?"

> ²⁰Yhwh has dealt with me in accordance with my faithfulness;
> in accordance with the purity of my hands he has recompensed me.

Here the two verbs that introduce the answer are both yiqtol. "Deal with" (*gāmal*) sometimes implies an act that corresponds to what the other person has done (e.g., 103:10; Deut. 32:6), but does not always have this implication (e.g., Prov. 3:30; 31:12). In itself, then, this verb would take us no further from v. 19. The parallel verb is in itself a rather common one (*šûb* hiphil) with various meanings and only contributes to the clarifying of the psalm's point by virtue of the *abb'a'* arrangement of the verbs and prepositional expressions in the line. This point is made more explicit in the first colon by the adverbial expression "in accordance with my faithfulness," which itself is then made more concrete by the parallel phrase "in accordance with the purity of my hands." The context in the other occurrence of the word "cleanness" (Job 22:30) makes clear that this implies moral cleanness as well as sacramental cleanness. It implies not having blood on one's hands (cf. Isa. 1:15–16) or in one's heart (Pss. 24:4; 73:1).

> ²¹For I have kept Yhwh's ways
> and not been faithless in leaving my God.

The top step of the section then occupies vv. 21–23 and focuses entirely on the faithfulness on the suppliant's part that made deliverance possible. The structure of the subsection corresponds to that in vv. 9–11 and 12–15 as it makes the point in general terms and then expands on its two aspects.

Thus within v. 21, "I kept Yhwh's ways" is first complemented by "I was not faithless to my God." The first refers to concrete obedience, the second to the principle of faithfulness; the first refers to "Yhwh," the second to "my God"; the first puts the point positively, the second negatively.

> ²²For all his decisions have been before me,
> and I have not put away his statutes from me.

"I kept Yhwh's ways" is spelled out further in the two parallel cola of v. 22, beginning with a "for" that picks up the "for" that opened v. 21. Yhwh's decisions and statutes expound the nature of Yhwh's ways. The phrase refers to the ways of which Yhwh approves (cf. 51:13 [15]; 81:13 [14]; 119:3; 128:1) rather than the ways Yhwh takes—though it might be assumed that there is a link with these (cf. 103:6–7). And keeping these ways depends on making sure they stay before one's eyes rather than putting them out of sight.

> ²³I have been a person of integrity with him
> and have kept myself from waywardness I might have done.

"I was not faithless to my God" is then spelled out in two further parallel cola. The suppliant claims to have been "whole" with God, to have been a person of *integrity, someone wholly committed. Again a negative complements the positive. Wholeness or integrity requires keeping oneself from *waywardness one might have done. "Keeping oneself" nicely rounds off the subsection that began with reference to "keeping" (v. 21).

> ²⁴So Yhwh has recompensed me according to my faithfulness,
> according to the purity of my hands before his eyes.

The beginning of vv. 24–27 signals a return to the theme of vv. 19–20, with v. 24 a resumptive line virtually repeating v. 20. The links will continue in the reference to purity (v. 26) and also to integrity (v. 25), which looks back rather to v. 23.

> ²⁵With the committed you showed commitment,
>   with the person of integrity you showed integrity,
> ²⁶With the pure you showed purity,
>   but with the crooked you showed refractoriness.

Nevertheless, vv. 25–26 make the point in new ways. Indeed, they invent several verbs to do so: at least, "show commitment" (*ḥāsad* hitpael) comes only here, "show integrity" (*tāmam*) comes in the hitpael only here, "show purity" (*bārar*) comes in the hitpael only here and later in Dan. 12:10, and "show refractoriness" (*pātal*) comes in the hitpael only here.³⁶

The worshipper has implicitly claimed to be a *committed person and has proved that Yhwh behaves in a committed way to such a person (cf. 16:10), but now the worshipper makes that explicit. Repeating the claim to be a person of *integrity and declaring that Yhwh has behaved with integrity toward such a person restates the point. So does repeating the claim to purity and declaring that Yhwh has behaved with purity. The worshipper has been characterized by commitment, integrity, and purity, and Yhwh has mirrored these qualities in delivering the suppliant.³⁷

After the three parallel cola in vv. 25–26a, we are ready for another in v. 26b, but its opening *w* signals that it will take us in another direction, to characterize people like the suppliants' attackers, and Yhwh's stance in relation to them. They are crooked (*'iqqēš*), twisted or twisting or devious people who turn a straight way, a way of integrity, into a distorted one (cf. Prov. 2:15; 28:6; and for the verb 10:9; 28:18). This is the psalm's first comment on the moral character of the suppliant's enemies, and in this respect vv. 24–27 go beyond vv. 19–20, their equivalent in the upward side of this stepped sequence. There is also another way in which the psalm marks the transition from characterizing Yhwh's relationship with the speaker to characterizing Yhwh's relationship with his enemy. It breaks the pattern of matching a verb describing Yhwh's act to a related adjective describing the person's act, though in substance it continues the pattern. Changing from *'iqqēš* to *pātal* keeps the "twisting" image, and words from the two roots appear as a pair elsewhere (Deut. 32:5; Prov. 8:8). It is thus a surprise and a risk to categorize Yhwh as refractory or twisting or devious or perverse (NRSV), though this should hardly be watered down to "wily" (NJPS) or "shrewd" (NIVI). The idea is that

---

36. This may make it unlikely that vv. 25–26 constitute an ancient wisdom saying (so Cross and Freedman, "Royal Song," 21).

37. On the claim to faithfulness and commitment before God, see on 17:1–5.

Yhwh can match the faithless in the capacity to throw a curve ball or bend a free kick.

> ²⁷For you are one who delivered a weak people,
> but lofty eyes you humbled.

Verse 27 in turn closes off vv. 24–27 as a subsection by summarizing the relationship between Yhwh's acts and the objects of them, both positive (v. 27a taking up vv. 24–26a) and negative (v. 27b taking up vv. 26b). In each colon the object precedes a yiqtol verb, so that the symmetrical arrangement contrasts with the opposing content. A distinctive feature of v. 27a is the reference to a people. Otherwise the psalm refers only to the speaker, presumably the people's leader. EVV translate vv. 25–29 in the present, thus reducing the disparity, but we have noted that the psalm makes much use of the yiqtol to refer to the past, and more likely the yiqtols here also do so. This one line then reflects the fact that the leader was fighting as the commander of his people. His deliverance was theirs. His *weakness was theirs. The fact that the line refers to their weakness rather than to any aspects of their moral character also makes for a link with the corresponding step in the first part of the section (vv. 19–20). There the leader's deliverance emerged simply from Yhwh's favor and was not explicitly based on the leader's character. Here it is similarly based on need, not on the people's character. Their weakness and deliverance contrast with the humbling of "lofty eyes." While this implies arrogance, it is as much a statement of fact about the position of the leader's enemies. They actually were in an exalted position and could take a sober look at weaker peoples and their leaders and come to the reasonable assessment that they could put them down. Yet that sober but lofty look was enough for Yhwh to decide to put these powers down.

> ²⁸For it is you who kept my lamp alight, Yhwh;
> my God illumined my darkness.

Verses 28–29 complete the sequence begun in vv. 16–18 with another simple testimony to the fact of deliverance, and like that first one it begins with a metaphorical statement (v. 28)[38] before going on to a more literal one. To speak in images, Yhwh brought light where there was darkness. The extinguishing of a person's lamp is an image for death (e.g., Job 18:5–6; 21:17), so the keeping alight of their lamp or its rekindling suggests keeping them alive or bringing them back

---

38. I follow LXX in seeing "Yhwh" as an invocation at the end of the first colon; 2 Sam. 22:29 has "For you are my lamp, Yhwh; Yhwh has illumined. . . ."

from near death or deathly danger (cf. Isa. 42:3). Yhwh's illumining the suppliant's darkness then restates the event in more original language. While the image is thus quite different from v. 16, the implication is the same.

> ²⁹For through you I rushed a barricade;
> through my God I leaped a wall.

Literally, how did Yhwh save the speaker's life? Verses 37–41 will speak of the leader's taking positive, aggressive action in relation to his foes, and v. 29 could be read that way. It might then recall 1 Sam. 30; also 2 Sam. 5; 1 Chron. 11. But thus far the psalm has spoken only of being rescued from attack, and I also read v. 29 thus.³⁹ The line speaks of the leader being able to escape from somewhere when apparently caught. It could then recall David's escape from Keilah (1 Sam. 23).

18:30–34. We move to statements about Yhwh rather than declarations addressed to Yhwh. First come two verses of present statement, in noun clauses and rhetorical questions. These are then buttressed by three verses of further statement about Yhwh's acts of deliverance and enabling, which provide the evidence for the present statement. Moral argument disappears; the past account simply concerns a demonstration of power.

> ³⁰God—his way has integrity,
> Yhwh's word is proven;
> he is a shield for all who take refuge in him.

The transition to a new section is marked in v. 30 by a tricolon whose description begins with another statement of Yhwh's *integrity, though it refers to the integrity of Yhwh's *way*. In the context, this denotes Yhwh's *way of acting in relation to the speaker (contrast v. 21). That is both a summary of what has preceded and an anticipation of what will follow. Likewise, Yhwh's word is presumably some word that relates to the speaker—perhaps Yhwh's commitment to the anointed (v. 50)—whose reliability the speaker's experience has proved. In turn the closing long colon explains further how that works out, by resuming statements from the opening declaration in v. 2 (shield, take refuge, on which/in him).

39. The verb *'āruṣ* could come from *rāṣaṣ* (crush, oppress) or *rûṣ* (run). The noun *gĕdûd* usually means "[military] company" but in PBH means "wall." So the first colon could mean "I have run [at]/crushed a wall/company." The occurrence of another word for wall in the subsequent colon suggests that the noun has the second meaning, and "running [at/over] a barricade" is both a more plausible expression than "crushing a barricade" and makes for a more plausible parallel to "leaping a wall."

> ³¹For who is God except Yhwh,
> and who is a crag apart from our God?—

A long line of rhetorical questions then buttresses the assertions. The first colon is longer than the second because the *kî* applies to both cola; beyond that, the two cola are exactly parallel. Whereas "God" in v. 30 was *hāʾēl*, here the term is *ʾĕlôah*, and the parallel expression is "a crag," which again resumes from v. 2.

> ³²The God who has girded me with strength
> and made my way whole,

With vv. 32–34 a series of participial statements then describe the way these characteristics of Yhwh have been embodied for the speaker.[40] We could see the participial statements as describing Yhwh's ongoing character, except that those finite verbs illustrate the psalm's regular alternating way of making past statements, and suggest that vv. 32–34 do refer to what has recently been happening.

Verse 32 first speaks of Yhwh as the leader's personal armorer, then spells out the implications of that by resuming talk of wholeness/integrity of way (cf. v. 30), but now it is the *integrity of the leader's way.

> ³³Who has made my legs like deer
> and stood me on my high places,
> ³⁴Who has trained my hands for battle
> so that my arms could bend a bronze bow.

How does that work out? The leader's way is whole because of the way he is able to plant his legs. Here a simile in the first colon combines with a metaphor in the second. He has energy or deftness that suggests a comparison with deer, and he can thus do the equivalent of climbing on high places as deer do.

Talk of legs then gives way to talk of hands and arms in two further parallel cola. But apart from the reference to similar body parts, the second colon goes beyond the first. How did Yhwh train his hands? By enabling his arms to bend a bow. A bronze bow would take some bending, and the expression may involve hyperbole, or the psalm may refer to a wooden bow strengthened with bronze, or by ellipse to a bow that shot bronze-tipped arrows.[41]

---

40. In each line a participial statement in the first colon is continued by a finite verb in the second, wayyiqtol (v. 32), yiqtol (v. 33), and weqatal (v. 34), in accordance with common practice. See GKC 116x.

41. Cf. R. Couroyer, "L'arc d'airain," *RB* 72 (1965): 508–14.

18:35–45. Verses 35–45 continue to describe Yhwh's acts but revert to addressing Yhwh. A long line again marks the beginning of the section. When this further testimony comes to an end in vv. 43–45, a redivision of those verses can plausibly move a tricolon from v. 43 to v. 45, so that the beginning and end of this section as a whole would be thus marked. In vv. 35–45 the psalm concretely mirrors the form of the lament in a prayer psalm, speaking of what "you" have done (vv. 35–36a, 39–40a, 43a), what "I" have done (vv. 36b–38a, 40b, 42), and what "they" have experienced (vv. 38b, 41, 43b–45). The psalm's relationship with this form is paradoxical. Yhwh has acted instead of abandoning the psalmist, the speaker has triumphed instead of being overwhelmed, and the enemy has been overwhelmed instead of triumphing. Thus, instead of lamenting in each of these directions, the psalm rejoices at each. One effect of this is to establish a strong tension between each of these sets of pronouns. But on one hand the tensions between "they" and "you" and between "they" and "I" are easily resolved; "they" lose out each time. On the other hand, the tension between "you" and "I" stands creatively unresolved. The section continues to emphasize the importance of "your" action, which has been in focus through vv. 1–34. But it also puts unusual emphasis on "my acts," also over against those of the army that is unmentioned.[42] Gerstenberger calls the victory declaration in vv. 37–38, 42 "preposterous."[43] Perhaps there is a link between this stress on "I" and the covert prominence of the first person in vv. 1–34, which reached its apogee in vv. 21–23, the very center of the step-structured section vv. 16–29. Any statement that "God acted for/through me" gives overt prominence to God but covert prominence to me, and the second feature gains in significance when the basis for it is *my* commitment.

As happens in a lament, the psalm does not systematically confine individual verses to one of these angles (see vv. 36, 38, 40; also v. 43 in MT). That itself mirrors the fact that these are not separate realities but complementary angles on one experience or event. The section thus speaks three times of "you," "I," and "they," suggesting a division into three subunits, vv. 35–38, 39–41, and 42–45, in each of which all three pronouns appear. Like the accounts of Yhwh's coming in vv. 7–15, the three subunits offer parallel accounts of events. They are for the most part not chronologically sequential ones. The speaker tells his story three times.

> ³⁵You have given me your shield that delivered me;
>   your right hand sustained me,
>   your response made me great.

---

42. Cf. Mays, *Psalms*, 94.
43. *Psalms*, 1:99.

In v. 35 (you), Yhwh's shield again reappears (cf. vv. 2, 30). NRSV "the shield of your salvation" could imply that Yhwh's deliverance was the suppliant's shield, but in such a construct phrase the implication is more likely that Yhwh's shield is the suppliant's deliverance: through Yhwh's shielding he is delivered. The parallel cola confirm this with their reference to Yhwh's right hand sustaining and Yhwh's response to the suppliant's prayer (cf. v. 6) making him great. If we conclude that v. 29 did not refer to aggressive action but constituted another testimony to the experience of preservation under attack, the last clause here becomes the first hint of such a reference, which will become prominent in this section.

> 36You have given my steps room beneath me;
> my ankles have not given way.

Verse 36 (you, my) continues to speak metaphorically, again as if the suppliant were a deer (cf. v. 33). The suppliant did not have to tread perilously narrow mountain trails. The second colon brings the transition from "you" to "I," or at least "my ankles," vividly suggesting the specific experience of losing one's footing at the edge of a constricted path.

> 37I pursued my attackers and overtook them;
> I did not turn before eliminating them.
> 38I struck them down and they were not able to rise;
> they fell beneath my feet.

In v. 37 (I) the leader's aggressive action comes into focus. It involved not merely successful defense but violent initiative, described in uncompromising terms. It meant pursuing without holding back—he was not merely trying to chase them away. It meant killing without mercy: there was to be no compromise. That continues into v. 38. It meant knocking people down in such a way as to make sure they never got up again: there was no attempt to minimize casualties. In case we have not got the point, the psalm adds, "They have fallen beneath my feet," and they stay fallen. In the midst of v. 38 thus comes the transition from "I" to "they." In the report of this slaughter, there is no suggestion of sadness or of regret at an appalling necessity.

> 39You have girded me with strength for battle,
> brought down my adversaries under my feet.

Indeed, v. 39 (you) turns quickly to a reaffirming of Yhwh's responsibility for events, going back to the beginning of the story to do so. It was Yhwh who made it possible for the leader to fight at all. Yhwh was indeed his personal armorer (cf. v. 32). Yhwh not merely rescued him when he had got into a mess but also took the initiative in commissioning him for battle, equipping him, and sending him on his way. The second colon takes the logic further. It was therefore Yhwh as much as the leader who put the adversaries down.

> ⁴⁰You have made my enemies turn tail for me,
>   and I have wiped out the people who were against me.

Verse 40 initially continues this "you," chronologically going behind v. 37; v. 40b resumes the "I" to summarize the consequential slaughter of the people who were *against me, described more fully in vv. 37–38. I follow LXX in taking Yhwh's "giving the enemies' neck" to denote causing them to turn their back (cf., e.g., Jer. 2:27), but it might denote causing them to bow down in submission or for slaughter (so KJV; cf. Gen. 49:8).

> ⁴¹They have cried for help but there was no one to deliver—
>   [cried] about Yhwh, but no one has responded to them.

Verse 41 (they) again goes behind events, not chronologically but causally. The second colon is commonly understood to suggest that they were crying *to* Yhwh, but this would be an unparalleled use of ʿal. That regularly denotes the subject of a cry, not its object (e.g., Exod. 8:12 [8]); one might even translate "against Yhwh" (cf. Job 31:38). The enemies are crying out about the way Yhwh is a threat to them, presumably crying to their gods. But there is no one to defeat Yhwh. By the regular ellipse in parallelism, "about Yhwh" in the second colon applies to the first, as "they cried for help" applies to the second as well as the first.⁴⁴ The verse contrasts their dealings with their gods with Yhwh's dealings with the leader. They cry out as he had (v. 6a), but no one responds (contrast v. 35). There is no one to deliver them (contrast vv. 2, 3, 27, 35). The similarity and contrast are also hinted at "sardonically"⁴⁵ by the similarity in appearance but contrast in meaning between the verbs *cry for help and *deliver.

> ⁴²I have ground them like dust on the wind,
>   like mud in the streets—I made them empty.

---

44. Cf. DG 132.
45. Alter, *Art of Biblical Poetry*, 32. Alter is commenting on the version in 2 Sam. 22:42, which uses a different verb (see translation note above on v. 41), but his comment also applies to the Ps. 18 version.

The third subsection does take the chronology further, adopting as its starting point in v. 42 (I), arranged *abb'a'*, the victories that were the conclusion of the previous subsections. Here it again restates the leader's action, paralleling vv. 37–38 and 40b, though it does so with at least one even more violent image. To grind something (*šāḥaq*) is to beat it very fine, like dust so light that the breeze can carry it off, or like the sand in the street that turns into mud. The enemies had planned to overcome the leader, but the leader had acted so as to make them and their plans empty or vain (*rîq* hiphil; see the noun in 2:1).[46]

> 43a–bYou rescued me from the attacks of people;
> you made me head of nations.

Once more the worshipper declares that this came about through Yhwh's act (you). Initially it is again described merely as a rescue, as if all Yhwh did was make possible an escape, not an annihilation. But reference back to that rescue is here a preliminary to a statement of its result. Further, in vv. 43–45 as a whole the immediate attackers disappear from view, and the testimony turns rather to the effect of the suppliant's extraordinary victory over them. Yhwh's act not only made escape and annihilation possible but also led to the leader's gaining sovereignty over a much wider range of nations. The scenario corresponds to that in Ps. 2.

> 43cPeople I did not know served me;
> 44aon hearing with their ear, they obeyed me.

This sovereignty extends far beyond the people involved in the conflict to faraway nations that the leader had previously not even known of (they). They heard of his victories and hastened to offer him their submission lest they should end up as his next victims (cf. 2 Sam. 8:3-12; 10:19).

> 44bForeigners withered before me;
> 45foreigners wilted
> and came trembling out of their strongholds.

The tricolon comprising vv. 44b–45 (they) closes off vv. 35–45 and continues the description of their action. Behind the offering of their submission was an overwhelming dismay at the news of the leader's victory. They withered or wilted like a plant (cf. 1:3; 37:2). They saw themselves

---

46. *HALOT* suggests that *rîq* might be a denominative verb; this usage, at least, might be denominative.

as strong, and they had confidence in their impressive fortresses, whose impressiveness is reflected in the word (*mimmisgĕrôtêhem*), easily the longest word in the psalm. But they find themselves creeping out of them knowing that they will be no match for this king who can rush barricades and leap walls (v. 29), as aggressor and not merely as fugitive.

18:46–48. The psalm closes with two short sections that correspond to its two short opening sections. First there is a final retrospective, corresponding to the introductory look back in vv. 3–6.

> ⁴⁶Yhwh is alive—my crag is to be worshipped;
> God my deliverance shall be on high,

The declaration that Yhwh is alive comes only here in the Psalms. Twice elsewhere Yhwh is referred to as the living God (42:2 [3]; 84:2 [3]), both in connection with Yhwh's being alive in the temple. Elsewhere that description affirms that Yhwh is lively and active, a solemn fact for people who slight Yhwh but an encouragement to people who turn to Yhwh in need (e.g., Josh. 3:10; 1 Sam. 17:26, 36; 2 Kings 19:4, 16). This declaration compares and contrasts with the Canaanite declaration "Baal is alive," both in its formulation and in the evidence it presupposes. It celebrates not an event reflected in happenings in nature but one reflected in happenings in the realm of politics.⁴⁷ It is the fact that Yhwh is alive and involved in a lively way in this realm that makes Yhwh "my crag" and "my deliverance" (picking up from v. 2). And therefore Yhwh is to be worshipped as one on high. The two verbs complement each other in subtle ways. *Worship implies bowing the knee, so that one verb suggests downward movement, one upward movement. One verb is a participle, the other a yiqtol, yet they rhyme (*wĕbārûk* and *wĕyārûm*). The second verb links with the first noun as well as with the first verb, for the nature of a rock is to be on high (cf. 61:2 [3]), and it is as one who is on high that Yhwh can be deliverance. Yhwh's exaltation reverses the exaltation of the people with lofty eyes and goes along with the exaltation of Yhwh's servant (the same verb, *rûm*, vv. 27 and 48).

> ⁴⁷God who has given me complete requital
> and subdued peoples under me,
> ⁴⁸Who has saved me from my enemies;
> yes, you put me on high above my adversaries,
> you rescued me from a violent man.

Verses 47–48 then provide the summary of Yhwh's acts that justifies this declaration. One might initially take the opening participles in each

---

47. Cf. Kraus, *Psalms,* 1:265.

verse (lit., "the one who gives," "the one who rescues") as statements of Yhwh's ongoing activity, but the wayyiqtol in v. 47b and the psalm's characteristic yiqtols in the second and third cola in v. 48 suggest that vv. 47–48 is all retrospective summary. The five cola are again subtly interwoven. Four regular-length cola embrace a two-word colon at the center. Two participles in the first and third suggest the division into verses and make the subsection end with a tricolon. The second and fourth link in making statements about lifting up and putting down, while the third and fifth link in making statements about deliverance. The third and fourth have parallel references to the leader's enemies, while the fourth and fifth link as a pair of strong affirmatives utilizing yiqtol verbs. The first and last link with their references to legal requital and lawless *violence. NRSV translates *něqāmâ* as "vengeance," NJPS as "vindication." The former suggests too much by way of strong feelings, the latter something too abstract. The word has a legal background and suggests God putting things right by seeing that people in the wrong are punished, but doing so with conviction, even passion.[48] Here again, then, the leader is claiming that Yhwh had been doing the right thing in putting down his adversaries. They were overturning the proper God-given order of the world. That made it necessary for Yhwh to subdue them under the feet of this leader to whom God is committed.

18:49–50. Like many testimony psalms, Ps. 18 closes by looking well beyond the immediate circumstances of Yhwh's act, both spatially and chronologically.

> [49]For this I will confess you among the nations, Yhwh,
> and make music to your name,

First, its *confession and making of *music for the honor of Yhwh's *name is relevant not only to Israel but also to the nations. It is striking that this war psalm is the first that envisages the declaring of Yhwh's praise among the nations. It is not explicit that the nations are drawn into this worship, though that is the normal point of such a declaration, and it will be explicit shortly in 22:22–31 [23–32] (cf. 47; 98; 118). In those other psalms, as elsewhere in the OT, the assumption is that Yhwh's acts of deliverance on behalf of Israel and its leader also have positive significance for other nations, in keeping with the original dynamic of Yhwh's promise to Abraham. And that is so even when the psalm rejoices in victory over other nations. The psalm does not imply that either God or Israel takes an intrinsically negative stance over against other peoples. Both parties are prepared to be tough when they meet opposition or at-

---

48. See (e.g.) *NIDOTTE*.

tack, but their capacity to do that is then an invitation to the rest of the world to see sense and bow down to Yhwh. For the two verbs, see 7:17 [18]. Paul uses v. 49 to express the significance of the preaching of the gospel to Gentiles (Rom. 15:9).

> ⁵⁰One who gives great acts of deliverance to his king,
>   keeps commitment to his anointed,
>   to David and his offspring forever.

Once again the basis for praise is expressed in participial phrases about *deliverance and *commitment in a final tricolon. Initially, one might assume that these continue the past reference of the ones in vv. 45–46, but the last word of the psalm makes us reconsider that. It establishes that the second participle has present reference, and suggests that the whole final verse looks beyond the immediate circumstances chronologically, as v. 49 does spatially. That also coheres with the assumption that it is the king who speaks throughout the psalm. Here he refers in the third person to Yhwh's king, Yhwh's *anointed, David's offspring, because he is no longer referring merely to his own experience but is universalizing in connection with the more general truth that his experience illustrates. (We may also infer that the king's scriptwriter raises his head over the parapet here.) The midrash comments that God's "mightily enlarging deliverance for his king" implies that deliverance will grow "little by little."[49] People who do not experience Yhwh's deliverance in the spectacular way the psalm describes need not lose heart.

Theological Implications

Psalm 18 offers no indication that it refers to something God will do in the future; it is not eschatological. It offers no indication that it refers to someone in the future; it is not messianic. It offers no indication that it points to Jesus of Nazareth; it is not christological. It is an expression of gratitude for something God has done for a military leader of Israel. To judge from the heading and the end, this person is the king (rather than, e.g., a general such as Joab), and specifically David. Even for David, Israel's greatest military hero, the portrait is larger than life, but that is the nature of reports of military triumph in the ancient and the modern world (and of testimonies), and as usual, God inspires fine examples of regular human forms of speech rather than devising new forms.

---

49. *Midrash on Psalms,* 1:269.

God has done four things for David: rescued him from a particular enemy, rescued him from enemies in general, enabled him actively to thrash his enemies, and thus made other peoples acknowledge him. The story in Samuel–Kings and Chronicles gives us accounts of how David indeed escaped from Saul and from other enemies, defeated other peoples, and won renown in his world. If we ask how he did that, the story suggests various answers. On different occasions he escaped and conquered because he could anticipate danger, because he had good friends and good officers, because he had good luck, because Yhwh told him what to do, because he was a good general, because he was brave, and because he trusted in Yhwh.

The psalm offers an analogous, though not identical, analysis. On the whole, its descriptions of Yhwh and its account of Yhwh's acts mean it puts much more emphasis on God's involvement. The picture of Yhwh's coming and acting in vv. 7–15 particularly stands out. There is nothing like it in the story, except on the occasion of two deliverances from the Philistines and victories against them. On one, David comments, "Yhwh broke through my enemies before me like waters breaking through." On the other, Yhwh told David he would hear "the sound of marching in the tops of the balsam trees," which would be a sign that "Yhwh has gone out before you to attack the Philistine army" (2 Sam. 5:20, 24). On both occasions, the Philistines attacked David, Yhwh guided him, and David experienced extraordinary deliverance that turned into an extraordinary triumph. But they were two different experiences. On the first occasion David simply defeated his opponents, though he recognizes Yhwh's hand in his being able to do so. On the second, he is aware of indications that Yhwh's own forces are involved in the battle, though the battle on the ground unfolds like any other. Both occasions contrast with the earlier triumph in 2 Sam. 5, David's extraordinary capture of Jebus, which involved no divine guidance or divine help, only human initiative and bravery.

In the psalm, vv. 7–15 represent a heightened version of the story's talk of the sound of marching in the balsam trees. It contributes to the way the psalm offers a heightened version of the four-level account of events that appears in 2 Samuel. At level one, human forces simply fight a battle (e.g., Ps. 18:37–38; 2 Sam. 5:6–9). Level two declares that it is Yhwh who makes that possible, for instance by making David the man he was (e.g., Ps. 18:32–36; 2 Sam. 5:10). Level three portrays Yhwh doing something against the odds, something humanly extraordinary (Ps. 18:16–19; 2 Sam. 5:17–21). At level four, events suggest an even more spectacular intervention on Yhwh's part (Ps. 18:7–15; 2 Sam. 5:22–25). This logical account of the levels corresponds to the order of events in 2 Samuel but reverses the order in Ps. 18—naturally enough, in that the point of a psalm is to give glory to God, so that God's act properly has greater prominence. But the psalm goes on to acknowledge the variety in the relationship between David's acts and Yhwh's.

The biggest tension between Ps. 18 and Samuel–Kings concerns David's character. Samuel–Kings does not portray David as a man of integrity, as the psalm does. A number of considerations may reduce this difficulty. First, it may be significant that David's moral collapse follows on the triumphs narrated in 2 Sam. 5. If one is to imagine the psalm being written with the younger David in mind, this disparity is lessened, though that explanation heightens the irony of the psalm when read in a much later setting in David's life, in 2 Sam. 22. Second, David's moral collapse was not accompanied by a religious collapse. We have noted that David seems always to have been committed to Yhwh rather than Baal or other deities, unlike successors who are unfavorably compared with him. Thus third, this emphasis fits with other larger-than-life aspects of the psalm. And fourth, if the psalm was written for David in the Second Temple period rather than during his lifetime, that fits this emphasis on David in Samuel–Kings and Chronicles.

At all these levels, like (e.g.) Samuel–Kings and Chronicles, Ps. 18 violently (!) confronts any claim that biblical faith could not see God involved in war. It affirms that Yhwh was indeed involved in (e.g.) David's capture of Jerusalem and his victories over the Philistines, and involved not merely in rescuing David but also in enabling him to act aggressively and kill people. A Christian might think (e.g.) that the psalm is mistaken and that Yhwh was not so involved, though that raises problems (e.g.) over the way Jesus treats the Psalms as Scripture. Or a Christian might think that God was so involved then but is no longer so involved, though one might then wonder why the change. A Christian might thus allegorize the psalm so that its battles refer to our battling against our own faults.[50] Or a Christian might think that the perspective of the psalm fits the NT attitude expressed in (e.g.) Rom. 13:4; Theodoret sees God acting thus in deliverances his people experienced when invaded from the north and the east in the fifth century.[51] That raises the question how we know when God is so involved, and it leaves the psalm open to misuse; but then so is any text.

---

50. Cf. Augustine, *Psalms*, 50–54.
51. *Psalms*, 1:126.

Psalm 19

The Fiery Cosmos and the Encouraging Law

Translation

The leader's. Composition. David's.

¹The heavens are announcing God's honor,
    the sky is declaring the work of his hands.
²Day to day it pours out speech,
    night to night it proclaims[a] knowledge.
³There is no speech, no words,
    whose voice is not audible.
⁴In all the earth their noise[b] has set out,
    at the end of the world their words.

    a. Soggin (*Old Testament and Oriental Studies*, 203–9) notes that *ḥiwwâ* is an Aramaism but doubts if this requires a postexilic date for vv. 2–7.
    b. *Qaw* usually means "line"; BDB translates "chord." Kraus (*Psalms*, 1:268) plausibly compares *qaw* in Isa. 28:10, 13, though that may involve explaining the unknown by the unknown (but see also Dahood, *Psalms*, 1:121–22), while NJPS refers to an Arabic verb *qawwâ*, "shout." All these may be onomatopeic. LXX "voice" may be a guess rather than signaling an original *qôlām*. Manfred Weippert emends in light of a Ugaritic noun *qar* meaning "voice" (see "Zum Text von Ps 19.5 und Jes 22.5," *ZAW* 73 [1961]: 97–99). Raymond J. Tournay ("Notules sur les Psaumes," in *Alttestamentliche Studien* [Friedrich Nötscher Festschrift], ed. Hubert Junker and Johannes Botterweck [Bonn: Hanstein, 1950], 271–80, esp. 271–74) sees the word as referring to a line of writing, God's message being written in creation rather than sounded in it.

For the sun he put a tent in them;[c]
   [5]it is like a groom coming out of his chamber.
It rejoices like a warrior to run the path—
   [6]its setting out is from one end of the heavens,
Its completed circuit is at their other end,[d]
   and there is nothing hidden from its ferocity.

[7]Yhwh's teaching has integrity,
   restoring life.
Yhwh's declaration is reliable,
   giving insight to the untaught.
[8]Yhwh's charges are upright,
   joying the heart.
Yhwh's command is clean,
   lighting up the eyes.
[9]Yhwh's reverence is pure,
   standing forever.
Yhwh's decisions are truthfulness;
   they are altogether faithful.
[10]They are more desirable[e] than gold,
   even than much fine gold,
Sweeter than honey,
   even juice from honeycombs.
[11]Yes, your servant takes warning from them;
   there are great results[f] from keeping them.

[12]Who can understand wanderings?[g]—free me from secret acts,
   [13]yes, withhold your servant from the willful.[h]
May they not rule over me; then I shall be whole
   and free of great rebellion.

c. I.e., the heavens.
d. Lit., "at their ends," perhaps pl. of extension.
e. GKC 126b sees the article on the ptc. as beginning a self-contained clause; *TTH* 135 (7), *DG* 112, and *IBHS* 37.5b see it simply as a relative separated from its antecedent.
f. EVV have "reward" for *'ēqeb*, but this positive connotation comes only from the context.
g. LXX renders the hapax *šĕgî'ôt* as "transgressions," and Jerome renders it "mistakes." Behind this difference is the existence of two verbs with overlapping meaning: *šāgag* refers to inadvertent error, and *šāgâ* can have that meaning but more often suggests a deliberate going astray. Interpreters commonly see the psalm as asking for the forgiveness of accidental faults (see esp. Jacob Milgrom, "The Cultic *šggh* and Its Influence in Psalms and Job," *JQR* 58 [1967–68]: 115–25, esp. 120–21). But LXX rather rightly connects the noun with *šāgâ* and assumes that its use here links with the verb's regular meaning. Further, while we may translate the noun as a numerical pl. "wanderings," we will eventually discover that vv. 12–13 work *abb'a'* and that "great rebellion" parallels "wanderings," which is thus more likely an intensive than a numerical plural.
h. *Zēdîm*; LXX "strangers" implies *zārîm*, foreigners or foreign gods.

> ¹⁴May the words of my mouth be acceptable
> and the talk of my heart come before you,
> Yhwh, my crag, my restorer.

Interpretation

Psalm 19 brings together a theme with which the Psalter opens and one with which it almost closes, a stress on attentiveness to Yhwh's teaching (see Ps. 1) and a stress on the cosmos's acknowledgment of Yhwh (see Ps. 148). The two themes recur in the Psalter (see esp. Ps. 119 for the one, Pss. 8 and 104 for the other) but generally appear separately. The Psalter as a whole simply interweaves them without laying down how to relate them, and similarly Ps. 19 simply juxtaposes them without telling readers how to relate them. So sharp is the disjunction between their treatment in the two parts of Ps. 19 that it may plausibly be maintained that these were originally two separate psalms or parts of psalms that have been combined,[1] as happened when parts of Pss. 57 and 60 were combined as Ps. 108. But if so, as is the case with Ps. 108, they are now one.[2]

There are verbal links between the two that might have encouraged the juxtaposition, as verbal links encouraged the juxtaposition of other whole psalms (e.g., Pss. 1 and 2; Pss. 3 and 4) without leading to their becoming one. The "light" language in the second part[3] may be an example. The heavens speak a word (*'ōmer*, vv. 2, 3), and v. 13 makes a plea about the suppliant's words (*'ēmer*). There is nothing hidden from the sun's ferocity (v. 6); the suppliant prays to be freed from the hidden (v. 12).[4] Between them, both parts also share verbal links with Ps. 18,

---

1. See (e.g.) Julian Morgenstern, "Psalms 8 and 19A," *HUCA* 19 (1945–46): 491–523, see 506–16.

2. For the view that they come from the same author, see (e.g.) Alfons Deissler, "Zur Datierung und Situierung der 'kosmischen Hymnen' Pss. 8 19 29," in *Lex tua veritas* (Hubert Junker Festschrift), ed. Heinrich Gross and Franz Mussner (Trier: Paulinus, 1961), 47–58, see 49–52.

3. On this see John H. Eaton, "Some Questions of Philology and Exegesis in the Psalms," *JTS*, n.s., 19 (1968): 603–9, see 604–5. Jonathan T. Glass ("Some Observations on Psalm 19," in *The Listening Heart* [Roland E. Murphy Festschrift], ed. Kenneth G. Hoglund et al., JSOTSup 58 [Sheffield: JSOT, 1987], 147–59) emphasizes sun imagery as an indication of the psalm's intrinsic unity. See also G. Vermes, "The Torah Is a Light," *VT* 8 (1958): 436–38; C. Dohmen, "Ps 19 und sein altorientalischer Hintergrund," *Bib* 64 (1983): 501–17; Walter Harrelson, "Psalm 19," in *Worship and the Hebrew Bible* (John T. Willis Festschrift), ed. M. Patrick Graham et al., JSOTSup 284 (Sheffield: Sheffield Academic Press, 1999), 142–47.

4. James R. Durlesser also notes aural links between the different parts of the psalm ("A Rhetorical Critical Study of Psalms 19, 42, and 43," *Studia biblica et theologica* 10

suggesting the basis for juxtaposing the two psalms. Psalm 18 opens with reference to Yhwh's servant and to Yhwh as "my rock," and Ps. 19 closes on these notes. The declaration about Yhwh's way being whole and Yhwh's word (*'imrâ*) proven (18:30 [31]) is followed by the declarations about the heavens speaking a word (*'ōmer*, 19:2, 3) and the plea about the suppliant's words (*'ēmer*, v. 14), and about Yhwh's teaching being whole and the suppliant praying for wholeness (vv. 7, 13). Yhwh's decisions appear in 18:22 [23] and in 19:9.

Many other connections between the two parts of the psalm are not made. It would have been easy to include in vv. 1–6 the term *'ēdôt* for the declarations or decrees written into creation, which v. 7 uses for the declarations or decrees in the Torah. It would have been easy to use the similar term *ḥuqqôt*, which also has both significances (e.g., Job 38:33; Ps. 18:22 [23]!). It would have been easy to include *daʿat* (v. 2) in vv. 7–11. It would have been easy to use the same verb for the sun's rejoicing and the heart's joying (vv. 5, 8). Indeed, if vv. 1–6 and 7–11 have a common origin, they read as if the author was avoiding using similar terms about the proclamation in creation and the nature of Yhwh's Torah. Verses 1–6 and 7–11 share a distinctive hymnic style in comprising theological statements without address either to God or to the congregation.[5] But there is no syntactic link between the two parts—no "also" or "but." There is a marked change of rhythm; whereas 3-3 is the norm in vv. 1–6 (though some lines are shorter or longer), for vv. 7–9 the rhythm changes to 3-2, though the end of the psalm reverts to long lines. All this makes it unlikely that vv. 7–13 were composed to follow vv. 1–6.[6] More likely two separate units have been brought together on the basis of linguistic links and, perhaps, the interest in the complementary relationship between proclamation in creation and the instruction that comes from Yhwh's Torah.

Verses 1–6 and 7–14 thus form the two parts of the psalm, though the second part also divides between praise of Yhwh's teaching in vv. 7–11 and plea in vv. 12–14. Neither part corresponds to the regular form of (e.g.) a hymn or prayer psalm, though their forms overlap with these. Instead of inviting praise of God, vv. 1–6 draw attention to it, and they implicitly provide the reasons for it. Verses 7–11 then compare with the praise that can form the background for a lament, and like a penitential psalm vv. 12–14b implicitly lament the suppliant's moral weakness and make a plea with regard to this need. The pressure of other people also surfaces in this plea, and the closing colon (v. 14c) implies a confession of trust in Yhwh.

[1980]: 179–97, see 181–86). On the psalm's structure, see Pierre Auffret, "De l'oeuvre de ses mains au murmure de mon coeur," *ZAW* 112 (2000): 24–42.

5. Cf. Gerstenberger, *Psalms*, 1:101.

6. Against Whybray's conclusion to a survey of attitudes to the question in *Reading the Psalms*, 42–47.

Whereas Ps. 18 begins with an invocation of God but by the end is addressing the world or the community or no one in particular (a fairly common development in the Psalms), Ps. 19 moves in the opposite direction. It begins by addressing no one in particular and does so through the first section and on through vv. 7–10 until it comes to address and plead with God in vv. 11–14; there is no address to the congregation, in the usual manner of Israelite praise. Michael A. Fishbane suggests that a concern with speech holds the three parts of the psalm together: in vv. 1–6 the cosmos speaks, in vv. 7–11 Yhwh speaks, in vv. 12–14 the psalmist speaks.[7]

The leader's. Composition. David's.

Heading. See glossary. In vv. 11, 13 the suppliant speaks as "your servant" and refers to the pressure of the willful (or of foreigners—see translation note on v. 13), and this might suggest that the psalm was written for David or for one of his successors, or was reapplied to such a person. To put it another way, David becomes an exemplar for spirituality.[8]

19:1–6. So the psalm begins with the way the cosmos proclaims God's glory, though God disappears by the time vv. 1–6 come to an end. We wonder at the regular, persistent, ferocious journey the sun makes each day, and we know that it speaks. But what does it say? Back at the beginning, we have been told that it declares God's honor by declaring itself God's handiwork, but nothing more has been said about the content of its proclamation. That the sky proclaims God's honor and God's handiwork is all we discover about the object of its proclamation, as vv. 1–6 focus more and more resolutely on the proclaiming and the proclaimer rather than the proclaimed. Thus vv. 3–4b have continued to speak in general terms of the way the heavens do their proclaiming, while vv. 4c–6 have gone on to focus more concretely on the proclaimer by speaking at such length about the sun. The point may be put rhetorically. The opening line of the psalm comprised subject, verb, and object. Verses 2–4b then focused entirely on expanding the verb, and vv. 4c–6 entirely on expanding the subject. The object virtually disappeared after the opening line, appearing only as the unnamed subject of a two-letter unstressed verb in v. 4c (the verb is hyphenated into its object):

v. 1	The heavens	declare	God's honor
vv. 2–4b		declare	
vv. 4c–6	The heavens		

7. *Text and Texture* (New York: Schocken, 1979), 86.
8. Cf. Leslie C. Allen, "David as an Exemplar of Spirituality," *Bib* 67 (1986): 544–46.

So a section that at first looked as if it would tell of how creation glorifies God has ended up glorifying creation. If vv. 1–6 concern natural revelation, perhaps that is the nature of natural revelation.

In vv. 4–6, v. 4a–b is a self-contained couplet, and v. 4c looks like a new start. Verse 5 involves two quite different though complementary similes, and I take v. 5a as completing a couplet with v. 4c. Verses 5b–6 are then a pair of couplets belonging together in an *abb'a'* sequence.

> ¹The heavens are announcing God's honor,
>   the sky is declaring the work of his hands.

Two opening long lines manifest an expansiveness that corresponds to their theme and claim. They complement each other while also being closely parallel internally.[9]

In v. 1 the parallelism of heavens and sky shows that the former are the physical heavens and not the metaphysical place of God's dwelling nor the heavenly beings, whom one might imagine doing some proclaiming. The second colon also clarifies how the heavens do this proclaiming of God's *honor—namely, by virtue of the fact that the heavens/sky are God's handiwork. That already hints that the psalm refers not merely to the empty firmament but also to the heavens with their planets and stars. The splendor of sun, moon, stars, and planets implies the splendor of the one whose hands made them, like a craft-worker. As Paul will put it, creation reveals God's eternal power and deity (Rom. 1:20). Like their English equivalents, the verbs for "announce" and "declare" (*sāpar* piel, *nāgad* hiphil) are more familiar when used to refer to human proclamation, specifically the telling of Israel's story (e.g., Pss. 44:1 [2]; 71:17–18; 78:3–4). If we understand our relationship to God as one that essentially involves faith, that distances us from creation because it cannot believe; but if we see our relationship with God in terms of praise, it makes us one with creation, for praise is also creation's role.[10]

> ²Day to day it pours out speech,
>   night to night it proclaims knowledge.

EVV usually render "day to day pours out speech. . . ," which is a rather obscure expression, but in any case the parallelism suggests that

---

9. Thus in v. 1, first "heavens" and "sky" correspond, singular complementing plural; "announcing" and "declaring" correspond, hiphil complementing piel; and the line as a whole works *abcc'b'a'*: "The heavens are announcing God's honor, and the work of his hands is declaring the sky."
10. So Westermann, *Living Psalms*, 255.

the sky is the subject of the verbs in v. 2.[11] Thus v. 2 takes v. 1 further in drawing attention to the fact that the announcing and declaring go on through the day and through the night, in different ways. As vv. 4–6 will go on to note, the splendor of the daytime sky is simply the sun. The splendor of the nighttime sky is much more variegated, as in the sun's absence other lights become visible. The daytime speech the sky pours out is presumably the speech about God's honor, to which v. 1 referred; the sun in its splendor speaks profusely and eloquently about its maker and about its maker's splendor. The further statement that the night sky proclaims knowledge is a more open-ended one. The parallelism between vv. 1 and 2 may mean that it refers again to conveying an awareness of the wonder of the hands that made the sky. But *da'at* in the Psalms often suggests *acknowledgment as well as awareness. Verse 2b then suggests that this proclamation in the sky pushes toward recognition of its maker and not merely awareness of its maker's existence. In this respect, too, v. 2 goes beyond v. 1. A concern with such acknowledgment of Yhwh anticipates the different focus of vv. 7–14 and makes it noticeable that some form of the verb *yāda'* does not appear there.

> ³There is no speech, no words,
>   whose voice is not audible.

Two more regular 3-3 lines in turn expand on v. 2. Verse 3a stands in tension with what precedes and thus raises a question, and with LXX and Jerome I take v. 3b to answer the question by qualifying the first.[12] Verse 3 as a whole thus underlines how eloquent is the heavens' testimony. LXX has the heavens' voice being "heard," but the psalmist might recognize that actually their testimony is not always heard, and the point of v. 3 is rather that it always makes itself open to being heard; the niphal participle is gerundive (cf. those in vv. 7, 10).

---

11. In v. 2 "day to day" and "night to night" correspond, as do "pours out" and "proclaims," and "speech" and "knowledge." This verse complements the first by using yiqtol verbs instead of participles. The verbs are again hiphil and piel, though in reverse order, so that between the two verses the verbs come in *abb'a'* sequence. Further, the one-word participial expressions give way to phrases (pours out speech, proclaims knowledge), with the subject of the proclamation (God's honor, God's handiwork) carrying over from the previous line.

12. NRSV "Their voice is not heard" takes the *bĕlî* clause as parallel to the preceding *'ên* clauses, but this seems to make v. 3 contradict v. 2 as well as to stand in tension with v. 4a–b. NRSV thus adds "yet" to open v. 4, to make sense of its translation in the context. The absence of a *w* at the beginning of v. 3b signals that this clause may not merely continue the *'ên . . . wĕ'ên* sequence, and the suffix on "their voice" referring back to v. 3a both supports this and supports the idea that the clause is relative.

> ⁴ᵃ⁻ᵇIn all the earth their noise has set out,
> at the end of the world their words.

The second line of expansion on v. 2 makes the point again positively and takes it further. How far has all that proclamation gone? Through all the earth, says the first colon. Whereas "heaven and earth" are elsewhere a regular pair, here one is the giver, the other the receiver. But has the heavens' noise really gone through all the earth? Yes, to the very end, the second colon affirms.[13]

Paul uses the words of this line (Rom. 10:18) to describe the spread of the gospel message through the world.

> ⁴ᶜFor the sun he put a tent in them;
> ⁵ᵃit is like a groom coming out of his chamber.

Three rhythmically less regular bicola now sharpen the focus once more. The topic of the proclamation is quite left behind, except as the unnamed subject of the verb "put" (presumably God). The process of proclamation is also left behind as they focus on the most impressive means of proclamation. This concentration on the sun in particular may reflect the prominence of the sun god in Egypt and Mesopotamia.[14] Any polemic is understated, but against that background, the psalm does not address the sun or sun god, like (e.g.) a hymn to Amon or to Shamash.[15] Here the sun is "merely" an entity for which the real God provides overnight accommodation. God is outside creation and sovereign provider for it.

God, then, put a tent in the skies for the sun to stay in overnight. So each morning the sun is like a groom emerging with a smile on his face from his room, ready for his wedding, or emerging with a smile from the marriage chamber (*ḥuppâ*; cf. Joel 2:16, where it denotes the bride's chamber) to do what he has to do out in the world.

---

13. In the two parallel clauses, the verb applies to both, so that they work *abca'c'*. The verb is qatal, continuing a pattern of variation running through the first four lines—participial clauses, then yiqtol clauses, then noun clauses, then qatal clauses. While the variation is rhetorical, between them they suggest a process that is continuous (v. 1), reiterated (v. 2), actual (v. 3), and factual (v. 4); cf. in part *TTH* 43. The line also continues a pattern of variation in the nouns: after speech, knowledge, words, and voice (*'ōmer, da'at, děbārîm, qôl*) the psalm now speaks of "noise" and "utterances" (*qawwâ, millîm*).

14. Odil Hannes Steck draws a contrast with the more wisdom-like ethos of vv. 1–4a (see "Bemerkungen zur thematischen Einheit von Psalm 19,2–7," in *Werden und Wirken des Alten Testament* [Claus Westermann Festschrift], ed. Rainer Albertz et al. [Göttingen: Vandenhoeck & Ruprecht, 1980], 318–24).

15. See *ANET* 367–68, 386–89.

> ⁵ᵇIt rejoices like a warrior to run the path—
> ⁶its setting out is from one end of the heavens,
> Its completed circuit is at their other end,
> and there is nothing hidden from its ferocity.

Or the sun is like a warrior enthusiastic about running the path ahead of him; thus nothing escapes the ferocity of this warrior (vv. 5b, 6c; cf. Judg. 5:31).[16] The intervening cola meanwhile describe the dimensions of this journey. Masculine singular "end" in v. 6a is complemented by feminine plural "ends" in v. 6b, and masculine "setting out" by feminine "completed circuit," these differences mirroring the complementary statements in the two cola. Reference to the beginning and end of the "path" implies reference to the journey as a whole and thus justifies the comment in v. 6c. The actual words take up those of v. 4a. It is by means of the sun's journey that the heavens' proclamation is effected. Their noise sets out through the sun's setting out from one end of the heavens. Their words come to the end of the world through the sun's coming to the end of its daily circuit of the heavens.

19:7–11. With a sudden transition, in vv. 7–9 six 3-2 lines glorify Yhwh's instructions to Israel, with vv. 10–11 as footnotes, in 2-2, 2-2, and 3-3 rhythm.[17]

> ⁷Yhwh's teaching has integrity,
> restoring life.
> Yhwh's declaration is reliable,
> giving insight to the untaught.
> ⁸Yhwh's charges are upright,
> joying the heart.
> Yhwh's command is clean,
> lighting up the eyes.
> ⁹Yhwh's reverence is pure,
> standing forever.
> Yhwh's decisions are truthfulness;
> they are altogether faithful.

Yhwh's "teaching" can refer to the work of prophets and thinkers as well as to *the* Torah (see 1:2), and to oral as well as written teaching,

---

16. LXX has merely "heat," but this would be the only instance of *ḥammâ* with that meaning: elsewhere it is a term for the sun itself, usually in parallelism with "moon." But the related verb *ḥāmam* (be warm) is sometimes hard to distinguish sharply from *yāḥam* (be hot), and *ḥammâ* here at least carries the resonances of *ḥēmâ* (heat) and suggests the raging fury of a warrior (e.g., Isa. 51:13; Dan. 8:6).

17. In v. 8a, I remove a *maqqēph* to produce this consistency.

while its application to Genesis–Deuteronomy as a whole indicates that in principle it could also refer to the story of Yhwh's acts with Israel. Here the parallelism with the nouns in the next five lines makes these possibilities less likely. First, while etymologically *'ēdût* might suggest declaration or testimony concerning what Yhwh has done,[18] in practice it always refers to solemn declarations concerning Yhwh's expectations (e.g., 78:5; 119:14). That is reinforced by the further parallelism with "charges" (*piqqûdîm*, appointments Yhwh has made or decisions Yhwh has taken about what should happen). This word comes only in the Psalms (e.g., 103:18; 119:4). The plural means that the description in vv. 7–8 embraces the concrete instructions in their specificity as well as the whole in its unity (teaching, declaration).[19] The fourth term, "command" (*miṣwâ*), continues that reference to specificity and makes most explicit that vv. 7–8 do refer to Yhwh's expectations, as the line-by-line parallelism spells out the implications of the initial general expression "teaching." The verses laud Yhwh's instruction about behavior.

Following on the four near-synonyms, in v. 9 comes the expression *yir'at Yhwh*, which usually means "reverence for Yhwh"; after that comes "Yhwh's decisions." The latter takes a natural place in this sequence, as do the predicates that follow these two subjects. "Reverence for Yhwh" does not so fit, and it is odd to describe reverence for Yhwh as pure and standing forever. That sounds more like another description of Yhwh's instructions. So more likely *yir'at Yhwh* is another subjective genitive, denoting reverence that Yhwh lays down, teaching that indicates what reverence for Yhwh looks like. Verse 9 thus adds another pair of terms referring to Yhwh's teaching as a whole and in its specificity. At the same time, the occurrence of the term "Yhwh's reverence" draws attention to the wisdom flavor of vv. 7–11 (cf. Job 28:28; Prov. 1:7).

The six terms for Yhwh's instructions are qualified by six descriptions of their nature, by means of four adjectives, a participle, and a noun. They are characterized by *integrity, reliability, uprightness, cleanness, purity, and truth. This is a puzzling list of qualities to attribute to God's instructions. It is persons or lives that are whole or have integrity (e.g., 18:23, 25, 30, 32 [24, 26, 31, 33]). It is persons or promises that are reliable or faithful (e.g., 89:28 [29], 101.6)—though commands are once so described (111:7). It is persons or conduct that are upright (e.g., 11:2, 7; 25:8)—though Yhwh's *mišpāṭîm* are so described (119:137; Neh. 9:13), as is Yhwh's word (Ps. 33:4). It is persons or hearts that are clean (e.g., Job 11:4; Ps. 24:4; and cf. 18:20, 24 [21, 25]). It is hearts and promises that are pure (e.g., 12:6 [7]; 51:10 [12]). *Truthfulness is a much more generally

18. Cf. Weiser, *Psalms*, 202.
19. Cf. Mays, *Psalms*, 99.

applicable term. But as a group, these descriptions either involve ellipse or metonymy or need to be seen as pregnant expressions. They affirm that the effects of God's instructions are whole, reliable, upright, clean, pure, and true. They produce people and lives of that kind.

The six participial phrases that occupy the alternating short cola in vv. 7–9 make analogous points. They come in pairs, as the verse division suggests, though this is more obvious with the second and third pairs. First (v. 7), Yhwh's instructions are life-giving, or more specifically life-restoring (the verb is *šûb* hiphil). They provide renewal for the *nepeš* (*person), as food does for the hungry (Lam. 1:11, 19) or a son for an old person (Ruth 4:15) or comfort or good news for the anxious (Lam. 1:16; Prov. 25:13) or Yhwh for people under attack (Ps. 35:17).[20] How do they do so? The parallel participial phrases in vv. 7b–8 will suggest they do so by offering the encouragement that a life of obedience does issue in a life of blessing, and by leading one into the experience of its doing so. Conversely, the closing line of this section (v. 11) will suggest some awareness of temptation to wrongdoing and of the way wrongdoing destroys one's life. Verse 7a already makes the equivalent positive point, that obedience restores life. It can make one a person of integrity.

The person who needs such restoring is one who has been behaving like a fool, but Yhwh's declaration also gives insight (*ḥākam* hiphil) to the untaught (v. 7b). Etymologically, the untaught (*petî*) is the open person, one whose mind has not yet been occupied by insight and is therefore in a vulnerable, dangerous position. Yhwh's declaration concerning what is true and what Yhwh expects gives shape to their mind. It protects them and other people. It makes them reliable instead of unprincipled and immature.

The heart therefore joys at Yhwh's charges (v. 8a). There is joy in knowing what God's will is and in therefore being able to do it and stay in the place of God's blessing. The point is restated in the declaration that God's command lights up the eyes (v. 8b). NRSV's "enlightening the eyes" obscures the point; the lighting up of the eyes is a mark of encouragement (e.g., Ezra 9:8).

Verse 9 adds that Yhwh's reverence, the revelation that encourages and gives content to reverence, stands forever, like Yhwh's promise or covenant oath. It is permanently reliable as a guide to the nature of Yhwh's will and thus as a guide to the way Yhwh makes the world work. To put it another way, Yhwh's *decisions (*mišpāṭîm*) are *faithful (*ṣādēq*) as well as true. They arise out of a relationship with the world and/or with

---

20. Such usage argues against the translation "restoring the *soul*" (cf. LXX). See further Jonathan D. Safren, "'He Restoreth My Soul,'" in *Mari in Retrospect*, ed. Gordon D. Young (Winona Lake, IN: Eisenbrauns, 1992), 265–71.

Israel, express the nature of that relationship, and further it. Elsewhere the hendiadys *ṣĕdāqâ/ṣedeq ûmišpāṭ* recurs (e.g., 33:5; 89:14 [15]; 97:2) and declares that God acts decisively and faithfully and that humanity is also called to do so. Verse 9 affirms that Yhwh's expectations form part of this profile. Yhwh makes firm and definitive decisions about how human conduct should be and about the consequences that will follow from sticking to these decisions, but these decisions embody Yhwh's faithfulness. The unexpected noun "*truthfulness" (following on adjectives and a participle) and the unexpected verb "are faithful" (following on participles) mark the end of the sixfold sequence in vv. 7–9.[21]

> [10]They are more desirable than gold,
>   even than much fine gold,
> Sweeter than honey,
>   even juice from honeycombs.

The affirmation in v. 10 naturally follows. In each line the second colon takes the first further—not just gold, but fine gold; not just honey, but honey dripping fresh from the comb. Like corn syrup, honey is the test for sweetness (e.g., Prov. 24:13); the second colon makes explicit that the psalm has in mind not merely the common date honey but the greater delicacy of bee honey. Yhwh's decisions are as desirable or delightful as these (*ḥāmad*, niphal participle). The same participle applies to wealth (Prov. 21:20), but these are more so.

Yhwh's instructions are delightful and sweet-tasting for the reason that has been implicit in the descriptions in vv. 7–9. These words of Yhwh are not merely the sweet nothings that lovers share, but neither are people expected to be attached to Yhwh's expectations for selfless reasons, as if obedience were its own reward. Apart from Prov. 21:20, the participle "desirable" (*neḥĕmād*) comes otherwise only in Gen. 2–3, where it describes the trees in the garden and then the fruit of the forbidden tree. Clearly Adam and Eve did not take the view that Yhwh's decisions were more desirable than its fruit; the psalm thus offers a different commitment. Adam and Eve ignored Yhwh's teaching and ended up needing their *nepeš* to be restored. They behaved like the untaught when confronted by the shrewd. They found themselves the victims of a negative "forever." They went after what their eyes reckoned desirable and found their eyes opened in a bad sense, and not lightened up. The psalmist can be quite open about the fact that Yhwh's instructions are delightful for very practical reasons. If only Adam and Eve had viewed Yhwh's warnings as more delightful than the fruit of the forbidden tree!

---

21. On the emphatic use of a noun rather than an adj., see GKC 141c.

In terms of their potential fruitfulness, in reality those warnings were thus delightful, but Adam and Eve did not view them thus.[22]

> [11]Yes, your servant takes warning from them;
> there are great results from keeping them.

Verse 11 underlines the point by declaring the suppliant's responsive commitment. The verb, *zāhar* II (niphal), suggests the way people heed the words of a watchman (e.g., Ezek. 33:4–6). But in the context it also conveys the resonances of *zāhar* I, "be bright."[23] Heeding their warnings guards people from the gloom and darkness of the divine chastisement that comes from wrongdoing.

Thus there is a great outcome from following them. In the context of the heading, Yhwh's servant is David, as is so in Ps. 18, but a similar psalm such as 119 makes much use of "Yhwh's servant" as a description of an ordinary Israelite, and Ps. 19 is equally open to being claimed by such suppliants.

19:12–14. Unexpectedly, the last three lines of the psalm comprise pleas. Verses 7–11 could give a rather confident impression of our relationship with God's expectations. We see the wisdom of them and thus naturally follow them. In reality, things are more complicated, as v. 11 has already implied with its reference to our need of warnings.

> [12]Who can understand wanderings?—free me from secret acts,
> [13a]yes, withhold your servant from the willful.

If God's expectations are so good for us, why does the point need such underlining? Why do we take so little notice of them?

EVV add a pronoun to suggest that v. 12 asks who can understand one's own individual wrongdoing, but this is not the psalm's point. It rather begins from a more general sense of puzzlement at the human inclination to go off the rails. The mystery of human sin is the fact that we all go astray even though we can see that God's expectations make sense, in the way vv. 7–11 have described.

LXX and Jerome assume that v. 12 then asks God to cleanse the suppliant from hidden or secret wrongdoings, but this obscures an issue in the Hebrew. The verb is not one meaning "cleanse" but *nāqâ* (piel), "acquit." The OT makes a number of references to acquitting the guilty, but always in order to affirm that God does not do so and that human

---

22. See further David J. A. Clines, "The Tree of Knowledge and the Law of Yahweh," *VT* 24 (1974): 8–14.

23. Cf. Mitchell Dahood, "An Ebla Personal Name and the Metaphor in Psalm 19,11–12," *Bib* 63 (1982): 260–63.

beings should not (e.g., Exod. 34:7; Job 9:28; 10:14). One person can certainly *forgive* another, and kings can *pardon* wrongdoers, and God can both forgive and pardon, but the OT does not use the law-court image in this connection because acquitting the guilty is an immoral act and one destructive of the community's foundations. It is therefore unlikely that the psalm is asking for cleansing in the sense of acquitting existent wrongdoing, even (or especially) secret or hidden wrongdoing.

But *nāqâ* (niphal) can denote being free or empty, and the piel verb here seems to have an equivalent meaning. The cleansing for which the psalm is asking is not forgiveness but the removing of the inclination to wrongdoing. That makes for a good link with the verse's opening question and a good lead-in to the parallel colon. Further, without a plea for acquittal for past sin, vv. 12–14 have more coherence. Their concern throughout is with a life of obedience that issues from the right attitude to God's expectations that vv. 7–11 have lauded. They are asking for strength, not forgiveness.

There may be two sorts of "secret acts" (lit., "hidden things") from which the psalm asks for such cleansing, both being aspects of what Yhwh's teaching forbids. They may be the secret plots that precede actual wrong deeds; hiding is involved when people are planning acts of deception or malice (cf. the cognate nouns in 10:8–9; 101:5). Hiding can also be involved when people are seeking help from other deities, especially since this often involves household rites rather than temple rites. The account of secret rites in Ezek. 8 includes reference to people bowing down to the sun, and such reference to temptation to seek help from other deities would follow well on vv. 1–6. The challenge of vv. 7–11 then concerns a religious life lived by Yhwh's word rather than one that follows the religious practices of other peoples.

In v. 13a the "yes" constitutes a resumptive beginning for a colon that reexpresses the plea in v. 12 and clarifies it further. The kind of people who are involved in secret plans to do wrong to someone or who secretly worship other deities are the "willful," people who do not feel any obligation to take any notice of Yhwh's instructions,[24] whose attitude thus contrasts with that expressed in vv. 7–11. They are people who work hard at getting people to turn away from Yhwh's teaching (cf. 119:21, 51, 69, 78, 85, 122). The plea constitutes another recognition that the person who sees the wisdom in Yhwh's teaching (vv. 7–11) is not thereby immune from the pressure to join people who walk another way. The masculine "willful" complements the feminine "hidden," the "hidden things" being the deeds and the "willful people" those who do them. In another context "sparing me from the willful" could imply protecting

---

24. See *NIDOTTE* 1:1095.

me from their attacks (cf. LXX?), but in this context it will signify a plea that I not be sucked into their willfulness (cf. Ps. 1). Yet these two needs may overlap. The willful lean on people to join them—or else.

> ^{13b}May they not rule over me; then I shall be whole
> and free of great rebellion.

Thus may they not force me to walk their way, in the manner of the process of which Yhwh warns Cain (Gen. 4:7). If one again follows the heading and sees "Yhwh's servant" as David, then this constitutes a plea that other willful rulers should not rule over Yhwh's designated ruler of Israel and push him into policies that involve rebellion against Yhwh, as was often the kings' experience. Yhwh's protecting him from that will make it possible for him to remain wholly committed to Yhwh (*integrity): the psalm picks up that opening metonymic description of Yhwh's teaching (v. 7).

The parallel colon redescribes that by picking up the more recent image of being free or clear—of *rebellion (cf. v. 12). Verses 12–13 thus turn out to work *abb'a'*, the outer cola forming a pair and the inner cola forming another pair. Having recourse to other deities is then the "great rebellion" of which v. 13c speaks (cf. Isa. 1:2). The phrase recalls the expressions "great sin/wrong/offense," referring to adultery and then to religious adultery, turning to another god (see Gen. 20:9; 39:9; Exod. 32:21, 30, 31; Ezra 9:7, 13; though the adjective is *gādôl*, not *rāb* as here).[25]

> ¹⁴May the words of my mouth be acceptable
> and the talk of my heart come before you,
> Yhwh, my crag, my restorer.

The psalm closes with a tricolon that repeats this plea. The first two cola work *abb'a'*: literally, "May be for acceptance—the words of my mouth—and the talk of my heart—before you." The first and last phrases thus apply to both cola, as is reflected in the standard prosaic translation "May the words of my mouth and the meditation of my heart be acceptable before you." The context suggests the "words" are not the words of the psalm or the psalmist's words in general, but the words one might address to another deity or the words that might be the means of doing wrong to another person. Words are commonly a means of wrongdoing in the Psalms, the link between secret plots and actual harm to people. So a plea that one's words may be acceptable to God is another

---

25. Cf. Jacob R. Rabinowitz, "The 'Great Sin' in Ancient Egyptian Marriage Contracts," *JNES* 18 (1959): 73; W. L. Moran, "The Scandal of the 'Great Sin' at Ugarit," *JNES* 18 (1959): 280–81.

plea for liberation and protection from wandering. The middle colon's reference to inward talk restates that again. Inward talk is the secret plot or the secret turning to another deity. "Acceptable" or "welcome" (*lĕrāṣôn*) commonly refers to the acceptability or welcome of a sacrifice (e.g., Lev. 1:3). The psalm presupposes that there is a link between the acceptability of one's sacrifices and the acceptability of one's (inner) words and prayers. Acceptable words and hearts without acceptable sacrifices are not enough; they would be too cheap, too ethereal, too otherworldly. But acceptable sacrifices without an acceptable mouth and heart are also not enough.

The final colon is both conventional and surprising. The description of Yhwh as *crag has recurred in Ps. 18 and makes for another link with that preceding psalm, and another link with the possibility of hearing the psalm on the lips of David. But the regular context for this description is when the suppliant needs protection. Here the focus lies on the possibility that other people need protection from us, and Yhwh is the crag in the sense of being one who enables us to stand firm against ourselves and our inclinations, or against the pressures of the willful, who seek to draw us into their wanderings. The description of Yhwh as restorer brings the first occurrence in the Psalter of the verb *gā'al*. A restorer (*gō'ēl*) is the next of kin within a family who takes action or spends resources in order to put things right when a family member is in trouble or has been wronged. Used of God, this verb thus puts us in God's family and implies God's accepting family obligations toward us when we are in trouble. "Restore me" therefore implies, "Do your duty by me"[26] by making things right for me.

Perhaps a further implication of this closing acknowledgment of Yhwh as rock and restorer is that it constitutes a recognition that the kind of commitment expressed in vv. 7–13 is a necessity if we are to find Yhwh behaving as rock and restorer. Once again this sets up a link with Ps. 18, which made the same assumption but reversed the balance between these. Psalms 18 and 19 thus complement each other.

Theological Implications

Traditionally, Ps. 19 has been understood to set natural revelation and special revelation alongside each other.[27] In broad terms that is an ap-

26. Rogerson and McKay, *Psalms*, 2:97.
27. See Aquinas's commentary (Ps. 18 in his enumeration); Calvin, *Psalms*, 1:307–33—though they do not use the actual terms "general revelation" and "special revelation"; also Michael Landon, "God and the Sciences," *ResQ* 38 (1996): 238–41. Sheri L. Clouda notes an interplay of a visual and a verbal revelation in the psalm ("The Dialectical Interplay

propriate understanding, though it requires nuancing if it is not to generate skewed interpretations of the psalm. First, the concept of revelation was an attempt to solve problems in post-Enlightenment thinking, and naturally the Scriptures do not directly address these questions. Their talk of revelation belongs in a different framework. Related to this is the fact that neither of the two main parts of the psalm talks in terms of "revelation," unlike (e.g.) the accounts of God's being revealed to Israel's ancestors or the prophets. Instead, the first part talks about announcing and declaring. The heavens do not reveal something that was hidden but draw attention to something that has always been apparent. Further, it is not nature in general that does this proclaiming, but the heavens in particular, because of their particular capacity in their impressiveness to draw attention to God's honor. And they do not reveal anything by way of ethical demands.

The second part does move from speaking of God as *'ēl* to speaking of God as Yhwh,[28] but otherwise it does not offer a revelation of further truths that could not be known from nature, such as the truths about God's purpose expressed in the story of Israel that came to a climax in Jesus. Rather, it talks about the nature of God's instructions—more specifically, about the profitability of these. We assume they refer to Yhwh's instructions to Israel in particular, though they do not say so. And in any case, God's instructions to Israel about matters such as morals, the organization of society, and worship are often quite similar to other peoples' beliefs and practices in such areas. Again the distinction between general and special revelation collapses.

Christian doctrine emphasizes that general revelation is not enough, and vv. 1–6 imply this, though in a different way. We have noted how they talk more and more about the proclamation and less and less about the object of the proclamation. The heavens resemble a preacher who reckons to draw attention to Jesus but inevitably draws attention to himself or herself. In other words, vv. 1–6 deconstruct. The heavens testify to God's splendor, but they more obviously testify to their own splendor and thus draw God's people into worshipping them. In contrast, vv. 7–11 recognize this problem from the beginning. They never pretend to be glorifying anything other than God's teaching. But their change to 3-2 rhythm (which corresponds to that of Ps. 119) suggests that the function of Yhwh's instructions is not triumphalist or supersessionist but is to remind God's people not to fall into the trap of worshipping the cosmos, and vv. 12–14 ask for Yhwh's help in making sure we follow them to that

---

of Seeing and Hearing in Psalm 19 and Its Connection to Wisdom," *Bulletin of Biblical Research* 10 [2000]: 181–95).

28. Cf. Mays, *Psalms*, 98.

end. But vv. 7–11 do offer a way out of the temptation to which vv. 1–6 refer. It is tempting to worship (e.g.) the sun, but Yhwh's teaching forbids that and promises that real life lies in resisting this temptation. If some people are inclined to bibliolatry, to the worship of Scripture (though I have never met one such), then they would need to face the warning that might also emerge from the second part of the psalm, that we must no more revere Scripture as if it were God than revere the sun as if it were God. Further, vv. 7–14 also deconstruct if read as implying that special revelation supersedes general revelation, because a revelation given only to Israel cannot bring about Yhwh's just reign in the whole world, over which the heavens make their proclamation.[29]

A further double contrast with Christian attitudes emerges in the psalm. Christians are often enthusiastic about the glory of nature but see Moses's teaching as an oppressive bondage. Psalm 19 finds God's revelation in the cosmos rather frightening in its fieriness, but is full of joyful enthusiasm for Yhwh's expectations. The psalm challenges Christian readers to see that Yhwh's instructions are designed to be life-giving. The letter of Yhwh's instructions is not designed to kill (contrast 2 Cor. 3:6).[30]

Finally, we observe that the psalm cannot be satisfied with comments on creation and revelation. At the end, it has to come to a plea for redemption.[31] Theodoret thus sees three kinds of divine law in the psalm: the law written into creation, the law given through Moses, and "the law of grace"(!).[32] Ross Wagner sees the psalm as starting from God in creation and moving through a response to God's revelation in the Torah to a climax in the plea of the human heart.[33] Arndt Meinhold sees it moving from words about God, via words of God, to words to God.[34]

---

29. Cf. Rolf Knierim, "On the Theology of Psalm 19," in *The Task of Old Testament Theology* (Grand Rapids: Eerdmans, 1995), 322–50, see 345.
30. Cf. Mays, *Psalms*, 99.
31. Cf. Fishbane, *Text and Texture*, 89.
32. *Psalms*, 1:133. He adds references to Rom. 1:20; 2:14; 8:2; Gal. 3:19.
33. "From the Heavens to the Heart," *CBQ* 61 (1999): 245–61.
34. "Überlegungen zur Theologie des 19. Psalms," *ZTK* 80 (1983): 119–36.

Psalm 20
A Blessing for the King

Translation

The leader's. Composition. David's.

¹May Yhwh answer you on the day of trouble,
  the name of Jacob's God set you on high.
²May he send your help from the holy place,
  sustain you from Zion.
³May he be mindful of all your grain offerings,
  enthuse over your whole-offering. (Rise)
⁴May he give you in accordance with your thinking,
  fulfill your every plan.
⁵May we resound at your deliverance,
  wave our flags[a] in the name of our God;
May Yhwh fulfill all your requests.

⁶Now I know
  that Yhwh is delivering his anointed.
He will answer him from his holy heavens
  with mighty acts of deliverance by his right hand.

⁷Some people extol chariotry and others horses,
  but we—we extol the name of Yhwh our God.

    a. LXX "be magnified" (cf. Syr) implies metathesis from the verb *dāgal* to the more predictable *gādal*. In later Hebrew usage *degel* refers to a company of troops (cf. *DCH*) and Tg, Sym, and Jerome translate on the basis of this meaning. An Akkadian cognate suggests "wait for" (cf. *DCH*).

⁸They—they are collapsing and falling;
    we—we are rising and lifting ourselves up.[b]
⁹Yhwh, deliver the king;[c]
    may he answer us on the day we call.

Interpretation

Reading through Ps. 20 soon establishes that vv. 1–5 belong together but that something new happens with v. 6. That is signaled first by the resumptive monocolon in v. 5c and then by the change of verb form in v. 6. Verses 1–5 are the words of a group of people (see v. 5a–b) to an individual, probably a leader in the context of some crisis: v. 9 will eventually imply that it is the king. In v. 6 an individual speaks and picks up from vv. 1–5 references to Yhwh's answering (v. 1), Yhwh's delivering (v. 5), and the holy place ($qōdeš$, v. 2, is also the word for "holy" in v. 6). So this person's "acknowledgment" is a response to vv. 1–5. The one who speaks seems to refer indirectly to himself in the third person in speaking of Yhwh's "anointed," meaning the king. In vv. 7–9 the reversion to first-person plural suggests that these are the words of the original speakers, who also refer to the anointed king in the third person.[1]

Commentators describe vv. 1–5 as a prayer,[2] but several considerations suggest this is not quite right. One expects a prayer to be addressed to God (v. 9a alone in the psalm is so addressed), or at least spoken in the jussive without any other overt addressee, so that God's overhearing makes God the de facto addressee (as in v. 9b); we might compare the bulk of Ps. 72. But vv. 1–5 here are addressed to the person for whom people are "praying," like the bulk of Ps. 91. In form, the verbs may be read equally as yiqtol or jussive. Like Ps. 91, vv. 1–5 here are thus less a prayer than a declaration of confidence in what Yhwh will do, or a promise, or a proclamation of God's blessing, like Eli's words to Hannah (1 Sam. 1:17).[3] The king's response in v. 6 corresponds to that. In vv. 7–9 the original speakers take up the king's declaration of commitment to Yhwh and close off the psalm with an actual prayer and a final wish or expression of confidence. The psalm is a dialogue

---

    b. I have translated the hitpolel verb as reflexive, though *HALOT* takes it as reciprocal, "help one another up," and LXX as passive, "be set upright."

    c. Weiser (*Psalms*, 205) renders, ". . . O King, who answers us . . . ," but this is a forced understanding.

    1. On the psalm's structure, see Pierre Auffret, "Qu'il te réponde, YHWH, au jour de détresse," *BN* 101 (2000): 5–9.

    2. E.g., Kraus, *Psalms*, 1:278.

    3. Cf. Gerstenberger, *Psalms*, 1:103–5; Seybold, *Psalmen*, 89; J. Kenneth Kuntz, "King Triumphant: A Rhetorical Study of Psalms 20 and 21," *HAR* 10 (1987): 157–76, see 159.

between people and king, though a priest might speak the people's part on their behalf.

The psalm has a number of verbal links with Ps. 18, so that we might reckon that the psalms have been (almost) juxtaposed so as to suggest that Ps. 18 offers testimony that the blessings in Ps. 20 have come about, or that Ps. 20 promises that Yhwh will do again what Ps. 18 testifies to. There the king speaks of Yhwh's "answer" making him great (18:35 [36]), and here the people promise that Yhwh will "answer" the king (v. 1). There the king speaks of being in trouble (*ṣar*, 18:6 [7]), and here the people refer to the day of trouble (*ṣārâ*, v. 1). There the king describes Yhwh as his haven on high (*miśgāb*, 18:2 [3]); here people promise that Yhwh will place the king in a haven, above the danger that assails him, inaccessibly high (*śāgab* piel, v. 1). There the king testifies to the way Yhwh sustained him (18:35 [36]); here people promise that Yhwh will sustain the king (v. 2). There the king makes music to Yhwh's name (18:49 [50]); here the people promise that the name of the God of Jacob will protect him. In v. 8 the enemies' falling compares with, and the people's rising contrasts with, the falling and non-rising of the king's victims (18:38 [39]).

An Aramaic prayer bears substantial similarity to Ps. 20:

> May Horus answer us in our troubles
> May Adonay answer us in our troubles
> O Bow in Heaven, Sahar.
> Send your emissary from the temple of Arash,
> and from Zephon may Horus sustain us.
> May Horus grant us our heart's desire
> May Mar grant us our heart's desire
> May Horus fulfill our every plan
> May Horus fulfill—may Adonay not withhold (even) in part—
>   every request of our hearts,
> the request of hearts which you, O El, have tested.
> We—O Mar, our God, Horus, YH, our god—are faint.
> May El Bethel answer us tomorrow.
> May Baal of Heaven, Mar, bless.
> Upon your pious ones are your blessings.[4]

---

4. I quote the text from Charles F. Nims and Richard C. Steiner, "A Paganized Version of Psalm 20:2–6 from the Aramaic Text in Demotic Script," in *Studies in Literature from the Ancient Near East* (Samuel Noah Kramer Festschrift), ed. Jack M. Sasson (New Haven, CT: American Oriental Society, 1984), 261–74. For varying views on its date and its relationship to the psalm, see Moshe Weinfeld, "*Ḥtqṣt hp'g'ny ('rmyt bktb dmwty) šl thlym k'* 2–8," *Eretz-Israel* 18 (1985): 130–40, 70*; K. A. D. Smelik, "The Origin of Psalm 20," *JSOT* 31 (1985): 75–81; Ingo Kottsieper, "Anmerkungen zu Pap. Amherst 63," *ZAW* 100 (1988): 217–44; idem, "Papyrus Amherst 63," in *Die Königspsalmen*, by Oswald Loretz (Münster: Ugarit, 1988), 55–75; Oswald Loretz, *Königspsalmen*, 15–54; Martin Rösel, "Israels Psalmen

The date of both the psalm and the Aramaic prayer, and their relationship, are matters of contention, so that we cannot comment with conviction on whether the psalm reworked the prayer or vice versa, but comparing the two is nevertheless illuminating. The prayer appeals to a number of gods, the psalm to one; likewise there are a number of sanctuaries from which an answer to the prayer might come, but only Zion from which Yhwh's answer will issue. This enables the suppliants to hedge their bets; it gives them choices. The psalm has only one hope. Related to this, second, the prayer is verbally more repetitive as it associates the same desire with different gods. The psalm speaks in more varied ways about what Yhwh will do, though its synonymous parallelism means that within lines it often says essentially the same thing in different words. It also makes more use of imagery and thus has a different effect for the suppliants and for God. Third, the prayer is indeed a prayer. Although much of it is expressed in the third person, it is concerned for "us," whereas the psalm is concerned for "our" leader, the king, and it takes the form of a blessing rather than a prayer. Further, with its reference to chariotry and horses, the psalm offers more concrete indications of a situation of need, and with its references to falling and rising, more concrete indications of what an answer to prayer or the fulfillment of the blessing would look like.

The psalm may have been used when a battle was expected; links with Ps. 18 (and 21) may support that. Then 2 Chron. 20 illustrates the kind of occasion, and Pss. 44 and 60 indicate the kind of prayers people then prayed, which a blessing such as Ps. 20 responds to, though we do not know what particular situation this might have been.[5] But alternatively the psalm may have been used on a regular liturgical occasion in view of the recurrent need for assurance that the king would be delivered if war should come. It need not indicate that the king currently faces a crisis. Either way, we do not know when it was written.

> The leader's. Composition. David's.

Heading. See glossary. The psalm involves a dialogue between people and king and could thus be used by the David of the day and his people.

20:1–5. The third-person yiqtols or jussives that dominate vv. 1–5 compare with those in the blessing in Num. 6:24–26, while Ps. 72 illustrates the interweaving of many such third-person forms with one or two actual prayers. In the OT, blessing is the task of leaders such

---

in Ägypten?" *VT* 50 (2000): 81–99; Ziony Zevit, "The Common Origin of the Aramaicized Prayer to Horus and of Psalm 20," *JAOS* 110 (1990): 213–28.

5. Cf. Rogerson and McKay, *Psalms*, 1:90.

as Moses, David, and other kings (e.g., Deut. 33; 1 Chron. 16:2), and of priests (e.g., Num. 6:24–26; Deut. 10:8; Ps. 118:26), while ordinary people have the capacity to bless one another (129:8) and to bless the king (72:14–15; 1 Kings 1:47; 8:66). Here the opening verses, with their promise of Yhwh's answering the king's prayer and accepting his gifts, might suggest a priest's blessing, but it becomes clear with v. 5 that if a priest speaks, he does so on the people's behalf.[6]

> ¹May Yhwh answer you on the day of trouble,
> the name of Jacob's God set you on high.
> ²May he send your help from the holy place,
> sustain you from Zion.

In each of the first two lines the second colon parallels the first but makes the point more specific.[7] Each first colon speaks of a concrete act, "answer" and "send help" being the two aspects to a response to a prayer that a person utters in a situation of need. First there is a declaration that God has heard and intends to act, then there is an act that puts this declaration into effect. Each second colon shows what the response looks like. The promise referring to the *name of Jacob's God makes a link with Jacob's testimony when he speaks of the God who answered him on the day of his trouble (Gen. 35:3).

Coming parallels with Isa. 30–31 suggest a comparison with its warnings about going down to Egypt for *help (30:1–2; 31:1–5). Yhwh will make such recourse unnecessary; perhaps the blessing contains a warning not to fall into that trap. What is the "holy place" from which this help comes? At first the second colon seems to clarify this, as it is supposed to do. Zion is the holy place. Yet in due course v. 6 will complicate this picture. Yhwh answers both from Zion, the holy place (*qōdeš*), and from "his holy heavens" (*šĕmê qodšô*). But Zion is itself the place where Yhwh decided to live, and it is a kind of outpost of Yhwh's home in heaven, so it is also the place whence Yhwh's acts issue. Mentioning Zion here will link with the fact that this is where congregation and king are gathered.

> ³May he be mindful of all your grain offerings,
> enthuse over your whole-offering. (Rise)

---

6. In vv. 1–5, every colon but the penultimate includes a word that ends with -*kā*, "you/your," and every colon but the first two in v. 5 includes a verb beginning with *y*, "may."

7. Verse 1 works *abca′b′*, the adverbial phrase "in the day of trouble" carrying over to the second colon in a way that leaves space for the longer subject. Qal verbs and piel verbs complement each other. The shorter v. 2 then works *abb′a′*.

Verse 3 further presupposes that Zion is where sacrifices are offered and blessings proclaimed, and where Yhwh will respond to the offerings the king makes to accompany his prayers, and will turn blessings from words into deeds.[8] That will happen because Yhwh is *mindful of the king's gifts. The idea is hardly that Yhwh's support can be bought: at least Ps. 50 (for instance) would deny that. The gifts are rather a sign of the king's serious turning to Yhwh in a situation of need. Verse 7 will hint at the possibility that the king might do otherwise, the possibility referred to in passages such as Isa. 30–31. But Yhwh cannot resist someone who does thus turn. In isolation, *minḥâ* might refer to offerings in general, but the second colon adds reference to the *whole-offering. More likely, then, the two cola refer to different kinds of offering. Leviticus 2, indeed, uses the term *'azkārâ* to refer to the portion of the grain offering that was itself burnt as an offering to Yhwh, to get Yhwh's attention or to signify the giving of attention to Yhwh. The verb in the second colon joins in reexpressing the point, though a little obscurely, but it seems that the people promise (lit.) that Yhwh will "recognize as fat" these offerings.[9] The fat was a delicacy that especially belonged to Yhwh (e.g., Lev. 3:16–17).

> [4]May he give you in accordance with your thinking,
>   fulfill your every plan.

Verse 4 continues the theme of Yhwh's answering the king's prayer and responding to his sacrifices.[10] Initially we might assume that the reference to the king's *lēbāb* denotes the right attitude of heart that must accompany a sacrifice, but the second colon clarifies the logic and indicates that it refers to thinking. The king's heart or *mind has been formulating plans, which one can do independently of Yhwh (again, cf. Isa. 30:1). The words assume that the king is not making this mistake.

> [5]May we resound at your deliverance,
>   wave our flags in the name of our God;
> May Yhwh fulfill all your requests.

It now becomes clearer who speaks in vv. 1–4: either the people as a whole or someone who represents them. It also becomes explicit that the trouble envisaged by vv. 1–4 does not affect the king alone but in-

---

8. It works *abb'a'* as in v. 2, pairs qal and piel as in v. 1, and also pairs plural and singular.

9. Taking *dāšan* as declarative piel; see *IBHS* 24.2fg, following Ernest Jenni, *Das hebräische Pi'el* (Zurich: EVZ, 1968).

10. It once more works *abb'a'* and pairs qal and piel.

volves the whole people, though it is not yet explicit why it does that. The king needs *deliverance, and when he has deliverance, the people will *resound. But what sort of deliverance is this? In theory the second colon may imply some clarification, though in practice it does so only incompletely. As well as resounding, the people will wave their flags or banners in God's *name. Such banner-waving comes in two contexts, both with military implications. In Num. 1–2 the banners belong to the army of Israel on the march. In the Song of Songs the context is more paradoxical, but the description of the woman as "awesome as women with banners" (or perhaps "armies with banners"; Song 6:4, 10) suggests military connotations.[11] So the people may speak as members of the army the king leads. But the location of this colon after the reference to celebrating the king's deliverance means it hardly denotes their waving their banners as they go into battle; perhaps they imagine waving them in triumph as they return home.

In v. 5c the blessing comes to an end with a further single clause. One would normally expect such a clause to form a tricolon with the two that precede, but here markers point rather to its being a self-contained single-colon line. Whereas v. 5a–b formed another 2-2 line that matched vv. 2–4, v. 5c is a regular three-stress line. In content, it resumes the third-person blessing form and sums up the blessing as a whole, the requests being those implied by the reference to "answer" (v. 1), to offerings (v. 3), and to desires (v. 4, where the verb "may he fulfill" recurs).

> [6]Now I know
> that Yhwh is delivering his anointed.
> He will answer him from his holy heavens
> with mighty acts of deliverance by his right hand.

20:6. Commentators commonly assume that the "I" responding to vv. 1–5 denotes the voice of a prophet or priest,[12] but it is more natural to take it as the voice of the person addressed in vv. 1–5, the king, who then speaks of himself in the third person as Yhwh's *anointed. When someone whose words may be trusted has uttered words of blessing or promise or response, then the appropriate reaction is trust and confidence (see, e.g., 1 Sam. 1:17–18).

It is unnecessary to hypothesize that the king's "now I know..." is a response to an unquoted oracle or an unmentioned liturgical event.[13] While "now I know..." can be a response to an event (e.g.,

---

11. The implications of Song 2:4 and 5:10 are more enigmatic.
12. E.g., Adam C. Welch, "Psalm xx," *ExpTim* 37 (1925–26): 407–10.
13. See Weiser, *Psalms*, 207–8.

Gen. 22:12; Judg. 17:13), the confession also corresponds to Jethro's at Sinai, which was a reaction to words from Moses (Exod. 18:11). In the context of the psalm, the confession constitutes a response to the people's words of blessing. Perhaps their being mediated by a priest gives them the authority to call forth such a response, or perhaps they derive that from a power that can also reside in the people's words. The king echoes their words in using the verb *deliver and the noun deliverance.[14] The verb is qatal, expressing the conviction that God is already beginning the act that implements the promise. The king echoes the promise again in using the verb "He will answer him," the same verb form as appeared in v. 1 except for the necessary change in suffix. We have noted that the reference to this answer coming "from his holy heavens" takes up the word *qōdeš* from v. 2, though it locates Yhwh's sanctuary in the heavens rather than on Zion. "His holy heavens" at first makes one think of Yhwh's metaphysical dwelling, but in that connection one would expect the construct phrase in the opposite order to suggest "his heavenly sanctuary" (which is NJPS's translation, indeed). But Ps. 18:7–15 spoke of the way Yhwh's answer came from his holy heavens in the form of an extraordinary demonstration of Yhwh's power within the cosmos as Yhwh intervenes in the world. Once again the psalm promises what Ps. 18 testifies to. Such will be the acts of *might coming from Yhwh's right hand that bring about deliverance.[15]

20:7–9. The reversion to "we" talk in vv. 7–9 suggests that these are again the words of the people or their representative.

> [7]Some people extol chariotry and others horses,
> but we—we extol the name of Yhwh our God.

First a long line (4-4) more overtly takes up the theme of trust as it recognizes the possibility that one might put confidence in chariotry and horses (cf. Isa. 31:1). But it uses a distinctive verb, referring not to trust but to prayer. The verb (*zākar* hiphil, with *bĕ* to introduce the object) again picks up the people's words, this being the hiphil of the verb translated "be mindful" in v. 3, while the reference to Yhwh's *name also picks up v. 1 (and v. 5), as does the juxtaposing of "Yhwh" and "our God" (compare "Yhwh" and "Jacob's God" there). The verb suggests people talking about and commemorating someone or something (cf.

---

14. Though the noun is *yeša'*, not *yĕšû'â* as in v. 5.
15. I have laid out v. 6 as two bicola, though the lines are prosaic, and it is arguably the two middle cola that stand in parallelism. Certainly the qatal and yiqtol/jussive verbs form a contrasting pair, affirming both that in a sense Yhwh has begun to act and that nevertheless Yhwh's act still lies in the future.

Josh. 23:7; Isa. 48:1; Amos 6:10; without *bĕ*, Pss. 45:17 [18]; 71:16; 77:11 [12]). There are people who do that for chariotry and horses, as Isaiah notes, but as a proper Israelite this king will do it only for Yhwh. The rhetoric recalls the way Isa. 30 critiques people's applying words such as "refuge," "shelter," and "protection" to Egypt as they put their trust in horses and chariotry. The king will not make that mistake but will extol only Yhwh.[16]

> [8]They—they are collapsing and falling;
> we—we are rising and lifting ourselves up.

In this neat line of contrasting parallelism, the verbs again are instantaneous qatals (plus a final wayyiqtol) portraying coming events as already actual. In connection with qatals the pronouns are unnecessary and are included for emphasis. Each line thus comprises a pronoun and two verbs of more or less synonymous meaning.[17]

> [9]Yhwh, deliver the king;
> may he answer us on the day we call.

The two cola complement each other as the first comprises address to God and the second reverts to the third-person form referring to God that characterized vv. 1–5.[18] In the first colon *deliver recurs from vv. 5, 6a, 6b, and the actual word "king" comes for the first time. The second colon then begins with a third variant on the suffixed verb that appeared in vv. 1 and 6, so that the verb forms an inclusion with v. 1. As there, the expression "on the day . . ." follows. If "the day of trouble" becomes "the day we call," it ceases to be the day of trouble.

---

16. William F. Smelik ("The Use of *hzkyr bšm* in Classical Hebrew," *JBL* 118 [1999]: 321–32) takes this expression to mean "swear by." Literally understood, this involves some tautology in Josh. 23:7 and Isa. 48:1 and a tortuous explanation of Ps. 20:7, but it might be an equivalent to the colloquial use of "swear by" to mean "place reliance on."

17. In the first colon, the two verbs would be capable of describing dramatic stages in the process of crumpling (cf. Judg. 5:27), but they are also capable of being more or less synonyms and here are linked by simple *w*, which suggests that they constitute two ways of describing the same event. In the second colon, *ʿûd* is a separate root from the common *ʿûd* meaning "witness." In one of the two uses of the polel (147:6), it is set over against bringing someone down, which suggests that despite the *w* consecutive the two verbs in v. 8b are also more or less synonyms.

18. MT implies, "Yhwh, deliver; may the king answer us on the occasion when we call" (cf. Jerome). The king might then be the divine King—so Tg, which takes this as an invocation and thus follows it with an imperative (cf. *Midrash on Psalms*, 1:292). LXX has "Lord, deliver the king, and listen to us on whatever day we call on you." It is surely right rather to divide the verse 3-3, though there is no need to emend the second colon to a second-person verb.

Theological Implications

The distinctive feature of Ps. 20 is the prominence it gives to the blessing of the king, the declaration to the king that God intends to respond to his prayers, sustain him, protect him, and give him victory. Blessing involves the avowal to someone that God has such intentions toward them. It is thus related to prayer in the sense that God wills that it play a role in the implementing of God's will in the world, but a blessing is not so much a request addressed to God as a declaration of what the blesser is empowered to say God will do. It is performative language, language that puts into effect what it speaks of. Blessing is God's means of implementing a purpose in people's life. The relationship of blessing can be two-way, and there is a relationship of codependence between people and king. King blesses people; people bless king.

In general terms, the people as a whole, and the priests in particular, know what is God's purpose for the king. In a context where it might seem uncertain whether that purpose will come about, their privilege and task is thus to declare to the king that God's purpose will indeed be fulfilled. God will accept his offerings and answer his prayer, protect him, help him, sustain him, and enable him to fulfill his plans. They are confident about rejoicing to see all that happen, trusting in God for it rather than in their military hardware. Such a declaration of God's intent has the natural effect of strengthening the king to face what he has to do. There is a dynamic interrelationship between people's blessing their leader when in need, the leader's confidence, and the people's confidence. Paradoxically, blessing does not make actual prayer redundant. Perhaps it does the opposite. On the basis of exercising the God-given responsibility to bless, priests and people can pray with more confidence for God to implement the blessing.

In the NT, too, believers have the capacity, responsibility, and privilege of blessing one another (Luke 2:34; 6:28; Rom. 12:14; 1 Cor. 4:12), and churches and pastors live in a codependent relationship similar to that of king and people. Their congregation, and groups such as elders or deacons or church councils, have the power, privilege, and responsibility to bless their pastor by declaring God's acceptance of his or her prayers, God's protection, help, and sustaining, and their own trust in God rather than in their church's resources. The pastor is dependent on their blessing. And they themselves are dependent on that blessing.

Psalm 21

The Implications of Someone Else's Deliverance

Translation

The leader's. Composition. David's.

¹Yhwh, in your strength may the king rejoice,
  In your deliverance how he may delight, so much![a]

²The desire of his heart you gave him,
  the request of his lips you did not withhold. (Rise)
³For you go to meet him with rich blessings,[b]
  you set on his head a crown of fine gold.
⁴When he asked life from you, you gave to him
  length of days forever and ever.[c]
⁵His honor is great because of your deliverance,
  splendor and majesty you put on him.
⁶For you make him an abundant blessing[d] forever,
  you gladden him with joy through your presence.

    a. In K both verbs could be either yiqtol or jussive, but in Q (and C) the second verb is *yāgel* (for K's *yāgêl*), which looks like a jussive. GKC 109k takes it as yiqtol, but it does not fit GKC's reasons for using such a form for a yiqtol, whereas jussive fits the psalm's third-person thanksgiving form. *TTH* 70 seems to take Q as jussive.
    b. Lit., "blessings of good," but the second word might then seem redundant, and this expression is likely an instance of the use of two nouns of related meaning to convey a superlative sense (see *IBHS* 14.5b).
    c. I take the asyndesis as subordinating the first clause to the second, and follow LXX, Jerome, and Tg in taking the second colon as comprising the object of the second verb, so that the colon involves enjambment (i.e., the syntactical unit continues to the second colon rather than ending with the first colon); EVV provide an object pronoun in the first colon.
    d. *šît* followed by two accusatives usually denotes making something into something else (cf. Tg; elsewhere, e.g., 84:6 [7]). "You give blessings to him" would require *lĕ*. With GKC 124e I take the pl. as intensifying.

⁷For the king is trusting in Yhwh,
   by the commitment of the Most High he does not falter.

⁸Your hand finds out all your enemies,
   your right hand finds out those who are against you.
⁹You make them like a blazing furnace
   at the time of^e your presence.
Yhwh swallows them in his wrath;
   fire consumes them.
¹⁰You destroy their offspring from the earth,
   their issue from humankind.
¹¹When^f they have directed evil against you,
   thought up a scheme, they do not succeed.
¹²For you set them back;^g
   with your bows you aim at their faces.

¹³Be on high, Yhwh, because of your strength.
   We will sing and make music to^h your might.^i

Interpretation

Like the preceding psalm, Ps. 21 implicitly works with the interwovenness of the destiny of king and people, and like Ps. 18 it rejoices in a recent deliverance of the king. But whereas Ps. 18 looked at matters wholly in light of this recent deliverance and Ps. 20 looks at matters wholly in light of his present need, Ps. 21 perfectly balances the king's recent deliverance and its ongoing implications, in a 7-7 *abb'a'* structure:

a The king's rejoicing (one line; v. 1)
   b Yhwh's past deliverance of the king (six lines; vv. 2–7)
   b' Yhwh's future victory over all enemies (six lines; vv. 8–12)
a' The people's rejoicing (one line; v. 13)

---

e. Francis J. Morrow ("Psalm xxi 10," *VT* 18 [1968]: 558–59) emends *lĕʿēt* to *lĕʿummat*, "before."

f. LXX translates *kî* as "for" and then takes the last verb as a relative clause, "[in which] they do not succeed," but this does not follow on very well from v. 10. BDB translates "although," but this is hard to parallel, esp. with a qatal verb.

g. Lit., "make them [into] a shoulder": the expression is odd, but it makes for a parallel with "made him [into] a blessing," and it almost parallels "make them like a blazing furnace." See GKC 117ii.

h. Both verbs can govern the theme of their praise as a direct object.

i. C has *gĕbûrōtêkā*, "your mighty acts"; cf. LXX and Jerome. We might take MT's sg. as abstract for concrete.

Because the destiny of king and people are interwoven, the psalm can be a thanksgiving for the king's recent deliverance, yet one actually uttered by the people who depend on the king and on whom the king depends. In the regular way of a thanksgiving, it begins with a commitment to praise, which on the people's lips takes the form of a jussive (v. 1). It goes on to recall the king's prayer and Yhwh's answer, closing with a third-person equivalent to a declaration of trust (vv. 2–7). It then draws inferences regarding Yhwh's ongoing and/or future victories (vv. 8–12) and closes with renewed praise (v. 13). The lines are all bicola, those in vv. 1–7 being all of above-average length: each has at least four words in each colon (except v. 5, which is 3-4)—though MT construes (e.g.) vv. 1, 6, and 7 as 3-3. In contrast, vv. 8–13 are all 3-3 (except v. 9, which comprises two 3-2 lines).

The psalm combines reference to the king's deliverance and to his majesty, and in light of the latter some interpreters have inferred that it related to his crowning or to an annual celebration of his kingship.[1] This makes it harder to do justice to the references to his deliverance. More likely the references to his majesty are one aspect of a declaration that Yhwh has responded to the king in ways that go far beyond his request. In the context of some crisis the king asked for his life to be preserved and for Yhwh to deliver him from his enemies (vv. 1, 2, 4). What Yhwh did was much more than that—gave him rich blessings and long life and not just survival; gave him splendor, honor, and majesty and not just escape from pressure; gave him joy and gladness and not just relief; and did all this on an ongoing basis (the verbs are yiqtol). This feature of the psalm may also link with its indeed being used for ongoing commemorations of Yhwh's deliverance, not simply in relation to a crisis that has just passed. The passing of time shows that Yhwh granted blessing, continuing life, and royal honor as well as one-time deliverance.

> The leader's. Composition. David's.

Heading. See glossary. The speaker in the psalm is the congregation, or a priest speaking on its behalf, talking about the king, and the heading may invite us to see the psalm as a response to the present David's experience, perhaps expressed in terms of the historical David's story. The heading may alternatively invite us to imagine it being used in connection with the actual David, whose experience provides a powerful illustration of the way Yhwh can not only rescue someone from his enemies but also give him ongoing royal majesty. Or it may invite us to

---

1. See, e.g., A. Anderson, *Psalms*, 1:179.

see it as to be fulfilled for the future David: the midrash makes the last assumption,[2] while Tg reads "the king Messiah" in vv. 1, 7, and Paul may reflect the psalm's language in 2 Thess. 1:8–9 (see below).

21:1. First, then, a priest declares the king's reasons for thanksgiving (implicitly shared by the people).

> ¹Yhwh, in your strength may the king rejoice,
>   In your deliverance how he may delight, so much!

At the heart of these two opening cola are matching *bĕ*-expressions and matching verbs. The first colon has the invocation "Yhwh" and the subject "the king," which also apply to the second. The second colon has the particle "how" and the adverb "so much," which also apply to the first—though in the rhetoric of the psalm, "delight so much" takes further the simple "rejoice."

Alongside the notion of Yhwh's *strength, reference to Yhwh's *deliverance makes explicit that strength is not merely a quality that Yhwh possesses, which would not be especially a reason for rejoicing, but a quality that Yhwh shows in action. "Deliverance" (cf. v. 5) also forms a concrete link with Ps. 20 (see 20:5, 6, 9). In v. 1 it is already implicit that the hope, blessing, expectation, and prayer of Ps. 20 have become reality.

21:2–7. The thanksgiving immediately and appropriately looks back to the king's prayer and Yhwh's answer. Verses 2–5 alternate lines of qatal verbs (vv. 2, 4) and lines of yiqtols (plus a noun clause) (vv. 3, 5). At first, one might hear v. 3 as having past reference, like the yiqtol cola in Ps. 18, but eventually the alternation of expressions suggests a movement between past statements and statements of ongoing truth and faith that these past statements warrant.

> ²The desire of his heart you gave him,
>   the request of his lips you did not withhold. (Rise)

The cola are exactly parallel. The second uses a rarer noun for "request" (actually a hapax) and a rarer and negatived verb to complement the familiar positive "you gave," while in substance the second colon complements "heart" with "lips." The words again link with Ps. 20, where the people promised that God would give to him according to his heart (v. 4). But in substance the reference to the king's heart's desire recalls the desire of David's *nepeš*, and later of Jeroboam's, to reign over Israel (2 Sam. 3:21; 1 Kings 11:37). *Rise here is a good example

---

2. *Midrash on Psalms,* 1:293.

of this word's occurrence at points that imperil any theory about what it might mean.

> ³For you go to meet him with rich blessings,
> you set on his head a crown of fine gold.

If we interpreted David's "desire" aright, the second of these parallel cola (eight words working *abcdb'ec'd'*) then restates v. 2—the language makes one think of David coming to Hebron or Jerusalem after winning many victories. The first colon may also suggest such an event, notwithstanding its yiqtol verb. As LXX's *prophthanō* recognizes, Yhwh does not merely wait for the king to arrive but goes out to meet him with blessings and with his crown: *qādam* (piel) suggests taking the initiative rather than reacting when someone arrives.

> ⁴When he asked life from you, you gave to him
> length of days forever and ever.
> ⁵His honor is great because of your deliverance,
> splendor and majesty you put on him.

Verse 4 returns to the king's prayer. Here the two expressions for the content of the request form a bracket around the line, the second occupying the whole second colon. The request for life is presumably a request for safe deliverance from enemies; the second colon thus goes far beyond the first rhetorically, as Yhwh's response goes far beyond the request. An Israelite or Judean king could be notoriously short-lived, and v. 4b may relate to that fact, though the promise of life lasting forever is a conventional Middle Eastern wish for a king (cf. 1 Kings 1:31, when David is on his deathbed; also Neh. 2:3; Dan. 2:4). In either context it suggests living to the absolute fullness of the length of human life, as opposed to being cut off in one's prime.³

Verse 5 then again describes how things are on an ongoing basis as a result of Yhwh's act. Here splendor and majesty spell out *honor.

> ⁶For you make him an abundant blessing forever,
> you gladden him with joy through your presence.

---

3. There is little indication outside the Psalms that a king or anyone else would have asked for eternal life or been granted it, so we should hardly interpret the poetic language of the Psalms in these terms (against Dahood, *Psalms*, 1:132). Nor is there any clear indication that the king or anyone else would have thought in terms of living on in one's descendants.

The double *kî* clause in vv. 6–7 continues the yiqtol clauses (adding a participial clause in v. 7a). In v. 6, each word in the first colon takes up from vv. 3–4. The idea of Yhwh's making (the verb is *šît* as in v. 3b) the king an abundant blessing is that Yhwh turns him into such an embodiment of multiple blessing that he becomes a standard whereby people seek blessing for themselves (cf. the idea of "being a blessing" in Gen. 12:2; Isa. 19:24; Zech. 8:13). The second colon then follows from the first. Perhaps the asyndeton again subordinates the resumptive colon to the new one: "Because you make him a blessing forever, you make him glad. . . ." The gladness issues from Yhwh's presence or *face because blessing comes as Yhwh looks with favor.

> ⁷For the king is trusting in Yhwh,
>   by the commitment of the Most High he does not falter.

We might once more take the first colon as leading into the second—it is because the king is trusting in Yhwh that he does not falter. But here the cola are linked by a *w*, which may rather indicate that they are parallel, the second restating the first. Not faltering or *falling down is then another way of referring to trust; or rather, the second colon indicates that the king's *trust is one that does not falter. This is a telling observation in light of the pressure on a king to put his trust elsewhere. But the second colon also goes beyond the first in indicating how the king can maintain such trust. He can do so because of Yhwh's own *commitment; the king receives lots of divine commitment to inspire trust. Yhwh is then both the object of trust and its subject, in the sense of its enabler. The repeated preposition *bĕ* (in/by) underlines the link between the cola.

Verse 7 has been seen as the center of the psalm and as linking the two halves, and it has even been called a refrain,[4] but structurally and substantially it rather closes off vv. 1–7. While it may suggest that the king's trust was the key to the deliverance that vv. 2–6 spoke of,[5] the location of this statement and the use of the participle rather suggest that ongoing unfaltering trust or ongoing trust and security are the fruit of Yhwh's deliverance as the *Most High, and an expression of or motivation for his rejoicing.

21:8–12. These lines more consistently maintain the yiqtol verbs that already dominated vv. 2–7 (only the acts of the enemies require a qatal,

---

4. E.g., J. Kenneth Kuntz, "King Triumphant: A Rhetorical Study of Psalms 20 and 21," *HAR* 10 (1987): 157–76, see 170; F. Charles Fensham, "Ps 21—a Covenant-Song?" *ZAW* 77 (1965): 193–202, see 195; Pierre Auffret, "Note sur la structure littéraire du Psaume xxi," *VT* 30 (1980): 91–93.

5. So Werner Quintens, "La vie du roi dans le Psaume 21," *Bib* 59 (1978): 516–41, see 535.

in v. 11). The particularity of Yhwh's acts for the king in a concrete context now provides the basis for generalizations about Yhwh's power that look beyond the experience of this king. LXX and Jerome translate the verbs as future, and no doubt the statements apply in the future. But translating as future risks implying that these statements do not apply now, when the logic of the psalm is that the concrete deeds Yhwh has already undertaken provide a basis for expecting Yhwh to act in the present. Verse 8, at least, begins in a way that might suggest the psalm is addressing the king, so that vv. 8–12 would be a blessing like the one in Ps. 20. But there is no indication of a change of addressee (v. 9 refers to Yhwh in the third person, but v. 7 has already illustrated the ease with which a psalm can do that when addressing Yhwh). Further, some of the language more suggests God's acts. For instance, the active right hand of the Psalms is usually Yhwh's (so in 18:35 [36]; 20:6 [7]); it is natural to take the fire of v. 9a and that of v. 9b to have the same reference, and to take the presence of v. 9 to be the same as that of v. 6. I infer that the psalm continues to address God.[6]

> ⁸Your hand finds out all your enemies,
>   your right hand finds out those who are against you.

The cola are exactly parallel, though the word order is *abcb'ac'*. "Right hand" gives specificity to "hand"; unusually, the verb is simply repeated; "those who are *against you" is a more poetic and much less everyday expression than "enemies" (*'ōyēb*).

> ⁹You make them like a blazing furnace
>   at the time of your presence.
> Yhwh swallows them in his wrath;
>   fire consumes them.

Each of these two shortest lines in the psalm (presumably hence MT's making them one verse) brings us up short in the manner of 3-2 lines, as Yhwh's fiery action brings up short those who are its victims. Verse 9a first makes the same point as v. 8 more metaphorically, again picking up the verb *šît*. Whereas Yhwh makes the king an embodiment of blessing, Yhwh makes enemies a blazing furnace. The statement is a kind of metonymy; they are not so much the furnace as the object in the furnace. The second colon then makes clear when and how Yhwh does that, through Yhwh's presence, which thus has quite different implications for the enemies from the ones it has for the king (v. 6). But

---

6. Fokkelman (*Major Poems*, 2:103) suggests that the section is systematically ambiguous, implying a "perfect synergy" between the king's acts and God's.

the colon also thus opens up a question: Why should Yhwh's presence have that effect?

While changing to third-person reference to Yhwh, v. 9b clarifies that. It again recalls Ps. 18:3–15 [4–16], which talked at some length about rage and about fire consuming, about Yhwh's presence (translated in 18:6 as "before him" but literally "to his face/presence"), and about swallowing (if we may assume that Belial carries this resonance in 18:4), though here in 21:9 Yhwh becomes the swallower. Yes, when people's cry comes to Yhwh's presence, this issues in consuming fire for their attackers. The two cola provide complementary descriptions of this event, the second explaining how Yhwh swallows the enemies (by fire consuming them). Thus "Yhwh" and "fire" form a pair, as do "swallow" and "consume," but "in his wrath" has no equivalent. It applies to both cola, but letting it do that makes the second colon stop abruptly and bring us up short in the way just noted.

> [10]You destroy their offspring from the earth,
> their issue from humankind.

Verse 10 reverts to more literal description. Secure deliverance requires not only the elimination of direct attackers but also the elimination of the next generation of attackers (cf. Ps. 137:9). The line makes the point poignantly, though apparently without sympathy: the next generation are their parents' "fruit" and "seed."

> [11]When they have directed evil against you,
> thought up a scheme, they do not succeed.

Verse 11 restates the point yet again, this time imagining the circumstances. Yhwh does not take the initiative in attacking people; Yhwh is responding to attack. The expression in the first colon is unusual, and the resumptive "when" clause (the *kî* carries over to this clause) puts the point more straightforwardly. The rhetoric of the latter part of the line compares and contrasts with that in v. 9. The line is the expected length, and the resolution of the issues raised by the main part of the line comes in a brisk final declaration, *bal-yûkālû*, "They-do-not-succeed."

> [12]For you set them back;
> with your bows you aim at their faces.

Two parallel cola then explain more literally how Yhwh brings that about. The first takes up the verb *šît* once more, with implications for the enemies like those in v. 9 rather than those for the king in vv. 3 and

6. The second colon describes how the turning in v. 10a comes about:[7] Yhwh shoots at them, and they wisely turn tail. The verb, however, also reverses the one in v. 10a, so that vv. 11–12 work *abb'a'*. The enemies take aim at Yhwh; Yhwh takes aim back. There is no contest.

> [13]Be on high, Yhwh, because of your strength.
> We will sing and make music to your might.

21:13. The psalm ends in the same way as Ps. 18. One might initially take the closing exhortation to Yhwh to be exalted (*rûm*) as referring to an act of self-assertion in keeping with the declarations in vv. 8–12 (cf. 89:13 [14]), but the verb more often refers to exaltation in the eyes of people. Further, the reference to Yhwh's strength forms an inclusion with v. 1. There the king rejoices in Yhwh's strength; here everyone does. The second colon confirms that this is the implication of the opening imperative, as the two cohortative verbs about singing and making *music parallel the imperative about being high (also with an -*â* ending). "Your *might" likewise parallels "your *strength," being a less common word; oddly, these two words do not otherwise appear together.

Theological Implications

Psalm 21 vividly illustrates how significant for the people of God as a whole are the deliverances of individual members, and particularly of leaders. The logic of the psalm is as follows. The king has experienced Yhwh's delivering him from his foes (vv. 2–5). That inspires his praise and his ongoing trust (vv. 1, 6–7). It also gives grounds for the conviction that Yhwh does/will overcome all those who oppose the divine purpose (vv. 8–12). And that inspires the people's praise (v. 13). The people who pray this psalm thus move from a distanced declaration and observation in the third person (vv. 1–7) to a general statement (vv. 8–12) and then to an explicit identification with that statement's implications (v. 13). Being in a position of leadership inevitably exposes a leader to danger but also drives the leader to prayer and provides the opportunity to prove God. If the people are aware of that process, it gives opportunity for them to join in the leader's praise and profit from the leader's experience.

Second Thessalonians 1:8–9 recalls v. 9 in the way it talks about flaming fire and eternal destruction "from the presence of the Lord,"[8] and the church uses the psalm at the Feast of the Ascension of Christ. Verses

---

7. Thus GKC 156d sees it as a circumstantial clause.
8. Cf. Kidner, *Psalms*, 1:104.

1–6 can be seen as further illustrated in the experience of Christ, in his dying (with its prayer), his resurrection, and his ascension. Death, resurrection, and ascension are victories over evil people and evil forces, and the second half of the psalm implies that God will also consume other evil people and evil forces.

Psalm 22

Prayer That Honors Two Sets of Facts

Translation

The leader's. On dawn help. Composition. David's.

¹My God, my God, why did you abandon me,
  far from my deliverance, my bellowing words?
²My God, I call by day, and you do not answer,
  by night, and I have no quietness.ᵃ

³But you sit as the holy one,
  the great praise of Israel.ᵇ
⁴In you our ancestors trusted,
  trusted and you rescued them.
⁵They cried out to you and they escaped;ᶜ
  they trusted in you and were not shamed.

⁶But I am a worm, not a human being;
  the reproach of others, despised by people.
⁷All who see me mock me,
  open their mouth wide, shake their head.
⁸"Commit it to Yhwh; he must rescue him,
  he must save him, since he likes him."

a. Tg omits the "and" before the verb and thus reads, "By night I have no quietness."
b. I take the pl. *tĕhillôt* as intensive.
c. The simple *w* plus qatal is anomalous (*TTH* 133) rather than frequentative (so GKC 112h).

⁹For you are the one who made me break out of the womb,
  making me trust[d] on my mother's breast.
¹⁰On you I was thrown from birth;[e]
  from my mother's womb you were my God.

¹¹Do not be far away from me, because trouble is near,
  because there is no one to help.
¹²Mighty[f] steers have surrounded me,
  strong ones of Bashan have closed about me.
¹³They have opened their mouth at me,
  like a tearing, roaring lion.[g]
¹⁴I have been poured out like water;
  all my bones have come loose.[h]
My heart has become like wax;
  it has melted inside me.
¹⁵My vigor has dried up like a piece of pottery,
  my tongue is stuck to my palate;
You put me in deathly dirt,
  ¹⁶for dogs have surrounded me.
An assembly of wrongdoers have encircled me,
  like a lion at my hands and my feet. [MT]
  [or, my hands and my feet have shriveled. (cf. Vrs)][i]

d. C has *mibṭaḥî*, "my hope" (cf. LXX, Jerome) for MT *mabṭîḥî*. I follow LXX and Jerome in referring *bāṭaḥ* (hiphil) to the attitude of trust rather than a position of security (NRSV).

e. Lit., "from the womb" (but here *reḥem*, not *beṭen* as in vv. 9a and 10b).

f. Applied to "steers," mighty is a more likely meaning for *rabbîm* than "many" (cf. BDB, though it does not cite this example).

g. There is no *k*, but for the adverbial usage to indicate the manner in which something happens, see GKC 118r.

h. Here the *w* plus qatal perhaps indicates that the second verb describes the same reality rather than referring to a chronologically subsequent event.

i. MT has *kā'ărî*; the versions presuppose a third-person verb, usually taken to be *kārû*. Of the several roots *kārâ*, the most common means "dig" (cf. LXX), but this gives poor sense. There is no basis for stretching it to mean "pierce," though that does facilitate its being applied to Jesus (see Calvin, *Psalms*, 1:373–75, with the translator's comments in the footnote). Jerome renders "bind," which gives good sense but with dubious basis: it is apparently based on a meaning of *kûr* in Arabic, "wind [a turban]" (cf. BDB on *kûr* and TDOT on *kārâ*). Aq "they disfigured" presupposes that the verb is Aramaic *kā'ār*. I rather take the verb to be *DCH*'s *kārâ* V (cf. NRSV; J. J. M. Roberts, "A New Root for an Old Crux," *VT* 23 [1973]: 247–53); Michael L. Barré prefers the translation "have gone lame" ("The Crux of Psalm 22:17c," in *David and Zion* [J. J. M. Roberts Festschrift], ed. Bernard F. Batto and Kathryn L. Roberts [Winona Lake, IN: Eisenbrauns, 2004], 287–306). For other possible interpretations, see L. C. Allen, "Cuckoos in the Textual Nest," *JTS*, n.s., 22 (1971): 143–50, esp. 148–50; John Kaltner, "Psalm 22:17b," *JBL* 117 (1998): 503–6; Brent A. Strawn, "Psalm 22:17b," *JBL* 119 (2000): 439–51; R. Tournay, "Note sur le Psaume xxii 17," *VT* 23 (1973): 111–12; Gregory Vall, "The Old Guess," *JBL* 116 (1997): 45–56.

¹⁷As I count all my bones,
  they take note and look over me.ʲ
¹⁸They divide my garments among themselves,
  cast lots for my clothing.

¹⁹But you, Yhwh, do not be far away;
  my strength, hasten to my help.
²⁰Save my life from the sword,
  my very self from the power of the dog.
²¹Deliver me from the mouth of the lion;
  may you have answered me from the horns of the buffalo. [MT]
  [*or*, my weakness from the horns of the buffalo. (cf. LXX)]ᵏ
²²I will tell of your name to my kindred,
  in the midst of the congregation I will praise you.

²³You who revere Yhwh, praise him;
  all you offspring of Jacob, honor him;
  be in awe of him, all you offspring of Israel.
²⁴For he has not despised,
  nor has he loathed, the lament of the weak.
He has not turned his face from him,
  but when he cried for help, listened to him.
²⁵From you will come my praise in the great congregation;
  my promises I will fulfill before the people who revere him.

²⁶Weak people will eat and have their fill;
  those who seek help from him will praise Yhwh;
  may your heart live forever.
²⁷All the ends of the earth must be mindful and turn to Yhwh;
  all the families of the nations must bow lowˡ before you.
²⁸For sovereignty belongs to Yhwh;
  he rules among the nations.
²⁹All the well-to-do of the earth have eaten and bowed low;
  all those who are going down to the dirt kneel before him,
  people who could not keep themselves alive.ᵐ
³⁰Their offspringⁿ will serve him;
  a generation to comeᵒ will be told of my Lord.

j. I take the asyndetic clause as circumstantial (cf. Briggs, *Psalms*, 1:203). *Rā'â b* can carry the connotation "feast the eyes on" (cf. 54:7 [9]; 59:10 [11]); the first verb in the clause, *nābaṭ b* (hiphil), has similar implications on its one other occurrence, 92:11 [12].

k. LXX implies a noun such as *'ĕnûtî* (cf. v. 24) for MT's *'ănîtānî*.

l. BDB takes *hištaḥăwâ* as hitpalel from *šāḥâ*, HALOT as eshtafel from *ḥāwâ*.

m. For *wĕnapšô lō' ḥiyyâ* LXX implies *wĕnapšî lô ḥayyâ*, "My spirit lives for him"; while the transition to first person is out of place, "The person who lives for him . . ." would be a good lead-in to v. 30.

n. The suffix carries over from *napšô*.

o. Linking *yābō'û* (the first word in v. 31 in MT) with what precedes (cf. LXX).

³¹They will tell of his faithfulness to a generation unborn,ᵖ
that he acted.

Interpretation

Psalm 22 is an individual's cry for help, closing with a particularly remarkable and extensive act of praise. There is thus a tension in the psalm. In isolation, vv. 1–21 imply that the suppliant is currently distraught, while vv. 22–31 imply that the worshipper is in a position to testify to Yhwh's deliverance. Verses 1–21 could stand alone as a prayer psalm, and vv. 22–31 might have been added to it later; they do not look as if they could stand alone as a thanksgiving.¹ The fact that vv. 1–21, the bulk of the psalm, describe the suppliant's need as a present reality makes it unlikely that the psalm as a whole belongs in the context of an experience of deliverance, to which vv. 1–21 look back; a suppliant would then use a thanksgiving psalm. Rather, the transition needs to be seen as cohering with a feature of the psalm as a whole. Throughout, it alternates between questions, protests, and laments on the one hand; and acknowledgments of Yhwh, statements of faith in Yhwh, and prayers to Yhwh on the other. The theme of "the possibility, efficacy and necessity of giving praise to God"² runs through the whole psalm. Verses 22–31 do not indicate that the suppliant has yet experienced Yhwh's deliverance. They do indicate that the suppliant knows Yhwh will deliver. This conviction may derive from hearing general declarations of Yhwh's acts and faithfulness or from someone's bringing a word from God between vv. 21 and 22, but such hypotheses are not directly evidenced and not really necessary.³

The awareness of the community in vv. 3–5 and 22–31 may signify that the suppliant prays this prayer in the company of others. But if so, for the most part the prayer avoids referring to them, for their presence would qualify the assertion of aloneness that characterizes vv. 1–21. We do not know anything of the particular circumstances that led to its composition, and neither can we tell what literal distress the psalm reflects. It speaks of rejection by the community, of the attacks of violent and life-threatening forces, and of personal disintegration, but it does

---

p. The niphal ptc. is gerundive.

1. But on vv. 27–31 as a self-contained entity, see Édouard Lipiński, "L'hymne à Yahwé Roi en Psaume 22,28–32," *Bib* 50 (1969): 153–68; Charles Krahmalkov, "Psalm 22,28–32," *Bib* 50 (1969): 389–92; Othmar Keel-Leu, "Nochmals Psalm 22,28–32," *Bib* 51 (1970): 405–13; Stéphane Guillet, "Louer Dieu dans la détresse," *Hokhma* 56 (1994): 1–16.
2. Ellen F. Davis, "Exploding the Limits," *JSOT* 53 (1992): 93–105, see 96.
3. Cf. Rudolf Kilian, "Ps 22 und das priesterliche Heilsorakel," *BZ* 12 (1968): 172–85; and in general the comments on "Prayer" in the introduction to this commentary.

this in allusive terms that prevent us from determining one concrete set of circumstances. It thereby makes the psalm usable by many people experiencing such pressures. It is simultaneously an expression of deep personal feeling and an artful, carefully structured composition.[4]

> The leader's. On dawn help. Composition. David's.

Heading. See glossary. Designating the psalm "David's" may imply that we are invited to imagine David using it when under pressure (e.g.) from Saul, or to imagine a later "David" such as Hezekiah using it in a setting such as that in 2 Kings 18–20. It is harder to imagine its being designed for use by the coming "David," though we will see how Jesus and the NT writers did apply it to him. "On dawn help" is presumably a tune or a way of singing. Although $'ayelet$ (help) is elsewhere the construct of the word for a hind (cf. EVV), in v. 19 $'ĕyālûtî$ means "my help" (but see comment; cf. $'ĕyāl$ in 88:4 [5]), and LXX, Tg make sense in inferring a reference to help here. Dawn is then the moment when help may arrive or the moment when one offers prayer and praise (cf. Tg; and 57:8 [9]). The midrash plays with both understandings, hind and help, partly in applying the psalm systematically to the situation of Esther.[5]

22:1–2. The psalm begins with two long lines, 4-4 and 5-3. Its laments and protests will again use the first, second, and third person to describe how I feel, what they have done, and what you (God) have done or not done.[6] But we may hypothesize that the last is the most agonizing form of expression, and this psalm wastes no time in coming to the point.

> [1]My God, my God, why did you abandon me,
>   far from my deliverance, my bellowing words?

So the psalmist goes straight for the sharpest point.

The first verse contains two remarkable sentences, which, although apparently contrary to each other, are yet ever entering into the minds of the godly together. When the Psalmist speaks of being forsaken and cast

---

4. Cf. N. H. Ridderbos's comments, "The Psalms: Style Figures and Structure," in *Studies on Psalms*, by B. Gemser et al., OtSt 13 (Leiden: Brill, 1963), 43–76, see 53.
5. See *Midrash on Psalms*, 1:297–326. Cf. Esther M. Menn, "No Ordinary Lament," *HTR* 93 (2000): 301–41, see 317–27. William L. Holladay also notes intertextual links with Jeremiah's confessions ("The Background of Jeremiah's Self-Understanding," *JBL* 83 [1964]: 153–64). Anton Jirku ("*'Ajjelet haš-Šaḥar*," *ZAW* 65 [1953]: 85–86) suggests that the title originally referred to a god. Morris Sigel Seale ("Arabic and Old Testament Interpretation," *ExpTim* 66 [1954–55]: 92–93) notes that the expression is a natural one within the context of Arabian poetry.
6. See Westermann, e.g., *Praise and Lament*, 64–71.

off by God, it seems to be the complaint of a man in despair.... And yet, in calling God twice his own God, and depositing his groanings into his bosom, he makes a very distinct confession of his faith.[7]

In this respect and in its beginning with a question, Ps. 22 compares with Ps. 10, though that is not originally a separate psalm, and with Ps. 13. In the invocation *ʾēlî* (cf. v. 10), however, it compares with 89:26 [27], where Yhwh invites the king to call on "my God." In 18:2 [3] the king does so after having had God listen and respond, and in 118:28 he praises "my God" for an act of deliverance (cf. Exod. 15:2). In 68:24 [25] the worshipper praises "my God" as the awesome, mighty one; in 63:1 [2] the supplicant expresses confident trust even though currently separated from "my God," and in 140:6 [7] also appeals with confidence to "my God." The expression encapsulates the personal relationship of supplicant and God. That is here belied by the Deity's inaction. Only 102:23–24 [24–25] comes near to the contradiction involved in the first colon.[8] "My God" and "abandon" do not fit easily in the same sentence. The fact that the term *ʾēl* by nature points to the awesome and mighty nature of God underlines the point. If the mighty and awesome creator God is with us, that solves problems.

So why is this not so? The "Why?" compares with those in other psalms (e.g., 10:1, which also relates to Yhwh's being "far off"; 42:9 [10]; 43:2; 44:23–24 [24–25]; 88:14 [15]). Yet there and here, what the supplicant actually wants is action, not explanation, and after this opening line the "Why?" disappears. The talk of Yhwh's abandoning the worshipper contrasts with the many expressions of conviction that Yhwh does not do that (e.g., 9:10 [11]; 27:9–10; 37:25, 33; 38:21 [22]; 71:9, 18; 119:8). It compares with the declaration of the enemies that Yhwh has done so (71:11); the supplicant has internalized their conviction and abandoned the conviction regularly expressed in the Psalms. The succeeding lines of the psalm will make clear that we should not infer that the supplicant would be satisfied if this "Why?" question were answered. The question is rhetorical and implies, "You should not have abandoned me, and I appeal to you to come back now." The expression of conviction in 38:21 [22] makes for especially poignant comparison because it goes on to ask that Yhwh not "be far off" (cf. 35:22; 71:12) and calls Yhwh "my deliverance." Psalm 22 implies an inability to frame such a prayer.

Elsewhere, Westermann comments:

---

7. Calvin, *Psalms*, 1:357.
8. The only other occurrence is the ironic appeal "my god" to an idol in Isa. 44:17; *ʾēl* appears in no other suffixed forms.

In this opening of Psalm 22, there is a fundamentally different understanding of man's relationship with God from the one that has grown up since the period of the Enlightenment. We describe the relationship as "belief" and equate the term with religion itself. But in a relationship with God viewed as belief, it is man who is the subject; one either believes in Him or not. In this respect the relationship with God in the psalms is quite other; there God is the subject, He it is who initiates the relationship. So even when a man despairs of God, he can never break free from Him, as we see clearly in Psalm 139.[9]

Perhaps that links with the fact that the suppliant does not say, "You seem to have abandoned me." The psalm is not talking about an apparent abandonment but a real one. It also contrasts with Weiser's comment: "The fundamental theme of the psalm . . . is really that of seeking God and of finding God."[10] We can accept that comment if we understand it in Hebrew terms, not our own. Seeking God means seeking to get God to act, and finding God is reaching that goal. Seeking and finding are not merely spiritual, inward acts of ours. To put it another way, the psalm is not asking that Yhwh be present with the suffering person merely in the sense of giving them a sense of God's presence. Abandonment lies in failing to act on the suppliant's behalf.

While poetically v. 1 is a well-formed 4-4 line, grammatically it is incoherent; EVV smooth the construction. LXX treats v. 1b as a noun clause: "My bellowing words are far from my deliverance,"[11] which makes for a good construction but poor sense. Grammatically "far from my deliverance" seems to be in apposition to "my God," while EVV rightly assume that "far from" applies to "my bellowing words" as well as to "my deliverance." EVV also gentrify the last phrase in translating "the words of my groaning." Actually, a *šĕ'āgâ* is the roar of a lion (e.g., Zech. 11:3).

> ²My God, I call by day, and you do not answer,
> by night, and I have no quietness.

In this contrasting neat parallel bicolon, "by day" parallels "by night," as "and you do not answer" parallels "and I have no quietness," the latter explaining the result of the former. "My God I call" then applies to the second colon as well as the first. "My God" is now the more common *'ĕlōhay* (e.g., 18:6, 21, 28, 29 [7, 22, 29, 30]). The greater familiarity of

9. *Living Psalms*, 84.
10. *Psalms*, 220.
11. Actually LXX seems to read *šĕgi'ōtay* (my transgressions) for *ša'ăgōtî* (my bellowing).

the noun means this suffixed form again draws attention to the mutual relationship of supplicant and Deity, which is belied by God's silence. "I call" is likewise a less agonized word than the "bellowing" of v. 1. A day-and-night calling on God might be a natural accompaniment to a day-and-night meditation (1:2), like day-and-night hearing from God and praising God (42:8 [9]; cf. 92:2 [3]). It corresponds to God's day-and-night protection (121:6) and accompanies the heavens' day-and-night proclamation (19:2 [3]). Day and night belong to Yhwh (74:16; cf. 139:11–12). But this day-and-night calling (cf. 77:2 [3]) issues from the experience of Yhwh's hand being heavy day and night (32:4), accompanies day-and-night weeping (42:3 [4]), and reflects people's day-and-night wrongdoing (55:10 [11]). But Yhwh does not answer, by day or by night (contrast 3:4 [5]). That does not fit the theory (20:1, 6, 9 [2, 7, 10]).

The closing clause refers to lacking quietness (*dûmiyyâ*; cf. NIVI), not lacking rest (NRSV) or respite (NJPS). The supplicant has no basis for giving up the bellowing that v. 1 refers to or even the calling that v. 2 speaks of. The link with v. 1 suggests that vv. 1–2 are parallel, in *aba'b'* order. The one addressed is *'ēlî* and *'ĕlōhay*, my mighty and personal God; this God's abandoning me is expressed in a refusal to answer my call, and thus my bellowing continues, and I cannot make a transition to silence. Psalm 22 concerns the theological mystery of "the deaf God."[12]

22:3–5. Verses 3–5 draw a contrast between the abandonment of vv. 1–2 and some other facts about Yhwh, and between the lament of vv. 1–2 and the praise that characterizes Israel. It goes on to refer back to the basis for that praise in Yhwh's deeds in the past. That is an unusual move for an individual prayer psalm.[13] Making this move also sets up a contrast between the "my" of vv. 1–2 and the "our" of v. 4. The psalmist is seeking to hold together the reality of personal present abandonment and the reality of the community's trust and deliverance. The past deliverance was as real as the present abandonment: the supplicant also does not say that Yhwh only *seemed* to rescue the ancestors.

> ³But you sit as the holy one,
>   the great praise of Israel.

I follow LXX and Jerome in understanding v. 3 as 3-2 rather than 2-3, which would imply, "But you are the holy one, enthroned on/inhabiting the great praise of Israel" (cf. KJV; NRSV; BDB). The idea of Yhwh's sitting enthroned in the heavens or in Zion is a familiar one (2:4; 55:19 [20]; 80:1 [2]; 99:1; 123:1; cf. 99:1–3 for the association with Yhwh's

---

12. Carroll Stuhlmueller, "Psalm 22," *Biblical Theology Bulletin* 12 (1982): 86–90, see 87.
13. Cf. Westermann, *Living Psalms*, 82.

being the holy one; also Isa. 57:15). Likewise, the idea that Yhwh *is* Israel's praise is a familiar one (Deut. 10:21; Jer. 17:14), but the idea of Yhwh's being enthroned on or inhabiting Israel's praise is unparalleled, and if either of these is the psalm's point, one might have expected it to be expressed more clearly. The fact that 3-2 is the more common line division supports the conclusion that LXX construes the line correctly.[14] The reminder that Yhwh is the holy one is a reminder that Yhwh is the powerful, transcendent, divine God. It underlines the fact that Yhwh has the power to deliver the suppliant but is not doing so. Moses' song of praise after the Israelites' deliverance at the Red Sea asks,

> Who is like you among the gods [*'ēlîm*], Yhwh?
> Who is like you, majestic in holiness,
> Revered in praises, doing a wonder? (Exod. 15:11)

The psalm is taking up the theme of Moses' song. Against that background, the psalm reaffirms that Yhwh is the sole *'ēl* and is my *'ēl*, that Yhwh is the holy one, and that Yhwh is Israel's great praise. In Moses' song *tĕhillôt* probably suggests praiseworthy deeds, as in v. 25 of this psalm (see also 35:28, where it parallels *ṣedeq*; 78:4, where it parallels *niplā'ôt*). Here in v. 3 it indicates the *praise that responds to such deeds.

> ⁴In you our ancestors trusted,
>   trusted and you rescued them.
> ⁵They cried out to you and they escaped;
>   they trusted in you and were not shamed.

In the context of such an allusion to Moses' song, vv. 4–5 explicitly suggest a reference to the deliverance from Egypt,[15] though in other respects the verbal links are not exact. Then the ancestors did (sometimes) believe in Yhwh (*'āman* hiphil, not *bāṭaḥ* as here; Exod. 4:31; 14:31; Ps. 106:12). There Yhwh delivered them (*yāša'* hiphil, not *pālaṭ* as here; Exod. 14:30; Ps. 106:8, 10). There they cried out (*zā'aq*, Exod. 2:23) and Yhwh listened.

Although the first two cola work by the second going beyond the first and completing its "story," the second two cola are parallel. The *cry is an expression of *trust; the escape means they are not shamed. That verb (*bôš*) can denote a sense of disappointment in oneself, which would make sense at this point (cf. NJPS), but vv. 6–8 suggest that the psalm is thinking more of the effect of God's act on other scornful people.

---

14. For possible emendations, see B. N. Wambacq, "Psaume 22,4," *Bib* 62 (1981): 99–100.
15. Cf. *Midrash on Psalms*, 1:315.

Admittedly the fact that crying out is an expression of trust means that one might have expected "trust" in the first colon and "cry out" in the second. The reversion to trust in the last colon rounds off this section of the psalm and makes that its most prominent feature. Presumably the repetition implies another contrast with the suppliant's experience: "I am trusting, trusting, trusting, but it does not work for me." Is there also an implication that bellowing, "My God, why did you abandon me?" is an expression of trust?

22:6–8. The "but you" of v. 3 is balanced by the "but I" that begins the new section, whose atmosphere returns to that of vv. 1–2. All three lines comprise two cola, each with four words. Further, the attitude of other people who effectively excommunicate the suppliant adds polemical poignancy to the suppliant's identifying with their mutual ancestors in vv. 4–5. The suppliant has identified with that community in a context when the present community resists such identification.

> ⁶But I am a worm, not a human being;
> the reproach of others, despised by people.

The suppliant thus offers four two-word self-descriptions. The first two come in two contrasting concrete noun phrases; a worm is a symbol of insignificance (Isa. 41:14; Job 25:6). The second colon comprises two parallel verbal phrases. The psalm does not indicate precisely why the suppliant has become the object of scorn, except that whatever started this process (illness? crop failure?) is now compounded by people's attitude.

> ⁷All who see me mock me,
> open their mouth wide, shake their head.

The first colon comprises a subject and a predicate, and the second colon adds two more predicates, so that v. 7b is internally parallel like v. 6b. The first colon makes a general statement, the second makes it concrete: staring open-mouthed (lit., they "spread out with the lip") and shaking the head are expressions of the scorn that v. 6a spoke of.

> ⁸"Commit it to Yhwh; he must rescue him,
> he must save him, since he likes him."

Here the two central clauses are parallel, so that the line works $abb'c$, with a movement within the first colon from addressing the suppliant to referring to the suppliant in the third person.[16] "Commit" is literally "roll"

---

16. Cf. GKC 144p. LXX, Syr, Jerome, and Tg tidy this by making the whole colon third person, in different ways.

(for this connotation, cf. 37:5; Prov. 16:3). "Rescue" picks up the verb from v. 4; what Yhwh did for the ancestors is exactly what the suppliant and the mockers agree Yhwh needs to do now. "Save" (*nāṣal* hiphil) is another exodus word (e.g., Exod. 3:8; 18:8–10). But the sharpest sting comes in the last clause: "if he likes him" (*ḥāpēṣ*). Other psalms speak with conviction about Yhwh's liking; Yhwh's deliverance is the evidence of this (18:19 [20]; 41:11 [12]). If Yhwh does delight in the suppliant, then deliverance will follow. But the suppliant can no longer have conviction about that, having been abandoned by Yhwh. The mockers' sarcastic affirmation, implying that Yhwh does not like him, corresponds to the suppliant's fear.

22:9–10. Two lines return to reflection on what Yhwh has done in the past—not now in bringing Israel into being but in bringing the suppliant to birth. They also add to the uncomfortable contrast between the suppliant's experience and the declaration in 27:10.

> ⁹For you are the one who made me break out of the womb,
>   making me trust on my mother's breast.

The suppliant certainly knows that birth is a "natural" process but also sees that at another level it comes about because Yhwh makes it happen. This is so not merely by the way Yhwh created humanity at the beginning, as if matters then proceed by inbuilt processes, but because of the way Yhwh is involved in the individual birth (I assume that v. 9 applies to humanity in general, not just to this person). Verse 9a pictures this process quite vividly. As a baby the suppliant did not merely leave the womb but burst out of it (cf. Job 38:8; 40:23); perhaps the imagery links with the way the breaking of the mother's waters heralds the birth. And Yhwh acted as midwife, first pulling the child out, then immediately setting it at its mother's breast with the instinctive *trusting expectancy of finding milk there.

> ¹⁰On you I was thrown from birth;
>   from my mother's womb you were my God.

Psalm 55:22 [23] speaks (a little allusively) of casting what is given to us on Yhwh in the conviction that Yhwh will then sustain us, and here presumably the idea is similar. The second colon then matches that and rounds off this little section with its further references to "my mother" (cf. v. 9b) and "from the womb" (cf. v. 9a). The closing *'ēlî 'attâ*, "You [were] my God," forms a powerful inclusion with the psalm's opening *'ēlî 'ēlî lāmâ 'ăzabtānî*, "My God, my God, why did you abandon me?"[17]

---

17. Cf. John S. Kselman, "'Why Have You Abandoned Me?'" in *Art and Meaning*, ed. David J. A. Clines et al., JSOTSup 19 (Sheffield: JSOT, 1982), 172–98, see 186.

22:11–18. The psalm's first explicit plea (v. 11) introduces its most substantial section of lament, which moves between "they" (vv. 12–13, 16, 17b–18) and "I" (vv. 14–15b, 17a) but once reverts to "you" (v. 15c).

> ¹¹Do not be far away from me, because trouble is near,
>   because there is no one to help.

This initial plea is indeed brief, occupying only a two-stress clause that soon gives way to two parallel reasons for the plea. In light of v. 1, perhaps the implication of the plea is "Do not *stay* far away," and the need for that is underlined by the reminder that trouble is *near* and the suppliant has no human *helper.

> ¹²Mighty steers have surrounded me,
>   strong ones of Bashan have closed about me.
> ¹³They have opened their mouth at me,
>   like a tearing, roaring lion.

For, while many human beings are in the scene, none count as helpers, but many count as bulls and lions. In the first line the *abb′a′* arrangement means that the verbs "surround/close about" the line, like the animals themselves. The second line makes matters worse than the first. Peril comes not merely from steers, which surround but have not yet done anything and may continue to do nothing if one stands still (for steers are not aggressive animals, and only here are they a figure for attackers). It comes from people who have their mouths open, ready to consume, like a lion ready to tear up its prey: lions are always a threat and regularly a figure for people who are aggressive and dangerous (e.g., vv. 16, 21; 7:2 [3]; 10:9; 17:12). One lion (v. 13) is more of a threat than a whole herd of steers (v. 12). Within each of these two lines, too, the second colon makes the situation worse. The threatening creatures are not mere ordinary steers but huge ones, the kind that flourish on the rich pasturage up in Bashan (cf. Amos 4:1). And the attackers resemble not a mere ordinary lion but a tearing, roaring one. By means of the animal imagery, "the poet paints a surrealistic picture of the vacancy left by God's retreat."[18] It portrays people's "inhuman cruelty."[19] Among some Middle Eastern peoples, demons were portrayed as wild and frightening animals,[20] and Israelites who thought in such terms could apply the psalm to the sense of being oppressed by demons as well as to human attackers or even their "inner demons."

18. Schaefer, *Psalms*, 54.
19. Davis, "Exploding the Limits," 98.
20. Cf. Keel, *Symbolism of the Biblical World*, 86, 97.

> ¹⁴I have been poured out like water;
> all my bones have come loose.
> My heart has become like wax;
> it has melted inside me.

The first-person implications of these attacks come in a series of images in the three lines of vv. 14–15b. All speak of the interaction between the self and the physical body.

Verse 14a offers two complementary images, though the first is puzzling. Normally it is one's blood or one's *nepeš* that is poured out (e.g., 79:10; Lam. 2:12), though Lam. 2:11 speaks of pouring out one's liver. Here most likely "I" is equivalent to "my *nepeš*" in the sense of "my life." The suppliant's life is ebbing away. That might imply that objectively the situation is getting more and more threatening, or that the suppliant's courage and hope are ebbing away. Both would no doubt be true, but the second colon likely implies that the second is more in focus. As we put it, "I am falling part," "I cannot hold myself together."

Verse 14b then reexpresses the point. The first colon stimulates a question: How has the suppliant's heart become like wax? The second explains: By melting as wax does in the flame (cf. 68:2 [3]; 97:5).

> ¹⁵ᵃ⁻ᵇMy vigor has dried up like a piece of pottery,
> my tongue is stuck to my palate;

The further image, of vigor drying up, comes only here; the nearest parallel is the saying that a broken spirit dries the bones (Prov. 17:22), taken up in the exiles' plaint that their bones have dried up (Ezek. 37:11). Bones can be an image for vigor (cf. 31:10 [11]). Etymologically and anatomically they are the strong parts of the body. Here, then, the psalm presupposes that the breaking of the suppliant's spirit has indeed withered the suppliant's vigor so that it is as dry as a piece of pot. The tongue sticking to the mouth can be a result of thirst (cf. Lam. 4:4) but here rather suggests an inability to speak (cf. 137:6; Job 29:10; Ezek. 3:26).

> ¹⁵ᶜYou put me in deathly dirt,
> ¹⁶ᵃfor dogs have surrounded me.

The only second-person lament in the section includes the first yiqtol since v. 11a, but in implications it contrasts with that. Yhwh is not doing what the suppliant there asked. Dirt stands for humiliation (because the ground is the opposite to exaltation; e.g., 7:5 [6]; 72:9; 113:7) and then for death (because both our bodies and our souls end up in the earth; v. 29; 30:9 [10]; 104:29). The dirt "of death" makes the connotation explicit here. The psalm began with God distressingly absent and inactive; worse, it continues with God distressingly present but active in a death-bringing way. The second colon reverts to the third person. Israelites did not have pet dogs, though they did have sheepdogs (Job 30:1). Here "dogs" implies hunting dogs[21] or wild dogs, scavengers in the dirt looking for something to eat (59:6, 14 [7, 15]; Jer. 15:3). The reference again implies that the suppliant is as good as dead.

> [16b]An assembly of wrongdoers have encircled me,
>   like a lion at my hands and my feet. [MT]
>   [*or*, my hands and my feet have shriveled. (cf. Vrs)]

Verse 16b–c returns to the human beings that the dogs stand for, who are waiting about, hoping to make a profit from the suppliant's death. In MT, the second colon then offers a further parallel, in which the scavengers are again likened to a lion, but in the ancient versions it makes a further statement about the withering of the suppliant's person.

> [17]As I count all my bones,
>   they take note and look over me.

The lament reverts to the first person to give another description of how near death the suppliant is: no more than a walking skeleton. That provides another way of accounting for people's looking on with satisfaction as these scavengers anticipate profiting from the suppliant's actual death.

> [18]They divide my garments among themselves,
>   cast lots for my clothing.

This is worked out concretely in the two parallel closing cola, in which the second explains how the action in the first was put into effect. The midrash imagines the people of Susa doing that to Esther and imagines her praying in accordance with what now follows.[22] Kraus quotes a Mesopotamian song: "The coffin lay open, and people already helped themselves to my valuables; before I was even dead, the mourning was already done."[23]

22:19–22. Once more there is a transition to something more positive. Three lines of plea, followed by the undertaking to praise Yhwh for responding to the plea, might seem to be closing off the psalm, though

---

21. Cf. ibid., 87.
22. *Midrash on Psalms*, 1:304–5, 321.
23. *Psalms*, 1:298.

actually it will take an unexpected turn. The proportion of actual plea in a prayer psalm (three verses out of twenty-one) is typical; confrontation of Yhwh has the main focus. Again, it is typical that the plea is dominated by an appeal for deliverance, expressed in several different ways but always vaguely rather than concretely. The psalm leaves Yhwh to work out what deliverance needs to look like (the need is to get Yhwh to decide to deliver), and its vagueness again facilitates the psalm's being appropriated by people in quite different situations. But most of the expressions here take up terms from vv. 1–18.

> ¹⁹But you, Yhwh, do not be far away;
> my strength, hasten to my help.

The transition is marked first by the opening *wĕ'attâ* (but you), which contrasts with the "they" of preceding cola, and then with its invocation, the first since vv. 1–2. This is also the first time the psalm has addressed "Yhwh," whose name has previously come only in scorn on the attackers' lips (v. 8). The colon then takes up the initial plea from v. 11, so that references to Yhwh's being far away feature at the beginning of the psalm (v. 1), at the beginning of the major section of lament (v. 11), and at the beginning of the main section of plea (v. 19). To parallel "Yhwh" is *'ĕyālûtî*, a hapax that I take to mean "my strength" (cf. Jerome), though LXX has "my help"; either way, these are significant parallels to "Yhwh." Corresponding to the negative "Do not be far away" is the positive "Hasten to my help," with the more regular word for *help. That appeal also takes up from v. 11. Tellingly, the new word here is "hasten."

> ²⁰Save my life from the sword,
> my very self from the power of the dog.

In spelling out the help the suppliant needs, the verb governing both cola is taken up from the lips of his attackers in v. 8 and now used without irony. "My life" (*nepeš*, *person) is then paralleled by "my very self," literally, "my only one" (*yāḥîd*; cf. 35:17). "I only have one life." And the impersonal "sword," a metaphor for violent death, is paralleled by "the power of the dog," representing the creatures slavering at the prospect of picking over the suppliant's remains.

> ²¹Deliver me from the mouth of the lion;
> may you have answered me from the horns of the buffalo. [MT]
> [*or*, my weakness from the horns of the buffalo. (cf. LXX)]

334

Working out the point once more, a verb that links with the suppliant's own noun "deliverance" in v. 1 is also reutilized without irony. It takes up two more animal images. Here the lion is paralleled by the wild buffalo, the singular by the plural, the mouth that consumes by the horn that tosses. I assume that further in MT the imperative is paralleled by a precative.[24] It seems artificial to assume that the psalm moves in the middle of the verse from an imperative to a report of an actual event and also that the report is then not taken further, at least not for several lines. The precise parallelism through the rest of the verse puts the reader on the track of the fact that the verb in the second colon is indeed a precative rather than a qatal. Either way, the verb expresses the matter pregnantly: "Answer me [and deliver me] from the horns of the buffalo."[25] The suppliant will not settle for the failure to answer, which v. 2 protested.

> [22] I will tell of your name to my kindred,
>   in the midst of the congregation I will praise you.

The promise then to give testimony to Yhwh's response to this plea comes in two neat parallel cola. As well as suggesting the importance of feeling part of the community rather than cast out by it, the immediate reference to "my kindred" and "the congregation" reflects how the praise of God is an essentially corporate enterprise because it involves giving glory to God before other people. Yet the psalmist's undertakings do not involve words especially associated with praise for personal acts of deliverance. Telling (*sāpar* piel) of Yhwh's *name, and (even more) *praising, are quite general words. If anything, they are more at home in hymnic praise than in thanksgivings. So the promises point to an ongoing life of praise that the suppliant will be able to resume, as much as to a one-off testimony. For that regular praise, too, praising God on one's own is an odd second best.

22:23–25. Like Ps. 6, the psalm now takes an extraordinary turn. The "praise" to which v. 22 had looked forward is summoned in the now (the word recurs in vv. 23, 25, and 26) as the suppliant now affirms without irony that Yhwh is Israel's great praise.[26] The lines reaffirm a relationship with the community from which people have been excluding the suppliant. They presuppose not that the suppliant must have *seen* the answer to the plea in vv. 19–21, but at least that the suppliant has *heard* it and

---

24. Cf. *IBHS* 30.5.4d.
25. Cf. GKC 119ff. George W. Coats ("The Golden Calf in Psalm 22," *HBT* 9 [1987]: 1–12) sees the buffalo (*rĕ'ēm*) as a divine throne like the golden calf, which is here a positive symbol.
26. Cf. Schaefer, *Psalms*, 55.

has thus made a transition to the conviction that Yhwh has responded, and that deliverance is therefore a reality. Perhaps the key factor was the appeal to Yhwh's name (see vv. 19 and 22).²⁷ We have noted that the psalm has been reticent with the actual name "Yhwh"; that will now recur in the suppliant's praise (vv. 23, 26, 27, 28).

> ²³You who revere Yhwh, praise him;
>   all you offspring of Jacob, honor him;
>   be in awe of him, all you offspring of Israel.

The move in the psalm is marked by a tricolon with three parallel cola, arranged $aba'b'b''a''$. Its immediate focus is actually on the kind of acknowledgment of Yhwh to which Israel as a whole is regularly committed: *praise, honor, and awe. The first suggests a wordless enthusiasm, the second a recognition of Yhwh's splendor, the third a sense of reverence, almost dread, and submission. The three parallel subjects first designate the worshippers by their commitment as a people of *reverence for Yhwh, and then twice by their status as descendants of Jacob-Israel: all of them are summoned to this worship.

> ²⁴For he has not despised,
>   nor has he loathed, the lament of the weak.
> He has not turned his face from him,
>   but when he cried for help, listened to him.

After the talk using the terms of regular worship, v. 24 makes clear that the promise (v. 22) and the summons (v. 23) do actually relate to the particularity of what Yhwh has done for this suppliant. These statements are then made by faith. The suppliant has not yet received any sign of Yhwh's responding. Both the suppliant and the congregation often have to let their ongoing praise be based only on what they know from Yhwh's great acts in the past. Yet by faith the suppliant makes this declaration in v. 24. Yhwh would be entitled to despise, or scorn (*bāzâ*), or to loathe and repudiate certain types of stances—notably, the prayer of someone who also had recourse to other gods. But Yhwh could hardly take that stance to "the lament of the *weak person" (*'ĕnût 'ānî*).²⁸ Thus Yhwh's declining to despise reverses the despising of other human beings (v. 6).

---

27. So John W. Wevers, "A Study in the Form Criticism of Individual Complaint Psalms," *VT* 6 (1956): 80–96.

28. I take the first noun, "lament," as derived from *'ānâ* I, "answer," since lament/supplication (cf. LXX, Tg) would be responsive; the psalmist is playing with the homonymy between *'ānâ* I and *'ānâ* III, "be weak" (in BDB's enumeration). I doubt whether we need to hypothesize further roots to explain the usage of similar words for sung prayer or praise in later Aramaic and Hebrew.

And Yhwh has not done so, the second line of v. 24 affirms—again, affirms by faith. The equivalent to the double "nor scorning" and "not loathing" is "not turning the *face" and rather "listening"; at last the point is made by a positive verb, following on the three negatives. And the equivalent to "the lament of the weak" as the basis for the response is the fact that the suppliant *cried for help.

> ²⁵From you will come my praise in the great congregation;
> my promises I will fulfill before the people who revere him.

I take v. 25 with what precedes rather than with what follows, since it continues and concludes the references to what concerns the suppliant personally; perhaps the long line hints at the end of a section. The two cola complement each other. On one hand, from Yhwh will come the suppliant's (reason for) *praise: here *těhillâ* refers to the divine act that deserves praise rather than to the human act of praise (contrast v. 3). The suppliant now speaks of this act as future, as it is. On the other hand, the movement of the suppliant's offerings is the opposite, from suppliant to Yhwh. The suppliant's practical expression of praise that responds to Yhwh's practical act deserving praise takes place "in the great congregation/before the people who *revere Yhwh," and is outwardly expressed in the offerings that fulfill promises made beforehand. The psalm has not referred to these, though they are implicit at the opening of this section since telling of Yhwh's name and praising Yhwh could hardly be realities without some solid accompaniment. As with human relationships, words are important, but they are not enough. One may thus assume that thanksgiving was routinely accompanied by a thank-offering (cf. 50:14–15; 65:1–2 [2–3]). Verse 25b makes a commitment to such a thank-offering when Yhwh has acted to deliver, as the suppliant knows Yhwh will. EVV render *neder* as "vow," a vow being a promise that is made with due solemnity. To English ears "vow" can suggest something more legal and legalistic than a *neder* need be—hence the translation "promise."

22:26–31. A testimony, even an anticipatory one, aims to glorify Yhwh and build up Israel's faith, and thus in the last section of the psalm the suppliant withdraws and leaves these two parties in focus. The movement compares with that in vv. 1–5,[29] which spoke of a disruption between the community's experience and that of the suppliant. Here the psalm seeks to put them in their right, creative relationship. The individual's experience should correspond to that of the community and should deepen its faith.

---

29. Schaefer, *Psalms*, 53.

> ²⁶Weak people will eat and have their fill;
> those who seek help from him will praise Yhwh;
> may your heart live forever.

Thus in a further tricolon the declaration in v. 24a (expressed in the qatal because it directly pertained to the suppliant) generates a declaration in the yiqtol by which other people are invited to live—but which is also the generalization by which the suppliant has to live for the moment. The first two cola put in parallelism *weak people[30] and people who *seek help from Yhwh, because that is what weak people have to do. Although ‘ānāw does not signify mere poverty, weakness in the sense of lack of status in the community would tend to link with poverty, so that one reason for the weak having recourse to Yhwh is for food. Yhwh's responsiveness then gives them reason for praise and for ongoing encouragement (the collocation of expressions recurs in 69:32 [33]). The setting of "the great congregation" suggests that the suppliant refers to celebratory sacrificial meals. "Weak people/people who have recourse to Yhwh" can refer to Israel as a whole, but in the context of the psalm it rather suggests a particular promise for those who are under pressure similar to the suppliant's experience. They are invited to live by faith as the suppliant is doing.

> ²⁷All the ends of the earth must be mindful and turn to Yhwh;
> all the families of the nations must bow low before you.

The implications of Yhwh's acts for the suppliant and others who seek help from Yhwh are now extended to the whole world (cf. Ps. 18). What Yhwh does for the weak demonstrates something important about Yhwh. The world needs to reflect and be *mindful about its significance, then to turn to Yhwh. The parallel expression "bow low" expresses the implications of that second verb in another way. EVV often render *hištaḥăwû* as "worship," but it refers to the physical act of prostration rather than the attitude that accompanies this act, and it can refer to a proper prostration before a human being. Be mindful, turn, and bow low are three very suggestive words to apply to other nations; elsewhere the Psalms so apply only the last (66:4; 86:9), though their point is made elsewhere by other verbs (e.g., 67; 98). So the nations are envisaged as thinking like Israel (e.g., 105:5) and turning like Israel (e.g., Lam. 3:40) as well as bowing like Israel.

> ²⁸For sovereignty belongs to Yhwh;
> he rules among the nations.

---

30. *‘Ănāwîm*; "weak" in v. 24 was *‘ānî*, but I assume there is no difference between the nouns' implications.

The explicit reason for such submission by the nations is that Yhwh does rule the whole world. Yhwh's action in this Israelite's life is a clue to the way Yhwh can act in the world as a whole. The point is made in two parallel clauses, one a noun clause and one a verbal clause.

> ²⁹All the well-to-do of the earth have eaten and bowed low;
>   all those who are going down to the dirt kneel before him,
>   people who could not keep themselves alive.

Another tricolon further itemizes this submission to Yhwh, in terms of social groups rather than ethnicity. Over against the weak are the well-to-do, literally, the fat, whom the psalm describes as eating and bowing low. The stress will lie on the latter; their bowing is an act recognizing the source of their sustenance. The middle colon then returns to the weak, here described as "those who are going down to the dirt." Elsewhere such expressions refer not to humanity as a whole in its mortality but to a particular group of people who are in danger of death at the moment, as the suppliant was (cf. v. 15) and the weak regularly are (cf. 28:1; 88:4 [5]; 115:17; 143:7). The third colon confirms that. It is not likely that the bowing and kneeling refer to something that happens in Sheol; at least, such an idea does not come elsewhere in the OT. Rather, all these groups come to bow to Yhwh because of what they see or hear of the suppliant, which encourages them to believe that their slide down into death could be halted. Yhwh's setting the suppliant on the way to deathly dirt (v. 15) was not the end of Yhwh's acts in this person's life, and that pattern can also apply to other people who still seem on the way to death but can find new encouragement and bow down to Yhwh.

> ³⁰Their offspring will serve him;
>   a generation to come will be told of my Lord.

Further, when people who cannot keep themselves alive turn to Yhwh, that will result not merely in their survival but in their having offspring who will also serve Yhwh. These "offspring" thus take up the story from the "offspring of Jacob/Israel" in v. 23. The second colon explains how this comes about. They, too, hear of what the psalmist's *Lord does for the weak. Their own existence would not have come about without it. Like (e.g.) Ps. 30, the psalm is beginning to look beyond the immediate temporal horizon as well as beyond the immediate geographical one.

> ³¹They will tell of his faithfulness to a generation unborn,
>   that he acted.

That process comes to a conclusion pointing out that what we have been talking about all along is Yhwh's *faithfulness, at first missed by the suppliant, then perceived in action—if only by faith for the moment. "Tell of" again takes up an earlier expression (see v. 22) and once more indicates that the chain of proclamation will be extended, from individual to community in the present, and from present to future. "That he acted" makes explicit that such faithfulness is not merely an abstract characteristic but a deed (we might translate ṣidqātô as "his faithful deed").

Theological Implications

It would be a shame if "Psalm 22 cannot be the prayer of just any afflicted Israelite."[31] It offers a most suggestive concrete expression of a mature spirituality that is able under pressure to hold on to two contradictory sets of facts. The Psalter presents it as a model for the prayer of ordinary Israelites or Christians when they experience affliction. It is particularly apposite for people who simultaneously experience the three forms of affliction that the psalm reflects. First, they may have the sense of being personally overwhelmed, feeling they are falling apart, nearing collapse, staring death in the face. Second, that may be so because they are experiencing persecution from other people. They may be scorned, despised, and mocked by people who are as powerful, hostile, and threatening as a herd of wild animals. That has often been the experience of Jewish people (commonly at the hand of Christians) and of Christians. The prominence of "they" in vv. 6–8, 11–18 contrasts with the emphasis on "you" at the psalm's opening. It signals that "Psalm 22's subject matter centers on the persecution of an innocent victim. . . . Our psalm's preoccupation with violent victimization suggests that human violence is the fundamental problem with which it wrestles." It illustrates the process of scapegoating, the way a group demonizes an individual in such a way as to justify group violence.[32] Third, they may be aware that God has abandoned them: God is not intervening to deliver them

---

31. So James L. Mays, "Prayer and Christology," *ThTo* 42 (1985): 322–31, see 329; cf. McCann, "Psalms," 765. But contrast Alfons Deissler, "'Mein Gott, warum hast du mich verlassen . . . !'" in *"Ich will euer Gott werden,"* ed. Helmut Merklein and Erich Zenger (Stuttgart: Katholisches Bibelwerk, 1981), 97–121, see 120; Stanley B. Frost, "Psalm 22," *Canadian Journal of Theology* 8 (1962): 102–15, see 109–11; Menn, "No Ordinary Lament," 302.

32. Stephen L. Cook, "*Relecture*, Hermeneutics, and Christ's Passion in the Psalms," in *The Whirlwind* (Jane Morse Memorial), ed. Stephen L. Cook et al., JSOTSup 336 (Sheffield: Sheffield Academic Press, 2001), 181–205, see 201–2.

(as their persecutors point out). God does not answer their prayers. The psalm encourages people to own that this is their experience and not to hide from it. It thus questions the common Christian way of encouraging people to cope with suffering by reassuring them that God is present with them in their suffering. God was not present with this suppliant and does not expect us to pretend that this is so when it is not.

Instead, in the context of that experience the psalm invites us to bear in mind a different, second set of facts. First, we remind God and ourselves of God's past acts of deliverance toward the people of God, specifically the acts of deliverance that brought the people into being. That grieves us, but it also encourages us and challenges God. Second, we remind God and ourselves of God's involvement in our individual lives, from the moment of our birth. That has similar significance. Third, we explicitly urge God to change, to be near to act rather than far away doing nothing, to deliver rather than leaving us to people's persecution. And fourth, we believe our own publicity. We believe in our own argument. We believe that God will respond, and we start talking that way.

The direct reference of the psalm is thus to the suffering of the faithful. One of the faithful who has taken it on his lips is Jesus, which reflects the depths with which it plumbs forsakenness and hope. This does not make him the primary referent of the text. It is not a prophecy. The NT use of the psalm "wrenches it out of its setting."[33] But that did enable it to illumine Jesus for the early church.[34] The allusions in the Gospels come in reverse order to their placement in the psalm, and generally do not make explicit a link with the psalm (John 19:24 is the exception). First, the soldiers divide the dying man's clothes among them by casting lots (Mark 15:24; cf. Ps. 22:18). Second, the passersby mock him and shake their heads as they taunt him (Mark 15:29; cf. vv. 7–8). Third, in the midst of being executed Christ takes up the psalm's opening words (Mark 15:34) and thus identifies himself as someone abandoned by God in the manner of a suffering Israelite. Much later in the NT, Hebrews puts v. 22, from the beginning of the last part of the psalm, onto the lips of Christ (Heb. 2:12).

It has been suggested that in taking up individual verses in this way, Jesus and/or the NT writers thought of the psalm as a whole as apply-

---

33. Sheldon Tostengard, "Psalm 22," *Int* 46 (1992): 167–70, see 167.
34. See Soggin, *Old Testament and Oriental Studies*, 152–65; Loren R. Fisher, "Betrayed by Friends," *Int* 18 (1964): 20–38; Hartmut Gese, "Psalm 22 und das Neue Testament," *ZTK* 65 (1968): 1–22; Harvey D. Lange, "The Relationship between Psalm 22 and the Passion Narrative," *CTM* 43 (1972): 610–21; John Reumann, "Psalm 22 at the Cross," *Int* 28 (1974): 39–58; J. R. Scheifler, "El Salmo 22 y la Crucifixión del Señor," *EstBib* 24 (1965): 5–83; Fritz Stolz, "Psalm 22," *ZTK* 77 (1980): 129–48; Tostengard, "Psalm 22"; Richard D. Patterson, "Psalm 22," *JETS* 47 (2004): 213–33, see 227–30.

ing to Jesus. This suggestion may imply an attempt to make premodern interpretation work on a basis that modern interpretation can accept. Yet it is illuminating to look at Jesus in light of the psalm as a whole.

First, Jesus's quoting of the psalm's opening suggests the awful reality of the cross. It means Jesus is cut off from the Father. This is not because he is bearing the Father's wrath against sin in the place of humanity (that would have to be argued on the basis of other texts). On the contrary, God is still identified with Jesus and is steadfastly watching him on the cross, totally identified with what Jesus is doing. In Christ, God is reconciling the world (2 Cor. 5:19). But God is holding back from acting to deliver Jesus and thus from gaining the relief that God as well as Jesus wants from the pain of this moment. Only if God is as steadfast as Jesus in accepting the terrible pain of this moment of holding back can God carry human sin to the uttermost.

If Jesus then identifies with vv. 3–5, that in turn identifies him with the Israelite people. His work belongs in the context of God's work with Israel. He came to renew Israel. Part of his hope lies in his place within Israel and his significance for Israel. That is part of the reason why God cannot abandon him forever.

Verses 6–8 then begin to make clear that Jesus's problem is the hostility of humanity. His affliction indicates God's willingness to let humanity go to the very end in rebelling against God. It also indicates Jesus's willingness to go to the end of being the embodiment of the love of God as God carries the sin of the world. In Jesus, God bears the totality of human rebellion.

In remembering vv. 9–10, Jesus would be recollecting his experience of being the child of Mary. When choosing the mother of the Lord, God had sought out a young woman who was willing to be totally available to God. It is frightening to think what difference it could have made for Jesus to be nurtured by the wrong mother! But he was nurtured by the right one. The psalm would testify to God's making him dependent on her and meeting his needs through her as he grew.

The center of the psalm is the lament in vv. 11–18. These lines powerfully express the rejection by humanity that the passion story itemizes. The powerful people who attack Jesus are religious and political leaders, whose position is characteristically imperiled by the teaching of Jesus.

Verses 19–22 then constitute the prayer that Jesus prayed and that God did not answer. In the literal sense, this stage of Jesus's suffering belonged in Gethsemane, and it was Ps. 22 that provided his words. On the cross Jesus in fact asks for no deliverance. What the psalm then hints is that without a plea from people with whom God is in covenant, there is no deliverance.[35]

Read on Jesus's lips, vv. 23–31 comprise his invitation to give praise for God's eventual response to that weak person, because that act of God promises that other weak people who call on God in their need will also eat and be satisfied. And this promise holds beyond his immediate company (people such as his disciples). The well-to-do and powerful (people like the writer of this commentary and most of its readers) who put him to death will bow down to his God, along with other people threatened with death—and their descendants.

---

35. So Cynthia L. Rigby, "All God, and Us," in *Psalms and Practice*, ed. Reid, 202–19, see 208.

Psalm 23
God as Our Shepherd and Host

Translation

Composition. David's.

¹My shepherd is Yhwh; I do not lack[a]—
    ²he makes me lie down in grassy pastures.
He guides me by completely restful[b] waters;
    ³he restores my life.
He leads me in faithful paths
    for his name's sake.
⁴Even when I walk in the darkest canyon,
    I do not fear disaster.[c]
Because you are with me; your rod and your staff—
    they comfort me.

a. Given the asyndeton, we might take the noun clause as circumstantial and translate "My shepherd being Yhwh, I do not lack" (cf. Theophile James Meek, "The Metrical Structure of Psalm 23," *JBL* 67 [1948]: 233–35), but in the context, at the beginning of the psalm, the noun clause makes too vital a statement to be tucked away thus. Cf. the comments on the opening clause in J. Mittmann, "Aufbau und Einheit des Danklieds, Psalm 23," *ZTK* 77 (1980): 1–23, see 1–3; Douglas J. Green, "The Good, the Bad and the Better: Psalm 23 and Job," in *The Whirlwind* (Jane Morse Memorial), ed. Stephen L. Cook et al., JSOTSup 336 (Sheffield: Sheffield Academic Press, 2001), 69–83, see 76.

b. Intensive pl.; see GKC 124e.

c. *IBHS* 38.2e and *TTH* 143 take this as an irreal conditional: "even if I were walking. . . ." GKC 107x, 159bb leave this open. It is the context (esp. v. 5) that suggests it is a real conditional (cf. DG 121.1).

⁵You lay a table before me
   in the presence of my enemies.
You bathe my head with oil;
   my cup amply satisfies.ᵈ
⁶Good and commitment will certainly chase me
   all the days of my life.
I will return to [MT]/dwell in [LXX]ᵉ Yhwh's house
   for long days.

Interpretation

Like Ps. 11, Ps. 23 is radically a psalm of trust, containing no actual plea. It manifests the same hopefulness that Ps. 22 eventually affirms, but it expresses itself in symbols, and it is even more difficult to tie down to a particular meaning or context.[1] The preciousness of the psalm derives in large part from its lyricism, which is part of what also makes us unable to tie it down. It leaves itself open to many applications.[2] Although the "I" envisaged by the psalm may be an ordinary individual, it is open to being appropriated by a leader such as a king[3] or a Second Temple leader, or by the community as a whole in any period.[4] The psalm's line division is less clear than is often the case, partly because there is little conventional parallelism in the psalm and its rhythm is particularly irregular.[5]

---

d. Lit., "My cup is a satiation." LXX and Jerome rightly infer that the cup fills and gives great enjoyment to the person (Briggs, *Psalms*, 1:210) rather than that the cup itself overflows (so EVV). Günther Schwarz ("'. . . Einen Tisch angesichts meiner Feinde'?" *VT* 20 [1970]: 118–20) reorders the cola.

e. MT has *wěšabtî* (and I will return), but the subsequent preposition *b* is surprising. LXX (cf. also Tg, Jerome) presupposes *wěšibtî* (and my dwelling), assimilating to 27:4.

1. See Felix Asensio, "Entrecruce de simbolos y realiades en el Salmo 23," *Bib* 40 (1959): 237–47; Susan Gillingham, *The Image, the Depths and the Surface*, JSOTSup 354 (Sheffield: Sheffield Academic Press, 2002), 45–78; Hugh S. Pyper, "The Triumph of the Lamb," *BibInt* 9 (2001): 384–92; Jörg V. Sandberger, "Hermeneutische Aspekte der Psalmeninterpretation dargestellt an Psalm 23," in *Neue Wege*, ed. Seybold and Zenger, 317–44; Ron E. Tappy, "Psalm 23," *CBQ* 57 (1995): 255–80; Robert Couffignal, "De la bête à l'ange," *ZAW* 115 (2003): 557–77.

2. Cf. Mark S. Smith, "Setting and Rhetoric in Psalm 23," *JSOT* 41 (1988): 61–66. John H. Eaton comments that modern understanding of the psalm may err on the side of the prosaic (see "Problems of Translation in Psalm 23:3ff.," *BT* 16 [1965]: 171–76).

3. So A. L. Merrill, "Psalm xxiii and the Jerusalem Tradition," *VT* 15 (1965): 354–60.

4. Cf. *Midrash on Psalms*, 1:334.

5. See the detailed study by Dennis Pardee, "Structure and Meaning in Hebrew Poetry," in *Sopher Mahir* (Stanislav Segert Festschrift), ed. Edward M. Cook (Winona Lake, IN: Eisenbrauns, 1990), 239–80.

At the level of imagery, vv. 1–4 hold together as they affirm Yhwh's caring by using the image of shepherding. That has caused this to be seen as the shepherd psalm. But vv. 5–6 leave that image behind and imply the different image of Yhwh's hospitality, though they also describe the suppliant in more literal and conventional fashion as a human being beset by enemies.[6] In vv. 1–4, "Yhwh" and "I" are literal realities, but the rest is metaphor. In vv. 5–6, I take it that the enemies are also a literal reality, and so may be Yhwh's house, though even if that is so, other questions about the relationship of literal and metaphorical also arise here: Does the psalm speak of a literal meal or a metaphorical one? Nevertheless, the second part of the psalm offers some control on the interpretation of the first part: Yhwh acts as our caring shepherd by the provision we receive in Yhwh's house, where we enjoy feasting and rejoicing as Yhwh exercises hospitality to us on occasions of worship. Although worship in spirit should not be excluded, the emphasis on the provision of food and drink (v. 5; cf. v. 2) suggests that interpretation should not be confined to this. Worship involves the whole person, and a relationship with Yhwh is not confined to religious life. Yhwh also acts as our protective shepherd in accompanying us out into the world, with its danger and hostility.

At the substantial level, both vv. 1–4 and 5–6 thus combine reference to Yhwh's continuing, steady provision and Yhwh's preserving the worshipper through the recurrent pressure of other people's attacks. In vv. 1–4 these come sequentially: first the continuous and steady (vv. 1–3), then the recurrent and protecting (v. 4). In vv. 5–6 they are interwoven in a way that makes them difficult to disentangle, though vv. 5a and 6a relate more to the recurrent and protecting, vv. 5b and 6b to the continuous and steady. The psalm thus almost has an $abb'a'$ structure:

a steady provision/shepherding (vv. 1–3)
  b protection/shepherding (v. 4)
  b' protection/hospitality (vv. 5a, 6a)
a' steady provision/hospitality (vv. 5b, 6b)

The $abb'a'$ structure is more complete in terms of the rhetorical way the psalm speaks of and to Yhwh:

---

6. Yair Mazor ("Psalm 23," *ZAW* 100 [1988]: 416–20) thus emphasizes the transition from animal imagery to human portrayal. Ludwig Köhler maintains that the shepherd image holds through the psalm (see "Psalm 23," *ZAW* 68 [1956]: 227–34); cf. Julius Morgenstern, "Ps 23," *JBL* 65 (1946): 13–24; Alfred Von Rohr Sauer, "Fact and Image in the Shepherd Psalm," *CTM* 42 (1971): 488–92; but this requires either forced reading or emendation.

a Yhwh is my shepherd (third person; vv. 1–3)
 b You are my shepherd (second person; v. 4)
 b′ You are my host (second person; v. 5)
a′ Yhwh is my host (third person; v. 6)

The two specific references to "Yhwh" in the first and last lines are part of this structure. In different ways these two third-person references and the twofold addressing of Yhwh as "you" give Yhwh considerable focus in the psalm.[7]

If Yhwh is the direct addressee in vv. 4–5, who is the addressee in vv. 1–3 and 6? The lines may be addressing the community of the faithful, implicitly encouraging them to live by the same trust that the worshipper expresses (cf. Ps. 22). They may be self-addressed, designed to build up the worshipper's own trust (cf. Pss. 42–43). They may have half an eye on addressing those persecutors who will see Yhwh providing for the worshipper (cf. Ps. 6). Whoever is this implicit direct addressee of vv. 1–3 and 6 will also be the implicit indirect addressee of the lines that formally address Yhwh.

Composition. David's.

Heading. See glossary. If "David's" invites us to imagine David using the psalm, his having been a shepherd would nuance the invitation. Both the image in vv. 1–4 and the reality in vv. 5–6 resonate with his story.[8]

23:1–4. The psalm declares trust in Yhwh as the shepherd who provides food and water and protects from danger. The first pair of lines (vv. 1–3a) and the last pair (v. 4) describe the first of these two key aspects of a shepherd's work, providing food and water and providing protection. The middle line (v. 3b–c) sums up the significance of his work in both these aspects.

> ¹My shepherd is Yhwh; I do not lack—
> ²ªhe makes me lie down in grassy pastures.

---

7. On the psalm's structure, see further Pierre Auffret, "Essai sur la structure littéraire du Psaume 23," *EstBib* 43 (1985): 57–88; C. M. Foley, "Pursuit of the Inscrutable," in *Ascribe to the Lord* (Peter C. Craigie Memorial), ed. Lyle Eslinger and Glen Taylor, JSOTSup 67 (Sheffield: JSOT, 1988), 363–83; N. A. van Uchelen, "Psalm xxiii," in *New Avenues in the Study of the Old Testament*, ed. A. S. van der Woude, OtSt 25 (Leiden: Brill, 1989), 156–62.
8. See Jack Lundbom, "Psalm 23," *Int* 40 (1986): 5–16.

Convention takes the opening clause as a statement about Yhwh, who is (among other things) my shepherd,[9] but succeeding lines suggest it is rather a statement about who shepherds the suppliant. Partly for defamiliarization I thus take it as the latter, the words being in the order predicate-subject. Whereas other people identified other gods as their shepherd or trusted in their own resources, for Israel, Yhwh fulfills that role.

The image of shepherding is not always a gentle, pastoral one, and it is often a despised occupation.[10] David pointed out to Saul that shepherds were rough and tough characters who needed to be brave and ruthless killers, which is what fitted him to take on Goliath (see 1 Sam. 17:34–36; cf. Exod. 2:17–19) and to turn into the ruthless killer he became. Nevertheless (or consequently), in the Middle East it was a term for a great king such as Hammurabi or Ashurbanipal,[11] and within the OT for the Persian conqueror Cyrus (Isa. 44:28).[12] It is also a term for a deity.[13] All that means that "shepherd" is an image for authority and power. The shepherd is the sovereign lord, the sheep is the vassal; it is not a cozy image.[14] But it does also suggest the capacity to take the flock's side against its attackers (Ps. 80:1–3 [2–4]; Jer. 31:10); sheep without a shepherd are in some danger (Num. 27:17; 1 Kings 22:17). Further, a shepherd also sees that sheep are fed and watered (Isa. 40:11), and that is the psalm's initial point. There are shepherds who neglect their flocks (see Ezek. 34), and Yhwh is not that kind of shepherd. Yhwh had seen that the people lacked nothing on their journey through the wilderness (Deut. 2:7; Neh. 9:21), and Moses had promised the same for the people's life in the land (Deut. 8:9). That is the testimony of Ps. 34:10 [11], though the worshippers of the Queen of Heaven claim to have had the opposite experience (Jer. 44:18).

The shepherd image thus applies naturally to the people as a whole rather than to individuals, to a flock rather than an individual sheep.[15]

---

9. It is then a clause of identification: so DG 49a. See further E. Pfeiffer, "Eine Inversion in Psalm xxiii 1bα," *VT* 8 (1958): 219–20; Rudolf Mosis, "Beobachtungen zu Psalm 23," *Gesammelte Aufsätze zum Alten Testament* (Würzburg: Echter, 1999), 275–94, see 276–82.

10. Cf. *Midrash on Psalms*, 1:327. On the shepherd in Ps. 23 and elsewhere in the OT, see Regine Hunziker-Rodewald, *Hirt und Hermas*, BWANT 155 (Stuttgart: Kohlhammer, 2001), esp. 168–88.

11. See *ANET* 164.

12. Thus Richard S. Tombach ("Psalm 23:2 Reconsidered," *JNSL* 10 [1982]: 93–96) notes that v. 2 uses terms that could be applied to a king's role.

13. See *ANET* 69, 71, 72, 337, 387–88.

14. See Beth Tanner, "King Yahweh as the Good Shepherd," in *David and Zion* (J. J. M. Roberts Festschrift), ed. Bernard F. Batto and Kathryn L. Roberts (Winona Lake, IN: Eisenbrauns, 2004), 267–84.

15. Cf. J. Severino Croatto's comments, "Psalm 23:1–6," in *Return to Babel*, ed. John R. Levison and Priscilla Pope-Levison (Louisville: Westminster John Knox, 1999), 57–62, see 59–60.

Specifically, as well as recalling the story of Israel's exodus and journey through the wilderness, the image will later allude to their arrival in Canaan and the building of the temple.[16] The worshipper boldly declares that Yhwh's shepherding, which naturally applies to the flock in general and is celebrated in Israel's story and in its worship, also applies to this individual sheep. This boldness has been reckoned to suggest a late date, though this does not seem logical.

Sheep commonly pasture in the wilderness (etymologically, *midbār* suggests pasturage), land that receives too little rainfall to support a settled population and sustain agriculture but grows enough grass to support flocks that keep on the move. It is the territory the community can afford to allocate to sheep. So a shepherd's task in the wilderness is to find the pastures for the flock (cf. 65:12 [13]; Jer. 9:10 [9]; 23:10; Joel 1:19–20; 2:22; also Amos 1:2). "Grassy" makes the point explicit. Causing the flock to lie down there rather than simply feed suggests ample provision. It implies that they have eaten, are satisfied, and have no need to move on to look for further grass: this pasture will provide the next meal, too. Lying down after feeding also hints at security (Ezek. 34:14–15; Zeph. 3:13; also Job 11:19; Isa. 17:2).

> [2b]He guides me by completely restful waters;
> [3a]he restores my life.

The second line completes an *abb´a´* sequence with the first line (MT's verse division reflects the parallelism between vv. 2a and 2b). The piel complements the hiphil, the plural noun complements the singular, and the prepositions complement each other. Substantially, v. 2b confirms that the shepherd provides drink as well as food. Guiding (*nāhal*) is the act of a powerful but caring party toward a weaker and needy party (31:3 [4]; Gen. 33:14; 2 Chron. 28:15; Isa. 40:11; 49:10; 51:18), just as Yhwh took Israel through the wilderness and into the promised land (Exod. 15:13). As well as knowing where the grass grows, a shepherd needs to know where to find the little pools of water that the rocks trap and the sun does not evaporate, or where it is possible to construct a small dam to hold the water. The traditional rendering "still water" makes sense

---

16. Tg refers the initial shepherding to the exodus and wilderness journey but then sees the psalm as having the exile in mind in v. 4; Qimchi takes up this idea and suggests that the psalm might relate to the return from the exile. David Noel Freedman similarly sees it as suggesting a second exodus, from the exile: see "The Twenty-Third Psalm," in *Pottery, Poetry, and Prophecy* (Winona Lake, IN: Eisenbrauns, 1980), 275–302; also Michael L. Barré and John S. Kselman, "New Exodus, Covenant, and Restoration in Psalm 23," in *The Word of the Lord Shall Go Forth* (D. N. Freedman Festschrift), ed. Carol L. Meyers and M. O'Connor (Winona Lake, IN: Eisenbrauns, 1983), 97–127. Cf. Bernard P. Robinson, "Pastures New," *Scripture Bulletin* 29 (1999): 2–10.

in a European context where many rivers and streams run through the countryside, but in a Middle Eastern wilderness the speed of streams is not a problem, and the OT makes no reference to it. "Water of restfulness" is rather water by which the sheep may rest, the idea being parallel to that in v. 2a. The sheep may drink and lie down by the pool, again knowing they can get up and have another drink. It is an idyllic idea, perhaps rarely experienced in real life.

"He restores my life" (*napšî*, my *person) is itself an expression that suggests reviving a person or an animal by giving them food and drink (see 19:7 [8]), so that it sums up the implications of v. 2 and parallels v. 1 in the *abb′a′* structure of vv. 1–3a. To spell out the prosaic implications of vv. 1–3a, as shepherd, Yhwh restores my life and sees that I lack nothing, by making sure I have food, water, and rest.[17]

> ³ᵇHe leads me in faithful paths
>   for his name's sake.

Verse 3b further complements vv. 1–3a but also anticipates v. 4 in summarizing the style of the shepherd's twofold work.

"Leading" (*nāḥâ*) is another word for Israel's journey through the wilderness (Exod. 13:17, 21; 15:13; 32:34; Deut. 32:12; Neh. 9:12; Pss. 77:20 [21]; 78:14, 53), though it is used more generally of Yhwh's leading, not least when people are under pressure from enemies (5:8 [9]; 27:11). That helps us to see why the psalm speaks of leading in paths of *faithfulness (*ṣedeq*; cf. leading with your *ṣĕdāqâ* in 5:8 [9]). These are not merely right paths in the sense of paths that lead to the right places, the places with grass and water. Nor is the psalm introducing a moral note and asking to be led to live the right kind of life. Faithful paths are paths consistent with the divine shepherd's faithfulness. The confession corresponds to the declaration in the Song of Moses that Yhwh is leading Israel with *commitment (Exod. 15:13).

The motivation "for his *name's sake" corresponds to that in 31:3 [4], but here it restates the first colon. Yhwh is a God characterized by faithfulness (e.g., 4:1 [2]). In a sense, that is the meaning of the name "Yhwh." So acting in faithfulness demonstrates that the name is a true reflection of the character.

> ⁴Even when I walk in the darkest canyon,
>   I do not fear disaster.
> Because you are with me; your rod and your staff—
>   they comfort me.

---

17. Timothy M. Willis ("A Fresh Look at Psalm xxiii 3a," *VT* 37 [1987]: 104–6) takes the line to refer more specifically to providing shelter.

These two lines thus complement the first two in describing the other way in which Yhwh's faithful leading works out. Both grass and water may well lie in or near canyons, not out in the open, where the water flows away and the sun dries up the grass. But canyons are also places of danger. Wild animals go there for the same reason as sheep, and the undergrowth, the shadow, and the rocks provide them with good hiding places from which to pounce on sheep. The word ṣalmāwet ([canyon of] deep darkness) is a suggestive one. It may originally have been pointed ṣalmût, but MT's pointing heightens its effect by making it suggest deathly shadow. In turn, "deathly" is likely a form of superlative, as is sometimes the case in English ("dead right"), yet here an apposite one because the darkness did threaten death (cf. English "dead tired").

But the sheep is not afraid when walking through a canyon, even a very dark one. The second line explains how this can be. The sheep knows that in its shepherd it has a courageous and tough person who is prepared to take on whatever threatens the flock. Like Yhwh's presence or absence (see on 22:1 [2]), having Yhwh "with" us is not merely a feeling. It does not signify mere presence but also action (e.g., Isa. 41:10). This presence expresses itself by aggressive action to defeat enemies and thus protect the one to whom Yhwh is committed (again, cf. Isa. 41:10).[18] So the shepherd's presence makes itself felt by means of rod and staff.[19] A rod is the object with which the Davidic ruler is to break up the nations (Ps. 2:9), with which Yhwh punishes Judah (Isa. 10:5), and with which a man might strike his servant so hard that he kills him (Exod. 21:20). The shepherd would carry one attached to his belt as the weapon with which to attack animals and thus protect the sheep.[20] His staff is the cane on which he might lean for support (e.g., Zech. 8:4), though it is also the means by which a shepherd might keep the sheep in order and knock down olives for them to eat. The two objects thus "comfort" the sheep in different ways.[21] "Comfort" (nāḥam piel) sometimes suggests emotional encouragement and sometimes action that changes a situation, and both would be relevant in this context. The psalm's links with the language of the exodus and of Isa. 40–55 make v. 4 also resonate with (c.g.) Isa. 40:1; again, what the psalm does is apply that community comfort to the individual.

18. Cf. Horst Dietrich Preuss, "'. . . Ich will mit dir sein!'" *ZAW* 80 (1968): 139–73.
19. On these, cf. E. Power, "The Shepherd's Two Rods in Modern Palestine and in Some Passages of the Old Testament," *Bib* 9 (1928): 434–42.
20. See Hannah W. Kinoti's comments from an African perspective, "Psalm 23:1–6," in *Return to Babel*, ed. Levison and Pope-Levison, 63–68, see 63–64.
21. Tg and Luther agree that the staff is the Torah, but Tg sees this as good news, Luther as bad news (*Selected Psalms*, 1:170–71).

23:5–6. Thus far the psalm has spoken purely metaphorically. Now it mixes metaphor with literal reality, though the bounds of literal and metaphorical are hard to discern.

> ⁵You lay a table before me
>   in the presence of my enemies.
> You bathe my head with oil;
>   my cup amply satisfies.

Presumably the enemies are literal, though it is prosaic to infer that the psalm's background must lie in an actual temple thanksgiving meal,[22] and the psalm has not referred to an act of deliverance that such a meal might celebrate. To lay a table for someone is to act as a gracious host (cf. Prov. 9:1–2), and it is what a king does (by means of his servants) for his extensive household (e.g., 2 Sam. 9:7–13). Verse 5a might then suggest the picture of the suppliant as a member of God's quasi-royal household, while other members of the community who are opposed to him in the manner of Ps. 22 look on with frustration and envy.[23]

Verse 5b then takes the image further in two ways. At this banquet the host pours perfumed oil on the guest's head (cf. Luke 7:46) and gives the guest a large cup of wine that well satisfies.

> ⁶Good and commitment will certainly chase me
>   all the days of my life.
> I will return to [MT]/dwell in [LXX] Yhwh's house
>   for long days.

When translated into theological terms, what all this means—the shepherding and the hospitality, the provision and the protection—is that *good and *commitment will always be pursuing me. EVV "follow" is a watered-down translation of *rādap*, which consistently means something more energetic (usually hostile; e.g., 7:1 [2]; 18:37 [38]; 69:26 [27]; 71:11; in 34:14 [15]; 38:20 [21] it refers to pursuing in a more positive sense). The verb thus carries two encouraging implications. One is that if wild animals/enemies (vv. 1–5) pursue us, good and commitment also do so. The other is that good and commitment follow us with energy. The personification of these aspects of God compares with the

---

22. Against E. Vogt, "The 'Place in Life' of Ps 23," *Bib* 34 (1953): 195–211. Dennis D. Sylva ("The Changing of Images in Ps 23.5, 6," *ZAW* 102 [1990]: 111–16) doubts whether vv. 5–6 refer to the temple at all.

23. Philip D. Stern ("The 'Bloodbath of Anat' and Psalm xxiii," *VT* 44 [1994]: 120–25) suggests that the psalm picks up motifs from the Anat story but has Yhwh keeping the enemies at bay instead of slaughtering them.

prayer in 43:3 for God's light and truthfulness to be sent out to lead us (*nāḥâ*, as v. 3b) to God's house; there, too, the context is the pressure of enemies persecuting the suppliant. In the present context the implication will be that it is here in God's house that the suppliant enjoys the hospitality described in v. 5. Chronologically, then, v. 6 no more follows on v. 5 than v. 4 follows on vv. 1–3. It rather describes Yhwh's care from a different angle.

The implication will be that these personified attributes of Yhwh—and thus Yhwh in person as the good and committed one—will indeed make sure that we get to Yhwh's house, and do so in order that we may stay there. Or rather, they imply that goodness and commitment will keep doing that, for they imply that we will keep needing to be chased in this way. Being in danger of not finding provender or of being attacked by enemies is not a once-for-all experience for people who belong to Yhwh. It is a recurrent one. But so is being chased and enabled to dwell with Yhwh. Through our life, for long days (the terms are parallel) Yhwh will ensure this.

In v. 6b, both "return to" and "dwell in" make partial sense but also raise problems, and it finally makes little difference which we follow.[24] MT implies that the worshipper's returning is a recurrent, not a once-for-all act, but it also implies that we return in order to stay for a while. LXX hardly implies that the worshipper sleeps in the temple every night, which could only apply to (e.g.) a Levite.[25] Perhaps the suppliant lives with an ongoing cycle of danger, deliverance, and dwelling. But references elsewhere (e.g., 27:4–5) suggest that the expression could be understood figuratively to refer to dwelling in the realm of Yhwh's provision and protection.[26]

Theological Implications

Although Ps. 23 has become associated with death and funerals, it is actually "a psalm about living," one that "puts daily activities, such as eating, drinking, and seeking security, in a radically God-centered

---

24. On the complementary nature of the readings, see Ernst A. Knauf, "Psalm xxiii 6," *VT* 51 (2001): 556.

25. Sigurdur Ö. Steingrímsson ("Der priesterliche Anteil," in *Text, Methode und Grammatik* [Wolfgang Richter Festschrift], ed. Walter Gross et al. [St. Ottilien: EOS, 1991], 483–519) argues that the author was a priest.

26. Cf. Otto Eissfeldt's comments in light of an Arad ostracon, "Bleiben im Hause Jahwes," *Kleine Schriften* (Tübingen: Mohr, 1973), 5:113–17; also Aubrey R. Johnson, "Psalm 23 and the Household of Faith," in *Proclamation and Presence* (Gwynne Henton Davies Festschrift), ed. John I. Durham and J. R. Porter (London: SCM, 1970), 255–71.

perspective."[27] The life of a member of God's people is lived between unfettered enjoyment of the presence of God and two aspects of the precariousness of life. One is uncertainty over whether we will have food to eat and water to drink. The other is the experience of hostility from other people. The implicit background of this psalm of trust is thus the reality explicitly reflected in many prayer psalms, that food and water are known to fail and enemies to threaten.[28] The psalm invites people into a declaration of trust that is both extraordinarily courageous and coldly rational. Yhwh, after all, is like a half-decent shepherd. This fact promises them provision and protection, what Luther calls "comfort in all *Anfechtungen*" (temptations, assaults, distress, and affliction).[29] It is for other psalms to handle the situations when Yhwh's shepherding fails. As Luther goes on to note, when that happens, this psalm invites people to keep trusting that Yhwh is our shepherd, holding on to God's word and promise.[30] They will then find that God acts on their behalf with "fierce tenderness,"[31] wielding rod and staff for them.

---

27. McCann, "Psalms," 767.
28. Cf. Westermann, *Living Psalms*, 130.
29. *Selected Psalms*, 1:155. Luther's thirty-page "brief" exposition of the psalm (152), mostly allegorical, was given "one evening after grace at the dinner table" (147); it presumably would have taken one and a half hours or more to deliver.
30. Ibid., 1:158–59.
31. Nancy J. Ramsay, "Counseling Survivors of Child Sexual Abuse," *Journal of Pastoral Care* 52 (1998): 217–26, see 219.

Psalm 24

Yhwh's Ownership of the World, Conditions for Approaching Yhwh, Admitting Yhwh to the City

Translation

David's. Composition.

¹To Yhwh belong the earth and what fills it,
  the world and the people who live in it,
²Because he is the one who has founded it on the seas,
  set it[a] on the rivers.[b]

³Who may go up to Yhwh's mountain,
  who may stand in his holy place?
⁴The innocent of hands and pure of heart,
  ones who have not lifted my self [L]/their selves [C][c] to emptiness
  and not sworn to deception.
⁵They may take a blessing from Yhwh,
  faithfulness from the God who delivers them.

   a. I take the yiqtol as having aorist reference (see the "Interpretation" for Ps. 18); it seems forced to take it as frequentative (so GKC 107b).
   b. There seems no need to take this as pl. of intensification, "the great river" (so GKC 124e).
   c. L *napšî*, "my person" (cf. LXX^A) makes the line closer to the command "You shall not lift my name to falsehood" (Exod. 20:7). C *napšô*, "his person" (cf. other LXX MSS, Jerome) makes the line closer to 25:1 and generates a smoother reading.

⁶Such is the company of those who have recourse to him,ᵈ
  those who seek your face—Jacob. (Rise)

⁷Lift your heads, gates,ᵉ
  lift yourselves, eternal doors,
  so that the glorious king may come in.
⁸Who is this, the glorious king?
  Yhwh, strong one and warrior,
  Yhwh, the battle warrior.
⁹Lift your heads, gates,
  lift, eternal doors,
  so that the glorious king may come in.
¹⁰Who is this, then,ᶠ the glorious king?
  Yhwh Armies,
  he is the glorious king. (Rise)

Interpretation

The psalm comprises three self-contained brief sections that are unusually unrelated to each other. The psalm is "baffling" in this respect.¹ Perhaps the sections are of independent origin, but if so, they now appear together as one psalm. Verses 1–2 declare that Yhwh established the world and therefore owns it. Verses 3–6 form a liturgy, comprising a question about the qualifications for entering Yhwh's presence, an answer, and a responsive declaration that the speakers fulfill the qualifications. Verses 7–10 form another liturgy, comprising a demand that gates open for a glorious king, a question about this king's identity, and an answer. Perhaps the whole is a processional liturgy, in which case vv. 1–2 might be the procession's song of praise as it stood outside the city gate before beginning the double liturgy.

> David's. Composition.

Heading. See glossary, though the words come here in the reverse of the usual order (cf. Pss. 101; 110). LXX adds "for the first day of the week," this being the psalm used on Sundays in the daily service in the second temple.² The idea that the psalm is "David's" might suggest it was given a link with David's bringing the covenant chest into Jerusalem

---

d. So Q *dōrĕšāyw*; K *dršw* implies "[the company] that has recourse to him."
e. LXX reverses subject and object: "Lift your gates, heads [i.e., leaders]."
f. The doubled enclitic *hû'-zeh* is even more emphatic than the *zeh* in v. 8.
1. Yair Mazor, "Psalm 24," *SJOT* 7 (1993): 303–16, see 303.
2. See Trudiger, *Psalms of the Tamid Service*, 54–75.

or with the Davidic king's regular celebration of Yhwh's taking up the position of king there.³

24:1–2. In two closely parallel lines, vv. 1–2 declare that Yhwh founded the earth securely and therefore owns it.

> ¹To Yhwh belong the earth and what fills it,
>   the world and the people who live in it,

This double noun clause begins with the predicate "Yhwh's [is]"; it appears only in v. 1a, but it carries over its force into the parallel colon. The rest of the two cola then comprise two double-noun phrases that form the subjects of the clause. In each, the opening noun refers to the earth or world, the framework for the whole. The noun in v. 1a is more familiar; the parallel noun in v. 1b is less usual and also more precise, indicating that we are really talking about the earth as the inhabited world. The second noun in each colon then refers to the contents of the frame: the noun in v. 1a again is more general, and the expression in the parallel colon sharpens it with its reference to people.

> ²Because he is the one who has founded it on the seas,
>   set it on the rivers.

A number of inferences could be drawn from this statement—for instance, that Yhwh has authority over the entire world, that Yhwh has responsibility for the entire world, that Yhwh must be acknowledged by the entire world. But v. 2 draws none of these. Instead, it declares the basis for the statement. Again the line begins with an expression that applies to both cola, though here it is not the predicate but the subject. The line leads into a prepositional phrase and a verb, and then another prepositional phrase and verb that comprise the parallel colon. Each time the preposition is ʿal, the noun is plural, and the verb is third person with a third-person feminine suffix, but a feminine noun complements the masculine, a yiqtol verb complements the qatal, and piel complements qal. The basis for Yhwh's ownership of the world is the fact that Yhwh established it on its foundations. We might paraphrase this by saying that Yhwh created the world; the reference to creation might link with the psalm's being used on the first day of the week.⁴ But the psalm makes a more concrete point. For the OT, often the question to which a statement about creation is the answer is a question about the world's security, and this statement corresponds to that interest. Beneath the

---

3. Marco Treves ("The Date of Psalm xxiv," *VT* 10 [1960]: 428–34) links it with the temple rededication in 164 BC.
4. Cf. Hill, *Prayer, Praise and Politics*, 158.

world are vast reservoirs of water, as evident from waters continually bursting through as rivers and springs. Is the earth, then, secure? Might it be washed away? By no means, the psalm declares. In creating the world, Yhwh acted rather like a skilled engineer building an edifice on a marshy base, who proceeds by driving piles deep down to make sure of a firm foundation. Yes, the world is secure, Yhwh made it so, and therefore Yhwh owns it.

24:3–6. Abruptly everything changes and we are asking a question about qualifications for coming into Yhwh's presence to make requests. By the end of the section it will be explicit that this is not a mere theoretical question: a group of people is waiting to discover whether they qualify. How do the questions link with what has preceded? The only verbal link is the name Yhwh, but it is a significant one. Verses 1–2 have asserted that Yhwh established the earth and is therefore sovereign over it. The question about the possibility of going into the presence of this God is therefore a solemn one. The section comprises a question (v. 3), an answer (vv. 4–5), and a further response by the questioners (v. 6). Like Ps. 15, the qualities this liturgy specifies are social and religious ones, not qualities in the realm of spirituality or purity, though the latter might be presupposed. But they do not form a list of qualifications that a gatekeeper could test, since most of them concern acts that take place in secret. This liturgy functions to put the ball back into the questioners' court. They have to examine themselves and accept responsibility for themselves. They cannot pass evaluation on to someone else.[5]

> [3]Who may go up to Yhwh's mountain,
> who may stand in his holy place?

The actual question is posed in two neatly parallel four-word cola, each comprising the word "who," a third-person singular yiqtol verb, a construct noun with the preposition *b*, and a noun depending on it. "Standing" follows on "going up," reference to the actual worship place follows reference to the mountain, and reference to "his holiness" follows on reference to "Yhwh." Talk of standing rather than bowing down suggests that the questioners come not simply to worship but also to make request. They take the posture a suppliant takes before a king.

> [4]The innocent of hands and pure of heart,
> ones who have not lifted my self [L]/their selves [C] to emptiness
> and not sworn to deception.

---

5. Cf. Crenshaw, *Psalms*, 158–59.

A tricolon responds to the question with a much briefer answer than the one in Ps. 15, though also one that may be broader insofar as it refers to attitudes toward God as well as toward other people. One way of seeing how it does that is to see it as covering these areas in *abb'a'* sequence: clean hands and swearing to deception refer to relationships with other people, while pure hearts and not lifting the self (*person) to *emptiness refer to attitudes toward God.[6] But this may tie the interpretation too tight. Certainly the first phrase covers proper outward conduct toward others; innocent hands are hands that are not covered in blood (cf. Exod. 21:28; Josh. 2:17–20; 2 Sam. 3:28; 14:9). But the second phrase, about proper inward attitude, may also refer to relationships with other people, since it is possible to be responsible for people's deaths without doing the killing oneself. Those who come before Yhwh must be persons whose relationships are honorable in their inner attitude and not just in the way they keep their hands clean, because the wrong inner attitude is also a threat to other people. Further, while both the second and third cola bring attitudes toward Yhwh into the equation, both also continue to have implications in connection with harming other people, for false oaths are another means of depriving people of their livelihood and even of their lives. In these two parallel cola the two parallel negatived third-person qatal verbs contrast with the positive adjectives in the first colon. They thus suggest that self-examination has to consider the negative and the concrete act as well as the positive and the person's general qualities. Further, one of the verbs is qal, the other niphal, and "to deception" corresponds to "to emptiness." "They have not lifted *my* person to emptiness" recalls the command not to lift Yhwh's name to emptiness (Exod. 20:7)—not to associate Yhwh's name with something empty or false such as a false report (Exod. 23:1) or a false testimony (Deut. 5:20; cf. also Job 31:5). "They have not lifted *their* person to emptiness" makes the same point in a slightly different way; "lifting up the self to someone/something" can suggest making oneself dependent (Ps. 25:1; 86:4; 143:8) or setting one's heart on something (cf. Prov. 19:18; Hosea 4:8), and either connotation is appropriate here. The phrase "to emptiness" suggests the purpose of their act; so does the parallel reference to swearing "to/for deception" (*l,* not *b*—contrast Gen. 27:35; 34:13). They swear oaths in order to achieve a deceptive end, in order to cheat and defraud. LXX makes the point explicit: "and have not sworn to the deception of their neighbor."

> [5]They may take a blessing from Yhwh,
>   faithfulness from the God who delivers them.

---

6. Cf. Schaefer, *Psalms,* 60.

A double promise is attached to those expectations, going beyond the question though perhaps only making explicit what was implicit in it. "Take" is again the verb *nāśā'*, translated "lift" in v. 4. "The one who is not carried away by fraud shall carry away a blessing from the Lord."[7] The "taking away" from the temple here applies to both cola, with "faithfulness" paralleling "blessing" and "the God who delivers" spelling out the implications of "Yhwh." Substantially, the collocation of blessing and deliverance is striking, as is the mediation of faithfulness. Blessing characteristically refers to God's involvement in the everyday recurrences of life, making it fruitful, whereas deliverance refers to God's more occasional involvement in the periodic crises of life.[8] But the collocation of these two recurs from 3:8 [9]. The verse implies that people are coming to meet with Yhwh to seek that ongoing blessing: they are not coming because there is a crisis. If their relationships with other people are honorable, then they will find Yhwh promising to make their lives fruitful. But the psalm also reminds them that Yhwh is their deliverer. That fact lies behind the promise of blessing: it is in having delivered that God blesses. It also lies in front of that promise—when new crises arise and disturb the life of blessing, God will again prove to be deliverer. And that is so because both blessing (*good fortune of) and *deliverance issue from the *faithfulness of Yhwh.[9]

> [6]Such is the company of those who have recourse to him,
>   those who seek your face—Jacob. (Rise)

The response to that account of the qualifications does not imply that "people who come here need to be people who have recourse to Yhwh,"[10] but "we acknowledge that people who want to have recourse to Yhwh and find Yhwh's blessing need to be that kind of people, and we are." It is yet another parallel bicolon, and this helps to explain a puzzle in it, the significance of "Jacob" at the end. "Jacob" is nominative and stands in parallelism with "company," as "those who seek your face" stands in parallelism with "those who have recourse to him."[11] "Jacob" makes explicit that the "company" (*dôr*) is more than a collection of unrelated

---

7. Jannie du Preez, "Mission Perspectives in an Old Testament Procession Song," *Missionalia* 18 (1990): 330–43, see 334.

8. See Claus Westermann, *Blessing* (Philadelphia: Fortress, 1978).

9. NRSV/NIVI "vindication" is hardly an appropriate rendering of *ṣĕdāqâ*, but NJPS's "a just reward" is no improvement; LXX's "mercy" is nearer.

10. Against Westermann, *Living Psalms*, 278.

11. NRSV mg takes it as vocative (cf. Tg, Jerome?), which is odd. LXX offers the easier reading: "who seek the face of the God of Jacob," though N. Tromp argues for its originality ("Jacob in Psalm 24," in *Von Kanaan bis Kerala* [J. P. M. van der Ploeg Festschrift], ed. W. C. Delsman et al. [Neukirchen-Vluyn: Neukirchener Verlag, 1982], 271–82). More likely

people: the word often means a "generation" and in the context of Israel thus suggests a group of related people. This company comprises the descendants of Jacob alive at a particular moment. They are the people who have recourse to or *seek help from Yhwh. Seeking Yhwh's *face has similar implications to that verb (cf. 27:8). It means not merely seeking a sense of being in God's presence, but also seeking to see Yhwh's face shining. It implies seeking that Yhwh should shine out in blessing on one's life. So "having recourse to Yhwh" or "seeking Yhwh's face" is another way of talking about seeking Yhwh's "blessing" and "deliverance," the expressions of Yhwh's faithfulness (v. 5).

24:7–10. Once again everything changes. Dialogue and question-and-answer format continue, but the nature of the dialogue and the participants are quite different, as are its presuppositions and frame of reference. Whereas the presupposition of vv. 3–6 was that Yhwh was on Mount Zion and that other people wished to come there, the presupposition of vv. 7–10 is that Yhwh is outside Mount Zion, and people are urging Yhwh's admittance. The verses take the form of four tricola. The almost identical sets of biddings in vv. 7 and 8 (each 3-3-3) make sense as the biddings of people standing outside the gates to which they refer. The questions in vv. 8a and 10a, also almost identical, make sense as the responses of gatekeepers. The statements in the second and third cola in vv. 8 and 10 then make sense as the answers of the earlier speakers who did the bidding.

> ⁷Lift your heads, gates,
>   lift yourselves, eternal doors,
>   so that the glorious king may come in.

The bidding's presupposition, then, is that Yhwh stands outside—outside Mount Zion, to judge from vv. 3–6.[12] It thus presupposes a variegated or dynamic rather than homogeneous or static understanding of Yhwh's

---

the line works *abcc'b'*, and the second-person reference to Yhwh ("your") complements the third-person reference ("him").

12. In this context it thus is hard to make sense of Alan Cooper's intriguing suggestion that vv. 7–10 refer to an assault by Yhwh on the realm of death ("Ps 24.7–10," *JBL* 102 [1983]: 37–60). Interestingly, this seems to be anticipated in the fourth-century account of "Christ's Descent into Hell," in *The Gospel of Nicodemus*, which applies the verses to Christ's breaking into hell (see Edgar Hennecke, ed., *New Testament Apocrypha*, vol. 1 [repr. London: SCM, 1973], 470–76; cf. David J. A. Clines, "A World Established on Water," in *The New Literary Criticism and the Hebrew Bible*, ed. J. Cheryl Exum and David J. A. Clines, JSOTSup 143 [Sheffield: JSOT Press, 1993], 79–90, see 88). For a more conventional mythic understanding, see Frank M. Cross, *Canaanite Myth and Hebrew Epic* (Cambridge, MA: Harvard University Press, 1973), 91–99; see also Loretz's comments, *Ugarit-Texte und Thronbesteigungspsalmen*, 263–67.

presence. Yhwh is not everywhere, or rather is not everywhere in the same way. This gains further significance from the setting of vv. 7–10 in the context of vv. 1–2, which implied Yhwh's power over the whole world as the one who established it. The bidding might presuppose that Yhwh has not yet taken up residence on Mount Zion. The dramatic setting would then be David's capture of Jerusalem, and the imaginary or dramatic voice asking, Who is this glorious king? might be that of a Jebusite resisting Yhwh's arrival. Or it might be David's subsequent moving of the covenant chest there. The psalm's understanding of Yhwh's presence is that Yhwh chooses to make a home in particular places within the world; since Sinai, Yhwh has had a mobile home, and David is now moving this from Gibeah to its new home in Israel's new capital (2 Sam. 5–6). A related possibility is that from time to time (perhaps at Sukkot) Israel celebrated and reenacted Yhwh's and/or the covenant chest's original move to Mount Zion. This theory would explain the presence of the psalm in the Psalter; if the psalm were composed for and used on just one occasion, we might expect to find it in Samuel–Kings rather than in the Psalter, where its presence suggests repeated use. But the bidding might alternatively presuppose that Yhwh and/or the chest had left Mount Zion to accompany Israel in fighting a battle, in the manner presupposed by (e.g.) 2 Chron. 20 (cf. 1 Sam. 4). Yhwh was to be expected to go out with Israel's armies (44:9 [10]; 60:10 [12]; 108:11 [12]). The OT's dynamic understanding of Yhwh's presence involves Yhwh's making that presence felt in action, and sometimes going to the scene to do so. Or perhaps the psalm presupposes the situation of the exile, when the glorious king abandoned Jerusalem, after which Isa. 52 proclaims the imminent reassertion of Yhwh's kingship and the return of the king.[13]

Whichever way, v. 7 bids the gates to open so that "the glorious king" may enter them, apparently by raising their lintels.[14] Only here is Yhwh "the glorious king" (lit., "the king of *honor"). Yet even if liturgically Yhwh stands outside, the term "eternal doors" implies a recognition that this place is associated with Yhwh's eternity. The gates were not especially old, but were the gates of the God who is from eternity to eternity.[15] In other words, "eternal gates/doors" involves a metonymy.

> [8] Who is this, the glorious king?
> Yhwh, strong one and warrior,
> Yhwh, the battle warrior.

---

13. Cf. Vicente Hueso, "El Salmo 24," *EstBib* 22 (1963): 243–53; Richard W. Reifsnyder, "Psalm 24," *Int* 51 (1997): 284–88.
14. So P.-R. Berger, "Zu Ps 24,7 und 9," *UF* 2 (1970): 335–36.
15. Cf. Keel's comments, *Symbolism of the Biblical World*, 172.

Verse 8 then asks—presumably rhetorically—after the identity of this glorious king. It is presumably the bidders of v. 7 who identify the king in military terms. In some sense, then, Yhwh comes as military victor—as (e.g.) one who has just won a victory such as the one described in 2 Chron. 20, or who is completing a victorious journey from Egypt to this new abode (cf. Exod. 15:1–18, where Yhwh is first described as a "man of war" and as one who "reigns" as king), or who is the victor over Babylon.

> ⁹Lift your heads, gates,
>   lift, eternal doors,
>   so that the glorious king may come in.

The bidding repeats from v. 7, again presumably rhetorically. For variation the verb in the middle colon is now qal, repeating the form in the first colon, rather than niphal as it was in v. 7.

> ¹⁰Who is this, then, the glorious king?
>   Yhwh Armies,
>   he is the glorious king. (Rise)

Verse 10 likewise repeats v. 8, with more marked verbal variation though with similar import. The first colon incorporates an extra pronoun. The third colon rounds off the psalm with a final affirmation of Yhwh's identity as "the glorious king." The middle colon introduces the title Yhwh Armies, *yhwh ṣĕbāʾôt*, which is a puzzling expression though a title with similar meaning to "Yhwh, strong one and warrior, Yhwh the battle warrior" (v. 8). LXX translates "Lord of the powers" (cf. Jerome), which suggests taking it as an example of a rare construction whereby a name can govern a construct or can be treated as a common noun.[16] The expression would then presumably imply "Yhwh who is God of the armies," an extended version of the title "Yhwh, God of the Armies." Some worshippers might take these armies to be Israel's earthly ones, though the OT is less inclined to associate Yhwh with earthly armies than with the heavenly army, the supernatural forces that Yhwh commands (1 Sam. 17:45 pointedly uses a different word to refer to Israel's forces). The great heavenly army (perhaps the plural is intensive) is one that Yhwh created and one that serves Yhwh (33:6; 103:21; 148:2). But elsewhere (e.g., 2 Sam. 5:10) LXX renders the title "Lord All-powerful," which suggests taking the plural as abstract and the compound expression as appositional. This would fit with the use of the extended phrase "Yhwh God Armies," where "God" is in the absolute rather than the

---

16. See JM 131o.

construct form (Ps. 59:5 [6]). The title would then imply "Yhwh Great Army" or "Yhwh Great Warrior."

Theological Implications

Although the three sections of the psalm are formally unrelated, they have somehow come to form parts of one psalm, and thus we can reflect on the interrelationship of their theological statements. The statements are three. Yhwh owns the world as the one who made it secure. People can properly come to seek Yhwh's blessing in the temple if there is integrity in their lives and their attitudes in relation to God and to other people. And such people can properly urge their own city to admit Yhwh the glorious king into its midst. The interrelationships of these convictions suggest that Yhwh is beneficent lord both of the realm of the cosmos as a whole and of the lives of individuals. In our context we may also need to observe that the latter is set in the context of the former. These convictions suggest that Yhwh both imposes sovereignty and seeks people's acquiescence in it. In our context, we may again need to recognize that the latter is set in the context of the former. They suggest that Yhwh can be both within the community and knocking on its door. In our context, we may need to see that the former is set in the context of the latter.

David Clines comments: "In subscribing to Ps. 24, we are writing a blank cheque for war."[17] But (to rework one of Clines's own points), that inference seems inconsistent with the psalm's own explicit demands regarding human behavior, in its middle section. It would be at least as plausible to suggest that in subscribing to Ps. 24, we are making war Yhwh's business rather than ours and writing a blank check for pacifism.

C. H. Spurgeon observes that all the peoples of the earth belonging to Yhwh makes nonsense of the suggestion sometimes made in his day that the "negro and other despised races . . . were not cared for by the God of heaven"; if a person is a human being, God claims that person.[18] He adds that since the world itself belongs to Yhwh, we are but "tenants at will" on it and had better behave as such. Jannie du Preez adds that because the whole earth belongs to Yhwh, "each habitation, workplace

---

17. "A World Established on Water (Psalm 24)," in *Interested Parties*, JSOTSup 205 (Sheffield: Sheffield Academic Press, 1995), 172–86, see 176. See further Francis Landy, "From David to David: Psalm 24 and David Clines," in *Reading from Right to Left* (David J. A. Clines Festschrift), ed. J. Cheryl Exum and H. G. M. Williamson, JSOTSup 373 (London: Sheffield Academic Press, 2003), 275–89.

18. *Treasury of David*, 1:374.

and place of worship are His" and observes how thus "the place of worship used in ancient Jebusite religion now becomes the sanctuary of Yahweh." Indeed, the gates of every place of worship in the world are to "stretch themselves in order that the rightful King may enter." And the people of God are called to bid them do so.[19]

---

19. "Mission Perspectives in an Old Testament Procession Song," 339–40.

Psalm 25
The Bases of Prayer from A to Z

Translation

 David's.

[ʾ] **¹**To you, Yhwh,
 I lift up my soul, my God,
[b] **²**In you I have trusted—may I not be shamed;
 may my enemies not exult over me.
[g] **³**Yes, may none of those who look to you be shamed;
 may those who are unfaithful without reason[a] be shamed.
[d] **⁴**Make me acknowledge your ways, Yhwh,
 teach me your paths,
[h] **⁵**guide me on the way in your truthfulness,
[w] And teach me, because you are the God who delivers me;
 I look to you constantly.
[z] **⁶**Be mindful of your compassion, Yhwh,
 and your great commitment, because they are of old.
[ḥ] **⁷**Do not be mindful of my youthful failures, or my rebellions;
 in accordance with your commitment be mindful of me yourself,
 for the sake of your goodness, Yhwh.
[ṭ] **⁸**Yhwh is good and upright;
 therefore he directs people who fail in the way.
[y] **⁹**He guides the weak on the way[b] with authority;
 he teaches the weak his way.

 a. For the use of *rêqām* to mean "without reason" rather than "without effect," cf. 7:4 [5].
 b. *Yadrēk* (guide on the way) is a jussive form, but the context suggests that this should not be pressed (cf. *IBHS* 34.2.1c).

[k] ¹⁰All Yhwh's paths are commitment and truthfulness
   for people who keep his covenant and his declarations.
[l] ¹¹For the sake of your name, Yhwh,
   pardon^c my waywardness because it is great.
[m] ¹²Who, then, is the one who reveres Yhwh?—
   he instructs him in the way he should choose.
[n] ¹³His life stays in goodness
   and his offspring possess the country.
[s] ¹⁴Yhwh's counsel is with those who revere him,
   and his covenant, in making them acknowledge him.
[ʿ] ¹⁵My eyes are ever toward Yhwh,
   because he is the one who brings forth my feet from the net.
[p] ¹⁶Face toward me, be gracious to me,
   because I am alone and weak.
[ṣ] ¹⁷The constraints of my heart have expanded;
   bring me forth from my pressures.
[r] ¹⁸Look at my weakness and my trouble
   and carry all my failings.
[r] ¹⁹Look at my enemies, how numerous they are,
   and at the violent opposition they show to me.
[š] ²⁰Guard my life and rescue me;
   may I not be shamed, because I rely on you.
[t] ²¹May integrity and uprightness watch over me,
   because I have looked to you.
   ²²God, redeem Israel
   from all its constraints.

Interpretation

This prayer psalm forms an incomplete alphabetical composition, like Pss. 9–10. It has no *q* line but two *r* lines; perhaps a word beginning with *q* originally opened v. 17, and many possibilities could be suggested. In vv. 1–2 and 5 I have followed LXX's colon division to produce a *b* line and a *w* line. The closing line stands outside the alphabetical pattern but (because v. 5 covers both *h* and *w*) nicely brings the psalm to twenty-two verses, the number of letters in the Hebrew alphabet. The alphabetical form suggests that the psalm is designed to cover the bases of prayer from A to Z. This gives it a distinctive power and dynamic, different from those psalms that may seem more expressive and emotional, though it may thereby raise the question whether we too easily assume that other psalms reflect unprocessed experience. They too process experience through poetic form. Psalm 25 has links with wisdom material in the

---

c. The weqatal follows on a quasi-purpose clause (GKC 112nn). DG 60c, 71d takes it as precative following on an extraposed phrase.

OT, notably its stress on the "way" and thus on the different "ways" a human life may take. These add to the likelihood that it was designed as a model prayer, one designed to teach people to pray, though this does not mean it could not also have been designed for use in corporate and individual worship, like other psalms. The alphabetical form being the psalm's structural principle, it has no further division into sections; my divisions are thus somewhat arbitrary, though they correspond to some approximate clustering of themes.[1] Its unity and interlinking are also furthered by the way a number of words are repeated within the psalm.[2]

Although we cannot know when it was written, we can imagine it being used in the Second Temple community in Judah. There individuals and communities were under pressure from the other communities surrounding them, whose individual lives were often interwoven with those of Judeans. To judge from prayers in (e.g.) Ezra 9 and Dan. 9, they were more preoccupied by awareness of their own moral shortcomings than the First Temple community. And to judge from (e.g.) Job, individuals within the community could be under pressure from others who passed judgment on their relationship with God. It compares with such Second Temple prayers in the unself-conscious way it interweaves pleas for rescue from trouble with pleas for forgiveness, without clearly relating these two realities of self-awareness. While vv. 16–22 eventually speak in the manner of a prayer designed for the midst of some crisis, the main part of the psalm does not do so. Its strong awareness of sin, its virtual lack of lament, its many statements of trust, and its desire for direction give it a distinctive flavor.

> David's.

Heading. See introduction.

25:1–3. Verses 1–3 constitute the psalm's initial looking to Yhwh and statement of trust.

> ['] ¹To you, Yhwh,
>   I lift up my soul, my God,

"Lifting up the soul" (*nepeš*, *person) suggests acknowledging dependence (see 24:4; cf. 86:4; 143:8), and the double invocation "Yhwh/my

---

1. Verses 1–3 and 20–22 correspond, but the psalm as a whole surely does not have a stepped structure (against H. Möller, "Strophenbau der Psalmen," *ZAW* 50 [1932]: 240–56; and Lothar Ruppert, "Psalm 25 und die Grenze kultorientierter Psalmenexegese," *ZAW* 84 [1972]: 576–82; who, significantly, offer two different stepped-structure outlines).

2. See further Auffret, *La sagesse a bâti sa maison*, 207–27.

God" underlines that. The metaphor of "lifting up" may suggest the inward equivalent to the physical lifting up of the hands (e.g., 28:2; 63:4 [5]) or eyes (e.g., 123:1) that are involved in prayer.

> [b] ²In you I have trusted—may I not be shamed;
> may my enemies not exult over me.

"In you I *trust" then expresses the point in another way. The specific reason for needing to trust is the possibility of being dishonored and disgraced in the community. The two cola make the point in two parallel wishes, one cohortative and one jussive, one negative and one positive. One might imagine an individual who experiences crop failure, business failure, illness, or bereavement, and has people assume that this raises questions about faithfulness to Yhwh, such as Job's friends raised. Or if Yhwh leaves an individual with these experiences, one might imagine these people questioning whether Yhwh is really the God to be worshipped. Such experiences radically imperil someone's place in the community as well as imperiling their understanding of God and of themselves and of the way God relates to them.

> [g] ³Yes, may none of those who look to you be shamed;
> may those who are unfaithful without reason be shamed.

The psalm raises this question not merely because this individual suppliant is at this moment under pressure from enemies but because such dishonoring is an ongoing or recurrent possibility for Israelites. Verses 15–21 will eventually suggest that the suppliant is indeed under such personal pressure; that makes it even more noteworthy that before focusing on this, the psalm sets the individual's destiny in the context of the life of other members of the community. The kinds of experiences noted in connection with v. 2 are, after all, common ones. Verse 3 makes the point by repeating twice more the verb in v. 2a. The two parallel cola are structured $abcc'b'a'$ so that the two identical verbs are juxtaposed at the center of the line.[3] *Looking to Yhwh is a key expression in the psalm (cf. vv. 5, 21). It is another way of referring to lifting up one's heart to Yhwh or trusting in Yhwh. Isaiah 49:23 declares that the plea here will be answered; for the participle here rendered "look to," see also Ps. 37:9; Isa. 40:31; Lam. 3:25; and Ps. 69:6 [7], which

---

3. In each colon, the subject is a participle, a suffixed form complementing an absolute form, and a negatived verb (lit., "May all those who look to you not be shamed") complements a positive one. A particle then opens the first colon, and an adverb closes the second.

works out the relationship of individual and community in this connection in a different way.[4] If we are to reckon that "being unfaithful without reason" is closely correlative to such waiting, then it might denote the kind of treachery that Job's friends practiced. While Job looked to Yhwh, they betrayed their relationship with him without real reason.

25:4–7. Two pleas, for teaching and for forgiveness, now interweave. The reference to waiting for Yhwh provides a link with vv. 1–3, but neither of the two pleas relates in a concrete way with the theme of vv. 1–3, and they may not especially relate to each other, though they may suggest that awareness of failure is a reason for the plea for teaching. Each pair of verses hangs together. In vv. 4–5, the first colon of v. 5 stands in parallelism with both cola in v. 4. In vv. 6–7, the first two cola and the last two especially stand together.

> [d] ⁴Make me acknowledge your ways, Yhwh,
>   teach me your paths,
> [h] ⁵ªguide me on the way in your truthfulness,

Three parallel verbs ask for instruction in Yhwh's way: "Make me *acknowledge,"[5] "Teach me" (which will recur in v. 5), and "Guide me in the way." The last phrase translates a verb (*dārak* hiphil) that picks up the earlier word "way" (*derek*), which itself stands in parallelism with "path." Each of the verbs suggests more than teaching in the sense of causing someone to understand something conceptually; they denote a teaching that affects the life. EVV take the reference to Yhwh's *truthfulness to make this more explicit, as suggesting that the suppliant wants to live in ways that correspond to the truthfulness, steadfastness, and consistency of Yhwh's ways. But the parallelism with what follows suggests that the phrase more likely supports a request to Yhwh to offer guidance by appealing to Yhwh's truthfulness, steadfastness, and consistency.

> [w] ⁵ᵇAnd teach me, because you are the God who delivers me;
>   I look to you constantly.

If these two cola also stand in parallelism and need interweaving, they suggest: "Because you are the God who constantly delivers me and for

---

4. For different views of the psalm's more general relationship with Ps. 37, see Ruppert, "Psalm 25"; and Norbert Lohfink, "Lexeme und Lexemgruppen in Ps 25," in *Text, Methode und Grammatik* (Wolfgang Richter Festschrift), ed. Walter Gross et al. (St. Ottilien: EOS, 1991), 271–95.
5. Not merely "make your paths known to me" (LXX); cf. v. 14.

whom I constantly wait." Or perhaps they suggest that the experience of *looking to Yhwh (and having Yhwh act) supports the affirmation that Yhwh is the God who *delivers. Or the link with vv. 1–3 may suggest the logic is the reverse: Yhwh's being a proven deliverer ("who delivers *me*," lit., "the God of my deliverance") is what makes it possible to take the constant waiting stance to which vv. 3 and 5 refer. What, then, is the significance of the "because" and the link with what precedes? Is it that these two cola indicate what *is* Yhwh's way, and therefore is the way in which to be led? Or do they indicate the way I need to be taught about, in order to live in trust that this will indeed be Yhwh's way with me? Or does the suppliant ask that the gift of being taught be added to the gift of being delivered?

> [*z*] ⁶Be mindful of your compassion, Yhwh,
>   and your great commitment, because they are of old.
> [*ḥ*] ⁷Do not be mindful of my youthful failures, or my rebellions;
>   in accordance with your commitment be mindful of me yourself,
>   for the sake of your goodness, Yhwh.

Analogous verbal patterns occur in these five cola. The only verb is *zākar*: there are two biddings to be *mindful and one *not* to be mindful. There are two appeals to Yhwh's *commitment, one accompanied by appeal to Yhwh's compassion, the other by appeal to Yhwh's *goodness. Between them these thus appeal to Yhwh's inherent instinct to act in grace and keep faithfulness whatever happens, to Yhwh's equally ancient womblike feelings for humanity in its neediness, and to Yhwh's practical beneficence and generosity. The suppliant's professed contrasting qualities are *failures, or shortcomings, and *rebellions, or assertiveness. The two terms contrast with each other as a negative falling short or lack of initiative, and a positive excess of initiative. Together they contrast with Yhwh's commitment and compassion, yet they also appeal to these. Likewise, the suppliant's "youthfulness" offers a contrast with Yhwh's antiquity. It thus might not refer to the suppliant's own young years: however young or old, the suppliant is a youngster compared with Yhwh, and makes that part of the basis for an appeal for compassion. But on the more usual understanding, the suppliant refers to shortcomings as a child who did not know better, and acts of rebellion as an adult for which there was no such excuse. The two verses are thus asking that Yhwh should not let the fact of shortcomings and rebellions be reason to stop showing the suppliant commitment and compassion in the form of practical goodness.

25:8–11. The same two themes continue, but (until the last colon) the pleas become generalizations.

> [*t*] ⁸Yhwh is good and upright;
> therefore he directs people who fail in the way.
> [*y*] ⁹He guides the weak on the way with authority;
> he teaches the weak his way.

Verses 8–9 again generate their own verbal patterns in the recurrence of reference to the *way and to the *weak, and they also extend the patterns in vv. 4–7 (good, fail, way, guide on the way, teach). The appeal to Yhwh's *goodness continues: goodness is inherent in Yhwh, like commitment and compassion, and so is uprightness. These two qualities are not seen as qualifying each other, as if in isolation goodness might be too soft and uprightness too hard. Rather, Yhwh's showing goodness is an expression of Yhwh's being upright. Indeed, whereas human uprightness can make people intolerant of failure, it increases Yhwh's commitment to people who *fail to walk in that right way of which vv. 4–5 spoke. So v. 8 also provides further reason for confidence that Yhwh will heed the appeal not to keep in mind failures and rebellion. Whereas the two cola in v. 8 thus link in linear fashion, the two in v. 9 are more classically parallel. The connections with what precedes also indicate why the *weak* need to be guided with *authority. The powerful need to be taught a commitment to proper *mišpāṭ*, but the weak need to be led in the way of *mišpāṭ* in the sense of having Yhwh apply *mišpāṭ* to their lives. In this context their being taught Yhwh's way means becoming more aware for their own encouragement that *mišpāṭ* is Yhwh's way, which is for their encouragement.

> [*k*] ¹⁰All Yhwh's paths are commitment and truthfulness
> for people who keep his covenant and his declarations.

Verses 10–11 take further the themes of vv. 4–9, though separately from each other, and they bring the psalm to its midpoint. They also recall the language of Exod. 34:6–10.⁶ The suppliant implicitly acknowledges a place among the kind of rebellious people described in Exod. 32–34 but pleads for Yhwh to take toward this "I" the stance Yhwh took to the people there—and to take this stance to the people as a whole now (e.g., v. 22).

In v. 10, talk of Yhwh's "paths" takes up the word from v. 4, talk of Yhwh's *commitment takes up the word from v. 6, and talk of Yhwh's *truthfulness takes up the word from v. 5. So this comment on "all" Yhwh's paths makes a powerful summary generalization. The second colon then indicates that even if the weak could not appropriately be required to

---

6. Cf. McCann, "Psalms," 777.

exercise *mišpāṭ*, this does not leave them without obligation. After the verb "keep," Yhwh's "covenant" will refer to the covenantal obligation that Yhwh imposes, which is identical with Yhwh's "declarations," the announced requirements of relationship with Yhwh.

> [*l*] ¹¹For the sake of your name, Yhwh,
>   pardon my waywardness because it is great.

The suppliant returns to the awareness of failure (cf. v. 7). Verse 10 might have given the impression that there is no hope for people who fail to live by the covenantal declarations. Yet the psalm knows well the paradoxical relationship between an absolute obligation to commitment and the possibility of casting oneself on Yhwh's mercy. Yhwh's character requires the expectation of commitment, but it also requires the manifestation of mercy. Thus the psalm with some boldness follows v. 10, which implicitly appeals to Yhwh's name, with an explicit appeal to Yhwh's *name that takes the argument in a different direction. "Pardon" (*sālaḥ*) is not the OT verb most commonly rendered "forgive" (see v. 18), though it is the nearest to a technical term for "forgive" in Hebrew,[7] used only with Yhwh as subject. "Pardon" is the cancellation of the significance of a wrong act that Yhwh alone can effect. Reference to the suppliant's *waywardness as "great" supports the view that v. 7a did not refer to mere youthful peccadilloes. Rashi suggests the neat argument that Yhwh's name being great makes it appropriate to pray for the forgiveness of great waywardness.

25:12–14. We may treat these three lines together in light of the recurrence of the description "those who revere Yhwh" in vv. 12 and 14, the dependence of v. 13 on v. 12, and the transition to first-person speech at v. 15.

> [*m*] ¹²Who, then, is the one who reveres Yhwh?—
>   he instructs him in the way he should choose.

One might expect the answer to the question to comprise a description of what is implied by revering Yhwh (cf. 24:3–6), but instead it comprises a description of what this revering leads to: hence, the line almost parallels the declaration that "reverence for Yhwh is the first principle of wisdom" (e.g., 111:10). The verse thus also parallels 24:3–6 in another way, in declaring the blessing that will come from such revering. The declaration about being taught Yhwh's way (v. 9) is reaffirmed in a promise about Yhwh's instructing the people in the way they should

---

7. Cf. J. J. Stamm in *TLOT* 798.

choose: showing them how to choose Yhwh's way rather than walking in the way approved by other deities or in the way of wrongdoing. LXX suggestively has Yhwh instructing in the way *Yhwh* chooses, but usage does not support this (cf. 119:30, 173). Rather, people have to choose their way; they need Yhwh to push them into making the right religious and moral choice. The problem about choice in accordance with Yhwh's will that the psalm has in mind is not the choice between various possibilities that might all be good (shall I be a lawyer or a rocket scientist?), but the choice between an option that is compatible with commitment to Yhwh and one that is not.

> [n] ¹³His life stays in goodness
> and his offspring possess the country.

The decision is to choose the way to life rather than the way to death: it will result in enjoying what is good. Each word in the second colon then clarifies the significance of the first. The *good the psalm is referring to is the practical goodness of staying in possession of the country (cf. 37:11). Following the reference to the one person's "life" (*person) by a reference to their family makes the second line better news than the first. The second colon also reassures us about the implications of the verb in the first, because "staying" (*lûn*) might mean only staying the night, but "possessing" (*yāraš*) implies a more sure, long-term occupancy.

> [s] ¹⁴Yhwh's counsel is with those who revere him,
> and his covenant, in making them acknowledge him.

Verse 14 then restates v. 12. Another way to say that Yhwh instructs people is to say that Yhwh's counsel is with them. The word for counsel (*sôd*) is somewhat allusive. It puzzled LXX, which renders "strength."[8] Jerome's "secret" is nearer (cf. 64:2 [3]), but "friendship" (RSV) is harder to parallel; for "counsel," see 83:3 [4]. Humanly speaking, without counsel things go wrong, but with a number of advisers they go well (Prov. 15:22); how much more difference will Yhwh's counsel make. The second colon restates once more what this counsel does, picking up the reference to *acknowledging (v. 4) and to Yhwh's covenant (v. 10). The line makes elegant use of parallelism as "his covenant" parallels "Yhwh's counsel" while the rest of the colon takes forward the point of the first colon in a different way. Prosaically put, Yhwh's counsel and covenant are with those who revere him, to make them acknowledge Yhwh.

8. On this, see *CP* 251–52.

25:15–19. First-person speech now again dominates the psalm, as it dominated vv. 1–7. There is no more talk of teaching or of mindfulness. Instead, the imagery of vision is more prominent: My eyes look to Yhwh (v. 15); I want Yhwh to face me and look at me (vv. 16, 18, 19).

> [ʿ] ¹⁵My eyes are ever toward Yhwh,
>   because he is the one who brings forth my feet from the net.

For the eyes to be "toward" Yhwh (cf. 123:2; 141:8) is to look to Yhwh for help or provision (cf. 34:5 [6]; 104:27; 145:15). I have taken the participial statement of faith in Yhwh in the second colon, which explains the orientation of the eyes, as referring to Yhwh's characteristic nature and action, but LXX may be right in understanding it as referring to a specific act of deliverance that Yhwh is about to do. It offers the most concrete indication thus far that the psalm envisages the attack of an enemy.

> [p] ¹⁶Face toward me, be gracious to me,
>   because I am alone and weak.

The converse of my eyes being toward Yhwh is that Yhwh's eyes are "toward me," which leads Yhwh to act in help or provision (34:15 [16]), or that Yhwh is "facing toward" me instead of facing away and not seeing me (cf. 69:16 [17]; 86:16; 119:132). So in raising our eyes to Yhwh, we are trying to catch Yhwh's eye, so that Yhwh will then be gracious to us: we are appealing not to our desert but to Yhwh's instinct to show favor when we deserve nothing (see 4:1 [2]). The "because" clause then provides another level of reason why Yhwh should act. On the one hand, the psalm presupposes the needs of someone who is on their own, which stands in some tension with the reference to "all" the people who wait for Yhwh (v. 3) and with other plurals in vv. 1–11. If we are to be prosaic, we may imagine the suppliant surrounded by attackers, with other faithful people far away. The suppliant is someone *weak (cf. v. 9), not someone powerful.

> [ṣ] ¹⁷The constraints of my heart have expanded;
>   bring me forth from my pressures.

The inner logic of the line reverses in that the reason for Yhwh's act comes first and the imperative second, and in this respect the line stands out within vv. 15–21. The first colon expresses itself somewhat paradoxically. "Expanding" (*rāḥab* hiphil) is usually a positive expression and elsewhere denotes Yhwh's act of deliverance. As an expression of grace (as here), Yhwh expands me when I am in constraint (4:1 [2]). Here it is the constraints that are being given plenty of room or scope.[9] Although constraints are often outward troubles (cf. v. 22), here they are constraints of the heart or inner anguish (cf. Gen. 42:21). In the second colon, "pressures" (*měṣûqôt*) is another term that etymologically suggests constraints; a further noun from this root appears set over against "expand" in Job 37:10.

> [r] **18**Look at my weakness and my trouble
> and carry all my failings.

Verse 18 introduces another visual term in asking for Yhwh to "look at" my *weakness (cf. vv. 9, 16) and my trouble (cf. 7:14, 16 [15, 17]; 10:7, 14). Somewhat surprisingly, the second colon then goes in quite another direction in reverting to the need for forgiveness. Here for the first time the Psalter uses that most common term for "forgive," *nāśā'*, which means "carry"[10] (cf. 32:1, 5; 85:2 [3]; 99:8), rather than the more technical term "pardon" (contrast v. 11). Its implication is that weakness, trouble, and sin are all facts about human experience that the suppliant needs God to handle by carrying them, coping with their implications, and accepting us as we are.

> [r] **19**Look at my enemies, how numerous they are,
> and at the violent opposition they show to me.

There is another direction the suppliant needs Yhwh to look—at the people who cause the trouble. Their numerousness contrasts with the suppliant's loneliness (v. 16). The second colon complements their numerousness with the lawless *violence of the way they oppose (be *against) the suppliant.

25:20–22. As a whole, v. 21 parallels v. 20 with its appeal for protection in the first colon and its "because" clause about the suppliant's stance in the second, while *"looking to" again takes up from vv. 2–3. Although v. 22 stands outside the alphabetical scheme, it completes three closing lines that pair with the psalm's three opening lines; like v. 3 it generalizes the previous two lines' appeal on behalf of "me."

> [š] **20**Guard my life and rescue me;
> may I not be shamed, because I rely on you.

---

9. NRSV's "relieve the troubles of my heart, and" presupposes *harḥēb w* for MT's *hirḥîbû*. One might achieve a similar end by taking MT as precative perfect.

10. Not "take away" except in the sense of "take away with him."

The imagery of sight may be in the background in vv. 20–21, as is hinted by EVV's use of verbs such as "watch," but the language more explicitly concerns the reality behind such imagery, the reality of protection. The formulaic nature of the psalm's language as a whole surfaces in the plea to "guard" and "rescue," for strictly, if Yhwh responds to the former plea, that makes the latter unnecessary. Talk of shame suggests that near the end of the psalm we are returning to the agenda at the beginning (see vv. 2–3), and *relying here is then equivalent to "trusting" there.

> [t] ²¹May integrity and uprightness watch over me,
>   because I have looked to you.

The *integrity and uprightness (*yōšer*) that must watch over the suppliant are personified attributes of Yhwh (cf. 43:3). While the psalms appeal more often to the suppliant's integrity and uprightness (e.g., 7:8, 10 [9, 11]; 26:1, 11; 36:10 [11]), they do also refer to Yhwh's integrity (cf. 18:30 [31]), and this psalm has already referred to Yhwh's being upright (v. 8).

> ²²God, redeem Israel
>   from all its constraints.

The "constraints" reappear from v. 17, but the line begins with a striking new verb, *redeem. The initial p on the verb takes the line outside the alphabetic structure, but it means that the initial, central, and closing verses (vv. 1, 11, and 22) begin ’*lp*, the letters of a verb meaning "learn" (the same applies in Ps. 34).[11] So this aspect of the psalm's structure affirms that its nature is to enable people to learn about prayer.

Theological Implications

What do they learn? Given that the psalm has no surface structure beyond its alphabetical form, what structure of thinking emerges from it?

1. Prayer involves constantly looking to Yhwh in expectant trust, constantly waiting for Yhwh to act, revering Yhwh, and taking refuge in Yhwh.

2. Prayer assumes the context of weakness, aloneness, constraint, pressure, suffering, attack, and danger. Indeed, pressure and constraint can have the last word in prayer (v. 22).[12]

---

11. Cf. Schaefer, *Psalms*, 61–62.
12. Cf. Brueggemann, *Psalms and the Life of Faith*, 199.

3. Prayer asks for Yhwh to be mindful of us, to look at us so as to be moved to act, to be gracious, to deliver, to vindicate, to protect, to rescue, to redeem, to give us the good things of life, and to expose people who are deceptive and unfaithful.

4. Prayer bases itself on Yhwh's name or nature, and thus appeals for Yhwh's truthfulness, action as deliverer, compassion, commitment, goodness, uprightness, judgment, and integrity to watch over us.

5. Prayer seeks that we should be made to acknowledge Yhwh and thus have Yhwh's guidance and direction with regard to the path we should choose, not so much to answer existential questions as to drive us to walk in the path of integrity in the way we thus acknowledge to be necessary, thereby giving us counsel and fulfilling covenant obligations. It assumes that the gift of Torah is part of God's saving work.[13]

6. Prayer acknowledges that we are moral failures but knows that Yhwh cares about people who fail in their commitment. It thus owns our need for Yhwh to put our failures and wrongdoing out of mind, to pardon these, and to carry them—deeds of long ago that we might not really be very responsible for, and deeds of our adulthood for which we have no excuse.

7. Prayer takes place in the context of our being part of the believing community, for which we also pray.

---

13. Cf. Mays, *Psalms*, 127.

Psalm 26
Prayer and Moral Integrity

Translation

David's.

¹Decide for me, Yhwh,
  because I—I have walked in my integrity,
And I have trusted in Yhwh;
  I do not slip.
²Probe me, Yhwh, try me,
  test my heart and mind.

³For your commitment is before my eyes;
  I walk about by your truthfulness.
⁴I have not sat with empty men;
  I do not go with deceivers.
⁵I am against the assembly of the wicked;
  I do not sit with the faithless.

⁶I will wash my hands in innocence
  and I will go around your altar, Yhwh,
⁷Letting people hear[a] the sound of thanksgiving
  and telling of all your awesome deeds.

a. Following Q *lašmiaʿ* = *lĕhašmîaʿ* (cf. Jerome; see also GKC 53q) rather than K's implicit *lišmōaʿ* (cf. LXX).

⁸Yhwh, I am dedicated to the abode that is your home,
   the place where your honor dwells.

⁹Do not take away my life with sinners,
   my existence with people of bloodshed,
¹⁰People with a scheme in their hands
   and their right hand full of bribery.
¹¹But I—I walk in my integrity;
   redeem me, be gracious to me.

¹²My foot stands on the level;
   in the great assembly I will worship Yhwh.

Interpretation

One can see why this prayer psalm was placed after Ps. 25.[1] With its reference to integrity and trust, it starts where its predecessor almost opens and closes (v. 1; cf. 25:2, 21), it goes on to refer to commitment and truthfulness (v. 3; cf. 25:10), and it pleads for Yhwh to redeem and be gracious (v. 11; cf. 25:11, 16). Like Ps. 25, it lacks any lament or the urgency that suggests a current crisis in the suppliant's life, and rather suggests a prayer that people could pray at any time. Unlike Ps. 25, however, it makes a claim to moral and religious integrity and does not plead for mercy in connection with moral and religious failure. It is the prayer of someone who meets the expectations of Ps. 1 concerning how and where one walks, sits, and stands. One could imagine its being used by pilgrims demonstrating that they meet the challenge of (e.g.) Pss. 15 and 24 as they look forward to worship in the temple.[2] But its extensive claim to integrity would also suit someone accused of wrongdoing, and this feature makes it somewhat resemble Pss. 7; 17; and 139.[3] Psalms 7 and 17 make similar use of the imperative of *šāpaṭ* and/or the noun *mišpāṭ* (7:6–8 [7–9]; 17:2) and acknowledge Yhwh's probing of heart and mind (7:9 [10]; 17:3), though they presuppose a more urgent need. In its lack of a sense of urgency, its openness to Yhwh's examination, and its commitment to repudiate the faithless, it more recalls Ps. 139. We do not know anything about its date or background.

1. Indeed, Theodor Lescow ("Textübergreifende Exegese," *ZAW* 107 [1995]: 65–79) argues that Pss. 24–26 form a "ring composition."
2. Cf. E. Vogt, "Psalm 26, ein Pilgergebet," *Bib* 43 (1962): 328–37.
3. Cf. W. H. Bellinger, "Psalm 26," *VT* 43 (1993): 452–61. See the introductory comments on Ps. 7 for the possible use of such psalms.

It begins and almost ends with three lines of plea for Yhwh's support (vv. 1–2, 9–11). The intervening six lines are then a substantial self-defense, a declaration of moral commitment (vv. 3–5) and religious commitment (vv. 6–8) that itemizes the double claim of vv. 1–2. The actual concluding line (v. 12) offers a summary relating to the double self-defense.

David's.

Heading. See introduction. The heading, too, corresponds to that of Ps. 25. One might imagine the young David appropriately praying the psalm, though not the mature David: Theodoret imagines him praying it before he was king and before he prayed Ps. 25.[4]

26:1–2. The psalm begins with a plea for Yhwh to act on the suppliant's behalf. Imperatives occupy three cola and reasons occupy the other three. But the order is $abb'b''a'a''$, and the verse division thus corresponds to a further aspect of the dynamic of this opening section, because the opening imperative and the ones in v. 2 have different functions. The action for which v. 1 asks will be based on successful completion of the action v. 2 invites, which will establish the truth in the claims of the three "because" clauses. In other words, the lines could appropriately be read in reverse order.

> ¹Decide for me, Yhwh,
>   because I—I have walked in my integrity,
> And I have trusted in Yhwh;
>   I do not slip.

LXX as usual renders the verb *šāpaṭ* forensically, as if it means "judges," but this implies too narrow an understanding. The psalm is indeed asking for vindication, but for more than that—for the exercise of Yhwh's *authority on the suppliant's behalf, which will also eventuate in redemption as an expression of grace (v. 11). The basis for the plea lies in three first-person verbs: "I have walked," "I have *trusted," "I do not slip." The first two appear in the verse's middle two cola, which work $abcb'c'$: after the "because I" (the "I" is emphasized), each colon comprises a b-expression and a first-person qatal verb. The link between Yhwh's deciding and the suppliant's moral *integrity recurs from 7:8 [9], while "integrity" itself recurs from 25:21. There the psalm appealed to Yhwh's integrity; here the psalm makes the complementary appeal to the suppliant's own integrity. In turn, this appeal to moral integrity is complemented by an appeal to

---

4. *Psalms*, 1:169.

the right religious attitude, the suppliant's *trust in Yhwh—rather than (e.g.) in other deities or in military resources. In the third, asyndetic, circumstantial[5] clause the verb is yiqtol rather than qatal; it qualifies both those preceding qatal verbs. "Slip" (*māʿad*) is a rare verb that suggests losing one's footing when (for instance) the path along the side of a mountain is narrow (cf. 18:36 [37]; 37:31; Job 12:5). Here it thus implies that the suppliant has to walk a narrow and tricky path in walking with integrity and maintaining trust in Yhwh, but has made sure of keeping on this path, and continues to do so.[6]

> ²Probe me, Yhwh, try me,
>   test my heart and mind.

The suppliant is willing to submit to having this bold claim closely examined. These further three verbs stand in even closer parallelism. In form they are all second-person imperatives: the first is qal with a suffix, the second is piel with a suffix, and the third is qal absolute.[7] The last verb (*ṣārap*) is the one that most often keeps its literal reference to smelting precious metal (cf. 66:10). The first (*bāḥan*) also occasionally keeps that reference (e.g., Job 23:10), but it is usually a metaphor. The middle verb (*nāsâ*) is a more general word for trying or testing a person or a thing (e.g., 78:18, 41, 56).[8] If the claim to integrity and trust is to be sustained, the suppliant is aware that it is the inner person that needs such testing. Someone who looks upright can be secretly involved in shady deals, and someone who looks committed to Yhwh can be secretly placing their trust elsewhere. The second colon thus goes beyond the first in the sharpness of its metaphor, with the vivid implicit allusion to the process of smelting, and in the object of the verb: not just the outer person but including (lit.) the kidneys and heart (see 7:9 [10]).

26:3–5. These three lines now itemize the claim to moral integrity, alternating between talk of movement and of sitting, in *aaʹbaʺbʹbʺ* order, which suggests both that there is a distinction between these two activities and that they are interlinked. In isolation the time reference of v. 3 (noun clause followed by weqatal clause) is hard to discern, but vv. 4–5 clarify it as they alternate between qatal verbs and yiqtol verbs. It then makes sense to see v. 3 as partially anticipating that pattern, the weqatal

---

5. Cf. GKC 156g.
6. On this claim, cf. 17:1–5.
7. K and Q are different forms of the impv. (see GKC 48i).
8. On references to such testing of metals in the Psalms, see Keel, *Symbolism of the Biblical World*, 183–86.

verb in v. 3b having similar significance to the yiqtols in vv. 4b and 5b, perhaps frequentative.[9]

> ³For your commitment is before my eyes;
> I walk about by your truthfulness.

First, the suppliant returns to "walking" (cf. v. 1), though the verb is now hitpael (hence, "walk about"). Letting something stand before your eyes suggests paying attention to it and approving of it (e.g., 5:5 [6]; 36:1 [2]; 101:3, 7). Yhwh's *commitment is thus an inspiration, or a summons to a responsive commitment. The second colon makes the point more specific. Having God's commitment before the eyes indicates the way the suppliant goes about that walk. The second colon further confirms that by linking *truthfulness with commitment, since these two form a moral pair (e.g., Prov. 3:3; 16:6; 20:28). The suppliant has walked about or set a course (NJPS) by these, letting them shape that course.

> ⁴I have not sat with empty men;
> I do not go with deceivers.

Reference to sitting follows on reference to walking (cf. 1:1). Sitting to make plans lies behind going about implementing them, and both stages now appear in the two parallel cola of v. 4.[10] The two parallel nouns governed by *'im* explain the need to avoid the kind of sitting and going to which the line refers, for they speak of liars (men of *emptiness) and deceivers ("secretive people," *'ālam* niphal), the second being characteristically the less usual word. The insistence on neither sitting nor going with liars and deceivers constitutes the opposite to walking with Yhwh's committed truthfulness before us.

> ⁵I am against the assembly of the wicked;
> I do not sit with the faithless.

Verse 5 also works *abb'a'* and begins by making the same point even more strongly as it speaks of being *against or repudiating the gathering where these people cook up their schemes. They are now identified as wicked (*bad) and *faithless (again, see 1:1). The suppliant runs in the opposite direction rather than sitting down with them. "Assembly" is *qāhāl*, often "congregation"; it appears in parallelism with *môšāb* ("seat," "home") in 107:32, which again suggests a link with 1:1; see also v. 12

---

9. See *TTH* 133, also 35, and GKC 112rr. Whereas LXX takes the weqatal as having past reference, Jerome takes it as a "proper" weqatal.
10. These work *abb'a'*, yiqtol complementing qatal.

below. The gang of thieves likes to see itself as a family, and anyone likes to feel part of the family. The verb "sit" (now yiqtol) rounds off vv. 4–5 and thus acts as a bracket around the two lines, and the "with" expression also parallels both cola in v. 4.

26:6–8. We move from moral commitment to religious commitment. The section continues from what preceded as it begins by making a connection with distancing oneself from the kind of wrongdoing vv. 3–5 referred to, but it brings that distancing into the context of worship. Each line makes clear that we have moved from the everyday world with its moral challenges to the religious world, the world of altar, proclamation, and Yhwh's dwelling. Further, we move from the everyday world negatively conceived to the religious world positively conceived, from a *qāhāl* that needs to be repudiated to a company that can be affirmed.

> ⁶I will wash my hands in innocence
> and I will go around your altar, Yhwh,

In Deut. 21:1–9 washing the hands is part of a rite that acknowledges a share in some communal guilt but proclaims one's personal innocence. Undertaken by priests, washing hands and feet can be a rite of purification in preparation for fulfilling one's worship role (e.g., Exod. 30:17–21).[11] Further, one can imagine that laypeople might have washed their hands as part of preparing themselves to approach the sanctuary.[12] But none of these seem very relevant in the present context. More significant is the similarity to 73:13 in a parallelism suggesting that there (and also here) the expression involves a catachresis: "Washing one's hands in innocence" denotes keeping one's hands innocent (of blood; cf. 24:4) and thus not needing to wash. The second colon presumably refers to what follows. Having maintained one's innocence (or received cleansing), one is in a position to join with the congregation in going around Yhwh's altar, (e.g.) to make the sacrifices that accompany praise, prayer, and thanksgiving. The cohortative expresses the suppliant's commitment. The midrash links this picture with 118:25–27 and the circling of the altar at Booths (Sukkot; *m. Sukkah* 4.5).[13]

> ⁷Letting people hear the sound of thanksgiving
> and telling of all your awesome deeds.

---

11. Cf. Paul G. Mosca, "Psalm 26," *CBQ* 47 (1985): 212–37, who sees v. 6 as indicating that the speaker in the psalm is a priest. But he notes that the text needs to be revocalized in v. 7 to make this thesis work.

12. Cf. L. A. Snijders, "Psaume xxvi et l'innocence," in *Studies on the Psalms*, by B. Gemser et al., OtSt 13 (Leiden: Brill, 1963): 112–30, see 121–22.

13. *Midrash on Psalms*, 1:361.

One of the occasions for sacrifice and worship would be when the suppliant gives testimony to what Yhwh has done in response to prayer, or without being asked. It does not do to keep quiet about this; when Yhwh acts, the beneficiary gives glory to God by telling the story of it before people, in the way thanksgiving psalms do, accompanying that with a thank-offering. The second colon formally parallels the first in beginning with another infinitive/gerund (piel complements the earlier hiphil) and going on to an object (direct complements the earlier indirect). But in content it moves from talk about what God has done in the worshipper's experience (the subject of thanksgivings and thank-offerings) to talk about Yhwh's awesome deeds (*revere), Yhwh's acts in creation and in delivering Israel (the subject of hymns and whole-offerings). It thus moves to another occasion for sacrifice and worship. The midrash refers it specifically to the Hallel Psalms, 113–18, connected with Passover and thus with the exodus.[14]

> [8]Yhwh, I am dedicated to the abode that is your home,
> the place where your honor dwells.

The *dedication is the antonym of the repudiation in the corresponding line of the previous section. The parallelism works differently from that of v. 7. "Yhwh, I am dedicated" applies to the second colon as well as the first; "the abode that is your home" then offers one description of the object of this love or dedication, while the entire second colon is occupied by a parallel description. The two descriptions then suggest both the ordinariness and the wonder of the temple. In the first ("the abode of your home," or less literalistically, "your home abode"), the word "abode" (*mā'ôn*), when not applied to Yhwh, refers to an animal's lair. Yet this homely refuge is also "the place of the dwelling of your honor." While "place" (*māqôm*) is an ordinary word, it often refers specifically to Yhwh's "place," the temple (e.g., 24:3; 132:5). "Dwelling" is then especially a word for the wilderness sanctuary, but also for the temple (e.g., 43:3; 46:4 [5]; 74:7; 132:5). And *honor takes the heightening further as the line works toward a lofty climax: lair, home, place, dwelling—honor![15]

26:9–11. We return to plea—two lines negative (though only one verb), one line positive (though two verbs, both in the second colon). The verbs thus bracket the section, and the three cola describing the people with whom the suppliant has perhaps been accused of associat-

14. Ibid.
15. LXX with "beauty" implies *nō'am* (cf. 27:4) for *mĕ'ôn* and suggests a different rhetorical structure, *abb'b"a*, the two lofty words forming a bracket around the three everyday words.

ing contrast with the one colon of the suppliant's self-description. The shape is thus *abb'b"ca'*.

> ⁹Do not take away my life with sinners,
> my existence with people of bloodshed,

The one verb thus governs both cola, and the two objects in the two cola stand in parallelism. The OT talks about death as being "taken away" or "gathered" (*'āsap*) to be with one's ancestors, but the qal verb often means "take away" in a more general sense and more specifically refers to the taking away of the life (*person), as here (cf. Judg. 18:25), or of the spirit (104:29; Job 34:14). The object in the second colon gives more precision to that in the first. The psalm presupposes that Yhwh's justice properly takes away the life of people of *bloodshed, whether by proper judicial process or by divine intervention that comes in the form (e.g.) of sudden fatal illness or accident, and the suppliant asks not to be swallowed up by that reality.

> ¹⁰People with a scheme in their hands
> and their right hand full of bribery.

Two parallel noun clauses then further characterize the people described as sinners and murderers and indicate how they go about their deeds, making a link with vv. 3–5. As usual in the Psalms, killing involves deceit, and the people who have ultimate responsibility for the deed are not the people who literally get the blood on their hands. Their hands are simply full of schemes and bribes, ways (e.g.) to get someone out of the way so as to appropriate their land (like Jezebel in relation to Naboth). These hands (*yad, yāmîn*) are very different from the hands of v. 6 (*kap*).

> ¹¹But I—I walk in my integrity;
> redeem me, be gracious to me.

But the suppliant is perhaps accused of belonging to such a company, and v. 11 first denies this, repeating the earlier claim (v. 1, though the verb is now yiqtol) to an *integrity in contrast to the moral failure of the scheming and bribing that brings death. The second colon completes the verbal bracket around vv. 9–11 with the two positive and rhyming imperatives that more than counterbalance the negative imperative in v. 9a and yet achieve extra force through their two-word succinctness, *pĕdēnî wĕḥonnēnî*—verbs picked up from toward the end of the previous psalm (25:16, 22).

> ¹²My foot stands on the level;
> in the great assembly I will worship Yhwh.

26:12. With v. 11, this final line completes an inclusion with v. 1.[16] In EVV's understanding, this stands in contrast with what precedes in declaring a confident faith that "my foot stands on level ground"—a declaration quite in place at the end of a prayer psalm but expressing a confident faith and hope that we have not previously heard. The psalm's dynamic then contrasts with its predecessor. The earlier part of Ps. 25 was characterized by confidence, but it moved to more urgent plea as it proceeded. The main framework of this psalm has been plea, and the center has been self-defense that buttressed the plea, but now it closes with confidence. By implication, the suppliant's plea was itself a statement of faith, and perhaps it is this that now makes an overt statement of faith possible. The first colon, then, is such an overt statement of faith,[17] of conviction that the apparent insecurity that vv. 1–11 has presupposed is not reality. The suppliant's foot does not stand in the kind of insecure place of which the Psalms often speak (e.g., 25:15; 31:8 [9]; 94:18; 116:8). And the second colon is a statement of hope, of the expectation of once again taking a place in a great assembly (*maqhēlîm*)[18] that contrasts with the assembly that the suppliant disavows (*qāhāl*, v. 5). (It may indicate that the yiqtol statements in v. 6 are statements about the suppliant's habits and desire, whether or not they can be present reality.)

But talk of "standing" completes the triple link of verbs with Ps. 1 (walk, sit, stand) and thus suggests a different sort of standing, the taking of a moral stance. And "the level" (*mîšôr*) can have a moral reference as well as a physical one (e.g., 45:6 [7]; 67:4 [5]; 27:11 and 143:10 are more ambiguous), in keeping with the regular meaning of *mêšārîm*. The final line might thus reaffirm and sum up the double commitment that the psalm has claimed.[19] Perhaps the psalm plays with the two meanings of *mîšôr* and expresses confidence that Yhwh will deal straight just as the suppliant has stood straight.

At the center of the line the two *b* expressions (translated "on" and "in") hold it together, one singular and one plural, and the two cola complement each other in other ways. They again combine reference to everyday life and worship life, and they complement reference to standing firm outside with bending on one's knees inside, given the link between the word for *worship (bārak)* and the knee (*berek*).

16. Cf. Fokkelman, *Major Poems*, 2:114.
17. Cf. *TTH* 14a.
18. I take the pl. as abstract, a pl. of majesty.
19. Cf. Augustine, *Psalms*, 64.

Theological Implications

"The activist mode of the I in Psalm 26 is remarkable."[20] While Ps. 25 reassures us that people who recognize their moral failure do not have to hold back from prayer, Ps. 26 reminds us that, ideally, people who pray need to be able to claim moral integrity and religious commitment, and must dissociate themselves from the faithless. The psalm surely presupposes that God's relationship with us is based first on God's acceptance of us, not on our deserving, but this underlines rather than undermines the need for people of whom God takes hold to commit themselves in integrity and trust. The fact that no one is flawless provides no basis for falling short in a fundamental commitment to right living in society and an exclusive trust in God. Further, the fact that we are called to associate with the faithless in order to bring God's love to them needs to be accompanied by a decisive repudiation of them in the sense that we have nothing to do with their way of thinking and acting. We are called to be in the world but not of the world, to walk, sit, and stand in a distinctive way. We cannot serve God and Mammon (Matt. 6:24).[21] People who lack moral integrity and trust in God can still pray for God to deliver them and may well find that God responds, but people who can claim moral integrity and trust in God have more basis for leaning on God to do so.

20. Hauge, *Between Sheol and Temple*, 153.
21. McCann, "Psalms," 784.

Psalm 27
Prayer Arising out of Testimony

Translation

David's. [Before his anointing (LXX).]

¹Yhwh is my light, my deliverance—
  whom should I fear?
Yhwh is the stronghold of my life—
  of whom should I be afraid?
²When evil people drew near to me
  to devour my flesh,ᵃ
My adversaries, my enemies—
  it was they who stumbled, fell.

³If an army should encamp against me,ᵇ
  my heart would not fear.
If a war should arise against me,
  in thisᶜ I trust.
⁴One thing I asked from Yhwh,
  for that I would inquire
To dwell in Yhwh's house
  all the days of my life,

---

a. RSV's "uttering slanders against me" infers the meaning from the presumed sense of an analogous expression in Dan. 3:8; 6:24.

b. Noun and verb are related, generating a paronomasia: *taḥăneh . . . maḥăneh*.

c. EVV imply "in this circumstance" (i.e., if there is a war), but the verb *bāṭaḥ* regularly governs a *bĕ* expression, so more likely "in this" refers to the person and activity of Yhwh described in vv. 1–6 (so Rashi).

Looking at Yhwh's delights
and making request[d] at his palace.
⁵For he would conceal me in his shelter[e]
on the day of evil,
Hide me in his tent,
lift me high on a crag.
⁶Now my head will lift high[f]
over my enemies all around me.
In his tent I will offer noisy sacrifices
as I will sing and make music to Yhwh.

⁷Listen to my voice as I cry out, Yhwh;
be gracious to me, answer me.
⁸For you my heart said,
"Inquire of my face."
I do inquire of your face, Yhwh;
⁹do not hide your face from me.
Do not push aside your servant in anger;
you have been my help.
Do not forsake me, do not leave me,
my God who delivers.
¹⁰If my father and mother leave me,
may Yhwh take me in.
¹¹Instruct me in your way, Yhwh,
lead me on a level path.
In view of my watchful foes
¹²do not give me over to the desire of my enemies.
For there have arisen against me false witnesses,
one who testifies for violence.

¹³Unless[g] I believed in seeing good from Yhwh
in the land of the living . . .
¹⁴Look to Yhwh;
be strong; may your heart take courage;
yes, wait for Yhwh.

---

d. The rare verb *bāqar* has this precise meaning only here; Rashi nicely sees it rather as a denominative from *bōqer* and takes it to refer to appearing there morning by morning (cf. NEB mg).

e. Q has *bĕsukkô*, K *bĕsukkâ*, which will then derive its suffix from the next line (cf. 31:20 [21]).

f. LXX, Sym, Jerome imply *yārîm* ("He will lift my head high") instead of *yārûm*.

g. Q gives the pointing of the Aramaic equivalent, which begins with *aleph* (cf. Tg; BDB). The diacritical dots on this word suggest that the Masoretes believed it should be omitted, with LXX, Aq, Sym. *Midrash on Psalms*, 1:373–74, offers homiletic comments on the diacritical dots.

Interpretation

Yet another psalm, headed simply "David's," combines declarations of trust with pleas, but in yet another profile. This time slightly more than half the psalm expresses trust, then the psalm goes on to cry out to Yhwh. The combination recalls that in Pss. 9–10. The first part presumably addresses the congregation, making a declaration of confidence based on a past event (vv. 1–2), then going through that logic again at greater length (vv. 3–6). It is thus thanksgiving-like, though it does not speak of the past events as if they are recent ones, and its appearance of confidence is compromised by the fact that most of its lines have the short second cola more characteristic of a lament. The second part (vv. 7–12) addresses Yhwh and indicates why the earlier part was looking back to past occasions of proving Yhwh. It utters a plea for deliverance now and gives the reason for it, as the earlier part expressed confidence and then indicated the basis for this confidence. The psalm's closing lines address the self in returning to urging confidence in Yhwh (vv. 13–14). Verses 1–6 could stand alone as a psalm of trust; we will note verbal links between the two parts that suggest vv. 7–14 might then have been composed to build on it, rather than being also an independent psalm.[1] The way the psalm speaks about the temple and its reference to a level path (vv. 4, 11) may have contributed to its being located after Ps. 26 (see 26:8, 12). We do not know its date.

> David's. [Before his anointing (LXX).]

Heading. See on Pss. 25 and 26. David's life would provide plausible illustrations for contexts in which the psalm as a whole might be prayed; LXX may invite us to think especially of the pressures Saul put on him, and may be inferring from v. 5 a link with 1 Sam. 21:1–6 [2–7].[2] Elisha's, Hezekiah's, or Nehemiah's life would provide other contexts (e.g., 2 Kings 6:15;[3] 18–19; Neh. 4).

27:1–2. So the brief opening section declares confidence and gives its grounds.

---

1. Cf. Lindström, *Suffering and Sin*, 152–54. Gunkel (*Psalmen*, 112–18) treats the two parts quite separately. Harris Birkeland ("Die Einheitlichkeit von Ps 27," *ZAW* 51 [1933]: 216–21) argues for the psalm's unity; so also A. H. Van Zyl, "The Unity of Psalm 27," in *De fructu oris sui* (A. Van Selms Festschrift), ed. I. H. Eybers et al. (Leiden: Brill, 1971), 233–51; Pierre Auffret, "'Mais YHWH m'accueillera,'" *EstBib* 60 (2002): 479–92; Hauge, *Between Sheol and Temple*, 119–43.
2. Cf. Theodoret, *Psalms*, 1:172–73.
3. Kidner, *Psalms*, 1:120.

> ¹Yhwh is my light, my deliverance—
> whom should I fear?
> Yhwh is the stronghold of my life—
> of whom should I be afraid?

The declaration that Yhwh is my *light is characteristically spelled out as implying that Yhwh is *deliverer. That being so, I have no reason to fear. Yet stating this somehow draws attention to the fact that evidently I do have reason for fear.

The statement about the *stronghold of my life, the strong one who makes sure I have safe refuge from danger or attack, makes the point about deliverance in another way. Similarly, the question in the second colon repeats the earlier second colon with the verb that often appears in parallelism with it, and thus again draws attention to the fact that I evidently have reason to be afraid.

> ²When evil people drew near to me
> to devour my flesh,
> My adversaries, my enemies—
> it was they who stumbled, fell.

These two lines form a further pair. In their case this is not because they stand in parallelism but because the first line is a temporal clause dependent on the main clause that follows. I follow LXX and Jerome in translating the qatal verbs in v. 2b as past rather than as present or future (with EVV). The use of the qatal suggests that v. 2 provides the basis for the conviction expressed in v. 1. Three descriptions of the suppliant's past foes balance the three descriptions of Yhwh in v. 1: they are *bad people, adversaries, and enemies. Two verbs describe their attacks (draw near so as to devour); two verbs describe their unexpected failure (stumble, fall). The postponing of those verbs until the end of the two-line sentence, after the threefold characterization and the doubled hostile verbs, builds up suspense through the verse. More specifically, the second line exhibits a distinctive form of parallelism in which both subjects come in the first colon and both verbs in the second (instead of "my adversaries stumbled, my enemies fell").[4] The congregation listening to this testimony is invited to picture the suppliant attacked by people who are as threatening as a devouring beast, but able to find somewhere to hide. More literally, these people fell over instead of consummating

---

4. Cf. Dahood, *Psalms*, 1:166. This is also reflected in the simple *w* linking the verbs, which are synonymous and/or form a hendiadys rather than describing two stages in a process.

their victory. The psalm combines the imagery of law court, battle, and hunting.[5] Thus the supplicant is not a person who trusts God because of some personal capacity for trust, because of being a person of faith, because of a capacity to laugh at dangers, or because of making an act of existential commitment to trust. That might be of no use to people who were not made that way. The supplicant is one who trusts in God because of something God did. That has more capacity to be an encouragement to others.

27:3–6. In the manner of a thanksgiving such as Ps. 30, the testimony then repeats itself in vv. 3–6, at greater length.

> [3]If an army should encamp against me,
>   my heart would not fear.
> If a war should arise against me,
>   in this I trust.

Another declaration of confidence like v. 1 occupies two further parallel lines.[6] The past experience of deliverance when enemies attacked, such as v. 2 described, is the basis for the *trusting conviction that the attack of another army would not be a problem.

> [4]One thing I asked from Yhwh,
>   for that I would inquire—
> To dwell in Yhwh's house
>   all the days of my life,
> Looking at Yhwh's delights
>   and making request at his palace.

Those two lines are then backed up by their own qatal statement. This time three lines run together to form one sentence, with the qatal verb coming first. LXX and Jerome again rightly translate it as past, and this time NRSV also does so. I take it thus to set the verse as a whole (indeed, vv. 4–5) in the past. In a way again characteristic of a testimony psalm, in vv. 4–5 the supplicant looks back to a prayer offered in the midst of danger (once more this parallels Ps. 30).

In the parallelism between the two cola in the first, "one thing" is taken up in "that," and "I asked" is taken up in "I would seek." "From Yhwh" applies in the second colon as well as the first, and the yiqtol in

---

5. Cf. Pietro Bovati, *Re-establishing Justice*, JSOTSup 105 (Sheffield: JSOT, 1994), 296–99.

6. In each, the first colon comprises an "if" clause, a third-person singular feminine yiqtol verb, the expression "against me," and the feminine singular subject. The two second cola then diverge and complement a third-person clause with a first-person one, a negatived expression with a positive one, a yiqtol expression with a participial one.

the second colon complements the qatal in the first. Given the parallelism, I take this yiqtol also to have past reference, perhaps frequentative. For the "one thing," compare Luke 10:41–42.[7]

The second colon takes up the theme of dwelling in Yhwh's house, which came in 23:6 LXX. Given that the psalm presupposes or allows for the possibility of being under military attack, that in itself implies that this dwelling does not denote a 24/7/52 staying in the physical temple courts—or does that only hyperbolically. On the other hand, the concreteness of some of the references to events in Yhwh's palace or tent also makes it implausible to understand this dwelling as solely a metaphor for being in Yhwh's presence. I take it, then, that the psalm moves easily between referring to Yhwh's permanent protective presence and to the freedom recurrently to seek Yhwh's guidance or offer Yhwh praise in the temple. The same Yhwh is sacramentally present in the temple and experientially present in the pressures of ordinary life. Here, however, initially the suppliant refers to the plea always to be free to go to the temple.[8]

The third sets two reasons for such a visit, in parallel cola, each comprising *l* plus an infinitive (the first qal, the second piel) followed by a *b* expression. Given the OT's hesitation about the idea of looking at Yhwh at all, the idea of looking at Yhwh's personal delightfulness (*nōʿam*, EVV "beauty") would be surprising, but the notion of looking at Yhwh's delightfulness is clarified by the phrase's other occurrence (90:17). It denotes the delightfulness of what Yhwh does for people rather than Yhwh's personal being. And this enhances the parallelism of the second colon, since the request to which it refers will denote seeking after Yhwh's intentions or will for the suppliant and the people. The line then concerns the suppliant's visiting Yhwh's *palace to seek to see what beautiful intentions Yhwh has.[9]

> ⁵For he would conceal me in his shelter
>   on the day of evil,
> Hide me in his tent,
>   lift me high on a crag.

The suppliant goes on to recollect what issued from the prayer. LXX suggestively renders all the verbs in v. 5 in the past. Verse 5 comprises two parallel lines. One could take these as separate sentences, but the

---

7. Cf. Luther, *First Lectures*, 1:127.

8. On this motif, see Rolf von Ungern-Sternberg, "Das 'Wohnen im Hause Gottes,'" *Kerygma und Dogma* 17 (1971): 209–23.

9. J. D. Levenson suggests that *nōʿam* refers to an affirmative response to a request for guidance ("A Technical Meaning for n'm in the Hebrew Bible," *VT* 35 [1985]: 61–67).

parallelism between the lines and the absence of a particle at the beginning of the second suggests the latter continues the "for" sentence. The parallelism is admittedly variegated. Whereas the first line comprises a colon about protection and a colon about the circumstances that make protection necessary, the second line comprises two further clauses about protection, parallel with each other. The two lines thus follow an *aba'a"* pattern, with the prepositional phrase applying to all three cola. What the suppliant asked, and what Yhwh promised, corresponded to the reality of which vv. 1–2 spoke, though v. 5 uses different imagery. The prayer was that in the day when people did *bad things (the day when bad people attack; v. 2), Yhwh should hide the suppliant the way Rahab hid the spies (Josh. 2:4), or the way a lion hides its prey in its shelter so that no other creature can get it. The prayer was that the suppliant should be concealed in Yhwh's tent. Here the psalm uses a term (*'ōhel*) that could apply to the temple itself, as it does in v. 6 (cf. 15:1), transferring to it a term that naturally applied to Yhwh's earlier mobile home in the wilderness. Yet the parallelism with "shelter" encourages us rather to take "tent" as another metaphor for a safe place.

The third version of the request confirms this as it uses a quite different image for safety, that of being lifted up onto a *crag. In isolation we might infer that this is a crag that Yhwh provides, but elsewhere Yhwh regularly *is* the crag (cf. 28:1; 31:2 [3]; 61:2–4 [3–5] combines these images). So more likely the psalmist is asking to be lifted high onto Yhwh and thus definitively protected. This in turn further nuances the parallelism in v. 5, for the two opening cola are closer in meaning than either is to this last colon. But the imagery is held together by shared links with the temple, the place of protection, whose physical nature symbolizes one form of protection. "When I am in the hiding place of his tent, it is as though I am on a rock on high" (Ibn Ezra).

> ⁶Now my head will lift high
>   over my enemies all around me.
> In his tent I will offer noisy sacrifices
>   as I will sing and make music to Yhwh.

The suppliant rejoices in the further outworking of that answer to prayer. Protection means triumph and also thanksgiving. The suppliant's head can lift up high as a result of the suppliant's being lifted high onto Yhwh's rock and thus given Yhwh's protection and victory over the enemies that were all around (see 3:3, 6 [4, 7]). And the appropriate thank-offering and thanksgiving can follow. The verb in the first line is yiqtol because it refers to an event that will come about through Yhwh's act; the verbs in the second line are cohortative because they refer to acts the suppliant is committed to. When Yhwh acts, we can raise our heads in a way that we cannot without that—and also raise our offerings and our voices. As the place where these offerings are made, Yhwh's "tent" must now be the temple itself. The offerings are "sacrifices of a shout." The *shout that accompanied the prospect of battle and encouraged boldness but also reflected apprehension (e.g., Zeph. 1:16) now accompanies the sacrifices, with quite different implications. The parallel colon complements the shouting with something more melodic, both vocal and instrumental (for the combination of shouting and *music, cf. 33:3).

27:7–12. Verses 1–6 would make a complete testimony psalm. We are thus not prepared for vv. 7–12, which turn from an expression of confidence to urgent prayer. As is sometimes the case in psalms (notably Ps. 89, as well Pss. 9–10), the praise that begins the psalm is not where the psalm is intending to go. The recollection of pressure, prayer, and divine response paves the way for further prayer under pressure while looking for a further divine response. As vv. 1–6 could be complete in themselves as a testimony psalm, so vv. 7–12 or 7–14 could be complete in themselves as a prayer psalm. But as vv. 1–6 gain extra resonances from their association with what follows, so the prayer gains extra purchase through its association with what precedes. And we now see why the earlier lines made their references to fear and why lines with a short second colon dominated them.

> [7]Listen to my voice as I cry out, Yhwh;
>   be gracious to me, answer me.

The three pleas are natural ones for a prayer, not least to begin a prayer. All three imperatives recur from 4:1 [2], though in the opposite order. So here the logic is first "Listen": that must come before all else, but it is not enough. The psalmist also needs a demonstration of *grace. And that will show itself in an answer.

> [8a–b]For you my heart said,
>   "Inquire of my face."

Although that line is thus somewhat conventional (though not therefore insignificant), v. 8a–b is otherwise. Its implication is apparently that the suppliant's heart speaks on Yhwh's behalf as the suppliant senses an internal voice speaking for Yhwh and saying, "Inquire of my *face." This internal voice is not just one that issues from the suppliant's individual spirituality, because the invitation it recalls is one addressed to the people of God; "Inquire" is plural (as, e.g., 105:4; Zeph. 2:3). The suppliant is recalling and taking up Yhwh's urging to the whole people. At the same time the verb recurs from v. 4 and constitutes Yhwh's invitation to come and inquire once more, as under that earlier experience of pressure.

> **8c**I do inquire of your face, Yhwh;
> **9a**do not hide your face from me.

The suppliant's response is initially to declare, "I have done so and am doing so." The second colon then uses parallelism particularly effectively in turning the question around. Yhwh's *face is again the object of the verb, but the colon suggests that the question about Yhwh's face is not what the suppliant is doing in regard to it, but what Yhwh is doing in regard to it. Yhwh had been committed to hiding the suppliant (v. 5), but now will it be Yhwh's face that is the object of hiding?

> **9b**Do not push aside your servant in anger;
> you have been my help.
> Do not forsake me, do not leave me,
> my God who delivers.

The further four cola comprise two parallel lines, in the manner of vv. 1, 2, and 5. In each line the opening colon contains the verb(s) in the second-person singular jussive, preceded by the negative *'al*. The first pictures Yhwh standing still but sending the suppliant away, like a king refusing the plea of a petitioner; it adds "in anger," which rephrases the notion of Yhwh's face being hidden. The second pictures Yhwh going away as the suppliant stands still, more like a friend walking off at the moment one especially needs support. The pair of cola that follow these two opening hortatory clauses (v. 9c and 9e) each back up the urging with reference to who Yhwh is. Both use abstract nouns to denote this, with a first-person suffix (lit., my *help, my God of *deliverance). The first comes in a clause describing what Yhwh has been in the past, the second in a vocative phrase affirming that this is also Yhwh's nature, or noting that this is what the suppliant needs Yhwh again to be. The suppliant's concern about Yhwh's rejection and wrath carries no implied awareness of sin (cf. Job).[10] If the suppliant needed to acknowledge guilt, this would surely need to be explicit.

> **10**If my father and mother leave me,
> may Yhwh take me in.

In the context of the urgings in vv. 7–9 and 11–12, the yiqtol in v. 10b is likely jussive. Our family, and specifically our parents, are people we

---

10. Against Weiser, *Psalms*, 251–52.

would most expect to stay committed to us when we are under attack and (e.g.) accused of some wrongdoing, so that reference to the possibility of their abandoning us is a figure of speech for total abandonment (cf. Job 19:13–14; Isa. 49:15). The verb for "take in" (*'āsap*) usually refers to gathering a collection of things or people, but it is suggestive that it can be used for taking an animal or a person into one's home for refuge (Deut. 22:2; Josh. 20:4; Judg. 19:15, 18). Thus the figure recalls the imagery of vv. 4–5.

> 11a–bInstruct me in your way, Yhwh,
> lead me on a level path.

A further parallel bicolon includes two singular imperatives (one hiphil, one qal) with first-person suffix, and two words for way/path. The first verb might suggest Yhwh's pointing from afar, but the second suggests that this instruction involves Yhwh's standing alongside. The invocation in the first colon then applies to both, and the second colon is filled out with a second noun. The *way/path is thus defined not merely theologically (it is Yhwh's) but also pragmatically (it is level). Yhwh's way/path here, then, is not right in the sense of moral (though no doubt it is that) but right in the sense of wise. The suppliant appeals to Yhwh in seeking the way of deliverance and victory.

> 11cIn view of my watchful foes
> 12ado not give me over to the desire of my enemies.

MT links "in view of my *watchful foes" with what precedes and thus produces two tricola out of vv. 11–12. I have rather taken these verses as three bicola. Verses 11c–12a (2-3) thus explicitly introduce the enemies whose activity has been implicit in vv. 7–11a. With regard to these assailants, the suppliant asks for action not merely because of them (because they are the cause of the trouble) but "in view of" them (*lĕmaʿan*; see 5:8 [9] for preposition and participle/noun). The second colon (v. 12a) further makes explicit (as if it were necessary) that these people are watching with ill intent rather than good intent. Further, it again makes explicit (as if it were necessary) what the suppliant wants Yhwh to do, or not to do, making it impossible for them to fulfill their desire (*nepeš*, *person).

> 12bFor there have arisen against me false witnesses,
> one who testifies for violence.

Verse 12b–c comprises the nearest thing to a lament in the psalm, and thus the nearest thing to a statement of its problem. Like Pss. 25 and 26, the psalm gradually works its way to becoming more explicit about its agenda. But v. 12b–c also draws attention to the brevity of this element in the psalm and the contrast with other prayer psalms where the ratio of plea to lament is the reverse of that here in vv. 7–12. In this line the verb applies to both cola, and each colon has a description of the foes, one plural, one singular. On one hand, they are *false witnesses, people who give testimony but whose testimony does not correspond to reality. They might, for instance, be accusing the supplicant of blasphemy or treachery, which are capital offenses. They are thus also people who (on the traditional understanding of *yāpēaḥ*) breathe out *violence: they breathe out words, but their words are lies and will bring about death (cf. the related verb *pūaḥ*, e.g., Prov. 6:19; 14:5, 25). But for the translation "who testifies to violence," see 35:11: they give testimony that will result in lawless violence. For description in terms of false witness (vv. 7–12) combined with description in military terms (vv. 1–6), compare Ps. 7.

27:13–14. The last two lines turn back from plea (vv. 7–12) toward statement of trust (vv. 1–6) yet appropriately locate themselves somewhere between these, in two different ways.

> ¹³Unless I believed in seeing good from Yhwh
>   in the land of the living . . .

The statement of trust is incomplete[11] as well as implicit. By saying "unless" the supplicant implies the reality of trust without declaring it, perhaps strongly implying it, as in the form of an OT oath that similarly lacks an apodosis.[12] But "there is something wistful, threatening, and defiantly faithful about this congery of statement and allusion. It is a fragmented mixture of anger, regret, and loyalty."[13] The line declares a characteristic OT conviction about the sphere of Yhwh's activity. It believes in Yhwh's *goodness, which means believing in Yhwh as one who gives people good things such as a long life rather than an early death, and freedom from enemies rather than oppression.[14] It believes in seeing these in the land of the living, not in some hypothetical other land or life (contrast Tg with "the land of eternal life"). It thus holds together body and spirit, experience of worldly good things with a life of worship and prayer such as the psalm describes. "Seeing Yhwh's goodness" is another way of referring to "looking at Yhwh's delights" (v. 4).

---

11. Cf. GKC 159dd, 167a.
12. Syr and Jerome thus render it by a strong affirmative; cf. *HALOT*. Jeffrey Niehaus ("The Use of *lûlē* in Psalm 27," *JBL* 98 [1979]: 88–89) sees this line as dependent on v. 12.
13. David R. Blumenthal, *Facing the Abusing God* (Louisville: Westminster John Knox, 1993), 184.
14. Cf. M. Mannati, "*Ṭûb-Y.* en Psaume xxvii 13," *VT* 19 (1969): 488–93.

> ¹⁴Look to Yhwh;
> be strong; may your heart take courage;
> yes, wait for Yhwh.

The psalm closes off with a tricolon of imperatives, which are singular and thus presumably addressed to the suppliant rather than to the congregation. In the absence of any indication that the speaker changes I take them as a threefold self-exhortation like those in Pss. 42–43 rather than (e.g.) the response of a prophet.[15] They are then another statement standing between plea and trust. The imperatives to trust imply that the suppliant is not trusting, yet the fact that the suppliant is uttering them implies the presence of trust. The actual verbs work *abb'a'*, with two exhortations to expectancy (using the same verb) forming a bracket around two exhortations to strength and courage (using different verbs with similar meaning). The framework of *looking to Yhwh to act makes it possible to be a person of strength and courage in the present, and conversely the presence of strength and courage makes it possible to be a person who can look for Yhwh to act. To be strong and take courage is the positive equivalent to not being fearful or afraid (1 Chron. 22:13; 28:20; 2 Chron. 32:7). At the close of the psalm, it thus corresponds positively to the occurrence of those verbs in its opening verse. This adds to the impression that these are the suppliant's words. That double exhortation to be strong and courageous recurs especially in exhortations to Joshua and the people on the edge of the land (Deut. 31:6, 7, 23; Josh. 1:6, 7, 9, 18) and in David's exhortations to Solomon (1 Chron. 22:13; 28:20). The psalm's addition of reference to the heart is distinctive and makes for another correspondence to the opening of the psalm (v. 3). The suppliant thus offers a self-reminder of the need to take the stance that Joshua and his people gloriously took in entering the land, and that Solomon took in building the temple. But the framework of reference to waiting also constitutes a reminder that this does not comprise an exhortation to a task in which the suppliant is alone, but to a task that has Yhwh's promises attached—the promises to which the earlier part of the psalm referred.

Theological Implications

Christian commentators commonly compare the psalm with Rom. 8:31–39. In doing so it is important not to transfer the psalm's confidence and the prayer wholly to the religious or spiritual sphere, so that it does

---

15. But contrast Mandolfo's arguments, *God in the Dock*, 58–63.

not continue also to embrace the secular and material sphere (perhaps the same is true with regard to Rom. 8 itself). The psalm testifies to the experience of God protecting from worldly attackers, prays for God to do so again, and urges the self to keep expecting God to do that. It thus establishes a close link between testimony or thanksgiving, prayer or plea, and self-encouragement. Testimony finds one aspect of its raison d'être in encouraging the testifier to pray with confidence and make a commitment to expectant hope. In prayer, we benefit from reminding ourselves of occasions when we have asked God to protect us and God has indeed delivered us, because this builds up our confidence to ask for God to do that again and our conviction that God will do so. When we ask how we can have expectancy, the answer is that it derives from reflection on experience and from prayer that builds confidently on experience.

Psalm 28

Praying for the Punishment of the Faithless

Translation

David's.

¹To you, Yhwh, I call;
  my crag, do not be deaf toward me,
Lest you keep silence toward me,
  and I become like people who go down to the Pit.
²Listen to the sound of my pleas for grace
  as I cry for help to you,
As I lift up my hands
  to your holy room.
³Do not drag me off with the faithless,
  with the people who cause harm,
People who speak peace to their neighbors
  but evil in their hearts.[a]
⁴Give to them in accordance with their effort,
  in accordance with the evil of their deeds;
In accordance with the work of their hands give to them;
  render their recompense to them.

a. I follow LXX in taking this phrase as a second object of "speak," which fits the usual pattern of parallelism, rather than as an independent clause, "but there is evil . . ." (Jerome).

⁵Because they do not consider
    the deeds of Yhwh,
The work of his hands,[b]
    he will tear them down and not build them up.

⁶Yhwh be worshipped,
    for he has listened to the sound of my pleas for grace.
⁷Yhwh is my strength and my shield;
    in him my heart trusts.
So I will be helped,[c] and my heart exults,[d]
    and I will confess him with my song.[e]
⁸Yhwh is his strength[f] and stronghold;[g]
    he is the deliverance of his anointed.

⁹Deliver your people, bless your possession,
    shepherd them and carry them forever.

Interpretation

Once more a psalm begins with that brief heading and offers yet another combination of plea and trust that virtually lacks lament. Like Ps. 26 it leaps straight into plea and focuses on an appeal not to share the fate of the faithless. Like Ps. 27, it divides just after half way, but it does so in reverse profile: plea precedes declaration of confidence rather than vice versa. Verses 1–4 comprise an appeal to Yhwh to lis-

    b. Jerome associates this colon with what follows rather than what precedes, which makes for more usual prosody but is hard to make sense of.
    c. But Patrick D. Miller, "Ugaritic *ġzr* and Hebrew *'zr* ii," *UF* 2 (1970): 159–175, takes this as an occurrence of *'āzar* II, "be strong" (cf. 33:20; 89:19 [20]; 115:9, 10, 11; 118:13).
    d. I take *wĕne'ĕzartî* as having a weqatal's proper future reference (and link it with what follows, with NJPS and NRSV but against MT, LXX, and Jerome). On the other hand, it is hard to take *wayya'ălōz*, which then follows, as having past reference, but a qatal could have present reference (cf. GKC 111r), and I take this wayyiqtol thus. Its relationship with what precedes is logical rather than chronological (cf. GKC 111l).
    e. The preposition *min* is odd; Mitchell Dahood repoints *ûmĕšîrî*, "and [with] my song" ("Ug *mšr*, 'song,' in Psalms 28,7 and 137,3," *Bib* 58 [1977]: 216–17); A. Gelston emends to *ûbĕšîrî* ("A Note on the Text of Psalm xxviii 7b," *VT* 25 [1975]: 214–16). LXX implies *ûmibbî*, "and from my heart."
    f. Usually *lāmô* would mean "their," but there is no pl. noun for it to refer to. On the other hand, it occasionally means "his" (see GKC 103f; JM 103f), and v. 8b does provide a referent for that. LXX could imply *lĕ'ammô*; I take this to be an attempt to understand or correct MT.
    g. MT associates "and stronghold" with the next colon, but this makes for an odd accumulation of nouns there and an odd division of the line.

| Heading | Psalm 28 |

ten (vv. 1–2) and act (vv. 3–4), v. 5 a response, vv. 6–8 praise to Yhwh for thus answering the plea, and v. 9 a closing plea for the people as a whole. Again the psalm incorporates a number of double lines (all until v. 9), and lines with a short second colon once more dominate the plea.

> David's.

Heading. See introduction. Verse 8 will eventually make a connection with the king and imply that the psalm comes from the period of the monarchy, though hardly that it is a royal psalm.

28:1–2. The psalm begins with an extended appeal to Yhwh to listen, in two double lines. While v. 1 and v. 2 both comprise complete sentences, v. 2 parallels v. 1 in content and also in its *abb'c* structure, and presses its agenda more sharply.

> ¹To you, Yhwh, I call;
>   my crag, do not be deaf toward me,
> Lest you keep silence toward me,
>   and I become like people who go down to the Pit.

The first two cola overlap only in the vocative, in which "my *crag" spells out an implication of "Yhwh." The second colon takes the first further. "To you I call" is complemented by "Do not be deaf toward me" (lit., "from me": not listening involves turning the ears away). "You" and "I" are symbolically at two ends of this opening line.

In the motivation line, the second colon again takes the first further, and the whole bicolon relates in that way to the opening line. The reference to "keeping silence" restates the verb in the previous colon, and "toward me" repeats the expression there, so that one can see v. 1 as a whole as working *abb'c*. The last colon in the verse provides the explicit motivation for the plea. Death involves going into a tomb or down into a grave or down into Sheol, the metaphysical Pit (strictly the "pit," *bôr*, is a cistern, a huge underground storage place for water that might be seen as like a huge grave pit and might be grave shaped, though much bigger).[1] The suppliant fears soon joining people who meet that fate; why this seems likely, we do not know. But it requires Yhwh's hearing if this is not to happen.

> ²Listen to the sound of my pleas for grace
>   as I cry for help to you,

---

1. See Keel, *Symbolism of the Biblical World*, 62–73; also the picture in Terence E. Fretheim, *Jeremiah* (Macon, GA: Smith & Helwys, 2002), 520.

> As I lift up my hands
> to your holy room.

Verse 2a–b then virtually reworks v. 1a–b, with a positive verb rather than the negative one and the more specific, sharper-edged, and rarer verb "*cry for help." It also adds the similarly more specific, sharper-edged, and rarer plural noun "pleas for *grace" (*taḥănûnîm*). So the psalm is pleading for an act of God's grace in the form of an act of deliverance.

In v. 2c–d the first colon begins with a *b* expression and thus parallels the one that precedes and gives v. 2 as a whole its own *abb′c* structure. Parallel to the suppliant's verbal cry is the physical gesture of raising the hands in appeal toward Yhwh's inner room in the temple, the *děbîr*, usually referred to as the "most holy place." Although one must allow for various practices in prayer, generally in Scripture it involves standing as before a superior, raising one's hands in appeal like a child in a classroom seeking to get the teacher's attention, or opening the hands in readiness to receive, and opening one's eyes to look to God.[2] Sitting, clasping one's hands in a more closed posture, and shutting one's eyes are harder to parallel. Yhwh as crag (v. 1) again comes in close association with the temple (cf. 27:3–4).

28:3–4. Another pair of double lines comprise a further extended appeal, now regarding the nature of the action the psalm looks for. The suppliant never quite complains about being under attack, and it may be that this plea simply concerns the possibility of being somehow caught up undeservedly in the fate that comes to faithless people deservedly, or it may imply the experience of being accused of wrongdoing, which brings that danger.

> ³Do not drag me off with the faithless,
> with the people who cause harm,
> People who speak peace to their neighbors
> but evil in their hearts.

Thus v. 3 begins by presupposing that the *faithless are to be dragged off, presumably to death (cf. v. 1, also 26:9); its second colon further defines the faithless as people who cause harm (see 5:5 [6]). Verse 3c–d makes more explicit wherein lies their faithlessness and how they go about causing harm, with the two cola offering a contrast. They are people who talk *šālôm* with their neighbors, talk as if they want peace with them and as if they seek their well-being. But in their hearts they talk trouble (the verb carries over to the second colon). Evil is the an-

---

2. See Keel, *Symbolism of the Biblical World*, 308–23.

tithesis of shalom (as in Isa. 45:7) and thus here refers not (directly) to moral evil but to something *bad that they plan should happen to the neighbors. The speaking in their hearts (i.e., thinking and planning) contrasts with the outward speaking. As usual the psalm assumes that community depends on honesty, on a correspondence between heart and word, and laments the lack of this on the part of some people.

> ⁴Give to them in accordance with their effort,
>   in accordance with the evil of their deeds;
> In accordance with the work of their hands give to them;
>   render their recompense to them.

An equivalent positive plea issues from that fact about the faithless. While wishing not to be swallowed up by their fate, the supplicant does wish them to be swallowed up by it. The two lines are again broadly parallel, repeating the expression "give to them." Within v. 4a–b, the second colon completes the first, while within v. 4c–d, the second colon more closely parallels the first. The words "effort," "deeds," and "work of their hands" combine to picture the faithless as being like people doing a hard week's work, and the point is underlined in the fourth colon by the use of the word "recompense." The supplicant wants to see these dedicated laborers properly compensated, "in accordance with" their work (the preposition k, three times). But the single word "evil" turns the whole verse upside down. While the antithesis with shalom suggested that in v. 3d ra' meant "something bad, harm, trouble," in this line the related noun $rōa'$ occurs in the setting of the recurrent expression "evil of their deeds" (e.g., Jer. 4:4), suggesting that it refers to moral evil. But the etymological link between the two makes a moral point. Troublemaking is evil.

> ⁵Because they do not consider
>   the deeds of Yhwh,
> The work of his hands,
>   he will tear them down and not build them up.

28:5. Verse 5 brings a change to a declarative form in which Yhwh is spoken of rather than addressed,[3] and the line bears some parallels with the prophetic word responding to a supplicant in 12:5 [6], though it is not as explicitly marked. Like 12:5 [6], it begins with reasons for Yhwh's action and then declares that Yhwh will indeed act. Significantly, its words parallel prophetic words in Jeremiah (e.g., Jer. 1:10; 24:6; 31:28). Indeed, we could imagine this whole psalm as Jeremiah's conversation

---

3. Cf. Ridderbos, *Psalmen*, 214–17; also Craigie, *Psalms 1–50*, 237, 239.

with Yhwh. In the statement of reasons, v. 5 evaluates the attitude of the faithless from another angle. In the way they look at their own deeds and the work of their hands (v. 4), they fail to consider Yhwh's deeds and the work of Yhwh's hands. There might be two senses in which this was true. First, they fail to take Yhwh's deeds as setting the pattern for their own. Faithlessness is an attitude toward other members of the community and toward God, and they are ignoring obligations to Yhwh as well as ignoring obligations to other members of the community. But second, they fail to take into account the way Yhwh will act toward them, the fact that Yhwh is indeed one who sees that people receive the reward for their deeds. The last colon would then follow from this declaration, in affirming that Yhwh will indeed act and not let them get away with their wrongdoing. It would be morally wrong for Yhwh to allow them to succeed and prosper through their plotting, rather than bringing them down. In principle, when there has been tearing down, there can be building up, as Yhwh affirms to Jeremiah, but these people deserve to be finally put down. A paronomasia brackets the verse: because they will not consider (*lōʾ yābînû*), Yhwh will not build up (*lōʾ yibnēm*). Another paronomasia recalls the opening plea and brackets vv. 1–5 as a whole: Yhwh's tearing down (*hāras*) means Yhwh has not been deaf (*ḥāraš*, v. 1).

28:6–7b. Again like Ps. 12, the psalm then makes a sudden transition in light of the word of response, first in the form of a statement of conviction and praise in the qatal and in noun clauses.

> ⁶Yhwh be worshipped,
>   for he has listened to the sound of my pleas for grace.

The praise begins with the Psalter's first occurrence of the expression "Yhwh be *worshipped" (but see 16:7; 18:46 [47]). It comes in a similar connection in 31:21 [22]; see also (e.g.) 124:6; 135:21; 144:1, and doxologies such as 72:18–19. It is especially at home in the praise of an individual responding to the concrete things Yhwh has just done for them, and it perhaps starts off as a cry of praise that someone issues as an immediate response to Yhwh's act, in everyday life (e.g., Gen. 24:27).[4] As happens in 31:21 [22], it is followed by the reason for this worship, as with other invitations to worship. Here v. 6b simply restates the first colon in v. 2, turning the request into a statement (oddly, NRSV obscures this by using different words to translate the equivalent expressions earlier). Yhwh has answered the suppliant's first prayer, for attentiveness, as that paronomasia in v. 5b suggests.

---

4. See Westermann, *Living Psalms*, 53–54, 176–77.

> ^{7a–b}Yhwh is my strength and my shield;
> in him my heart trusts.

Verse 7a–b completes another of the pairs of lines that characterize this psalm, reversing the order of the logic so that the two lines work *abb′a′*. The closing colon "in him my heart *trusts" balances "Yhwh be worshipped" (v. 6a), while "Yhwh is my *strength and my shield" states the basis for or content of that trust. The reference to trust might reflect the fact that the suppliant has *heard* Yhwh's answer but not yet *seen* it (hence the need to keep exercising trust). But the word order, with "in him" coming first, may rather place the usual emphasis on the question of whom or what one trusts rather than on whether one trusts or doubts.

28:7c–8. Two further paired lines go on to relate to the second plea, for Yhwh to grant protection from the fate of the faithless.

> ^{7c–d}So I will be helped, and my heart exults,
> and I will confess him with my song.

In light of the knowledge that Yhwh has listened and responded in word, the suppliant expresses confidence that Yhwh will act and *help, which is further reason for praise. This opening statement of confidence then applies to both cola, whose two clauses about praise parallel each other. One has an impersonal subject ("my heart") and one has "I" as subject; one has present reference and one expresses the commitment to future worship that often appears in such contexts; one verb points to the suppliant's attitude and one points to the glory this *confession brings Yhwh.

> ⁸Yhwh is his strength and stronghold;
> he is the deliverance of his anointed.

A sequence of parallels with the preceding two-line section about Yhwh having listened to the plea comes to completion, since each section has reference to worship, offers reasons for worship in a finite verb (one appropriately past, one appropriately future), and includes noun clauses. Indeed, these noun clauses overlap in content with those in v. 7, asserting that Yhwh is strength (*'ōz*) and adding that Yhwh is a stronghold (*mā'ôz*)—which will have similar significance to describing Yhwh as a shield (v. 7a). Yhwh is a strong one whose strength is applied to the protection of the anointed king. In isolation, the reference to Yhwh's *anointed could suggest that this is a royal psalm, but everything so far (especially vv. 3–4) has rather indicated an ordinary individual, and v. 8

therefore associates this individual with the anointed as the people's leader. The individual's security comes from membership of this people led by this leader. *Deliverance balances *help in the opening colon of this section (v. 7c), but it also pairs with "strength" in the parallel colon; forms of these words come in Exod. 15:2, suggesting that the suppliant is rejoicing in Yhwh as the God of the Red Sea deliverance.

> ⁹Deliver your people, bless your possession,
>   shepherd them and carry them forever.

28:9. The closing line returns to plea, along the lines of Pss. 3; 12; 14; and 20. The concluding plea is the converse of the main plea in vv. 3–4: it asks for blessing that is the opposite of the trouble it seeks for the faithless.[5] This sole single line in the psalm does have enough verbs to make a double line and does comprise four parallel clauses, but they (probably) make up only two cola in which the general "your people" is paralleled by the more concrete "*possession." The punctiliar "*deliver" gives way to ongoing blessing, shepherding, and carrying, though these verbs again relate to the exodus-wilderness story. As well as being the occasion when Yhwh delivered, that was when Yhwh blessed (e.g., Num. 6:24; 24:1), when Israel became Yhwh's possession (e.g., Exod. 34:9), when Yhwh acted as Israel's shepherd (Ps. 74:1–2), and when Yhwh carried Israel, in more than one sense (Exod. 19:4; 32:32). Like Ps. 3, the "I" who speaks in this psalm here prays for the people as a whole. This plea thus constitutes another expression of the suppliant's relationship with the people as a whole and a claim to belong to this people and thus to the realm of God's blessing rather than to that of faithless people who are on the way to trouble.

Theological Implications

In light of Jesus's command to forgive our enemies, Christians are inclined to look askance at people who pray for the punishment of others. The psalm calls us to be wary lest such willingness to forgive wrongdoing that has been done to us turn into indifference to the wrong done to other people. The proper stance to such wrongdoing is to want to see it punished, and Jesus promises that people who seek such justice will see it (Luke 18:1–8),[6] in the manner of the prophetic response in the psalm. Further, expressing a desire for that implies a commitment

---
5. Cf. Rogerson and McKay, *Psalms*, 1:128.
6. Cf. Kidner, *Psalms*, 1:123.

of one's own toward doing right and a dissociation from wrongdoers. It also implies that one leaves punishment to God rather than taking matters into one's own hands. In response to the knowledge that God promises recompense for wrongdoing, one can be worshipful, trusting, and prayerful.

Psalm 29
The Power of Yhwh's Voice

Translation

Composition. David's. [For the conclusion of Tabernacle(s) (LXX).]

¹Bestow on Yhwh, divine beings,
  bestow on Yhwh honor and strength.
²Bestow on Yhwh the honor of his name;
  bow low to Yhwh in his holy majesty.

³Yhwh's voice[a] was over[b] the waters;
  the glorious God thundered,
  Yhwh over the mighty waters.
⁴Yhwh's voice was with power,
  Yhwh's voice was with majesty.

⁵Yhwh's voice is breaking cedars,
  Yhwh is breaking up[c] the cedars of Lebanon,
⁶Making them[d] jump like a calf, Lebanon and Sirion,
  like young buffalo.

   a. Ernst Vogt argues that this is an instance of *qôl* being an interjection, "Listen" ("Die Aufbau von Ps 29," *Bib* 41 [1960]: 17–24, see 17).
   b. Or perhaps "against" (so Carola Kloos, *Yhwh's Combat with the Sea* [Leiden: Brill, 1986], 52).
   c. I take the *w*-consecutive here and in v. 6 as continuing the participial construction (see GKC 116x).
   d. The suffix is explained by "Lebanon and Sirion" later in the line. See *CP* 32–33 on the possibility that this is enclitic *m* (cf. DG 27). MT reads the line as 2-4; *CP* 32–33 takes it as 3-3.

⁷Yhwh's voice is dividing flames of fire;
⁸Yhwh's voice convulses the wilderness.
Yhwh convulses the wilderness of Kadesh;
⁹Yhwh's voice makes deer convulse[e]
and strips[f] forests.

And in his palace each one in it[g] is saying:
¹⁰"In honor Yhwh took his seat over[h] the flood,
and Yhwh took his seat[i] as king forever."

¹¹"May Yhwh give strength to his people;
may Yhwh bless his people with well-being."

Interpretation

Psalm 29 sharply raises a question that arises in a number of psalms. Who is the implied speaker and who the implied addressee? In laments and thanksgivings the implied speaker is an individual Israelite, or the community as a whole, or its leader. In laments the addressee is Yhwh. In thanksgivings and declarations of trust it is Yhwh and/or the community. Other psalms seem to be addressed to the king (e.g., Ps. 20) or the community (e.g., Pss. 1; 2; 19; 24), and there is a secondary sense in which all psalms address the community as they tell it how to pray.

   e. Jerome has "makes them go into labor," a common meaning of the verb. But this seems irrelevant in this context, and the verb is used simply for continuity with v. 8, where "convulse" is simply a stronger expression than "jump" (v. 6). The deer are jumping about in fright. NRSV "oaks" for "deer" generates better parallelism with the next colon, but this requires at least the repointing *'êlôt* for *'ayyālôt* (cf. *Midrash on Psalms*, 1:383). NJPS mg similarly but conversely provides "brings ewes to early birth" as an alternative translation for the second colon, based on Arabic usage of the two words (cf. *HALOT* on *ḥāśap* and *ya'ărâ*). But while the two cola are formally parallel, in substance they take up the references to animals and trees in vv. 5–6 to complete the stepped structure. Thus one reference to animals and one to trees is appropriate here.
   f. It seems impossible to take this as a proper *waw*-consecutive, whether we understand the verb form as regular yiqtol (which would require us to translate it "and stripped") or as a yiqtol with past meaning (because the verb still does not have a consecutive relationship with the previous verb). We have to treat it as if it were a simple, non-consecutive *waw*. See *IBHS* 31.1.1e.
   g. I take the palace to be antecedent to the suffix on *kullô*.
   h. The preposition is *l*, which in Ugaritic could mean "from," i.e., "since" (*IBHS* 11.2.10c).
   i. I take the *w*-consecutive as following on the seat-taking in the previous line—it is the same seat-taking as that to which the previous colon refers, but this colon has subsequent implications in mind. It would make little difference if we assume that the wayyiqtol has present implications (so *TTH* 79). "Will sit" (LXX, Jerome) is harder to justify, though again in substance this makes little difference.

Formally, Ps. 29 addresses divine beings in the way a hymn such as Ps. 96 addresses Israelite worshippers, in order to summon them to worship (Ps. 96 also overlaps in content with Ps. 29). But its distinctiveness in being addressed to other divine beings makes one ask what else is going on here. Perhaps the psalm indirectly addresses the community; it tells the community how to think about the other divine beings that their neighbors acknowledge and that Israel often acknowledges. The implied speaker is then someone such as a priest or prophet, as is the case in (e.g.) Pss. 1 or 2. Perhaps it indirectly addresses Yhwh, telling Yhwh of the community's commitment.

The psalm has a stepped structure:[1]

  a Challenge to acknowledge Yhwh's honor and might (vv. 1–2)
    b Declaration that Yhwh in honor asserted sovereignty over the waters (vv. 3–4)
      c Declaration that Yhwh showed power in the world (vv. 5–9b)
    b′ Recognition that Yhwh in honor reigned over the flood (vv. 9c–10)
  a′ Plea regarding Yhwh's might (v. 11)

The psalm is dominated by 4-4 lines. In general this does not mean these say more than the 3-3 lines that dominate elsewhere, because this psalm is less inclined to let terms from one colon carry over into the next (as does happen in vv. 6 and 9a–b). Rather, the terms recur. Thus vv. 1, 7–8a, 10, and 11 could easily be turned into six-word lines by judicious omission of expressions that appear in both cola. Instead, the lines work by "stepped parallelism" in which elements in one line recur with new continuations, and by "extended parallelism" in that this can go on over three cola (see vv. 1–2, 3–4, 5–9b).[2] That form of parallelism is more characteristic of Canaanite poetry,[3] and a number of the statements in the psalm parallel aspects of Canaanite theology. The Canaanite pantheon included a number of divine beings, and the senior god Baal Hadad was a god revealed in the storm. Baal won a victory over the

---

1. For other understandings of the structure, see Kemper Fullerton, "The Strophe in Hebrew Poetry and Psalm 29," *JBL* 48 (1929): 274–90; Dario Gualandi, "Salmo 29 (28)," *Bib* 39 (1958): 478–85; Elpidius Pax, "Studien zur Theologie von Psalm 29," *BZ* 6 (1962): 93–100; Pierre Auffret, "Notes conjointes sur la structure littéraire des psaumes 114 et 29," *EstBib* 36 (1977): 103–13; idem, "Notes complémentaires sur la structure littéraire des Psaumes 3 et 29," *ZAW* 99 (1987): 90–93; idem, "Voix de YHWH dans la splendeur," *BN* 112 (2002): 5–11.
2. Westermann, *Living Psalms*, 230.
3. See Dahood, *Psalms*, 1:175.

Sea and came to be enthroned as a result. The geographical references in the psalm can be understood to relate to northern Canaan.[4] Indeed, T. H. Gaster suggested that Ps. 29 is an adaptation of a Canaanite hymn to Hadad; it might then be very old.[5] We do not have any examples of Canaanite psalmody so there is no direct evidence for or against this possibility and no other evidence regarding the psalm's date. The psalm may simply reflect the way understandings of Baal could contribute to the articulation of faith in Yhwh. In some contexts the psalm would function as a polemical statement over against Canaanite faith (even if implicitly so, since its form is that of a hymn),[6] which was a longstanding source of temptation to Israelites.[7] Eighteen times the psalm uses the name "Yhwh."

Composition. David's. [For the conclusion of Tabernacle(s) (LXX).]

Heading. See glossary. LXX's addition makes a nice link with the modern hypothesis that Tabernacles (Sukkot) involved a celebration of Yhwh's becoming king (see v. 10).

29:1–2. The psalm begins with a pair of lengthy and stately lines (4-4, 4-4) urging recognition of Yhwh, somewhat in the manner of a hymn; the reasons for this recognition will come in a moment. Each colon begins with a second-person plural imperative (the same imperative three

---

4. Rendsburg sees the psalm as of northern Israelite origin (see *Linguistic Evidence*, 35–38).

5. Apparently he first published the view in "The Earliest Known Miracle-Play?" *Folklore* 44 (1933): 379–90 (cf. Loretz, *Ugarit-Texte und Thronbesteigungspsalmen*, 80, 235). See also T. H. Gaster, "Psalm 29," *JQR* 37 (1946–47): 55–65; Frank M. Cross, "Notes on a Canaanite Psalm in the Old Testament," *BASOR* 117 (1949): 19–21; Aloysius Fitzgerald, "A Note On Psalm 29," *BASOR* 215 (1974): 61–63; Christian Macholz, "Psalm 29 und 1. Könige 19," in *Werden und Wirken des Alten Testaments* (Claus Westermann Festschrift), ed. Rainer Albertz et al. (Göttingen: Vandenhoeck & Ruprecht, 1980): 325–33; Klaus Seybold, "Die Geschichte des 29. Psalms und ihre theologische Bedeutung," *TZ* 36 (1980): 208–19; Hans Strauss, "Zur Auslegung von Ps 29 auf dem Hintergrund seiner kanaanäischen Bezüge," *ZAW* 82 (1970): 91–102; Andreas Wagner, "Ist Ps 29 die Bearbeitung eines Baal-Hymnus?" *Bib* 77 (1996): 538–39; but contrast B. Margulis, "The Canaanite Origin of Psalm 29 Reconsidered," *Bib* 51 (1970): 332–48; P. C. Craigie, "Psalm xxix in the Hebrew Poetic Tradition," *VT* 22 (1972): 143–51; idem, "Parallel Word Pairs in Ugaritic Poetry," *UF* 11 (1979): 135–40; idem, *Psalms 1–50*, 241–49; Kloos, *Yhwh's Combat*, 98–112; Loretz, *Ugarit-Texte und Thronbesteigungspsalmen*, 76–248. On the possible redaction history of the psalm, see also Siegfried Mittmann, "Komposition und Redaktion von Psalm xxix," *VT* 28 (1978): 172–94.

6. See Johannes F. Diehl et al., "Von der Grammatik zum Kerygma," *VT* 49 (1999): 462–86, see 486.

7. Actually, the psalm constitutes an unfortunate polemical statement, Norman C. Habel and Geraldine Avent suggest, because it confirms the impression that the earth is God's suffering victim ("Rescuing Earth from a Storm God," in *Earth Story*, ed. Habel, 42–50).

times, then a different one in the fourth colon) and continues with "to Yhwh." The middle two cola follow that with the object of the verb, the first colon with a vocative phrase, the last colon with a prepositional phrase. So there are overlapping links between the first, second, and third cola over against the fourth, and the second and third over against the first and fourth; the fourth stands as most distinctive over against the others and brings the section to a climax.

> ¹Bestow on Yhwh, divine beings,
>   bestow on Yhwh honor and strength.

The exhortation to "bestow" (*yāhab*) *honor on Yhwh appears elsewhere only in 96:7–8 (cf. 1 Chron. 16:28–29; Deut. 32:3). There, too, it is "honor and strength" that are to be bestowed on Yhwh. The exhortation may relate to several different temptations. Other beings, including human beings, have their own honor and strength, and the exhortation urges them to surrender these to Yhwh. It then does not concern the mere "ascribing" of honor and strength to Yhwh (recognizing that Yhwh has these) but the giving over of honor and strength that at the moment we possess.[8] Another temptation is that our attachment to our own honor and strength may make us reluctant to acknowledge Yhwh's, so that we rather appropriate Yhwh's honor to ourselves and not merely hold on to our own. Yet another is that we may ascribe honor and strength to entities other than Yhwh—for instance, to other heavenly beings or to political entities. Both Pss. 29 and 96 oppose that. What is more extraordinary about Ps. 29 is that the imperative itself addresses not human worshippers but "divine beings," literally, "sons of gods." It is the first appearance of the gods (*'ēlîm*) in the Psalter. Whereas singular *'ēl* is rather an exalted and powerful term for the one God Yhwh (e.g., 16:1; 19:1 [2]), plural *'ēlîm* (cf. Exod. 15:11) or *'ĕlōhîm* (Ps. 82:1) or *bĕnê 'ēlîm* (89:6 [7]) denotes heavenly beings subordinate to Yhwh, as each of these psalms shows in different ways. These are presumably the same beings as are termed *bĕnê 'ĕlōhîm* in Job 1:6; 2:1, members of the court of heaven and members of Yhwh's household there who assist Yhwh in different ways in determining what happens on earth. The use of the word corresponds to that in other Middle Eastern languages. There it can connote "not only major deities but also a wide variety of other phenomena: monstrous cosmic enemies; demons; some living kings; dead kings or the dead more generally; deities' images and standards as well as standing stones; and other cultic items and places"—in fact,

---

8. The absence of suffixes on the nouns surely does not count against this understanding (against Kloos, *Yhwh's Combat*, 34).

anything that is not regular humanity.[9] We therefore need to distinguish between English use of the word "god" and Middle Eastern use of terms such as these. The OT does not tell us how these divine beings came into existence and in what sense they are "children of gods/children of God," though Ps. 82:7 does assert that despite this status they can "die like human beings." Hence, as well as being subordinate to Yhwh, they are metaphysically different from Yhwh, who is the sole God with no possible beginning and no possible end.

Although Ps. 29 formally addresses these divine beings, its real audience may rather be Israelites inclined to worship other deities, as most Israelites were for much of OT times. In urging the divine beings to give honor to Yhwh, it is placing this exhortation before such Israelites.[10]

> ²Bestow on Yhwh the honor of his name;
> bow low to Yhwh in his holy majesty.

Verse 2 makes specific a concern with acknowledging the *honor of Yhwh's *name—that is, the honor suggested by the name Yhwh which points to who Yhwh is. After the threefold "bestow," v. 2b offers the parallel "bow low" (see on 22:27 [28]). Bestowing honor is a substantial act of worship; bowing low is a symbolic one evidently regarded as at least as significant (since it comes at the end of this sequence of verbs). "Holy majesty" (*hadrat-qōdeš*) is likewise parallel to "the honor of his name"; both are construct phrases, the suffix on "his name" also applying to "holy majesty," as LXX recognizes. KJV brings out the grammatical parallelism between these two expressions in translating this last phrase "the beauty of holiness," though this abandons the realization in LXX and Jerome that here the second noun functions adjectivally. The translation "beauty" also suggests the assumption that the phrase describes the worshippers, which is even less plausible here than in Ps. 96. The word *hădārâ* and related words regularly denote majesty or splendor, and here the phrase refers to Yhwh's holy majesty, Yhwh's majesty as the holy one.[11]

---

9. Mark S. Smith, *The Origins of Biblical Monotheism* (New York: Oxford University Press, 2001), 6.

10. An alternative first colon in LXX and Jerome understands the *'ēlîm* to be *'êlîm* (rams), the objects rather than the subjects of offering, while the *Midrash on Psalms* focuses on the idea that the addressees are *'illēm*, "dumb" (*Midrash on Psalms*, 1:380). On theological interpretation in Psalm 29 LXX, see N. A. van Uchelen, "De LXX-Interpretatie van Ps 29," *NedTT* 24 (1969–70): 171–81.

11. In Ugaritic *hdrt* may mean something like "appearance," and Kraus (*Psalms*, 1:345) sees this as the meaning of *hădārâ* here; see also the discussion in P. R. Ackroyd, "Some Notes on the Psalms," *JTS*, n.s., 17 (1966): 392–99. But the "long linguistic chain" between

> ³Yhwh's voice was over the waters;
> the glorious God thundered,
> Yhwh over the mighty waters.
> ⁴Yhwh's voice was with power,
> Yhwh's voice was with majesty.

29:3–4. The two longest sections of the psalm, vv. 3–4 and 5–9b, correspond to the reasons for praise in a hymn, which are simultaneously the content of the praise. Here they are both the bases for urging other heavenly beings to bestow honor on Yhwh and the content of the recognition urged on them. Both sections relate to the power of Yhwh's voice, on earth as it is in heaven. Verses 3–4 directly concern heaven. The five cola are all parallel.

The first colon states the theme. The second and third repeat the first in an expansive form, adding that Yhwh is a glorious God (a God of *honor), that the voice thundered, and that the waters are mighty. The fourth restates the first and third; the fifth restates the first and second. Psalm 29 finds God's majesty reflected in the fury of the storm as Ps. 8 finds it in the way the cosmos reflects God's assertion of authority over against resistant powers, and as Ps. 19 points to the ferocious heat of the sun over which God is also sovereign.[12]

"The waters" stand for tumultuous forces that threaten to overwhelm the regular order of life, in the way that a flood can overwhelm people, land, and even cities. They can stand for such tumults as we experience them in political life (e.g., 18:16 [17]; 46:3 [4]; 124:4–5) and personal life (e.g., 32:6; 69:1–2, 14–15 [2–3, 15–16]). They can also stand for such tumults as supernatural realities (e.g., 74:13; 93:4), the forces over which Yhwh asserted control at creation (e.g., 33:7; 74:13; Isa. 51:10). In the context of the summons to the heavenly beings in vv. 1–2, one would naturally think of such supernatural forces, and the qatal verb in the second colon here fits with that; the time reference of the noun clauses in the other cola follows from that. The section as a whole refers back to Yhwh's self-assertion at the Beginning. In stories told by Israel's contemporaries, the divine beings often had trouble asserting authority over such primordial entities. The psalm urges the divine beings to recognize Yhwh's authority because Yhwh had no such difficulty. Like an authoritative teacher entering an unruly classroom, Yhwh spoke, and the forces that were so brave and outspoken hushed.

---

the Ugaritic word and this proposed meaning of the Hebrew word has "more than one weak link" (Kidner, *Psalms*, 1:125; cf. Craigie, *Psalms 1–50*, 242–43).

12. I rework Rogerson and McKay's point (*Psalms*, 1:130); they make a contrast between the way Ps. 8 speaks of the peaceful calm of the night sky and Ps. 19 speaks of the beneficence of the sun's warmth. I doubt if the psalmist saw these that way.

> ⁵Yhwh's voice is breaking cedars,
>   Yhwh is breaking up the cedars of Lebanon,
> ⁶Making them jump like a calf, Lebanon and Sirion,
>   like young buffalo.
> ⁷Yhwh's voice is dividing flames of fire;
>   ⁸Yhwh's voice convulses the wilderness.
> Yhwh convulses the wilderness of Kadesh;
>   ⁹ᵃ⁻ᵇYhwh's voice makes deer convulse
>   and strips forests.

29:5–9b. The psalm turns from the past to the present: the verbs are participles and yiqtols, making it clear that the psalm is not merely talking about the original creation or the heavenly realm. The length of the section suggests that the real agenda lies here. The psalmist wants the divine beings (and fellow Israelites who actually sing or hear the psalm) to take seriously Yhwh's lordship in this realm. The section apparently invites people to imagine a vision or a scene in the psalmist's imagination, where a tumultuous thunderstorm is taking place, and it makes us reconsider the significance of the "waters" of vv. 3–4 and allow for their being present realities within this world. When thunder reverberates through the natural world on earth, it is an echo of Yhwh's thundering in the heavens, and an aftershock of Yhwh's thundering at the Beginning. It thus witnesses to the assertion of sovereignty of vv. 3–4. The thunder and lightning Yhwh generates reinforce the conviction that Yhwh asserted sovereignty over the waters at the Beginning. The comments start from realities of natural life, and specifically of the thunderstorm. A thunderstorm can cause huge trees to fall or strip them of their foliage. It can make the ground seem to shudder.[13] It can light up the scene with flashes of forked lightning. It can make animals panic. The psalm hears the voice of Yhwh in the sound of the thunder, but also sees this whole drama as a reflection of Yhwh's power exercised at the Beginning, and perhaps as exercised in political events. There is no implication that this is an act of punishment.[14]

The four lines form two pairs, vv. 5–6 and 7–9b. In the first pair, the lines are linked by *w*-consecutive and by the double reference to Lebanon. The second pair is held together by the repeated references to Yhwh's voice, to

---

13. There is no need to hypothesize reference to an earthquake, which would confuse the picture (see on 18:7 [8]).

14. John Day ("Echoes of Baal's Seven Thunders and Lightnings in Psalm xxix . . . ," *VT* 29 [1979]: 143–51) sees a parallel between the sevenfold thundering voice of Yhwh in Ps. 29 and Baal's "seven lightnings, . . . eight storehouses of thunder"; but the parallel requires some inference, since neither text actually applies the number "seven" to thunder or a voice.

convulsing, and specifically to the convulsing of the wilderness. Both pairs comprise 4-stress cola until they close with 2-stress cola (vv. 6b, 9b).

In v. 5 the two cola are parallel, with *šābar* piel building on *šābar* qal, and "cedars of Lebanon" giving specificity to "cedars" and also topping that, because Lebanese cedars are so impressive. In v. 6 the cola are again parallel but with a substantial carryover from the first colon into the second, and with "young buffalo" topping "calf." In vv. 7–9b the patterns are more complex. Verses 7 and 8a are parallel statements about Yhwh's voice, with a yiqtol verb succeeding a participle; prosaically put, the wilderness is the scene of both forked lightning and the ground's shuddering, both brought about by Yhwh's voice. But v. 8b also parallels v. 8a, indeed more closely; the relationship between these two cola is like that between the cola in v. 5, with the second again giving specificity to the first by naming the wilderness. In turn v. 9a parallels vv. 7 and 8a with its reference to Yhwh's voice, and parallels vv. 8a and 8b in its use of the verb *ḥûl*, but it varies it by using the polel rather than the hiphil. Verse 9b, however, parallels v. 9a in the same way as the second colon in v. 6 parallels the first, with a substantial carryover.

The section hangs together as a stepped structure:

    Trees (v. 5)
        Animals (v. 6)
            Wilderness (vv. 7–8)
        Animals (v. 9a)
    Trees (v. 9b)

It thus says nothing about humanity as it speaks of mountain heights and empty wilderness, of trees and animals of the wild, of the far north (Lebanon and Sirion, another name for Hermon, as in Deut. 3:9) and the far south (Kadesh, though in a Ugaritic context this would suggest Kadesh on the Orontes). It recalls Job 38–40 with its reminder that there are vast tracts and aspects of Yhwh's world that are quite irrelevant to humanity and to which humanity is quite irrelevant. But there, too, Yhwh is sovereign.

> ⁹ᶜAnd in his palace each one in it is saying:
> ¹⁰"In honor Yhwh took his seat over the flood,
>   and Yhwh took his seat as king forever."

29:9c–10. Once more the scene changes and reverts to the heavens. Yhwh's *palace is located in the heavens, above the waters, over which Yhwh asserted sovereignty (cf. 104:1–9). The context tells us that the reference is to Yhwh's heavenly palace (cf. Tg) rather than its earthly equivalent. We have had no reference to Jerusalem and its temple: the scene in vv. 1–2 was Yhwh's court in the heavens, Yhwh's palace there. "Each one" then denotes each of the divine beings there. They are now doing what vv. 1–2 bade them to do and repeating in their own words the psalmist's words in vv. 3–4.

MT takes "honor" as the last word of v. 9 and as the object of "saying," though the meaning is not clear; there are no other examples of a shout comprising "Honor." Nor is the connection with what follows very clear. I rather take "honor" as the first word in v. 10[15] and as used adverbially, as in 8:5b [6b]. The isolated last colon of v. 9 then becomes the introduction to the words of "each of them." These words of the divine beings occupy v. 10, which becomes a 4-4 line like those in vv. 1–2, 5–9, 11, with overlapping parallelism. "Yhwh took his seat" appears in both cola, the suffix "his" carrying over from the first to the second. "In honor . . . over the flood" likewise carries over from the first to the second, while "as king forever" retrospectively clarifies and modifies the first colon.

If one reads the psalm linearly, the divine beings are presumably offering their recognition in light of what they have seen on earth. The impressiveness of what results on earth from Yhwh's voice resounding there makes them bestow honor on Yhwh as they were bidden. But the stepped structure of the psalm may make a linear reading inappropriate. More likely vv. 9c–10 simply give a response to vv. 1–2 in light of vv. 3–4. The divine beings witnessed Yhwh's assertion of sovereignty over the waters, and it is this that puts them in a position to give the testimony they now give. The logic of the psalm may then be that it puts human worshippers in the position of having two bases for acknowledging Yhwh's sovereign honor, the testimony of these divine beings and the evidence from within the world that vv. 5–9b offer.

The divine beings' way of making the affirmation in vv. 3–4 is to talk of Yhwh taking up a seat in *honor, and the second colon then makes explicit that Yhwh does so as king; the seat is a throne. The language parallels the way a hymn such as Ps. 96, noted above, goes on to declare that Yhwh began or has begun to reign (96:10). LXX and Jerome, for instance, recognize that the psalm asserts not merely that Yhwh *is* king or *is* enthroned (contrast EVV), but that there was a specific moment when Yhwh asserted sovereignty over the dynamic powers that might resist that sovereignty and took a seat on a throne. The same applies to this psalm. That moment might be linked to the creation of our world, as Ps. 74 implies, though this is not explicit here or in Ps. 96. But anyway, the psalm asserts that there was such a moment, and that it had permanent consequences. That

---

15. So Margulis, "Canaanite Origin of Psalm 29," 335; David Noel Freedman and C. Franke Hyland, "Psalm 29," *HTR* 66 (1973): 237–56, see 253.

assertion of authority would then last "forever." The tumultuous waters will never be able (successfully) to reassert themselves.

> [11] "May Yhwh give strength to his people;
> may Yhwh bless his people with well-being."

29:11. The psalm closes with a further 4-4 line with overlapping parallelism.[16] LXX and Jerome take these verbs as indicative; I have taken them as jussive, with EVV. What is their significance as jussives? Psalms sometimes close with a petition that seems only tangentially related to the theme of the psalm as a whole; the preceding Ps. 28 is an example, and so might this be. But there is no actual indication of a change of speaker from vv. 9c–10. Further, "strength" paired with "honor" in v. 1, so that "strength" here looks like the completion of an inclusion in vv. 9c–11 with vv. 1–2. More likely, then, v. 11 continues and concludes the divine beings' words in vv. 9c–10, their response to the challenge in vv. 1–4.

It is the divine beings who affirm that Yhwh should give strength to Yhwh's people; this affirmation implies that Yhwh possesses strength and is therefore in a position to do so. They are thus ascribing strength to Yhwh, as v. 1 bade them to do. As members of Yhwh's heavenly court, they share in the task of making decisions regarding events on earth and in implementing these decisions. Their particular responsibility is to do so in a way that recognizes their commitment to particular peoples whom they represent: Chemosh, for instance, argues for Moab's cause in cabinet meetings (cf. the account of the "leaders of the nations" in Dan. 10). But what they are now doing—extraordinarily—is arguing on behalf of Israel! In urging that Yhwh give *strength to Israel, they are actually bestowing strength on Yhwh as well as ascribing it, in that they are implicitly making their resources available to Yhwh in connection with taking Israel to its destiny—specifically by blessing Israel with *well-being. This would have particular point if the psalm was used at Sukkot in anticipation of the beginning of the rainy season and the new agricultural year.

Theological Implications

Psalm 29 offers distinctive forms of challenge and encouragement to worshippers who use it. It affirms that the power of Yhwh is so great that it has won the recognition of the other divine beings. That happened before creation, but if there is any doubt whether it is so, the testimony

---

16. "Yhwh . . . his people" recurs, "blessing" complements "giving," while "well-being" complements "strength."

of nature dispels it, because the power of events such as thunderstorms reflects that same power. When Israelites are tempted to think that other deities are more powerful than Yhwh, they must resist the temptation, because these deities themselves have already responded to a challenge to recognize Yhwh as the only real God. And when it seems that the power of another people can overcome Israel, this cannot be so, because that other people's representative god is there in heaven arguing for Yhwh's blessing of Israel.

Psalm 30

How to Give Your Testimony

Translation

Composition. Song for the dedication of the house. David's.

¹I will exalt you, Yhwh, because you put me down[a]
   but did not let my enemies rejoice over me.
²Yhwh my God,
   I cried for help to you and you healed me.
³Yhwh, you brought me up from Sheol;
   you kept me alive from going down to the Pit. [Q]
   [you restored me to life from among people going down to the Pit.
      (K)][b]

⁴Make music to Yhwh, people committed to him;
   confess his holy remembrance.
⁵For there is an instant in his anger,[c]
   a life in his acceptance.

   a. BDB takes this verb as the sole occurrence of *dālâ* piel, which would literally mean "draw water." But this verb surely cannot be reduced to the meaning "draw up" (with the emphasis on "up" rather than "draw"), and appeal to v. 3 hardly helps; the suppliant was not drawn from Sheol like water from a well. To obtain the meaning "raise," it would be better to hypothesize a different verb with that meaning—cf. *DCH*'s *dālâ* III. I take this rather as the piel of *DCH*'s *dālâ* II, "hang down," with a similar meaning to that of *dālal* "be low" (and cf. *dal* "poor").

   b. K implies *miyyôrdê*; Q has *miyyārĕdî*, an anomalous form of the inf. Verse 9 has the regular form.

   c. LXX and Jerome have "There is wrath in his anger," perhaps implying *rōgez* for *regaʿ*.

In evening weeping takes up lodging,
    but at morning there is resounding.

⁶I myself had said when I was doing well,
    "I will never fall down."
⁷Yhwh, in your acceptance
    you had established strength for my mountain.[d]
You hid your face;
    I became terrified.

⁸On you, Yhwh, I was calling;
    to my Lord I was pleading for grace.[e]
⁹"What is the profit in my being killed,
    in my going down to the Abyss?
Can dirt confess you,
    proclaim your truthfulness?
¹⁰Listen, Yhwh, be gracious to me;
    Yhwh, become a helper to me."

¹¹You turned my mourning into dancing for me;
    you undid my sackcloth and girded me with joy,
¹²So that my heart[f] may make music to you and not wail,
    and, Yhwh my God, I may confess you forever.

Interpretation

Psalm 30 is a textbook example of a thanksgiving or testimony psalm, with an overlapping double structure:

Opening commitment to praise (v. 1)
Recollection of prayer and of Yhwh's act of deliverance (vv. 2–3)
Invitation to praise (v. 4)
Basis for that praise (v. 5)

Recollection of past flourishing and its reversal (vv. 6–7)
Recollection of prayer (vv. 8–10)
Recollection of Yhwh's act of deliverance (v. 11)
The aim of that in ongoing praise (v. 12)

    d. Apparently this is a way of saying, "You established me with the strength of a mountain."
    e. These yiqtols might have their more usual future reference and be part of the suppliant's recollection, looking back to the determination formulated then. But this interpretation would be a little tortuous.
    f. *Kābôd*; see 7:5 [6] and the comment. The "my" is supplied from the context.

If the testimony was given in the context of the temple, it presumably accompanied a thank-offering, but in other contexts it would stand alone.

The psalm has a close verbal relationship with Ps. 6, almost as if it was written for use by someone who has had Ps. 6 answered. As well as sharing some common expressions, it refers to healing (v. 2; cf. 6:2 [3]); Yhwh's remembrance/celebration (*zēker*, v. 4; cf. 6:5 [6]); terror (v. 7; cf. 6:2–3 [3–4]); and the lack of confession in the realm of death (v. 9; cf. 6:5 [6]).

> Composition. Song for the dedication of the house. David's.

Heading. See glossary. We have called this a testimony psalm, and as such it expresses an individual's thanks for Yhwh's deliverance; the heading presumably refers to a reuse of the psalm in a different connection. Its content might seem better suited to the dedication of an individual's house (cf. Deut. 20:5) than the temple. But as individuals can use communal psalms, so communities can use individual psalms, and one can imagine thanksgiving psalms being used at the dedication of David's temple (see 1 Kings 8:63),[1] at the rededication after the exile (see Ezra 6:16–17), and after the desecration by Antiochus Epiphanes (see 1 Macc. 4:52–59). The midrash links it with all three events.[2] But it was the last of them that generated *the* Dedication Festival, Hanukkah (cf. John 10:22). The desecration by Antiochus had issued from the people's commitment to Yhwh rather than from their abandoning of Yhwh, so that of these dedication occasions it is the one that would link best with Ps. 30. The psalm was subsequently used at Hanukkah (see *Soperim* 42a).

30:1–3. The worshipper immediately gets down to the business of thanksgiving, with three lines that each incorporate invocation of Yhwh and then put the focus on Yhwh's past acts: You did not let my enemies rejoice, you healed, you brought up, you preserved.

> ¹I will exalt you, Yhwh, because you put me down
> but did not let my enemies rejoice over me.

Like some other thanksgivings (Pss. 34, 107, 138), the psalm starts with a commitment to praising Yhwh, and it will close with another such commitment. The "I" immediately marks the psalm as a thanksgiving rather than a hymn, because its distinctive nature will be to give personal testimony to what Yhwh has done for an individual. "I" has little place

---

1. Slomovic notes links with 1 Chron. 21, which leads into the account of the building of the temple ("Historical Titles," 369).
2. *Midrash on Psalms*, 1:390–91.

in a hymn, which focuses resolutely on Yhwh. In a sense the claim to be able to exalt (*rûm* polel) Yhwh is an odd one that might seem to reverse the relationship between humanity and God. God *is* on high; humanity does not put God there. Indeed, Yhwh is the one who exalts (9:13 [14]; 18:48 [49]; 27:5). Yet this commitment suggestively follows the exhortation to ascribe or give splendor to Yhwh (Ps. 29). Like divine beings, human beings can have their splendor and their exaltation, as fathers or elders or teachers or kings, and the psalm begins by implicitly renouncing such exaltedness and owning our insignificance compared with Yhwh's. Suggestively, the verb "exalt" can elsewhere occur in parallelism with a verb such as "bow low" (99:5, 9); exalting Yhwh correlates with a willingness that I should be lowered. Here the "because" clause indicates that Yhwh did the lowering. After the commitment and the invocation, formally the two cola parallel each other, both with piel verbs, but one positive and one negatived; one has "me" as direct object, and one has "my enemies" as direct object and "me" as indirect object. But in substance the two clauses are sequential and summarize the suppliant's testimony by recalling the way Yhwh first put down, then raised up (cf. vv. 6–11). If Yhwh had left the suppliant in a lowly state, then the enemies could have rejoiced, but Yhwh did not do that (cf. Ps. 41). But the enemies are less prominent than they are in a lament such as Ps. 6: "The enemies have lost all significance once the threat they pose is averted."[3]

> ²Yhwh my God,
>   I cried for help to you and you healed me.

In letting the invocation occupy the whole short first colon, v. 2 gives special prominence to "my God," the new element over v. 1, which further indicates that the suppliant is not preoccupied by Yhwh's putting down and reaffirms a personal commitment to make Yhwh "my God." As the lead-in to the second colon, it also more specifically responds to the evidence of Yhwh's commitment in the act of deliverance. The two verbs in the second colon provide another encapsulation of the thanksgiving: I *cried for help; you healed. "Healed" may indicate that the suppliant had been ill or had been injured in some way (cf. 41:3–4 [4–5]), but the psalm does not go on to refer to a physical ailment and thus leaves itself open to being used in connection with other forms of restoration, such as the verb can also denote (e.g., 147:3).

> ³Yhwh, you brought me up from Sheol;
>   you kept me alive from going down to the Pit. [Q]

3. Westermann, *Living Psalms*, 170.

> [you restored me to life from among people going down to the Pit. (K)]

Verse 3 gives yet another summary of what Yhwh had done, or spells out the implications of the healing that made it impossible for the enemies to rejoice. On the Pit, see 28:1. So real here is the way *Sheol can overwhelm someone who is technically still alive that Yhwh had actually to reach down into Sheol and lift "me" out (*napšî*, *person). That suggests that in the parallel colon K makes better sense. It was too late merely to preserve the suppliant's life (*ḥāyâ* piel or hiphil; e.g., 33:19), as Q implies is what is needed. The suppliant was as good as dead, was standing in the doorway of Sheol among other dead people, and needed bringing back to life (see the use of that verb in, e.g., 2 Kings 8:5). Yhwh reversed the direction of that journey from down to up. Characteristically, the thanksgiving makes Yhwh the subject of the sentences, so that these are more acts of confession than thanksgiving statements with "I" or "we" as the subject, and the emphasis lying on my/our feeling of gratefulness.[4] Verses 1–3 work this out in a striking way. "I" have the first word, and vv. 1–2 begin with anti-thanksgiving and recollection of "my cry," but Yhwh's act of deliverance, with Yhwh the subject of the verbs, gets more and more prominence until it entirely takes over v. 3.

30:4–5. Psalm 30 "celebrates not only God's saving power but [also] the efficacy of speech—both speech to God in prayer and praise of God in thanksgiving. There is, then, a submerged logical link between the summarizing account of the effect of prayer in lines 2–3 and the exhortation to sing and praise in line 4." This "foregrounding of language" will continue to the very last line of the testimony.[5] As usual, the thanksgiving gives glory to Yhwh before other people, so that it is also a testimony. The thanks are directed to Yhwh but are given in public so that other people overhear. Perhaps the suppliant takes family and friends to the temple to witness the thank-offering and hear this thanksgiving, which now turns to address those others directly. Three lines of invitation to join in praise thus accompany the three lines of thanksgiving. But a striking feature of vv. 4–5 is that in isolation we would reckon it to be a hymn of praise. The "I" disappears, and it has the two features of a hymn, the invitation to praise and the reasons for it, in terms of the characteristic nature or acts of Yhwh rather than specific acts on behalf of the worshipper. The act that is the basis for this suppliant's *thanksgiving* is the basis for the whole community's *hymn*, because the event evidences Yhwh's

---

4. So Westermann, e.g., ibid., 168–69; cf. the section on "Thanksgiving or Testimony" in the introduction to this commentary.

5. Alter, *Art of Biblical Poetry*, 134–35.

characteristic nature and acts. Yet the overlap with thanksgiving in a situation such as this makes the suppliant invite the people themselves into *confession* or testimony. In this sense they identify with the suppliant. What Yhwh did for this person, Yhwh did for them.

> ⁴Make music to Yhwh, people committed to him;
>   confess his holy remembrance.

Verse 4 is a neat 3-3 line with the same verbs complementing each other as in 17:17 [18], though in reverse order—one suggesting the *musical means of expression, the other the *confessional content of the expression. The first colon includes the subject of both verbs. Here *committed more clearly points to people's commitment to Yhwh as opposed to their commitment to other members of the community. The second colon spells out the implications of "Yhwh": it is "his holy remembrance." EVV have "name," but the word is not *šēm* but *zēker*, the name as something people make mention of and thus celebrate in worship (cf. 6:5 [6]).

> ⁵For there is an instant in his anger,
>   a life in his acceptance.
> In evening weeping takes up lodging,
>   but at morning there is resounding.

Verse 5 explains why Yhwh's act on behalf of one person is good news for other people, in two further neat parallel lines. Both contrast two facts. Yhwh's act of deliverance for an individual provides further evidence regarding who Yhwh is, evidence that is thus significant for people in general. The general truths that this act evidences relate to the way Yhwh is and to the way human experience therefore is. On the one hand, his anger is short-lived, his love long-lasting. The double statement generalizes from the opening words about Yhwh putting down but not leaving down. As is the case in the story of Job and in Ps. 6, it is inappropriate to infer from the reference to Yhwh's anger that Yhwh's putting down was a punishment for the suppliant's wrongdoing. The awareness that Yhwh was angry was an inference from the experience of being put down, or another way of describing that. As far as we can see, like Job the suppliant does not know why Yhwh might have been angry and has no awareness of wrongdoing that could explain this anger. The psalm's focus of concern is rather the fact that whatever the reason, the anger was momentary compared with the acceptance or welcome or delight (*rāṣôn*)—which also emerges from the person of Yhwh rather than being something earned. The suppliant knows that we normally live as people on whom God looks with love, affection, and delight, and to whom God behaves with those characteristics. When you know that, it is possible to put up with a short inexplicable experience of being under God's wrath.

To put it another way, the transition from weeping to joy can happen overnight. At night you could be deathly ill, and in the morning you could have recovered; I take this as a figure of speech, another way of describing how quickly Yhwh can heal. As "instant" paired with "life" and "anger" with "delight," here "evening" pairs with "morning" and "weeping" with "resounding." Both weeping and *resounding can be happy or sad, but the context makes clear that these tears signify pain, hurt, and worry, and this resounding signifies triumph and joy. In a vivid metonymy the suppliant pictures the weeping as lying down to sleep for the night instead of the weeper doing so, and pairs that figure of speech with an ellipse: one would expect "resounding gets up," but instead "the person gets up resounding."

30:6–7. The psalm could have stopped at v. 5, but vv. 6–12 repeat the story. Augustine notes that the psalmists are inclined thus to repeat themselves: "It is not enough for them to declare once for all the object of their joy."[6] The story of what Yhwh has done needs telling more than once, more than one way. Verses 6–7 give more detail on the experience, first by going behind Yhwh's act and describing how things had been and how things went wrong, in three more lines of diminishing length. They abandon parallelism and subordinate poetic form to the telling of a disquieting story. In the first two lines, each second colon completes the sentence begun in the first; in the last line, the second colon follows on from the first in linear fashion.

> [6]I myself had said when I was doing well,
> "I will never fall down."

So the suppliant looks back to when things were fine, literally, "in my ease/prosperity" (*běšalwî*). I follow LXX and Jerome in taking this as an objective statement about how things actually were (cf. Rashi). Modern translators and commentators understand it to suggest complacency, but there is no basis for that in the usage of related words (this particular form is a hapax). There seemed no reason why that state of God-given well-being should not continue forever. "I could not imagine anything tripping me up." While *fall down (*môṭ*) can imply the false confidence of a faithless person (10:6), or the commitment of the faithful person (15:5), it most often refers to the security of the person who belongs to

---

6. *Psalms*, 19.

Yhwh (16:8; 21:7 [8]; 46:5 [6]; 62:2, 6 [3, 7]; 125:1). Again, there is thus no reason to take the verb to suggest that the suppliant had lapsed into false self-confidence.

> ⁷Yhwh, in your acceptance
> you had established strength for my mountain.
> You hid your face;
> I became terrified.

Verse 7a confirms that one can rule out an implication of wrongful complacency in v. 6. "It was Yhwh who in love had put me in that position of strength." The way of expressing the point is odd, but evidently the suppliant was not living in self-confidence.

Nevertheless, everything did collapse, the psalm makes clear, in two horrified brief asyndetic cola. The hiding of Yhwh's *face is indeed a frightening notion. It is not a mere spiritual sense that God has become inaccessible, but an experience of God withdrawing blessing and protection. This found expression in being put down by illness and virtually surrendered to Sheol. And because it had such devastating implications, it was a terrifying experience. One wonders whether interpreters see the suppliant as acknowledging sinful self-reliance in v. 6 because this makes Yhwh's turning away explicable. The suppliant rather finds it inexplicable, but is no longer troubled about it because it was short-lived.

30:8–10. A further distinctive feature of this second telling of the suppliant's story is the extended recollection of the prayer that issued from the turning of Yhwh's face with its terrifying consequences—with the usual illogic, for it was a bold act to appeal to someone whose face had turned away. This recollection is the longest section in the psalm, hinting at the wonder of the fact that God did answer prayer; the prayer itself occupies three lines. LXX and Jerome read the verbs in v. 10 as past rather than as imperative, which would associate it with vv. 11–12 and make the psalm comprise five three-line sections.

> ⁸On you, Yhwh, I was calling;
> to my Lord I was pleading for grace.

The introduction to the recollected prayer comprises two parallel cola, one addressing God in the second person, one speaking of God in the third person. The combination again reflects the dual nature of the psalm as both a thanksgiving and a testimony. Identifying God as "Yhwh" points to God's personal nature; identifying God as my *Lord appeals to the servant-master relationship that obligates the master as well as the servant. "Pleading for *grace" (*ḥānan* hitpael; cf. *tĕḥinnâ* in 6:9 [10]) nuances the simple "call."

> [9] "What is the profit in my being killed,
>   in my going down to the Abyss?
> Can dirt confess you,
>   proclaim your truthfulness?"

The first two lines of the prayer combine brisk, urgent 2-2 cola, both manifesting an overlapping parallelism. In v. 9a, "What is the profit?" applies to both cola; in v. 9b, "dirt" is the subject of both verbs, and "your truthfulness" is the object of both. To put it another way, "going down to the Abyss" spells out the implications of "my being killed," and "proclaim your truthfulness" spells out "confess you." It is Yhwh's *truthfulness that one can *confess when Yhwh has answered one's prayer. "Dirt" suggests people who have returned to the dirt from which they were made (Gen. 3:19). On the logic of the argument, again see 6:5 [6]. Whereas v. 3 portrayed the suppliant as at Sheol's gate or having already gone down to the Pit, here the psalm rather speaks of being in danger of this fate, using the term Abyss (see 16:10). "My being killed" is literally "my blood," which would often point to violent death and suggests the kind of danger coming from an injury that could have led to death rather than an illness.[7]

> [10] "Listen, Yhwh, be gracious to me;
>   Yhwh, become a helper to me."

Verse 10 gives us the actual plea, with the characteristic double desire that Yhwh may listen and act. Mediating between "listen" and "become a *helper" is "be *gracious" (compare the noun in v. 7). It is the graciousness of Yhwh that makes listening issue in decisive action.

30:11–12. Although the second version of the testimony goes into great length over the prayer, it says nothing concrete about what Yhwh did in answering, by way of healing or deliverance. As it focused on the prayer in vv. 8–10, so in two long internally parallel lines it now focuses on the praise that Yhwh's act made possible.

> [11] You turned my mourning into dancing for me;
>   you undid my sackcloth and girded me with joy,

Two cola portray the immediate effect of Yhwh's act, bringing a transformation from negative to positive. The turning from mourning to

---

7. Cf. *bloodshed, but here the word is sg.

dancing was the reverse of the transformation when Jerusalem was destroyed (Lam. 5:15). While "mourning" (*mispēd*) can denote grieving for some loss other than death, it usually refers to mourning someone's death (e.g., Gen. 50:10). This makes a link with the death-like nature of the suppliant's experience. "I had been grieving over my own death like people when Jerusalem fell, but now I am dancing like people when the community was restored" (cf. Jer. 31:13). An outward expression of mourning was the wearing of ordinary, non-celebratory clothing (sackcloth would be the equivalent of working clothes as opposed to festive garments). Now it is as if Yhwh personally undid the ties on the sackcloth, like a parent undressing a child, and put over the shoulders something bright and festal, the clothing for a wedding rather than a funeral. The psalm actually refers to joy rather than joyful clothing (no doubt both would apply), and this makes for a link between the beginning and end of the line as this joy replaces mourning.

> ¹²So that my heart may make music to you and not wail,
> and, Yhwh my God, I may confess you forever.

The first-person verb in the second colon parallels the two third-person verbs in the first colon, "so that" applies to the second colon as well as the first, and the invocation "Yhwh my God" and the qualifier "forever" apply to the first colon as well as the second. The first colon also continues the contrast that characterized v. 11, through its antithesis of music and wailing. I thus take the second verb as *dāmam* II, "wail," not *dāmam* I, "be silent." Admittedly silence can imply grief, and further, when standing in the doorway of death, the suppliant stood at the entrance of the realm where there is no music or testimony, only silence; there is nothing to be said or sung in that realm. But wailing has similar implications and makes for a better parallel with the preceding cola. Either way, when God has acted, all that is transformed. *Music and *confession become natural. This last line also holds together the nature of the psalm as thanksgiving and testimony. It addresses Yhwh, which makes it thanksgiving. But it does so aloud, because the thanksgiving is also a testimony or confession designed to glorify Yhwh in such a way that other people can hear (cf. v. 4, from which the verbs "make music" and "confess" recur). Yhwh's act of deliverance is so wonderful that its ripples spread out from the suppliant to other people and also spread out through time. Indeed, the suppliant sees this as one of Yhwh's aims in the act of deliverance ("so that . . .").[8] The suppliant implicitly promises to let them keep doing so, so that the rest of life is shaped by this experience.

---

8. It is a shame to water down *lĕma'an* to "with the result that" (JM 169g).

Theological Implications

The life of a believer is lived between poles of experience: put down—brought up; going down to the Pit—restored to life; instant—life; anger—delight; evening—morning; tears—resounding; delight—hiding of the face; strength—terror; mourning—dancing; sackcloth—joy; making music—wailing. Sometimes we are on the way from joy to sackcloth, and we lament. Sometimes we are on the way from sackcloth to joy, and we give thanks and testify. For that experience, this textbook example suggests that thanksgiving or testimony

- is explicitly personal,
- tells a story,
- addresses God in joy,
- addresses other people in wonder,
- links the story with issues of life and death,
- tells the story again when once does not seem enough,
- draws the inferences for faith from the individual's experience,
- invites the rest of the community to join in, and
- expects that this experience will shape one's ongoing testimony.

Psalm 31

When a Prayer Needs to Be Prayed Twice

Translation

The leader's. Composition. David's.

¹I rely on you, Yhwh—
  may I never be shamed;
  in your faithfulness rescue me.
²Incline your ear to me,
  save me quickly.
Be a crag, a stronghold[a] for me,
  a fastness,[b] to deliver me,
³For you are my cliff, my fastness,
  and for the sake of your name you lead me, guide me.
⁴You take me out of the net that people have hid for me,
  for you are my stronghold;
⁵into your hand I entrust my spirit.

You have redeemed me, Yhwh,
  true God.
⁶I have been against people who hold fast to empty vanities; [MT]
[*or,* You have been against people who hold fast to empty vanities;
     (LXX, Jerome, Syr)]
I—I have trusted in Yhwh.

a. Lit., "a crag of stronghold," a crag that is a stronghold, or just a strong crag.
b. Lit., "a house of fastness" (abstract or intensive pl.).

⁷I shall joy and rejoice in your commitment,
    you who have looked at my weakness,
    acknowledged me when I was in straits.
⁸You have not delivered me into the hand of the enemy;
    you have stood my feet in a wide place.

⁹Be gracious to me, Yhwh,
    because I am in straits.
My eye wastes away through aggression,
    my spirit and my insides.
¹⁰Because my life is used up by sorrow,
    my years by groaning.
My strength has failed because of my waywardness [MT, Jerome]/
    weakness [LXX, Sym],
    my limbs have wasted away.
¹¹Before[c] all my foes I have become a reproach,
    and to my neighbors, very much,[d]
And a terror to my acquaintances, people who see me in the street—
    they flee from me.
¹²I am disregarded like a dead person, out of mind;
    I have become like a vessel, perishing.
¹³For I have heard the defamation[e] of many,
    alarm on every side,
As they scheme together against me—
    they have plotted to take my life.
¹⁴But I—I have trusted in you, Yhwh;
    I have said, You are my God.
    ¹⁵My times are in your hand;
Save me from the hand of my enemies, from my pursuers;
    ¹⁶shine your face on your servant;
    deliver me, out of your commitment.
¹⁷Yhwh, may I not be shamed, because I have called on you;
    may the faithless be shamed,
    may they go wailing[f] to Sheol.
¹⁸Lying lips must be silenced,
    that speak assertively against the faithful,
    with pride and contempt.
¹⁹How much good you have had,[g]
    that which you have hidden away for people who revere you,

  c. The parallelism suggests *min* means something like "before," not "because of" (NJPS) or "more than" (Tg).
  d. For possible emendations of *mĕʾōd*, "very much," see (e.g.) UBS.
  e. "Whispering" (EVV) looks like etymologizing (see BDB); "defamation" fits all the occurrences of *dibbâ*.
  f. Or "silent"; see on 30:12 [13].
  g. I take the noun clause to derive its tense reference from the past reference of the rest of the verse.

> Which you have done for people who rely on you,
> > before human beings.
> [20]You protect them securely in your presence[h]
> > from human plots.
> You hide them in a shelter
> > from contentious tongues.
>
> [21]Yhwh be worshipped,
> > because he has shown the wonder of his commitment to me[i]
> > as[j] a city besieged.
> [22]I—I had said in my alarm,
> > I am cut off from before your eyes.
> But on the contrary, you listened to the sound of my plea for grace
> > when I cried for help to you.
> [23]Dedicate yourselves to Yhwh, all his committed ones;
> > Yhwh guards the true,
> > but abundantly requites the one who acts with pride.
> [24]Be strong; your heart may take courage,[k]
> > all you who are waiting for Yhwh.

Interpretation

Psalm 31 compares with Ps. 22 in a number of respects. It is a prayer psalm arising out of pressing need that pleads for deliverance but interweaves its pleas with declarations of trust in Yhwh and laments at the present situation with its distress, and before the end it makes a marked transition to praise that speaks of the prayer as having been answered. But such past-tense declarations about Yhwh's acts already appear in vv. 1–8 (esp. vv. 5b, 7–8). While these might refer to an earlier experience of Yhwh's deliverance that is part of the basis for laying hold of Yhwh, it is more natural to take them as the first anticipatory references to the act of deliverance that the suppliant needs now. Verses 1–8 thus constitute a prayer that could be complete in itself, with pleas for God to listen and deliver, statements of trust and commitment, declarations that God has responded, and anticipations of joyful response to that. Verses 9–24 then go through this sequence again, though with a different profile. They begin with a plea leading into substantial lament (vv. 9–13), go on to further pleas

h. Lit., "you hide them in the hiding place of your presence/face."
i. Lit., "he has made wonderful his commitment to me."
j. Cf. GKC 119i; or "in."
k. "Be strong, and he will encourage your heart" (cf. KJV) is grammatically possible, but the logic would surely be the reverse: "He will encourage your heart, and you can then be strong."

interwoven with statements of trust (vv. 14–20), and close with worship and exhortation based on God's having heard and responded (vv. 21–24). The two parts of the psalm might have been composed separately,[1] though a number of expressions recur: "rely" (vv. 1, 19), "may I not be ashamed" (vv. 1, 17), "in your hand" (vv. 5, 15), "trust" (vv. 6, 14), "commitment" (vv. 7, 16, 21). These may make it more likely that the two parts were composed in relation to each other; if composed separately, they now stand together.

The lament in vv. 9–13 emphasizes how long the suppliant's affliction has been going on, and this might suggest that vv. 9–24 were composed because the deliverance Yhwh had promised has not arrived. Such interpretations understand the psalm as a reflection of something going on in the psalmist's psyche. But there is more than one reason for hesitating over an interpretation that takes the psalm as if it were the transcript of a process (nor need it reflect a liturgy, though it might do so). One is that it takes no account of the parallel with other psalms that go through their "story" twice, not least the immediately preceding one, Ps. 30 (cf. also, e.g., Pss. 42–43, which does that three times; also praise psalms such as Pss. 95 and 100). This suggests that repetition of this kind may simply be part of the rhetoric of prayer. It is natural to go through the "story" more than once.

The conventional nature of the psalm's language also warns against trying to infer from it what was going on inside the psalmist—or outside. The description of the situation of need embraces "battle, ensnaring, illness, reviling, isolation, persecution, threat of murder, enemies that are presumptuous against God," a list whose complexity also makes for a parallel with Ps. 22 and other psalms.[2] It shares particular links of imagery and language with (e.g.) Pss. 4; 7; 18; 28; and 71 (see vv. 1–3); with Ps. 6, which gives this psalm another point of connection with Ps. 30 (see on vv. 9–10); and also with Jeremiah's laments (see vv. 9–13 in the psalm). The ancient versions further extend these parallels.[3] We should perhaps not assume that one person experienced all those pressures but that a prayer might take up imagery from varying contexts in order to express itself in familiar words and images. "Intensely personal sentiment" is thus expressed in "stereotyped words and formulae" that reflect a "rich, shared tradition of prayer in Israelite worship from which the

---

1. For more complex theories about the psalm's origin, see (e.g.) Westermann, *Living Psalms*, 174. Contrast Luis Alonso Schökel, "En la mano de Dios," *EstBib* 56 (1998): 405–15.
2. Eaton, *Psalms*, 93.
3. See (e.g.) the notes in *BHS*.

poet can freely draw."⁴ The use of familiar imagery might alternatively mean that the prayer was designed for many people to pray in different contexts and therefore uses images that might be familiar to the people who would use it. Indeed, Eberhard Bons thus describes it as a kind of "fictional" text, a portrait of what peril, prayer, and deliverance can look like, drawn for the encouragement of the faithful.⁵

> The leader's. Composition. David's.

Heading. See glossary. LXX adds "of alarm" (cf. v. 22), suggesting a link with 1 Sam. 23:26, where David was alarmed by Saul's pursuit of him, but Yhwh rescued him.

31:1–5a. The psalm leaps straight to the heart of the matter with a plea for hearing and deliverance that appeals to the characteristics of Yhwh's relationship with the supplicant. The imagery compares with Pss. 7; 18; and 27.

> ¹I rely on you, Yhwh—
> may I never be shamed;
> in your faithfulness rescue me.

Such a declaration of *reliance is a standard way to begin a prayer psalm (see 7:1 [2]). The second and third cola, arranged $abb'a'$, are then complementary in substance and form: a first-person verb and a second-person verb, a cohortative and an imperative, a negative and a positive, a *l* expression (forever) and a *b* expression (in your *faithfulness). The suppliant's problem is other people's attacks, which imply the need of rescue. These attacks apparently presuppose or lead to the claim that Yhwh has abandoned the suppliant, which explains the reference to shame. That is another topic that recurs in psalms, not least at the beginning (e.g., 25:2–3).

> ²Incline your ear to me,
> save me quickly.
> Be a crag, a stronghold for me,
> a fastness, to deliver me,

Verse 2 elaborates on v. 1, first with the plea for Yhwh to listen that frequently and logically precedes the plea to save (cf. 28:1–2; 30:10 [11]; and for this verb, *nāṭâ* hiphil, 17:6). The parallel colon thus complements

---

4. Rogerson and McKay, *Psalms*, 1:138; cf. Kraus, *Psalms*, 1:361; and for lists of parallels, Craigie, *Psalms 1–50*, 259–60.
5. *Psalm 31—Rettung als Paradigma* (Frankfurt: Knecht, 1994), 256–57.

the first. Its plea for speed perhaps clarifies v. 1; at the moment people are getting away with attacks that mean shame, and the suppliant does not want this to continue "forever."

Verse 2b makes the point again by the use of some familiar vivid noun images, *crag, stronghold (see 27:1), and fastness (see 18:2 [3]).

> ³For you are my cliff, my fastness,
>   and for the sake of your name you lead me, guide me.

NRSV and NIVI take v. 3 as a further request, but the verbs are now yiqtol rather than imperative, and taking them as requests involves ignoring the copula that begins v. 3b. Verse 3 looks more like buttressing for vv. 1–2. The nature of the verbs supports this, for leading and guiding are not quite what are needed at this moment. The suppliant is continuing to point to reasons for Yhwh to listen and act, and these include Yhwh's habitual practice of leading and guiding (cf. NJPS). Again, for "cliff" see 18:2 [3]. The two cola thus complement each other in offering different descriptions of Yhwh's relationship with the suppliant, in a double noun clause and a double verbal clause. For leading and guiding for the sake of your *name, see 23:2–3.

> ⁴You take me out of the net that people have hid for me,
>   for you are my stronghold;
> ⁵ªinto your hand I entrust my spirit.

Verses 4–5a first complete an *abb'a'* sequence running through vv. 3–4, with another verbal clause complemented by another noun clause. Again, then, the psalm is appealing to Yhwh's characteristic way of relating to the suppliant, and thus seeking for Yhwh once more to act this way. For the metaphor of hiding a net, as if the person were an animal or a bird that hunters were trying to catch, see 9:15 [16]. "You are my stronghold" takes up v. 2, as "you are my fastness" did (in v. 3). Verse 5a then continues the yiqtol verbs, and I therefore take it as continuing the statement of the ongoing relationship between the suppliant and Yhwh. Indeed, it rounds off vv. 1–5a by pairing with the declaration of reliance that opened v. 1, though it also constitutes an unexpected further colon that forms a tricolon with v. 4.⁶

31:5b–8. The qatal verbs in this section suggest the crisis is over. Yhwh has responded. Admittedly, the fact that vv. 5b–8 are part of a prayer,

---

6. "Entrust" represents an unusual use of *pāqad* (hiphil), though see Lev. 6:4 [5:23]; 1 Kings 14:27; Jer. 40:7; 41:10 for illuminating comparable literal uses of the verb. Likewise "spirit" (*rûaḥ*) is an unusual way to refer to a person's soul or being or dynamic or life (one might have expected *nepeš* or *ḥayyîm*), but cf. 32:2; 34:18 [19]; 78:8; 104:29–30.

along with vv. 1–5a, implies that the actual deliverance still lies in the future, and this is the clearer given that vv. 9–24 follow. But the suppliant knows that Yhwh has heard the prayer in vv. 1–2 and has responded, and thus speaks as if deliverance is achieved.

> ⁵ᵇYou have redeemed me, Yhwh,
> true God.

I have reckoned that v. 5b–c forms a complete line and that the sharp transition to a qatal verb marks it as the beginning of the suppliant's statement regarding what Yhwh has done—that is, what Yhwh has made a commitment to doing (cf. 6:8–9 [9–10]; there is another such sharp transition in Ps. 22).[7] The invocation "*true God" suggests that in *redeeming, Yhwh has acted in accordance with the convictions expressed in vv. 3–4.

> ⁶I have been against people who hold fast to empty vanities; [MT]
> [or, You have been against people who hold fast to empty vanities;
>   (LXX, Jerome, Syr)]
> I—I have trusted in Yhwh.

Verse 6 looks behind this act of redemption to the attitude the suppliant has shown, which Yhwh has vindicated (MT), or to the attitude that God has shown (LXX). MT's text perhaps implies a recognition that the suppliant has not yet actually seen the act of redemption, since it implies the need to keep up the attitude of repudiation.[8] The verbs are again qatal, and I have taken them as fientive and thus as referring to the past, though it would make little difference to take them as stative and as referring to the present (EVV). Negatively, the suppliant and/or Yhwh have had nothing to do with people who pay regard to idols. They have been *against them; for the use of *šāmar* (hold fast to), compare Jon. 2:9 (though there the verb is piel); Isa. 56:1; Hosea 12:6 [7] (though there the reference is to relationship priorities). "Empty vanities" combines two words of similar meaning (*hebel* and *šāwʾ*) to emphasize the value judgment on the gods other than Yhwh, gods represented by images: they have no substance or power to correspond to their outward form (*emptiness). Luther renders as "supervain."[9] Perhaps the suppliant was being accused of having recourse to other deities. This was an accusation easy to make and hard to disprove because such practices could be part of personal, rather

---

7. Thus the context does not suggest that *pādîtâ* is precative (against *IBHS* 30.5.4d).
8. So Gerstenberger, *Psalms*, 1:138.
9. *First Lectures*, 1:139.

than corporate, religion; they could be a capital offense and the accusation thus be life-threatening. Yhwh's answer vindicates the suppliant's profession of having nothing to do with such religious practices. The parallel colon then puts the point positively in terms of *trust, or (if we follow LXX) indicates that the suppliant is not one who is open to Yhwh's repudiation.

> ⁷I shall joy and rejoice in your commitment,
>   you who have looked at my weakness,
>   acknowledged me when I was in straits.

Verse 7 first looks forward to rejoicing in Yhwh's deliverance, in the way a lament often does. The yiqtol verb thus refers to that future rejoicing that will be properly appropriate when the redemption that Yhwh has promised becomes actuality. The act of redemption will be a proof of Yhwh's *commitment and thus a vindication of the descriptions in vv. 1–5a. Verse 7b–c then comprises two parallel cola that more concretely spell out the nature of that commitment as they again look back on the suffering that the suppliant knows is coming to an end. The two second-person qatal verbs are parallel; I assume that both indicate that Yhwh not merely became aware (see, know) but also focused and responded (looked, *acknowledged). The two expressions for trouble complement each other in the way they work syntactically, one being the object of the verb, the other being governed by a preposition. They also complement each other as metaphors in referring to "*weakness" and "straits"; as in 4:1 [2] the context (see v. 8) suggests that the suppliant is aware of the etymological meaning of ṣārôt (straits).

> ⁸You have not delivered me into the hand of the enemy;
>   you have stood my feet in a wide place.

Verse 8 concludes the psalm's description of these acts that are past in that Yhwh has determined on them, using two contrasting clauses, one negative, one positive. The reference to a wide place parallels 4:1 [2] and suggests that v. 8b links especially with v. 7c. Yhwh's act of redemption has moved the suppliant from trying to walk a narrow cliff-side path, where it is hard to maintain a footing (especially when under attack from people who are trying to push one off), to a broad place where one ceases to be in that danger. We might infer that v. 8a links with v. 7b. The weakness made it hard to overcome enemies, but Yhwh has preserved the suppliant from ending up in their power. Not being delivered into the hand of the enemy also pairs with entrusting the spirit to the hand of Yhwh (v. 5).

31:9–13. The prayer restarts with a plea, but after the opening colon the section comprises lament at the suppliant's affliction, a lament designed to motivate Yhwh to respond to that plea for grace. The lament is distinctive for its near-exclusive focus on "I." There is no accusing of Yhwh, and not till the last line are there sentences with other people as the subject. Verses 9c–10 directly talk about the way the experience affects the suppliant, the point being that the affliction is going on for so long. Verses 11–12 talk about the attitude this affliction produces in people in the community. Verse 13 explains the link between these: enemies either treat the suppliant in the way the friends treated Job and thus cause the community to reject him, or more likely they cause the affliction itself and thus the rejection. After the introductory line, the whole lament is expressed in parallel cola (v. 11 tests the rule). That adds to the force and pathos of the statement: everything is said more than once. Yhwh cannot escape from this portrayal. Most lines have short, 2-stress second cola.

> ⁹Be gracious to me, Yhwh,
>   because I am in straits.
> My eye wastes away through aggression,
>   my spirit and my insides.

The plea for *grace could come at the very beginning of a psalm (e.g., 4:1 [2]; 51:1 [3]), while the first description of the suppliant's need takes up from v. 7 (though the form there was the pl. of *ṣārâ*; here it is *ṣar*). The line thus makes explicit that the suppliant still has the problem that v. 7 spoke of as if it were solved. The whole section will spell out the nature of the "straits" the suppliant is still in.

For the first colon of v. 9c–d, see 6:7 [8]; the wasting comes about because the eye is continually looking for deliverance but not seeing it. The second colon then adds the spirit (*person) and the insides as further subjects of the verb. Perhaps the psalm is sampling from a well-known prayer and then adding that this wasting is affecting not merely the eye but the whole person, which is described from two angles as the spirit or soul or heart, and the insides or stomach. Both these can be connected with longing or waiting or desiring (for *nepeš*, see 10:3; 33:20; 42:1–2 [2–3]; and for *beṭen* see Prov. 13:25; 18:20).[10]

---

10. The pairing of *nepeš* and *beṭen* reappears in 44:25 [26], and **BDB** takes them to refer to soul and body, but *beṭen* elsewhere refers to the insides (cf. 17:14), sometimes explicitly the womb (cf. 22:9–10 [10–11]; 58:3 [4]; 71:6; 127:3; 139:13; while 132:11 suggests a male equivalent).

> ¹⁰Because my life is used up by sorrow,
>   my years by groaning.
> My strength has failed because of my waywardness [MT, Jerome]/
>   weakness [LXX, Sym],
>   my limbs have wasted away.

Verse 10a–b reinforces the point. First, "used up" (*kālâ*) complements "wastes away." This verb, too, often has eyes or soul as its object (e.g., 69:3 [4]; 73:26), but it has different connotations with life or time or days as subject (cf. 102:3 [4]). "Groaning" (*ʾănāḥâ*) is another expression that takes up from Ps. 6 (see v. 6 [7]; there are only nine further occurrences).

Then v. 10c–d further reinforces. "Fails" (*kāšal*) is another parallel to "wastes away" and "used up"; "wastes away" itself reappears in the second colon, rounding off these three lines, with this line alone having two verbs. "Strength" is the strength to keep going in these circumstances (cf. 38:10 [11]; Isa. 40:29, 31), while "my limbs" makes yet another link with Ps. 6 (see v. 2 [3]). But 32:3 clarifies the logic of this line: what makes the limbs waste away is the groaning by which one expresses a longing for deliverance but sees none (cf. Prov. 14:30; for the converse, 15:30). The reading "because of my *weakness" (*bāʿŏnî* or *bĕʿonyî*), implied by LXX and Sym, coheres with the immediate context and with the rest of the psalm and takes up from v. 7. MT's "because of my *waywardness," *baʿăwōnî*, introduces a new idea that does not appear elsewhere in the psalm. If people are inclined to assume that trouble always links with sin or that no one can ever truly claim to be committed to God, LXX reminds them that the former is not so and that the latter can be. If people are inclined to exclude or forget the possibility that all our lives are affected by our wrongdoing and that our trouble can be increased by it, MT reminds them of that.

> ¹¹Before all my foes I have become a reproach,
>   and to my neighbors, very much,
> And a terror to my acquaintances, people who see me in the street—
>   they flee from me.

In v. 11 four parallel descriptions of people's attitude to the suppliant constitute one sentence. Naturally the suppliant is a reproach (*ḥerpâ*; see 15:3) to enemies: they abuse the suppliant for presumed wrongdoing such as alleged adherence to other deities (v. 6). "I have become a reproach" applies to the words that follow as well as those that precede; the parallelism perhaps implies that the enemies are also neighbors, as would commonly be the case in a community.¹¹ "A terror to my acquaintances" forms a third expression parallel to those in the two preceding cola, constituting a stronger expression that brings the sequence to a climax. While some people can talk as if they are superior to the suppliant, other people imagine themselves caught by the same fate.

We would not have been surprised if v. 11c had been an extra colon that closed off a tricolon, but it actually is the beginning of a further bicolon that hangs on to the preceding one by enjambment. This further bicolon has a structure similar to the preceding one, with "people who see me in the street" belonging to the expressions on both sides. It stands in apposition to "my acquaintances" but is then the subject of "They flee from me." People stand back from such an embodiment of hurt, almost as if the experience might be catching.

> ¹²I am disregarded like a dead person, out of mind;
> I have become like a vessel, perishing.

Verse 12 puts the point yet again, in a separate sentence, with "I have become" acting as a bracket around vv. 11–12. In itself v. 12 is structurally a pair of neatly parallel cola with two first-person qatal verbs (one niphal, one qal), two *k*-phrases, and two further expressions that qualify the *k*-phrases. "Out of mind" thus qualifies "dead person," not the verb "disregard" (*ignore), which already contains that idea. The suppliant's point is not merely that the dead are eventually forgotten but that people who are reckoned to have died as a judgment on their wrongdoing are deliberately forgotten. "Perishing" suggests the fate of many vessels, especially household vessels that are commonly made of clay.

> ¹³For I have heard the defamation of many,
> alarm on every side,
> As they scheme together against me—
> they have plotted to take my life.

Is the suppliant being overly gloomy? Verse 13 argues not. The opening clause carries over into the second colon; "defamation of many" and "alarm on every side" are parallel objects of the verb. The suppliant hears the defamation of many people on all sides, and this causes alarm, because it may result in conviction for wrongdoing. We could take vv. 13a–b and 13c–d as separate sentences, but I have rather reckoned that they repeat the enjambment structure of v. 11. The first colon thus continues the description of people's scheming against the

---

11. The line as a whole works *abcb'a'*, "neighbors" pairing with "foes" and "very much" with "all."

supplicant, with "together" (*yaḥad*) corresponding to "many," "on every side" adding further emphasis to the way forces are combining, and the closing "against me" making explicit what is implicit in v. 13a–b. The last colon then also makes explicit the deathly implications of all this. "Alarm on every side" may be a proverbial saying: it becomes a key phrase in Jeremiah (see Jer. 6:25; 20:3–4, 10; 46:5; 49:29; cf. also Lam. 2:22).

31:14–20. After the lament the suppliant reverts to the kind of stance that characterized vv. 1–5a. Declarations of trust in vv. 14–15a and 19–20 thus bracket further pleas, using the imperative (vv. 15b–16), the cohortative (v. 17a), and the jussive (vv. 17b–18). Those correspond to the three directions of a lament, regarding Yhwh's action, the suppliant's experience, and the actions of other people. Compared with the actual lament in vv. 9–13, then, "I" has rather little prominence. Unusually, the section begins with four tricola: a declaration of trust, an imperative plea, a cohortative and jussive plea, and a further jussive plea. Each of these tricola closes with a short, two-word colon. The section concludes with two double bicola, expressing the suppliant's further trusting conviction.

> ¹⁴But I—I have trusted in you, Yhwh;
> I have said, You are my God.
> ¹⁵ᵃMy times are in your hand;

In this opening statement of *trust, "I" is thus indeed initially prominent. The three cola become shorter and shorter. If the suppliant has been accused of seeking help from other gods, the emphatic declaration of personal trust in Yhwh counters that. The first two cola are parallel in being verbal statements that say the same thing in different words. The third is then a noun clause expressing the content of the suppliant's trust. To put it another way, the second colon develops the declaration that the suppliant trusts in *Yhwh* as opposed to anyone else. The third develops the declaration that the suppliant *trusts* in Yhwh as opposed to being unsure about whether it is possible to do so. The only preceding reference in the Psalter to "times" has concerned times of pressure (9:9 [10]; 10:1), and such a significance fits here (though Tg interprets as "times of my rescue"). The suppliant is affirming that times of pressure such as the ones this psalm reflects are under Yhwh's control.

> ¹⁵ᵇSave me from the hand of my enemies, from my pursuers;
> ¹⁶shine your face on your servant;
> deliver me, out of your commitment.

On the basis of that declaration of trust, the second tricolon moves to plea. The first colon makes the basic point: the suppliant asks to be rescued from enemies who are in pursuit. The second participle makes the first more concrete: it indicates the way the enemies are causing trouble. Verse 16 then goes behind the plea. Verse 16a does so by speaking of the attitude of *face that issues in an act of rescue. The third colon parallels the more everyday verb "rescue" (*nāṣal*) with the more theological verb *deliver but then buttresses the plea in a different way by appealing to Yhwh's *commitment.

> ¹⁷Yhwh, may I not be shamed, because I have called on you;
> may the faithless be shamed,
> may they go wailing to Sheol.

The third tricolon expresses the plea in first-person and in third-person terms. While the suppliant might be asking not to experience the shame of not having one's prayer answered, in the context shame is more likely the experience threatened by the enemies' act itself. They accuse the suppliant of shameful deeds such as praying to another God, and the suppliant asks for deliverance from that threatened shame. Calling on Yhwh and having Yhwh respond will itself disprove the enemies' accusations, since Yhwh would hardly respond if the suppliant were indeed one who prayed to other gods. The situation is one in which there has to be shame somewhere: either the suppliant or the enemies are *faithless people. Thus the converse of a plea not to be shamed is a plea that the enemies may have that experience as their accusations are shown to be false. Likewise, the situation is one that must generate death somewhere. They are accusing him of acts that carry the death penalty. If their accusations are proved false, they will make themselves liable to the death penalty.

> ¹⁸Lying lips must be silenced,
> that speak assertively against the faithful,
> with pride and contempt.

The fourth tricolon takes further that plea about the enemies. Here the first colon makes a complete statement, the second qualifies the subject of the statement, and the third further qualifies that. The line characterizes the enemies' speech in four ways: It is *false. It is assertive or excessive (*'ātāq*): the word suggests advancing boldly and freely. It is proud, *lofty, majestic, and impressive. It is contemptuous (the noun *bûz*). It does not care either for the rights of the suppliant or for the community it is deceiving.

> ¹⁹How much good you have had,
>   that which you have hidden away for people who revere you,
> Which you have done for people who rely on you,
>   before human beings.

A double bicolon (v. 19) then makes a transition to a further statement of confidence. Initially the focus shifts to grounds for trusting God that lie in the past. The psalm thus continues to invite comparison with Ps. 22, where the suppliant contrasts present experience and both national past and personal past (see 22:4–5, 9–10 [5–6, 10–11]). In the past for people such as the suppliant, Yhwh has already stored up *good. Indeed, Yhwh has already done such good for such people. The middle two cola are parallel: In the past Yhwh has stored up and done good for people who *revered and *relied on Yhwh. The opening colon leads into that statement, and the last colon gives it further emphasis: anyone could see this expression of goodness. So present experience of bad will not have the last word.

> ²⁰You protect them securely in your presence
>   from human plots.
> You hide them in a shelter
>   from contentious tongues.

If v. 20 had then asked why that was not happening now, it would have been closer to Ps. 22, but instead the suppliant takes Yhwh's past acts as reliable clues to Yhwh's present acts. The past acts produce a generalization about Yhwh's activity. The two lines are exactly parallel in structure and in meaning, and we might take them as two long parallel cola.[12] The first line's additional reference to Yhwh's presence or face underlines the personal nature of the protection Yhwh provides. It issues from the fact that Yhwh's *face turns toward the person in need (cf. v. 16). The general declaration relates to the particular circumstances that the psalm has described and in substance represents a reaffirmation of the trust expressed in vv. 1–5a.

31:21–24. Once again the psalm makes a transition to statements declaring that Yhwh has responded to the plea, as happened in vv. 5b–8. It then finally invites other people to share in the conviction the suppliant has received.

---

12. Each comprises a second-person singular yiqtol verb (one hiphil, one qal) with a third-person plural suffix, a *b* expression, and a *mē* expression introducing a construct phrase.

> ²¹Yhwh be worshipped,
>   because he has shown the wonder of his commitment to me
>   as a city besieged.

The participle "[be] *worshipped" recalls 18:46 [47], from the end of a testimony uttered when the suppliant has *seen* Yhwh's answer, and also 28:6, where the suppliant has so far only *heard* it, as is the case here. In the suppliant's experience, Yhwh's doing a wonder still lies in the future, but it is actual in Yhwh's decision-making, and so the psalm again speaks of it as already performed. In this psalm one can see how the process of internal and external argument traced in vv. 9–20 has brought the suppliant through the facing of tough realities but has also set alongside them reasons for trust, and this makes newly possible the kind of affirmation that vv. 5b–9 already made. Indeed, it generates an extraordinary form of this affirmation, for "wonders" are usually God's great acts for the people, not acts for ordinary individuals (see 9:1 [2], which uses the niphal participle, much the most common form of *pālā'*). It is as if the suppliant were a city besieged and about to fall, but Yhwh has miraculously rescued it.

> ²²I—I had said in my alarm,
>   I am cut off from before your eyes.
>   But on the contrary, you listened to the sound of my plea for grace
>   when I cried for help to you.

The testimony-like recollection continues, going backward through the story in the manner of Ps. 30. After the account of the (promised) deliverance comes the account of the need, the prayer, and the response to the prayer, though not in that order. First, there was the sense of being lost (v. 22a–b). The verb *gāraz* comes only here, but it has similar meaning to *gāzar*, which suggests being cut off from Yhwh's hand or activity (88:5 [6]) and therefore finished (cf. Lam. 3:54; Ezek. 37:11). Here the suppliant felt similarly cut off from Yhwh's sight, invisible to God, with the same results, yet had gone in for something like the contradiction that appears in 22:1 [2], and even though feeling cut off from God's attention had *cried for help to God (the verb in 30:2 [3]). The psalm indeed incorporates a "yet," but it is a "yet" about God, not about the suppliant's own prayer. "But on the contrary" (*'ākēn*) thus contrasts reality with what someone had earlier said inside, or had thought (e.g., Job 32:8; Isa. 49:4).[13] When I cried for help, "you listened"; this is the characteristic joyful realization toward the end of a prayer

13. See BDB.

psalm: see (e.g.) 6:8, 9 [9, 10]; 22:24 [25]; 28:6 (where "plea for *grace" also comes).

> ²³Dedicate yourselves to Yhwh, all his committed ones;
> Yhwh guards the true,
> but abundantly requites the one who acts with pride.

The closing lines turn from thanksgiving to Yhwh such that other worshippers overhear, to overt addressing of other worshippers. This begins with a challenge about their attitude to Yhwh. The experience to which the suppliant testifies is grounds for urging other people who are *committed to Yhwh to *dedicate themselves to Yhwh. (This might seem tautologous, but the implication will be that they are committed to Yhwh by virtue of being members of Yhwh's people, and they are urged to make that commitment a reality in this way.) The experience of the one justifies a challenge to all. It illustrates a generalization about Yhwh that the rest of v. 23 expounds. The second colon parallels the first, again putting the point positively and characterizing dedication as involving being *true—in the context, true to Yhwh. "Yhwh guards" thus provides the basis for the exhortation "dedicate yourself." But the second and third cola more directly and systematically link together as positive and negative.[14]

> ²⁴Be strong; your heart may take courage,
> all you who are waiting for Yhwh.

The final line comprises a different form of exhortation. It concerns the way people relate to life rather than to God. Or rather, it urges a certain attitude to life on the basis of another aspect of a relationship with God. That emerges in the further generalization in the closing colon. The people addressed are "all who wait for Yhwh." The psalm testifies to a past *waiting in anticipation of *hearing* a response, and to a continued waiting in anticipation of *seeing* a response; once more the "all" invites the community as a whole into the same stance. The implication is that waiting for Yhwh is the key to strength and courage of heart, because waiting for Yhwh implies the certainty that Yhwh is going to act. One might again compare Isa. 40:28–31, noted in connection with v. 10b, though the words are different, and also Isa. 41:6. But the line as a whole is especially close to Ps. 27:14 (see the comments).

---

14. The subject of both cola is "Yhwh," so that the other two words in the second colon have four words to balance them in the third. A piel participle balances the qal participle in the second, but it is also given extra emphasis by the "abundantly." Then singular "one who acts with pride/*loftiness" (see v. 18) balances plural "the true."

Theological Implications

"Psalm 31 is the model of prayer that is confident of being heard"[15]—not because the suppliant has such great faith but because of the one the suppliant trusts in.[16] It is an example of a prayer that needs to be prayed twice. That might be because it has received no answer. It might be because the actual situation stays the same—and thus gets worse. Or it might be because this is required by the complexity of the tale that needs telling, or the depth of the feelings that need expressing, or the greatness of the God who needs to be acknowledged. So one statement is insufficient. Perhaps it is the confidence expressed in vv. 5b–8 that makes it possible and necessary to do the lamenting in vv. 9–13 and to pray the prayer in vv. 14–20.

In Luke 23:46, Jesus uses v. 5a to express trust as he accepts his imminent death. It is therefore important to note that in the psalm, one entrusts one's spirit to God not merely in light of life's imminent end but also in light of the conviction that life will continue. Jesus likewise knew he was to receive his spirit back; he was not giving it up forever. In other words this is not a statement that simply accepts the end of life, but one that also works with the fact that God can and will continue to give us life. Thus "Into your hands I entrust my spirit" (v. 5a) and "My times are in your hand" (v. 15a) are two ways of saying the same thing.[17] Further, the psalm is not one that provides only Jesus with words for prayer. When Pope John Paul II visited Yad Vashem in 2000, he began and ended his address with Ps. 31:12b–14 and commented, "Here . . . we are overcome by the echo of the heart-rending laments of so many." But we know that "evil will not have the last word. Out of the depths of pain and sorrow, the believer's heart cries out: 'I trust in you, O Lord; I say, "You are my God." ' "[18]

---

15. Kraus, *Psalms*, 1:365.
16. Mays, *Psalms*, 143.
17. Schaefer, *Psalms*, 77.
18. http://www.vatican.va/holy_father/john_paul_ii/travels/. Follow the link "Jubilee Pilgrimage to the Holy Land" under 2000 and click "Visit to the Yad Vashem Museum." See also John C. Edres, "Psalms and Spirituality in the 21st Century," *Int* 56 (2002): 143–54.

Psalm 32
When Suffering Issues from Sin

Translation

David's. Instruction.

¹The good fortune of the one whose rebellion is carried,
  whose failure is covered over!ᵃ
²The good fortune of the person
  for whom Yhwh does not count waywardness,
  and in whose spirit there is no deceit!

³When I kept quiet, my limbs wasted
  through my anguish all day long.
⁴For day and night
  your hand was heavy on me.
My strength wanedᵇ
  as in the summer heat. (Rise)
⁵I acknowledgedᶜ my failure to you, did not cover over my wrongdoing;

   a. Lit., "who is carried [as to] rebellion, . . . covered over [as to] failure." For the sake of rhyme, the spelling of *nĕśûy* from *nāśaʾ* (as if it came from *nāśâ*) is assimilated to that of *kĕsûy*.
   b. Lit., "my moisture turned"—though *lāšād* comes only here and in Num. 11:8 and is of uncertain meaning.
   c. Lit., "I caused you to know." The hiphil yiqtol *ʾôdîʿăkā* makes for a comparison with *ʾôdeh* ("I will confess") in the next line, but the context suggests the first yiqtol must refer to a past act, the same act then referred to by a qatal in the parallel clause (see the interpretation of Ps. 18). Verse 4 has also illustrated this pairing of tenses. In that case one could take the yiqtol *tikbad* as having a past imperfect meaning, but in light of v. 5 that, too, may also be a simple past.

I said, "I will confess my rebellions to Yhwh,"
and you did carry^d my sinful wrongdoing.^e (Rise)
⁶Therefore every committed person should plead with you
when he is found,
Yes,^f when he is overwhelmed, by mighty waters;
they will not reach him.
⁷You are a shelter for me;
you preserve me from distress;
with shouts of rescue you surround me.

⁸I will instruct you and teach you^g in the way you should go;
I will counsel you—my eye is upon you.^h

⁹Do not be like a horse or a mule,
without insight,
Whose advanceⁱ must be curbed^j with bridle and bit,
or it will not come near you.^k
¹⁰There are many pains for the faithless,^l
but the person who trusts in Yhwh—commitment surrounds him.
¹¹Joy in Yhwh,
rejoice, faithful people,
resound, all you upright of heart.

Interpretation

The psalm is a thanksgiving or testimony, whose nature is thus to bring home in public worship the implications for other people of what

d. The "did carry" represents the fact that the pronoun appears: "*You* carried."

e. EVV render *ʿāwōn* as "guilt" here instead of by a term such as "iniquity" that they have used in vv. 2 and 5; NJPS uses "guilt" throughout, which is more consistent. I have reckoned that NJPS is right that the word here likely has the same meaning as earlier but that like the words used in parallelism with it, *ʿāwōn* more likely refers primarily to the worshipper's act, which is described in the three different ways analyzed in connection with vv. 1–2.

f. For the meaning of *raq*, cf. 91:8 with the comment in *HALOT*; also KJV. For possible emendations of this elliptical verse, see (e.g.) A. S. van der Woude, "Zwei alte cruces im Psalter," in *Studies on Psalms*, by B. Gemser et al., OtSt 13 (Leiden: Brill, 1963), 131–36.

g. The simple *w* links two verbs that refer to the same act rather than being sequential.

h. I take this as a noun clause, though it is usually taken as a circumstantial clause, "my eye [being] upon you" (e.g., *TTH* 161.1).

i. I take *ʿedyô* as a noun *ʿădî* from *ʿādâ* I, not *ʿādâ* II; cf. George Castellino, "Psalm xxxii 9," *VT* 2 (1952): 37–42—though he emends to turn the word into a verb. A. A. Macintosh ("A Third Root עדה in Biblical Hebrew?" *VT* 24 [1974]: 454–73) derives it from *ʿādâ* III, meaning "speed."

j. Lit., "[is] for curbing" (see *TTH* 204).

k. Lit., "There is no coming near you."

l. Rather than "Many are the pains . . ."; see JM 141b.

Yhwh has done for the worshipper. This particular testimony has two distinctive features. First, the topic of the testimony is a particular form of deliverance, the experience of forgiveness and release that came from owning up to sin after attempting to deny it. Second, the didactic element in the testimony is especially marked. Thus the psalm starts with a generalization concerning the implications for other people of the worshipper's experience (vv. 1–2), and only subsequently goes on to recount that experience (vv. 3–5), then reaffirms its significance (vv. 6–7). Less expectedly, a word from Yhwh to the worshipper follows (v. 8). The psalm closes as it began, with further didactic generalizations and with explicit exhortation to wisdom and invitation to other people to rejoice in Yhwh, on the basis of what this testimony implies (9–11).

> David's. Instruction.

Heading. See glossary. On this first occurrence in the Psalter, it is tempting to link *instruction with the occurrence of the verb *śākal* (hiphil) in v. 8. Like many other terms in the headings, such as *composition, "instruction" could apply to many more psalms than the ones actually so labeled, but in this instance at least, it draws attention to the fact that the psalm is designed to offer God-given enlightenment on a relationship with God and on the way to pray. That fits with the instructional tone of vv. 1–2 and 8–10. If one wished to imagine David praying it, then his eventual confession after his affair with Bathsheba and his murder of Uriah would make a telling context.

32:1–2. The two opening lines of generalization are parallel, and each is also internally parallel. Although such generalizations have a natural place in a thanksgiving psalm as it brings home its implications for other believers, such psalms more commonly begin with the worshipper's personal declaration or with an invitation to other people to join in praise (Pss. 73 and 92 are exceptions). These two lines are also distinctive for taking the form of proverbs (cf. 1:1).

> ¹The good fortune of the one whose rebellion is carried,
>   whose failure is covered over!

The two short cola about *good fortune offer two descriptions of the nature of sin and forgiveness. Sin is like *rebellion against an authority, or *failure to achieve a target one has aimed at or should have aimed at. Forgiveness involves carrying that rebellion (perhaps the implication is that it is too heavy for the rebel to do so), accepting the cost of it in oneself and thus not letting it destroy the relationship (see 25:18).

That is obviously a hugely humble act for an authority. Or forgiveness involves covering a person's shortcoming (cf. 85:2 [3]) so that it does not appear in a record sheet (contrast Neh. 4:5 [3:37]) or does not cause public shame (cf. Prov. 12:16) or is not a subject of public outcry (contrast Ezek. 24:8). That involves some unexpected concern for the person who has failed (cf. Prov. 10:12; 11:13; 17:9). No wonder, then, that the psalm comments on the good fortune of the person who has this experience. And how extraordinary that it declares the good fortune not of the faithful person (like Ps. 1) but of the faithless person, not of the torah-keeper but the torah-breaker.[1]

> ²The good fortune of the person
> for whom Yhwh does not count waywardness,
> and in whose spirit there is no deceit!

Verse 2 then begins with two cola (or one long colon) comprising a parallel declaration to those in v. 1 and offering yet another image for sin and forgiveness. Sin is also *waywardness; forgiveness involves Yhwh not counting the wrong deeds we do. Perhaps Yhwh simply does not think about them but puts them out of mind, leaves them out of account. Perhaps Yhwh even declines to view them as wrongdoing, makes excuses for us, or treats them as uncharacteristic mistakes. Between them, the pairs of three terms in vv. 1–2b "specify the full dimensions of human evil" but also "indicate the completeness of the divine deliverance from evil which makes happiness possible."[2] Verse 2a–b would thus make a satisfactory complete line, though rhythmically an odd one. An unexpected further colon turns out to bring the line to a more telling conclusion. Verse 2c is in fact parallel to v. 2b and thus makes vv. 1–2 comprise four parallel statements about "good fortune," but v. 2c makes a new point about the person who is so fortunate, a point that will be crucial to the psalm that now unfolds.

In speaking of deceit, v. 2c is hardly suggesting that the person of good fortune must be clear of deceit in the whole of life, which would be hard to reconcile with the acknowledgment of rebellion, failure, and wrongdoing. Rather, the worshipper is declaring that there needs to be the kind of openness in relationships that acknowledges those realities rather than trying to deceive anyone about them. Good fortune requires the divine love that carries, covers over, and declines to count. But it also requires the human openness that declines to try to deceive. This openness needs to operate toward other people and God. On the one hand,

1. Spurgeon, *Treasury of David*, 2:81.
2. Craigie, *Psalms 1–50*, 266.

"deceit" (*rĕmiyyâ*) usually suggests falsehood in relation to other people (52:4 [6]; 120:2–3; Mic. 6:12), and one can imagine that the worshipper's rebellion, failure, and wrongdoing could have involved such falsehood in relationship with other members of the community, deceit of the kind the psalms often attack. The cover-up of sin that the psalm will go on to describe would also involve such deception. But on the other hand, the psalm will also acknowledge an attempt to avoid owning up to God about sin, and this deception, too, imperils the experience of "good fortune." (Of course, many deceivers do experience good fortune; the Psalter contains much testimony to that fact but still reckons that this generalization is worth making.)

32:3–5. Verses 3–5 give the background to vv. 1–2 and in particular to that extra colon in v. 2. They constitute the account of what happened, which is the characteristic marker of a thanksgiving or testimony. In this sense they are the kernel of the psalm.[3] There was the experience of anguish, the act of turning to Yhwh, and Yhwh's response.

> ³When I kept quiet, my limbs wasted
> through my anguish all day long.

Keeping quiet is not a mark of OT piety. OT piety makes a noise, either in lament and prayer or in thanksgiving and praise. There is something suspicious about a person keeping quiet. It gives the impression that something is being concealed. We do not yet know what is going on here. We do learn that internal anguish and outward wasting accompanied silence. The silence did not put a stop to the outward wasting; indeed, perhaps it caused it. The psalm then testifies to the way soul and body interact. When things are wrong inside, they have a way of affecting our bodies. Only noise can bring an end to anguish and wasting, the vocal protest to Yhwh that the psalms keep modeling or the confession voiced in this psalm. These drive Yhwh to act and thus remove the reason for lament and the cause of wasting. Silent confession will not do, either.[4]

> ⁴For day and night
> your hand was heavy on me.
> My strength waned
> as in the summer heat. (Rise)

---

3. So Bernd Willmes, *Freude über die Vergebung der Sünden* (Frankfurt: Knecht, 1996), 54.
4. Robert Jenson, "Psalm 32," *Int* 33 (1979): 172–76, see 173.

Verse 4 amplifies the point. The quietness indeed led to the wasting, but although this may have come about through natural processes, it also came about through the pressure of Yhwh's hand. It was pressure like that which brought about a terrible epidemic in Ashdod as a sign of Yhwh's rebuke of the people there for the presumption of the Philistines (1 Sam. 5:6–7, 11). This thus marks the worshipper as someone on the receiving end of Yhwh's rebuke and implies some wrongdoing. The second line marks time but expresses once more in innovative terms how severe was the wasting. In the heat of summer, one does not have to stay in the sun for long for one's body moisture to evaporate, and that is the psalm's image for the suppliant's inner and outward withering.

> ⁵I acknowledged my failure to you, did not cover over my wrongdoing;
> I said, "I will confess my rebellions to Yhwh,"
> and you did carry my sinful wrongdoing. (Rise)

After such talk of wasting, anguish, and withering, we might expect an account of a prayer and of an act of God that put the situation right. In v. 5 there comes the beginning of such a turning point in the story. Breakthrough comes because the worshipper turned to God, though this turning takes a different form from what is characteristic of a lament: "I acknowledged" and did not "cover over" but determined to "confess." The two long cola are parallel, the first also internally parallel (we could reckon it a 2-2 line in its own right, but the length of the second and third cola in v. 5 suggests that the first is an opening 4-stress colon to go with them). The three nouns recur from vv. 1–2. So does the verb "cover over" (for which compare Job 31:33; Prov. 28:13), though with some irony. If the worshipper covered over wrongdoing instead of acknowledging it, then Yhwh would not cover it over. Because the worshipper did not cover it over or stopped doing so, Yhwh has done so. *Confess is a familiar verb in a new context, with similar meaning to the similar-sounding *acknowledge in the previous line. Usually we are acknowledging truths about God and God's relationship with us (e.g., 4:3 [4]; 9:20 [21]; 20:6 [7]) and confessing (e.g., 6:5 [6]; 7:17 [18]; 9:1 [2]; 18:49 [50]; 28:7; 30:4, 9, 12 [5, 10, 13]). Here for the first time we are acknowledging and confessing truth about us. Presumably the psalm is referring to some communal worship event when the worshipper made this confession, perhaps accompanying it with a sacrifice. The three verbs for confession complement the three for sin and the three for forgiveness, and mediate between them.

The extra long colon that then closes v. 5 is unexpected and brings the verse to a climax. It transpires that it is not the human act that brings about the move from withering to good fortune. The human act is a necessary but not a sufficient condition for that move. There is no restoration without human turning to Yhwh, but there is no restoration without divine turning to the worshipper. Sometimes Yhwh's turning comes first, and Yhwh hopes this may stimulate human turning (e.g., Isa. 44:22). Sometimes human turning comes first and stimulates divine turning (e.g., Jon. 3:10—though Jonah knew that Yhwh was already itching to turn). The verb "carry" again recurs from v. 1, along with the words that come in the phrase (lit.) "the wrongdoing of my failure." The colon thus resumes the content of vv. 1–2 except that it refers to the single act that supports the generalization enunciated there. The worshipper had to do nothing to gain Yhwh's forgiveness but confess. Yhwh pays the price for our forgiveness in being willing to "carry sinful wrongdoing."

32:6–7. Confession opens the floodgates of a dam; "the waters subside and the pressures diminish."[5] We might therefore have expected reference to relief from the physical difficulties described in vv. 3–4, but these are forgotten in the concern with their cause, which has now been dealt with. The psalm returns to generalization, addressed to Yhwh but meant for other people to overhear. The first generalization works out an implication of the worshipper's experience for people in general. The second works out its implications for the worshipper's own ongoing relationship with Yhwh. The two thus correspond to the implications drawn in Ps. 30 in vv. 4–5 [5–6] and then 11–12 [12–13].

> [6]Therefore every committed person should plead with you
>   when he is found,
> Yes, when he is overwhelmed, by mighty waters;
>   they will not reach him.

First, every *committed person should *plead with Yhwh rather than making the mistake of staying silent (v. 3). The second colon is elliptical, but it is followed by another *l* phrase, suggesting that the verse's two middle cola are parallel: literally, "at the time of the finding, / Yes, at the rushing, of mighty waters." "The time of" then applies to the third colon as well as the second and "mighty waters" applies to the second as well as the third, "mighty waters" being the postponed subject of the finding. The expression thus refers to these waters' coming to overwhelm (cf. the use of this verb *māṣā'*, "find," in 116:3; 119:143).[6] The result of pleading

---

5. Craigie, *Psalms 1–50*, 267.
6. NIVI assumes that Yhwh is the object of "find" and renders "while you may be found," but one would at least then expect the niphal (e.g., Isa. 55:6; 65:1; Jer. 29:14), and the context does not otherwise point to this notion. NJPS more plausibly assumes that Yhwh is the subject of "find"; the idea of finding out wrongdoing is a more common one (e.g., Pss. 17:3; 36:2 [3]) and fits well into the context. The idea then is that we should face up to situations with Yhwh when our wrongdoing has been detected and thus avoid

with Yhwh will be that "mighty waters" may seek and find and rush at us, but they will not touch us (*nāgaʿ* hiphil).

> ⁷You are a shelter for me;
>   you preserve me from distress;
>   with shouts of rescue you surround me.

The implicit ground for that promise is the worshipper's own experience, here expressed as its own generalization in light of the one-time event. The three cola make the point three times, first in a noun clause and then in more closely parallel verbal clauses. Each of these has a second-person singular yiqtol (one poel, one qal) with a first-person singular suffix. The image of shelter takes up from that of mighty waters (cf. Isa. 28:17; 32:2). It is because Yhwh is a shelter that the waters cannot find/reach us. The middle colon puts the point more generally; the word for "preserving" (*nāṣar*) looks rather like the word for "distress" (*ṣar*), which highlights the contrast in their meaning. Then "surround" is again what waters are inclined to do (Jon. 2:3, 5 [4, 6]). The third colon thus suggests a contrast between the threatened surrounding by the waters and the actual surrounding by "shouts of rescue," or perhaps "a great shout of rescue" (intensive plural)—the shout or shouts of Yhwh coming to rescue (*resound). Mighty waters can be a figure for enemies, an imagery that may run through vv. 6–7, and the surrounding shouts of rescue then contrast with the surrounding shouts of attack (109:3).

> ⁸I will instruct you and teach you in the way you should go;
>   I will counsel you—my eye is upon you.

32:8. The worshipper hardly continues to address Yhwh, nor does the worshipper address someone else. While the psalm does imply that this repentant sinner could leap into being a teacher, the "you" is singular, and there is no individual whom one can identify as addressee; further, "My eye is upon you" sounds more like Yhwh's words. So the conversation partners are the same as in vv. 3–7, but Yhwh now responds to the worshipper. Whereas words from Yhwh to assure a suppliant of being heard do not appear in laments where we might expect them, words from Yhwh sometimes appear unexpectedly in psalms of praise such as Ps. 95, and so it is here (perhaps we should expect words from God to be unexpected and to take unexpected form).

In the two parallel lines, the three first-person clauses are all parallel. Yet another trio of expressions follows up previous ones, suggesting a

---

going through the kind of experience the worshipper went through, described in vv. 3–4. But the statement is again quite elliptical.

complete commitment to personal teaching on Yhwh's part, to keep the suppliant on the right path in the future. The earlier part of the psalm has indicated that in some respects the worshipper had not been walking in Yhwh's way. After the wrongdoing and the confessing, Yhwh effectively offers the resources to ensure that the worshipper will not fall into the same mistake again. The closing noun clause makes a different point and thus brings the line to a climax, albeit perhaps an ambiguous one. Yhwh's eye upon us suggests attentiveness. But why is Yhwh so attentive? Is Yhwh being caring, so as to help us along the way the previous colon referred to? Or is Yhwh checking up on us? Perhaps Yhwh does both, and we choose which form of attentiveness wins out.

32:9–11. For the first time the addressees are explicitly plural, in v. 9a and again in v. 11, and vv. 10–11 refer to Yhwh in the third person. I take it that the worshipper thus once again speaks, initially in response to Yhwh's word, but didactically pointing out the implications of this word for the community. The psalm thus closes as it began with the worshipper addressing the people who have listened to the testimony. But the plurals enclose singular pronouns and nouns in vv. 9b–10, which encourage people to see the verses' application to them as individuals and not to hide behind the community.

> ⁹Do not be like a horse or a mule,
>   without insight,
> Whose advance must be curbed with bridle and bit,
>   or it will not come near you.

The exhortation perhaps pushes the ambiguous statement at the end of v. 8 in the solemn direction. The comparison with a horse or mule is unique; the horse is usually a symbol of strength, but the line recalls the general point of that closing section of Ps. 95, warning worshippers about failing to obey Yhwh.

> ¹⁰There are many pains for the faithless,
>   but the person who trusts in Yhwh—commitment surrounds him.

In itself v. 10 is another quite general observation in didactic style, unrelated to the specific content of the testimony, and making the converse point to the generalizations in vv. 1–2. In the context it may also provide us with a clue to the nature of the worshipper's secret failure, wrongdoing, and rebellion. This *faithlessness was the sin other psalms deny, the deceit (see v. 2) of indulging in some forbidden religious practice rather than trusting in Yhwh. Like many other Israelites, the worshipper had thought that this was the key to security, but now knows that this is not so. It produced trouble rather than avoiding trouble. Thus the implication of this testimony is that such faithlessness issues in pains, whereas trust in Yhwh turns out to work. Commitment *to* Yhwh (v. 6) opens one to the commitment *of* Yhwh. That is the way in which the surrounding of a shout that brings one person's rescue (v. 7) becomes the surrounding of a *commitment to anyone who *trusts Yhwh. Further, the worshipper has discovered that unfaithfulness to Yhwh is not the one sin that cannot be forgiven.

> [11]Joy in Yhwh,
>   rejoice, faithful people,
>   resound, all you upright of heart.

That being true, the *faithful can rejoice in Yhwh. The closing line comprises three parallel two-stress cola, each beginning with a second-person plural imperative. The first two refer to the meaning of the sound the people may make, the third to the *resounding itself. The first goes on to specify the object of rejoicing; the second and third specify the subjects of it. As the closing verb tops the first two by being hiphil rather than qal, so the closing noun expression tops the previous ones by its complexity: it has only one stress in MT, but it involves three words and adds "all" to what precedes. Threefold praise matches threefold sin, threefold confession, threefold forgiveness, threefold teaching, and threefold protection.

Theological Implications

Different groups of Christians may take one of two opposed positions about the link between sin and suffering. Some are inclined to emphasize passages of Scripture stressing this link, others focus on passages that deny a link. Both positions suggest oversimplified accounts of Scripture as a whole. Both Testaments allow that there can be a connection. In the NT, Jesus implies the link when he declares the forgiveness of the disabled man who had been lowered through the roof (see Mark 2:1–12), as does Paul in his comment about illness and death in Corinth (see 1 Cor. 11:29–30; Paul actually quotes the psalm in another connection in Rom. 4:7–8). On the other hand, Jesus denies the link in the case of the man born blind (see John 9:3), as the story of Job denies it in the case of Job. The Psalms, too, imply that both perspectives can be true. Many of the laments and thanksgivings in the Psalter presuppose that people suffer without their having sinned (not that they are denying that the sufferers have sinned at all; they are denying that there is some particular sin that has merited this particular suffering). Other laments and thanksgivings, such as Ps. 32, imply that there can be a link.

The friends of someone who is ill do them no service if they behave like Job's friends and insist that the person's trouble must mean they have sin to repent of; this may not be so. But they also do the person no service if they rule out this possibility. The worshipper who offered this testimony had tried to do that, but found it was counterproductive. It made the situation worse. The psalmist "recognises in this [silence] the really sinful thing about his past. The silence was the seed of death in his existence in this past."[7] The testimony is that in the end confession was good for the soul, and also for the body.

---

7. Karl Barth, *Church Dogmatics*, IV/1 (Edinburgh: T&T Clark, 1956), 576.

Psalm 33
The Creator and the Lord of History

Translation

¹Resound because of Yhwh, faithful ones;
  praise is to be desired[a] of the upright.[b]
²Confess Yhwh with the lyre,
  make music to him with the ten-stringed harp.
³Sing him a new song,
  play well[c] with a shout.

⁴For Yhwh's word is upright;
  his every deed is characterized by truthfulness.
⁵He is dedicated to faithfulness in exercising authority;[d]
  the earth is full of Yhwh's commitment.[e]
⁶By Yhwh's word the heavens were made,
  all their army by the breath of his mouth,
⁷Gathering the waters of the sea as in a dam/wineskin,
  putting the deeps in storerooms.[f]

  a. I derive *nā'wâ* from *'āwâ*, but it is hard to distinguish between forms from (e.g.) *'āwâ* (desire), *nā'â* (be lovely), and *nāwâ* (praise). Cf. 93:5; 147:1.
  b. In Ugaritic the initial *l* could denote the vocative, "O upright," and this would open up further possibilities for *nā'wâ* (see *NIDOTTE* on *n'h*; cf. *IBHS* 11.2.10i; Mitchell Dahood, "Vocative *lamedh* in the Psalter," *VT* 16 [1966]: 299–311, see 305). But it is doubtful whether a Hebrew speaker would read it that way.
  c. Lit., "do well [in] playing."
  d. The pronominal subject of the ptc. is omitted; cf. GKC 116s.
  e. Or "Yhwh's commitment fills the earth"; *mālē'* can be transitive or intransitive.
  f. The participial expressions could be taken as clauses, but one would then expect them to have present meaning (cf. v. 5); it is harder to take them as if they had their own past reference rather than deriving that from their relationship with a past main verb in v. 6.

⁸All the earth should revere Yhwh,
   all the world's inhabitants be in awe of him.

⁹For he is the one who has spoken, and it has come to be;
   he is the one who has commanded, and it has stood up.
¹⁰Yhwh has frustrated the plan of nations,
   foiled the intentions of peoples.
¹¹Yhwh's plan stands forever,
   the intentions of his mind to all generations.
¹²The good fortune of the nation that has Yhwh as its God,
   the people he chose as his possession!

¹³From the heavens Yhwh has looked,
   seen all humanity,
¹⁴From his dwelling place he has watched
   all earth's inhabitants.
¹⁵The one who shapes their mind, each one, [MT]
   [or, The one who shapes their mind alone, (LXX)][g]
   is the one who discerns all their deeds.
¹⁶A king does not deliver himself by his great army,
   a warrior does not rescue himself by his great strength,
¹⁷A horse is a falsehood for deliverance—
   with its great might it does not save.
¹⁸No, Yhwh's eye is on people who revere him,
   on people who wait for his commitment,
¹⁹To rescue them[h] from death,
   to keep them alive when food is gone.

²⁰Our spirit hopes for Yhwh;
   he is our help, our shield.
²¹For in him our heart will joy,
   for in his holy name we trust.
²²Yhwh, may your commitment be over us,
   in keeping with the way we wait for you.

Interpretation

Psalm 33 comprises 22 lines, but these do not begin with the successive letters of the alphabet.[1] While the number of lines might be chance,

g. MT has *yaḥad*; LXX implies *yāḥîd*.
h. *Napšām*, "their *person."
1. William Wallace Martin ("The Thirty-Third Psalm as an Alphabetic Psalm," *AJSL* 41 [1924–25]: 248–52) does reconstruct it so that it is alphabetical. Cf. also the comments in Pierre Auffret, *Hymnes d'Égypte et d'Israël*, OBO 34 (Göttingen: Vandenhoeck & Ruprecht, 1981), 72–73.

since other psalms have 21 or 23 lines, worshippers familiar with prayers such as Lam. 5 (cf. also Prov. 2) might assume that the form suggests comprehensive teaching on the praise of Yhwh, in the form of an act of praise. The opening follows the form of a hymn in comprising a bidding to praise (vv. 1–3) and reasons for praise (vv. 4–7). There follows another, indirect bidding to praise (v. 8) followed by further reasons, occupying the bulk of the rest of the psalm (vv. 9–19). The close is a declaration of trust and a prayer (vv. 20–22). Thus this is a "song about God," who is mentioned in almost every line "until the last line when he is finally addressed."[2] The more the psalm goes on, the less it sticks by the strict form of a hymn, though that is true of many examples of the genre, and this may be because it is also focusing on achieving the 22-verse total. It has sufficient links with other parts of the OT for Alfons Deissler to speak of it as having an anthological character.[3]

It has no heading, though LXX has "David's" and 4QPs[q] "David's. Song. Composition." The experience of David and that of many subsequent Davidic kings would illustrate vv. 10–19 and/or would be a challenge to them: the two great embodiments of David's household in Isaiah's day, Ahaz and Hezekiah, would illustrate both the challenge and the experience. But the absence of a heading highlights the way v. 1 follows on 32:11 and turns Ps. 33 into a response to its exhortation. Psalm 33 also incorporates a declaration about "good fortune" (v. 12) like the ones that open Ps. 32, and closes in a way similar to that psalm with its references to joy, trust, and commitment. In keeping with the relationship between thanksgiving and praise, following on Ps. 32 it offers the ongoing hymnic praise that is given new energy by the experience to which thanksgiving testifies.[4] Commentators have attempted to guess at the way its lines were shared by priest, choir, and people, but there are no markers in the text to tell us whether or how this happened: contrast (e.g.) Ps. 118.

33:1–3. The opening exhortation to praise comprises three 3-3 parallel lines, each also internally parallel to make six parallel cola. The bidding notes how Yhwh is the topic or reason for the worship (v. 1)[5] and its object (vv. 2, 3). It notes its nature, though its reference to *confessing is slightly odd because strictly that term belongs more in a thanksgiv-

---

2. Fokkelman, *Major Poems*, 2:131.
3. "Der anthologische Charakter des Psalmes 33 (32)," in *Mélanges bibliques* (André Robert Festschrift; Paris: Bloud & Gay, 1957), 225–33. Cf. Seybold, *Psalmen*, 137. On literary features of the psalm, see Jean Marcel Vincent, "Recherches exégétiques sur le Psaume xxxiii," *VT* 28 (1978): 442–54.
4. See further Gerald H. Wilson, "The Use of 'Untitled' Psalms in the Hebrew Psalter," *ZAW* 91 (1985): 404–13, see 405–7.
5. Cf. the use of *b* after *rānan* (piel) in (e.g.) 20:5 [6]. Qimchi infers that God is the only proper cause for resounding and praise.

ing/testimony psalm. On the other hand, its emphasis on sound does belong in a hymn; thanksgivings focus on words, whereas for hymns importance attaches to both noisiness (*resound, *praise, *shout; v. 1, 3b) and *music (vv. 2–3).⁶ The music in turn involves both instruments and singing. Far from implying that the motive and the goal of praise are more important than the means,⁷ the psalm makes no reference to the motive of the praise but typically holds together the goal or content and the outward means. In praise the motives and desires of the worshipper disappear in a concern to put the focus on Yhwh. Music, noise, and reference to the person of Yhwh are equally intrinsic to praise. "We can turn ourselves into a fine-sounding and harmonious instrument and sing the praises of God through all our faculties, both of sense and of intellect."⁸

> ¹Resound because of Yhwh, faithful ones;
> praise is to be desired of the upright.

Verse 1 is a twofold description of the people invited to join in, people who are *faithful and upright. Both terms apply to the people of God because they are the people of God, though no doubt they implicitly challenge people to live up to their name. That is what God has called them to be. Parallel to the imperative in the second colon is a much more unusual formulation: "Praise is to be desired" of such people.

> ²Confess Yhwh with the lyre,
> make music to him with the ten-stringed harp.

Verse 2 then combines the content of the praise with its musical means, bringing together reference to two instruments, the *lyre and then the *harp, here one with ten strings (cf. 144:9; also 92:3 [4]).

> ³Sing him a new song,
> play well with a shout.

The first explicit reference to singing then combines with another reference to "playing" (*nāgan* piel, lit., "touch," i.e., "pluck") and a reference to shouting. In 40:3 [4] and 144:9 the "new song" could be new because it corresponds to something new Yhwh has done, and in 96:1; 98:1; 149:1 it might relate to a new awareness of Yhwh's acting with sovereign authority, delivering the people, and putting down their foes. Perhaps v. 3 is a

---

6. Westermann, *Living Psalms*, 210–11.
7. So McCann, "Psalms," 810.
8. Theodoret, *Psalms*, 1:202–3.

conventionalized version of the latter. Perhaps Yhwh's acts as creator, sovereign, and deliverer always deserve new songs. Perhaps new songs contrast with old "worldly" songs, or perhaps the expression involves metonymy: a new person sings a new song.[9]

33:4–7. The "for" characteristic of a hymn introduces the first set of reasons for this new song. The two pairs of lines (broadly parallel in content though less so in form) expound two such reasons, the general nature of Yhwh's relationship with the world, and the way Yhwh made the world at the beginning. Again each line is internally parallel.

> [4]For Yhwh's word is upright;
>   his every deed is characterized by truthfulness.
> [5]He is dedicated to faithfulness in exercising authority;
>   the earth is full of Yhwh's commitment.

In support of the opening bidding, vv. 4–5 first declare that Yhwh has the characteristics attributed to the people who were bidden to praise, though they also add to these. As well as being upright and *faithful, Yhwh is *true and *committed. Yhwh thus more than matches our best human aspirations. The two lines also nuance these points. It is actually Yhwh's *word* that is upright. Given Hebrew's lack of a word for "promise," the context may suggest that this word of Yhwh's is a declaration of intent about the future, a common meaning in the Psalms (e.g., 56:4 [5]; 105:42; 106:24; 119:25). Such a word of Yhwh is straightforward and reliable. Yhwh's promises do not deceive. In parallelism with that observation, Yhwh's deed is one that fulfills such undertakings: that is the sense in which it has the character of truthfulness.

The second line declares that Yhwh is not merely truthful and thus faithful but is also *dedicated to *faithfulness—enthusiastic about faithfulness, given to faithfulness. The point is expressed in another way by speaking of this as a dedication to the faithful exercise of *authority (lit., "to faithfulness and authority"). Further, Yhwh is not only faithful but also *committed. That looks behind faithfulness to the act of commitment that precedes it. It also looks beyond regular faithfulness to the commitment that keeps going when the other party ceases to be faithful. Yet more, it is the earth that is full of Yhwh's commitment. How might that be? One embodiment of it might be that Yhwh shows a commitment to Israel wherever the people are, in (e.g.) Egypt or in Babylon. That fits the second half of the psalm. Another might be that the whole world experiences Yhwh's commitment, along lines suggested by the Noah covenant (Gen. 9).

---

9. For both these ideas, cf. Luther, *First Lectures*, 1:154.

> ⁶By Yhwh's word the heavens were made,
>   all their army by the breath of his mouth,

That might fit the lines that immediately follow, as well as prompting a rereading of vv. 4–5 as a whole. It was by that word of Yhwh to which v. 4 referred that the heavens were made, along lines suggested by Gen. 1 as Yhwh commands and things come into being, and also along lines characteristic of Egyptian and Mesopotamian thinking.[10] The act of creation was an instance of Yhwh's word and deed proving upright and truthful. In the second colon we might have expected reference to the earth being made, but instead we find reference to the heavenly army, the stars and planets by means of which God exercises authority on earth. Again the line thus prompts a rereading of what precedes. Yhwh's self-giving to faithfulness in exercising authority is expressed through this army. On the other hand, alongside the reference to Yhwh's word the reference to Yhwh's breath parallels the allusion to Yhwh's deed in v. 4. It thus expresses more than the truism that words involve breath. Yhwh's breath (*rûaḥ*) suggests Yhwh's dynamic power, which can mean destruction (Job 15:30), as it did for Tiamat in *Enuma Elish*, but here it means creation. The world came into being by an authoritative word and by the exercise of dynamic power.

> ⁷Gathering the waters of the sea as in a dam/wineskin,
>   putting the deeps in storerooms.

The participles then give us a (partial) account of the creation of the earth. Although the creation of the heavens is described in positive terms, the creation of earth is expressed as the containing of negative forces. The great negative force is the dynamic power of the waters that surround the land, reside in the heavens, and lie under the land, all of which can overwhelm the land with floods when let loose. Creation meant Yhwh containing these terrifying forces by means of the sky and the land. The psalm hints at several comforting images for this containment. Israelites were used to constructing little dams in the wilderness to hold the tiny quantities of water that could sometimes be retained from a winter storm (see on 23:2b–3a); to Yhwh, all the world's oceans are just such a little pond, securely restrained by the shores of the sea. But the word for "dam" is most familiar as a way of describing the "heap" of waters at the Red Sea crossing or the Jordan crossing (78:13; Exod. 15:8; Josh. 3:13, 16); Yhwh's containing the waters at creation was as effective as that.

---

10. Cf. Kraus, *Psalms*, 1:376–78.

Further, instead of the word for "dam/heap" (*nēd*), LXX, Jerome, Tg, and Sym imply the word for "bottle" (*nōd* = *nōʾd*); to Yhwh, containing these waters was no more problematic than filling a bottle (the psalm may be referring to the wineskin-like nature of a cloud; cf. Job 38:37).[11] Or the deeps are a resource that Yhwh keeps in a heavenly closet, under secure control but ready for dispensing in appropriate ways when needed. Providing for the earth and protecting it in this way is an expression of Yhwh's dedication to decisive faithfulness, and it instances the way the earth is full of Yhwh's commitment.

> [8]All the earth should revere Yhwh,
> all the world's inhabitants be in awe of him.

33:8. As praise psalms often do, the psalm issues a resumptive bidding, expressed in parallel cola. "The earth" is spelled out as "the world's inhabitants," and "revere" as "be in awe." Such biddings to the world can be expressed as imperatives, which is more vivid, but the jussive maintains the realistic perspective that the psalm is actually addressing Israelites; it is glorifying Yhwh in their eyes by speaking thus of the whole world (imperatives and jussives are mixed up in Pss. 96–100). As the earth is full of Yhwh's commitment (v. 5), so it is appropriate that the whole earth should *revere Yhwh. On the other hand, succeeding verses will speak of the nations as having divergent aims from Yhwh's, and both possible aspects of the verbs "revere/fear" (*yārēʾ*) and "be in awe/dread" (*gûr*) are relevant here. The nations may choose which applies.

33:9–12. As in vv. 4–7 reasons follow, in four further lines, each internally parallel. But the focus changes to Yhwh's ongoing sovereignty in political affairs. In vv. 9–10 the psalm uses qatal verbs, but they are gnomic qatals.[12]

> [9]For he is the one who has spoken, and it has come to be;
> he is the one who has commanded, and it has stood up.

Verse 9 takes up the language of v. 6 and initially seems to refer to creation, though it would be odd for this to be purely a resumptive point. But the language of v. 9 applies to political events in Isa. 48:5, 13, where the heavens stand to attention—compare Ps. 33:6. We will shortly discover that the qatal verbs of v. 9 continue into v. 10, while the verb "stand" itself recurs in v. 11. Verse 9 is the beginning of a declaration about Yhwh's regular involvement in the world, which manifests the

---

11. Cf. Keel, *Symbolism of the Biblical World*, 215.
12. DG 57c; see further GKC 106k.

same dynamics as the creation. In politics as in creation, Yhwh speaks and things happen; Yhwh commands and things stand to *attention*.

> ¹⁰Yhwh has frustrated the plan of nations,
>   foiled the intentions of peoples.
> ¹¹Yhwh's plan stands forever,
>   the intentions of his mind to all generations.

Verses 10–11 make the point negatively and then positively. "Plan" (*'ēṣâ*) and "intentions" (*maḥšĕbôt*) again recall Isaiah (e.g., Isa. 14:24–27; 46:10–11; 55:7–9), as does the declaration that Yhwh's undertaking "stands forever" (Isa. 40:8). The two nouns are thus common ones, while the verbs are much less common. As a generalization the psalm makes the point that Second Isaiah applies to the situation of the exiles.

> ¹²The good fortune of the nation that has Yhwh as its God,
>   the people he chose as his possession!

Second Isaiah would also be comfortable with the point in v. 12, though it is more an implication of the prophet's words than a thought that occurs there. Here the point is made as a proverbial formulation about *good fortune. The formulation comes as a conclusion (cf. Pss. 2; 84; 127; 137; 144; also 34:8 [9]) rather than the opening to a psalm (cf. Pss. 1; 32; 41; 112; 128). For the first time, too, a psalm comments on the good fortune of a people rather than that of individuals. Even in connection with a people, however, one might expect a proverbial formulation to be capable of applying to any nation. Paradoxically, this proverbial formulation can apply to only one people. That might be so as a point of pure logic: Yhwh could only be committed to one people. The second colon makes the point more sharply. There is only one people Yhwh chose. Talk of Yhwh's choice of Israel is surprisingly rare in the Psalms (only 135:4 otherwise refers to the choice of Israel) but is again more common in Isa. 40–55 (e.g., 41:8–9; 44:1–2; 48:12). There, too, Israel is Yhwh's *possession (47:6). The formulation in the line as a whole is a variant on that of the covenant relationship whereby Yhwh is Israel's God and Israel is Yhwh's people (cf. Isa. 40:1).

33:13–19. The remainder of the psalm's statements about Yhwh expand on the point in vv. 9–11. First they make a generalization about Yhwh's relationship with the world (vv. 13–15; cf. v. 9). They go on to apply that point to political questions (vv. 16–17; cf. vv. 10–11). Then they note the significance of this generalization to Yhwh's own people (vv. 18–19; cf. v. 12). It is the sequence in vv. 9–12 and 13–19 that suggests v. 12 is the conclusion of vv. 9–11, rather than the introduction to vv. 13–19.

> ¹³From the heavens Yhwh has looked,
>   seen all humanity,
> ¹⁴From his dwelling place he has watched
>   all earth's inhabitants.

The verbs are again gnomic qatals. The two lines parallel each other; within v. 13 the two cola also manifest overlapping parallelism, but in both lines one colon alone would not make a complete sentence. Thus in v. 13 the verbs are parallel but the prepositional phrase and the subject in v. 13a apply also to the second colon, while in v. 13b the object applies also to the first. In v. 14 the second colon simply provides the first with its object. Between the two lines the two "from" phrases are then parallel, the one giving a location, the other giving its significance; Yhwh's dwelling place is in the heavens. The two object phrases are also parallel. "All humanity" is literally "all the sons of the human," so that the formal parallel with "all the inhabitants of the earth" is very close, and together these phrases underline the completeness of Yhwh's seeing. The three verbs in turn emphasize the intent of Yhwh's looking, seeing, and watching, coming to a climax with a rare verb, *šāgaḥ* (it otherwise occurs only at Isa. 14:16; Song 2:9). Once more they imply that Yhwh does not know everything by inherent omniscience but is capable of discovering everything when desiring to do so.

> ¹⁵The one who shapes their mind, each one, [MT]
>   [*or*, The one who shapes their mind alone, (LXX)]
>   is the one who discerns all their deeds.

Verse 15 then makes up for what might seem a shortfall in vv. 13–14. They have expatiated on the location, activity, and object of the watcher, but said nothing about the nature of this watcher except that it is "Yhwh." Verse 15 remedies that. EVV take it as an enjambment, but the second colon repeats the point in vv. 13–14 and then looks redundant. More likely the line is a further self-standing sentence, a noun clause in which the resumptive subject is "the one who discerns all their deeds" ("all" recurs again, further to underline that point). The point of the line is thus to add that the watcher is the original shaper, their creator. Specifically, Yhwh shapes people's *mind; that implies the ability to look into it.

> ¹⁶A king does not deliver himself by his great army,
>   a warrior does not rescue himself by his great strength,
> ¹⁷A horse is a falsehood for deliverance—
>   with its great might it does not save.

The point here initially seems unrelated, though vv. 18–19 will make the link clear. Again the two lines are parallel; the first is also internally parallel, and in the second the two cola complement each other in a different way as the second restates the first. To put it another way, in v. 16 the two cola are formally parallel but substantially complementary, while in v. 17 they are formally distinct but substantially parallel. Over the four cola, the elements come in threes. The two lines concern a king (in his capacity as commander-in-chief), a warrior, and a horse (the most impressive piece of military equipment in Israel's world). They concern their capacity to deliver, rescue, or save: in the first line (v. 16) the parallel verbs are both niphal (one a participle, the other a yiqtol); in the second (v. 17) "deliver" reappears as a noun and the further verb is piel. The first line thus speaks of human beings' incapacity to find their own escape, while the second line speaks of the horse's incapacity to meet the need for deliverance. The ineffective means of such escape are an army, strength, and might: the king may have no personal strength or might but has an army, whereas a warrior or a horse has these. Each is qualified by "great"; but none does anyone any good. The striking noun applied to the horse could apply to all. They are all a *falsehood.

> ¹⁸No, Yhwh's eye is on people who revere him,
>   on people who wait for his commitment,
> ¹⁹To rescue them from death,
>   to keep them alive when food is gone.

The link between vv. 13–15 and vv. 16–17 is that the aim of Yhwh's watching (vv. 13–15) is not merely (say) curiosity or a desire to catch people out. Yhwh especially wants to keep an eye on Israel in order to make sure that they find rescue (cf. vv. 16–17) when they need it. People who rely on strength, might, and cavalry do not find rescue, because the key to rescue lies in that watching eye, expressive of divine *commitment. On the human side, the key to rescue thus lies not in the accumulation of those resources but in an attitude of *revering (cf. v. 8) and *waiting. There is a creative tension between these two. The former implies humble submission to Yhwh, accepting whatever Yhwh sends and doing whatever Yhwh says; the latter implies expecting Yhwh to do a new thing, and specifically not to leave us where we are in need, and it implies pressing Yhwh to act on our behalf. The additional reference to sustenance when there is no food makes more concrete the way Yhwh may preserve life in time of war, when people might be under siege or an army might devastate their land and/or consume their supplies, and starvation might be a real possibility.[13]

33:20–22. The hymn ends with a declaration of present hope and future praise and trust, and a prayer for this hope to be vindicated. Such are not the routine features of a hymn, but they are not outside the parameters of the variety exhibited by the hymns.[14] Insofar as it is a three-line sequence in which the worshippers reassert the prominence they had at the beginning, it forms an inclusion with vv. 1–3, though its own nature is rather different from that opening exhortation to praise. Indeed, vv. 20–22 do express the personal attitude that vv. 1–3 did not express as they focused on Yhwh.

> [20]Our spirit hopes for Yhwh;
> he is our help, our shield.

Verse 20 takes up the reference to the community's *nepeš* (*person) in v. 19a, here translated "spirit," and in substance takes up the references to rescue and waiting in vv. 18b and 19a. The *nepeš* that Yhwh rescues can therefore live in hope of proving Yhwh as *help and *shield. The two ideas go together: Yhwh is a help by being a shield. The noun clause in the second colon provides the reason for the verbal statement in the first. Hope (*ḥākâ* piel) is an unusual verb but similar in meaning to (e.g.) *yāḥal* (*wait).

> [21]For in him our heart will joy,
> for in his holy name we trust.

I take the transition to a yiqtol verb to signify a real move from talking about present reality to talking about a commitment for the future, such as often features toward the end of a praise psalm. The psalmist expects people to have reason to carry on praising Yhwh as Yhwh proves a reliable shield and help, and thus to have reason to carry on *trusting.[15] As *holy (cf. 105:3; 106:47; 111:9; 145:21), Yhwh's *name represents the very being of the holy one and thus points to God's awesomeness (cf. 86:11; 99:3; 102:15 [16]). There is a certain paradox, then, in being able to *trust* in this name.

---

13. The pair of lines manifests yet another poetic pattern. Both are internally parallel and together form one complete sentence; although v. 18 could stand on its own, v. 19 could not do so. In v. 18, the first words, "No, Yhwh's eye [is]," apply both to "on those who revere him" and to the parallel expression. In v. 19, the two object clauses (*l* plus infinitive) relate first to death, then to life.

14. See Westermann's comments, *Praise and Lament*, 130.

15. The two clauses are neatly parallel, with a pair of instances of "for," a pair of complementary *b* expressions, and a pair of complementary verbs (yiqtol and qatal).

> ²²Yhwh, may your commitment be over us,
> in keeping with the way we wait for you.

In the psalm's closing wish (v. 22), the worshippers take up the statement of conviction about people who *wait for Yhwh's *commitment (v. 18b) and turn it into a prayer. Asking for this commitment to be "over" us perhaps links with the image of a shield in v. 20.

Theological Implications

Geoffrey Wainwright describes Isaac Watts as "bolder" than John Calvin in following the long Christian tradition of "trinitarian reading of Psalm 33," specifically of v. 6.[16] I prefer to describe Calvin as bolder than Watts in resisting that tradition, which is a good way to express something about the Trinity but risks missing the psalm's own contribution to Christian theology and spirituality. This is a hymn that covers praise from A to Z. Its fundamental affirmation is that all Yhwh's words and deeds are characterized by uprightness, truthfulness, faithfulness, decisiveness, and commitment (vv. 4–5). That can then be spelled out in different directions. Yhwh's creation of the world illustrates it, manifesting there an easy sovereignty and a control of other powerful and dangerous forces, and therefore being a reassurance to humanity (vv. 6–7). Yhwh's involvement in international events illustrates it, again manifesting sovereignty and control over forces that work in other directions and therefore being a reassurance to Israel (vv. 9–12). In particular, Yhwh's capacity to bring deliverance illustrates it, making nonsense of people's trust in other impressive-looking resources, and therefore offering an invitation to reverence and expectation in relation to Yhwh (vv. 13–19). Over against the scriptural texts with which it has close links, Ps. 33 brings out the implicit lessons of the Genesis creation story and declares that the affirmations in Isaiah about Yhwh's involvement in international events are not confined to particular contexts but are standing truths about Yhwh. They are thus not merely eschatological;[17] they chiefly concern not a sovereignty that Yhwh will one day exercise but a sovereignty that God has exercised and does exercise.

---

16. "Psalm 33 Interpreted of the Triune God," *Ex auditu* 16 (2000): 101–20, see 112.
17. Against McCann, "Psalms," 811. Markus Witte ("Das neue Lied," *ZAW* 114 [2002]: 522–41) sees the psalm as concerned with time as a whole, with past, present, and future in their interrelation.

The frame of the psalm suggests an equivalent comprehensiveness about our human response to God. Worship involves looking away from ourselves to an object. It involves the making of music and noise. But when we have seen who Yhwh is, it involves an expression of reverence, hope, joy, and trust.

Psalm 34

Deliverance by Yhwh and Reverence for Yhwh

Translation

> David's. When he disguised his good sense before Abimelech, he threw him out, and he went.

[ʾ] **1**I will worship Yhwh at all times;
  continually his praise will be in my mouth.
[b] **2**My spirit exults itself in Yhwh;
  the weak should listen and rejoice.
[g] **3**Extol Yhwh with me;
  let us exalt his name together.

[d] **4**I sought help from Yhwh and he answered me,
  rescued me from all my terrors.
[h] **5**People look to him and they will shine;
  [w] their faces are not[a] to be ashamed. [MT]
[(h)] Look to him and shine; (Jerome, Aq, Syr; cf. LXX)]
  [(w) your faces are not to be ashamed. (LXX, Jerome, Syr)]
[z] **6**This was a weak man who called,[b]
  and Yhwh listened
  and delivered from all his troubles.

a. On the negative *ʾal,* see GKC 109e.
b. Or "this weak man called" (cf. JM 143i).

[h] ⁷Yhwh's aide camps
    around people who revere him and delivers them.
[ṭ] ⁸Sense and see how good Yhwh is;
    the good fortune of the man who relies on him.
[y] ⁹Revere Yhwh, his holy ones,
    because there is no lack for people who revere him.
[k] ¹⁰Apostates/lions[c] have been in want and starved,[d]
    but people who seek help from Yhwh will lack no good thing.
[l] ¹¹Come, children, listen to me,
    I will teach you reverence for Yhwh.
[m] ¹²Who is the person who delights in life,
    loves days for seeing good things?
[n] ¹³Guard your tongue from what is bad,
    your lips from speaking deceit.
[s] ¹⁴Turn away from bad and do good;
    seek well-being—pursue it.

[ʿ] ¹⁵Yhwh's eyes are toward the faithful,
    and his ears to their cry for help.
[p] ¹⁶Yhwh's face is against people who do what is bad,
    to cut off their memory from the land.
[ṣ] ¹⁷People cry out and Yhwh listens;
    from all their troubles he rescues them.
[q] ¹⁸Yhwh is near people who are broken inside;
    he will deliver the crushed in spirit.
[r] ¹⁹Many are the bad experiences of the faithful,
    but Yhwh will rescue him from them all,
[š] ²⁰He guards all his bones;
    not one of them is broken.
[t] ²¹A bad thing will finish off[e] the faithless;
    those who are against the faithful will suffer punishment.[f]
   ²²Yhwh redeems the life of his servants;
    all those who rely on him—none will suffer punishment.

c. "Lions" is otherwise the meaning of *kĕpîrîm* in the OT, but "apostates" is suggested by the root's meaning in later Hebrew (cf. *HALOT* on *kāpār*, *DTT* on *kāpar*). In this context this gives better sense than "lions" (despite J. J. M. Roberts, "The Young Lions of Psalm 34,11," *Bib* 54 [1973]: 265–67).

d. The verbs are further gnomic qatals, like those in Ps. 33:9–14.

e. For this implication of the polel, see Theodore H. Robinson, "Note on Psalm xxxiv.21," *ExpTim* 52 (1940–41): 117.

f. The verb *'āšam* covers the range of "commit an offense," "be guilty," and "pay the penalty."

Interpretation

Psalm 34 holds together three features, rather like Ps. 33. First, as Ps. 33 utilizes the form of a hymn, Ps. 34 utilizes the form of a testimony (we should hardly call it a thanksgiving, since there is not one line addressed to Yhwh). It thus begins with a declaration of intent and an invitation to other people to join in, and with some account of the way the worshipper prayed in a situation of need and Yhwh listened and acted (vv. 1–6). But this account, the central feature of a testimony or thanksgiving, is brief, and it soon gives way to a focus on generalizations about Yhwh and on driving home implications for the listeners—as Ps. 33 moves away from the form of a hymn. Second, in each case the psalm thus lets one feature of its type of psalm dominate to an unusual extent, and in each case the effect is to put the emphasis on teaching rather than on worship. Here *tôrâ* (instruction) thus takes over from *tôdâ* (thanksgiving); again we note that not one line of the psalm is addressed to Yhwh. Indeed, the teaching comes for a while to focus more on the human attitude that will open itself to Yhwh's act of deliverance than on the act of deliverance itself. Third, this emphasis is underlined by using the form of an alphabetical psalm. Like some other such psalms (cf. Pss. 9–10; 25), the form is not quite regular. Here v. 5 covers two letters, and v. 22 is thus supernumerary in relation to the alphabetic sequence.[1] As before, the teaching covers the subject from A to Z and seeks to "wrest some kind of order and coherence out of the variety and seeming disconnectedness of the experiences of everyday life."[2]

> David's. When he disguised his good sense before Abimelech, he threw him out, and he went.

Heading. See introduction (on "David's"). The heading links the psalm with an occasion when David had fled from Saul and taken refuge with a Philistine king, but then came to be afraid of that king (1 Sam. 21:10–12 [11–13]). Fear is a rare experience for David, who normally is surrounded by others' fear and is a cause of it. In 1 Samuel the king is

---

1. See the comments on 25.22; further H. Wiesmann, "Ps. 34," *Bib* 16 (1935): 416–21; Pierre Auffret, *Hymnes d'Égypte et d'Israël*, OBO 34 (Göttingen: Vandenhoeck & Ruprecht, 1981), 89–91; David Noel Freedman, "Patterns in Psalms 25 and 34," in *Priests, Prophets and Scribes* (Joseph Blenkinsopp Festschrift), ed. Eugene Ulrich et al., JSOTSup 149 (Sheffield: JSOT, 1992), 125–38.

2. Anthony R. Ceresko, "The ABCs of Wisdom in Psalm xxxiv," *VT* 35 (1985): 99–104, see 102; see further Victor A. Hurowitz, "Additional Elements of Alphabetical Thinking in Psalm xxxiv," *VT* 52 (2002): 326–33. Leon J. Liebreich looks at the psalm in light of words that recur ("Psalms 34 and 145 in the Light of Their Key Words," *HUCA* 27 [1956]: 181–92).

Achish of Gath, but introducing the name of Abimelech, king of Gerar, in the psalm reinforces the point, since he was an earlier Philistine king whom Abraham and Isaac also attempted to deceive because of their fear (the fear is more explicit in the Isaac story) (Gen. 20; 26). Readers are thus encouraged to imagine how Abraham, Isaac, or David might have conquered fear by learning the lesson of this psalm, and/or how they might do something different with their fear. The psalm puts great emphasis on fear/reverence in relation to Yhwh, and sees this as the key to deliverance in the kind of danger Abraham, Isaac, or David were in. A more precise parallel with the David story, which apparently suggested the link, lies in the expression "disguised his good sense" (*ṭāʿam*), which comes in 1 Sam. 21:13 [14] in connection with David's acting crazy. The psalm uses this unusual word in urging people to use their good sense (v. 8). It also commends praise (*tithallēl*, v. 2) as an alternative to acting crazy (*wayyithōlēl*, 1 Sam. 21:13 [14].[3]

34:1–3. The initial commitment to praise that characterizes a testimony occupies three lines, each 3-3.

> [ʾ] ¹I will worship Yhwh at all times;
>   continually his praise will be in my mouth.

The two parallel cola manifest neat variations. One is a verbal clause, one a noun clause that takes its time reference from the verbal clause. *Worship suggests a bodily posture, *praise an audible noise. "Continually" balances "at all times," the two words receiving emphasis through coming together at the center of the line.

> [*b*] ²My spirit exults itself in Yhwh;
>   the weak should listen and rejoice.

The two cola form asyndetic statements, though they are related in substance, and we might see the first as subordinate to the second. Reference to the spirit (*person) complements the reference to body and voice in v. 1, while the hitpael of *hālal* (*praise) complements the noun *tĕhillâ* in v. 1. The testimony implicitly addresses the *weak, who are encouraged to shape their attitudes by it; the second colon thus states the object of the line as a whole. It also makes clear that this object is not merely to transmit teaching but also to see teaching have its fruit in joy. Perhaps that is why teaching such as this appears in the Psalms rather than in a

---

3. See Patrick W. Skehan, "A Note on Ps 34,1," *CBQ* 14 (1952): 226. On the effect of the heading, see also Paul M. Gaebelein, "Psalm 34 and Other Biblical Acrostics," in *Sopher Mahir* (Stanislav Segert Festschrift), ed. Edward M. Cook (Winona Lake, IN: Eisenbrauns, 1990), 127–43, see 133–34; Kent Harold Richards, "Psalm 34," *Int* 40 (1986): 175–80.

teaching book such as Proverbs, though the latter does emphasize the joy of the parents of the wise (e.g., Prov. 23:15–16, 24–25).

> [g] ³Extol Yhwh with me;
>   let us exalt his name together.

Verse 3 again comprises parallel cola with variations, like v. 1.[4] Both the verbs are spatial: one speaks of enlarging Yhwh, the other of raising Yhwh. In suggesting what worship does to Yhwh, they thus complement vv. 1–2 by suggesting what worship is as expressed by the worshipper. And the two calls for togetherness in v. 3 complement the two expressions for continuance in v. 1. Praise is concentrated in the body of worshippers as well as spread out in time.

34:4–6. In the proper manner of a testimony, the psalm goes on to speak of an experience of Yhwh acting, which is relevant not just for the person who had this experience but for others. The worshipper was a weak person, imperiled by frightening circumstances, who prayed. Yhwh listened, answered, and rescued. Each of the two narrative lines (vv. 4, 6) works in linear fashion, the first colon's story being continued in what follows. The two lines complement each other through one being in the first person, one in the third, but in content they are parallel. Both comprise three clauses and both outline the worshipper's whole story, or almost do so: paradoxically, v. 6 goes further back than v. 4 (as happened in the second version of the story in Ps. 30). As a tricolon, v. 6 forms an emphatic ending to the recounting of the individual's experience. The intervening line, v. 5, which makes a general statement, is internally parallel in doing so.

> [d] ⁴I sought help from Yhwh and he answered me,
>   rescued me from all my terrors.

Thus v. 4 succinctly sums up the nature of a testimony: I prayed (*seek help), God responded, God acted. The response to a prayer consists in words and deeds, and the second colon thus gives precision to the first in making explicit that God's response was not merely a matter of deed but of word. To judge from the other occurrences of the word "terror" (*měyūrâ*; Prov. 10:24; Isa. 66:4), God delivered from the object of dread, not merely from the feeling of dread (contrast *māgôr* in Ps. 31:13 [14])—though dealing with the former will deal with the latter.

> [h] ⁵People look to him and they will shine;
>   [w] their faces are not to be ashamed. [MT]

4. Here the words come in *abca′b′c′* order; a polel cohortative complements a piel imperative, "together" complements "with me," and "his *name" complements "Yhwh."

> [(*h*) Look to him and shine; (Jerome, Aq, Syr; cf. LXX)]
> [(*w*) your faces are not to be ashamed. (LXX, Jerome, Syr)]

MT makes a statement or promise while the ancient versions suggest a command or encouragement, but both apply to other worshippers the message of the testimony. In substance "looking to Yhwh" is similar to "seeking help from Yhwh," but the verb makes its point by means of concentrated visual imagery. First there is looking (the opening qatal verb is a generalization like those in 33:9–11). That issues in a change in the appearance of the person who looks: by a feedback process, the object of their look affects them. The second colon then again makes explicit something implicit in the first, that this appearance need now show no trace of shame, which would arise if not being rescued implied that they have gone against Yhwh.

> [*z*] ⁶This was a weak man who called,
>   and Yhwh listened
>   and delivered from all his troubles.

In reverting to testimony, v. 6 first identifies the worshipper as *weak, in this context a general expression that need not specifically indicate (e.g.) oppression by human beings in power, though it might do so. Beyond that, the three clauses correspond closely to those in v. 4.

34:7–14. Any division of vv. 7–22 may be arbitrary, but this first half is dominated by imperatives, whereas the second half comprises entirely statements. The notion of *revering Yhwh recurs in vv. 7, 9, and 11. It is a common motif in the teaching in Proverbs, but following on vv. 4–6 it may carry the specific implication of seeking help from Yhwh, since one of the indications of truly acknowledging Yhwh is looking to Yhwh for help rather than turning to other deities. Interwoven with these allusions to revering Yhwh are references to the notion of the *good, in vv. 8, 10, 12, and 14. The good constitutes the pleasant things that make life enjoyable (vv. 10, 12); indeed, they make life possible since they include (e.g.) deliverance from attack. They come from Yhwh, who is good (v. 8). And they come to the person who does good (v. 14). The collocation suggests a link between the theological and the experiential; Yhwh's goodness lies in a generosity that gives good things. It suggests a link between the theological and the behavioral; doing the good thing is a matter of taking the right attitude to Yhwh. It also suggests a link between the behavioral and the experiential; doing good leads to enjoying good.

> [*ḥ*] ⁷Yhwh's aide camps
>   around people who revere him and delivers them.

So revering Yhwh implies seeking help from Yhwh, and it thus leads to deliverance (v. 7). Here Yhwh's aide is the agent of that. In the Psalter, Yhwh's aide (*mal'āk*) appears only in Pss. 34 and 35 (the word comes in the plural elsewhere), in both places with military implications. Yhwh's aide is one involved in the defense of people who belong to Yhwh and in attack on their attackers (35:5–6). To speak of this aide "camping around" people who need defending presumably implies that he is the leader of a substantial host (cf. 2 Kings 6:17).

> [*ṭ*] ⁸Sense and see how good Yhwh is;
> the good fortune of the man who relies on him.

Verse 8 brings the first imperative in this section, with similar implications to those of the statement in v. 7, or implying an inference that can be drawn from it. That is, sensing (or tasting) and seeing that Yhwh is good re-expresses the idea of seeking help from Yhwh or revering Yhwh. If we may press the image of "taste," it underlines the sensuous side to the "good" that the psalm invites people to enjoy. First Peter 2:3 picks up its language to make a point about our inner relationship with God as involving tasting that God is good;⁵ it is therefore important to let the psalm's own statement stand as one about God's involvement with our outward, bodily life. The two cola are parallel in substance though not in form. The second constitutes an exclamation about *good fortune parallel to the imperative in the first (and to the statements in v. 7), and *reliance parallels reverence and sensing/tasting as an attitude to Yhwh.

> [*y*] ⁹Revere Yhwh, his holy ones,
> because there is no lack for people who revere him.

The further imperative makes the point yet again, twice reusing the verb *revere, which opens and closes the line. "His holy ones" (cf. 16:3) restates the point once more, in that holiness is the position of the people whom the *holy one has chosen and taken. Revering Yhwh thus involves behaving in a way that corresponds to one's position as someone brought into association with the holy one. To say that such a person experiences no lack is the negative way of saying that they have every good thing.

> [*k*] ¹⁰Apostates/lions have been in want and starved,
> but people who seek help from Yhwh will lack no good thing.

---

5. On the use of Ps. 34 in other early Christian writings, see Lars O. Eriksson, *"Come, Children, Listen to Me!"* (Stockholm: Almqvist, 1991).

The point is made yet once more in two contrasting statements. On the one hand, for all their fierce strength, lions have been known to run out of food, and because they turn away from Yhwh, so have apostates. On the other, for all their lack of resources, people who *seek help from Yhwh have all they need. "Lack" picks up from the previous line and the promise of "good" from v. 8, while "seek help" reinforces the testimony (v. 4) and makes explicit that it applies to people in general.

> [*l*] ¹¹Come, children, listen to me,
>   I will teach you reverence for Yhwh.

A resumptive exhortation urges people to be open to learning about this reverence for Yhwh that makes Yhwh the one from whom we seek help rather than having recourse to other deities. The exhortation, and the emphasis that runs through the psalm, presupposes that this attitude is not an instinctive or easy one. People are always tempted to reckon that they have to take control of their own destinies and needs and/or to look to resources other than Yhwh. The invitation to "children" comes in Proverbs (e.g., 4:1; 5:7), though Proverbs more often issues its invitation to "my child[ren]" (e.g., 1:8; 2:1; 3:1, 11, 21).

> [*m*] ¹²Who is the person who delights in life,
>   loves days for seeing good things?

Verse 12 might then for a moment hold us in suspense, or perhaps we should infer that motivation is key to the instruction that the psalm offers. The question is, What do you really want? The psalm does not see reverence for Yhwh as a way of limiting human love for life and its good things. On the contrary, it is the key to them. Only here does the OT talk about delighting in life; usually it rather emphasizes delighting in Yhwh or in Yhwh's word or in obedience to Yhwh (1:2; 40:8 [9]; 73:25; 119:35). The Psalter as a whole thus holds these together. The parallel line underlines the this-worldliness of the point. The question is, Does someone enthuse about having a long life for seeing good things from Yhwh? (see the introduction to vv. 7–14).[6]

> [*n*] ¹³Guard your tongue from what is bad,
>   your lips from speaking deceit.

---

6. R. Couroyer ("Idéal sapientiel en Égypte et en Israël," *RB* 57 [1950]: 174–79) notes an interesting near-parallel to this line in an Egyptian tomb inscription.

For the person who responds to that question, there follows the promised further explication of reverence for Yhwh. It is a neat parallel line, with the verb applying to both cola, the object each time a part of the body, and the last element in each colon a *min* expression. Previous lines have emphasized the good, and the antonym has thus hovered in the background. Now it comes into the foreground (vv. 13, 14, 16, 19, 21). *Bad, in parallel with "good," covers both the unpleasant and the wrong and implies a link between them. Bad behavior generates bad experience. At this first appearance, this badness is a matter of speech, and the second colon goes on to make more explicit its nature. Badness in speech is speech that is dishonest. In other contexts one might take this to refer to dishonesty in relationships with other people (cf. 5:6 [7]; 10:7), and 1 Pet. 3:10–12 applies vv. 12–16 in that way. In the present context it more likely refers to dishonesty in relation to God (cf. Ps. 17:1). It is possible to profess reliance on Yhwh but to be turning to other deities in the privacy of one's home.

> [s] ¹⁴Turn away from bad and do good;
>   seek well-being—pursue it.

So one is to turn away from such badness and do good, not following kings who failed to "turn away" from other deities (e.g., 2 Kings 3:3; 10:29, 31). The second colon works out the implication of this, restating that implicit invitation in v. 12. Do you want to seek *well-being for yourself—indeed, not just to seek it but also to give your energy to chasing after it? Turning away from badness and doing good is the key.

34:15–22. The closing eight lines further develop the promises attached to the imperatives in vv. 7–14. Thus these last eight lines are more about Yhwh and less about attitudes toward Yhwh. They also reintroduce the stress on "all" from vv. 1–6: rescue from all troubles (vv. 17–18), protecting all bones (v. 20), vindicating all those who take refuge (v. 22).

> [ʿ] ¹⁵Yhwh's eyes are toward the faithful,
>   and his ears to their cry for help.

A statement about Yhwh's eyes is already implicitly a statement about Yhwh's concern and Yhwh's instinct to deliver. When Yhwh's eyes see the *faithful distressed, that leads to action (33:18–19). The parallel second statement makes that more explicit with its reference to the ears to which a *cry for help comes (10:17; 17:6; 18:6 [7]; 31:2 [3]).

> [*p*] ¹⁶Yhwh's face is against people who do what is bad,
> to cut off their memory from the land.

Verse 16 begins with the converse point about Yhwh's *face. "This is a terrible word. If we believed it to be true, . . . who would doubt that we would go about far more carefully?"[7] To have Yhwh's face against you presages calamity, and the second colon makes explicit something this will mean. Human beings often like to think they will be remembered; if their memory is kept alive, there is a sense in which they are kept alive. We find it a solemn prospect to think of being forgotten, as if we had never lived or might as well not have lived. We celebrate a good life and a good person; we want to forget a bad life, a bad person. Yhwh will see that this forgetting is a bad person's fate. Israelites would expect their memory to be kept alive in their family and on the land that bears their name; the faithless will lose their land and thus lose that reminder of their life (cf. Ps. 109).

> [*ṣ*] ¹⁷People cry out and Yhwh listens;
> from all their troubles he rescues them.

The fate of the needy is the opposite; v. 17 recapitulates v. 15 and repeats from v. 6 and then from v. 4. When people *cry out, they ask for Yhwh to listen and act. The first colon declares that Yhwh indeed listens; the second again reassures us that Yhwh's response does not stop there but goes on to action.

> [*q*] ¹⁸Yhwh is near people who are broken inside;
> he will deliver the crushed in spirit.

Verse 18 turns to people's inner need. The first expression is literally "broken of heart," but the breaking of the heart carries too-specific or too-narrow connotations in English. Nor do the two expressions that come here denote a positive "spiritual brokenness." They rather suggest the overwhelming depression and discouragement often voiced in the Psalms. In modern cultures such crushing can accompany outward success. In a traditional culture it is more likely the accompaniment and consequence of the outer pressure that the psalm otherwise speaks of. It links with rejection in the community. The deliverance the psalm promises is thus the same rescue from troubles of which previous lines spoke. That outward deliverance will also bring inner healing. So when the psalm speaks of Yhwh drawing near the people who are broken,

---

7. Luther, *First Lectures*, 1:161.

it envisages Yhwh doing so in order to act (cf. 69:18 [19]; 145:18–19). The second colon makes this explicit. Yhwh draws near not merely to offer people comfort in their affliction but also to *deliver them from their affliction. Yhwh makes people feel better about bad situations not merely by changing their attitude to the situations but by changing the situations.

> [r] ¹⁹Many are the bad experiences of the faithful,
>   but Yhwh will rescue him from them all,

The psalm continues to make clear that it is not unrealistic about whether troubles come to the *faithful, nor does it assume that it is always bad deeds that lead to bad experiences. It does declare that a bad experience (indeed, many of them) is not the end, because Yhwh rescues from them all (that word also again recurs).

> [š] ²⁰He guards all his bones;
>   not one of them is broken.

In doing so, Yhwh looks after the faithful person at every point. "All" comes yet again. The psalm *does* make extravagant claims for Yhwh's protection.

> [t] ²¹A bad thing will finish off the faithless;
>   those who are against the faithful will suffer punishment.

The psalm also makes an extravagant claim about the experience of the *faithless person. Whereas the *faithful survive and triumph over a series of bad experiences, just one bad experience (or one bad deed) is the death of the faithless. The second colon explains how that works itself out in what happens to people who are *against the faithful, though it does not explain how the exposure of guilt and the paying of a penalty happens. This may take place in a divine court or in a human one. Either way, justice will be done.

> ²²Yhwh redeems the life of his servants;
>   all those who rely on him—none will suffer punishment.

The closing promise summarizes the message of the psalm as a whole. On the one hand, Yhwh *redeems—this word has not come before in the psalm, but it makes the same point as other verbs such as "rescue" or "deliver." The second colon again spells out how that works, by making a contrast with the previous line. Yhwh's redemption ensures that the faithful do not stand guilty or pay a penalty, in any court. The other respect in which the last line summarizes the whole lies in its account of the appropriate response to those facts, that one is to *rely on Yhwh (see v. 8). *All* (that word again) who do this are delivered.

Theological Implications

As a theological A–Z, Ps. 34's one timeless statement is that Yhwh is good. That is not so much a moral statement as a relational one: Yhwh is good in relation to us. That expresses itself in the fact that Yhwh's ears and eyes are turned our way. When we are in need, Yhwh is near, to answer prayer and to do that in two respects: listening to prayer and acting in response to prayer. This answer involves rescue, deliverance, protection, redemption. It brings vindication and makes our face shine rather than being shamed. It promises us the good things of life rather than lack, and promises us a full and long life, an experience of shalom. It also involves seeing that evildoers have the opposite experience.

As an A–Z of spirituality, Ps. 34 presupposes that the life of the holy ones, the servants of Yhwh, the weak and faithful, involves facing many terrors and troubles. It involves an experience of inner crushing. That being so, it urges us to seek help from Yhwh, to look to Yhwh, to revere Yhwh, to rely on Yhwh, to cry for help to Yhwh. It urges us to be honest rather than deceptive in our turning to Yhwh. It declares that one act of God for us draws us into continuing thanksgiving and testimony. These involve the body that kneels and the mouth that enthuses wordlessly. They exalt Yhwh before other weak people and win their rejoicing because they know that this God is also their God.

The Psalter as a whole emphasizes that weak people often do not experience Yhwh this way. Yhwh is often strangely far away and inactive. It nevertheless includes Ps. 34 and similar psalms to affirm that it speaks truth that those experiences must not be allowed to overwhelm. And it challenges people in situations like Abraham's, Isaac's, and David's to live by its theology and spirituality.

Psalm 35
How to Respond to Attack

Translation

David's.

¹Contend, Yhwh, with the people who contend with me,
  fight with the people who fight with me.
²Take hold of buckler and body shield,
  arise as[a] my help.
³Draw spear and pike[b]
  to meet my pursuers.
Say to me,
  "I am your deliverance."
⁴The people who seek my life
  must be shamed and confounded.
The people who plan calamity for me
  must fall back and be disgraced.
⁵They must be like chaff before wind,
  with Yhwh's aide driving.
⁶Their way must be darkness and slipperiness,
  with Yhwh's aide pursuing them.

a. On the *b* see GKC 119i; JM 133c.
b. LXX and Jerome understand *sĕgōr* as impv. from *sāgar*, "shut," which takes the form in the natural way but requires one to read in much to make sense. To refer to a weapon, the word may need repointing (cf. *BHS*). On the form of the weapon, see Keel, *Symbolism of the Biblical World,* 221.

⁷For without cause they have hidden a pit for their net for me,
    without cause they have dug it for my life.
⁸Devastation must come upon him that he does not recognize;
    the net that he hid must catch him;
    as his devastation, he must fall in it.
⁹But my spirit will rejoice in Yhwh,
    joy in his deliverance.
¹⁰All my bones will say,
    "Yhwh, who is like you?—
One who saves a weak person from someone stronger than him,
    yes, a weak and needy person from someone who robs him."

¹¹Lawless witnesses arise;
    they ask me about things I do not know.
¹²They repay me bad in return for good,
    bereavement for my spirit.
¹³I myself, when they were ill—
    sackcloth was my clothing.
I afflicted myself with fasting
    while my plea would keep returning to my bosom.
¹⁴As if mourning for my friend or brother I walked about,
    as if mourning like a mother^c I bowed down, gloomy.
¹⁵But at my stumbling, they rejoiced and gathered together,
    gathered together against me.
Assailants^d I did not know
    tore at me and would not be silent,
¹⁶As the most profane twisted mockers,^e
    in grinding^f their teeth against me.
¹⁷My Lord, how long until you see?—
    restore me from their great devastation,^g
    my life from the lions/apostates.
¹⁸I will confess you among the great congregation;
    among a mighty people I will praise you.

   c. I follow J. Gerald Janzen ("The Root *škl* and the Soul Bereaved in Psalm 35," *JSOT* 65 [1995]: 55–69) in understanding the expression as a subjective genitive, not an objective one, in light of the reference to parental bereavement in v. 12b.

   d. *Nēkîm* comes only here. BDB translates *nēkeh* as "handicapped," but this fits ill in the context, and one wonders why the psalm did not use *nākēh*. LXX *mastiges* (whips) and Tg "those who crushed me with their words" suggest an active rather than a passive connection with *nākâ*. D. Winton Thomas ("Psalm xxxv.15f.," *JTS*, n.s., 12 [1961]: 50–51) emends to *makkîm* to gain this meaning.

   e. Lit., "as the profane ones of the mockers of twisting." In 1 Kings 17:12 *māʿôg* means "a loaf," but that hardly fits here. I take the word as from a second root *ʿûg*, meaning "be bent" (cf. *HALOT*; but I take the genitive as descriptive rather than objective).

   f. Inf. abs. used in place of the finite verb.

   g. *Šōʾêhem* is the only occurrence of *šôʾ*, apparently a m. equivalent of *šōʾâ*; I take it as intensive pl.

¹⁹They must not rejoice over me, the people who attack me falsely;
    the people who are against me without cause glint their eye.
²⁰For they do not speak for well-being,
    but against quiet people in the land.
They plan lying words
    ²¹and they have opened wide their mouth against me.
They have said, "Hurrah, hurrah,
    our eyes[h] have seen."
²²You have seen, Yhwh—do not be silent;
    my Lord, do not stay far away from me.
²³Stir yourself, wake up, to decide for me,
    my God and my Lord, to contend for me.
²⁴Decide for me in accordance with your faithfulness, Yhwh my God;
    then they must not rejoice over me.
²⁵They must not say inside, "Hurrah, our longing;"
    they must not say, "We have devoured him."
²⁶The people who rejoice at my calamity
    must be ashamed and disgraced all at once.
The people who act great against me
    must be clothed in shame and confusion.
²⁷Those who delight when faithfulness is shown to me will resound
        and rejoice;
    they will say continually, "Yhwh is great,
    the one who delights in the well-being of his servant,"
²⁸As my tongue talks about your faithfulness,
    every/all day your praise.

Interpretation

This lengthy individual prayer relates to a sense of being under attack. "We see a great deal of calamity here. . . . Much struggle is needed before the I, relieved, can start singing out."[1] Three times the psalm laments attacks, pleads for Yhwh to act, and looks forward to praising Yhwh as deliverer. While vv. 1–10 could stand on their own, vv. 11–18 and 19–28 lack an invocation and therefore could hardly do so. The threefold structure compares with Pss. 42–43, though this prayer is longer; perhaps it is no coincidence that Ps. 43 with its opening invocation can become a self-existent whole, but Ps. 42:6–11 without an opening invocation does not.

The three sections of Ps. 35 describe attack in a variety of terms. Verses 1–10 speak of physical attack, both military and hunting, though

---

h. The traditional reading *'ênēnû*, "our eye" (e.g., Norman H. Snaith, *Spr twrh nby'ym wktwbym* [London: British and Foreign Bible Society, n.d.], 971), for L's *'ênênû* looks like a correction to match the sg. verb.

1. Fokkelman, *Major Poems,* 2:135.

the latter is elsewhere a figure for the former.[2] Verses 11–18 then speak of personal attack that follows on the suppliant's experiencing some personal calamity. Verses 19–28 speak of deliberate false accusation. If we are to look for a literal situation that the psalm reflects, then we might plausibly think in terms of false accusation precipitated by the suppliant's ill-fortune, and reckon that in vv. 1–10 the psalm uses the imagery of battle and hunting to describe that experience. The imagery of battle suggests aggressiveness and danger. The imagery of the hunt suggests stealth and cleverness. The background of the psalm would then parallel that of Job. If we take the battle imagery literally as our starting point, the psalm becomes a royal psalm, but as a whole it makes less sense.

The references to Yhwh's aide (vv. 5, 6) and to apostates/lions perhaps encouraged the placing of this psalm after Ps. 34: see 34:7 [8] (the only other reference to Yhwh's aide in the Psalter) and 34:10 [11].

David's.

Heading. See introduction. The reference to David may have in mind the time he was attacked and pursued by Saul (see esp. 1 Sam. 24, with David's self-defense there): the psalm would start from a literal understanding of the imagery in the first section.

35:1–10. The first section jumps abruptly into an exhortation to Yhwh to take violent action on the suppliant's behalf (vv. 1–3). It is then dominated by jussives with the same implication (vv. 4–6, 8), interrupted by just one line describing the attacks (v. 7). It concludes with three lines looking forward to the experience of testifying to deliverance (vv. 9–10). Thus vv. 1–3 are all second person, vv. 4–8 all third person, and vv. 9–10 first person (though indirectly).

> ¹Contend, Yhwh, with the people who contend with me,
>   fight with the people who fight with me.
> ²Take hold of buckler and body shield,
>   arise as my help.

The opening imperative lines in vv. 1–3 all have the short second cola characteristic of a lament, and each line is shorter than the last (the third only in terms of syllables), progressively underlining the urgency of the suppliant's plea. The first line is a neat parallel bicolon, each colon using an imperative and a related noun or participle to urge Yhwh to fight, repeating the key words to suggest poetic justice.[3]

---

2. Cf. Keel, *Symbolism of the Biblical World*, 89.
3. Watson, *Classical Hebrew Poetry*, 239.

The second line goes behind that initial bidding to the concrete first act that the suppliant needs Yhwh to undertake in order to get ready to fight and thus *help. On the two words for "shield," see 5:12 [13]; presumably a warrior would not take up both at the same time but take up a buckler or body shield, or a buckler as big as a body shield. To think of Yhwh needing a shield may seem odd, and interpreters suggest that the shield is for the protection of the suppliant. A warrior might have a shieldbearer, but a warrior takes up a shield for his own protection, not for someone else's; the psalm surely includes the idea because it is intrinsic to being a warrior. Even Yhwh does not go out to battle without a shield.

> ³Draw spear and pike
> to meet my pursuers.
> Say to me,
> "I am your deliverance."

The third and fourth lines expand further on the exhortation to get ready for battle. On the one hand, v. 3a bids Yhwh to take up offensive as well as defensive weapons. Again one is hardly to imagine Yhwh taking up both spear and pike at the same time; the bidding is hyperbolic. Verse 3b balances v. 2b, *deliverance paralleling help, but it goes even further behind the opening bidding, back to the word of Yhwh that will precede the preparation in vv. 2–3a and the subsequent action in v. 1. In other words, the suppliant is asking, "Speak to me (*napšî*, *person) to reassure me; put on your weapons; arise; and act to deliver." While the imagery of vv. 1–3 would be appropriate to a person such as a king involved in military conflict, it could equally suggest someone whose life is in danger as a result of personal attack within the community and who is bidding Yhwh to act in warrior-like fashion against such attackers. It is an aspect of exodus faith that Yhwh is a warrior (Exod. 15); Ps. 35 claims that theology for the individual as well as for the people as a whole. "Contend" (v. 1) can be legal language (cf. v. 23) or military language (e.g., Ps. 18:43 [44], "attacks"); it is thus a useful root here in light of the psalm's immediate use of military imagery and its subsequent use of legal imagery.

> ⁴The people who seek my life
> must be shamed and confounded.
> The people who plan calamity for me
> must fall back and be disgraced.

Next vv. 4–6 give four lines of imprecation. Each is longer than the last, reversing the movement in vv. 1–3 and suggesting another way of increasing intensity as the lines unfold. Here the focus moves from the suppliant's need and Yhwh's capacity for action to the attackers' fate.

The lines are not internally parallel, but the first pair of lines parallel each other, and so do the second pair.

Thus each of the two lines within v. 4 comprises a pair of verbs of similar meaning, then a participial phrase describing the subject. Of these verbs, one refers to actual defeat, to "falling back," while three refer to the consequence: shame, confounding, and disgrace. If the psalm reflects conflict within the community, we can see that shame will be the corollary to the suppliant's own vindication and the failure of those planning trouble and seeking the suppliant's death.

> ⁵They must be like chaff before wind,
>   with Yhwh's aide driving.
> ⁶Their way must be darkness and slipperiness,
>   with Yhwh's aide pursuing them.

Verses 5 and 6 then both begin with the jussive of *hāyâ* to introduce a clause describing the attackers' fate. Each second colon makes Yhwh's aide the subject of a participial clause. In Ps. 34:7 [8] Yhwh's aide fulfills the defensive side to the role of protector and deliverer; here he fulfills the corresponding aggressive side. The aide does not fit the image of an angel (EVV) in Christian spirituality, being a strong and assertive figure, as he was at the exodus (Exod. 14:19; 23:20, 23; 33:2).[4] It is a further indication that the suppliant is asking for a personal experience of the pattern of Yhwh's acting at the exodus. The simile of chaff being blown away is a familiar one (e.g., 1:4; Job 21:18), more frightening for people who watched this process during each harvest.

After the simile in v. 5, a metaphor in v. 6 pictures the attackers, disgraced by the community and in danger of paying the penalty for their plotting against the suppliant's life, having to run for their own lives (or is this literal reality, not metaphor?). They have to do so in the dark, coping (among other things) with the slipperiness of the rocky paths through the mountains (cf. Jer. 23:12), and pursued not merely by the suppliant's friends or other members of the community but especially by that divine aide. The picture recalls Zedekiah's frightened and unsuccessful flight from Nebuchadnezzar (2 Kings 25). There is some poetic justice about the picture, too. The attackers have been pursuing the suppliant (v. 3); now positions are reversed. Yhwh's aide "is either our salvation or our doom" (cf. Exod. 23:20–22).[5]

> ⁷For without cause they have hidden a pit for their net for me,
>   without cause they have dug it for my life.

---

4. Cf. Schaefer, *Psalms*, 86.
5. Kidner, *Psalms*, 1:142–43.

In this sole line of lament in the first section of the psalm, the parallelism takes an unusual form; one would expect something like "For without cause they have hidden their net for me, dug a pit for my life." There was no need to repeat "without cause" (the expression could carry over from the first colon) so that the repetition gives the point great emphasis; vv. 11–18 will elaborate on it, and vv. 19–28 will begin by repeating the expression itself. The unusual rhetorical combining of pit and net (placed on or in the pit) also emphasizes the danger the attackers put the suppliant in.

> ⁸Devastation must come upon him that he does not recognize;
>   the net that he hid must catch him;
>   as his devastation, he must fall in it.

In light of the lament, v. 8 then returns to jussives, though it moves abruptly from using the plural for the attackers to referring to one individual, for vividness. Initially the line thus seems not to continue directly from what precedes, but with its talk of devastation ($šô'â$, the modern Hebrew word for the Holocaust) it actually takes up a notch the preceding description of personal disaster. This is to come on its victim in such a way that he never sees it coming and therefore can take no evasive action. The second, parallel colon then does make a link with the preceding line (v. 7), taking up the words "net" and "hid." The plea asks for some poetic justice; he is to fall into his own trap. In imagery these two cola are thus different, though the second explicates the first, explaining how it will come about, so that the two cola form a pair.[6] These two cola would themselves have been enough to comprise a line longer than any in vv. 4–6. But they are followed by a third parallel colon that holds them together and summarizes them, from the first taking up the word "devastation" and from the second the notion of a pit and net into which the attacker must fall. This brings the imprecation in vv. 4–6 to an unexpected further climax with a three-colon line longer than all that have preceded.

> ⁹But my spirit will rejoice in Yhwh,
>   joy in his deliverance.

Verses 9–10 close off the first section with the prospect of joy in deliverance, which in a time of crisis a suppliant regularly holds up before God and the self. In substance they are thus first person, though formally

---

6. They also do so formally, manifesting an $abb'a'$ order: a third-person feminine yiqtol verb with a third-person masculine suffix and a noun followed by a relative clause, then these same elements in reverse order.

they are not, since the subjects of the verbs are "my spirit," or "self" (*person) and "my bones." Again each of the three lines is longer than the last, reversing the movement in vv. 1–3 at the close of that section. Joy and praise will become more and more expansive as the suppliant celebrates what Yhwh will have done.

Verse 9 comprises two parallel cola, with a common subject, a third-person feminine singular yiqtol verb, and a *b* expression. The second makes explicit that in this context the reason for rejoicing and joying in Yhwh is Yhwh's *deliverance. That word picks up from v. 3, which will have been proved true. Although the suppliant has prayed at great length about the attackers' downfall, perhaps it is significant that the object of this rejoicing is not their downfall but this deliverance. The psalm was not looking for downfall for the sake of vengeance but because this is necessary to bring release and reprieve.

> ¹⁰All my bones will say,
> "Yhwh, who is like you?—
> One who saves a weak person from someone stronger than him,
> yes, a weak and needy person from someone who robs him."

The further two lines point in the same direction. Reference to the bones nicely accompanies reference to the spirit. Both suggest the whole person, but *nepeš* may point more to the inner person while the bones suggest the outer, the body as a whole. While the *nepeš* will have escaped the pit and the net, the body will feel that directly. The rhetorical question "Who is like you?" recurs in connection with declarations of the way Yhwh acts to deliver people when they pray (e.g., 71:19; 86:8) and the way Yhwh acted in creation and in Israel's history (e.g., 89:8 [9]; Exod. 15:11; 1 Chron. 17:20). It sets Yhwh off over against gods that could be represented by lifeless images (e.g., Jer. 10:5–7). That is explicated in the closing line with its two parallel cola, similar in structure to v. 9. The opening participle applies to both cola and again makes the point about deliverance or rescue; broadly, v. 10a expands on v. 9a and v. 10b expands on v. 9b. But following on v. 10a, the activity of rescuing is defined as Yhwh's distinguishing trait, the feature that makes Yhwh incomparable. The rest of the two cola identifies the objects of rescue (the *weak, then the weak and *needy, meaning the weak person who is therefore needy). They finish with parallel *min* expressions identifying the kind of person from whom such people need rescue. The closing reference to robbery brings the section to a slightly surprising concrete conclusion. The earlier verses have made clear that the suppliant will not be thinking of a burglar who steals someone's stereo but of a swindler who deprives someone of their land and home, and potentially their life (cf. the comment on 17:4b–5).

The generalization about Yhwh as rescuer will be one that has been proved again by the suppliant's experience; by implication, the out-loud rejoicing and saying will not merely signify the suppliant's feeling of relief but will also give testimony to the rescue's implications for other people, whose faith in that generalization should be deepened by the suppliant's testimony. The rhetorical question "Who is like you?" again recalls exodus faith (Exod. 15:3, 11), so that once more the suppliant is claiming the application of that gospel to the life of the individual, though vv. 9–10 also imply a feedback process whereby Yhwh's exodus-like act toward the individual in turn builds up the community's faith. It is characteristic of prayers in the Psalms to expect that, but this is to look some distance into the future; at the moment the suppliant has reason to be preoccupied with having the generalization personally proved.

35:11–18. The second section works its way toward another plea (v. 17) and a more explicit declaration of how the suppliant will give testimony to Yhwh (v. 18); but in the meantime it focuses on lament at the way the attackers have been behaving. Verses 11–16 thus constitute a vast expansion on v. 7. This lament dominates the second section as imprecation dominated the first.

> [11]Lawless witnesses arise;
> they ask me about things I do not know.

The nature and methods of the attackers become more explicit in v. 11. They are people giving testimony against the suppliant, and as (lit.) "witnesses of *violence" they are doing so in an outrageous, lawless way that aims to end in bloodshed. "Arise" is a verb that can describe witnesses standing to speak (e.g., 27:12, which also speaks of testimony that issues in bloodshed). The second colon details what happens when they arise: they proceed by means of a cross-questioning concerning events that the suppliant knows nothing about.

> [12]They repay me bad in return for good,
> bereavement for my spirit.

The four lines in vv. 12–14 underline the lamentable nature of this by making claims about the suppliant's own conduct in relation to these attackers. While these have some formal similarity to claims to past commitment to Yhwh that a psalm sometimes incorporates as reason for Yhwh to respond, in substance they are different. They speak of the suppliant's past behavior in order to highlight the attackers' wrongdoing. Not only do their claims have no substance; their attacks also contrast with the suppliant's behavior. The contrast concerns grief or bereavement: the grief they now cause, and the grief the suppliant shared with them.

Thus in v. 12 the *bad with which they repay that *good is described as a kind of bereavement that they cause. The word (*šěkôl*) literally denotes specifically the loss of children, often a consequence of war (cf. 137:8–9; Isa. 47:8–9; Lamentations),[7] so that the colon makes a link with the war talk of the first section.

> [13] I myself, when they were ill—
> sackcloth was my clothing.
> I afflicted myself with fasting
> while my plea would keep returning to my bosom.

More generally, the reference to bereavement of spirit (*person) points up the contrast with what has preceded: the suppliant had donned the clothes of deep grief when the attackers were ill. The reference to their illness perhaps implies that it was the onset of the suppliant's illness that gave the attackers the reason or pretext for their action, on the basis of the assumption that this marked the suppliant as under Yhwh's punishment. Donning sackcloth was a way of drawing God's attention to their need.

That was taken further by fasting, another sign of grief; in this situation, eating is too much of a frivolity. The psalm assumes that merely to *feel* sadness is not enough; because we are physical creatures and not just minds and spirits, it would be odd not to express sorrow in (e.g.) abstention from food and thus afflicting one's spirit or one's self (*person). Alongside fasting there was explicit prayer for their healing. The expression "my *plea would keep returning to my bosom" appears only here; it is perhaps a metonymy, reflecting the way one may beat one's chest in prayer (cf. Nah. 2:7 [8]).[8] It may simply allude to the way the suppliant was continually praying (the verb is yiqtol), or it may suggest that for a while the prayer went unanswered and the suppliant undertook further self-abasement on behalf of the people who are now attackers. In the context it is hardly a wish that the prayer may be ineffective, since the next line continues the recollection of a positive stance in relation to the attackers.

> [14] As if mourning for my friend or brother I walked about,
> as if mourning like a mother I bowed down, gloomy.

---

7. Cf. Briggs, *Psalms*, 1:305.
8. Cf. ibid., 1:306.

That line (v. 14) works *aba'b'*. The verb that closes the first colon, "I walked about," raises the question "How?" and is given precision by the verb at the end of the second: "I bowed down, gloomy"—perhaps a reference to dark clothing or smearing with dirt. Similarly, the expression "one mourning" in the second colon explicates the *k* expression in the first (lit., "like [one mourning] a friend, like [one mourning] a brother"). That second *k* expression also intensifies the first, with its reference not merely to one mourning a friend or brother but to a mother mourning for her dead child. Yes, there was great intensity about the way the suppliant had cared about these people in their misfortune, who are now deliberately causing the suppliant trouble.

> ¹⁵But at my stumbling, they rejoiced and gathered together,
>   gathered together against me.
> Assailants I did not know
>   tore at me and would not be silent.

The three lines in vv. 15–16 make explicit the contrast in their response to the suppliant's need. They laughed; then they gathered together. Why did they do that? In explicating this, the parallel colon in v. 15a begins by repeating the verb and then answers the question with its "against me." Verse 15b takes the description further, describing these assailants as muggers who tore at the suppliant like wild animals. That makes this sound like a physical attack, but the further comment that they would not be silent suggests that it is a verbal attack rather than a physical one. They would not stop accusing the suppliant.

> ¹⁶As the most profane twisted mockers,
>   in grinding their teeth against me.

Verse 16 fits with this. They are utterly profane people. They mock a person who is down. And they thus show themselves twisted people. All that expresses itself in grinding their teeth, a gesture of hostility (cf. 37:12) with more threat than it sounds.

> ¹⁷My Lord, how long until you see?—
>   restore me from their great devastation,
>   my life from the lions/apostates.

Two final lines close the section with a plea and with the anticipation of praise. The plea opens with the invocation "my *Lord" and a question about time such as often appears in a lament. As is often the case, the question is abrupt (see 6:3 [4]); here that abruptness means it occupies just one colon, the second and third cola in the line forming a pair. The shortness of the question corresponds inversely to the length of the oppression. EVV's understanding of the particle "How long?" suggests some irony. Usually, Yhwh's seeing is a positive thing (e.g., 25:18–19; 31:7 [8]); like Yhwh's listening, it leads inevitably to action. Not so here, then, and the suppliant wants to know long will that be so—or rather, wants it to stop being so. But "How long?" is *kammâ*, not the usual *'ad-mātay*, and I follow LXX in assuming that it implies something like "When?" rather than "How long?"—"How long until you look?" not "How long will you look?" What will it be like when Yhwh sees, or stops simply seeing and starts acting? The psalm has spoken of devastation as the desired fate of the attackers; here it describes this as the suppliant's current experience at their hands, which is presumably part of the background to that earlier jussive plea. The third colon then provides a parallel object for the verb (another word for "life") and a parallel *min* expression, in *abb'a'* order. The first *min* expression is impersonal, the second personal; for *kěpîrîm* (see 34:10 [11]), the description of the attackers as profane suggests that "apostates" again fits, though the reference to "tearing" also makes "lions" possible.

> ¹⁸I will confess you among the great congregation;
> among a mighty people I will praise you.

The anticipation of praise in parallel cola[9] looks forward to and implicitly promises *confession and *praise (the one verb suggesting content, the other sound), apparently in a great festive setting in the temple.

35:19–28. The third section returns to a variant on the balance of the first, combining jussives concerning the rejoicing of the attackers (vv. 19, 24b–26), supporting lament (vv. 20–21), second-person plea (vv. 22–24a), and jussives concerning the rejoicing of the faithful (vv. 27–28).

> ¹⁹They must not rejoice over me, the people who attack me falsely;
> the people who are against me without cause glint their eye.

The opening jussive (v. 19) begins by taking up the fact that the attackers have rejoiced at the suppliant's stumbling and insisting that it must not be allowed to continue. EVV assume that the "not" in the first colon carries over into the second.[10] But in substance the second colon

---

9. Two first-person singular yiqtol verbs (one hiphil, one piel) with second-person singular suffix, two *b* expressions, two adjectives, all with similar meanings, come in *abcb'c'a'*.

10. Cf. GKC 152z; JM 160q. Structurally the line works *abb'a'*, two third-person yiqtol verbs with a direct or indirect object, and as their subjects two plural participial expressions with a first-person singular suffix and an adverbial qualifier.

has a different meaning from the first. While "without cause" complements *falsely, "glint the eye" is a gesture with some power, rather like a curse (cf. Prov. 6:13; 10:10), and it refers to what the people who are *against the suppliant are already doing, not something the suppliant prays they may not do.

> ²⁰For they do not speak for well-being,
>   but against quiet people in the land.
> They plan lying words
>   ²¹and they have opened wide their mouth against me.
> They have said, "Hurrah, hurrah,
>   our eyes have seen."

The description of the attackers continues in vv. 20–21. MT takes these as two tricola. In the first, the second and third cola balance the first. On the one hand, these people do not speak in such a way as to encourage and develop the *well-being of those they attack or of the community as a whole. On the contrary, the way they speak is characterized by falsehood designed to put down peace-loving people.[11] This general reference will really have in mind the suppliant individually, as is confirmed by the further tricolon in the wayyiqtol and qatal, speaking more directly of the suppliant. The second and third cola again balance the first. The wide opening of their mouths suggests their telling huge lies, and the second and third cola give information on those lies: They said they had seen certain things happen with their own eyes.

So MT. But the exclamation *heʾāḥ* normally expresses joy, and that points rather to these two verses comprising three bicola.[12] The first two cola (v. 20a–b) make a straightforward contrast. The two cola at the center (vv. 20c–21a) make a general statement and then show how it applies to the suppliant. The third line (v. 21b–c) declares the attackers' pleasure in seeing the suppliant's trouble—perhaps the trouble that has already come, perhaps the trouble they anticipate.

> ²²You have seen, Yhwh—do not be silent;
>   my Lord, do not stay far away from me.

Verses 22–24 comprise the psalm's most extensive plea. It is given additional force by the six invocations involving three nouns in the

---

11. I have followed the conventional understanding of the hapax *rigʿê* (quiet people), though it is really quite uncertain, yet supported by *HALOT*'s comment that "to find peace, more precisely to look for peace, should really be the genuine base meaning of the root *rgʿ*." LXX and Jerome assume it is something to do with anger.

12. Cf. Gunkel, *Psalmen*, 145.

three possible pairings: "Yhwh/my Lord," then "my God/my Lord," then "Yhwh/my God." In v. 22 it first takes up the assailants' own verb and observes that Yhwh has also done some seeing—or rather (since they are lying) has done some true seeing. In speaking thus it is also taking up the verb from v. 17. The suppliant goes on to speak of Yhwh being deaf or dumb—*ḥārēš* can have either meaning and the ideas are closely linked, since either implies the other. As v. 17 implied, Yhwh either does not hear the suppliant's prayer or does not respond to it. The parallel colon expresses the point in another way in appealing for Yhwh not to stay far away. When Yhwh draws near, that means action, but at the moment Yhwh fails to do so. The psalm asks for that to be put right and for the proper combination of seeing, hearing, speaking, drawing near, and acting.

> ²³Stir yourself, wake up, to decide for me,
>   my God and my Lord, to contend for me.

If we find v. 22 rather bold, v. 23 is more so. It comprises two hiphil imperative verbs, two *l* expressions, and two invocations, and it could have worked *abca'b'c'*, but instead it works *aa'bcc'b'*. The first effect is to make the exhortation even more bold as the line opens with the two scandalous imperatives (LXX reduces them to one). "Stir yourself" (*hāʿîrâ*) is the only occurrence of the hiphil of *ʿûr* in such an imperative, though the further effect is to make it rhyme with the companion verb (*hāqîṣâ*); the qal and hiphil of the two verbs come together in 44:23 [24]. Putting the two invocations next to each other perhaps mitigates against any disrespect implied by the imperatives, but it also strengthens the plea by underlining the special relationship between the suppliant and "my God," "my *Lord." Where there is a such a relationship, bold pleas are possible. The final element in the line is a reference to the aim the suppliant needs Yhwh to pursue—literally, "for my *decision/for my cause." The latter noun picks up the verb "contend," repeated in the psalm's very first colon. What the suppliant needs is vindication.

> ²⁴Decide for me in accordance with your faithfulness, Yhwh my God;
>   then they must not rejoice over me.

Verse 24 first takes up that reference to a decision by using the verb "*decide" and qualifies it with a reference to Yhwh's *faithfulness, in accordance with the way these two ideas often come together to suggest the exercise of authority in a way that manifests faithfulness or an attitude of faithfulness that expresses itself in decisive action. Verse 24a also announces a theme that will recur (see vv. 27–28). Another double invocation occupies the middle of the line, and the second colon repeats the opening of v. 19. It is formally a beginning to the jussives that will occupy vv. 25–27, but this initial jussive is subordinate to the imperative in v. 24a (we might take v. 24b as a purpose clause, but one would then expect the negative *lō'*, not *'al*).

> ²⁵They must not say inside, "Hurrah, our longing;"
> they must not say, "We have devoured him."

Verses 25–26 develop the jussives about the attackers, first in parallel negative declarations. The opening verb is repeated, but the qualifying expression (lit., "in their heart") carries over from the first to the second. In substance their statements are similar, and they use the same metaphor, though formally they differ.

> ²⁶The people who rejoice at my calamity
>   must be ashamed and disgraced all at once.
> The people who act great against me
>   must be clothed in shame and confusion.

The two wishes, positive in form though negative in content, are expressed in two parallel lines, arranged *aba'b'*. So these characterize the attackers as people rejoicing in the suppliant's misfortune (*bad) and magnifying themselves over the suppliant. The order suggests that the self-magnifying would follow on the calamity (e.g., the suppliant's being found guilty and punished by the community), which would give them the opportunity to enhance their position. The alternative destiny urged by the suppliant contrasts with that. It expresses the reality of shame in a number of ways. It uses two verbs (*bôš*, *ḥāpar*) and two nouns (*bōšet*, *kĕlimmâ*), recycling terms from v. 4. It underlines the power of the verbs by adding "all at once" (*yaḥdāw*), which binds the verbs together and thus combines their force, and it underlines the nouns by picturing the shame as a clothing that covers and clings to the attackers. The total effect is to portray a sharp contrast between the exaltation of themselves and the humiliation of the suppliant that they intend, and the reversal that the suppliant looks for.

> ²⁷Those who delight when faithfulness is shown to me will resound
>   and rejoice;
> they will say continually, "Yhwh is great,
>   the one who delights in the well-being of his servant."

The tricolon concerning other people expresses the contrast in another way. LXX and Jerome take the opening colon to imply that there are people who hope to see the suppliant vindicated, and it might be likely that there were many ordinary people who sympathized with the suppliant's plight but were just as helpless. Rhetorically, however, this psalm like others portrays the suppliant as quite alone, and more likely, then, the colon refers to the delight that will be expressed when the suppliant's vindication comes about. Characteristically, the psalm expresses the conviction that this one-time act of Yhwh's will make an ongoing difference to a broad number of people, not just stimulate gladness on the part of one person that will be forgotten tomorrow. The act confirms the community's conviction about Yhwh and builds up its ongoing trust. People's delight in the suppliant's vindication as Yhwh acts in *faithfulness then turns out to echo Yhwh's own delight in this servant's *well-being, which stands in contrast to the attitude of the attackers (v. 20) and the prospect of calamity (v. 26). Their rejoicing contrasts with the rejoicing that the suppliant prays against (vv. 19, 24). If we are right to infer that their delight is one that looks back on Yhwh's act, perhaps Yhwh's delight also looks back with satisfaction on the fact that the suppliant is now enjoying well-being rather than trouble.

The tricolon builds up its force as it develops. The second colon indicates the content of people's joyful *resounding, in a preliminary description of Yhwh that offers another contrast: in v. 26 they make themselves great, but in v. 27 Yhwh is the only great one. The third colon elaborates on that conviction. Between them, the first and third colon thus define Yhwh's greatness. Whereas the attackers' purported greatness lies in their malicious, undeserved harassment, Yhwh's greatness lies in doing the right thing by someone in need and acting for the sake of this servant's well-being.

> ²⁸As my tongue talks about your faithfulness,
> every/all day your praise.

I take the last line as a circumstantial clause explaining how the corporate rejoicing in v. 27 will come about. The suppliant will be unable to stop *talking about that act of vindication and *faithfulness and will do so every day and/or all day, which will encourage the "continually" of the community's rejoicing. All these words that vv. 27–28 envisage contrast with the words that the suppliant deprecates (e.g., vv. 20–21, 25). The subject and verb in the first colon also apply to the second, and the adverbial expression in the second also applies to the first. Thus only the object appears in both cola, "your faithfulness" and "your praise" being parallel. Yhwh's being faithful is indeed a key topic of Yhwh's praise.

Theological Implications

The psalm focuses particularly resolutely on its prayer against the suppliant's attackers. It thus starts as it means to continue, asking for Yhwh to fight on behalf of one who cannot fight (vv. 1–3), then asking for devastating reversal for the attackers (vv. 4–8), and looking forward to praising Yhwh for deliverance from them (vv. 9–10). It draws a contrast between the suppliant's past behavior and that of the attackers (vv. 11–16) and again appeals for deliverance and looks forward to testifying to receiving it (vv. 11–18). It asks Yhwh to wake up and take action so that the attackers are covered in shame (vv. 19–26), and looks forward to the faithful joining in praise when Yhwh brings this about.

Many of the psalm's motifs reappear in Jeremiah (e.g., 18:20, 22; 20:7, 11; 23:12),[13] reflecting the way such psalmody shaped Jeremiah's spirituality and theology and suggesting the way Yhwh's speaking to Jeremiah affirmed that spirituality and theology. Jesus then explicitly utilizes this psalm, identifying with the position of the suppliant (John 15:25). In contrast, modern commentators are routinely uncomfortable with the psalm. One comments, "It is clear that such an attitude is not identical with Christian *ideals* but, on the other hand, the psalmist lived in the pre-Christian era."[14] Strangely, Jesus was apparently not embarrassed by the psalm and gives no hint of seeing himself as having superseded it, suggesting that once again this is a problem about us as interpreters of the psalm. Neither do christological interpreters of the psalm such as Augustine or Luther hesitate, though of course they do go in for some allegorizing of it.[15] Likewise, the psalm is regularly used in healing rites in Kenya.[16] Nor is praying for one's enemies Christian as opposed to Jewish.[17]

Admittedly, if the battling the psalm asks Yhwh to undertake is legal battling and legal defeat, that may take some of the edge off the stance that bourgeois modernity dislikes. Then "God's judicial activity appears . . . as an alternate form of his aggressive engagement on behalf of right and righteousness."[18] Yet we should not let this reduce the encouragement

---

13. Cf. Terrien, *Psalms*, 311.
14. A. Anderson, *Psalms*, 279. Cf. Félix Asensio's discussion ("Sobre la marcha del salmo 35," *EstBib* 31 [1972]: 5–16). Its starting point is Theodoret's remarks about the psalm being written under the law, not under grace (*Psalms*, 1:216–17), though (as his editor notes) Theodoret is somewhat incoherent in his comments on this issue.
15. See Augustine, *Psalms*, 79–86; Luther, *First Lectures*, 1:165–69.
16. See Philomena Mwaura, "The Old Testament in the Nabii Christian Church of Kenya," in *Interpreting the Old Testament in Africa*, ed. Mary Getui et al. (New York: Lang, 2001), 165–69.
17. See (e.g.) the comments on v. 13 in Rosenberg, *Psalms*, 1:123.
18. Keel, *Symbolism of the Biblical World*, 207–8.

the psalm gives people to bring to God their urgent desire to see attackers shamed. The psalm is an expression of fear and rage that urges God to take action to remove the causes of fear and rage. Christians are rather inclined to ask God to remove the fear and rage from their hearts, but the psalm invites the inference that this would be inappropriate (or at least a second best). The fear and rage can be deep and proper responses to ways other people are behaving. The fear and rage are designed to do something with, not to be evaded. They are not designed to drive the people under attack to action, but they are designed to drive them to prayer. Perhaps if that happens, the anxiety and rage will calm; but this is the route to such calming, not some supernatural act that takes away these proper feelings before they have done their work.

In a sense the psalm thus expresses less-cool faith than many others. Yet it also articulates a particularly consistent expectation that one will be given reason for thanksgiving and testimony, and makes a commitment to offering it. In its own way, Ps. 35 insists on looking in the face two sets of facts, like Ps. 22. It looks in the face the fact of vicious attack and serious danger, and it looks in the face the fact that Yhwh is a powerful and delivering God and surely will act to put down attackers. Thus there is no hint of despair in this psalm, yet it makes clear that the moment for that praise lies in the future, not in the present (even if we grant that looking forward to offering such praise in the future is a paradoxical form of actual praise, an anticipatory celebration of what Yhwh is going to do). The suppliant *withholds* praise now.[19] Praise is an indication of recognition that Yhwh has acted. At the moment Yhwh has not acted. It would be meaningless to praise now. It would not be true to the actual situation. The present is a moment for protest, but the moment for praise will come.

Commentators and Western Christians rarely need the deliverance and reversal the psalm pleads for, except after a particularly partisan book review; but we should not therefore refuse this form of prayer to the many people in the world who are in a less fortunate position, not least because of their treatment by Western Christian nations. Further, being ourselves not under attack, we are urged by the psalm to put ourselves into the position of people who are thus under attack. The psalm implies that if we are not incensed by persecution and oppression and do not want to urge God to put down the attackers, there is something wrong with us.

---

19. Brueggemann, *Message of the Psalms*, 65.

Psalm 36
Human Faithlessness and Divine Commitment

Translation

The leader's. Yhwh's servant's. David's.

¹The rebellious utterance of the faithless[a] is in the midst of my heart [MT]/his heart [LXX, Jerome, Syr];
   there is no awe for God before his eyes,
²For it flatters him in his eyes,
   with regard to his wrongdoing being found out and opposed.
³The words in his mouth are harmful and deceptive;
   he has given up acting wisely and doing good.
⁴He thinks up harm on his bed;
   he sets himself on a path that is not good;
   he does not reject evil.

    a. Lit., "the utterance of rebellion belonging to the faithless." I take the genitive as adjectival and the *l* as denoting "belonging to" or "on the part of," *l* being used to avoid too long a construct chain (BDB 513b) and/or because a second genitive would have had a different meaning from the first. Briggs sees rebellion as personified, like sin in Gen. 4:7, and inspiring the faithless to wrongdoing (*Psalms*, 1:317); cf. R. J. Tournay, "Le Psaume xxxvi," *RB* 90 (1983): 5–22, see 10–11. LXX's "The rebel speaks of sinning . . ." perhaps implies *něʾum pōšēʿa liršōʿa*. Craigie (*Psalms 1–50*, 290) takes *něʾum* as a heading, but it would be an odd term to describe vv. 1–4 (contrast 110:1).

> ⁵Yhwh, your commitment stands in the heavens,
>   your truthfulness extends to the skies.
> ⁶Your faithfulness is like the majestic mountains,
>   your authority like the great deep;
> You deliver human being and animal;
>   ⁷Yhwh, how valued is your commitment.
> Divine beings and human beings
>   take refuge in the shadow of your wings.
> ⁸They drink their fill of the rich fare of your house;
>   you let them drink at your lovely river.
> ⁹For with you there is a living fountain;
>   in your light we see light.
>
> ¹⁰Prolong your commitment to the people who acknowledge you,
>   your faithfulness to the upright of heart.
> ¹¹The foot of the lofty must not come on me
>   or the hand of the faithless make me flee.
> ¹²There, the people who do harm are falling;
>   they are being thrust down and they will be unable to get up.

Interpretation

The psalm divides into three sections. Verses 1–4 comprise a comment on the attitude and life of the faithless, of a kind that might have appeared in Proverbs. Verses 5–9 address God with a confession of faith in God's commitment and of delight in God's provision. Verses 10–12 address God with a plea to keep showing that commitment. Eventually, then, this becomes a prayer psalm, but it takes its time about revealing that this is where it is going. Initially it focuses on two sets of facts. First it simply describes the nature of wickedness, which is something the psalmist is deeply concerned about (v. 1a)—but we do not know why, though the concern might be, for instance, to teach people to be wary of such behavior. Then in vv. 5–9 it simply offers Yhwh praise in a way that is also deeply felt, but again we do not know why, though out of context this might purely be an act of worship. It is only with the plea in vv. 10–12 that the psalm comes together as we discover the suppliant's own anxiety.

It thus transpires that initially the psalm is seeking to gain Yhwh's attention not merely by means of personal pressure, but also on the basis of the general facts about wickedness that vv. 1–4 describe. It is then reminding Yhwh and the self of Yhwh's characteristics because these also turn out to relate to the suppliant's need: they are both reasons to keep trusting and reasons for Yhwh to respond to the prayer. The psalm may express the awareness, praise, and anxiety of someone under actual pressure from the faithless, or may simply fear the day when that pressure will come. It is not impossible that in its diversity the psalm utilizes various earlier material, though the verbal links between the sections[1] mean that the author must have combined these with great skill; they form one whole.

> The leader's. Yhwh's servant's. David's.

Heading. See glossary and the heading to Ps. 18, the only other psalm where "Yhwh's servant's" comes.

36:1–4. Verses 1–4 describe the stance of the *faithless—perhaps one individual or perhaps a concrete description of a kind of person of which there are many representatives.

> ¹The rebellious utterance of the faithless is in the midst of my heart [MT]/his heart [LXX, Jerome, Syr];
>   there is no awe for God before his eyes,

The overwhelming majority of references to an "utterance" ($ně’um$)[2] refer to the words of a prophet or of God, so there is some irony about the *faithless making an "utterance" (cf. Jer. 23:31), especially since it is an utterance of *rebellion. The expression is unique, but it fits the literary originality of the psalm with its creative combining of the forms of wisdom, praise, and prayer. Perhaps that links with the fact that this rebellious utterance on the part of the faithless is (in MT) "in the midst of my heart" or "in the depths of my *mind." "In the midst of me" or "in my heart" are two ways of saying the same thing, so the compound expression suggests that this utterance has really had an effect on the speaker. If we follow LXX, then the rebellious utterance is deep within such people, deeply ingrained. The second colon goes on from the first by explaining what the rebellious utterance indicated. The psalms usually refer to *reverence for God; "awe" ($paḥad$; cf. 119:120) is a rarer and more powerful expression to match the intensity of the first colon. Why do people need to keep awe for God "before their eyes"? One implication might be that we need to focus intently on it; it cannot be taken for granted. Another might be that failure to do so will issue in our experiencing the negative con-

---

1. On such literary features, see John S. Kselman, "Psalm 36," in *Wisdom, You Are My Sister* (Roland E. Murphy Festschrift), ed. Michael L. Barré (Washington, DC: CBA, 1997), 3–17.
2. Technically a ptc., "something uttered."

sequences. Romans 3:18 makes lack of awe for God the climax in a portrayal of the nature of sin.³

> ²For it flatters him in his eyes,
>   with regard to his wrongdoing being found out and opposed.

Verse 2 explains how this rebellious faithlessness manifests itself, with another irony. The statements of the faithless are slippery—one cannot get hold of them; they are slick and smooth, but unreliable. The faithless flatter in the sense of deceiving (LXX). Their eyes focus on being plausible rather than on being awed. But the irony is that the persons they are flattering are—themselves. Their rebellious utterance deceives them into reckoning they can avoid being found out and opposed or repudiated (*against). Beneath the surface are the psalmist's feelings and implicit fear: What if the faithless person is right that it is possible to avoid being found out and denounced?

> ³The words in his mouth are harmful and deceptive;
>   he has given up acting wisely and doing good.

Verse 3 turns to the externally directed nature of this slipperiness. The problem lies specifically in the person's words, which are calculated to cause *harm and do so by deceptiveness. The second colon comments that he has thus turned his back on wisdom and thereby on *goodness (the verb implies that he once did act with wisdom and goodness). The faithless person does not see a link between wisdom and goodness and reckons it possible to be wise (shrewd, clever) in pursuing one's own gain without needing to be good, which would mean (e.g.) being generous to other people rather than taking advantage of them or plotting against them. The psalm itself assumes a link between wisdom and goodness, a link that also embraces the reverence for Yhwh with which the psalm began (cf. Prov. 1:1–7, which links these three). Indeed, the further sections of the psalm will imply that this is key. There is an intrinsic link between wisdom and goodness: the wise thing is the good thing, the good thing is the wise thing. But sometimes that linkage needs Yhwh's reinforcing. It is thus significant that in working for a wisdom that ignores goodness, the faithless person is also ignoring Yhwh.

> ⁴He thinks up harm on his bed;
>   he sets himself on a path that is not good;
>   he does not reject evil.

---

3. Cf. Kidner, *Psalms*, 1:146.

A tricolon restates the point again and brings the section to an end. *Harm in the first colon picks up from v. 3a, *good picks up from v. 3b, so that the second colon parallels the first. That comes out also in the pairing of the planning one does in the privacy of one's bedroom (cf. 4:4 [5]) and the execution one does when leaving home to implement the plans. But the third colon also parallels the second, repeating its content in introducing reference to not rejecting evil (*bad), the antonym of good, another way of saying he sets himself to do no-good. Formally, positive verb and negated adjective are thus complemented by negated verb and positive adjective.

36:5–9. In a marked contrast, without any marker (such as "but") to suggest a transition, suddenly the psalm is addressing Yhwh, as a psalm should, rather than describing the faithless person. The portrayal of Yhwh contrasts with that of this person, a rebellious, faithless, slippery, harmful, deceptive evildoer. Yhwh is characterized by *commitment, *truthfulness, *faithfulness, *authority, and *deliverance. Aquinas comments on the contrast: "There are some who ascribe their sins to God, saying that they sin of necessity; and they appropriate their goods to themselves, saying that they have them from their own power. David does the opposite."[4]

> [5]Yhwh, your commitment stands in the heavens,
>   your truthfulness extends to the skies.
> [6a–b]Your faithfulness is like the majestic mountains,
>   your authority like the great deep;

Verses 5–6b expound on the magnitude of those characteristics. The sense in which Yhwh's commitment stands in the heavens is explained by the parallel declaration that Yhwh's truthfulness extends to the sky. Both stand so tall, they reach so far, that they stretch to the very sky. There is no limit to them. To be slightly more down-to-earth, Yhwh's faithfulness is like the highest mountains, if we follow Tg in taking the expression "like God's mountains" as a superlative.[5] But perhaps we should translate that phrase literally. A mountain of God like Zaphon (cf. Isa. 14:13) reaches right into the sky and forms a link between earth and heaven. Verse 6b parallels that opening colon again; it may be referring to the deep in the sky where Yhwh keeps the rain (cf. 33:7), or it may make the point in a different way by looking down instead of up (cf. 135:6). As deep as one can imagine looking into the unfathomable deep, one can never plumb the depths of the decisive authority with which Yhwh's faithfulness is implemented, or reach a depth where it ceases to operate. Some of the

---

4. Aquinas on the psalm (Ps. 35 in his numbering).
5. Cf. Rashi; *IBHS* 14.5b.

resonances of that assertion come from the fact that the deep is the realm where one might find tumultuous powers that resist Yhwh's authority and that are therefore a threat to the world's welfare (cf. 148:7). To say that Yhwh's commitment, truthfulness, faithfulness, and authority extend up to the heavens and down to the depths is a merism affirming that they also cover everything in between, in the realm where human beings and animals actually live. In Amos 9 and by implication in Ps. 139, Yhwh's capacity to reach up to the heavens or down to the bottom of the sea or down to Sheol is bad news; there is no escaping Yhwh's authority. But for the upright confronted by the faithless, it is good news.

> 6cYou deliver human being and animal;
>   7aYhwh, how valued is your commitment.

I take v. 6c as the beginning of another line, completed in v. 7a.[6] It adds reference to the fact that Yhwh is deliverer—of humans and animals, bringing the first half of this section to a close with a summary of the significance of vv. 5–6b and another reference to Yhwh's commitment. This motif forms an inclusion around vv. 5–7a.

> 7bDivine beings and human beings
>   take refuge in the shadow of your wings.

The second half of the section (vv. 7b–9) begins by taking the previous line further. It is not just human beings and animals that look to Yhwh. Subordinate divine beings (the kind mentioned in, e.g., 82:1 [2]; 95:3) as well as human beings do so. Yet the mention of such divine beings also brings a transition to a more homely way of speaking of God than the exalted picture of vv. 5–6b. Yhwh is transcendent, but also close.[7] The language of refuge is usually a metaphor for *relying on Yhwh, but v. 7b spells out the image in a way that suggests it is not a dead metaphor (cf. 5:11 [12]; 11:1; 17:8).

> 8They drink their fill of the rich fare of your house;
>   you let them drink at your lovely river.

Verse 8 thus makes clear that the resources of the temple are the psalm's world of thought, though they also move the thinking onward. In itself taking refuge would first suggest simply relief from deprivation, but taking refuge with Yhwh implies much more than that. It means not just survival but also rich provision. Yhwh is not only powerful

---

6. Cf. Seybold, *Psalmen*, 149.
7. Terrien, *Psalms*, 315.

protector but also generous host (cf. Ps. 23). At a sacrificial meal in the temple, people would literally drink and eat their fill of Yhwh's rich fare. The combination of verb and noun is striking. The verb *rāwâ* denotes drinking one's fill, and the noun *dešen* denotes fat, in solid or liquid form. So the expression points to the moist succulence of the food. The second of the two parallel cola also makes clear that the line speaks metaphorically if also literally. People may literally enjoy a rich banquet in Yhwh's presence; on other occasions they figuratively drink from Yhwh's river.

> [9]For with you there is a living fountain;
> in your light we see light.

Verse 9 takes the description further. Since there is no river on the temple mount, so there is no running spring, but there and elsewhere people refresh themselves with what Yhwh provides. Indeed, Yhwh usually *is* the fountain (Jer. 2:13; 17:13), and that may be the assumption here. Yhwh is one who makes refreshment flow, because this refreshment comes from Yhwh. The last clause restates and summarizes the point in another metaphor: *light is another image for provision and blessing. Yhwh's provision and blessing is real provision and blessing, because it is Yhwh's. Yhwh provides for the people's needs in the temple and also in everyday life. As Yhwh's face shines out upon them, that issues in people seeing the gifts that issue from Yhwh's grace and generosity.

36:10–12. Three neat lines of parallel cola continue to address God and talk about commitment and faithfulness, but these come to be the subject of plea rather than of praise. Likewise, they talk further about faithlessness and harm in the manner of vv. 1–4, but these too come to be the subject of plea rather than of teaching—or is it lament? The talk of richness in vv. 7–9 is forgotten; the suppliant's need is more basic.

> [10]Prolong your commitment to the people who acknowledge you,
> your faithfulness to the upright of heart.

The interesting verb *māšak*, which usually denotes drawing something along or stretching something, here applies to both cola. The psalm asks for the continued extending of *commitment and *faithfulness for the benefit of people who *acknowledge Yhwh, people who are upright of heart—that is, really upright, not people who pretend to be upright but in their heart are planning wrongdoing. So even here, the suppliant is not yet speaking as a suppliant. This is not yet overtly plea for oneself, but plea for other people, intercession.

> ¹¹The foot of the lofty must not come on me
> or the hand of the faithless make me flee.

Spelling out an implication that also turns out to have underlain vv. 1–4, v. 11 refers once more to the *faithless, whom the first colon also terms people of *loftiness, people in an exalted position. Faithlessness on the part of the powerless is not too threatening, and the gaining of an exalted position by people who are faithful to Yhwh and to the community will be a positive blessing, but faithlessness and loftiness are a lethal combination (cf. 10:2). The line specifically refers to these people's hand and foot, the foot that treads others down and the hand that drives them away from the community or out of the city or off the land that is their livelihood. But tellingly, the object of this driving and treading is now "me." This is the first appearance of a first-person singular part of speech since the psalm's opening colon, and it reveals that vv. 1–4 were not concerned merely with the objective wrongdoing of the faithless or with the harm they do to other people. Verse 11 need not suggest that the faithless who are in their exalted position are already doing wrong to the suppliant, but it implies that this is where things seem to be going.

> ¹²There, the people who do harm are falling;
> they are being thrust down and they will be unable to get up.

In contrast, the verbs are now qatal, implying that the wrongdoers' downfall is actually happening before the suppliant's eyes—that is, the eyes of faith.[8] There is thus some formal tension between vv. 10–11 and v. 12. The suppliant pleads for Yhwh to be faithful and to deliver, and simultaneously believes that Yhwh is doing so. Verse 12 complements and goes beyond vv. 10–11 in another sense, for it presupposes that faithfulness and deliverance also require the actual putting down of the people who do *harm (who reappear from vv. 3–4). The first verb describing their fate makes the general point about their fall, though it might raise the questions "How?" and "How finally?" In the second colon, the pual verb $dōḥû$ implies answers to both questions: as a passive verb it implies that there is an agent behind this fall (they do not just stumble), and as a resultative pual it draws attention to the result of the event, which is then made even more specific in the closing clause. Their fall is certain and final.

---

8. Gerstenberger (*Psalms*, 1:156) takes them as precative.

Theological Implications

In life, two parties can seem to occupy two different universes. On one hand there are people who rebel against Yhwh, who are faithless to Yhwh and to others, who bring harm to others, who spend their time planning deception, and who are in an exalted position that they can use to put their plots into effect. On the other hand there is Yhwh, who is characterized by commitment, truthfulness, faithfulness, authority, and thus the capacity to deliver, protect, and provide generously. In section 1 only the faithless person was present to the psalmist, and thus to us (the declaration "There is no awe for Yhwh before his eyes" [v. 1] is the exception that proves the rule; it refers to Yhwh, but only in negative terms). In section 2, only Yhwh was present to the psalmist, and thus to us. Section 3 brings the parties together by urging Yhwh to take responsibility for the difference between the characters in sections 1 and 2 and to assert authority on behalf of the suppliant over the faithless.

Christian faith uses the expressions in vv. 7–9 to refer to "spiritual" blessings: Jesus means eternal life, living water, bread of life, light for the world (John 3:16; 4:10; 6:35; 8:12). While the metaphorical nature of the psalm opens it to such applications, we need to be wary of missing the down-to-earth implications of these terms through reinterpreting it in light of the NT. The psalm declares that God provides rich material provision and bodily protection and invites us to ask for these.

Psalm 37

The Weak Will Take Possession of the Land

Translation

    David's.

[ʾ] ¹Do not be vexed at evil people;
    do not fret at people who act meanly,
²For like grass they soon wither,
    like green herbs they shrivel.
[b] ³Trust in Yhwh and do good,
    dwell in the land and feed on truthfulness.ª
⁴Take delight in Yhwh
    so that he may give you the requests of your heart.
[g] ⁵Commit to Yhwh your wayᵇ—
    trust in him, he will act,
⁶And will bring out faithfulness to you like light,
    a decisionᶜ for you like midday.
[d] ⁷Be still before Yhwh,
    wait patientlyᵈ for him.

  a. *Rāʿâ* usually means "feed on" or "tend"; the former fits the context. *Rāʿâ* II, "befriend," or *rāʿâ* III, "strive for," would be rare or unique. Jerome takes *ʾĕmûnâ* adverbially, which would make little difference.
  b. C has *dĕrākeykā*, "your ways."
  c. C has *mišpāṭeykā*, "decisions for you."
  d. Taking *hitḥôlēl* as from *ḥîl* II, a byform of *yāḥal* (*DCH*), not the common *ḥûl/ḥîl*, "writhe" (against BDB); cf. Jerome *expecta*, Aq *apokaradokei*, Tg *ʾôrîk*; also LXX *hiketeuson*.

Do not be vexed at the person who makes his way successful,ᵉ
    at the one who acts on his schemes.
[*h*] ⁸Drop anger, abandon fury;
    do not be vexed, only to do evil.ᶠ
⁹For evil people get cut off, but people who look to Yhwh—
    they take possession of the land.
[*w*] ¹⁰So yet a little while and there will be no faithless person,
    and you will look at his place and there will be no one.
¹¹But the weak—they will take possession of the land
    and delight in abundance of well-being.
[*z*] ¹²The faithless schemes in relation to the faithful
    and grinds his teeth against him;
¹³The Lord laughs at him,
    because he has seen that his day will come.
[*ḥ*] ¹⁴Faithless people have drawn the sword,
    directed their bow,ᵍ
To bring down the weak and needy,
    to slaughter people who are upright in their way.
¹⁵Their sword will enter their own heart,
    their bows will break.
[*ṭ*] ¹⁶Better is the little of the faithful
    than the abundance of many faithless people, [MT]
    [*or,* than the great abundance of the faithless, (LXX, Jerome)]ʰ
¹⁷For the arms of the faithless will be broken,
    but Yhwh upholds the faithful.
[*y*] ¹⁸Yhwh acknowledges the days of people with integrity,
    and their possession will last forever.
¹⁹They will not be shamed in bad times;
    in days of famine they will eat their fill.
[*k*] ²⁰For the faithless perish,
    Yhwh's enemies,
Like the most valuable of pastures/lambs they are consumed,
    in smoke they are consumed.
[*l*] ²¹The faithless person borrows and cannot repay,
    but the faithful is gracious and gives,
²²For the people blessed by him/who bless him take possession of
    the land,
    but the people belittled by him/who belittle him are cut off.ⁱ
[*m*] ²³By Yhwh a man's steps have been made firm
    when he delights in his way.

e. Or "is successful in his way."

f. *Rāʿaʿ* hiphil, which can hardly mean "to cause harm to oneself" (see on 15:4); and see the next line (v. 9a).

g. See on 7:12 [13].

h. MT has *rabbîm*; LXX, Jerome imply *rāb*.

i. MT has passive participles, but LXX implies pointing as active: *mĕbārĕkāyw* and *mĕqalĕlāyw*.

²⁴If he falls, he is not hurled headlong,
    because Yhwh upholds [him with] his hand.
[n] ²⁵I have been young and now I am old,
    but I have not seen a faithful person abandoned
    or his offspring seeking bread.
²⁶Every day he is gracious and lends,
    and his offspring are a blessing.
[s] ²⁷Turn from evil and do good,
    and dwell forever.
²⁸For Yhwh dedicates himself to acting with authority
    and does not abandon the people committed to him.
[ʿ] They are kept forever,
    when the offspring of the faithless are cut off.
²⁹Faithful people will take possession of the land
    and dwell in it forever.
[p] ³⁰The mouth of the faithful talks insight,
    his tongue speaks with authority.
³¹His God's teaching is in his heart;
    his feet do not waver.
[ṣ] ³²The faithless person watches for the faithful
    and seeks to kill him.
³³Yhwh does not abandon him into his hand
    or let him be condemned when he is on trial.
[q] ³⁴Look to Yhwh
    and keep his way.
He will exalt you to take possession of the land;
    when the faithless are cut off, you will see.
[r] ³⁵I saw a faithless person, terrifying,
    arousing himself, like a flourishing native tree/cedar.[j]
³⁶But he passed on/someone passed by/I passed by[k] and there—he was gone;
    I sought him and he could not be found.
[š] ³⁷Watch the person of integrity, see the upright person, [MT]
    [or, Watch integrity, see to uprightness, (LXX, Jerome)][l]
    because there is a future for the man of peace,
³⁸But rebels are destroyed all at once;
    the future of the faithless is cut off.
[t] ³⁹The deliverance of faithful people comes from Yhwh,
    their stronghold in time of trouble.

j. Lit., simply "a native," but the adj. "flourishing" always applies to trees. LXX suggests *ʾerez* (cedar) for *ʾezrāḥ*.

k. MT has third person; LXX, Syr, Jerome, 4Q171 (4QpPsª) have first person.

l. For MT's *tām* and *yāšār*, LXX and Jerome imply the abstract nouns *tōm* and *yōšer*, which are easier with the verb *šāmar* but harder with *rāʾâ*. John Kselman ("Two Notes on Psalm 37," *Bib* 78 [1997]: 252–54) argues for "way of integrity, . . . way of uprightness," understanding *derek* from v. 34.

⁴⁰Yhwh helps them and rescues them,
   rescues them from the faithless and delivers them
   because they rely on him.

Interpretation

This alphabetic psalm comprises a homily[1] such as might have appeared in Proverbs. The posture of an old man (v. 25), likely a stylized one rather than one to be taken too literally,[2] corresponds to that of the teachers in Proverbs instructing younger people. The individual lines in the homily would be quite in place as sayings in Proverbs. The form of individual lines or pairs of lines and the nature of the argument corresponds to those of Proverbs, such as the exhortation with reasons in a *kî* clause (e.g., vv. 1–2) or with a promise about consequences (e.g., vv. 3–4), the contrast between the behavior and destiny of the faithful and the faithless (e.g., vv. 21–22), the "x is better than y" form (v. 16), and the appeal to experience (vv. 25, 35–36). Yet there is no particular reason to reckon that the preacher has taken over actual sayings from the tradition rather than devising new examples to fit the alphabetical form.

This form provides the homily with its structural principle. There is no development of thought through it but a series of observations illustrating its central conviction that Yhwh looks after the faithful, while the faithless perish. The sections into which I have divided the psalm are therefore somewhat random. Most letters have two bicola (*ḥ* has three; *n* has a tricolon and a bicolon, *t* a bicolon and a tricolon); usually only the first line begins with the relevant letter, though sometimes this letter reappears. The alphabetical form corresponds to the psalm's thesis that there is an order about the world.

In its setting in the Psalter, Ps. 37 takes up the theme of Ps. 1, with which it has a number of verbal links such as delight, Yhwh's teaching, reciting, the comparison with a tree, succeeding, and more common motifs such as the "way" and the antithesis of faithful-faithless. Psalm 1 provided a controversial principle within whose affirmations to view the laments that follow. We have now come a long way since Ps. 1, and much of the journey has indeed disconfirmed what Ps. 1 asserted. Psalm 37 reaffirms the perspective of Ps. 1 a quarter of the way through the Psalter, insisting that the experience generating the laments not be allowed to overwhelm the convictions stated in Ps. 1. Psalm 73 will do the same again at the beginning of book III of the Psalter. (There is no

---

1. Cf. Gerstenberger, *Psalms*, 1:158; Michael Jinkins, "The Virtues of the Righteous in Psalm 37," in *Psalms and Practice*, ed. Reid, 164–201, see 181.
2. Cf. Gerhard von Rad, *Wisdom in Israel* (London: SCM, 1972), 37–38.

way of determining whether someone deliberately arranged the Psalter that way, but that is how it is.) There is no need to choose between a liturgical and a literary background for the psalm.[3] The homily may well have its background in worship, but it also fulfills a function in the Psalter as part of an account of how life with God works. For Pss. 1; 37; and 73 (like, e.g., Pss. 91 and 119) are statements of faith acknowledging that there is evidence to clash with them, but nevertheless urging an attitude of trust. They insist on what *must* be so, even if things often look otherwise.

The homily thus presupposes that there are people tormented by the prosperity of the faithless. They are not living with the kind of poverty that means they do not have enough to eat, but they see these other people doing better than they are, and see themselves as the actual or potential victims of the schemes of these others. Among the contexts in which one can imagine the homily being used are the inequalities within the Judean or Ephraimite community in the monarchic period such as feature in the Prophets and in the time of Nehemiah, and the conflicts with other communities reflected in the time of Ezra and Nehemiah. The key motif of possession of the land would relate to a family's allocation within the promised land as a whole or to the Judean community's vulnerability in relation to other Persian provinces.

The Qumran Psalms Pesher, 4Q171 (4QpPs^a), includes a substantial exposition of the psalm and encourages the community to live by its promises as they are under pressure from other groups, to believe in God's putting these others down, preserving the community through the coming crisis, and giving it authority in Jerusalem.[4] I assume that its differences from MT are hardly evidence for a different original text.[5] Jesus similarly takes up v. 11 and makes it one of his Blessings (Matt. 5:5).

David's.

Heading. See introduction. In the monarchic period it was the king's responsibility to see that Israel was the kind of society that is here described. When the Messiah comes, it will likewise be his responsibility.

37:1–6. Do not be vexed, trust, delight, commit.

---

3. As Gerstenberger (*Psalms*, 1:158) seems to imply.
4. See (e.g.) *The Dead Sea Scrolls: Study Edition*, ed. Florentino García Martínez and Eibert J. C. Tigchelaar (Leiden: Brill, 2000), 1:342–47; J. M. Allegro, "A Newly-Discovered Fragment of a Commentary on Psalm xxxvii from Qumrân," *Palestine Exploration Quarterly* 86 (1954): 69–75; Dennis Pardee, "A Restudy of the Commentary on Psalm 37 from Qumran Cave 4," *Revue de Qumran* 8 (1972–75): 163–94; Maurya P. Horgan, *Pesharim: Qumran Interpretations of Biblical Books* (Washington, DC: CBA, 1979), 192–226.
5. Against Craigie, *Psalms 1–50*, 295–96.

> [ʾ] ¹Do not be vexed at evil people,
>   do not fret at people who act meanly,
> ²For like grass they soon wither,
>   like green herbs they shrivel.

The ʾ lines begin with a negative, *ʾal* (recurring to open the second colon), specifically with an exhortation not to be vexed, which recurs in vv. 7 and 8. The homily thus includes three of the four OT occurrences of *ḥārâ* hitpael (Prov. 24:19 is the other, used in the same connection). The verb usually refers to anger and often appears in combination with *ʾap*. It perhaps points to the heat of anger, to anger blazing (not merely kindling),[6] to the way anger can make a person hot inside. The hitpael specifically suggests hot anger turned in on oneself because it cannot receive expression to the person toward whom one might wish to express it. So the parallel verb in v. 1 is *qānāʾ* (piel), which may also suggest something like heat, the redness that strong feelings bring to the face, the passion of jealousy or anger. Jealousy fits here. The object of these strong feelings are *bad people (*měrēʿîm*). Slightly more specifically, they are people who act meanly (*ʿawlâ*; cf. *ʿāwel* in 7:3 [4]).

The basis for not being vexed or fretting is that wrongdoers are short-lived. Formally the second line parallels the first in combining two verbs with two prepositional phrases, but here verbs and prepositional phrases are reversed so that the two lines work *abbʾaʾ*. The evil wrongdoers are like grass. Formally the simile raises suspense and poses the question "How so?" but in reality the audience knows the answer to that question because the regular characteristic of grass in such figures is that it withers quickly (e.g., 90:5–6; 103:15; 129:6). If the teacher had wanted to raise suspense, this would have been possible by placing "green herbs" in the first colon, because these words are less familiar in comparisons; their associations are with food (e.g., 23:2; Gen. 1:11–12, 30). The verbs, too, are unfamiliar.[7] The homily is thus clear rather than subtle in the way it reminds its hearers of a familiar (alleged) fact, though it does seek to keep their interest in the way it does so.

> [b] ³Trust in Yhwh and do good,
>   dwell in the land and feed on truthfulness.
> ⁴Take delight in Yhwh
>   so that he may give you the requests of your heart.

---

6. So BDB 60.

7. The first is *yimmālû* from *mālal*, a rare byform of *ʾāmal*; the second, *yibbôlûn*, is an unexpected form from *nābēl*; the forms generate paronomasia.

The *b* lines open with a compressed antithesis to vv. 1–2. On one hand, instead of being possessed by negative feelings about wrongdoers, people who do what is bad, they urge people to *trust in Yhwh (*bāṭaḥ*) and do *good. "In" is even the same preposition as "at" (*bĕ*). Focus not on them but on God and on your own life. Perhaps we should infer that like wrong/bad, doing good denotes a stance over against other people—such as openness and generosity rather than deceptiveness and hostility. The second colon then continues the imperatives, but they represent the kind of imperatives that indicate the result of a previous imperative and thus offer a concealed promise.[8] *If you trust in Yhwh and do good, then you* will *dwell in the land and feed on truthfulness.* The two clauses are closely related. Being able to eat depends on having land, on a family having its allocation within the promised land, or on being able to stay in the land of Canaan; either way, this makes it possible to grow one's food and thus eat. One thus feeds on *truthfulness—perhaps on Yhwh's truthfulness, because Yhwh proves truthful in caring for the person who does good; perhaps on one's own truthfulness, because being able to eat is a fruit of that.

"Take delight" continues the alimentary image (cf. Isa. 55:2; 66:11), though it then brings listeners up doubly short. First it does so by making Yhwh the object of the delight that is commended (cf. Job 27:10). People are not to become too enthusiastic about mere material provision. It also does so by eventually changing our first perception of the syntax. We could initially take the first colon as a continuation of the promises disguised as exhortations. It then promises that people who trust in Yhwh will find that they do have reason to delight in Yhwh, presumably because of Yhwh's provision. But the second colon turns out to be a purpose clause (or a result clause) dependent on this opening imperative, which suggests the imperative is indeed an exhortation. People are being urged to delight in Yhwh now, not later when they have experienced Yhwh's blessing. Delight in Yhwh is a more affective version of trust in Yhwh or a more affective version of the idea of *seeking help from Yhwh that appears elsewhere. It is also a positive affective equivalent to being vexed and fretting. The remedy for negative feelings that come from looking at others is to look at Yhwh and let appropriate feelings arise. In turn, receiving the requests of our heart is equivalent to staying in the land and feeding on/in truthfulness. They are requests (a noun from *šā'al*), not merely desires (NRSV). To let them stay as desires is to risk their not being fulfilled (James 4:2). But they are indeed the requests of the heart: the listeners are invited to bring their deepest longings to Yhwh so that they can be fulfilled (perhaps translating as a

---

8. Cf. GKC 110c; *IBHS* 34.4c.

result clause would make the psalm a little too unequivocal). The line as a whole is parallel to v. 3.

> [*g*] ⁵Commit to Yhwh your way—
>   trust in him, he will act,
> ⁶And will bring out faithfulness to you like light,
>   a decision for you like midday.

The *g* lines lead to listeners being invited to roll (*gālal*) their way, or destiny, or future, onto Yhwh (cf. 22:8 [9]), which makes the point about trust once more in yet other words. Or they are invited to reveal their way to Yhwh (*gal* from *gālâ* piel, implied by LXX, Tg). Either way, the significance of the unusual vivid word is then broadly confirmed in the second colon by the repetition of the more prosaic *trust. Initially the promise attached to this exhortation is expressed briskly and austerely, "He will act," though the verb (*'āśâ*) does recur from vv. 1 and 3, so that Yhwh's act is set against the act of wrongdoers and in response to that of right-doers.

So what will Yhwh do? Verse 6 expresses the promise more vividly, though not more concretely, in a *wāw*-consecutive. The verb applies to both cola, which work *abcc'b'*. The two nouns are the recurrent combination of *faithfulness and *authority/decision; in this order the second promises that the first will be implemented with the required energy. These are thus set over against the wrongdoing with which the homily began. They form another reason not to be vexed. They might seem a commonplace, and before and after them thus comes a pair of similes in "not only–but even" order. Yhwh's decisive faithfulness will not only be like *light, but also/even like the bright light of midday.

37:7–15. Be still, drop anger; the weak will take possession of the land, the bows of the faithless will break.

> [*d*] ⁷Be still before Yhwh,
>   wait patiently for him.
> Do not be vexed at the person who makes his way successful,
>   at the one who acts on his schemes.

The *d* lines stimulate the idea that the listeners next be urged to be still (*dāmam*) before Yhwh (more literally, "for Yhwh"), another suggestive expression of trust. Being still implies a willingness to submit to Yhwh (see 4:4 [5]) and not to take action to resolve matters that need resolving (62:5 [6]). Thus it implies waiting, as the parallel verb makes explicit.

The second line in turn makes explicit that stillness and patient waiting are also the opposite of being vexed (see v. 1).[9] It is tempting to be vexed at the person who is successful and go-ahead (the homily moves from talking about people in the plural to focusing on an individual example; it will alternate between these). That is true even if they are entirely honorable people, but one would assume that the homily refers to people who are successful by shady means, and words such as "schemes" (*mězimmâ*) usually refer to plans to cause people trouble (cf. v. 12; this noun in 10:2; 21:11 [12]); v. 9 will confirm that the homily refers to evil people. Indeed, it is hard to be successful and go-ahead without treading on a few people.

> [*h*] ⁸Drop anger, abandon fury;
>   do not be vexed, only to do evil.
> ⁹For evil people get cut off, but people who look to Yhwh—
>   they take possession of the land.

The *h* lines lead to the use of the hiphil of the verb "drop" (*rāpâ*), of which "abandon" is then a more familiar synonym. Both expressions relate to anger, and they are then complemented by yet another exhortation not to be vexed, now strengthened by the reminder that it only leads to wrongdoing. The infinitive of the hiphil "do evil" (*bad) picks up the use of the participle (v. 1) and the antonym "good" (v. 3). It thus warns the listeners that getting vexed at evildoers can result in joining them rather than manifesting the opposite qualities—perhaps because jealousy makes them join in their evildoing, perhaps because it makes them take vengeance into their own hands instead of being still and waiting for Yhwh to act.

That exhortation is thus buttressed by a reminder of what happens to *bad people who have joined other wrongdoers instead of standing firm as people who *look to Yhwh to act. As the two cola contrast these two groups, they also contrast their destiny. The parallelism thus suggests that it is from the land that evildoers are "cut off"; that is also the context for the subsequent references to being cut off in vv. 22, 28, and 34, though not in v. 38. The expression may also imply that they lose their lives, but the emphasis lies on the fact that this happens in such a way that they lose their place on the land and thus lose their capacity to maintain their lives and/or lose their place of rest there. "Take possession" is *yāraš*, which will recur in vv. 11, 22, 29, and 34. The verb could suggest simply possessing without an implication of dispossessing, but it commonly implies dispossessing others, and here the context does sug-

---

9. That verb governs both cola, which provide it with two parallel objects introduced by *bě*—or rather, one object described in two ways.

gest this because of the recurrent link with the cutting off of the wicked. The idea then is that whereas at the moment the wicked are doing so well that they may be in a position to take over the land of others, that situation is due to be reversed.

> [w] ¹⁰So yet a little while and there will be no faithless person,
>   and you will look at his place and there will be no one.
> ¹¹But the weak—they will take possession of the land
>   and delight in abundance of well-being.

The *w* lines, beginning with a syntactically unnecessary *w*, constitute a two-line restatement of v. 9; every colon begins with *w*. "Yet a little while" restates the promise in v. 2 that the prosperity of the faithless will not last long. The *faithless appear for the first time; they will reappear in vv. 12, 14, 16, 17, 20, 21, 32, 35, 38, 40. The second colon restates the first more emphatically, with a reference to the faithless person's "place"—another reference to the land from which the faithless is cut off.

Verse 11 in turn introduces us to the *weak, though this is evidently the group that has been present from the beginning in all but name. While in itself "weak" carries no affirming connotation, the weak are often set over against the faithless, but the implication is that the faithful are people who are weak rather than that the weak are people committed to Yhwh. As the faithless are removed from their place, the weak are in a position to take it over. And that in itself will lead them toward multiple shalom. Their taking delight in Yhwh (v. 4) will indeed issue in taking delight in the good things that Yhwh gives. The ʿānāw (weak) becomes the subject of ʿānag (delighting).

> [z] ¹²The faithless schemes in relation to the faithful
>   and grinds his teeth against him;
> ¹³The Lord laughs at him,
>   because he has seen that his day will come.

The *z* lines lead to the appearance of the verb "scheme" (zāmam; cf. the noun in v. 7). For the first time the homily explicitly antithesizes the *faithful and the *faithless and juxtaposes the two words: the Hebrew words rāšāʿ and ṣaddîq are not linked in the manner of these two English words, but in content they do represent opposites. And for the first time the homily indicates that the experience lying behind the psalm is not merely the objective fact that the faithless prosper when they should not, but that in doing so they attack the faithful. "The faithless" is subject of both clauses; in the second, "grinding the teeth" is either an accompaniment to the scheming of the first (one may grind one's teeth in formulating a plan) or the means of taking it further (cf. 35:16). Either way it suggests a concrete threatening action that bodes ill for the victim.

Verse 13 sets the *Lord's laughter asyndetically and thus sharply against that: the faithless think they are so clever and powerful, but to God they seem quite otherwise. The Lord's laughter is thus promise and inspiration (cf. 2:4), and also confession (59:8 [9]) and example to be followed (52:6 [8]). Yhwh "has seen" what will happen to the faithless; the verb is more concrete than "knows" (NJPS) and the tense more concrete than "sees" (NRSV). Yhwh has taken a look into the future; Yhwh can do so as the one who determines it. Yhwh is therefore in a position to laugh. The statement thus presupposes that Yhwh has determined that the faithless person will fall. "His day" is more likely Yhwh's day than the faithless person's day.

> [$ḥ$] ¹⁴Faithless people have drawn the sword,
>   directed their bow,
> To bring down the weak and needy,
>   to slaughter people who are upright in their way.
> ¹⁵Their sword will enter their own heart,
>   their bows will break.

Uniquely, there are three $ḥ$ lines, beginning with reference to the sword (*ḥereb*) that the *faithless may wield; the second colon then accompanies that with the bow they may draw. If these weapons of war are metaphors for the more devious weapons the faithless actually use, then the words draw attention to the fatal effect of whatever these weapons are.

Verse 14b makes that explicit. They bring down the *weak and *needy; the parallel colon itself then makes explicit that they indeed not merely cause a wound from which people may recover, but kill them. There is a terrible contrast between the two ends of the line. We are talking about people who are upright with regard to their way. In their own lives and in their relationship with the community, they walk tall. But the faithless cause them to fall (*nāpal* hiphil). Thus what the faithless do directly conflicts with what is proper, with the right ordering of reality.

Verse 15 must therefore follow, also beginning with reference to the sword and thus with a $ḥ$. That inversion of what is proper cannot be allowed to stand. The line speaks of no divine intervention such as v. 13 may imply. By a process of propriety written into the way life works, the sword by which the faithless seek to invert what is right will mysteriously turn and lodge itself in the heart of the one who wields it, and the bow will mysteriously break rather than complete its dastardly deed. Even these inanimate objects prove part of a moral structuring of reality and behave with a personal seemliness that the faithless lack.

37:16–26. Yhwh upholds and acknowledges; the faithless perishes, the faithful thrives.

> [ṭ] ¹⁶Better is the little of the faithful
>   than the abundance of many faithless people, [MT]
>   [*or*, than the great abundance of the faithless, (LXX, Jerome)]
> ¹⁷For the arms of the faithless will be broken,
>   but Yhwh upholds the faithful.

The *ṭ* lines permit the reappearance of *ṭôb* (better), though the word is used in a more down-to-earth sense than was the case in v. 3 (good). Like "x is better than y" proverbs (e.g., Prov. 16:8, 16, 19, 32), this saying does not tell us how it can be true. How can little be better than more?

The next line gives the answer to the question. It is not (for instance) that goodness—a faithful relationship with the community and with God—is its own reward. Verse 17 puts the point concretely in declaring that on the one hand, the faithless will have their arms broken, though it also thereby puts the point a little obscurely. Singular "arm" can signify strength, suggesting here people's capacity to act against the faithless, but the plural is rarer and less focused in meaning. We might infer an irony and reckon that the faithless will not be able to carry their (ill-gotten?) gain. The verb is niphal, which might add to the irony, as if the arms break under the pressure of the abundance, and/or might suggest that their selfishness has its natural result: their very excess makes them unable to enjoy it, as is the experience of Western cultures that have so much but do not enjoy it. Or the niphal might imply an agent, and thus raise the question as to this agent's identity, which the parallel colon answers with an active participle paralleling the niphal yiqtol. Structurally the line works *abcc′b′d*, the very last word without correspondent in the first colon thus being the one that answers its implied question. If Yhwh is upholding you, a little is enough. If Yhwh is not doing so, even abundance will not be enough. The idea parallels Deut. 8:3.

> [y] ¹⁸Yhwh acknowledges the days of people with integrity,
>   and their possession will last forever.
> ¹⁹They will not be shamed in bad times;
>   in days of famine they will eat their fill.

Verses 18–19 begin with three *y* words—acknowledges, Yhwh, days. *Acknowledging people's days implies taking note of them and supporting them. The people to whom this applies are people of *integrity, which once more links with faithfulness (cf. 7:8 [9]). The second colon suggests the implication of this acknowledgment. The "days" referred to are days in the land or days on their land; Yhwh will ensure that these days never end.

Verse 19 spells this out further. In bad times a family might lose its land. If the land does not produce enough for the family to survive, it may have to borrow from people who are better off, using its land as collateral. And unless its fortunes improve considerably, it ends up forfeiting this collateral. The homily promises that Yhwh will see that people of integrity do not fall into this spiral. In bad times, when the rains fail or enemies ravage, Yhwh sees that they find ways of surviving so that they are not shamed, reduced to having to mortgage their land and themselves. The second colon spells out the point. If there *are* poor harvests, they will do all right and still have plenty to eat, and thus avoid this spiral.

[k] ²⁰For the faithless perish,
    Yhwh's enemies,
    Like the most valuable of pastures/lambs they are consumed,
        in smoke they are consumed.

The two *k* lines begin with *kî* (for), but the preacher works harder with this letter for the second line where four of the five words begin with *k*.¹⁰ The *kî* makes a link with what precedes: the destiny of the faithless is again the other side to the destiny of the people of integrity. The faithless will find no way through those days of famine. The inevitability of that is underlined by describing them as Yhwh's enemies, which might mean that their faithlessness suggests hostility to Yhwh or that it earns hostility from Yhwh or both.

The simile in the second line again links with the context, especially if we may understand "pastures" (*kārîm*—a rare word, perhaps chosen because of the *k*) more broadly than as pasturage for sheep. The burning up of pastures by the sun or by enemies or by accidental fire would cause famine. If the simile relates rather to lambs and the way they are consumed as sacrifices, the link is less specific. Being consumed in smoke is a contracted way of saying that they are consumed and go up in smoke.

[l] ²¹The faithless person borrows and cannot repay,
    but the faithful is gracious and gives,
²²For the people blessed by him/who bless him take possession of the land,
    but the people belittled by him/who belittle him are cut off.

---

10. The exception is "in smoke," which could so easily have been "like smoke" (*kĕʿāšān*)—to which, indeed, many Hebrew MSS change it.

The *l* lines introduce the topic of borrowing (*lāwâ*), which is also related because the bad times are the times when people have to borrow. I take the faithless person's defaulting on a debt not as a sign of wickedness but rather as a further sign of receiving the due reward for faithlessness, because the defaulting will threaten harsh consequences (see 2 Kings 4:1; Neh. 5; Amos 2:6–7). Faithless people will never be able to get out of the poverty trap. The second colon then offers the contrast that the faithful will be in a position to be *gracious and generous—in lending (cf. v. 26) and even in giving what one does not expect to be paid back.

The companion line explains the difference between these two destinies in the familiar terms. The "him" is presumably Yhwh, who is the one who blesses and belittles or is blessed and belittled; the word for belittle (*qālal*) is less fierce than the more technical word for cursing (*'ārar*). Blessing is a *word* that results in an *event*; in the case of the opposite verbs, cursing refers more to the powerful word, belittling more to its aim or result. The act of blessing adds to people, making them prosperous and fertile; the act of cursing cuts them down, making them unsuccessful and unproductive. Thus the result of blessing and belittling/cursing is the usual antithesis, ability to enjoy ongoing possession of the land or being cut off from it.

> [*m*] ²³By Yhwh a man's steps have been made firm
>   when he delights in his way.
> ²⁴If he falls, he is not hurled headlong,
>   because Yhwh upholds [him with] his hand.

The *m* lines lead to an opening that refers to Yhwh (*myhwh*, "from Yhwh") but goes on to another *m* word, a rare word for steps (*miṣ'ădê*). Yhwh enables people to keep a firm footing, because of "delighting" in them (*ḥāpēṣ*). In other contexts such delight might issue simply from God's grace, but in the context of this homily, it is likely that the people Yhwh delights in are the faithful, mentioned (for instance) in the *l* and *n* lines on either side. This point would be explicit if the colon refers to the *man's* delighting in *Yhwh's* way, but the pronouns are again ambiguous.

The image of steps continues in v. 24, the two lines being parallel, *aba'b'*. The homily is not wildly unrealistic. It recognizes that the faithful do fall; to make sense in the context, EVV have "stumble," but the word is *nāpal*, the regular verb for "fall." But the faithful do not fall in such a way that they fail to get up again, or they do not get hurled out of the land (cf. this verb, *ṭûl*, in Jer. 16:13; 22:26, 28). How is that? The second colon explains; "upholds" (the participle *sōmēk*) recurs from v. 17.

Yhwh takes the hand of people who fall and lifts them up, or gives them a hand, supports them *with* a hand.

> [n] ²⁵I have been young and now I am old,
>   but I have not seen a faithful person abandoned
>   or his offspring seeking bread.
> ²⁶Every day he is gracious and lends,
>   and his offspring are a blessing.

The *n* lines are distinctive for comprising a tricolon as well as a bicolon and for making an assertion that often outrages Christians. The *n* word is "young man" (*na'ar*); in the first colon the preacher claims a lifetime's experience on the basis of which to make the pronouncements in the second and third cola. Since the preacher has just referred to the fact that the faithful do fall, we should perhaps take the statement as hyperbole. It then still makes a declaration for the faithful to hold on to when Yhwh does abandon them for a while (see 22:1 [2]). If we read it in the context of that preceding recognition that Yhwh does let people fall but does not let them be finally thrown out of the land, this would fit the final colon's reference to their offspring begging for food. The statement is another formulation of the promise that the weak will enter into possession of the land. They will therefore be in a position to feed their offspring and pass it on to them so that they continue to eat.

Verse 26 then puts the point positively. The faithful not only have enough for themselves and their families but are in a position to be gracious (cf. v. 21) and to lend (the hiphil of *lāwâ* "borrow"—cf. v. 21). Lending properly involves simply lending—the Torah forbade making money through lending (e.g., Exod. 22:25 [24]). It is not a form of investment (see on 15:5). Lending might seem less generous than giving, though it might also offer more recognition of the other person's humanity. Instead of making others the recipients of charity, lending gives them the opportunity to reestablish themselves and hold their head high. Yhwh's support of the faithful enables them to play that role in the community. Like the negative point in v. 25, this blessing extends beyond one faithful person to the next generation. Because it inherits the land that Yhwh has enabled the faithful person to possess, it is also in a position to be a blessing, to be a means of the blessing of food coming to other needy people.

37:27–33. Turn from evil and do good.

> [s] ²⁷Turn from evil and do good,
>   and dwell forever.
> ²⁸ᵃ⁻ᵇFor Yhwh dedicates himself to acting with authority
>   and does not abandon the people committed to him.

The *s* lines begin "turn": turn aside rather than turn back (*sûr*, not *šûb*), turn from *bad/evil (cf. vv. 1, 8, 9) to *good (cf. v. 3). The "dwelling" thus made possible will be the dwelling in the land that v. 3 also promised; the "forever" continues the developing emphasis on perpetuity (vv. 25–26). Verse 27 thus mostly recycles familiar material except for the required *s* word.

In beginning with *"dedicates himself" and reference to acting with *authority, v. 28a then introduces terms new for this homily, though familiar elsewhere. The opening colon thus promises that Yhwh acts decisively in the world and does not sit inactive. But how does Yhwh exercise that authority? Most commonly *faithfulness is the word to explain that, and here the second colon could be seen as a definition or illustration of the nature of faithfulness. It also provides a negative to complement the positive of the first colon. Yhwh does not abandon (the verb from v. 25). The people *committed to Yhwh are secure.

[ʿ] ²⁸ᶜThey are kept forever,
　　when the offspring of the faithless are cut off.
²⁹Faithful people will take possession of the land
　　and dwell in it forever.

Unexpectedly, the ʿ lines fail to begin with the appropriate letter, though after the introductory preposition it is the first root letter in the opening expression, *lĕʿôlām* (forever). The combining of the second *s* line and the disguised ʿ line as v. 28 reflects the fact that the ʿ lines reformulate once more the promise that opened v. 28. As well as declaring that Yhwh's faithfulness will never come to an end, the new promise about the people who are committed to Yhwh adds the positive "keep" to the negative "not abandon." The second colon then makes the corresponding negative point about the faithless, restating familiar points though making a new point explicit. We have had promises regarding the offspring of the faithful; here is the warning about the offspring of the faithless. Because their parents lose their place on their land, they too lose theirs, and thus lose their livelihood and potentially their lives.

Verse 29 then reiterates the equivalent promise for the faithful (cf. Prov. 2:21–22). The first colon relates to their gaining possession of the land, but raises the question "For how long?" The second answers with both its verb (They will dwell in it) and its temporal expression (another "forever"). The next-to-last word is another word for "forever" (*lāʿad*), pairing with the word that began the two lines both in meaning and in being an ayin (ʿ) word preceded by a preposition. The very last expression, "in it" (*ʿāleyhā*), does finally begin with an ayin.

> [*p*] ³⁰The mouth of the faithful talks insight,
>   his tongue speaks with authority.
> ³¹His God's teaching is in his heart;
>   his feet do not waver.

The *p* lines at last encourage a new thought, that the mouth (*peh*) and tongue of the faithful *talk insight and speak with authority. Another aspect of the lifestyle of faithful people is that their faithfulness is expressed in the way they speak, which they do in a way that combines insight with *authority (for that word, cf. the comment on God in v. 28a). The distinctive pairing of insight and authority is unusual, though the words come together in the programmatic statement about insight in Prov. 1:2–3.

Verse 31 then restates that point. With its reference to Yhwh's teaching, the first colon also takes further a parallel with Ps. 1 (1:2), which speaks of reciting Yhwh's teaching (cf. v. 30 here). But v. 31 adds that Yhwh's teaching is in the heart of the faithful, not merely on their lips (cf. Deut. 30:14). It is written into their inner being and therefore shapes their life. The final colon adds that it also affects the walking aspect of their life. The feet (lit., "the steps") continue to stay firm in walking the right way. The context suggests that here the verb *māʿad* does not mean "slip" in the sense of accidentally losing one's balance but refers to making moral mistakes (cf. 26:1; contrast 18:36 [37]). The faithful avoid slipping off the right road.

> [*ṣ*] ³²The faithless person watches for the faithful
>   and seeks to kill him.
> ³³Yhwh does not abandon him into his hand
>   or let him be condemned when he is on trial.

The *ṣ* lines introduce the verb *ṣāpâ* (watch), which in turn returns to the theme of the faithless as an actual threat to the faithful (cf. vv. 12–15). Initially there might be some ambiguity about the use of the verb, because its meaning is usually positive: the participle, used here, regularly denotes a lookout. Is the faithless watching to see what will happen to the faithful? It is the second colon that makes explicit that the faithless is watching in order to seize an opportunity to harm the faithful.

Verse 33 sets another factor sharply and asyndetically against that. Once more the psalm declares that Yhwh does not abandon (cf. vv. 25, 28). In the process it does also presuppose that something like abandonment may appear to be happening. The faithful can find themselves in the hand or power of the faithless for a while. They do fall (v. 24), but Yhwh does not leave them there. The second colon specifies the context in which the threat and the deliverance may happen. Characteristically in the Psalms, the peril of the faithful is that they are brought before the community court in the manner of Naboth, threatened with the loss of their land. They may be there on some false charge, or the faithless may (e.g.) be insisting on foreclosing on a loan. Either way, the faithful are in their power. But Yhwh will see that the court finds in their favor. It will see through the fraud or insist that the faithless not press their rights.

37:34–40. There is a future for the man of peace.

> [*q*] ³⁴Look to Yhwh
>   and keep his way.
>   He will exalt you to take possession of the land;
>   when the faithless are cut off, you will see.

The *q* lines suggest an exhortation to *look to Yhwh (cf. v. 9). The second colon makes clear that such looking does not imply inactivity, yet the activity it involves is not an attempt to seize control of one's destiny but an attempt to keep Yhwh's way, in the conviction that Yhwh is keeping our way (v. 28).

Once more the second line attaches to the challenge a promise about possession of the land for the faithful and the cutting off of the *faithless, with nuances at the beginning and end. One is the promise of exaltation, which contrasts with the threat of being put down or being humiliated or found guilty (vv. 14, 19, 33). The other is the promise of seeing the fall of the faithless (cf. v. 10, with a different verb), which Yhwh has already seen (v. 13). The faithless may not gloat, but they will thereby know that Yhwh has acted.

> [*r*] ³⁵I saw a faithless person, terrifying,
>   arousing himself, like a flourishing native tree/cedar.
>   ³⁶But he passed on/someone passed by/I passed by and there—he was gone;
>   I sought him and he could not be found.

The *r* lines lead to a recurrence of "see" (*rā'â*), now referring to a past experience of the seeing that v. 34 promised (cf. the "not seeing" of v. 25). The two occurrences of the verb are juxtaposed as the last word of v. 34 and the first word of v. 35, emphasizing the link. The preacher's past seeing is a basis for the listeners' believing that they will see. In itself a faithless person might be nothing to worry about, but the faithless the psalm concerns itself with are the faithless with power, the "terrifying"

(*ʿārîṣ*) or ruthless. Such people assert themselves[11] against the faithful and look like a flourishing native tree, thriving as it grows in just the soil it needs, or a flourishing cedar, the great model of an impressive tree.

Yet v. 36 speaks of how this person passes on or people in general pass on or the preacher passes on, and the one who was apparently unassailable is gone. The second colon underlines the point by giving more detail on the personal testimony.

> [*š*] ³⁷Watch the person of integrity, see the upright person, [MT]
> [*or*, Watch integrity, see to uprightness, (LXX, Jerome)]
>   because there is a future for the man of peace,
> ³⁸But rebels are destroyed all at once;
>   the future of the faithless is cut off.

"Seeing" recurs in the *s* lines, following another occurrence of *šāmar* (watch; cf. vv. 28, 34) that suggests another way to expound the theme. In using this verb, LXX and Jerome envisage the preacher encouraging the listeners to "guard" integrity, and then to look to uprightness, an entirely plausible exhortation, whereas MT implies a more concrete form of looking, to see what happens to people of integrity and uprightness. The preacher who promised seeing in v. 34 and testified to seeing in vv. 35–36 now invites the listeners to keep their eyes open and see what goes on. Specifically, they may mark and see what happens to the person of *integrity (cf. v. 18), who is then defined as the upright person, and further in the parallel colon as "a man of peace." That expression occurs only here, but "the man of my peace" is "my friend" (e.g., 41:9 [10]) in the sense of one who behaves in loyal fashion. He is the sort of person who not only speaks peace but acts peace and keeps covenantal commitments, as opposed to seeking to bring trouble and ignoring such commitments (cf. 28:3; 55:20 [21]). The second colon also clarifies what the listeners will be expecting to see happen to such people: they have a future. It is another way of declaring that they will keep possession of the land and enjoy security.

Verse 38 again offers the contrast of destruction, coming suddenly (cf. vv. 2, 10, 36); the victims of this are newly designated *rebels. The second colon puts it in a way that picks up from v. 37 and thus makes the contrast more concrete; it will mean the cutting off of a future. That might be a metalepsis for being cut off from the land and thus having no future. But sometimes *ʾaḥărît* implies more specifically "posterity," and that would fit here—and perhaps retrospectively in v. 37.[12]

---

11. I take *ʿārâ* here as a byform of *ʿûr*. LXX takes it as a byform of *ʿālâ* (cf. Craigie, *Psalms 1–50*, 296) or reads it as a form of *ʿālâ*.

12. See BDB 31.

> [*t*] ³⁹The deliverance of faithful people comes from Yhwh,
>   their stronghold in time of trouble.
> ⁴⁰Yhwh helps them and rescues them,
>   rescues them from the faithless and delivers them
>   because they rely on him.

Finally the *t* lines begin with *deliverance—or almost do so; the word itself is actually preceded by the copula *w* (cf. the ʿ line, v. 28b). Deliverance as a familiar theme might seem predictable, though the psalm has not so far used such words, and to produce a *t* it uses an unusual form from the root, *těšûʿâ*. The parallel term, *stronghold in time of trouble, makes the point more concretely, as in 27:1.

The second line further spells out the implications. *Help and rescue are additional ways to speak of deliverance, while the second colon completes an *abbʹaʹ* sequence in v. 40a–b. We do not expect a third colon, though at the end of the psalm a tricolon neatly closes it off. What does one need to do to be delivered/rescued/helped? *Rely on Yhwh.

Theological Implications

The homily's alphabetical form means it does not build an argument into its formal structure but rather keeps returning to a number of points.

1. It has a pastoral concern, to encourage a change of attitude on the part of the listeners. They are inclined to fret at the fact that wrongdoers do well in life—maybe better than the faithful. Indeed the faithless are a threat to the faithful: they scheme against them. The faithless are the strong, the faithful the weak.

2. In that situation, the preacher wants the faithful to drop anger and rather to trust Yhwh, delight in Yhwh, commit things to Yhwh, be still before Yhwh, wait for Yhwh.

3. While believers might simply waste energy fretting at the prosperity of the faithless, they might also be tempted to join them. The homily also wants to stiffen their resolve in walking the right way—to do good, not be tempted into doing wrong even if that seems to be what pays.

4. It wants them to settle for the relatively little that they have now, because the abundance of the faithless will turn out to be short-lived. Their modest position is more secure than the prosperity of the faithless.

5. The present prosperity of the wicked makes it look as if there is no moral order in the world. The homily assures people that there *is* such

an order. There is an inbuilt moral link between acts and consequences. The sword of the faithless finds its way into their own heart.

6. But the homily urges trust in *Yhwh*, not in a moral order. Yhwh is faithful. Yhwh is the subject of a sequence of active verbs—give, act, bring out, support, acknowledge, exalt, help, rescue, deliver. The moral order is the way Yhwh works things out. The link between these is the fact that Yhwh laughs because Yhwh has seen what is going to happen.

7. The homily's key individual motif is land. Positively, the faithful will enjoy permanent possession of the land, and thus enjoy such abundance of well-being that they are enabled to share with other people. Negatively, the fate of the faithless is to be cut off from the land, which in effect means being cut off—period.

8. The homily knows that the faithful do fall and do fall into the hands of the faithless. It promises that Yhwh sees they get up again and do not stay down.

Commentators often emphasize that Ps. 37 needs to be seen in light of less reassuring teaching such as that of Job or Jesus. This is a code way of saying that Ps. 37 is not true, a device to sideline it. It also misses the point in a number of ways. The psalm's perspective is confirmed, not denied, by the story of Job at its beginning and end. Jesus also confirms it when he encourages people, "Strive first for the kingdom of God and his righteousness, and all these things [food, drink, and clothes] will be given to you as well" (Matt. 6:33 NRSV). He also takes one of his blessings from v. 11. A standard translation of that blessing speaks of the meek inheriting the earth (Matt. 5:5). Psalm 37 offers a twofold contrast. On the one hand, the people who inherit are the weak. While the psalm makes clear that they are expected to be people committed to Yhwh, its good news is that God's promise emerges from God; it is not a response to human deserving. It is not earned by meekness; it is a divine response to human need. On the other hand, what these people inherit is the land, not the earth. The psalm encourages no excessive expectations. Its promise is modest. It promises that families will have the piece of land they need to grow the crops they need, and that people will thus be able to sit under their vines and fig trees. And/or it promises that a community will have the land it needs to live its community life and will not have its land taken over by other powers that want to extend their holdings, still less build themselves an empire. It thus implies a warning about people who occupy more land than they need for their family to grow their food, or about colonizing powers that appropriate the land of other peoples.[13]

---

13. Cf. Brueggemann, *Psalms and the Life of Faith*, 249–53.

Psalm 37 explicitly acknowledges that this does not always work out—indeed, if that were not so, it would not have needed to be written. It insists that we do not let the negative experiences of believers obscure the fact that God is committed to making a moral order work out. "Oh, such shameful disloyalty, mistrust, and damnable unbelief! We refuse to believe these rich, powerful, and comforting promises of God. When we hear a few threatening words from the wicked, we begin to tremble at the slightest threat. May God help us to obtain the true faith which we see the Scriptures demanding everywhere!"[14] Thus people who are disturbed by the prosperity of the wicked and their own poverty should "drink this Psalm by way of potion."[15]

---

14. Luther, *Selected Psalms*, 3:229.
15. Augustine, *Psalms*, 91.

Psalm 38
Suffering and Sin

Translation

Composition. David's. For Commemoration. [Concerning the Sabbath. (LXX)]

¹Yhwh, do not in your wrath rebuke me,
  or in your fury chastise me.

²For your arrows—they have come down into me,
  and your hand has come down on me.
³There is no soundness in my flesh because of your rage;
  there is no well-being in my bones because of my failure.
⁴For my acts of waywardness have passed over my head;
  like a heavy burden, they are too heavy for me.
⁵My wounds smell and fester
  because of my stupidity.

⁶I am quite bent, bowed down;
  all day I walk about dark,
⁷Because my loins are full of burning/dishonor;
  there is no soundness in my flesh.
⁸I am quite numb and crushed;
  I howl because of the growling in my heart.
⁹My Lord, all my desires are before you,
  my moaning is not hidden from you.

¹⁰My heart has taken flight, my strength has abandoned me;
    the light in my eyes, too[a]—it has gone from me.

¹¹My friends and neighbors—
    they stand away from me in my affliction.
The people near me have stood far off,[b]
    ¹²and people who seek my life lay traps.
People who aim at trouble for me speak of destruction
    and talk lies[c] all day.
¹³But I am like a deaf man, who cannot hear,[d]
    like a dumb man, who cannot open his mouth.
¹⁴I have become like a man who does not hear,
    in whose mouth there are no rebukes.
¹⁵For I wait for you, Yhwh;
    you yourself will answer, my Lord, my God.
¹⁶For I said, "They must not rejoice over me,[e]
    those who exalted themselves against me when my foot faltered."

¹⁷For I am poised for stumbling
    and my pain is before me continually.
¹⁸For I recognize my wrongdoing,
    I am anxious because of my failure,
¹⁹And my mortal enemies are powerful—
    Many are those who are against me with falsehood.
²⁰Those who repay evil for good
    attack me for pursuing good.[f]

²¹Do not abandon me, Yhwh;
    my God, be not far off from me.
²²Hasten to my aid,
    my Lord, my deliverance.

Interpretation

This prayer psalm begins and ends with pleas, for Yhwh's wrath to be withdrawn (v. 1) and for Yhwh to deliver rather than abandon (vv.

---

a. Lit., "them, too." On the construction, see JM 146d.

b. Yiqtol and qatal forms of the same verb alternate in v. 11b–c without apparent difference in meaning.

c. GKC 124e takes this as intensive pl., "base deceit." On "destruction" (also pl.), see on 5:9 [10].

d. The verb is first person, thus perhaps: "For I am like a deaf man—I cannot hear."

e. Lit., "For I said, 'Lest they rejoice over me'"—an idiomatic use of *pen* after the verb "say" (see BDB; GKC 152w).

f. K *rdwpy* and Q *rādĕpî* are variant forms of the inf. with suffix (see GKC 61c).

21–22). The main part divides into two sections that lament first the suppliant's sickness (vv. 2–10) and then the stance taken by other people (vv. 11–19). These laments incorporate some declaration of trust in God and some self-defense (vv. 15, 20), but also some recognition of the suppliant's sin (vv. 3, 5, 18). One might outline the psalm as a stepped structure, though there is some arbitrariness about the location of the divisions within vv. 2–10 and 11–20:

Plea (v. 1)
    Protest at sickness and confession of sin (vv. 2–5)
    Protest at sickness and expression of trust (vv. 6–10)
    Protest at other people's attacks and expression of trust
      (vv. 11–16)
    Protest at other people's attacks and confession of sin (vv. 17–20)
Plea (vv. 21–22)

Psalm 38 perhaps comes here because it picks up words from Ps. 37 such as "talk" (*hāgâ*, v. 12; cf. 37:30) and the unusual word for deliverance (*těšû'â*, v. 22; cf. 37:39). Further, it has twenty-two lines, like an alphabetical psalm, which might be chance, but its position following Ps. 37 encourages readers to recognize this feature of the psalm (cf. the "Interpretation" for Ps. 33). It includes a number of repetitions that contribute to its unity, such as "rebuke" (vv. 1, 14), "come down" (vv. 2a, 2b), "there is no soundness in my flesh" (vv. 3, 7), "because of" (vv. 3a, 3b, 5), "failure/wrongdoing" (vv. 3–4, 18), "heavy/be heavy" (v. 4, twice), "quite" (vv. 6, 8), "before" (vv. 9, 11 [see comment], 17), "abandon" (vv. 10, 21), "stand" (vv. 11b, 11c), "far off" (vv. 11, 21), "hear" (vv. 13, 14), "good" (vv. 20a, 20b). Those repetitions link with another feature. It is hard to imagine this carefully expressed and structured poetic piece being composed by a person who is undergoing the suffering and attacks described in the psalm.[1] Indeed, it is hard to imagine someone having all these symptoms.[2] The psalm was more likely created by someone who knows about sin and suffering and is well-acquainted with the Israelite tradition of prayer, and is thus in a position to compose a prayer that people undergoing suffering could use to express their pain, their trust, their repentance, and their plea. This would explain both the variety in the imagery and the general nature of the confession.

    1. See Rogerson and McKay, *Psalms*, 1:181.
    2. Cf. Craigie, *Psalms 1–50*, 304. Watson (*Classical Hebrew Poetry*, 320) thus sees it as characterized by hyperbole.

Briggs suggested that the allusions to sin are secondary, and Lindström has revived this argument.³ Even if one or other of their constructions of an earlier version of the psalm is correct, we are left with the question of interpreting the psalm as it stands. Its distinctiveness suggests that we should not conform it to other psalms that do not make the link between sin and suffering.

> Composition. David's. For Commemoration. [Concerning the Sabbath. (LXX)]

Heading. See glossary. "David's" would raise the possibility of using the psalm in connection with the nation's affliction, which Isa. 1:5–6 portrays as that of an individual human being in terms that parallel the psalm. "Commemoration" (*zākar* hiphil) can be a general word for praise (cf. 20:7 [8]); the infinitival expression here comes in 1 Chron. 16:4. But it is not clear how this would relate to the psalm that follows. On the other hand, Sirach links the commemoration or token offering (*'azkārâ*; Lev. 2:2, 9, 16; 5:12; 6:15 [8]; 24:7; Num. 5:26) with prayer for healing and confession (Sir. 38:9–11). The general understanding of the *'azkārâ* within the OT does not especially illumine the psalm, not least because of the unclarity about its significance.⁴ But if the *'azkārâ* had come to be linked with healing and confession, the heading could well designate the psalm as appropriate in this connection.

> ¹Yhwh, do not in your wrath rebuke me,
>   or in your fury chastise me.

38:1. An opening plea. An invocation of Yhwh and a negative particle, both of which apply to both cola, lead into two precisely parallel clauses comprising the preposition *bĕ*, a word for "anger" with a second-person singular suffix, and a second-person singular verb (one hiphil, one piel) with first-person singular suffix. The first verb is rather mild, but the second is more painful and more obviously leads into what follows in the psalm. The word order puts some emphasis on the prepositional phrases and could imply that the suppliant grants the appropriateness of some rebuke or chastisement but asks that Yhwh not get too enthusiastic about it, and/or recognizes the educative nature of suffering but asks that this not be combined with punishment. Yet the companion plea that closes the psalm does not suggest a mere request for suitably moderate or pedagogical rebuke/chastisement. The suppliant wants de-

---

3. Briggs, *Psalms*, 1:335–36; Lindström, *Suffering and Sin*, 239–44. Both extend this argument through Pss. 38–41, Lindström more systematically (*Suffering and Sin*, 239–323).
4. See (e.g.) John E. Hartley, *Leviticus*, WBC (Dallas: Word, 1992), 30.

liverance and re-establishment. As a whole the psalm also clarifies that it is not asking Yhwh not to get wrathful, not to start punishing (as v. 1 in isolation could suggest). It presupposes that wrathful chastisement is already a reality; the psalm is asking Yhwh to stop. The wording is quite similar to that in 6:1 [2]. The most marked difference is the appearance of "wrath" (*qeṣep*) instead of "anger" (*'ap*); a word that nearly always refers to divine wrath thus replaces a word that often denotes human anger. This makes for a difference in the relationship of the two cola. In Ps. 6 the reference to fury (*ḥēmâ*) makes the second colon heighten the first with its allusion to anger. In Ps. 38 the reference to fury makes the second colon clarify that the divine wrath is not a cool objective matter but a hotly felt one.

38:2–5. Four bicola of lament take up the interaction between Yhwh's wrath, the suppliant's suffering, and the suppliant's wrongdoing. Wrath and suffering are the focus in vv. 2–3a, wrongdoing and suffering in vv. 3b–5.

> ²For your arrows—they have come down into me,
> and your hand has come down on me.

The wrath is mediated in down-to-earth actual experience by Yhwh's arrows and Yhwh's hand. The two cola are parallel, ordered *abcb'c'a'*. The second clause thus follows a word order we might expect, but the first opens with the subject and gives it emphasis. The verb in both cola is the unusual *nāḥat*, niphal then qal, but with slightly different implications. The arrows come down and penetrate the person, yet perhaps the descent of the hand onto the person is more devastating. The idea of Yhwh shooting arrows may go back to the portrayal of Resheph, the master divine archer at Ugarit, who shoots illness at people.[5]

> ³There is no soundness in my flesh because of your rage;
> there is no well-being in my bones because of my failure.

The consequences and causes are described in two long balancing cola (4-4).[6] On one hand there is no wholeness or health (*mĕtōm*, related to the word for *integrity) and no *well-being in the suppliant's flesh or bones—that is, in the entirety of the outward person, the covering of flesh and skin, and the inner person with the firmness embodied in the bones that should signify firmness and strength. The cause of this can

---

5. See (e.g.) Dahood, *Psalms*, 1:235; also *DDD*.
6. Each comprises a noun clause beginning "There is no" (*'ên*) that leads to a word for health, a *b* expression referring to an aspect of the person, and a *mippĕnê* expression to denote a cause.

be described in two ways. To say that the trouble issues from Yhwh's rage restates v. 1. Wrath suggests the distinctive power of divine anger; fury suggests its burning force, rage or indignation (*za'am*) points to the personal sense of outrage expressed in the reaction of someone who feels affronted by a party that has failed to meet obligations. And this links with the other way of speaking about causes. Trouble has come "because of my failure." The formal similarity of the two *min* expressions conceals a substantial dissimilarity between "your rage" and "my failure"—though these two are assumed to be linked: the psalm does not say "because of the consciousness of my sin" (as if it were talking about a psychological process) but "because of my sin."[7] It is because Yhwh is enraged at the suppliant's *failure or shortcomings. This link is unusual for the Psalms and thus brings the long line to an unexpected conclusion.

> [4]For my acts of waywardness have passed over my head;
> like a heavy burden, they are too heavy for me.

Verses 4–5 expand on v. 3, v. 4 proceeding more metaphorically, v. 5 more concretely. They particularly take up the unexpected admission that closed v. 3. But reference to Yhwh's anger and Yhwh's punitive activity now disappears from the psalm. The focus lies on that other form of causality, "my failure," and its consequences; when Yhwh reappears, it will be as the one who listens to prayer and can respond and deliver.

So now the reality that overwhelms is not Yhwh's anger or hostile action but the suppliant's acts of *waywardness. They are a crushing burden. When Christians speak in such terms, they often refer to the psychological burden of sin or to its effect on our relationship with God. In the present context, the psalm's point is a different one. The overwhelming and burdening it describes is the effect of sin on the body in the form of the total loss of health and well-being to which v. 3 has referred. The two cola in v. 4 are parallel, with "for my acts of waywardness" applying to both. Their verbs are parallel, with one qatal governing a direct object, the other yiqtol governing an indirect object. The first verb implies a simile along the lines of "like a waterfall," "like waves and billows," "like a flood" (cf. 42:7–8 [8–9]; Isa. 8:8). The explicit simile in the second colon then parallels that implicit one in the first. Schematically put, we see:

For my acts of waywardness	[like a deep flood]	have passed over	my head;
	like a heavy burden	are too heavy	for me.

7. Against Luther, *Selected Psalms*, 3:157.

Images such as overwhelming floods are usually a figure for the wrath of God that engulfs people. The fact that here it is "my acts of waywardness" that overwhelm me highlights the difference in perspective that began in v. 3b.

> ⁵My wounds smell and fester
> because of my stupidity.

Verse 5 makes the point again, with the second colon completing the first and the line as a whole paralleling each of the cola in v. 4. The first colon thus gives a more concrete description of what the lack of soundness or well-being looks and smells like, and the second explains this in terms of the suppliant's "stupidity" (*'iwwelet*). Such terms are characteristic of Proverbs (e.g., 5:23; 14:1, 3, 8, 17, 18, 24, 29) rather than of Psalms (only 69:5 [6]). The word suggests indiscipline, self-deceit, and impatience, and the recognition that intelligent people make just as foolish decisions and choices as less intelligent people; the only difference is that the disaster they bring to themselves and other people may be bigger. The suppliant is aware of having behaved in ways that were religiously and/or relationally stupid—stupid in relation to God and/or to other people. Perhaps v. 20 implies that the suppliant's relationships with other people have been honorable and that the focus lies on failure, wrongdoing, and stupidity before God. The psalm invites suppliants to be exceptions to the rule that "people's stupidity ruins their way, and their heart rages against Yhwh" (Prov. 19:3).

38:6–10. Five more bicola of lament further describe the suppliant's suffering (vv. 6–8) and conviction about Yhwh's relationship with that (vv. 9–10). Talk of the suppliant's sin as well as of Yhwh's wrath thus disappears for a while—or rather goes underground, as we shall see.

> ⁶I am quite bent, bowed down;
> all day I walk about dark,

In describing this suffering, vv. 6–8 start again with the outward and move toward the inward. First there is the suppliant's outward disposition, the reality that other people see. Verse 6 begins with an irony or a paronomasia or two. "I am bent" (*'āwâ* niphal) is the verb from which "acts of waywardness" in v. 4 (*'āwōn*) comes; waywardness involves bending one's way, perverting it. Although v. 6 thus does not talk directly about sin, it may hint that the suppliant's bentness of body issues from bentness of life.[8] Then "I am bowed down" is a verb (*šāḥaḥ*) that usually

---

8. I take it that there is one root *'āwâ* (so *HALOT*), though if historically there were two (so BDB), this makes no difference in the way the psalm brings the two words into association.

denotes prostrating oneself in humility before God or before a human being. Fortunately the psalm indeed suggests that the suppliant is bowed down before God, as well as physically bowed down. In the parallel colon with the description in terms of color rather than of posture, the reference to a gloomy appearance may make the point again. The suppliant goes around like someone mourning, which could include mourning for sin and not just gloom at suffering. The cola work *abbʿaʾ*, two verbs and then an adverbial expression, an adverbial expression and then two verbs, with the four verbs showing some variety—niphal and qal qatal, then qal participle and piel.

> ⁷Because my loins are full of burning/dishonor;
> there is no soundness in my flesh.

The ambiguity continues. Are the suppliant's loins full of burning (EVV) or of dishonor (LXX, Jerome)? The noun *niqleh* (strictly, a niphal participle) can be derived from *qālâ* I, "roast" ("burn" more generally in cognate languages), or from *qālâ* II, "belittle." The suppliant burns with fever but also burns with shame. The second colon parallels the first in content though not in form, and generalizes the point. It repeats the opening of v. 3, but does "soundness" also now carry the overtones of *integrity?

> ⁸I am quite numb and crushed;
> I howl because of the growling in my heart.

The pattern of v. 6a in turn reappears: two verbs (though here both are niphal and joined by *w* rather than asyndetic) followed by "quite" (*ʿad-mĕʾōd*). But the nature of the two verbs is to allude more to the inner state of the person than to the outward bearing. "Numb" (*pûg*) is a rare verb as likely to suggest an inner numbness or paralysis as an outer one (cf. Gen. 45:26). "Broken" (*dākâ*) is likewise a rare byform (of *dākāʾ*) that also suggests an inner crushedness corresponding to an outer one (cf. 10:10)—it is used for outer and inner brokenness in 51:8, 17 [10, 19]). Both these verbs make for a remarkable contrast with the words in the second colon. "Howl" (*šāʾaq*) is unexpected because it usually denotes the roaring of a lion or a warrior; only here does it suggest shouting out in distress (though *šĕʾāgâ* is used in this sense in 22:1 [2]; 32:3; Job 3:24). The more familiar meaning of the word is emphasized by the reference to "growling," which is also commonly used of lions and perhaps literally refers to the growling of a lion over its prey as opposed to its roaring as it pounces.⁹ There is thus some suggestive tension

---

9. Cf. BDB 980.

between the two cola. The suppliant is numb yet shouting out, crushed yet growling. In our terms, it might seem that the talk of a growling heart makes the inner aspect to the suppliant's suffering most explicit, but we should perhaps see a parallel with the burning in the loins. The suppliant is indeed crushed in heart but also feels a physical pain inside, which generates a moan or growl.

> [9]My Lord, all my desires are before you,
> my moaning is not hidden from you.

Verses 9–10 are then a surprise. Yhwh has been portrayed as one acting in wrath against the suppliant, and quite justly. Suddenly the psalm is asserting that Yhwh sees the desires and hears the moaning of the suppliant. The line addresses Yhwh as my *Lord, and the way the lines unfold suggests this is an occurrence of *'ădōnāy* where the suffix has the personal meaning. Before (*neged*) Yhwh are not only the suppliant's sins (90:8) and outward cry (88:1 [2]) but also the suppliant's desires (cf. 10:17; 21:2 [3]). These are the desires expressed in words, but reference to them implies Yhwh's capacity to look behind the words to the inner person. That might be a frightening capacity, but here the suppliant views it as good news. The Lord can see the depth of longing to get out of this affliction. The privacy of the inner being can be public to Yhwh, and the suppliant is happy for that scrutiny, believing that Yhwh's knowledge of those desires in their fervency can only work in the favor of the person praying.

The second colon parallels the first, producing an *abcc'b'* line; further reference to outward moaning accompanies reference to inner desire. Moaning (*'ănāḥâ*) is the self-expression of Israel in Egypt, of Job, and of Lamentations (Exod. 2:23; Job 3:24; 23:2; Lam. 1:4, 8, 11, 21, 22)—an impressive company (cf. Ps. 6:6 [7]; 31:10 [11]). The negative verb accompanies the earlier positive prepositional expression and offers a litotes, the negative statement implying a strong positive one: one can imagine Yhwh reacting, "No, they are certainly not hidden!" Like any decent praying person in the OT, the suppliant has made no secret of those deep longings for relief from the pain that vv. 2–8 have described. Yhwh knows all about them.

> [10]My heart has taken flight, my strength has abandoned me;
> the light in my eyes, too—it has gone from me.

Lest there should be any lingering doubt, v. 10 summarizes them again in another long, 4-4 line that systematically expounds the sense that everything has gone from the suppliant's life. The first verb (*sāḥar*) is usually taken to mean something such as palpitate; its form is unique, repeating the last two root letters, a form that might suggest rapid, repeated movement.[10] But the verb elsewhere denotes to go on a journey, and the parallelism within v. 10a and between the two cola rather suggests the idea that the suppliant's heart has indeed gone off on a journey. It refers to that human experience of there seeming to be a hole in one's insides in a time of grief, pain, or loss—as if one's heart had been removed. The succeeding clause complements that with its generalization about the suppliant's strength disappearing. "That, too, has slipped out of my body and gone off somewhere else." Then the parallel colon makes the point in another way by speaking of the light in the eyes having gone. The putting out of the light is a conventional figure for death (e.g., Job 18:5–6), but here the psalm typically re-mints it with its reference to the light of the eyes, not the light in the tent or house that is extinguished. Again, in English we have the expression "The light seemed to have gone off" inside someone, as we look into their eyes. The life has gone. The point is expressed in a jerky way that corresponds to the disjointed nature of the suppliant's experience. Yes, heart, strength, and light are gone.

38:11–16. Surprisingly or not, the focus now changes markedly. So far, there have been only two people in the picture, the suppliant and Yhwh, but friends and enemies now come to be prominent. On the other hand, it is characteristic of prayer psalms to talk about the involvement of other people in one's troubles; in this sense that change is not surprising. In other respects vv. 11–16 continue the tone of vv. 6–10 in focusing on current suffering in a way that hints at an acknowledgment of wrongdoing (but that will not become explicit again until vv. 17–20) and in addressing Yhwh with a statement, but not a plea.

> [11a–b]My friends and neighbors—
> they stand away from me in my affliction.

Thus three lines (vv. 11–12) turn first to friends and enemies. The first responses of human beings to the illness of others are often withdrawal (cf. Luke 23:49)[11] or attack. "Friends" are literally people who love me or are *dedicated to me, or people whom I love or have dedicated myself to.[12] "Neighbors" are fellow members of my community, who as such also owe a commitment to me. The two words might be describing the same people. But these people (lit.) "stand

---

10. GKC 55e. D. Winton Thomas ("A Note on *libbî sĕḥarḥar* in Psalm xxxviii 11," *JTS* 40 [1939]: 390–91) suggests that the verb is a different *sāḥar*, meaning "bewitch."

11. Cf. Kraus, *Psalms*, 1:414.

12. That is, the suffix may be subjective, "I am the one who dedicates myself," or objective, "I am the one others dedicate themselves to."

from before my affliction." My affliction and my desire to be out of it are "before" Yhwh (v. 9), but these friends apparently cannot bear having this affliction "before" them. It is a common enough human reaction to suffering. Suffering is too hard to be in the presence of, too threatening, too anxiety-making. "Affliction" (*nega'*) is etymologically a "touch," a marked understatement, though the noun always means something like a blow.[13]

> ¹¹ᶜThe people near me have stood far off,
> ¹²ᵃand people who seek my life lay traps.

Verse 11c–12a begins by restating the point, with a more explicit irony. Our friends and neighbors are the people who are supposed to be near us—they *are* near us, by virtue of being members of our family and community. But these near ones stand far off! The second colon then may refer to more active enemies or may refer to the same people, who are now actively attacking as well as distancing themselves. One's enemies will also be members of one's community or even of one's family. They are not merely failing to attempt to make the situation better, (e.g.) by praying with the suppliant. They are trying to make it worse, perhaps by praying against the suppliant, because they "know" that the suppliant is a marked sinner and believe that they are doing God's work in bringing God's punishment, like Christians attacking gays or abortion doctors.

> ¹²ᵇPeople who aim at trouble for me speak of destruction
> and talk lies all day.

The first colon parallels v. 12a (supporting MT's verse division). The subject is again a participial clause, but the predicate turns from action to speech. That might seem an anticlimax after reference to laying traps, but speaking of destruction (to one another) will be the way they lay traps. Verse 12c restates the point, *talking deceit being the way they speak of destruction.

> ¹³But I am like a deaf man, who cannot hear,
> like a dumb man, who cannot open his mouth.
> ¹⁴I have become like a man who does not hear,
> in whose mouth there are no rebukes.

---

13. Jerome renders "leprosy," but neither this Hebrew word nor the rest of the psalm's description of the illness provides a basis for inferring that the psalm refers to a specific illness. BHS suggests removing the word, but it recurs in Ps. 39:11 [12], suggesting that it was also part of Ps. 38 when the Psalter was compiled.

Verses 13–14 begin to describe the way the supplicant copes with these attacks, specifically the words. They do so in two lines parallel to each other as well as internally parallel. The "But I" with which the lines start advertises a contrast with what precedes: the subject through vv. 11–12 was those other people, the subject through vv. 13–14 is "I," and two lines of noun clauses contrast with two lines of verbal clauses. Each of the two lines begins by describing the supplicant as one who simply does not listen to what people say. We already know this is not true, and succeeding lines will make that clearer. The supplicant certainly listens. But the two opening cola more precisely make a *comparison* with someone who cannot hear, and the two second cola give precision to where the similarity lies. The supplicant is like someone who does not hear in the sense of not making any response to the words of the enemies; it is as if the supplicant had not heard them.

In v. 14, the second colon makes explicit what kind of response the supplicant does not give and picks up the psalm's opening verb, "rebuke" (*yākaḥ*). It is almost as if the supplicant is behaving toward others in the way that opening line had asked Yhwh to behave. The line also points to an aspect of the general significance of the complaints at and prayers against other people that appear in many psalms. The Psalms expect people who have been wronged to say and do nothing to the people who have wronged them, and to that end they encourage them to speak forcefully to God about these people. The protest and lament of the Psalms give people opportunity to express their anger, but to do so to God rather than to the people who deserve it.

> **15**For I wait for you, Yhwh;
> you yourself will answer, my Lord, my God.

More specifically, vv. 15–16 indicate what the supplicant takes as the appropriate response. This is not rebuking people who have let us down or attacked us but waiting for Yhwh. The "for" with which v. 15 begins (obscured by EVV) is significant: because the supplicant is *waiting for Yhwh, the attitude of silence can be maintained. The second colon explains why it is possible to wait, or clarifies what is the object of waiting. Waiting is not a vague hanging on to see if something will happen, but a keen anticipation of what we know will happen. The threefold invocation of Yhwh, my *Lord (cf. v. 9), and my God functions both to build up the supplicant's conviction that Yhwh will answer and to remind Yhwh forcefully of the personal and relational reasons why Yhwh must do so.

> **16**For I said, "They must not rejoice over me,
> those who exalted themselves against me when my foot faltered."

Verse 16 introduces the motivation behind the waiting, and perhaps implicitly indicates the content of the prayer about which the supplicant was confident of an answer. Not responding to the attackers was not an indication of a cool dismissiveness. The supplicant was anxious about the possibility that the whole experience of chastisement would end in shame, with the attackers who have made it an occasion for attacks and plots continuing to rejoice at the suppliant's *falling down. That might refer once more to the suppliant's sickness, or it might refer to moral or religious downfall (e.g., going after other gods) that led to it.

38:17–20. The section pairing with vv. 2–5 again describes the suffering that characterizes current experience and acknowledges wrongdoing, expanding on the basis for the anxiety expressed in v. 16.

> ¹⁷For I am poised for stumbling
> and my pain is before me continually.

The supplicant is on the cliff's edge (v. 17). The point is expressed paradoxically: (lit.) "I am made firm [*kûn*] for stumbling." As before, a supplicant might say that to signify an awareness of being "prone to stumble" in a moral or religious sense, or to indicate a fear of being found guilty before the community and being executed or cast out for one's failure. The second colon gives the evidence for this. Not only are "all my desires *before* God" (v. 9), but also, "My pain is *before* me continually." While this might refer to outer pain, the psalm has come to speak more of inner pain, and that leads particularly well into v. 18. So the pain is the sense of divine chastisement and/or human abandonment and/or moral or religious guilt, and this pain is in danger of pushing the supplicant over the edge.

> ¹⁸For I recognize my wrongdoing,
> I am anxious because of my failure,

The reversion to a public acknowledgment of wrongdoing and failure, resuming that in vv. 3–4, is a surprise. The second colon goes beyond that recognition to inner anxiety (the verb *dā'ag*). Perhaps the implication is that the anxiety may be what tips the supplicant over the edge. Perhaps the fact of sin might be what makes Yhwh quite willing to let the supplicant go. Perhaps the underlying fact of sin makes it inevitable that a cause-and-effect process works itself out, and that the supplicant does fall over the edge. Perhaps it is simply that the supplicant professes not merely to give public acknowledgment of sin but also to feel inwardly troubled by it.[14]

---

14. Cf. NRSV's "I am sorry," though the word does not directly denote regret or repentance.

> ¹⁹And my mortal enemies are powerful—
>   Many are those who are against me with falsehood.
> ²⁰Those who repay evil for good
>   attack me for pursuing good.

The return once more to the attacks of the enemies in vv. 19–20 is another surprise. Perhaps the supplicant is recognizing two sorts of factors that could mean stumbling, both the sin that v. 18 acknowledged and the attacks of other people that vv. 19–20 go on to. Morally, the sin would be the cause of the downfall; practically, it would be these attacks that brought it about. This still leaves a tension with v. 20. How can the supplicant both acknowledge sin and complain to Yhwh about the enemies' attacks? Perhaps the implication is that the enemies are at fault because they were not the people the supplicant had sinned against. If the conflict is a private matter, the supplicant's position then parallels Judah's position in the time of Isaiah, when it has to acknowledge the sin that led to the Assyrian invasion, but might still protest to Yhwh at the wrongness of the Assyrians' action. It would also parallel Judah's position in the time of Ezra and Nehemiah, when it has to acknowledge the sin of mixed marriages but might still protest to Yhwh at the pressure from the other Persian provincial officials. But perhaps this tension is simply another sign that the confession of sin is conventional in the sense that it expresses the same awareness Christians have when they feel a discomfort at the Psalms' assertions about having lived a faithful life. This supplicant is aware of being a sinner and is aware of having no real grounds of complaint when trouble comes. This, too, does not alter the fact that the enemies are in the wrong.

In v. 19 the two cola are neatly parallel.[15] Numerousness thus complements powerfulness, but the unusual elements in the two cola are the two nouns used adverbially, which are syntactically similar and thus complete the neat parallelism, but have quite different precise meanings in relation to the line. The first really functions to fill out the line; the second reasserts the theme of deceit from v. 12.

In v. 20 the second colon simply completes the first. Although a sense of being in the right is implicit in the complaints about the enemies, here comes the (double) claim to have lived a good life—indeed, to have "pursued" *good, presumably the good of the people who are now at-

---

15. They come in *abcc'a'b'* order—lit., "and those who attack me [with regard to my] life are powerful, and many are those who are *against me [with regard to] *falsehood." 4QPsª has *ḥinnām*, "without reason," for *ḥayyîm* "[with regard to my] life" (cf. NRSV), perhaps conforming to Ps. 69:[4] 5.

tacking. Evidently a sense of having done wrong is compatible with a sense of having done what is good. This again hints that the failure the psalm refers to is religious wrongdoing.

38:21–22. The psalm finishes as it began, with plea.

> ²¹Do not abandon me, Yhwh;
>   my God, be not far off from me.

The first line takes the negative form of v. 1. The two parallel negatived verbs have similar meaning, but the first rather suggests, "Do not go away," and the second, "Do not stay away," and moreover, "Do not be inactive"—because the notion of Yhwh's nearness and distance suggests activity and inactivity.

> ²²Hasten to my aid,
>   my Lord, my deliverance.

The final verb then goes beyond that in being positive, in asking not only for action but for action *now*, and in adding that what is needed is *help. The unspecificity of the plea is even more remarkable than usual because there is no request for healing. For all that, particularly striking is the way the two lines are dominated by invocations. Four times the psalm calls on God, as "Yhwh," "my God," "my *Lord," and "my deliverance." As the last of these makes explicit, the nature of these invocations is to back up the pleas.

Theological Implications

Unlike the previous so-called "Penitential Psalms," Pss. 6 and 32, this prayer psalm does incorporate an expression of penitence. It acknowledges sin in terms of *failure or shortcoming, *waywardness, and stupidity—a negative falling short, a positive but twisted activity, and the outworking of a mind gone awry. This expression of penitence does come intermingled with other elements in the psalm and is not central to it, but the psalm's chief theological significance lies in its distinctive linking of sin and suffering.

The community prose prayers in Ezra 9 and Neh. 9 might suggest two possible links between an awareness of affliction, an acknowledgment of sin, and a claim to have acted rightly. Ezra 9 holds together a corporate experience of reversal and bondage, an awareness of sin over the centuries, and a particular recent act of wrongdoing that leads to the prayer, but it is set in the context of recurrent tensions with the neighboring Persian provinces for which the Judean community does not feel responsible. Nehemiah 9 belongs in a similar setting without the awareness of a recent act of wrongdoing. They thus illustrate how one can combine a general sense of sinfulness and failure in relation to God (and perhaps an awareness of a specific failure in this relationship) with the conviction that one has not behaved too badly in relation to other people. One can also combine with these awarenesses the realization that present negative experiences link with the general sinfulness (and if appropriate, the specific sin) and also a plea that Yhwh nevertheless relieve that affliction. Psalm 38 supports the idea that communities might pray in this way, and it implies that individuals might also do so.

Commentators often refer to the "ancient" belief that there is a link between sin and suffering, and suggest that more mature OT insight moved beyond this belief. Craigie thus comments, "The first consequence of sickness is to create a sense of guilt and distance from God," while "the second consequence is the development of a sense of alienation from fellow human beings."[16] The psalm might thus testify to the conviction that the suppliant's sickness resulted from sin, but the presence of the psalm in the Psalter need not indicate that the Psalter accepts that view, only that part of the freedom of the people of God is to express such convictions.[17] The suppliant's conviction is that sin produced suffering, not that suffering produced awareness of sin. And this is not simply an ancient belief. The belief that there is such a link and the belief that often sin and suffering are unrelated seem to have coexisted since ancient times and still coexist today; both appear in the NT (see the comments on "Theological Implications" on Ps. 32). The many psalms that protest because suffering comes undeserved warn us against reckoning that the two are always linked; Ps. 38 and other psalms warn us against denying that there is ever a link.

The link takes two forms, suggested by those two prose prayers. Our suffering can link with specific failures in our relationship with God: for instance, we may overwork and become ill. It can also link with the more general fact that we fail in our relationship with God and/or share in the failure of our communities. This understanding corresponds to the conventional Christian view that sees all the people of God as sinners and always needing to confess their sin; this view stands over against the one also appearing in Scripture that sees the people of God as fundamentally committed to God and sees wrongdoing as an aberration characterizing distinctly wicked people. The psalm's stepped structure also coheres with its distinctive stance in relation to suffering. This structure means there

16. Craigie, *Psalms 1–50*, 304.
17. Ibid., 303.

is no movement toward resolution in the psalm, as there is in Pss. 6 or 22. It goes round in circles. That may make it a psalm appropriate for ongoing illness, as opposed to illness that eventually is cured. It faces the consequences in terms of what chronic illness does to relationships with God and with other people. For instance, people may find it easier to pray for someone when they first grow ill, but harder to pray when they do not recover, and more inclined then to reckon that they must (e.g.) be wrong in their relationship with God.

Psalm 39

Living in Light of the Fact That We Will Die

Translation

The leader's. Jeduthun's.[a] Composition. David's.

1I said, I will keep watch on my ways
    so as not to sin with my tongue.
I will keep[b] a muzzle on my mouth
    while the faithless is still before me.
2I kept dumb, in silence;
    I kept quiet more than it was good,
And my pain—it stirred,
    3my mind became hot within me.
As I talked, fire burned;
    I spoke with my tongue.

4Yhwh, make me acknowledge my end—
    the number of my days, what they are;
    I want to acknowledge how passing I am.
5There, you have made my days handbreadths;
    my span is as nothing before you.

---

  a. One might translate "The leader, Jeduthun's." K, LXX, Jerome have "Jedithun's."
  b. LXX might imply *ʾāśîmâ*, "I will put," for MT *ʾešmĕrâ*; this is more straightforward but loses the first of the many repetitions in the psalm.

Yes, every human being, standing firm, is altogether breath; (Rise)
⁶yes, a man goes about in the shadow/as a shadow.ᶜ
Yes, it is for a breath that people hustle;
he heaps things up, but does not know who gathers them.
⁷So now, what do I look to, my Lord?—
my hope is in you.

⁸Rescue me from all my rebellions;
do not make me the reproach of the fool.
⁹When I kept dumb, I would not open my mouth,
because you were the one who acted.
¹⁰Turn away from me your affliction;
because of the hostility of your hand I—I am undone.
¹¹With rebukes for wrongdoing you have chastised a man
and consumed like a moth what he loves;ᵈ
yes, every human being is a breath. (Rise)
¹²Do listen to my plea, Yhwh,
do give ear to my cry for help;ᵉ
do not be silent at my tears,
Because I am a sojourner with you,
a transient like all my ancestors.
¹³Smear [your eyes]/look awayᶠ from me so that I may smile,
before I go and there is nothing of me.

Interpretation

The psalm again follows the previous one because of verbal links, and also a similar underlying concern including the unusual awareness that sin lies behind an illness. This psalm, too, speaks of being dumb (vv. 2, 9; cf. 38:13 [14]), before you (v. 5; cf. 38:9 [10]), hope (v. 7; cf. 38:15 [16]), my Lord (v. 7; cf. 38:9, 15 [10, 16]), opening the mouth (v. 9; cf. 38:13 [14]), your hand (v. 10; cf. 38:2 [3]), affliction (v. 10; cf. 38:11 [12]), rebukes (v. 11; cf. 38:1 [2], 14 [15]), chastise (v. 11; cf. 38:1 [2]), and being deaf (v. 12; cf. 38:13 [14]). Like Ps. 38, it also likes repetitions: keep/keep watch (v. 1), my mouth (vv. 1, 9), my tongue (vv. 1, 3), I kept dumb (vv. 2, 9), acknowledge (vv. 4a, 4c), my days (vv. 4, 5), breath (vv.

---

c. BDB takes this as an idiosyncratic instance of the word *ṣelem* that means an image, but that involves a stretch of the word. More likely the noun is a homonym from *ṣālam* II (cf. discussion in *HALOT*).

d. I have taken the qatals as gnomic.

e. The verbs have the -*â* sufformative (see 5:1 [2]).

f. *Hāšaʿ* looks like a form from *šāʿaʿ* suggesting "smear," but it is usually reckoned rather to derive from *šāʿâ*, "look" (e.g., Seybold, *Psalmen*, 162). It might then need emending to *šĕʿēh* (see BDB). MT perhaps invites hearers to keep both expressions in mind.

5, 6), "Yes, every human being is a breath" (vv. 5, 11), go (vv. 6, 13); and it has more occurrences of "yes" (*'ak*) than any other chapter in the OT.[1] The psalm's style is asyndetic (vv. 2a, 10a) and elliptical: (e.g.) "a breath they hustle" (v. 6) presumably means, "They hustle, but it is only for a breath [something transitory]." Further elliptical expressions (vv. 2a, 5b) are harder to interpret.

In other respects the general nature of the psalm is rather different from that of Ps. 38. It makes no reference to Yhwh's wrath, offers no detailed descriptions of bodily ailment, and shows less concern with sin but much concern with the brevity of human life. Although it uses the form of a personal reflection on experience, this is a means of offering a theological meditation. Its form may involve more "biographical stylization" than an indication that the psalm is a transcript of an actual process.[2]

The psalm comprises recollections, questions, and pleas. In the first part (vv. 1–3) the suppliant recollects seeking to maintain silence but being unable to hold back from speaking. The second part (vv. 4–7) articulates comments about the brevity of human life. The third part (vv. 8–13) is dominated by pleas relating to the experience of illness.

> The leader's. Jeduthun's. Composition. David's.

Heading. See glossary. Jeduthun was one of the three senior temple music leaders in David and Solomon's day, with Asaph and Heman (1 Chron. 16:41–42; 2 Chron. 5:12); another Jeduthun was a seer in Josiah's day (2 Chron. 35:15). For the link with David, 1 Chron. 29:15 is especially significant. There David likens the people to sojourners and transients like their fathers (cf. v. 12) and goes on to speak of their days (cf. v. 5) as like a shadow (cf. v. 6), without hope (cf. v. 7). The psalm could thus be imagined to spell out the implications of David's comments on that occasion. The psalm might be older than Chronicles, the heading younger.

39:1–3. The suppliant imaginatively recollects a personal decision to keep silence (v. 1), an initial success in doing so (v. 2), but an increasing internal pressure to speak (v. 3).

> ¹I said, I will keep watch on my ways
>   so as not to sin with my tongue.
> I will keep a muzzle on my mouth
>   while the faithless is still before me.

---

1. Cf. Ridderbos, *Psalmen*, 289.
2. Kraus, *Psalms*, 1:417. See further Otto Kaiser, "Psalm 39," *Gottes und Der Menschen Weisheit*, BZAW 261 (Berlin: de Gruyter, 1998), 71–83.

In v. 1a, the second colon completes the first and clarifies a question it raises: What "ways" does the suppliant need to watch? The answer is "ways of speech," which can easily be expressions of sin. In the Psalms that can be so in relation to other people, since the faithless do wrong by plotting against others and uttering words of deceit; but this psalm is more concerned with sin against Yhwh, with a failure to take the kind of stance commended in Ps. 37. It recalls the possibility that Job might sin by charging God with wrong (Job 1:22; 2:10).

Verse 1b gives further precision to the resolve. How can one avoid sinning with one's tongue? By muzzling one's mouth so that one cannot open it. Its second colon also completes its first, with a rather allusive adverbial phrase. Is the faithless person a temptation, causing trouble and tempting the suppliant to respond? Is it someone who will attack the suppliant for saying things that seem (e.g.) blasphemous, in the manner of Job's friends? The suppliant will keep silence both because of God (v. 1a) and because of other people (v. 1b).

> 2a-bI kept dumb, in silence;
> I kept quiet more than it was good,

MT takes vv. 2–3 as two 2-2-2 lines, but the last colon of v. 2 and the first of v. 3 look like a pair and I take the two verses as three 2-2 lines. First, v. 2a–b relates how the suppliant apparently kept the muzzle on for a while. Although restraint in speech is commended in Proverbs, otherwise keeping silent is a very unusual OT determination: noise characterizes OT praise and prayer. Outside this psalm the verb *'ālam* never occurs to describe voluntary silence except as an attribute of Yhwh's servant who is silent under attack (Isa. 53:7), though Job also apparently kept silence for a week (2:13). The parallel verb *ḥāšâ* is likewise never used to describe voluntary silence except in Ecclesiastes' meditation (3:7). In the context the succeeding phrase suggests "more than good,"[3] denoting the recognition that silence under affliction is not actually a good thing.

> 2cAnd my pain—it stirred,
> 3amy mind became hot within me.

The middle line then marks the transition from silence to speech. Like a cap on a geyser, a muzzle can work only until the pressure from inside becomes overwhelming. The suppliant's silence involved sitting

---

3. Out of the context "from good" is the obvious meaning for *miṭṭôb*, but this makes poor sense. "To no avail" (NRSV) or "even about good" (cf. NIVI; cf. Tg "from the words of the Torah") are hard to justify. It has been suggested that *ṭôb* is here a word for "speech," which provides a much easier sense. See DCH on *ṭôb* and *ṭābab*.

on pain, and the OT's general stance regarding silence recognizes that pain will not be sat on; it has ways of expressing itself indirectly if we silence it directly. The word order in the first colon emphasizes the way the suppliant's pain insisted on speech. The second colon repeats the point in different imagery.

> ³ᵇAs I talked, fire burned;
> I spoke with my tongue.

The third line may repeat the point, as *talk (which can mean speaking under one's breath to God) might not be incompatible with silence. Indeed, the suppliant may have in mind open speech before other human beings more than the speech to God that follows, which might not count as breaking the vow to which v. 1 referred.[4] As the suppliant thus talked quietly to God about the pain, then, the fire burned strongly within, and speech became inevitable, as it became for Job. And such speech will be uttered before human beings, even if addressed to God. "With my tongue" thus closes off v. 3 as it closed off v. 1a.

39:4–7. We might expect vv. 4–7 to tell us the content of the speaking v. 3 referred to, but they do not seem to do that. There would have been no reason to hesitate to say what appears here. More likely vv. 8–13 are the words the suppliant could not hold back; vv. 4–7 are a further preparation for uttering that prayer.

> ⁴Yhwh, make me acknowledge my end—
> the number of my days, what they are;
> I want to acknowledge how passing I am.

In EVV v. 4 has the psalm asking for knowledge of how short a human life is, but the suppliant already seems to know the answer to that question: the shortness of human life is part of the background to the section. It might be that making the inquiry is a veiled way of complaining about the answer that the suppliant knows, or simply an introduction to such a complaint as is implied in vv. 5–7.[5] More likely the suppliant is asking not for information but for the willingness to live with the facts, for the grace to *acknowledge and accept the nature of human life.[6] The suppliant's current experience of suffering and its possible mortal implications bring home the brevity of human life, and human beings often

---

4. Cf. Ridderbos, *Psalmen*, 283–85.
5. Richard J. Clifford ("What Does the Psalmist Ask for in Psalms 39:5 and 90:12?" *JBL* 119 [2000]: 59–66, see 61) suggests that the psalmist is asking about the end of the affliction.
6. Cf. Luther, *First Lectures*, 1:185.

need help to accept that reality. The second colon makes more explicit the meaning of "my end," how long my life is to be, and when it is to come to an end (cf. Job 6:11). If *yādaʿ* does here mean "acknowledge," that probably implies that the "what" clause is an indirect question, not a direct one. Either way, this will be an example of a question where "what" carries the implication "not very much" (e.g., 30:9 [10]; 56:4 [5]). The unexpected third colon makes that explicit, with the verb picking up from the first colon and the object clause summarizing the second colon. "Passing" (*ḥādēl*) comes tellingly from a verb meaning "cease, come to an end." The comments on the shortness of human life hardly suggest that the supplicant is old;[7] most people in the culture did not live to old age, so a relatively young person would be more aware of this brevity than are people in modern cultures.

> 5a–bThere, you have made my days handbreadths;
> my span is as nothing before you.

Verse 5a–b expands on the point that became more explicit through v. 4, but it now brings Yhwh into new associations with the matter. Yhwh is not merely the one who must help the supplicant acknowledge the facts. First, Yhwh is the one who made the facts what they are. If one wants to measure something relatively small (e.g., in making furniture) one may measure it in handbreadths (e.g., Exod. 25:25; 1 Kings 7:26). Yhwh has given this supplicant a life that is measurable on that scale. It is only a few inches long. The second colon underlines the point, not by comparing the duration of the supplicant's life with the duration of Yhwh's life but by asserting that the brevity of human life makes it unimpressive to Yhwh.[8]

> 5cYes, every human being, standing firm, is altogether breath; (Rise)
> 6yes, a man goes about in the shadow/as a shadow.
> Yes, it is for a breath that people hustle;
> he heaps things up, but does not know who gathers them.

Verses 5c–6 generalize the comment on this individual's life, the threefold asseverative *ʾak* ("Yes") holding the two lines together.[9] The first colon declares (lit.), "Yes, every human being standing firm [is] every breath." Presumably the idea is that even human beings who stand firm, people in good health who look destined to live a long life (unlike the supplicant?), are quite evanescent and might die at any moment. The idea of

---

7. Against Craigie, *Psalms 1–50*, 310.
8. Cf. Terrien, *Psalms*, 332.
9. For this line division, cf. Fokkelman, *Major Poems*, 3:60.

being "[mere] breath" will recur in vv. 6 and 11 (cf. 62:9 [10]; 144:4; Job 7:16). The parallel colon, v. 6a, then restates this in describing a person as living life "walking about in the shadow" (ṣelem), the shadow of death (ṣalmāwet; cf. 23:4 KJV), or "walking about as a shadow," something that has no substance.

The subsequent line takes the point further. People hustle and seethe and busy themselves (hāmâ), but it is only for a breath, for things that are transitory. The parallel colon puts the matter more concretely, though also figuratively. They heap things up the way one hopes to heap up grain at the harvest (cf. Gen. 41:35, 49), but they do not know who will actually gather the harvest in; after all, the farmer may have a heart attack during the harvesting. It is a common theme in Ecclesiastes that people may work hard but not enjoy the results (e.g., 2:18–23; and cf. Luke 12:16–20).

> ⁷So now, what do I look to, my Lord?—
> my hope is in you.

The supplicant is aware of therefore standing helplessly and vulnerably before Yhwh, my *Lord. There is a telling parallelism and contrast between the two cola. The verb qāwâ (*look to) and the noun tôḥelet (*hope) come from synonymous roots, but they are used in such a way as to effect a contrast. In the first colon the supplicant talks in terms of looking for something from Yhwh—but what can one look for? For nothing with certainty, and whatever blessing one might look for could turn to dust if (e.g.) one did not live to enjoy it. The answer to the opening question thus might turn out to be "nothing." One needs a paradigm shift, focusing on "Who?" instead of "What?" This is the movement between the two cola. Instead of looking for *something*, the supplicant hopes in *someone*. The brevity of human life does not lead to a determination to enjoy it while we can; it leads the supplicant "to God and nothing but God."[10] The context shows this hardly implies hoping *for* someone in the sense of hoping for a personal relationship with Yhwh that makes up for not having fullness of earthly life. Subsequent verses will confirm that the supplicant does not expect to escape from eventual death but does hope for an escape from what prevents the enjoyment of life before death.

39:8–13. Now comes something more like the kind of plea one would expect from someone experiencing pain and confronted by the faithless, a plea for God to listen and deliver, though the psalm continues to be distinctive in the way it works out these motifs. The supplicant speaks as

---

10. W. A. M. Beuken, "Psalm 39," *Heythrop Journal* 19 (1978): 1–11, see 4.

one under God's punishment for sin and acknowledges being a sinner, but asks for God to show mercy.

> ⁸Rescue me from all my rebellions;
> do not make me the reproach of the fool.

In Christian parlance "rescue from my rebellions" would suggest "Stop me from rebelling" or "Rescue me from the guilt that follows from my rebelling," but in this context the supplicant is asking for Yhwh's deliverance from the calamity that has come as the punishment of rebelliousness. The second colon thus parallels the first, because the public experience of calamity will lead to the scorn of people such as the fool or the faithless (v. 1). To put it another way, the scorn of the community will add to the nature of the calamity, because as well as (e.g.) the personal experience of illness it brings a breakdown of relationship with the community. That is the more so when the scorners are the fools or the faithless, which implies that for all the acknowledgment of rebelliousness and wrongdoing, the supplicant does not reckon to belong to the category of faithless fool. The implication, perhaps, is a claim that the wrongdoing to which v. 11 refers, and even "all my rebellions," are relatively isolated failures in a life characterized by faithfulness and insight; they are not the typical actions of the faithless fool. The acknowledgment of sin thus parallels that of Job, who is nevertheless a fundamentally committed person.

> ⁹When I kept dumb, I would not open my mouth,
> because you were the one who acted.

Verse 9 returns to the failed silence of vv. 1–2, repeating the verb from v. 2.[11] There the supplicant had not quite given an explanation for silence, except the fact of the presence of the faithless. Here the second colon gives an explanation, though it is not a particularly coherent one. The assumption that more often underlies the Psalms is that Yhwh's being the one who acted is not the reason for silence but the reason for speaking out: we are speaking to the one whose attitude we want to change. If submission to whatever Yhwh chooses to do is a higher ideal, the psalm is confirming that it may be an unattainable one, but that this is okay.

> ¹⁰Turn away from me your affliction;
> because of the hostility of your hand I—I am undone.

---

11. *TTH* 8 assumes that the meaning in v. 2 is past, but in v. 9 present (cf. NRSV). We would surely need indication that the meaning changes (contrast NIVI).

The psalm's usual stance is more the one expressed here. The suppliant has been the victim of Yhwh's "touch" (see 38:11 [12]). The parallelism makes explicit that this is a more painful experience than the word's etymology would suggest. Although the cola are formally dissimilar and the second provides the background for the first, there is a deep structural parallelism between them, reflected in the *abcc'b'a'* order. The two expressions for affliction/hostility of hand stand together at the center of the line, both with a second-person suffix. Outside them stand two expressions referring to the suppliant, "from against me" and the semantically redundant "I." Outside these and opening and closing the line are the verbs, a second-person imperative hiphil and a first-person qatal qal.

> ¹¹With rebukes for wrongdoing you have chastised a man
> and consumed like a moth what he loves;
> yes, every human being is a breath. (Rise)

Verse 11 begins as if it were to comprise simply a parallel bicolon, though not a simple one, as its parallelism is again subtle. The first colon is longer because it opens with an adverbial expression applying to both cola, while the second includes a simile that has no equivalent in the first. Diagrammatically put, v. 11a–b works as follows:

With rebukes for wrongdoing	you chastise		a man
	and consume	like a moth	what he loves.

The first colon raises the question how Yhwh chastises, which the second answers. "Loves" (*ḥāmad*) can be positive (e.g., 19:10 [11]; 68:16 [17]) or negative (e.g., Prov. 1:22; 12:12), but here looks morally neutral; the point is that the things people love are the obvious targets for Yhwh in these circumstances. The line would thus be quite self-contained, and the unexpected third colon therefore carries some emphasis, even though it comprises a partial repeat from v. 5, as v. 9 repeated the opening of v. 2.

> ¹²Do listen to my plea, Yhwh,
> do give ear to my cry for help;
> do not be silent at my tears,
> Because I am a sojourner with you,
> a transient like all my ancestors.

The appeal to listen to my *plea in v. 12a–c is again to be expected in a protest psalm, but its location here is odd; an appeal to listen to a plea belongs to the beginning of a psalm (e.g., Pss. 4; 17; 54; 55; 61; the nearest to an exception is 84:8 [9]). "Give ear" heightens the parallelism because it is a less-common verb; it likewise generally comes at the beginning of psalms (e.g., Pss. 5; 17; 54; 55; again, contrast 84:8 [9]). "*Cry for help" likewise heightens "plea," being another less-common word and a particularly vivid one. Like the first two cola in v. 11, these two cola would make a fine complete line with the invocation to Yhwh at the center, so we are once more surprised by the further parallel clause, which also heightens matters yet again. The verb does so by urging Yhwh not to be deaf or silent.[12] The noun also does so as tears follow on a plea and a cry for help. The idea of being deaf to tears would be an odd one, though the interwovenness of the content of the three cola will reduce that. Prosaically put, the line urges Yhwh to listen and give ear and not be deaf to the plea and cry for help accompanied by tears that attest to the genuineness of plea and cry. "It is a Rabbinic saying that there are three kinds of supplication, each superior to the other; prayer, crying, and tears. Prayer is made in silence, crying with a loud voice, but tears surpass all. 'There is no door through which tears do not pass,' and, 'The gates of tears are never locked.'"[13]

The second line provides the motivation for this appeal. The suppliant was used to the idea of there being resident aliens in the community who owned no land and were dependent for their life on living by their wits or casual employment or performing services or charity. They were thus especially vulnerable in tough times. Such a person is a "sojourner and transient with you" (cf. Lev. 25:6, 35, 40, 45, 47). That is also Israel's position in relation to Yhwh, to whom the land of Canaan actually belongs; it means they cannot sell it (Lev. 25:23). The psalm takes up that idea and reminds Yhwh of it in order to make a different point, though a point that could emerge from looking at Lev. 25 as a whole. Yhwh expected Israelites to care about resident aliens but also described Israel as a whole as having that position. The psalm brings those two ideas together and urges Yhwh to live by that expectation. The suppliant's position is emphasized by the double description that is the only element repeated in both cola:

For	a sojourner	am I with you,
	a transient	like all my ancestors.

The central element in the line applying to both cola is the phrase "with you." Being "with" Yhwh has similar implications to English staying

---

12. See on 35:22.
13. Kirkpatrick, *Psalms*, 206–7; cf. *t. Berakot* 32b.

"with" someone, when we mean in their home.[14] Etymologically, a sojourner (*gēr*) is a person who is somewhere temporarily, and a transient (*tôšāb*) is a "dweller," so that one might have thought that "transient" implied a more secure status than "sojourner"; but the words are not used that way, and in the parallelism here it is the less-common word that provides the heightening in the second colon. The closing phrase suggests a further link with the Torah, since "sojourner and transient" was Abraham's self-description in relation to the Hittites who occupied the land where he lived (Gen. 23:4). David also generalizes this description of the ancestors (1 Chron. 29:15) in a way that meshes with the psalm, because he refers to the inherent nature of human life as involving days that are like a shadow. That link also draws attention to the fact that in the psalm the basis for the appeal is an ambiguous fact. Being a sojourner and transient sets up a claim, but it is a limited claim. The sojourner will never be a landholder; the human being will not live forever.

> [13]Smear [your eyes]/look away from me so that I may smile,
> before I go and there is nothing of me.

It is paradoxical that the psalm's final appeal is then that Yhwh should look away from the suppliant, unlike Israelites looking at sojourners and transients so as to have compassion on them. It also contrasts with the appeal for attention in v. 12a. But the trouble is that the suppliant does have Yhwh's attention. This is an appeal like Job's (Job 7:19; 14:6). The look might seem less threatening than the hand (v. 10), but reality may be the opposite: the look reveals the attitude, and the attitude is determinative, for good or ill. Thus LXX paraphrases "Let me go," and Jerome, "Spare me." Perhaps the implication is that the suppliant gets more than a fair share of attention; perhaps the wrongdoing that the psalm confesses is no worse than other people's, but the suppliant is paying for it as other people do not. The psalm takes something like Ecclesiastes' approach to life. It recognizes that life is short, but it does not therefore simply give in to despair, and it commends enjoyment of life while it lasts. The prospect of death is accepted; the prospect of total gloom until death is not. It would be nice to have Yhwh's attention withdrawn, to have the hostile hand withdrawn, so as to smile before death comes. Since Israelites regularly assume that people continue to exist in Sheol, it is unlikely that "There is nothing of me" implies non-existence (the expression is in any case similar to the one used of Enoch).[15] It does

---

14. Cf. Dahood, *Psalms*, 1:242.
15. Cf. John Muir, "The Significance of *'yn* in Genesis v 24 and Psalm xxxix 13," *ExpTim* 50 (1938–39): 476–77.

imply non-existence on earth, where they experience the only existence worth having, when one compares it with existence in Sheol.

Theological Implications

The psalm combines emphases from both Job and Ecclesiastes, though it is nearer Ecclesiastes in its framework of thinking. Both Job and Ecclesiastes imply some sense that it is best to keep quiet before God. Job submits in quietness to his first experience of terrible loss, and to his second, until after a week of silence he curses the day of his birth. Ecclesiastes advises us to be restrained in the way we speak before God, who is (after all) in heaven, whereas we are on earth; we do not want to speak as fools (Eccles. 5:1–7). Yet neither live by their own advice. Job eventually breaks his silence on a gargantuan scale, and God both rebukes him to his face and commends him to his friends on the basis of the way he has spoken the truth rather than the kind of folly they have spoken (Job 42:7–8). Ecclesiastes writes a whole book that surely counts as utterance "before God" (the phrase in 5:2 [1]), and bold utterance, and the book's appendix shuffles its feet in anxiety about its contents (12:9–14), but the book as a whole found a welcome into God's book. Analogously, the psalm both commends silence and declines to exercise it. Indeed, it speaks loudly not just to give the supplicant release but also for the sake of dialogue with God, for other people to hear, and to help the silenced find a voice.[16]

Job and Ecclesiastes both imply that we are all sinners, but they refuse to let that be a way of explaining why suffering comes to particular individuals. Even if it is the case that Job is a sinner (cf. Job 9:1–2; 10:14–15), that cannot possibly explain why he has suffered the way he has. Even if it is the case that everyone sins, that cannot explain the nature and distribution of the suffering Ecclesiastes sees in the world. The supplicant acknowledges being a rebel, but confesses no concrete rebellion and asks for no forgiveness. In a general sense suffering reflects the fact of being a sinner, and one cannot say it is undeserved, yet one can still appeal for relief from it. The fact of sin does not explain why such trouble comes to this particular person: what about all the other faithless fools who look on at this person? It is humanity in general that sins and experiences God's chastisement (v. 11).

Job and Ecclesiastes both reflect on the insecurity and brevity of human life, though it is a more prominent theme in Ecclesiastes. The supplicant in the psalm emphasizes this brevity, in the hope that this will persuade

---

16. So Walter Brueggemann, "Voice as Counter to Violence," *CTJ* 36 (2001): 22–33.

Yhwh at least to make it possible for a person to enjoy the short life one has as a sojourner with Yhwh (to whom life belongs). That is why the suppliant looks to Yhwh in hope (v. 7). "Death in this poem is not a chaotic power which intervenes in this life and which YHWH is called upon to save the sufferer from, . . . but the irrevocable boundary of individual life."[17] Ecclesiastes thus urges people to live in light of the fact that we are going to die, and the psalm asks for the grace to own this fact. It invites us to live life in light of the fact that we are on our way to death—which does not imply living in gloom and fear but making the most of every day because we know our days will not last for long.

It might seem that knowing of Jesus's rising from death, which means that people who belong to Jesus will also rise to a new life, would change all this, but it does not seem to do so. Christian believers also do not accept suffering with equanimity. And in principle that is fine, because it suggests a proper high evaluation on this earthly life that God gave us. The NT takes up the words of v. 12 to describe our position on earth as sojourners and transients (Heb. 11:13; 1 Pet. 2:11). It is therefore important to value the psalm's distinctively different perspective.[18] To put it another way, the only way to the resurrection is via Gethsemane; Ps. 39 is a prayer Jesus might have prayed there, and one that believers on the way to resurrection still pray.[19]

---

17. Lindström, *Suffering and Sin*, 261.
18. Cf. Craigie, *Psalms 1–50*, 311.
19. See Ellen F. Davis, "Prisoner of Hope," in *The Art of Reading Scripture*, ed. Ellen F. Davis and Richard B. Hays (Grand Rapids: Eerdmans, 2003), 300–305.

Psalm 40

Testimony Warrants Plea

Translation

The leader's. David's. Composition.

¹I looked keenly for Yhwh;
    he bent down to me
    and listened to my cry for help.
²He lifted me up from the roaring pit,
    from the overflowing mud,
And set my feet on a cliff—
    he steadied my legs.[a]
³He put in my mouth a new song,
    a praise song to our God.
Many will see and revere
    and trust in Yhwh.

⁴The good fortune of the man who has made Yhwh his trust
    and has not attended to the defiant and people who turn to
        falsehood!
⁵You—you have done many things,
    Yhwh my God,

a. The qatal verb interrupting the wayyiqtol sequence explicates the previous wayyiqtol and sums up where we have got to, slowing the action (so Diethelm Michel, *Tempora und Satzstellung in den Psalmen* [Bonn: Bouvier, 1960], 17–18, as quoted in *IBHS* 33.2.1a).

Your awesome deeds and your thoughts for us—
> there is no one to set alongside you.[b]
Were I to proclaim and tell,[c]
> they are too many to recount.

⁶Sacrifice and offering you did not want[d]—
> you dug ears for me;
> whole-offering and purification offering you did not ask for.
⁷Then I said, "Here, I have come;
> in the written scroll it is inscribed for me."
⁸I wanted to do what is acceptable to you, my God;
> your instruction was within my heart.

⁹I heralded your faithfulness in the great congregation;
> there, I would not close my lips,
> Yhwh, you know.[e]
¹⁰I did not hide your faithful act within my heart;
> I told of your truthfulness in deliverance.
I did not conceal your true commitment
> before the great congregation.

¹¹You, Yhwh,
> do not close up your compassion from me;
> your true commitment continually protects me.
¹²For there surrounded me evils
> without number.
My wrongdoings caught up with me
> and I could not see.
They were more than the hairs of my head;
> my heart failed me.

¹³Be pleased,[f] Yhwh, to save me;
> Yhwh, hasten to my help.

b. The verb *'ārak* usually means "set in order," and "there is no setting [of them] in order" would make for good parallelism with the next line, but *'ēleykā* is then difficult; for "set alongside, compare," cf. 89:6 [7]; Isa. 40:18.

c. I take the asyndetic colon as the protasis of a condition with the apodosis to follow (GKC 159e; JM 167a), rather than as the apodosis of an unstated condition (GKC 108f).

d. In other contexts the stative verb *ḥāpēṣ* could have present reference here and in v. 8 (for v. 8 cf. NJPS; NRSV; GKC 106g; JM 112a; JM 57d [i]), but here vv. 6–8 are more coherent if we take the whole section to refer to the past.

e. Some LXX MSS see the first word in v. 10 as the object of "you know," which makes good sense when they read that word as "*my* faithful act"; v. 10a then reads, "I did not hide your truthfulness within my heart; I told of your deliverance." But this sentence division is harder with MT's "*your* faithful act."

f. *Rāṣâ* is usually transitive (e.g., 44:3 [4]), but here the verb takes up the significance of the cognate noun in v. 8.

¹⁴May they be shamed and disgraced altogether,
   the people who seek after my life, to terminate it.
May they fall back and be dishonored,
   the people who want trouble for me.
¹⁵May they be desolated because of their shameful deceit,
   the people who say of me, "Hey, hey!"
¹⁶May they rejoice and be glad in you,
   all the people who seek help from you.
May they say continually, "Yhwh be great"—
   the people who are dedicated to your deliverance.
¹⁷As I am weak and needy,
   may my Lord take thought for me.
You are my help and my rescuer;
   my God, do not delay.

Interpretation

Again a psalm pleads for deliverance from affliction that issues from sin, and once more its logic is complex. Verses 1–12 describe a past experience of Yhwh's deliverance (Rashi interprets it systematically of the exodus, Red Sea deliverance, and Sinai). They comprise five sections, marked by the fact that each begins with a long line, a tricolon (vv. 1, 6, 9, 11) or a 4-4 line (v. 4). But then this testimony turns out to be the introduction to a further plea for deliverance, in vv. 13–17. The dynamic of the psalm thus compares with that of Pss. 9–10; 27; and 89, where lengthy praise material turns out to be preparation for a prayer of protest. Verses 1–12 could stand on their own as a testimony psalm, and might have done so before vv. 13–17 were added,[1] though vv. 1–12 are idiosyncratic in the way they recall Yhwh's deliverance and may make more sense if they inherently lead in to vv. 13–17. This would fit with the way some roots in vv. 1–12 recur in vv. 13–17 (*ḥšb*, vv. 5, 17; *ḥpṣ*, vv. 6, 8, 14; *rṣh*, vv. 8, 13; also *těšû'â*, vv. 10, 16). Conversely vv. 13–17 could stand on their own as a prayer psalm; they do stand on their own in a variant form as Ps. 70, though as a unit they then manifest an "unusual brevity and terseness."[2] Whatever its prehistory,[3] Ps. 40 as we have it is a suggestive complex entity, though whether it is a "liturgy"[4] is another question. There is no particular indication that more than one person

---

1. E.g., Gunkel, *Psalmen*, 171. Contrast Nic. H. Ridderbos, "The Structure of Psalm xl," in *Kāp hê: 1940–1965*, ed. P. A. H. de Boer et al., OtSt 14 (Leiden: Brill, 1965), 296–304.
2. Kraus, *Psalms*, 2:67.
3. On the possible redactional history of the psalm, cf. Georg Braulik, *Psalm 40 und der Gottesknecht* (Würzburg: Echter, 1975).
4. See (e.g.) John H. Eaton, *Kingship and the Psalms* (London: SCM, 1976), 42–44.

or group was involved in its recitation. It may have been part of a wider worship event—but then, so may many psalms.

> The leader's. David's. Composition.

Heading. See glossary. If we are to imagine a link with David's life, then his time as an outlaw would be appropriate. The similarity between vv. 6–8 and Samuel's words linked to his rejection of Saul in favor of David (1 Sam. 15:22–23) would also be striking if one sought to connect the psalm with David. But the move between "I" and "we" might indicate that the Davidic king prayed the psalm in connection with a need that also involved the whole people.

40:1–3. The psalm thus opens with five brisk lines of testimony to an experience of Yhwh's deliverance. Strictly, the first four lines are the testimony, relating four stages in what Yhwh did—listening, rescuing, establishing, and thus putting a new song in the mouth; the fifth line draws an inference.

> ¹I looked keenly for Yhwh;
>   he bent down to me
>   and listened to my cry for help.

The first of the five lines actually begins with a colon that stands on its own, emphasizing the way "I *looked" by using the idiom that emphasizes a verb by prefacing the regular qatal with the infinitival form of the same verb (lit., "[in] looking I looked"). The repetition hints, "It is not in the power of Israel to do anything but wait for the Holy One, blessed be He, to redeem them in reward for saying *I waited patiently for the Lord*."[5] The testimony then begins to relate how Yhwh responded to that waiting. First Yhwh bent down to pay attention and listened to my *cry for help. "What cry for help?" we might ask. Like Ps. 30, the psalm testimony begins in the middle of things. As in that psalm, it will not be till later that we discover why the cry for help was necessary and why the suppliant was in the pit (see v. 12; cf. 30:6–7 [8–9]).

> ²He lifted me up from the roaring pit,
>   from the overflowing mud,
> And set my feet on a cliff—
>   he steadied my legs.

---

5. *Midrash on Psalms*, 1:432; it adds reference to Isa. 25:9; Zech. 9:12; Lam. 3:25; and other passages in the Psalms, including (in connection with the repetition) 27:14.

But listening to prayer is not enough—or does not count as proper listening until it issues in a response. The Psalms teach that prayer is not a matter of conforming our will to God's but of conforming God's will to ours. One aspect to Yhwh's action was to rescue the suppliant from the pit of roaring, the mud of flood; the verb applies to both cola, and the two *min* phrases are parallel. The two noun phrases mix two images;[6] more straightforwardly the psalm might have spoken of the clay pit and the roaring flood. A mud pit would refer literally to the kind of place in which Jeremiah was confined (Jer. 38), a pit that could be used as a cistern and was thus open to the sky and sometimes full of water, but that at other times would just have a layer of mud at the bottom. Jeremiah could easily have died there. Metaphorically, the pit then refers to the grave and to Sheol (Ps. 28:1; 30:3 [4]). This image could therefore be conflated with that of the roaring flood, likewise a familiar image for death-threatening dangers. The only other occurrence of the word for flood (*yāwēn*), in 69:2 [3], has similar significance;[7] and for "roaring" (*šā'ôn*), see 65:7 [8].

Necessarily complementing the rescue is the positive re-establishment of the person. The cliff (*sela'*) is not a rock in the midst of the river, on which a person might find refuge from the flood, but a mountain fastness where a person might find refuge from foes (18:2 [3]; 31:3 [4]; 71:3). The image has thus changed from v. 2a. Climbing such a cliff is itself a hazardous act, but Yhwh steadied the suppliant's steps and did not let them falter. Usually that expression refers to faltering in one's walk with Yhwh (17:5; 37:31; 44:18 [19]; 73:2), and that resonance would add a significant further implication in the second colon. Yhwh not only kept him safe physically but also kept him firm religiously.

> [3]He put in my mouth a new song,
>   a praise song to our God.
> Many will see and revere
>   and trust in Yhwh.

That in turn would add to the link with v. 3a. An act of deliverance is never complete until it has led to the worshipper offering the kind of testimony that we are reading. The opening phrase "he put in my mouth" applies to both cola, and the verb then has two parallel objects. The song may be a renewed song, because the worshipper may well not have been singing when overwhelmed by the flood, and also a fresh song, because

---

6. Thus LXX tries to makes sense by understanding the roaring pit as the "pit of misery" and the overflowing clay as "miry clay" (cf. Jerome and EVV for the latter).

7. Dictionaries give the meaning "mud," but this seems to be a mistaken inference from the parallelism here; it does not make sense in 69:2 [3].

the experience of Yhwh's deliverance gives the worshipper a fresh story to sing. A testimony is by definition a new song, not a repetition of an old one. The second object makes explicit that this is not merely a song but also a *praise song, and a praise song in honor of Yhwh, not of human beings (see v. 4) and not of some other deity—for only Yhwh delivers from death. Kraus sees the line as testifying to Yhwh's inspiring the actual song the suppliant sings, which would be in keeping with the assumption about the inspiration of "prophetic" praise elsewhere,[8] but the more simple understanding of the words is that Yhwh put the song in the suppliant's mouth by undertaking the act that "inspired" it. The movement to the first-person plural would fit well if the suppliant is a representative figure such as the king.

In turn yet again, one person's praise song has not completed its task until it has drawn in other people. We might expect "Many will hear" rather than "Many will see," but no doubt many did see the deliverance to which the song testified and now see the suppliant restored and giving this testimony; and "see" (*yir'û*) makes for a paronomasia with "revere" (*yîrā'û*). The second colon spells out the implications, making explicit that the second verb indeed suggests a positive *reverence, not a negative fear. The event and the song draw others into *trust that this individual's experience could be repeated for them (cf. 30:4–5 [5–6]).

40:4–5. Four further lines spell out that implication.

> [4]The good fortune of the man who has made Yhwh his trust
> and has not attended to the defiant and people who turn to falsehood!

The lines[9] open in v. 4 by declaring the *good fortune of any person who does *trust in Yhwh along the lines just envisaged, and sets alongside that an antithesis. The antithesis manifests an ambiguity recalling the one in 4:2 [3]. It could refer to attending or turning (*pānâ*) to other human beings, and specifically human beings characterized by deception. The verb often denotes having regard for someone and thus acting in their support (e.g., 25:16; 69:16 [17]). This would make sense here and point to a suggestive development between the cola, as the psalm would declare the good fortune of people whose trust in Yhwh expresses itself in not supporting wrongdoers—as if that were a way to buttress one's security. The defiant (*rāhāb*) would then be people who act assertively

---

8. *Psalms*, 1:425.

9. *BHS* makes v. 4 two whole lines, and in terms of numbers of words that is justified, but v. 4a is hard to construe as a complete poetic line, whereas v. 4 as a whole works as a bicolon. This understanding is confirmed by the patterning whereby a long line announces the beginning of a new section.

and uproariously, perhaps the embodiments of the dangerous power of floodwaters (as Rahab was the embodiment of stormy assertiveness; 89:9–10 [10–11]). In the internal parallelism of the colon, they will also be people who turn aside to falsehood. Like *pānâ*, the word for "turn aside," *śûṭ*, is an unusual one; it suggests turning in a wrong direction (the variant *śāṭâ* refers to sexual unfaithfulness). That would all make sense of the colon as a whole. But with a human subject *pānâ* more characteristically denotes attending or turning to other gods or other religious resources (e.g., Lev. 19:4; Deut. 31:18, 20). The defiant will then be entities who are asserting themselves against Yhwh. They might be supernatural, like Rahab; LXX renders "vanities," a word it uses for other gods. But they might still be human, like the "people who turn to falsehood" in the sense of turning to such false deities.

> ⁵You—you have done many things,
>   Yhwh my God,
> Your awesome deeds and your thoughts for us—
>   there is no one to set alongside you.
> Were I to proclaim and tell,
>   they are too many to recount.

Three lines then declare the facts about Yhwh that back up that declaration about the wisdom of trusting in Yhwh, and probably confirm that v. 4 draws a contrast between trusting Yhwh and trusting other deities (see esp. v. 5c–d). With emphasis the worshipper turns for the first time to address Yhwh, the *trustworthy one. There is little parallelism within the lines, but more parallelism between them. Verse 5a–b declares the many things Yhwh has done; the "us" makes clear that the psalm is still generalizing and not talking about Yhwh's particular acts for this worshipper. Verse 5c–d expands on what kind of deeds they were, not merely numerous but wondrous and well-thought-out actions; they thus make Yhwh an incomparable God, worth trusting indeed. Verse 5e–f again expands on the first, this time in connection with the point it made about the numerousness of these acts.

40:6–8. A long line again signals a movement in the psalm, back from general statement to individual narrative. The narrative continues from where vv. 1–3 left off and thus speaks further of the proclamation the worshipper made before the congregation, though it is a while before that becomes wholly clear.

> ⁶Sacrifice and offering you did not want—
>   you dug ears for me;
>   whole-offering and purification offering you did not ask for.

Thus v. 6 reverts to the worshipper's response to the experience of deliverance, but begins with a negative, with the response that Yhwh was not so interested in; the point is then repeated in the parallel statement in the third colon. The line refers to four of the main kinds of offering for which Lev. 1–4 offer instructions, though the *whole-offering comes first there. Since the OT generally assumes that Yhwh did want these offerings, it seems likely that the contrast between what Yhwh wanted and did not want is expressed hyperbolically: the psalm means, "Yhwh was less concerned for that than for this." The comparison often made with 1 Sam. 15:22–23 supports this inference, since Samuel's point there is that sacrifice is less important than obedience, not that it is totally unimportant. But the fact that the psalm mentions so many of the main forms of sacrifice means it does make the point quite emphatically. The intervening positive statement "You dug ears for me" is obscure but is traditionally assumed to mean that Yhwh has opened up the worshipper's hearing so as to be able to agree to do what Yhwh wants in place of bringing offerings. Perhaps the idea is that Yhwh has made the hole in the suppliant's head where ears could be placed.[10]

> [7]Then I said, "Here, I have come;
>   in the written scroll it is inscribed for me."
> [8]I wanted to do what is acceptable to you, my God;
>   your instruction was within my heart.

The next two lines maintain suspense by telling us at some length that this surgical procedure worked, but not yet telling us what form of action Yhwh actually was looking for. While there is some parallelism between the cola in each line (more especially the second), the parallelism between the lines is also significant. Each first colon continues the narrative form resumed in v. 6 but makes the worshipper the subject, as will continue to be the case through vv. 9–10. The commitment expressed in each first colon forms a corollary to the declarations about Yhwh's desires in v. 6. The worshipper came before Yhwh as one might in order to offer a sacrifice (v. 7a). But that was not the main point of the coming; the worshipper came with a "wanting" that corresponded to Yhwh's "wanting," came to do Yhwh's will, wanting to do what is "acceptable" (v. 8a; cf. v. 6a). The word ($rāṣôn$) often refers to sacrifices that take the right form and are therefore

---

10. Some LXX MSS have "body" rather than "ears," perhaps attempting to make sense of the Hebrew by taking the ears to stand for the whole body. This facilitates the application of the passage to Jesus (Heb. 10:5–7). Pierre Grelot argues that "body" is read back into LXX from Hebrews ("Le texte du Psaume 39.7 dans la Septante," *RB* 108 [2001]: 210–13).

welcomed; here that word is applied to another form of acceptability and delightfulness to Yhwh.

Each second colon in vv. 7–8 then tells us further about this will, though still without revealing its nature.[11] Whatever the date of the psalm, in some form the regulations for sacrifices will probably have stood as written instructions inscribed on a scroll; we know of no written scroll containing Yhwh's instruction (*tôrâ*) that did not include such regulations. The psalm declares that there is other instruction standing inscribed in a written scroll and expressing Yhwh's particular will for the worshipper. The words in v. 7b put extraordinary emphasis on the written nature of these instructions—*mĕgillâ, sēper, kātûb*. Verse 8b then uses the actual word *tôrâ*, in which the regulations for sacrifice would certainly be embodied, but evidently uses the word for these other instructions and adds that they are not (merely) written in a scroll but also written into the worshipper's inner being (cf. Jer. 31:31–34).[12]

> ⁹I heralded your faithfulness in the great congregation;
>   there, I would not close my lips,
>   Yhwh, you know.
> ¹⁰I did not hide your faithful act within my heart;
>   I told of your truthfulness in deliverance.
> I did not conceal your true commitment
>   before the great congregation.

40:9–10. Yet again the long line signals a new beginning. It is presumably vv. 9–10 that now tell us what Yhwh's instruction required.[13] Yhwh's desire was that the worshipper should give especially open testimony to the act of deliverance that vv. 1–3 spoke of. We do not know how commonly someone who received an answer to prayer would actually show up in the temple to offer a sacrifice and/or to give testimony. The stress on that activity suggests that this worshipper felt a particular compulsion, or thought the point needed emphasizing; vv. 13–17 may explain why this is so. A noteworthy testimony psalm such as Ps. 30 emphasizes the public significance of the act, but Ps. 40 puts even more emphasis on it—more than on the event of deliverance itself. The three lines again manifest some internal parallelism but also stand parallel to each other. Essentially they make the same

---

11. The parallelism between the lines makes it less likely that v. 7b refers to the suppliant's own written testimony.

12. The context surely does not support the view that this scroll is the psalm itself (against Seybold, *Psalmen*, 168–69).

13. On form-critical grounds Westermann argues for present-tense translation in vv. 9–10 (*Living Psalms*, 184–85), but past tense is the more natural implication of qatal verbs and makes good sense, especially in light of vv. 13–17, as he notes.

statement three times, with variations. The first and last line refer to the great congregation before which this testimony needed to be given; there was to be no subdued offering of sacrifice on a quiet Thursday afternoon when few people were present. The lines combine ṣedeq and ṣĕdāqâ (*faithfulness and faithful act) and 'ĕmûnâ and 'emet (*truthfulness and true), and also add *commitment and *deliverance. All these the worshipper heralded (bāśar, the verb for bringing good news, something one does with a loud voice so that everyone can hear) and told of, and negatively did not hide in the heart or conceal or close lips on (cf. v. 3). The yiqtol verb "would not close" perhaps suggests that the worshipper spoke not only loud but also long and repeatedly. What Yhwh had done could not be the subject of mere inner reflection and thankfulness. The parenthesis "Yhwh, you know" prepares the way for the appeal that will eventually come in vv. 13–17. Yhwh has no basis for acting as if the suppliant had given no proper response to the previous act of deliverance.

40:11–12. At the close of the testimony, the suppliant once more returns to the beginning. Indeed, it relates an aspect of the story that we might have expected to be interwoven with vv. 1–3—though Ps. 30 again illustrates how the retelling of one's experience in a testimony psalm need not come in linear order and later in the psalm can jump back to retell the earlier events.

> [11]You, Yhwh,
>   do not close up your compassion from me;
>   your true commitment continually protects me.

In isolation the two verbs might be understood as a prayer and a wish. The translation of v. 11b preserves the ambiguity; v. 11c might alternatively be rendered "may your steadfast commitment. . . ." Verse 12 (translated by perfect tense verbs rather than simple pasts) would then refer to the suppliant's present trouble. In the context, however, the long line marks v. 11 as the beginning of a new section within the testimony formed by vv. 1–12. Further, vv. 11–12 are not included with vv. 13–17 when the latter appear separately elsewhere as a prayer psalm (Ps. 70). These two facts suggest that v. 11 is not a prayer but a general statement, supported by the particular experience on which v. 12 will give us more information—and to which vv. 13–17 themselves will then implicitly appeal. "You, Yhwh" resumes from v. 5 and applies to both succeeding cola, which are then otherwise parallel and arranged abb'a'. A third-person positive verb complements and goes beyond a second-person negated one, with the effect emphasized further by the addition of "continually." "Your true commitment" (lit., "your *commitment and your *truth") likewise complements "your compassion," with the compound expression going beyond the simple one.

> ¹²For there surrounded me evils
>   without number.
> My wrongdoings caught up with me
>   and I could not see.
> They were more than the hairs of my head;
>   my heart failed me.

Verse 12 thus provides not a first statement of the suppliant's current difficulties, as EVV suggest, but a final summary of past difficulties whose resolution evidenced the declarations in v. 11. Here again is some parallelism between the cola but also parallelism between all three lines. Verse 12a–b leaves unclear what the psalm means by "evils." We might initially assume that these are the *bad things that happened to the suppliant, but v. 12c–d suggests they may additionally or rather be the bad things the suppliant did. Either way, when evils overwhelmed, this meant that wrongdoings were overwhelming. That fits with Pss. 38–39, where also the combination of a claim to proper obedience to Yhwh (cf. vv. 6–10 here) coexists with an acknowledgment of sin. The verbs suggest the activity of a powerful army pursuing, catching up, and then surrounding, in such a way that the one attacked cannot even see. They presuppose the inherent power of wrongdoings to bring about trouble, also an idea that appeared in Ps. 38. Verse 12e–f restates from v. 12a–b the point about the number of the troubles/wrongdoings, and then restates from v. 12c–d the point about their effect on the suppliant—here not in terms of outward sight but in terms of inner being.

40:13–17. An unexpected final section turns to urgent prayer. But the recollection of Yhwh's past deeds encourages that, as does the recollection of the suppliant's faithfulness in fulfilling the obligation to declare this faithfulness to the congregation. The prayer is book-ended by two single lines of second-person request, but it is dominated by six lines of third-person clauses. LXX and Jerome take these as wishes rather than merely statements of confidence, surely rightly in this context. The first five of the six lines are parallel; the predicate each time occupies the first colon and thus precedes the subject, which occupies the second. Three relate to the people the psalm prays against, two relate to the people the psalm identifies with, and one final third-person line has the suppliant as the overt subject. But underneath the surface, these six lines comprise three relating to the attackers and three relating to the suppliant.

> ¹³Be pleased, Yhwh, to save me;
> Yhwh, hasten to my help.

Thus the prayer begins with a second-person couplet. Yhwh has in the past been pleased to act in a favorable way to this people (44:3 [4]); the psalm asks for Yhwh to take that stance again. We do not know why the supplicant needs rescue, though succeeding lines will make some of that clear. The second colon parallels the first, producing an *abcb′c′a′* line. The divine name is simply repeated, "hasten" adds urgency to "be pleased," and the noun *help with a first-person suffix and preceded by *l* complements an infinitive with a first-person suffix and preceded by *l*.

> ¹⁴May they be shamed and disgraced altogether,
> the people who seek after my life, to terminate it.
> May they fall back and be dishonored,
> the people who want trouble for me.
> ¹⁵May they be desolated because of their shameful deceit,
> the people who say of me, "Hey, hey!"

Verses 14–15 then constitute three parallel expressions of a desire relating to the supplicant's attackers. In each line their fate is described in two synonymous or overlapping ways, as shame and disgrace, falling back and dishonor, shame and desolation. Each second colon then describes what makes them deserve this: they are seeking the supplicant's death, they want calamity for the supplicant (contrast the "wanting" of vv. 6, 8), they say "Hey, hey," suggesting "Hurrah, hurrah"—an expression of enthusiasm,[14] when the supplicant rather deserves sympathy. Unless they change, either the supplicant will be overwhelmed by curse, calamity, and death, or these people must be shamed for their deceitfulness.[15] The supplicant's prayer is rather milder than what they are seeking. They are seeking trouble and death. The supplicant is merely seeking divine rescue, which will thus mean they are exposed as who they are.

> ¹⁶May they rejoice and be glad in you,
> all the people who seek help from you.
> May they say continually, "Yhwh be great"—
> the people who are dedicated to your deliverance.

---

14. Cf. Tg's "We rejoice at his ruin, we rejoice at his affliction" (Stec, *Targum of Psalms*, 86).

15. On *ʿēqeb*, see Dahood, *Psalms*, 1:251–52, but I see no need to repoint the word.

There follow two expressions of a desire relating to people like the suppliant. A movement from individual to community has characterized the testimony: what happened to the suppliant was significant for believers in general. Here the logic is the reverse. The psalm expresses a desire in general terms, but its real concern is that this should work out for the suppliant. The two lines are again parallel. Rejoicing and being glad in Yhwh (another double expression, paralleling the more negative ones in vv. 14–15) expresses itself in declaring that Yhwh is great—which develops the point that this joyful rejoicing is not merely joy but joy in Yhwh. And that declaration will characterize not merely a one-time testimony but an ongoing life (cf. 30:12 [13]). Likewise, *seeking help from Yhwh is further defined as being *dedicated to Yhwh's *deliverance. In this case the first phrase helps to explain the second. Being dedicated to Yhwh's deliverance implies giving oneself to it in reliance and dependence.

> ¹⁷As I am weak and needy,
>   may my Lord take thought for me.
> You are my help and my rescuer;
>   my God, do not delay.

The third positive expression of desire makes overt what was implicit in v. 16, that the suppliant was naturally the real focus in v. 16. Here the wish occupies the second colon instead of being brought up into the first with the subject to follow. Once more the first colon uses a pair of terms, this time a painful pair, *weak and *needy. They expose the powerlessness of this one person in face of the attacks of multiple foes. The wish is that my *Lord may "take thought" for me. The psalm suggestively reuses a verb (*ḥāšab*) with which Psalms typically refer to faithless people "thinking up" schemes (e.g., 10:2; 21:11 [12]). The suppliant's attackers are evidently doing that; the psalm asks Yhwh to do some thinking and come up with a better plan than theirs.[16]

Finally the psalm reverts to a direct prayer and thus to the form of v. 13. Its content also takes up that opening plea. The word *help recurs, "rescue" (*pālaṭ* piel) is parallel to the earlier "save" (*nāṣal* hiphil), "my God" is parallel to "Yhwh," and "do not delay" is parallel to "hasten."

Theological Implications

Hebrews 10 appeals to Ps. 40 in order to gain some understanding of Jesus, and in this connection specifically appeals to the psalm

---

16. LXX takes the verb as yiqtol, but in the context this is less likely.

as providing a basis for reckoning that Jesus abolishes sacrifice.[17] We have recognized that it is unlikely that the psalm itself thinks sacrifice is dispensable. Rather, it argues that sacrifice cannot take the place of testimony.

Generally, lament leads into testimony. Here "the sequence is wrong. A complaint should not come after the joy of a new song." But this shows that "the move from disorientation to new orientation is not a single, straight line. . . . In our daily life the joy of deliverance is immediately beset and assaulted by the despair and fear of the Pit." But this is a realism that continues to be set in profound trust.[18] Even after experiences of God's deliverance, "there will come days of tribulations, and of greater tribulations. . . . Let no one promise himself what the Gospel does not promise."[19]

When believers have sought God's help and had God deliver them, but have then had trouble recur and need to come to God again in a similar way, the psalm suggests part of the basis on which they may do so. Its crucial emphasis is the expectation that they have given proper recognition before God for their previous deliverance. Actually, our healing hardly becomes complete until we have done so (Luke 17:11–19). But the psalm implies another aspect of the importance of this. Asked about the significance of a blind man's illness, Jesus commented that it lay in the way God was about to be glorified in the man's healing (John 9:3). It might be an exaggeration to say that the healing happened for God's sake *rather than* for the man's, but it would be not much of an exaggeration. Analogously, if an Israelite sought and received God's deliverance and did not come to stand in the midst of the people of God to give God the glory, at least half of the point of that deliverance disappears. If we receive God's deliverance or healing and never say so publicly, we forfeit one basis on which to seek God's deliverance or healing the next time around.

---

17. On the christological use of the psalm in Heb. 10, see Braulik, *Psalm 40*, 272–308.
18. Brueggemann, *Message of the Psalms*, 131.
19. Augustine, *Psalms*, 128.

Psalm 41

The Good Fortune of the Person Who Thinks

Translation

The leader's. Composition. David's.

¹The good fortune of the person who thinks about the poor;ᵃ
　on the day of trouble Yhwh rescues him.
²Yhwh keeps him and preserves him,
　and he is called fortunateᵇ in the land.
You cannot give him to the desire of his enemies.
　³Yhwh sustains him on his sickbed;
　you transform the entire place where he lies in his suffering.

⁴I myself said,ᶜ "Yhwh be gracious to me;
　heal me, for I have failed you.
⁵My enemies speak of trouble for me:
　'When will he die and his name perish?
⁶If he comes to visit,
　he speaks emptiness.

   a. LXX and Tg add a second word for "poor," perhaps implying (e.g.) *wĕ'ebyôn*, "and needy," but likely an expansion based on 40:17 [18] (Kirkpatrick, *Psalms*, 216).
   b. Following Q *wĕ'uššar*; K *y'šr* might imply *yĕ'aššēr*, "he gives [him] good fortune" (cf. LXX, Jerome, Tg).
   c. Understanding the psalm as a prayer psalm would imply we need to translate the qatal as "I say." Many of Gerstenberger's parallels for this (*Psalms*, 1:175) are questionable, and hardly any are as stark as this one would be.

His heart collects harm for himself;
   when he goes outside, he speaks it.'
⁷Together all the people who are against me whisper about me;
   they think up trouble against me.
⁸'A pestilence from Belial is infused into him;
   in that he has lain down, he will not rise again.'
⁹Yes, my friend,
   one in whom I trusted,
One who ate my bread,
   has exalted himself against me as a cheat.ᵈ
¹⁰But you, Yhwh, be gracious to me,
   raise me up and I will be friends with them."

¹¹By this I came to know that you were pleased with me,
   that my enemy does not shout over me,
¹²As I—in my integrity you upheld me
   and made me stand before you forever.

Interpretation

Like Ps. 40:1–12, this testimony contains the elements one would expect, but in a distinctive form. It parallels Pss. 1 and 32 in beginning with a generalization, about "the good fortune" of a certain kind of person (vv. 1–3), and that gives an opening didactic tone to the psalm. Yet this opening section also incorporates verbs that address Yhwh in confession of faith. As something like appeals or statements of trust, these might lead into a prayer, and vv. 4–10 do report a prayer, but it is a report of a prayer, not a prayer the suppliant is praying now. It thus leads into an account of the way Yhwh responded to the prayer (vv. 11–12).¹ It is this testimony in vv. 4–12 as a whole that provides the basis for the generalization with which the psalm starts; its didactic tone is merely an enhanced form of something implicit in the nature of testimony itself with its concern for the congregation to learn the lesson from a testimony.² "The middle verses re-live [the ordeal] in all its intensity, to bring out the true value of the compassion praised in the prologue and the vindication celebrated in the epilogue. . . . Only

---

d. LXX renders "has magnified his heel," and translations traditionally try to make sense of this by paraphrasing "has lifted his heel"; but lifting the heel is not the obvious way (e.g.) to describe tripping someone. I rather take *higdîl* as internal hiphil, a common usage esp. to describe the conduct of enemies (cf. 35:26; 38:16 [17]; 55:12 [13]). *'Āqēb* is then not the noun "heel" but the noun or adj. "betrayer, cheat, supplanter" (cf. 49:5 [6]). Cf. Tg.

1. Craigie (*Psalms 1–50*, 319) sees vv. 1–3 as the priest's words to a suppliant, but the second-person verbs addressed to God in vv. 2b and 3b complicate such a reading.
2. Cf. Weiser, *Psalms,* 343.

the body of the psalm can reveal how heartfelt is the beatitude with which it opens."[3]

> The leader's. Composition. David's.

Heading. See glossary. Although there are no accounts of David being ill (only of Michal pretending that he is; 1 Sam. 19:11–17), in general one can imagine David testifying to Yhwh's deliverance along these lines; one can also imagine subsequent kings using it.

41:1–3. In this opening section, Yhwh is named in each line (the name will come again in v. 4). In isolation the verbs in vv. 1b, 2a, and 3a might be taken as jussives (and the qatal in v. 3b as precative), but following on the statement in v. 1a, they are more likely statements. The combining of yiqtols (vv. 1b, 2a, 3a) and a qatal (v. 3b) then suggests we translate the whole as present.

> [1]The good fortune of the person who thinks about the poor;
> on the day of trouble Yhwh rescues him.

The declaration about *good fortune in v. 1 is an implicit invitation to attentiveness. "Think about the *poor person," it implies; "there is something to learn there."[4] That invitation is counterintuitive; *śākal* "usually describes the practical wisdom of the man of affairs,"[5] and such a person does not assume there is much to be learned from the poor. Practical wisdom says that all we have to look after is ourselves; the psalm (like much of Proverbs) declares that there are other things to be said. The verb recalls the heading *Instruction; see Ps. 32 and the occurrence of the verb in that psalm (32:8). Here, the second colon clarifies the first by indicating what it is that we have to learn from the experience of the poor. Yhwh helps those who cannot help themselves. We will discover that the psalm is not propounding a theological theory that seems in conflict with the evidence but offering an inference from experience. The poor person is the person giving this testimony.

> [2a–b]Yhwh keeps him and preserves him,
> and he is called fortunate in the land.

---

3. Kidner, *Psalms*, 1:161.
4. "Thinking about the poor person" is usually taken to suggest "taking thought *for* the poor person" (e.g., NJPS), but there are no parallels for such a use of the verb *śākal* (cf. Weiser, *Psalms*, 343).
5. Kidner, *Psalms*, 1:161.

Meanwhile vv. 2–3 further spell out the way Yhwh looks after the poor. Initially, v. 2a–b completes an *abb'a'* pair with v. 1. "Keeping" and "preserving" spell out the implications of "rescuing"—when the day of trouble comes, Yhwh sees that trouble does not overwhelm them and that life continues. "Preserves" is literally "keeps alive" or "brings [back] to life." The second colon then returns to the point about good fortune, adding the recognition of it to the fact of it, which was asserted in v. 1a.

> ²ᶜYou cannot give him to the desire of his enemies.
> ³Yhwh sustains him on his sickbed;
> you transform the entire place where he lies in his suffering.

The third line then moves to combine speech about Yhwh with address to Yhwh in the opening and closing cola of this tricolon, which brings the psalm's first section to an end. The alternating forms of speech reflect the nature of the psalm as both thanksgiving (addressing God) and testimony (addressing other worshippers). The opening colon also unexpectedly uses the modal negative *'al*,[6] suggesting a strong statement about what is possible for Yhwh. Other people's negative attitude is one form of trouble from which Yhwh rescues the poor person and in which Yhwh preserves. They want to see him die rather than recover, because of what they can gain from it (see vv. 4–10). The second and third cola begin to explicate how Yhwh rescues. "Yhwh" applies to both cola, which are then otherwise parallel, *abcb'a'c'*. The verbs are third-person yiqtol and then second-person qatal, the first (*sā'ad*) being less familiar but the second taking the point further: Yhwh does not merely sustain but also changes the situation; the "entire" underlines that. The two words for a bed denote the nature of the physical structure (something with a frame)[7] and the nature of what one does there (lie down).

41:4–9. This middle section then turns to relate the prayer the worshipper prayed, whose answer provides the evidence for the claim in vv. 1–3 (cf. the recollection of such a prayer in 30:6–10 [7–11]). I have reckoned that after the opening verb of speech, all seven lines report this prayer, and they could in fact stand alone as a prayer psalm.[8] The prayer then includes two internal quotations from the suppliant's enemies, in vv. 5b–6 and 8. This understanding makes sense of the alternating between plural and singular in vv. 5–8, and also of vv. 9–10, which are not a present lament and plea but a recollected one.

---

6. See GKC 109e.
7. See BDB.
8. It has been argued that in fact they once did so (e.g., Lindström, *Suffering and Sin*, 299–323).

> ⁴I myself said, "Yhwh be gracious to me;
> heal me, for I have failed you.

The two cola in v. 4 follow an *abb´c* sequence. The parallelism between "be *gracious" and "heal" is natural enough, the second verb giving precision to the first. The closing clause is then a surprise, because we have the impression from vv. 1–3 that this worshipper could come before Yhwh with head held high. The motif that has characterized Pss. 38–40 reappears here. An awareness of sin coexists with a sense of freedom to appeal to Yhwh for healing or deliverance, with an implication that in a general sense our sickness reflects the fact that we are sinners, but that this does not imply a concrete link between a particular shortcoming and a particular illness. Indeed, paradoxically, the fact of being a moral failure becomes a reason why Yhwh should be gracious and heal: after all, if there were no failure, there would be no need for grace.

> ⁵My enemies speak of trouble for me:
> 'When will he die and his name perish?

Likewise, the supplicant does not treat the attacks of enemies as the just result of this failure but as reprehensible. Verses 5–6 offer the first report of their words. The *bad thing they speak of (v. 5a) might be the evil they attribute to the supplicant (which v. 6 will go on to describe), but here the second colon suggests that it is the trouble they plan, or at least hope for; the word "trouble" thus has the same meaning as in v. 1. The perishing of the *name may simply signify that the dead person is forgotten, but it may also suggest that his land is open to appropriation—a sharper reason for their hoping for his death.

> ⁶If he comes to visit,
> he speaks emptiness.
> His heart collects harm for himself;
> when he goes outside, he speaks it.'

EVV take v. 6 to refer to the enemies, but the continuing of the singular (obscured in NRSV and NIVI) suggests that v. 6 continues to be the enemies' words about the supplicant. They are boldly accusing the supplicant of behaving in the way they themselves behave, speaking about someone who is "all words." The point is then taken further in the parallel line. This *emptiness means saying one thing but thinking and planning another. So the supplicant is (the enemies say) mentally collecting *harm for himself—not harm that will rebound but harm he plans to undertake when the moment is right. Speaking empty pleasantries inside gives way to speaking true intentions—harmful intentions—when one is outside.

> ⁷Together all the people who are against me whisper about me;
> they think up trouble against me.

Verses 7–8 repeat the sequence of vv. 5–6, again first introducing the words, then reporting them. The speakers might be simply whispering to one another (cf. 2 Sam. 12:19), but the root *lḥš* more often refers to whispering incantations (e.g., 58:5 [6])[9] and is perhaps an onomatopoeic word suggesting hissing and originally referring to snake charming.[10] The second colon would fit with this if it indicates the content and aim of the whispering. Again "trouble" (*bad) is the aim of the people who are *against the supplicant. The unity of their incantations seems to add to their power and make them all the more frightening ("Where two or three gather together . . .").

> ⁸'A pestilence from Belial is infused into him;
> in that he has lain down, he will not rise again.'

Verse 8 thus parallels vv. 5b–6 and indicates the content or implication or bottom line of their whispers. Having done their work, they can rest content about the position of the supplicant and about what will now ensue. I follow KJV in linking *dĕbar* not with the common *dābār* (word, thing) but with the less-common *deber*, meaning a pestilence, which appears in a similar context in 91:3, 6. That fits the talk in the present context of sickness and incantation, and the subsequent reference to Belial (see on 18:4 [5]). The attackers might themselves have described the sickness as coming from Belial, or this might be the supplicant's conviction about the source of any power they possessed. They might have understood themselves to be acting as Yhwh's servants in seeing that a sinner receives the appropriate punishment. Thus this pestilence is poured or infused into the supplicant as a result of their incantation.[11] The link with Belial can also point to its deathly nature: the reference to not rising again further parallels 18:4 [5]. The sickbed will become the deathbed.

> ⁹Yes, my friend,
> one in whom I trusted,

---

9. Cf. Theodor H. Gaster, "Short Notes," *VT* 4 (1954): 73–79, see 74.
10. In Isa. 26:16 it may refer to regular prayer, but the passage is obscure.
11. A byform of the word for "infuse" appears in association with the word for "whisper" in Isa. 26:16, but again the text is difficult.

> One who ate my bread,
> has exalted himself against me as a cheat.

The suppliant offers a final description of the baneful conduct of the attackers. Here they are individualized as one person, in the way EVV take to be happening in v. 6; but the content and the first-person suffixes now make it clear that it is the suppliant who speaks about being under attack. "My friend" is "the man of my *šālôm*," someone who should have been committed to my shalom or someone with whom I had a covenanted relationship. The parallel colon offers a complementary description: it is someone I trusted. Verse 9b offers a third description: it is someone who has been in the habit of accepting my hospitality, like a lover (Prov. 9:5) or someone for whom I accept responsibility (Neh. 5:14–18) or a member of my family (Job 42:11; contrast Isa. 4:1) or—more ironically—like an enemy whom I have treated as a friend (Prov. 25:21). These three descriptions build up the enormity of the final colon in the two lines. Admittedly, we should perhaps be able to guess long before the end of the two lines that this is where they are going, for each OT occurrence of "man of my shalom" denotes people who should behave in a way that furthers someone else's shalom but fail to do so (Jer. 20:10; 38:22; Obad. 7). "People who ate my bread" can have the same implication (Obad. 7). And maybe the suppliant should have been wise enough not to *trust anyone so unequivocally (cf. Jer. 17:5–10). So here, one who should have sought to make things work out well for the suppliant is instead seeking to make trouble. *This* is the person who has behaved in a Jacob-like way toward me ("Jacob" resembles the word for "cheat") by means of self-assertion, aiming to cheat me out of my position in society and/or of my land and/or of my life.[12]

> ¹⁰But you, Yhwh, be gracious to me,
> raise me up and I will be friends with them."

41:10. The recollected plea concludes with a form of the double wish that often appears in prayer psalms. The first colon recapitulates the opening colon of the plea (v. 4a), adding the invocation "you." The second colon begins by continuing that positive request, taking up the enemies' declaration that there will be no more rising from bed and asking that on the contrary Yhwh may bring about such a rising. It then goes on to ask for the chance to *šillēm* (piel) the person who has failed in *šālôm*.

That is usually taken as a variant on the common negative wish in a psalm, asking for the opportunity to repay the attackers instead of

---

12. John 13:18 applies the line to Judas's betrayal of Jesus.

making the more regular request for Yhwh to do so. It is not clear that the result would be a more unpleasant experience for the attackers than being punished by God, though David himself did reckon there was less risk in falling into divine hands than into human hands (2 Sam. 24:14). Nevertheless, this might seem not a very Christian prayer, though in his christological interpretation of the psalm, Augustine is quite comfortable with Jesus praying it.[13] The psalm might then provide another indication that there are no limits to what we can say to God and ask of God, and another illustration of the way in which disapproving of aspects of a request does not stop God from responding to the plea—even if God does grant deliverance but not that opportunity, as vv. 11–12 may imply. Perhaps this last colon thus also pairs with the opening line of the plea, which acknowledged falling short of God's desires. The suppliant does not pretend to be sinless and prays in the state he or she is in.

But all that presupposes that the traditional understanding of the verse is right, whereas *Midrash Tehillim* had already noticed that it stands in tension with the OT's usual expectation that Yhwh, not the suppliant, is the one who requites (which also underlines how there is nothing distinctively Christian about unease at such a prayer).[14] The midrash thus suggests in light of Prov. 20:22 that the psalm refers to repaying evil with good.

I understand the verb in light of the cognate noun in the previous verse; it is an example of the denominative verb *šālam*, not the root verb *šālēm*. The suppliant is promising to seek right relations with the people who have broken friendship.

41:11–12. The worshipper concludes the thanksgiving by relating how God answered that prayer.[15]

> ¹¹By this I came to know that you were pleased with me,
>   that my enemy does not shout over me,

Being a moral and religious failure evidently does not prevent the worshipper from pleasing Yhwh; Yhwh's pleasure need not depend on the worthiness of its object but issues from within Yhwh. The evidence or outworking of Yhwh's delight was an act of grace whose ongoing re-

---

13. *Psalms*, 131.
14. *Midrash on Psalms*, 1:438.
15. Out of context, we could understand the verbs in v. 11a as stative (so NRSV, NIVI) and translate the verbs in v. 12 as perfect (cf. GKC 111r; JM 118p; *TTH* 79), though it seems arbitrary to translate v. 11a as "I shall know" (cf. NJPS, NEB). But the fact that qatal verbs dominate vv. 11–12 as a whole suggests we should read the two lines as continuing the worshipper's story (cf. LXX, Jerome).

sults are first described in v. 11b, which explains the "by this" of v. 11a.[16] The act of grace means that the enemies are now in no position to take a triumphant stance over against the suppliant (*shout).

> [12]As I—in my integrity you upheld me
> and made me stand before you forever.

In turn the final line explains further the nature of this act of grace, suggesting different implications. In keeping with vv. 1–3, though not with the plea, the worshipper now speaks as a person of *integrity and implies that this integrity was the basis of Yhwh's act of upholding. The worshipper has been vindicated over against the attackers. The description of Yhwh's act initially speaks not of "lifting up," as one might have expected, but of "holding up" (*tāmak*). In one sense the worshipper had been down if not out (vv. 8, 10). But that had not meant a final downfall. Yhwh had proved to be one who upheld. The second colon does then speak of raising up or setting up (*nāṣab* hiphil), though the verb does not presuppose that the thing that is set up was previously cast down. Rather, "making me stand" goes beyond "upholding" in suggesting a firm establishing that will make it even harder for anyone to put this worshipper down on another occasion. That is especially the case because the worshipper now stands permanently before Yhwh, always before Yhwh's eye and the object of Yhwh's care.

Theological Implications

The location of Ps. 41 at the close of book I draws attention to parallels and contrasts with Ps. 1 at its beginning. Both open with a comment on the good fortune of certain sorts of people. Psalm 1 declared the good fortune of the person who paid attention to Yhwh's teaching. The trouble is that most of the psalms in between have placed a question mark by any straightforward understanding of that declaration. They comprise protest after protest at the fact that life does not work out like that. Indeed, many of them embody in themselves the tension between such a declaration and the facts of experience. Psalm 41 does so in the affirmations in vv. 1–3 and the experience reflected in vv. 4–10. The psalm as a whole thus faces two realities, like (e.g.) Ps. 22, but its declaration also nuances the declaration in Ps. 1 in light of all that has come in between. There is good fortune in paying attention to Yhwh's teaching; there is also good fortune in paying attention to what happens

---

16. Cf. BDB 471b.

to people for whom Ps. 1 seems not to work out, because such paying of attention reveals that this experience does not mean Yhwh has simply gone away. Yhwh acts faithfully either in preserving from trouble or in rescuing from trouble.

This collocation accompanies another, the declaration that good fortune belongs to people who walk in Yhwh's way (1:1, 6), and the declaration that it belongs to people who recognize that Yhwh takes action on behalf of the poor (41:1-2). The implication will be that walking in Yhwh's way involves taking action on behalf of the poor.[17]

Yet another collocation emerges from the fact that Yhwh acted to rescue because of being pleased with this poor person (v. 11). That recalls the earlier reference to people finding pleasure in Yhwh's teaching (1:2). While Ps. 41 appeals to Yhwh's grace, and does so specifically in the context of awareness of moral or religious failure (vv. 4, 10), it also suggests that the basis for Yhwh's being pleased to deliver was the suppliant's integrity (vv. 11-12). In other words, the suppliant's pleasure in Yhwh's teaching led to a commitment to embodying it in life. There is no necessary clash between the worshipper's two self-assessments, as sinner and as person of integrity. The worshipper is someone who falls short of Yhwh's ultimate standards, yet over against the standards of those enemies can claim to be a person of integrity. The fact that we all come to God as sinners means that "'Heal me, LORD, for I have sinned against you' [is] simply the right way to pray for restoration."[18] But we need also to be people who are fundamentally committed to integrity in our relationships with God and with other people.

---

17. McCann, "Psalms," 848.
18. Mays, *Psalms*, 171-72.

Psalm 41:13
Coda to Psalms 1–41
Yes, Yes!

Translation

[41:13]Yhwh be worshipped, the God of Israel, from eternity to eternity. Yes, yes!

Interpretation

[41:13]. This prose declaration is not part of the psalm that it follows (notwithstanding the verse number with which it is provided) but an act of praise at the end of book I of the Psalter (cf. the codas that follow Pss. 72; 89; and 106). It may reflect the liturgical response to Scripture in the synagogue, but if so this highlights the fact that in the present context it is a sign of the way that the psalms have now become part of a book. "Yes" is *'āmēn*, which entered European languages as a Hebraism, but etymologically means something like "Surely." It signifies a personal commitment to the preceding affirmation.

Theological Implications

The coda invites readers to pause and look back over what we have thus far read about Yhwh the eternal God of Israel. It presupposes that the Psalms are simultaneously theology and doxology. They are full of declarations about this God that invite a response—not merely study but especially *worship and serious affirmation.

Glossary

The following comments relate to words marked * in the commentary. Entries mostly refer to passages from Pss. 1–41 but are generally not exhaustive.

Acknowledge (*yāda'*). The verb commonly refers to knowing facts or knowing people, and it is usually so translated in EVV. But it often implies "acknowledging" or "recognizing" with the will and not merely the mind—so that knowing implies taking notice of and committing oneself (9:10, 20 [11, 21]; 14:4; 25:4; 37:18). Yhwh can be the subject of the verb with this meaning (1:6; 31:7 [8]).

Against, Be (*śānē'*). EVV render "hate," but like *'āhēb* (*dedicate oneself to, love) it denotes an attitude and an action as much as an emotion (5:5 [6]; 9:13 [14]; 11:5; 26:5). Often the connotation is "repudiate": it suggests having nothing to do with someone or something (31:6 [7]).

Anointed (*māšîaḥ*). See 2:2; 18:50 [51]; 20:6 [7]; 28:8. Not a participle, like the English word, but a noun; it designates an ongoing status rather than drawing attention to an event—we could invent the word "anointee" to translate it. It occasionally refers to a priest but more usually to a king. In Qumran documents it comes to refer to a future king or future priest, but in OT times it refers to an actual one. Human beings literally anointed a king, pouring or smearing oil on him (e.g., 1 Kings 1:34), but God sometimes commissioned such an anointing (e.g., 1 Sam. 16:3) so that metaphorically it was God who anointed him (e.g., 1 Sam. 10:1). Such a king is then "Yhwh's anointed" (e.g., 1 Sam. 24:6 [7]), someone who was once appointed by Yhwh and sacramentally designated, dedicated, and inaugurated, and who therefore has special status as Yhwh's appointee, one who rules on Yhwh's behalf. He is the means of Yhwh's rule being exercised.

Authority (*mišpāṭ*). Leadership and decision-making exercised with power and legitimacy (17:2; 25:9; 36:6 [7]). EVV usually translate "justice," and *mišpāṭ* is indeed ideally exercised with justice, but this is not always so; it can be exercised unjustly. In this sense the older translation "judgment" is better, since there can be unjust judgment. This is reflected in the characteristic pairing of *mišpāṭ* with *ṣĕdāqâ* or *ṣedeq* (*faithfulness; e.g., 33:5): authority needs to be exercised with *ṣĕdāqâ*, but that does not always happen. The pairing safeguards the quality of the exercise of authority. In turn *mišpāṭ* safeguards

Glossary

the decisiveness of a commitment to faithfulness. It is not merely a matter of intending faithfulness or affirming the importance of faithfulness but also of implementing it. Further, the exercise of *mišpāṭ* is not intrinsically a juridical matter; the word covers the exercise of authority in general. Thus the parent verb *šāpaṭ* means "decide"—decide *for* as well as decide *against* (see, e.g., 7:8 [9]; 9:4, 8 [5, 9])—and *mišpāṭ* means a decision taken by someone who has authority.

Bad (*ra'*). The word covers a range similar to the English word in that it can refer both to the bad things that happen (trouble, calamity; 10:6; 23:4; 27:5) and to the bad things that people do (wickedness, wrong; 34:13, 14, 16 [14, 15, 17]).

Bloodshed (*dāmîm*). The word for blood is used in the plural in connection with murderous attacks on other people (e.g., 9:12 [13]; 26:9); the plural perhaps expresses affective value.[1] But "person of bloods" need not be merely a synonym for "slayer"; it often denotes not people who directly shed blood, but people who want or scheme for the death of someone (5:6 [7]).[2]

Committed, commitment (*ḥāsîd, ḥesed*). Commitment implies pledging oneself to someone when one has no prior obligation to do so, or keeping such a pledge of commitment no matter what happens—as when the other person does not keep the pledge and thus forfeits any right to such commitment. EVV have "steadfast love" and other words. God's commitment is thus a basis for prayer, trust, and hope in crises, and a topic to talk about (6:4 [5]; 13:5 [6]; 17:7; 23:6; 40:10 [11]). The human response to God's goodness to us is to be *ḥāsîd* in relation to God (32:6; 37:28). A *ḥāsîd* is someone who keeps commitment and lives faithfully, against the odds, if necessary. It is the opposite of behaving falsely (12:1–2 [2–3]; 18:25–26 [26–27]). Commitment can link with the idea of covenant, but there is no intrinsic link between the two ideas: "commitment" and "covenant" do not commonly occur in the same context.

Composition (*mizmôr*). *Zāmar* (make music) and its derived nouns refer more to the making of music than specifically to the singing of songs (*šîr*), to melodies rather than words (e.g., 33:2), or to singing with instruments rather than a cappella. Insofar as they do refer to music with lyrics, the nouns suggest "songs" rather than "psalms": they imply no presupposition that the music relates to worship or prayer (cf. *zāmîr* in 2 Sam. 23:1; Isa. 25:5). While the OT uses the verb itself only of worship music, the more general use of the derived noun suggests that *zāmar* would also be the general term for making music.

Confess (*yādâ* hiphil). Giving testimony to the truth of something. This may be the truth about what God has done for the speakers (so that the verb is often translated "give thanks"; 30:4, 9, 12 [5, 10, 13]), or the truth about what the speakers have done (confession of sin; 32:5). By its nature such confession is a public act. The verb is the one from which the noun *tôdâ* (thanksgiving) comes. In confessing the good things Yhwh has done, one is giving thanks for them, and vice versa.

Crag (*ṣûr*). EVV render "rock," but the word refers not to a large stone but a high cliff in the mountains where a bird or wild animal can find security (18:2 [3]; 27:5; cf. 1 Sam. 24:2 [3]).

Cry for help (*šāwa', šaw'â, šewa'*). These words for "cry" have spelling similar to the word for "deliver" (*yāša'*), helping them to convey the idea of calling out with a particular aim, to get help from God (28:2; 30:2 [3]; 40:1 [2]) or from someone else able to help (72:12).

---

1. So *TDOT*.
2. See N. A. van Uchelen, "'*Nšy dmym* in the Psalms," in *The Priestly Code and Seven Other Studies*, by J. G. Fink et al., OtSt 15 (Leiden: Brill, 1969), 205–12.

Glossary

Cry, cry out (*ṣāʿaq, ṣĕʿāqâ*; also *zāʿaq, zĕʿāqâ*). The cry out of oppression or other wrong done to one, which issued from Abel, from Sodom's victims, and from Israel in Egypt (9:12 [13]; 22:5 [6]; 34:17 [18]).

David's (*lĕdāwid*). See the introduction.

Decide, decision (*šāpaṭ, mišpāṭ*). See *authority.

Dedicate oneself (*ʾāhēb*). EVV render "love," which is sometimes appropriate, but the word commonly indicates an act of the will or a commitment rather than (merely) a feeling (see 4:2 [3]; 11:5, 7). The antonym of "be *against."

Deliver, deliverance, deliverer (*yāšaʿ, yĕšûʿâ, yešaʿ, môšîaʿ*). EVV render "save/salvation/savior," but these words are inclined to suggest an act that delivers people from the wrath of God and gives them eternal life. While the Psalms, like other parts of the OT, are concerned for a living, personal relationship between people and God, they do not speak of that as *yĕšûʿâ*. "Deliverance" denotes action that rescues people from the attack of wicked people or from illness (18:2, 3, 27, 35, 41, 46, 50 [3, 4, 28, 36, 42, 47, 51]).

Emptiness, empty (*šāwʾ*). Emptiness is a moral, relational, and religious category. It denotes things with no moral, relational, or religious substance (12:2 [3]; 24:4; 26:4; 31:6 [7]; 41:6 [7]). Gods other than Yhwh (and their images) are empty because there is no substance equivalent to their outward impressiveness. Speech that is empty or worthless is speech that is only words: there is no reality equivalent to it. If the empty words relate to the past, the events or acts they spoke of never happened (e.g., Exod. 23:1). If they relate to the future, the events or acts they speak of will never happen (e.g., Lam. 2:14).

Face (*pānîm*). See 4:6 [7]; 11:7; 16:11; 17:15; 21:6 [7]; 24:6; 27:8; 31:16 [17]); it is also the word that most often lies behind the word "presence" in EVV (17:2; 31:20 [21]). It is the face that turns and looks, that notices and acts in love, commitment, generosity, deliverance, and blessing. The shining of the face implies looking on people with a life-giving smile, with love and generosity, and acting accordingly. If someone can be prevailed on to smile at a suppliant, all else will follow. So seeking God's face means seeking for God to look at us in such a way as to act thus, and seeing God's face means seeing such prayers answered as we experience vindication and deliverance. On the other hand, hiding the face, turning the face from people's oppression and need, means ignoring that need, a terrifying act because it means there will be no deliverance or blessing (10:11; 13:1 [2]; 22:24 [25]; 27:9; 30:7 [8]). But it is a comforting act when Yhwh's face is averted from our sin (51:9 [11]), and when Yhwh's face is against wrongdoers (34:16 [17]).

Fail, failures (*ḥāṭāʾ, ḥaṭṭāʾ*). These expressions are routinely translated "sin" (e.g., 25:7; 32:5; 38:3 [4]; 39:1 [2]). In everyday usage the verb suggests missing a target (Judg. 20:16) or missing one's way (Prov. 19:2), so that in a religious context it would imply a coming short of Yhwh's expectations or a failure to live up to them. Such shortcoming or failure does not imply doing one's best and failing but a reprehensible failure to do what was required, a missing the way for which we are responsible.

Faithful, faithfulness (*ṣaddîq, ṣĕdāqâ*). Acting in the right way in relation to people with whom one is in a relationship (e.g., 1:5, 6; 7:9, 11 [10, 12]; 11:3, 5, 7; 22:31 [32]). EVV "righteous, just, righteous, righteousness" thus lose the relationship connotations of the words. They do not directly refer to individual personal morality or to social justice as we understand that idea. They do not suggest treating everyone in the same, just way but doing the right thing by one's relationships or community.

Faithless, faithlessness (*rāšāʿ, rešaʿ*). The antonym of *faithful/faithfulness. The conventional English translation "wicked" is rather general. To be *rāšāʿ* is to fail to keep one's commitments to God and/or to other people (e.g., 10:2, 3, 4, 13, 15; 17:9, 13; 32:10).

593

Fall down/falter (*môṭ*). One aspect of the significance of "falling down" appears when it is defined as experiencing adversity (*ra'*; 10:6) or set against its opposite, which is "doing well" (*šalwâ*; 30:6 [7]) or being firmly established like the very creation (104:5). But *môṭ* is also used to refer to falling down morally or religiously, wavering in one's commitment (17:5).

Falsehood, false (*šeqer*). See 7:14 [15]; 27:12; 31:18 [19]; 33:17; 35:19; 38:19 [20]. Falsehood is what does not correspond to reality. It is testimony that does not correspond to what happened, or an image that corresponds to no reality and thus cannot save, or a promise that does not come true.

Good (the noun *ṭûb*, the adjective *ṭôb*). Since these words are wide-ranging antonyms of *ra'*, they can refer to doing what is good as opposed to what is wicked (14:1, 3; 27:13; 34:8, 14 [9, 15]; 37:3), and also to experiencing what is good as opposed to what is bad, experiencing blessing (4:6 [7]; 21:3 [4]; 23:6; 31:19 [20]; 34:10, 12 [11, 13]). Perhaps the two ideas come together in the implication that goodness entails generosity (25:13). Doing good suggests kindness, doing good to someone rather than doing what is merely objectively right (cf. 4:6 [7]; 16:2; 21:3 [4]; 23:6).

Good fortune of (*'ašrê*). EVV have "Blessed/happy is/are . . . ," but the Hebrew is a noun exclamation, without a verb. This construct plural is the only form in which the word occurs (a similar noun *'ošer* comes once, in Gen. 30:13). It is not numerical plural but intensive plural.[3] Further, it does not mean "blessing" in a merely "spiritual" sense, though it would include that: the expression would hardly be applied to godless people merely because they did well in life. But it is a less religious-sounding or liturgical word than the English word "blessed." It suggests that people's whole lives work out well. The contexts of the declaration suggest it has two aspects. Positively, Yhwh gives all good things (84:11–12 [12–13]; cf. 112:1–3; 128; 144:15). Negatively, Yhwh sees that people are delivered from trouble and preserved in crises (32:1–2; 33:12; 34:8 [9]; 40:4 [5]; 41:1 [2]; 65:4 [5]; 94:12). It "is not a wish and not a promise. . . . It is a joyful cry and a passionate statement."[4]

Grace, be gracious, prayer for grace (*ḥēn, ḥānan, tĕḥinnâ, taḥănûnîm*). The positive, generous attitude a person shows to someone else when there is no existent relationship or desert that the latter could appeal to. In human relationships, it corresponds to the way we may ask someone else to "do us a favor." The noun hardly occurs in the Psalter (see 45:2 [3]; 84:11 [12]), but "be gracious" is a frequent plea in prayers (4:1 [2]; 6:2 [3]). It appeals to the fundamentals of God's nature; there is nothing further back in God to appeal to than this. A *tĕḥinnâ* (6:9 [10]; 55:1 [2]) is then a plea for grace, an appeal to Yhwh's nature as one who acts with favor and grace toward people irrespective of what they deserve but because that is indeed Yhwh's nature (cf. *taḥănûnîm*).

Harm, harmfulness (*'āwen*). It has been argued that "people who do harm" (*pō'ălê 'āwen*; 6:8 [9]; 14:4; 28:3) are people who use words to cause harm to someone by the manipulation of demonic power, but the Psalms' language is too general to infer this or any other specific and precise connotation for the phrase.[5] It simply denotes causing harm to someone. But the language's generality means that psalms where it appears are open to being used by people under various forms of verbal attack that threaten their well-being and life.

---

3. Cf. BDB 80–81.

4. Martin Buber, *Right and Wrong* (London: SCM, 1952), 51 = *Good and Evil* (New York: Scribner's, 1952), 53. Waldemar Janzen ("*'Ašrê* in the Old Testament," *HTR* 58 [1965]: 215–26) renders "enviable."

5. See, e.g., *TDOT* or *NIDOTTE* on *'āwen*.

Harp (*nēbel*). Perhaps a variant on the *lyre. It sometimes explicitly had ten strings, whereas the lyre had fewer, and the harp may have been a louder and/or deeper instrument.[6]

Haven (*miśgāb*). The verb *śāgab* means "to be [inaccessibly] high up" (20:1 [2]; 59:1 [2]; 69:29 [30]). A *miśgāb* is thus a place that is inaccessibly and therefore safely high up (9:9 [10]; 18:2 [3]; 46:7, 11 [8, 12]; 59:9, 16, 17 [10, 17, 18]; 62:2, 6 [3, 7]).

Help (*'āzar, 'ēzer, 'ezrâ*). The context in (e.g.) 10:14 shows how helping does not denote assisting people who are doing their part but delivering people when they are helpless, people such as the wretched or the orphan who have no protection and no resources (cf. 22:11 [12]; 30:10 [11]). "Help" is thus a rather feeble equivalent for *'ēzer*, which suggests a powerful person taking decisive action of behalf of a weak person who is in dire need. In English, without "help" we might manage okay but a little less comfortably; in Hebrew, without *'ēzer* we would often be dead (cf. 33:20; 70:5 [6]; 124:8 in their context).

Holy, holiness (*qādôš, qōdeš*). Holiness points to the distinctiveness and separateness of God over against humanity. God's holiness denotes God in person: thus God speaks "by his holiness," that is, "by himself" (60:6 [8]). God *is* the holy one (22:3 [4]; 71:22). Holiness then points to the distinctiveness and separateness of places that belong to God (2:6; 3:4 [5]; 5:7 [8]; 11:4) and of people who belong to God (16:3; 34:9 [10]). It is not directly a moral category—it is more like "divine" over against "human" than "righteous" over against "wicked"—though because Yhwh *is* a moral character, it comes to have moral implications (see 15:1 and 24:3 in their contexts).

Honor (*kābôd*). EVV "glory." The word suggests the visible splendor of a monarch or some other important person, glorious in an impressive array (24:7–10). The visible honor is then assumed to be an appropriate outward expression of the figure's intrinsic majesty—though this may not always be so (49:16–17 [17–18]).

Hope (*tiqwâ, tôḥelet*). Nouns from *qāwâ*, *look to, and *yāḥal*, *wait. They can denote the attitude of hoping or waiting (39:7 [8]) or the object of expectation, the thing hoped for (9:18 [19]; 62:5 [6]; 71:5).

Ignore (*šākaḥ*). EVV often have "forget," but the verb indicates a deliberate act of putting out of mind (9:12 [13]; 10:11). It is the antonym of "be *mindful."

Instruction (*maśkîl*). If we assume that this word in headings comes from the verb *śākal*, then "instruction" is one possible meaning (that is, this is a psalm that offers a pattern for prayer or praise), though "contemplative poem" and "skillful poem" are other possibilities.[7]

Integrity (*tōm*; the common adjectives are *tāmîm* and *tām*). For *tāmîm*, LXX has the negative *amōmos* (faultless; cf. Jerome and EVV), but this gives a misleading impression since the Hebrew word suggests not the absence of something but a positive giving of the entire person to live Yhwh's way. It was a characteristic of Noah and an expectation of Abraham (Gen. 6:9; 17:1). The noun denotes a positive wholeness, completeness, or soundness—in the Psalms, usually of a moral kind (7:8 [9]; 15:2; 26:1, 11; 37:18, 37; 41:12 [13]). In suggesting a positive wholeness of commitment, the words do not imply sinlessness: it is possible to be a person of integrity without being sinless.

Lead, leader (*nāṣaḥ, měnaṣṣēaḥ*). Leading describes a musical role in 1 Chron. 15:21, and the "leader" might thus be the music director. "The leader's" perhaps then refers

---

6. See Joachim Braun, *Music in Ancient Israel/Palestine* (Grand Rapids: Eerdmans, 2002), 22–24; Keel, *Symbolism of the Biblical World*, 346–49.
7. See BDB 663–64.

to a collection of psalms. But the leader might be a king or priest who represented the people in worship.[8]

Light (*'ôr*). When the light shines out from Yhwh's face, that suggests people will experience blessing and deliverance (4:6 [7]; 27:1; 44:3 [4]; 97:10–11). Light is thus associated with material good, yet material good set in the context of a relationship with Yhwh (36:7–9 [8–10]; 43:3; 56:13 [14]; 89:15 [16])—like friends enjoying a magnificent meal, but enjoying it because they love each other.

Loftiness (*ga'ăwâ*). A common theme in Psalms (see 10:2; 31:18, 23 [19, 24]; 36:11 [12]) and Isaiah. "Arrogance" (EVV) begs two questions, because this and related words start off by denoting an objective position of exaltedness, and because it is not an inherently negative one. God is characterized by *ga'ăwâ*, and Israel can be too (e.g., Deut. 33:26, 29). But human *ga'ăwâ* threatens a twofold problem. Human beings may become proud of their exalted position, their majesty and power. And even if they do not, their possessing exalted power and majesty can mislead other people. They can think they are God, and even if they do not so think, they can look like God. For both reasons they may need to be stopped from occupying their lofty position for too long. The possession of power by the faithless enables them to pursue the weak, but this also involves their pretending to a godlike position. The Psalms appeal to that so as to provide Yhwh with further motivation for action. Recognition of Yhwh's deity is compromised by the exaltedness that enables the lofty to do what they do.

Look to (*qāwâ*). An attitude of expectancy or waiting, looking for something to happen. For the qal, see 25:3; 37:9; for the piel, 25:5, 21; 27:14; 37:34; 39:7 [8]; 40:1 [2]; see also *hope, and *wait for. Individually and corporately, people recognize that they have little control over their lives: they cannot control whether they recover from an illness, nor can they control their political destiny. Indeed, when they attempt to do either, they are subject to critique. Their vocation is to live life in the expectation that Yhwh is going to act, and to live straining their eyes to see that act.

Lord (*'ădōnāy*). The word looks as if it would mean "my lords," but it usually refers to Yhwh. There are two ways of understanding the ending.[9] The plural may be honorific, a plural of majesty, so that the expression means "my Lord." This fits (e.g.) 16:2; 22:30 [31]; 35:17, 22, 23; 38:9, 15, 22 [10, 16, 23]; 39:7 [8]; 40:17 [18]). But Ugaritic had a similar sufformative to this -*āy* with an emphatic or intensifying sense, and this sufformative might function simply to reinforce the meaning of the word; an English equivalent might be "*the* Lord." Vrs render it simply "the Lord." This fits (e.g.) 2:4; 37:13.

Lyre (*kinnôr*). To judge from the OT and from archaeological discoveries, the most common Israelite musical instrument, an equivalent of a guitar or banjo, but freestanding or handheld. It could be plucked or strummed.[10]

Might (*gĕbûrâ*). The decisive power and strength of a warrior (*gibbôr*). Yhwh is girded with might like a fighter girded with weaponry (65:6 [7]).

Mind (*lēb, lēbāb*). Anatomically the "heart" but dynamically the inner person as opposed to the outer (4:4 [5]; 10:6, 11, 13), sometimes the locus of the emotions (4:7 [8]), more often the locus of thought and intention (7:10 [11]; 10:17; 11:2), even the spirit or morale (69:20 [21]).

---

8. For other possible understandings of *mĕnaṣṣēaḥ*, see Tate, *Psalms 51–100*, 4–5.

9. See, e.g., *IBHS* 7.4.3ef, which reckons that the second understanding is always correct.

10. See Braun, *Music in Ancient Israel/Palestine*, 16–19; Keel, *Symbolism of the Biblical World*, 346–49.

Mindful, Be (*zākar*). EVV often have "remember," but the verb indicates a deliberate act of applying the mind/being mindful, and thus changing one's thinking and acting in light of that (9:12 [13]; 25:6–7; 63:6 [7]). It is the antonym of *ignore.

Morning (*bōqer*). "In the morning" may suggest rising early with energy and commitment to be involved in praise or prayer, or may suggest morning as the moment of God's action or the moment when one discovers God has acted (5:3 [4]; 30:5 [6]; 46:5 [6]; 49:14 [15]; 59:16 [17]).

Most High (*'elyôn*). In ordinary usage the word denotes something high (e.g., Neh. 3:25) and thus designates Yhwh as the exalted one. It could suggest Yhwh's exaltation over the world and over other deities, and might point especially to Yhwh's power (cf. Ps. 7:17 [18]; 18:13 [14]). It was apparently a title of God as worshipped by the pre-Israelite people of Jerusalem and came to be an honorific title for Yhwh (cf. Gen. 14:18–22; also Num. 24:16).

Music. See *composition.

Name (*šēm*). Even if a name does not have intrinsic meaning, it points to the identity of the person, but in some societies names have meanings that point to the person's nature or destiny or their parents' hopes for them (e.g., Grace, Hope). Thus to know, acknowledge, or praise the name is to know, acknowledge, or praise the person (7:17 [18]; 9:10 [11]). The exaltation of the name suggests the exaltation of the person (5:11 [12]; 8:1, 9 [2, 10]). Conversely, to eliminate the name is to eliminate the person (9:5 [6]). For Yhwh's name to act is for Yhwh to act, and the fact that the name sums up the person's character means that a key act under pressure is to call on Yhwh's name and thus summon Yhwh in person. The actual uttering of the name makes the presence of the person a reality, just because the name expresses who the person is (20:1, 5, 7 [2, 6, 8]). Acting for the sake of the name implies acting in accordance with who the person truly is, and demonstrating that (23:3; 25:11).

Needy (*'ebyôn*). In the Psalms the needy characteristically appear in the company of the *weak (9:18 [19]; 12:5 [6]; 35:10; 37:14; 40:17 [18]; 49:2 [3]; 69:33 [34]; 70:5 [6]). The context often makes clear that in the Psalms the word suggests not so much poverty itself as the vulnerability that issues from poverty. It is then the special responsibility of the king to look after their interests (72:4, 12, 13).

Palace (*hêkāl*). Both *hêkāl* and *bayit* refer to Yhwh's dwelling, but the first designates it as a palace, the second as a house. Either can refer to Yhwh's dwelling in the heavens (11:4; 18:6 [7]; 29:9; 138:2) or to that on earth (27:4; 48:9 [10]; 65:4; 68:29 [30]; 79:1). The psalmist comes to the earthly temple and bows to the heavenly one. But the standard translation "temple" for either word is misleading. Hebrew does not have a word equivalent to temple (hence the need to call it a *holy* palace), unless it is a word such as *miqdāš* (sanctuary; 73:17). As is the case with other expressions, Hebrew uses ordinary words to refer to religious matters rather than developing a special religious vocabulary. Designating the temple on earth or that in the heavens as a house or a palace draws attention to the fact that both are essentially dwelling places, places where people know Yhwh is present and thus (in the case of the earthly one) can be found.

Person (*nepeš*). *Nepeš* can refer to the inner person (the spirit) or the outer person (the body) or the whole person, the whole being. In 7:2 [3] lion-like attackers tear apart my *nepeš*. In Ps. 35 the suppliant asks God to speak reassuringly to my *nepeš* and restore it, and refers to people whose *nepeš* (longing) is to see the suppliant dead and who are seeking my *nepeš* (my life). They have dug a pit for it and are seeking bereavement for it. The psalm speaks of afflicting my *nepeš* and looks forward to it rejoicing in God's deliverance (vv. 3, 4, 7, 9, 12, 13, 17, 25). In Ps. 42:1–6 [2–7] the whole *nepeš* strains toward God and thirsts for God, the suppliant's *nepeš* is poured out, and the suppliant asks the *nepeš* why it is downcast.

Plea, plead (*tĕpillâ, pālal* hitpael). This law-court language pictures the suppliant as standing before a court and asking for mercy, on one's own behalf or on someone else's. Applied to prayer (4:1 [2]; 5:2 [3]; 32:6; 66:19–20; 72:15), it thus suggests an appeal for God to intervene, for oneself or for someone else. It implies an appeal to Yhwh's nature as someone who treats people in the right way, and it implicitly asks that the suppliant or the person on whose behalf one prays be given his or her rights. Yet it also implies that a suppliant "does not employ the language of an accuser," but that "the one praying adopt the posture and attitude of a suppliant."[11]

Poor (*dal*). Someone who lacks resources and is thus *needy and *weak (72:13; 82:3–4) and dependent on others taking notice of them (41:1 [2]).

Possession (*naḥălâ*). Etymologically "inheritance," but the word can refer to something belonging to God (28:9; 33:12) or something that can be given (2:8; 47:4 [5]); its emphasis lies on the certainty of possession rather than the means whereby it was obtained.

Praise (*hālal* piel and hitpael; *tĕhillâ*). An onomatopoeic word that suggests making a lalalalala-sound or ululating. The hitpael ("exult oneself") draws more attention to the implications of the praise for the person doing the praising. Both can be used for praising or exulting in what deserves praise and exultation (22:22–26 [23–27]; 44:8 [9]), and in what does not (e.g., wealth or other deities; 10:3; 49:6 [7]; 52:1 [3]; 97:7).

Rebel, rebellion (*pāšaʿ, pešaʿ*). See, e.g., 32:1, 5; 51:1, 3, 13 [3, 5, 15]. Traditionally translated "transgress/transgression," but one "rebels" against a person who is in authority (cf. the parallelism in 5:10 [11]).

Redeem, redemption (*pādâ, pidyôn*). The verb can refer to paying the price to regain something that is forfeit (cf. 49:7–8 [8–9]), but like the English word "redeem," it comes to emphasize the freedom rather than the price-paying (49:15 [16]; cf. 25:22; 26:11; 31:5 [6]; 34:22 [23]; 55:18 [19]; 69:18 [19]). Although the usage sometimes implies the expenditure of effort, generally it abandons the idea of cost (though see 44:26 [27]) and focuses on the act of deliverance whereby Yhwh takes someone as a personal possession and/or liberates them. Being Yhwh's servants puts us under the protection of a master who acts decisively for us and buys us back if that is needed.

Rely on (*ḥāsâ bĕ*). What a person does in relation to something that provides protection, such as a fortress (31:1–4 [2–5]). In relation to God, it is commonly what the Davidic king does (18:2, 30 [3, 31]), but it also characterizes the relationship between Israel and God.[12] Mediating between the natural image of taking refuge and the metaphor of reliance is the fact that the wings of the cherubim dominate the temple's inner sanctuary, while carvings of cherubim appear elsewhere in the temple. Though the cherubim function mainly to provide Yhwh with transport, it would not be surprising if they also suggested protection. This verb could then denote taking refuge in the temple, though we should not press the image. None of the occurrences of the verb mention the temple and all apply the verb directly to Yhwh. Since the temple was a place of asylum, then, more likely this has become a metaphor for finding refuge with Yhwh in a more general sense. Relying on Yhwh is thus similar to *trusting in Yhwh;[13] contrast *ḥāsâ bĕ* with *ḥāsâ bĕṣēl kĕnāpêkā*, "take refuge in the *shade of your wings" (17:7–8; 36:7 [8]; 57:1 [2]; 63:7 [8]), or *ḥāsâ taḥat*, "take refuge under" (91:4).

---

11. Chrysostom, *Psalms*, 1:83.
12. See *TDOT*.
13. Cf. BDB 90b.

Resound, resounding (*rānan, rinnâ*). Probably an onomatopoeic word, presumably n-n-n-n, it signifies a kind of sound, an inarticulate noise or cry that can signify (e.g.) praise and joy (30:5 [6]; 47:1 [2]) or protest and grief (17:1; 61:1 [2]). EVV "shout for joy" thus spells out something not implicit in the word itself, which emphasizes sound rather than verbal content.

Revere, reverence (*yārē', yir'â*). These words cover the range of both negative "fear" (3:6 [7]; 55:5 [6]) and positive "reverence" (5:7 [8]; 111:10), but the latter is more common in the Psalms. The same double significance attaches to *pāḥad* and *gûr*, which suggest something stronger ("dread" and "be in awe").

Rise (*selâ*). Dictionaries usually connect the word *selâ* with the root *sālal*, "rise." It comes at the end of lines in psalms without any consistent patterning. While it sometimes comes at the end of sections (Ps. 66), it often comes in the middle of a section or in the middle of a sentence (Pss. 67; 68). It may be a liturgical or musical direction ("raise the voice"?), but we do not know. I understand that David Allan Hubbard advocated the theory that it was what David said when he broke a string, which is the most illuminating theory because there is no logic about when you break a string, and there is no logic about the occurrence of *selâ*.

Seek help from (*dāraš, biqqēš*). Treating someone or something as a resource of guidance and strength. Looking to Yhwh in this way is a marker of being seriously committed to Yhwh; it is the opposite of looking to the traditional gods of the land (22:26 [27]; 34:4, 10 [5, 11]; 77:2 [3]; 105:4). "Seek" Yhwh (EVV) gives a misleading impression.

Shade of your wings (*ṣēl kĕnāpêkā*). See 17:8; 36:7 [8]; 57:1 [2]; 63:7 [8]. The image may have at least three backgrounds: the wings of a mother bird sheltering a baby bird, the cherubim in the temple, and the picture of the heavens as wings, specifically as the sun with wings (cf. Mal. 4:2 [3:20]).[14] But the first of these is the one that most clearly relates to providing shade or protection.[15]

Sheol (*šĕ'ôl*). The place where dead people are, a nonphysical equivalent to the grave or the tomb. It is not a place of punishment (except insofar as people are taken there before their time because of their wrongdoing; 9:17 [18]; 31:17 [18]; 49:14–15 [15–16]; 55:15 [16]) but just a place where people exist rather than really live, as bodies do in their graves. God does not intervene there, and therefore there is nothing to praise God for there (6:5 [6]). If the name originally had a meaning related to (e.g.) the verb *šā'al* (ask), there is no indication that this now influences the meaning of the name; it is simply a place name. It can be used metaphorically to refer to death itself, and insofar as death comes to overwhelm us in life (e.g., if we are seriously ill), then it is as if we are already overwhelmed by Sheol and need to be delivered from it (18:5 [6]; 30:3 [4]).

Shield (*māgēn*). A handheld protection for the main part of the body and thus a natural and recurrent image for protection, sometimes accompanied by reference to Yhwh's being a help or a deliverance (3:2–3 [3–4]; 18:2, 30, 35 [3, 31, 36]; 33:20; 144:2).[16]

Shout (*tĕrû'â, rûa'*). Perhaps onomatopoeic words, they signify a shout (e.g.) of joy or triumph (27:6; 33:3; 47:5 [6]). They can also refer to the blast of a horn.[17] EVV "shout of joy" or "triumph" spell out something not explicit in the words themselves. In either case the expression refers to the noise (e.g., a part of worship).

---

14. Cf. Keel, *Symbolism of the Biblical World*, 27–30.
15. Cf. Silvia Schroer, "'Under the Shadow of Your Wings,'" in *Wisdom and Psalms*, ed. Brenner and Fontaine, 264–82.
16. Cf. Keel, *Symbolism of the Biblical World*, 222–24.
17. So Westermann, *Living Psalms*, 211.

Glossary

Strength (*'ōz*). The notion of Yhwh's strength is an important one in the Psalms, where nearly half the word's occurrences come. Insofar as it means "strength," *'ōz* links with the verb *'āzaz* and related words. There are a number of passages (46:1 [2]; 59:9, 16, 17 [10, 17, 18]; 62:7, 11 [8, 12]) where some translators render "protection," in the conviction that the noun here links with the verb *'ûz* (see "stronghold" below).

Strings (*nĕgînōt*). The verb *nāgan* means to pluck strings and thus to play a stringed instrument such as a lyre, and in headings to psalms (e.g., Pss. 4; 6; 54) this noun thus signifies the accompaniment that goes with certain prayers.

Stronghold (*mā'ôz*). A refuge from danger or attack, such as a high rock (cf. 28:8; 31:2, 4 [3, 5]; 37:39; also 43:2 in the context of Yhwh's sending "light" to bring me back home). Readers might link *mā'ôz* with *'āzaz* (be strong) or *'ûz* (take refuge), though the collocation of *mā'ôz* and *'āzaz* in 52:7 [9] suggests the former. Modern opinions also differ as to the word's etymology, but both connotations are apposite.

Talk (*hāgâ, hāgût*). EVV sometimes translate by words such as "meditate" (1:2), but the verb can be used for ordinary talk between human beings (2:1; 37:30; 38:12 [13]) and also for religious talk that presupposes an audience (35:28; 63:6 [7]). It thus denotes not merely inner meditation but also speaking or reading out loud, in a way that others can hear. Thus at 1:2 cf. LXX's *meletaō* and even more *phtheggomai* in Aq, Sym. The use with the preposition *bĕ* hints at the speaker's personal identification with the object of the talking or meditation.[18]

True, truth, truthfulness (*'ĕmet, 'ĕmûnâ*). The words suggest a consistency between what someone says, means, and does, and a steadfastness, faithfulness, and reliability in doing what we say (15:2; 25:5, 10; 26:3; 31:5 [6]; 36:5 [6]). Thus Yhwh's truthfulness is a special subject of thanksgiving/testimony (30:9 [10]; 40:10 [11]; 71:22). Expressions such as "true God" are more literally "God of truthfulness."

Trust (*bāṭaḥ bĕ, mibṭaḥ*). The question about trust is where we put it. The question it raises is not whether we trust or doubt or mistrust or fear: ideally trust is the antonym of fear, but the two can coexist (see 56:3–4 [4–5]). It is what we put our trust in, whether in Yhwh (13:5 [6]; 31:6, 14 [7, 15]) or in armaments (44:6 [7]) or in wealth (52:7–8 [9–10]; 62:8–10 [9–11])—or even in other people who seemed trustworthy (41:9 [10]). The noun *mibṭaḥ* similarly suggests the object of trust (40:4 [5]; 65:5 [6]; 71:5).

Violence (*ḥāmās*). The word can refer to more general lawlessness or outrage (e.g., Gen. 6:11, 13), but the references in the Psalms all make sense on the basis of the assumption that the word denotes violence that is lawless and outrageous, often because it is exercised by means of the law (7:16 [17]; 11:5; 18:48 [49]; 25:19; 58:2 [3]; 72:14). Thus false witnesses are "witnesses of *ḥāmās*," witnesses whose testimony will issue in wrongful violence to the accused (35:11; cf. 27:12; 55:9 [10]).

Wait (*yāḥal* piel). Like *qāwâ*, the verb suggests an attitude of expectancy or waiting, *looking for something to happen; see 31:24 [25]; 33:18, 22; 38:15 [16]; 42:5, 11 [6, 12]; 43:5; 69:3 [4]; 71:14. See also *hope. The verbs refer to waiting *for* God rather than waiting *on* God.

Watchful foe (*šōrēr*). The translation follows NJPS and combines two possible understandings of *šōrēr* (5:8 [9]; 27:11; 54:5 [7]; 56:2 [3]; 59:10 [11]). Jerome assumes it relates to the verb *šûr* and thus suggests people who watch for me (with hostile intent). LXX renders "enemies," which rather suggests a link with Akkadian *šâru*.[19]

---

18. Cf. Jesús Arambarri, "Zu einem gelungenen Leben: Psalm 1,2," in *"Jedes Ding hat seine Zeit . . ."* (D. Michel Festschrift), ed. Anja A. Diesel et al., BZAW 241 (Berlin: de Gruyter, 1996), 1–17.

19. See BDB and *HALOT* respectively.

Way (*derek*). The way of God is the way God acts in the world, a way that has integrity (18:30 [31]), a way of commitment and truthfulness (25:9–10) that expresses itself in delivering people (67:2 [3]). Yhwh's way is thus our encouragement and hope (5:8 [9]) and a way we need to come to know more and more (27:11).

Waywardness (*ʿāwōn*). See 32:2, 5; 51:2, 5, 9 [4, 7, 11]. There are two roots *ʿāwâ*, one meaning "twist," one meaning "go astray"—not in the sense of accidentally losing one's way but of deliberately choosing the wrong road. A passage such as Jer. 3:21 suggests that people could be aware of the latter connotation of *ʿāwōn*. Sin involves skewing one's way.[20] But *ʿāwōn* might also suggest the first idea, the idea of perversity: people are twisted or crooked in their ways.

Weak (*ʿānî, ʿānāw*). Someone who is vulnerable and powerless, often as a result of circumstances such as having no surviving family. Such people are thus open to being victimized and hounded by the contrivances of others in the community who feel no obligation to its weaker members but who rather use their weakness to their own advantage. NRSV translates as "afflicted" (9:12 [13]), "poor" (9:18 [19]; 10:2, 9), "oppressed" (10:12), and "meek" (10:17); NIVI as "afflicted" (9:12, 18 [13, 19]; 10:17), "weak" (10:2), and "helpless" (10:9, 12); NJPS as "afflicted" (9:12, 18 [13, 19]) and "lowly" (10:2, 9, 12, 17). These first instances of the words in the Psalter in Pss. 9–10 show that they do not denote an inner humility, nor do they point to a group or party within the community as a whole.[21] Further, here as elsewhere "weak" is a way Israel characterizes itself over against other peoples when it wants to call on or glorify Yhwh's help (68:10 [11]; 74:18–23; 149:4). The broader idea of the weakness and vulnerability of the individual and of Yhwh's commitment to punishing anyone who sheds the blood of such a person has become a figure to characterize the attitude of strong, oppressive nations to a weak, vulnerable one, and Yhwh's involvement in this situation. The weak individual, too, is one who lacks power or resources, rather than someone who is either poor or humble.

Well-being (*šālôm*). A wide-ranging term that covers peace in the sense of freedom from war, safety, friendship, blessing, and prosperity (28:3; 29:11; 35:20, 27; 37:11, 37; 38:3 [4]).

Whole-offering (*ʿōlâ, kālîl*). The two words point to the nature of these offerings. They are sacrifices that go up (*ʿālâ*) to God in their totality (*kol*): the whole animal is burnt, so the offerer gets no benefit from the offering at all. The former is more common than the latter; both come in 51:19 [21].

Worship (*bārak* qal passive participle and piel). When Yhwh is the subject, the verb means "bless," but this meaning seems odd when Yhwh is the object. Rather, the verb then links with *berek* ("knee") and indicates bowing the knee before Yhwh (16:7; 28:6; 66:8, 20).

---

20. See *TLOT* 862–66.
21. See Kraus, *Psalms*, 1:93–95.

Bibliography

For any work that relates to an individual psalm, such as textual notes, the footnotes contain bibliographical detail; a later reference to the same work in the treatment of the same psalm uses a short title. This bibliography comprises more general works, which are always referred to by a short title in the footnotes. I refer to the commentaries of Ibn Ezra, David Qimchi, and Rashi simply by their names, the reference being to their treatment of the passage under discussion as it appears in editions of the Rabbinic Bible, *Miqrā'ôt Gĕdôlôt*. I refer to Thomas Aquinas's commentary without page reference because it is published in English only on the Internet.

Allen, Leslie C. *Psalms 101–150*. Rev. ed. Word Biblical Commentary. Nashville: Nelson, 2002.

Alter, Robert. *The Art of Biblical Poetry.* New York: Basic Books, 1985.

Anderson, Arnold A. *Psalms*. New Century Bible. 2 vols. London: Oliphants, 1972.

Anderson, Bernhard W. *Out of the Depths*. Rev. ed. Philadelphia: Westminster, 1983.

Aquinas, Thomas. *See* Thomas Aquinas.

Athanasius of Alexandria. *Letter to Marcellinus concerning the Psalms*. http://www.fisheaters.com/psalmsathanasiusletter.html.

Auffret, Pierre. *La sagesse a bâti sa maison*. OBO 49. Göttingen: Vandenhoeck & Ruprecht, 1982.

Augustine of Hippo. *Expositions on the Book of Psalms*. Vol. 8 of *A Select Library of Nicene and Post-Nicene Fathers of the Christian Church*, edited by Philip Schaff. 1st series. 1886–89. Repr., Grand Rapids: Eerdmans, 1989. http://www.ccel.org/fathers2/NPNF1-08/TOC.htm.

Brenner, Athalya, and Carole Fontaine, eds. *Wisdom and Psalms*. A Feminist Companion to the Bible, 2nd series, 2. Sheffield: Sheffield Academic Press, 1998.

Briggs, Charles A., and Emilie Grace Briggs. *A Critical and Exegetical Commentary on the Book of Psalms*. International Critical Commentary. 2 vols. Repr., Edinburgh: T&T Clark, 1986–87.

Broyles, Craig C. *The Conflict of Faith and Experience in the Psalms*. Journal for the Study of the Old Testament: Supplement Series 52. Sheffield: JSOT Press, 1989.

Brueggemann, Walter. *Israel's Praise*. Philadelphia: Fortress, 1988.

———. *The Message of the Psalms*. Minneapolis: Augsburg, 1984.

———. *The Psalms and the Life of Faith*. Minneapolis: Fortress, 1995.

Buttenwieser, Moses. *The Psalms*. Repr., New York: Ktav, 1969.

Calvin, John. *Commentary on the Book of Psalms*. 5 vols. Repr., Grand Rapids: Eerdmans, 1948–49.

Cassiodorus Senator. *Explanation of the Psalms*. 3 vols. New York: Paulist Press, 1990–91.

Chrysostom, John. *Commentary on the Psalms*. 2 vols. Brookline, MA: Holy Cross Orthodox Press, 1998.

Craigie, Peter C. *Psalms 1–50*. 2nd ed. With supplement by Marvin E. Tate and W. Dennis Tucker. Word Biblical Commentary. Nashville: Nelson, 2004.

Crenshaw, James L. *The Psalms*. Grand Rapids: Eerdmans, 2001.

Dahood, M. *Psalms*. Anchor Bible. 3 vols. Garden City, NY: Doubleday, 1966–70.

Eaton, John. *Psalms*. Torch Bible Commentaries. London: SCM, 1967.

Fokkelman, J. P. *Major Poems of the Hebrew Bible*. Vols. 2 and 3. Assen: Van Gorcum, 2000 and 2003.

Gerstenberger, Erhard S. *Psalms and Lamentations*. Forms of the Old Testament Literature. 2 vols. Grand Rapids: Eerdmans, 1988–2001.

Goldingay, John. *Songs from a Strange Land*. Leicester, UK: Inter-Varsity, 1978.

Goulder, Michael D. *The Prayers of David*. Journal for the Study of the Old Testament: Supplement Series 102. Sheffield: JSOT Press, 1990.

———. *The Psalms of the Sons of Korah*. Journal for the Study of the Old Testament: Supplement Series 20. Sheffield: JSOT, 1982.

Gunkel, Hermann. *Introduction to Psalms*. Completed by Joachim Begrich. Macon, GA: Mercer University Press, 1998.

———. *Die Psalmen*. 5th ed. Göttingen: Vandenhoeck & Ruprecht, 1968.

———. *The Psalms*. Philadelphia: Fortress, 1967.

Habel, Norman C., ed. *The Earth Story in the Psalms and the Prophets*. Sheffield: Sheffield Academic Press; Cleveland: Pilgim, 2001.

Hauge, Martin R. *Between Sheol and Temple*. Journal for the Study of the Old Testament: Supplement Series 178. Sheffield: Sheffield Academic Press, 1995.

Hilary of Poitiers. *Homilies on the Psalms*. In vol. 9 of *A Select Library of Nicene and Post-Nicene Fathers of the Christian Church*, edited by Philip Schaff and Henry Wace, 236–48. 2nd series. Repr., Grand Rapids: Eerdmans, 1989. http://www.ccel.org/fathers2/NPNF2-09/Npnf2-09-20.htm.

Hill, Edmund. *Prayer, Praise and Politics*. London: Sheed & Ward, 1973.

Ibn Ezra. *Těhillîm*. In *Miqrā'ôt Gědôlôt*. Repr. in *Psalms*, by A. J. Rosenberg. 3 vols. New York: Judaica, 1991.

Jerome [Eusebius Hieronymus]. *The Homilies of Saint Jerome*, vol. 1, *1–59 on the Psalms*. Washington, DC: Catholic University of America Press, 1964.

Johnson, Aubrey R. *The Cultic Prophet and Israel's Psalmody*. Cardiff: University of Wales, 1979.

———. *Sacral Kingship in Ancient Israel*. Cardiff: University of Wales, 1955.

Keel, Othmar. *The Symbolism of the Biblical World*. New York: Seabury, 1978.

Kidner, Derek. *Psalms*. Vol. 1, *Psalms 1–72*. Vol. 2, *Psalms 73–150*. Tyndale Old Testament Commentary. London: Inter-Varsity, 1973–75.

Kirkpatrick, A. F. *The Book of Psalms*. Cambridge Bible for Schools and Colleges. Repr., Cambridge: Cambridge University Press, 1910.

Kraus, Hans-Joachim. *Psalms*. Vol. 1, *Psalms 1–59*. Vol. 2, *Psalms 60–150*. Minneapolis: Augsburg, 1988–89.

Lindström, Fredrik. *Suffering and Sin*. Stockholm: Almqvist, 1994.

Loretz, Oswald. *Psalmstudien*. Beihefte zur Zeitschrift für die alttestamentliche Wissenschaft 309. Berlin: de Gruyter, 2002.

———. *Ugarit-Texte und Thronbesteigungspsalmen*. Münster: Ugarit, 1988.

Luther, Martin. *First Lectures on the Psalms*. 2 vols. Vols. 10 and 11 of *Luther's Works*, edited by Hilton C. Oswald et al. St. Louis: Concordia, 1974–76.

———. *Selected Psalms*. 3 vols. Vols. 12–14 of *Luther's Works*, edited by Hilton C. Oswald et al. St. Louis: Concordia, 1955–58.

Mandolfo, Carleen. *God in the Dock*. Journal for the Study of the Old Testament: Supplement Series 357. London: Sheffield Academic Press, 2002.

Mays, James L. *Psalms*. Interpretation. Louisville: Knox, 1994.

McCann, J. Clinton, Jr. "The Book of Psalms." Vol. 4 of *The New Interpreter's Bible*, edited by Leander E. Keck et al., 639–1280. Nashville: Abingdon, 1996.

Midrash on Psalms, The. 2 vols. New Haven, CT: Yale University Press, 1959.

Miller, Patrick D. *Interpreting the Psalms*. Philadelphia: Fortress, 1986.

Mowinckel, Sigmund. *The Psalms in Israel's Worship*. 2 vols. Oxford: Blackwell, 1967.

Peterson, Eugene. *Answering God*. Repr., San Francisco: Harper, 1991.

———. *Where Your Treasure Is: Psalms That Summon You from Self to Community*. Grand Rapids: Eerdmans, 1993.

Qimchi, David. *Těhillîm*. In *Miqrā'ôt Gědôlôt*. Repr. in *Psalms*, by A. J. Rosenberg. 3 vols. New York: Judaica, 1991.

Raabe, Paul R. *Psalm Structures*. Journal for the Study of the Old Testament: Supplement Series 104. Sheffield: JSOT Press, 1990.

Rashi. *Těhillîm*. In *Miqrā'ôt Gědôlôt*. Repr. in *Psalms*, by A. J. Rosenberg. 3 vols. New York: Judaica, 1991.

Reid, Stephen Breck, ed. *Psalms and Practice*. Collegeville, MN: Liturgical Press, 2001.

Rendsburg, Gary A. *Linguistic Evidence for the Northern Origin of Selected Psalms*. Atlanta: Scholars Press, 1990.

Ridderbos, N. H. *Die Psalmen*. Beihefte zur Zeitschrift für die alttestamentliche Wissenschaft 117. Berlin: de Gruyter, 1972.

Rienstra, Marchiene Vroon. *Swallow's Nest: A Feminine Reading of the Psalms*. Grand Rapids: Eerdmans, 1992.

Rogerson, J. W., and J. W. McKay. *Psalms*. Vol. 1, *Psalms 1–50*. Vol. 2, *Psalms 51–100*. Vol. 3, *Psalms 101–150*. Cambridge Commentary on the New English Bible. Cambridge: Cambridge University Press, 1977.

Rosenberg, A. J. *Psalms*. With translation of Rashi and other commentaries. 3 vols. New York: Judaica, 1991.

Schaefer, Konrad. *Psalms*. Berit Olam. Collegeville, MN: Liturgical Press, 2001.

Seybold, Klaus. *Introducing the Psalms*. Edinburgh: T&T Clark, 1990.

———. *Die Psalmen*. Tübingen: Mohr, 1996.

Seybold, Klaus, and Erich Zenger, eds. *Neue Wege der Psalmenforschung*. Freiburg: Herder, 1994.

Slomovic, Elieser. "Toward an Understanding of the Formation of Historical Titles in the Book of Psalms." *Zeitschrift für die alttestamentliche Wissenschaft* 91 (1979): 350–80.

Soggin, J. Alberto. *Old Testament and Oriental Studies*. Rome: Biblical Pontifical Institute, 1975.

Spurgeon, C. H. *The Treasury of David*. 6 vols. Repr., London: Marshall, 1963.

Stec, David M. *Targum of Psalms*. Collegeville, MN: Liturgical Press, 2004.

Tate, Marvin E. *Psalms 51–100*. Word Biblical Commentary. Dallas: Word, 1990.

Terrien, Samuel. *The Psalms*. Grand Rapids: Eerdmans, 2002.

Theodoret of Cyrrhus. *Theodoret of Cyrus: Commentary on the Psalms*. Translated by R. C. Hill. 2 vols. Washington, DC: Catholic University of America Press, 2000–2001.

Thomas Aquinas. *Commentary on the Psalms*. http://www4.desales.edu/~philtheo/loughlin/ATP/.

Trudiger, Peter L. *The Psalms of the Tamid Service*. Vetus Testamentum Supplements 98. Leiden: Brill, 2004.

Ulrich, Eugene, et al. *Qumran Cave 4.XI: Psalms to Chronicles*. Discoveries in the Judaean Desert 16. Oxford: Clarendon, 2000.

Watson, Wilfred G. E. *Classical Hebrew Poetry*. 2nd ed. Journal for the Study of the Old Testament: Supplement Series 26. Sheffield: JSOT Press, 1986.

Weiser, Artur. *The Psalms*. London: SCM; Philadelphia: Westminster, 1962.

Westermann, Claus. *The Living Psalms*. Grand Rapids: Eerdmans; Edinburgh: T&T Clark, 1989.

———. *The Praise of God in the Psalms*. Richmond: Knox, 1965. Enlarged ed. published as *Praise and Lament in the Psalms*. Atlanta: Knox, 1981.

Whybray, R. Norman. *Reading the Psalms as a Book*. Journal for the Study of the Old Testament: Supplement Series 222. Sheffield: Sheffield Academic Press, 1996.

Zenger, Erich. *A God of Vengeance?* Louisville: Westminster John Knox, 1996.

Subject Index

abandonment, 204, 340–41
Anderson, Bernhard W., 68
anger, 66–67, 503–4
Aquinas, Thomas, 82n7, 509
Aramaic prayer, 302–3
Athanasius of Alexandria, 9, 23
attacks or persecution. *See also* wars and warfare
  Psalm 5, 127, 132, 133
  Psalm 6, 64, 135, 141
  Psalm 12, 201
  Psalm 14, 212, 214–15, 217
  Psalm 17, 238, 245–46
  Psalm 18, 258–59
  Psalm 22, 340
  Psalm 35, 489–90, 503–4
  Psalm 38, 538, 545–48
  responses to, 127, 132, 135
Augustine of Hippo, 90, 429, 587
Auvray, Paul, 87n18
Avent, Geraldine, 414n7

babies and sucklings, cries of, 156, 161
Babylon, 33–35, 68
Basil, bishop of Caesarea, 9
Bathsheba, 453

Birkeland, Harris, 391n1
blessings, 301–3, 309
Bons, Eberhard, 438
Booths/Shelters festival, 51–55, 414
Briggs, Charles A., 539
Brueggemann, Walter, 58n65, 68

Calvin, John, 473
Canaanites, 74–75, 138, 259, 277, 413–14
Cassiodorus, 80n1
Childs, Brevard S., 23n7
Christian nations, 105, 106, 504
Christology
  Cassiodorus and, 80n1
  deliverance and, 318–19
  Hilary of Poitiers and, 80n1
  Psalm 1, 80n1
  Psalm 2, 105–6
  Psalm 16, 234
  Psalm 21, 318–19
  Psalm 33, 473
  Psalm 35, 503
Chrysostom, 99n12, 118
Clines, David, 364
commentaries, 7–8
commitment, 204, 209, 256–58

commitments, moral, 223–25, 381, 382–84, 387, 388
confession, and Psalms, 64–65
cosmos's acknowledgment of God
  God as creator, 71
  Psalm 19, 284, 285, 286–90, 298
  Psalm 33, 473
Creach, J. F. D., 103

daily life, and faithfulness, 234–35
David
  authorship of Psalms and, 26–30
  deliverance from attacks and, 279–81
  Psalm 3, and story of, 109
  Psalm 18, and story of, 254–56, 279–81
  and Psalm 18, origin of, 254–56
  Psalm 22, and story of, 324
  Psalm 23, and story of, 347
  Psalm 24, and story of, 356–57

Subject Index

Psalm 26, and prayers of young, 381
Psalm 27, and story of, 391
Psalm 31, and story of, 437
Psalm 32, and story of, 453
Psalm 33, and story of, 464
Psalm 34, and story of, 477–78
Psalm 35, and story of, 490
Psalm 40, and story of, 569
Psalm 41, and story of, 582
death
 Canaanites' beliefs about life and, 74–75, 138, 259, 277
 Egypt, and beliefs about, 74
 human beings and, 565
 Jesus, and rising from, 565
 Psalm 16, 234
 Psalm 39, 555, 557–59, 565
 Psalms on life and, 73–75
dedication occasions, 425
Deissler, Alfons, 464
deliverance
 David and, 279–81
 from Egypt, 257, 328
 Job and, 114
 and king, anointed, 311–12
 Psalm 3, 108–9, 114–15
 Psalm 7, 144–45, 152
 Psalm 9, 25
 Psalm 10, 25
 Psalm 18, 259–65, 265–71
 Psalm 21, 311–13
 Psalm 31, 438–42
 Psalm 34, 477, 486
 Psalm 40, 568, 569–71, 572–74, 575–76, 579
doxology, 69, 590

Eaton, John H., 45, 123n15, 251n1, 345n2
Ecclesiastes, 8, 90, 559, 563, 564–65
Egypt
 beliefs, 101n14, 262n23, 289
 deliverance from, 257, 328
 faithfulness and, 184
 life and death beliefs, 74
 Psalm 33, 467
 Psalm 34, 482n6
 psalmody and, 32–33, 68
 refuge in, 304, 308
 suffering in, 138
evangelistic preaching (kerygma), 22
evil. See attacks or persecution

faithfulness
 daily life and, 234–35
 Egypt and, 184
 Proverbs and, 88
 Psalm 1, 84–86
 Psalm 9, 170–74, 176–77
 Psalms 9–10 and, 166–70, 184, 185–86
 Psalm 10, 183–84
 Psalm 11, 188, 191–94
 Psalm 17, 237–38, 239–40
 Psalm 18, 265–71
 Psalm 36, 506, 509–11, 513
 Psalm 37, 517–18, 525–28, 531–35
 Psalm 41, 582–83, 588
faithless way of life
 Proverbs and, 82
 Psalm 1, 86–87, 88–90
 Psalms 9–10, 179–82, 184, 185, 186
 Psalm 10, 179–82
 Psalm 12, 196–97
 Psalm 28, 403–4, 409–10
 Psalm 36, 506, 507–9, 513
 Psalm 37, 518, 521–22, 533–35

Psalm 41 life, 588–89
 response of God to, 199–200
falsehoods. See attacks or persecution
fear, 8, 178, 468, 477–78, 503–4
Fishbane, Michael A., 123n16, 286

Gaster, T. H., 413–14
God
 acts of, 271–78, 318
 admitting God to the city, 364–65
 answers to prayers and, 581, 587–88, 589
 attributes of, 237, 245–46, 271–78
 becoming king, and Sukkot festival, 414
 commitment to anointed king by, 72–73
 conditions for approaching, 356, 358–61
 as creator, 71
 home of, 71–72
 honor of, 286–88, 415–16, 420
 images of, 237, 245–46, 271–78, 318
 involvment of, 70–71
 as king, 184, 185
 and Messiah, commitment to, 72–73
 ownership of world by, 356, 357–58, 364
 power of voice of, 412–14, 421–22
 role of, 184–85
 servants of, human beings as, 25, 154, 158–59, 254, 507
 word from God, 63
 Zion and, 71–72
good fortune
 Proverbs and, 81, 88
 Psalm 1, 81–82, 581, 588–89
 Psalm 2, 95
 Psalm 32, 453, 454, 581

607

Psalm 33, 469
Psalm 40, 571
Psalm 41, 581, 582, 588
Gunkel, Hermann, 44, 46, 204

Habel, Norman C., 414n7
Hanukkah, 425
Harrelson, Walter, 155n3
healing, 110, 136, 425, 496, 503
Hilary of Poitiers, 80n1
honor
  God's, 286–88, 415–16, 420
  Psalm 4, 120, 141
  restoration of, 111
Huie-Jolly, Mary R., 105n28
human beings
  authority over animate creation and, 154, 159–60
  capacity to name God and, 155n3
  conditions for approaching God by, 356, 358–61
  cries for help and, 323
  death and, 565
  feelings of being overwhelmed and, 340
  qualifications for staying with God and, 219, 223–25
  restoration of honor and, 111
  as servants of God, 25, 154, 158–59, 254, 507
hunting, and Psalm 7, 152

illness, experience of, 554, 555, 559–64
Israel, nation of
  Psalm 2, 96, 97–99, 100–103, 104, 105
  Psalm 38, 539

Jeduthun, 555
Jeremiah, 85–86, 570
Jesus
  and death, rising from, 565

protest psalms and, 63–64
Psalm 6, 63
Psalm 8, and aspects of, 160
Psalm 22, 64, 341–43
Psalm 35, 503
Psalm 42, 63
Psalm 42 and, 63
Job
  deliverance from attack and, 114
  prayers and, 49
  suffering and, 136, 139, 461, 564–65
John Paul II, 450
Jonah, 63
judgment and judicial procedures, 87–88, 152, 184, 186

Kaiser, Otto, 157n13
kerygma (evangelistic preaching), 22
king, anointed
  blessings for, 301–3, 309
  commitment by God to, 72–73
  deliverance from attack and, 311–12
  God as king, 184, 185
  God becoming king during Sukkot festival, 414
  monarchy period and, 404, 518
  Psalm 2, 25, 96, 99–100, 104–6
  Psalms 9–10 and, 185
  Psalm 20, 301–3, 309
  Psalm 37, 518
  Psalm 37, and period of, 518
  Psalm 41, 582
  role of, 184, 185
Köhler, Ludwig, 158n15, 346n6
Kraus, Hans-Joachim, 53, 54, 119n6, 333, 416–17n11, 571

laments at community life, 197, 199–201, 237, 242–43
Letter to Marcellinus (Athanasius), 23
life and death, 73–75. See *also* death
Lindström, Fredrik, 391n1, 539
Lohfink, Norbert, 136n4
Loretz, O., 154n2
Luther, Martin, 9, 104n26, 141, 354n29

Mandolfo, Carleen, 117n1, 120n8, 149n10
Mazor, Yair, 346n6
McKay, J. W., 146n6, 417n12
Meinhold, Arndt, 299
Mesopotamian beliefs, 289, 333, 467
Miller, Patrick D., 184
monarchy period, 404, 518
moral commitments, 223–25, 381, 382–84, 387, 388
Mowinckel, Sigmund, 46n54, 47–48, 51–52, 68

New Testament, and interrelationship with Psalms, 75–78
New Year festival, agricultural, 51–55, 414
Niehaus, Jeffrey, 399n11

Old Testament
  Psalms as "microcosm" of, 9
  wisdom material, 367–68
ownership of world by God. See cosmos's acknowledgment of God

pacifism, 365
pastors, and blessings for, 309
Peterson, Eugene, 22, 103, 104

Subject Index

pleas
  cry for help, 323
  feelings of being overwhelmed and, 340
  Psalm 5, 127–28, 133
  Psalm 9, 166–68
  Psalms 9–10, 174–75, 177–79, 182–83
  Psalm 10, 184–86
  Psalm 12, 197, 199–201
  Psalm 16, 237
  Psalm 17, 237–39, 240–42, 243–45
  Psalm 19, 285–86, 294–97, 299
  Psalm 28, 403–4, 409–10
  Psalm 38, 537, 538, 539–40, 550
  Psalm 39, 555–57
  Psalm 40, 571–72
  Psalm 41, 586–87
  silence from, 555–57
pleasure, taking, 83–84
power issues, 68, 412–14
praise. *See also* doxology
  doxology of Psalms, 69, 590
  human capacity to name God and, 155
  power of, 68
  prayer, and interrelationship with, 67–69
  Psalm 8, 25, 154, 155–58, 160
  Psalm 9, 170–77
  Psalms 9–10, 166–68, 184, 186
  Psalm 10, 183–84
  Psalm 18, 278–79
  Psalm 21, 313, 315, 318
  Psalm 22, 63, 323, 341–43
  Psalm 33, 464, 473, 474
  Psalm 41, 590
prayers
  attacks or persecution and, 141
  bases of, 368, 377–78
  God's answers to, 581, 589

praise, and interrelationship with, 67–69
prayed twice, 436
Psalm 4, 117–18, 124
Psalm 25, 368, 377–78
Psalm 26, 381–82, 385–87
Psalm 27, 391–93, 396–99
Psalm 34, 478–79
Psalm 36, 506–7, 511–12
Psalm 40, 568, 576–78
Psalm 41, 581, 583–86
Psalms and, 23–24, 60–64
Preez, Jannie du, 364–65
promises
  Psalm 1, 80–81, 90–91
  Psalm 12, 201, 202
  Psalm 20, 302, 303
  Psalm 37, 518, 529, 534, 535
prophecies, and Psalms, 56–57
protests, and Psalms, 62–63
Proverbs
  faithfulness and, 88
  faithless way of life, 82
  good fortune and, 81, 88
  silence from pleas and, 556
  structure and, 517
  teachings and, 81
  wisdom and, 8
  wrongdoers and wrongdoing, 213
Proverbs, compared with Psalm 37, 517
Psalm 1
  Christology and, 80n1
  exhortations and, 80–81, 90–91
  faithfulness and, 84–86
  faithless way of life and, 86–87, 88–90
  good fortune and, 81–82, 95, 581, 588, 589
  judgment and judicial procedures, 87–88
  pleasure, taking, 83–84

promises and, 80–81, 90–91
Psalm 2, and connection with, 94–95
structure of, 80
teachings and, 25, 80–81, 83, 90–91
theological implications of, 90–91
translation of, 79
verses 1–3, 81–86
verses 4–5, 86–88
verse 6, 88–90
wrongdoers and wrongdoing, 25, 82–83
Psalm 2
  Christian nations and, 105, 106
  Christology and, 105–6
  God's response to plans of Israel, 25, 96, 100–101, 104
  good fortune and, 95
  implications of plans of Israel, 25, 96, 101–3
  and Israel, nation of, 105
  and king, anointed, 25, 96, 99–100, 104–6
  plans of Israel, 25, 96, 97–99, 105
  Psalm 1, and connection with, 94–95
  structure of, 96–97, 101, 102, 103
  theological implications of, 103–6
  translation of, 92–93
  verses 1–3, 96, 97–99
  verses 4–6, 96, 99–100
  verses 7–9, 96, 100–101
  verses 10–12, 96, 101–3
  violence and, 104
Psalm 3
  and David, story of, 109
  deliverance from attack and, 108–9, 114–15
  Psalm 4, compared with, 108, 117
  structure of, 113
  summary of, 25, 108–9

609

Subject Index

theological implications of, 114–15
translation of, 107–8
verses 1–2, 109–10
verses 3–6, 110–12
verses 7–8, 112–14

Psalm 4
honor and, 120
prayers and, 117–18, 124
Psalm 3, compared with, 108, 117
structure of, 118
summary of, 25
theological implications of, 124
translation of, 116–17
trust and, 124
verse 1, 118–19
verses 2–5, 119–22
verses 6–8, 122–24

Psalm 5
attacks or persecution and, 127, 133
pleas and, 127–28, 133
structure of, 127, 129, 130
summary of, 25
theological implications of, 133
translation of, 125–26
trust and, 127, 128–32, 133
verses 1–2, 127–28
verses 3–7, 128–30
verses 8–9, 130–31
verses 10–12, 131–32

Psalm 6
attacks or persecution and, 64, 135, 141
Jesus and, 63
summary of, 25
theological implications of, 141
translation of, 134–35
verses 1–3, 135–37
verses 4–7, 137–39
verses 8–10, 139–41

Psalm 7
deliverance from attack and, 144–45, 152

hunting and, 152
judicial procedures and, 152
structure of, 146, 147, 150, 151
summary of, 25
theological implications of, 152
translation of, 142–44, 146n6
verses 1–2, 145
verses 3–5, 145–46
verses 6–9, 146–48
verses 10–16, 148–51
verse 17, 151
wars and warfare and, 152

Psalm 8
babies and sucklings, cries of, 156, 161
human authority over animate creation and, 154, 159–60
human beings as servants of God and, 25, 154, 158–59
and Jesus, aspects of, 160
praise and, 25, 154, 155–58
structure of, 154n2, 159
summary of, 25
theological implications of, 160–61
translation of, 153–54, 417n12
verses 1–2, 154, 155–58
verses 3–4, 154, 158–59
verses 5–8, 154, 159–60
verse 9, 154, 160

Psalm 9. See also Psalms 9–10
deliverance from attack and, 25
praise and, 170–74, 176–77
Psalm 10, 35n34
theological implications of, 184–86
verses 1–4, 170–72
verses 5–10, 172–74
verses 9:19–10:2, 177–79

verses 11–12, 174
verses 13–18, 174–77
Psalms 9–10. See also Psalm 9; Psalm 10
faithfulness and, 166–70, 184, 185–86
faithless way of life and, 179–82, 184, 185, 186
and God, role of, 184–85
justice and judicial procedures, 184, 186
and king, role of, 184, 185
pleas and, 166–68, 184–86
praise and, 166–70, 184, 186
Second Temple period and, 169
structure of, 166, 168, 178, 179, 180
theological implications of, 184–86
translations of, 162–64

Psalm 10. See also Psalms 9–10
deliverance from attack and, 25
faithless way of life and, 179–82
Psalm 9, 35n34
theological implications of, 184–86
verses 3–11, 179–82
verses 12–15, 182–83
verses 16–18, 183–84
verses 9:19–10:2, 177–79

Psalm 11
faithfulness and, 188, 191–94
theological implications of, 194
translation of, 187–88
trust and, 188, 189–91, 194
verses 1–2, 189–90
verse 3, 190–91
verses 4–7, 191–94

Psalm 12
attacks or persecution and, 201–2

Subject Index

faithless way of life and, 196–97
laments at community life and, 197, 199–201
pleas and, 197, 199–200
promises and, 201, 202
structure of, 197n3, 198
theological implications of, 201–2
translation of, 195–96
verses 1–2, 197–98
verses 3–4, 198–99
verses 5–6, 199–200
verses 7–8, 200–201
violence and, 202
word from God and, 63

Psalm 13
abandonment and, 204
commitment, 204, 209
structure of, 204
theological implications of, 209
translation of, 203–4
verses 1–2, 205–7
verses 3–4, 207
verses 5–6, 208–9

Psalm 14
attacks or persecution and, 212, 214–15, 217
faithfulness and, 211, 212, 217
Second Temple period and, 212
structure of, 214
teachings and, 211
theological implications of, 217
translation of, 210–11
verses 1–2, 212–14
verses 3–5, 214–15
verses 6–7, 215–17
wrongdoers and wrongdoing, 211–14, 217

Psalm 15
moral commitments and, 223–25
qualifications for staying with God, 219, 223–25
structure of, 219n3
theological implications of, 223–25

translation of, 218
verse 1, 220
verses 2–5, 220–23

Psalm 16
Christology and, 234
death and, 234
pleas and, 237
theological implications of, 233–34
translation of, 226–27
trust and, 227–28, 234
verses 1–2, 237
verses 2–4, 228–30
verses 5–11, 230–33

Psalm 17
attacks or persecution and, 238, 245–46
faithfulness and, 237–38, 239–40
image and attributes of God and, 237, 245–46
laments at community life and, 237, 242–43
pleas and, 237–39, 240–42, 243–45
structure of, 238
theological implications of, 245–46
translation of, 235–36
verses 1–2, 238–39
verses 3–5, 239–40
verses 6–9, 240–42
verses 10–12, 242–43
verses 13–15, 243–45

Psalm 18
and David, story of, 254–56, 279–81
deliverance from attack and, 251–53, 279–81
human beings as servants of God and, 254
origin of, 254–56
Second Temple period and, 281
structure of, 259, 265, 267, 273, 276
theological implications of, 279–81
translation of, 247–51
verses 1–2, 256–58
verses 3–6, 258–59

verses 7–15, 259–65, 280
verses 16–29, 265–71
verses 30–34, 271–72
verses 35–45, 273–77
verses 46–48, 277–78
verses 49–50, 278–79

Psalm 19
cosmos's acknowledgment of God and, 284, 285, 286–90, 298
pleas and, 285–86, 294–97, 299
revelation and, 298
structure of, 287, 296
teachings and, 284, 285, 286, 290–94, 298–99
theological implications of, 297–99
translation of, 282–84
verses 1–6, 286–90
verses 7–11, 285, 286, 290–94
verses 12–14, 286, 294–97

Psalm 20
Aramaic prayer and, 302–3
blessings and, 301–3, 309
and king, anointed, 301–3, 309
promises and, 302, 303
structure of, 304n7, 305nn8,10
theological implications of, 309
translation of, 300–301
verses 1–5, 303–6
verse 6, 306–7
verses 7–9, 306–7

Psalm 21
Christology and, 318–19
deliverance and, 311–15, 315–18
praise and, 313, 315, 318
structure of, 311–12
theological implications of, 318–19
translation of, 310–11
verse 1, 313
verses 2–7, 313–15
verses 8–12, 315–18
verse 13, 318

611

Subject Index

Psalm 22
  abandonment and, 340–41
  cry for help, 323
  Jesus and, 64, 341–43
  praise and, 63, 323, 341–43
  Psalm 31 compared with, 436–37
  structure of, 327, 331, 336
  translation of, 320–23
  verses 1–2, 324–27
  verses 3–5, 327–29, 342
  verses 6–8, 329–30, 342
  verses 9–10, 330, 342
  verses 11–18, 331–33, 342
  verses 19–22, 333–35, 342–43
  verses 23–25, 335–37, 343
  verses 26–31, 337–40, 343

Psalm 23
  and David, story of, 347
  and host, God as, 346
  and language, poetic, 42–43
  Luther's exposition of, 354n29
  shepherd imagery and, 346, 347–51
  structure of, 345, 346–47, 349, 350
  theological implications of, 353–54
  translation of, 344–45
  trust and, 345, 353–54
  verses 1–4, 346, 347–51
  verses 5–6, 346, 352–53

Psalm 24
  admitting God to the city, 356, 361–64
  approaching God, conditions for, 356, 358–61, 364
  and David, story of, 356–57
  ownership of world by God and, 356, 357–58, 364
  pacifism and, 365
  structure of, 359
  theological implications of, 364–65
  translation of, 355–56
  verses 1–2, 356, 357–58
  verses 3–6, 356, 358–61
  verses 7–10, 356, 361–64

Psalm 25
  and prayers, bases of, 368, 377–78
  Second Temple period and, 368
  structure of, 367, 368, 369
  theological implications of, 377–78
  translation of, 366–67
  verses 1–3, 368–70
  verses 4–7, 370–71
  verses 8–11, 371–73
  verses 12–14, 373–74
  verses 15–19, 375–76
  verses 16–22, 368
  verses 20–22, 376–77
  wisdom material in OT and, 367–68

Psalm 26
  and David, prayers of young, 381
  moral commitments and, 381, 382–84, 386, 388
  prayers and, 380–82
  religious commitments and, 381, 384–85, 387, 388
  structure of, 381, 382, 383, 386
  translation of, 379–80
  verses 1–2, 381–82
  verses 3–5, 381, 382–84
  verses 6–8, 381, 384–85
  verses 9–11, 381, 385–87
  verse 12, 381, 387

Psalm 27
  and David, story of, 391
  prayers and, 391
  structure of, 395, 400
  thanksgiving/testimony and, 391, 401
  theological implications of, 400–401
  translation of, 389–90
  trust and, 391–96, 399–400
  verses 1–2, 391–93
  verses 3–6, 391, 393–96
  verses 7–12, 391, 396–99
  verses 13–14, 391, 399–400

Psalm 28
  faithlessness and, 403–4, 409–10
  monarchy period and, 404
  pleas and, 403–4, 409–10
  structure of, 408
  theological implications of, 409–10
  translation of, 402–3
  verses 1–2, 404–5
  verses 3–4, 404, 405–6
  verses 5, 404, 406–7
  verses 6–8, 404, 407–9
  verses 9, 404, 409
  wrongdoers and wrongdoing, 409–10

Psalm 29
  Canaanite poetry compared with, 413–14
  power of God's voice and, 412–14, 421–22
  structure of, 412, 413
  translation of, 411–12
  verses 1–2, 414–17
  verses 3–4, 417–18
  verses 5–9b, 418–19
  verses 9c–10, 419–21
  verse 11, 421

Psalm 30
  dedication occasions and, 425
  Hanukkah and, 425
  thanksgiving/testimony and, 424–25, 433
  theological implications of, 433
  translation of, 423–24
  verses 1–3, 424, 425–27

Subject Index

verses 4–5, 424, 427–29
verses 6–7, 424, 429–30
verses 8–10, 424, 430–31
verses 11–12, 424, 431–32
Psalm 31
  and David, story of, 437
  deliverance and, 438–42
  prayers prayed twice and, 436, 450
  Psalm 22 compared with, 436–37
  structure of, 438, 439, 444
  translation of, 434–36
  trust and, 450
  verses 1–8, 436, 438–42
  verses 9–13, 442–45, 450
  verses 9–24, 436–37
  verses 14–20, 445–47, 450
  verses 21–24, 447–49
Psalm 32
  and David, story of, 453
  good fortune and, 453, 454, 581
  and sin, suffering issues from, 453, 460–61
  teachings and, 453
  thanksgiving/testimony and, 64, 452–53, 459–60, 461
  theological implications of, 460–61
  translation of, 451–52
  verses 1–2, 453–55
  verses 3–5, 453, 455–57
  verses 6–7, 453, 457–58
  verse 8, 453, 458–59
  verses 9–11, 453, 459–60
Psalm 33
  cosmos's acknowledgment of God and, 473
  and David, story of, 464
  good fortune and, 469
  headings and, 35n34
  praise and, 464, 473, 474
  structure of, 463–64
  theological implications of, 473–74
  translation of, 462–63

Trinity and, 473
verses 1–3, 464–66
verses 4–7, 464, 466–68, 473
verses 8, 464, 468
verses 9–12, 464, 468–69, 473
verses 13–19, 464, 469–72, 473
verses 20–22, 464, 472–73
Psalm 34
  and David, story of, 477–78
  deliverance and, 477, 486
  prayers and, 478–79
  structure of, 477, 479n4
  teaching and, 477, 480–83
  thanksgiving/testimony and, 477, 483–86
  theological implications of, 486
  translation of, 475–76
  verses 1–3, 477, 478–79
  verses 4–6, 477, 479–80
  verses 7–14, 480–83
  verses 15–22, 483–86
Psalm 35
  attack or persecution and, 489–90, 503–4
  Christology and, 503
  and David, story of, 490
  fear and rage against attackers and, 503–4
  healing rites and, 503
  Jeremiah compared with, 503
  Jesus and, 503
  structure of, 493n6, 497, 498, 500, 501
  theological implications of, 503–4
  translation of, 487–89
  verses 1–10, 490–95
  verses 11–18, 495–98
  verses 19–28, 498–502
Psalm 36
  faithfulness and, 506, 509–11, 513

faithless way of life and, 506–9, 513
human beings as servants of God and, 507
prayers and, 506–7, 511–12
theological implications of, 513
translation of, 505–6
verses 1–4, 506, 507–9
verses 5–9, 506, 509–11
verses 10–12, 506, 511–12
Psalm 37
  faithfulness and, 525–28, 531–35
  faithless way of life and, 518, 521–22, 533–35
  monarchy period and, 518
  promises and, 518, 529, 534, 535
  Proverbs compared with, 517
  structure of, 517, 519, 527, 531
  theological implications of, 533–35
  translation of, 514–17
  trust and, 518–21, 533–34
  verses 1–6, 518–21
  verses 7–15, 521–24
  verses 16–26, 525–28
  verses 27–33, 528–31
  verses 34–40, 531–33
Psalm 38
  attacks or persecution and, 538, 545–48
  and Israel, nation of, 539
  pleas and, 537, 538, 539–40, 550
  self-defense and, 538
  sins and, 538–39, 540–42, 550–52
  structure of, 538, 540, 543, 549n15
  theological implications of, 550–52
  translation of, 536–37
  trust and, 538, 542–45

613

Subject Index

verse 1, 537, 539–40
verses 2–5, 538, 540–42
verses 6–10, 538, 542–45
verses 11–16, 538, 545–48
verses 17–20, 538, 548–50
verses 21–22, 538, 550
Psalm 39
death and, 555, 557–59, 565
and illness, experience of, 554, 555, 559–64
Jeduthun and, 555
pleas and, 555–57
sins and, 554–55
structure of, 561
theological implications of, 564–65
translation of, 553–54
verses 1–3, 555–57
verses 4–7, 555, 557–59
verses 8–13, 555, 559–64
Psalm 40
and David, story of, 569
deliverance and, 568, 569–71, 572–74, 575–76, 579
good fortune and, 571
pleas and, 571–72
prayers and, 568, 576–78
sacrifices and, 579
structure of, 575, 577
thanksgiving/testimony and, 568, 574–75
theological implications of, 578–79
translation of, 566–68
verses 1–12, 568, 569–71
verses 4–5, 571–72
verses 6–8, 572–74
verses 9–10, 574–75
verses 11–12, 575–76
verses 13–17, 568, 576–78
Psalm 41
and David, story of, 582
faithfulness and, 582–83, 588
faithless way of life, 588–89

God's answer to prayers and, 581, 587–88, 589
good fortune and, 581, 582, 588
and king, anointed, 582
pleas and, 586–87
praise and, 590
prayers and, 581, 583–86
structure of, 583
thanksgiving/testimony and, 581
translation of, 580–81
verses 1–3, 581, 582–83
verses 4–9, 583–86
verses 4–10, 581
verses 4–12, 581
verse 10, 586–87
verses 11–12, 581, 587–88, 589
verse 13, 590
worship and, 590
Psalm 42, 63
Psalm 44, 64
Psalm 60, 63
Psalm 73, 63
Psalm 95, 49
Psalm 100, 49
Psalm 118, 42
Psalm 119, 81
Psalm 130, 64
Psalm 139, 43
Psalm 143, 64
Psalm 150, 23
psalmody, of Middle East, 32–35
Psalms
authorship of, 26–32
community worship and, 58–60
dates for, 30
as doxology, 69, 590
fivefold division of, 23
as form of intercession, 65–66
forms of speech and, 44–46
history and, 24, 25, 30–31, 35–37
imagery and, 43–44
individual worship and, 58–60

invitation to worship and, 49–50
and language, poetic, 42–44
life and death, 73–75
literary sanctuary and, 8
as "microcosm" of OT, 9
multi-points of view in, 42
number of psalms, 21
original functions of, 21
as poetry, 37–46
praise and, 46–49
prayer and, 23–24, 60–64
prophecies and, 56–57
protests and, 62–63
reasons for praise and, 50–51
rhythm and, 37–42
role of, 21–23
Second Temple period and, 35
self-knowledge and, 43
spirituality and, 58–69
structure and, 517
structure of, 37–40
Sukkot festival and, 51–55, 414
thanksgiving/testimony and, 55–56
title of book of, 25–26
wisdom and, 57–58
worship and, 46–51, 590
Psalter. *See* Psalms

rage, 66–67, 503–4
Rashi, 568
religious commitments, and Psalm 26, 381, 384–85, 387, 388
Rendsburg, Gary A., 414n4
revelations, 176, 287, 297–98, 299
reverence, and fear, 468, 477–78
Rienstra, Marchiene Vroon, 32
Rogerson, J. W., 417n12

sacrifices, 579
Second Temple period, 35, 169, 212, 281, 368

Subject Index

self-defense, 538
Shelters/Booths festival, 51–55, 414
Sheol doctrine, 74–75, 234
shepherd imagery, 346, 347–51
sins
  Ecclesiastes, and suffering issues from, 564–65
  and illness, experience of, 554
  Job, and suffering issues from, 564–65
  Psalm 32, 453, 460–61
  Psalm 38, 538–39, 540–42, 550–52
  Psalm 39, 554–55
  suffering and, 453, 460–61, 551–52
Sirach, 539
Smelik, William F., 308n16
Spurgeon, C. H., 364
Stern, Philip D., 352n23
suffering
  in Egypt, 138
  Job and, 136, 139
  sins and, 453, 460–61, 551–52
Sukkot festival, 51–55, 414
Sylva, Dennis D., 352n22

Tabernacles festival, 51–55, 414
teachings
  fear and, 8, 178
  Proverbs and, 81
  Psalm 1, 25, 80–81, 83, 90–91
  Psalm 14, 211
  Psalm 19, 284, 285, 286, 290–94, 298–99
  Psalm 32, 453
  Psalm 34, 477, 480–83
  role of Psalms in, 22, 23
thanksgiving/testimony
  Psalm 27, 391, 401

Psalm 30, 424–25, 433
Psalm 32, 453, 459–60, 461
Psalm 34, 477, 483–86
Psalm 40, 568, 574–75
Psalm 41, 581
Psalms and, 55–56
sacrifices and, 579
Theodoret of Cyrrhus
  on deliverance from attacks, 281
  on individual person, 82n4
  Psalm 26, and prayers of young David, 381
  on Psalm 29, 30
  on Psalm 35, 503n14
theology and theological implications. *See also under specific psalms*
  Canaanites and, 277, 413–14
  New Testament, and interrelationship with Psalms, 75–78
  Psalms as "microcosm" of OT, 9
  Psalms as theology, 69–78, 590
Thomas Aquinas, 82n7, 509
Thompson, Thomas L., 156
Tombach, Richard S., 348n12
Trinity, 473. *See also* Christology
trust
  Psalm 3, 108, 110–11
  Psalm 4, 124
  Psalm 5, 127, 128–32, 133
  Psalm 11, 188, 189–91, 194
  Psalm 12, 197, 200–201
  Psalm 16, 227–28, 234

Psalm 23, 345, 353–54
Psalm 27, 391–96, 399–400
Psalm 31, 450
Psalm 37, 518–21, 533–34
Psalm 38, 538, 542–45
Psalms and, 65, 67, 68, 69

Uriah, murder of, 453

violence, 104, 202. *See also* attacks or persecution; wars and warfare
Vogt, Ernst, 352n22, 411

Wagner, Ross, 299
Wainwright, Geoffrey, 473
wars and warfare, 152, 365
Watts, Isaac, 473
Weiser, Artur, 52–53
Westermann, Claus, 22, 44, 68, 574n13
Willis, Timothy M., 350n17
wisdom, 8, 57–58, 367–68
women, and authorship of psalms, 31–32
worship
  community worship, 58–60
  cult and, 47–48
  individual worship, 58–60
  invitation to worship, 49–50
  Psalm 41, 590
  Psalms and, 46–51, 590
wrongdoers and wrongdoing, 25, 82–83, 211–14, 217, 409–10

Zenger, Erich, 66
Zion, as home of God, 71–72

615

Author Index

Abusch, I. T. 34n32
Achtemeier, E. R. 135n1
Ackroyd, P. R. 416n11
Adam, K. P. 253n6
Albertz, R. 414n5
Albrektson, B. 204nh
Allegro, J. M. 518n4
Allen, L. C. 286n8, 321ni
Alter, R. 38n44, 39n45, 80n2,158n14, 206n11, 275n45, 427n5
Althann, R. 135n2
Anderson, A. A. 124n18, 240n6, 312n1, 503n14
Anderson, B. W. 23n9, 68
Anderson, G. W. 82n8
Aquinas, T. *See* Thomas Aquinas
Arambarri, J. 600n18
Arbez, E. P. 87n18
Arbuckle, G. A. 49n57
Asensio, F. 160n19, 345n1, 503n14
Athanasius of Alexandria 9, 23
Auffret, P. 80n2, 97n6, 110n4, 117n1, 127n1, 135n1, 154n2, 187nb, 204n3, 219n3, 237nl, 285n4, 301nd, 315n4, 347n7, 368n2, 391n1, 413n1, 463n1, 477n1
Augustine of Hippo 90, 212n3, 281n50, 387n19, 429, 503, 503n15, 535n15, 579n19, 587
Auvray, P. 87n18
Auwers, J.-M. 253n6
Avent, G. 414n7

Bail, U. 32n24, 137n6
Barré, M. L. 117ne, 219n3, 349n16
Barth, K. 461n7
Basil of Caesarea 9
Bauer, U. F. W. 83n10
Becking, B. 93nl
Beckwith, R. T. 36n36
Beentjes, P. C. 80n3
Behler, G. 226nd
Bellinger, W. H. 189n4, 380n3
Bennett, R. A. 211nf, 212n2
Berger, P.-R. 169n6, 195nf, 362n14
Bergmeier, R. 82n5
Berry, D. K. 252n3, 258n16
Bertolet, A. 93nn
Beuken, W. A. M. 559n10
Beyerlin, W. 157n9, 157n13, 219n2
Birkeland, H. 391n1
Blumnethal, D. R. 399n13
Boer, P. A. H. de 157n10, 204nh, 568n1
Boers, H. W. 234n14
Bons, E. 438
Bovati, P. 152n12, 393n5
Bratcher, R. G. 146n5
Braulik G. 568n3, 579n17
Braun, J. 595n6, 596n10
Brenner, A. 32n24
Briggs, C. A. 182n17, 231n8, 244n13, 253n6, 322nj, 496n7, 505na, 539

Briggs, E. G. 182n17, 231n8, 244n13, 253n6, 322nj, 496n7, 505na, 539
Brownlee, W. H. 94n1
Brueggemann, W. 23n6, 58n65, 62n68, 67n77, 68, 71, 172n10, 179n15, 186n20, 377n12, 504n19, 434n13, 564n16, 579n18
Buber, M. 594n4
Budde, K. 211n1
Bullough, S. 80n2
Buttenwieser, M. 119n5

Calvin, J. 232n11, 297n27, 321ni, 325n7, 473
Capps, D. 65n74
Cassiodorus 26n11, 80n1, 223n11
Castellino, G. 452ni
Ceresko, A. R. 477n2
Childs, B. S. 23n7, 29n18, 160n20
Chrysostom, J. 99n12, 118, 598n11
Clements, R. E. 219n1
Clifford, R. J. 557n5
Clines, D. J. A. 104n24, 294n22, 361n12, 364
Closen, G. E. 94nn
Clouda, S. L. 297n27
Coats, G. W. 335n25
Cohen, M. 236nk
Cole, R. L. 94n1
Collins, C. J. 155n3
Cook, G. 101n14
Cook, S. L. 340n32

Cooper, A. 361n12
Coppens, J. 135n1
Couffignal, R. 345n1
Coughenour, R. A. 201n10
Couroyer, R. 272n41, 482n6
Craigie, P. C. 11n1, 38n44, 228n3, 241nn8–9, 260n20, 406n3, 414n5, 417n11, 438n4, 454n2, 457n5, 505na, 518n5, 532n11, 538n2, 551, 558n7, 565n18, 581n1
Creach, J. F. D., 85n14, 103, 216n10
Crenshaw, J. L. 358n5
Croatto, J. S. 348n15
Cross, F. M. 252n5, 253n6, 269n36, 361n12, 414n5
Crüsemann, F. 213n7, 217n13
Culley, R. C. 108n2

Dahood, M. 11n1, 117ne, 294n23, 314n3, 392n4, 403ne, 413n3, 462nb, 540n5, 563n14, 577n15
Davis, E. F. 323n2, 331n19, 565n19
Davison, L. W. 32n22
Day, J. 418n14
de Boer, P. A. H. *See* Boer, P. A. H. de
Deissler, A. 284n2, 340n31
Diehl, J. F. 414n6
Dohmen, C. 284n3
Donner, H. 153na
Dubarle, A. M. 94nn
Du Preez, J. 360n7, 364, 365n19
Durlesser, J. R. 284n4
Dürr, L. 117n2

Eaton, J. H. 45, 123n15, 251nl, 284n3, 345n2, 437n2, 568n4
Edres, J. C. 450n18
Eissfeldt, O. 353n26
Enciso, J. 168n4
Eriksson, L. O. 481n5
Eshel, H. 166n3

Fensham, F. C. 315n4
Fenske, W. 234n14
Fiedler, D. K. 161n24
Fishbane, M. A. 123n16, 286, 299n31
Fisher, L. R. 341n34
Fitzgerald, A. 414n5
Fokkelman, J. P. 40n46, 96n5, 101n18, 146n7, 316n6, 387n16, 464n2, 489n1, 558n9
Foley, C. M. 347n7
Freedman, D. N. 252n5, 253n6, 269n36, 349n16, 420n15, 477n1
Frei, H. W. 83
Fretheim, T. E. 404n1
Frost, S. B. 340n31
Fullerton, K. 413n1

Gaebelein, P. M. 478n3
Gaster, T. H. 414, 414n5, 585n9
Gelineau, J. 41, 42
Gelston, A. 403ne
Gemser, B. 219n1, 452nf
Gerstenberger, E. S. 32n22, 37n39, 49n58, 54, 63n71, 101n14, 119n5, 159n17, 161n22, 189n2, 192n8, 205n6, 255n10, 273, 285n5, 301n3, 440n8, 512n8, 517n1, 518n3, 580nc
Gese, H. 341n34
Gillingham, S. E. 345n1
Gitay, Y. 80n2
Glass, J. T. 284n3
Goehrling, F. 89n20
Goldingay, J. 38n43
Gordis, R. 166n2
Goulder, M. D. 27n14, 160n19, 211n1
Gray, G. B. 166n2
Green, D. J. 344na
Greenberg, M. 33n29
Grelot, P. 573n10
Gualandi, D. 244n12, 413n1
Guillet, S. 323n1

Gunkel, H. 44, 46, 47, 48, 90n22, 204, 219n1, 254n9, 391n1, 499n12, 568n1
Gunnel, A. 82n6

Habel, N. C. 414n7
Hamp, V. 153na
Haney, R. G. 98n10
Hardmeier, C. 138n8
Harrelson, W. 155n3, 284n3
Hartley, J. E. 539n4
Hauge, Martin R 129n7, 388n20, 391n1
Hennecke, E. 361n12
Hilary of Poitiers 80n1
Hill, E. 357n4
Høgenhaven, J. 94n1
Holladay, W. L. 94nn, 324n5
Hollis, S. T. 32n26
Horgan, M. P. 518n4
Hubbard, R. L. 152n13
Hubmann, F. D. 226nd
Hueso, V. 362n13
Huie-Jolly, M. R. 105n28
Hulst, A. R. 160n20
Hunt, J. H. 34n32
Hunziker-Rodewald, R. 348n10
Hurowitz, V. A. 477n2
Hutton, R. R. 144n2
Hyland, C. F. 420n15

Ibn Ezra, A. 82n6, 154, 256n14, 395, 602
Irsigler, H. 204n4
Irvine, S. A. 210nc
Irwin, W.A. 126nl, 222

Jacobson, R. A. 197n3
Jänicke, H. 209n16
Janzen, J. G. 196nf, 488nc
Janzen, W. 594n4
Jenson, R. 455n4
Jerome [Eusebius Hieronymus] 12, 87, 91n24, 93nn, 101, 110n5, 112, 116nc, 121n10, 123n17, 125nc, 125ne, 126nl,

617

142na, 150, 159, 163ng,
163ni, 164nl, 164no,
164nq, 165nu, 165nx,
171, 171n9, 187na,
188nf, 191n6, 205n9,
216, 218nd, 227nj,
230n6, 233, 235nb, 236,
236nd, 236ng, 236nj,
238n2, 239, 239n5, 240,
248nh, 250nd, 257,
283ng, 288, 294, 300na,
308n18, 310nc, 311ni,
316, 321nd, 321ni,
327, 329n16, 334,
345nd, 345ne, 355nc,
360n11, 363, 379na,
383n9, 390nf, 392, 393,
399n12, 402na, 403nb,
403nd, 412ne, 412ni,
416, 416n10, 420, 421,
423nc, 429, 430, 434,
435, 440, 443, 468, 475,
480, 487nb, 499n11,
501, 505, 507, 514na,
514nd, 515, 515nh, 516,
516nk, 516nl, 525, 532,
543, 546n13, 553na,
563, 570n6, 576, 580nb,
587n15, 595, 600
Jinkins, M. 517n1
Jirku, A. 324n5
Johnson, A. R. 60n66,
129n7, 140n11, 220n4,
353n26
Jones, G. H. 100n13
Junker, H 166n2

Kaiser, O. 157n13, 555n2
Kaiser, W. 234n14
Kaltner, J. 321ni
Keel, O. 44n49, 228,
260n20, 262n23,
263n28, 264n31,
331n20, 333n21,
362n15, 382n8, 404n1,
405n2, 468n11, 487nb,
490n2, 503n18, 595n6,
596n10, 599n14,
599n16
Keel-Leu, O. 323n1

Kidner, D. 29n17, 83n9,
112n6, 147n8, 239n4,
241n7, 251n1, 318n8,
391n3, 409n6, 417n11,
592n5, 508n3, 582n3,
582n5
Kilgallen, J. J. 234n14
Kilian, R. 323n3
Kimhi, D. *See* Qimchi, D.
King, L. W. 34n31
Kinoti, H. W. 351n20
Kirkpatrick, A. F. 562n13,
580na
Kleber, A. 93nl
Kloos, C. 411b, 414n5,
415n8
Knauf, E. A. 353n24
Knierim, R. P. 299n29
Köhler, L. 158n15, 346n6
Koole, J. L. 219n1
Körbert, R. 94nn
Kottsieper, I. 302n4
Krahmalkov, C. R. 323n1
Kratz, R. G. 84n12
Kraus, H. J. 46n55,
53, 54, 82n5, 119n6,
122n12, 161n23, 196n1,
211nnd–f, 228n1,
232n11, 234n15,
277n47, 282nb, 301n2,
333, 416n11, 438n4,
450n15, 467n10,
545n11, 555n2, 568n2,
571, 601n21
Kruse, H. 153nb
Kselman, J. S. 104n4,
116ne, 330n17, 349n16,
507n1, 516n1
Kugel, J. L. 38n44
Kuntz, J. K. 260n21,
262n24, 301n3, 315n4
Kunz, L. 99n6
Kwakkel, G. 145n3

Lack, R. 80n2
Lamott, A. 197
Landon, M. 297n27
Landy, F. 364n17
Lange, H. D. 341n34
Lescow, T. 380n1
Leveen, A. 165ns

Leveen, J. 143nh, 243n11
Levenson, J. D. 394n9
Liebreich, L. J. 477n2
Lindars, B. 97n6
Lindblom, J. 226nd
Lindström, F. 136n3,
391n1, 539, 565n17,
583n8
Lipinski, E. 84n13, 323n1
Lohfink, N. 136n4, 370n4
Löhr, M. 166n2
Longenecker, R. N. 77n91
Loretz, O. 87n18, 139n9,
154n2, 205n5, 302n4,
361n12, 414n5
Louis, C. 160n19
Lowth, R. 38n44
Lund, Ø. 156n4
Lundbom, J. R. 347n8
Luther, M. 9, 22n2, 90n21,
104n26, 141, 208n13,
351n21, 354, 354n29,
394n7, 440, 466n9,
484n7, 503, 503n15,
535n14, 541n7, 557n6

Macholz, C. 146n5, 414n5
Macintosh, A. A. 94nn,
143nl, 452ni
Mandolfo, C. 117n1,
120n8, 149n10, 400n15
Mannati, M. 123n17,
188n1, 226nd, 399n14
March, W. E. 196nj
Margulis, B. 414n5,
420n15
Marti, K. 163ng
Martin, W. W. 463n1
Mays, J. L. 58n65, 161n21,
208n13, 273n42,
291n19, 298n28,
299n30, 340n31,
378n13, 450n16,
589n18
Mazor, Y. 346n6, 356n1
McCann, J. C. 36, 37n39,
89n20, 109n3, 127n4,
130n10, 185n19,
245n15, 255n10,
340n31, 354n27, 372n6,

388n21, 465n7, 473n17, 589n17
McCarthy, C. 164no
McKay, J.W. 146n6, 224n12, 297n26, 303n5, 409n5, 417n12, 438n4, 538n1
Meek, T. J. 344na
Meinhold, A. 299
Menn, E. M. 324n5, 340n31
Merendino, R. P. 80n2
Merrill, A. L. 345n3
Michel, D. 566na.
Milgrom, J. 283ng
Miller, P. D. 49n58, 94n1, 137n5, 184, 196nf, 223n9, 403nc
Mitchell, D. C., 89
Mittman, J. 344na
Mittmann, S. 414n5
Moenikes, A. 101n14
Möller, H. 368n1
Moloney, F. J. 160n19
Moltmann, J. 22n5
Moran, W. L. 296n25
Morgenstern, J. 94nn, 189n2, 284n2, 346n6
Morrow, F. J. 311ne
Mosca, P. G. 384n11
Mosis, R. 348n9
Mowinckel, S. 46n54, 47, 48n56, 51, 52, 68, 226nd, 263n28
Muir, J. 563n15
Murphy, R. E. 35n33
Mwaura, P. N. 503n16

Nasuti, H.P. 37n39, 64n73
Neuberg, F. J. 211ne
Neumann-Gorsolke, U. 160n20
Niehaus, J. J. 399n12
Nimms, C. F. 302n4
Nogalski, J. D. 29n16
Nordin, J. 161n20

Ogden, G. S. 181n16
Olofsson, S. 93nn

Pardee, D. 345n5, 518n4
Patterson, R. D. 341n34

Pax, E. 413n1
Peels, H. G. L. 229n5
Petersma, A. 93nn
Peterson, D. L. 87n19
Peterson, E. H. 22, 23n10, 38n44, 67n78, 70, 103, 104n22
Pfeiffer, E. 348n9
Pitkin, B. 153nb
Ploeg, J. P. M. van der 243n11
Power, E. 351n19
Press, R. 101n14
Preuss, H. D. 351n18
Prinsloo, G. T. M. 196n2
Pyper, H. S. 345n1

Qimchi, D. 135, 218nc, 349n16, 464n5, 602
Quintens, W. 315n5

Rabinowitz, J. R. 296n25
Rad, G. von 517n2
Ramsay, N. J. 354n31
Rashi 122n13, 187na, 213n5, 373, 389nc, 390nd, 429, 509n5, 568, 602
Reifsnyder, R. W. 362n13
Rendsburg, G. A. 166n2, 228n2, 414n4
Reumann, J. H. P. 341n34
Richards, K. H. 38n44, 87n19, 478n3
Ricoeur, P. 68
Ridderbos, H. N. 324n4, 406n3, 555n1, 557n4, 568n1
Rief, S. C., 82n6
Rienstra, M. V. 32n2, 137n6
Rigby, C. L. 343n35
Ringgren, H. 96n2
Roberts, J. J. M. 321ni, 476nc
Robinson, A. 94nn
Robinson, B. P. 349n16
Robinson, T. H. 476ne
Rogerson, J. W. 224n12, 297n26, 303n5, 409n5, 417n12, 438n4, 538n1

Rogland, M. F. 79na
Rösel, C. 37n39
Rösel, M. 302n4
Rosenbaum, S. N. 162nc
Rosenberg, A. J. 503n17
Ross, M. 64n72
Rowley, H. H. 97n6
Rubinkiewicz, R. 78n92
Rudolph, W. 156n5
Ruppert, L. 368n1, 370n4

Safren, J. D. 292n20
Sandberger, J. V. 345n1
Sarna, N. A. 114n10
Sasson, V. 97n7
Sauer, A. V. R. 346n6
Schaefer, K. 137n7, 193n9, 194n10, 252n4, 331n18, 335n26, 337n29, 359n6, 377n11, 450n17, 492n4
Schedl, C. 226nd
Schiefler, J. R. 341n34
Schmidt, W. H. 159n18
Schmitt, A. 234n14
Schmuttermayer, G. 253n6, 257n15
Schniedewind, W. M. 31n21
Schnutenhaus, F. 260n19
Schökel, L. A. 437n1
Schroeder, C. O. 112n7
Schroer, S. 599n15
Schwarz, G. 345nd
Seale, M. S. 324n5
Seybold, K. 23n8, 32n25, 36n36, 98n11, 121n10, 204n2, 233n13, 301n3, 414n5, 464n3, 510n6, 554nf, 574n12
Sfair, P. 153na
Sheppard, G. T. 94n1
Sibinga, S. 135n1
Simpson, W. G. 165ny
Skehan, P. W. 163nd, 478n3
Slomovic, E. 144n2, 425n1
Smelik, K. A. D. 302n4
Smelik, W. F. 308n16
Smith, M. S. 157n7, 345n2, 416n9

Snaith, N. H. 489nh
Snijders, L. A. 384n12
Soggin, J. A. 80n2, 96n3, 135n2, 153na, 157n7, 282na, 341n34
Sonne, I. 94nn, 189n2
Sperling, S. D. 34n31
Spurgeon, C. H. 114n12, 364, 454n1
Stamm, J. J. 373n7
Stec, D. M. 116ne, 122n13, 213n6, 577n14
Steck, O. H. 289n14
Steiner, R. C. 302n4
Steingrímsson, S. Ö. 353n25
Stern, P. D. 352n23
Stewart, D. K. 253n6
Stolz, F. 341n34
Strauss, H. 414n5
Strawn, B. A. 321ni
Strugnell, J. 166n3
Stuhlmueller, C. 327n12
Sylva, D. D. 352n22

Tagliacarne, P. 80n2
Tanner, B. L. 32n24, 348n14
Tanner, M. 157n7
Tappy, R. E. 345n1
Tate, M. E. 38n44, 154n1, 228n3, 596n8
Taylor, R. A. 78n92
Terrien, S. 253n6, 503n13, 510n7, 558n8
Theirry, G. J. 164no
Theodoret of Cyrrhus 30, 30n20, 82n4, 87n17, 213n4, 238n2, 281, 299, 381, 391n2, 465n8, 503n14
Thomas, D. W. 146n5, 488nd, 545n10
Thomas Aquinas 21n1, 82n7, 297n27, 509, 509n4, 602

Thompson, T. L. 156n6
Tigay, J. H. 93nh, 146n4
Tombach, R. S. 348n12
Torrey, C. C. 211n1
Tostengard, S. A. 341n33, 341n34, 341n34
Tournay, R. J. 153na, 228n3, 230n7, 282nb, 321ni, 505na
Trebolle Barrera, J. C. 32n22
Treves, M. 97n6, 357n3
Tromp, N. 360n11
Trudiger, P. L. 356n2
Trull, G. V. 234n14
Tsumura, D. T. 172n11

Uchelen, N. A. van 347n7, 416n10, 592n2
Ungern-Sternberg, R. von 394n8

Vall, G. 321ni
VanderKam, J. C. 92nf
van der Ploeg, J. *See* Ploeg, J. P. M. van der
Vang, C. 102n19
Van Leeuwen, R. C. 158n16
van Uchelen, N. A. *See* Uchelen, N. A. van
Van Zyl, A. H. 391n1
Vermes, G. 284n3
Vesco, J. L. 256n11
Vincent, J. M. 464n3
Vogels, W. 80n2
Vogt, E. 352n22, 380n2, 411na
von Rad, G. *See* Rad, G. von
von Ungern-Sternberg, R. *See* Ungern-Sternberg, R. von

Wagner, J. R. 299
Wainwright, G. 473

Wallis, G. 160n20
Wambacq, B. N. 328n14
Watson, W. G. 38n44, 197n3, 213n8, 490n3, 538n2
Watts, J. W. 104n25
Weinfeld, M. 302n4
Weiser, A. 45n52, 52, 53, 54, 104n23, 119n5, 220n5, 224n13, 291n18, 301nc, 306n13, 326, 397n10, 581n2, 582n4
Welch, A. C. 306n12
Wénin, A. 94n1
Wernberg-Møller, P. 196nj
Westermann, C. 22, 44, 48, 55n64, 62n67, 63n69, 64, 68, 108n1, 119n7, 205n7, 206n10, 287n10, 324n6, 325, 326n9, 327n13, 354n28, 360n8, 360n10, 407n4, 413n2, 426n3, 427n4, 437n1, 465n6, 472n14, 573n13, 599n17
Wevers, J. W. 336n27
Whybray, R. N. 37n39, 285n6
Wieppert, M. 282nb
Wiesmann, H. 477n1
Wilhelmi, G. 101n17
Willis, J. T. 94n1, 96n4, 219n1
Willis, T. M. 350n17
Willmes, B. 455n3
Wilson, G. H. 36nn36–37, 464n4
Witte, M. 473n17
Woude, A. S. van der 452nf

Zenger, E. 36n36, 66, 94n1, 202n11
Zevitt, Z. 303n4
Zolli, E. 196nj, 229n5

Index of Scripture and Other Ancient Writings

Old Testament

Genesis
1   159, 160, 467
1–2   159
1:11–12   519
1:21   160
1:30   519
2–3   293
3:8   262n25
3:19   431
4:7   296, 505na
5:1–3   161
6:9   595
6:11   600
6:11–12   213
9   466
9:1–2   161
9:6   161
12:1–3   95, 105
12:2   315
14:18–22   597
16:12   210nb
17:1   595
18–19   194
19:17   190
19:24   193
20   478
20:9   296
21:16–17   156n6
22:12   307
23:4   563
24:27   407
24:56   85
27:35   359
28:12   262
30:13   594
33:14   349
34:13   359
35:3   304
39:9   296
41:35   559
41:49   559
42:21   376
44:15   210nc
45:26   543
46:2   232
49:8   275
50:10   432

Exodus
2:10   266
2:17–19   348
2:23   138, 328, 544
2:23–24   259
2:24   199
3:7   183, 259
3:8   330
4:31   328
6:1   257
6:5   199
8:8 MT   275
8:12   275
8:18 MT   121
8:22   121
9:4   121
11:7   121
12   51
13:3   257
13:9   257
13:14   257
13:16   257
13:17   350
13:21   350
14–15   260
14:13   98, 172
14:19   492
14:30   241, 328
14:31   328
15   31, 47, 491
15:1–18   363
15:2   325, 409
15:3   495
15:6   172, 206, 207, 226nd
15:7   241
15:8   467
15:9   172, 206, 207
15:10   266
15:11   226nd, 328, 415, 494, 495
15:11–13   241
15:13   349, 350
15:17   173
15:18   173, 183
16   205
16:3   233
16:28   205
17:14   172
18:8–10   330
18:11   307
19   260
19:4   262n25, 409
19:18   261
19:25   116nd
20:3   229, 230
20:7   230, 355nc, 359
20:18–21   262
21:20   351
21:28   359
22:24 MT   528
22:24–26 MT   223
22:25   528
22:25–27   223
23:1   359, 593
23:4   206
23:13   230
23:18   230
23:20   492
23:20–22   492
23:23   492
25–40   220
25:25   558
29:26   193
30:17–21   384
32–34   372
32:21   296
32:30   296
32:31   296
32:32   409
32:34   350
33:2   492
33:16   121
33:20   245
34:6–10   372
34:7   295
34:9   409

Leviticus
1–4   573
1:3   297
2   305
2:2   539
2:9   539
2:16   539
3:16–17   305
5:12   539
5:23 MT   439n6
6:4   439n6
6:8 MT   539
6:10 MT   230
6:15   539
6:17   230

Index of Scripture and Other Ancient Writings

7:33   230
19:4   572
19:18   257n15
23   51
24:7   539
25   562
25:6   562
25:18–21   124
25:23   562
25:35   562
25:35–38   223
25:40   562
25:45   562
25:47   562

Numbers

1–2   306
5:11–28   144
5:26   539
6:24   409
6:24–26   123, 206, 303, 304
6:25   207
10:35–36   113, 147
11:8   451nb
12:8   245
14   205
14:11   205
14:27   205
20:11   266n34
20:14–21   60
24:1   409
24:7   266n34
24:16   597
24:20   172
27:17   348

Deuteronomy

1:28   184
1:29   184
2:7   348
3:9   419
4:11   262
4:12   245
4:15   245
4:25   210na
5:19 MT   262
5:20   359
5:22   262
6:7   82
7:21   184
8:3   525
8:7–20   144
8:9   348
9:4–5   172
9:12   214
9:16   214
10:8   304

10:21   328
11:4   172
11:16   214
11:28   214
16   51
20:5   425
21:1–9   384
22:2   398
23:20   223
28:29   79nc
29:22 MT   193
29:23   193
30:14   232, 530
31   51, 53
31:6   173, 184, 400
31:7   400
31:8   173
31:14   98
31:18   572
31:20   572
31:23   400
32:3   415
32:5   269
32:6   267
32:9   231
32:10–11   241
32:11   262n25
32:12   350
32:25   156
33   304
33:26   596
33:28   124

Joshua

1:5   173
1:6   400
1:7   400
1:8   79nc, 86
1:9   184, 400
1:18   400
2:4   395
2:17–20   359
3:10   277
3:13   467
3:16   467
7:12–13   87n16
20:4   398
23:7   308, 308n16

Judges

4–5   260
5   31, 47
5:27   308n17
5:28   213
5:31   290
9:4   97
15:11   210nc
17:2   116nd, 165ns

17:13   307
18:5   79nc
18:25   386
19:15   398
19:18   398
20:16   593

Ruth

4:15   292

1 Samuel

1   49, 51, 63
1–2   137
1:17   301
1:17–18   306
1:21–22   207
2   31, 47
2:1   118
2:5   137
4   362
5:6–7   456
5:11   456
10:1   591
15   146
15:22–23   569, 573
16:3   591
17:7   132
17:26   277
17:34–36   348
17:36   277
17:45   363
18:29   206
19:11–17   582
21:1–6   391
21:2–7 MT   391
21:10–12   477
21:11–13 MT   477
21:13   478
21:14 MT   478
22–24   257
23   271
23:26   438
24   144n2, 190, 490
24:2   257, 592
24:3 MT   257, 592
24:6   591
24:22   257
24:23 MT   257
26   190
30   271
30:25   100
3:21   313
5   271, 280, 281
5–6   362
5:6–9   280
5:10   280, 363
5:17–21   280
5:20   280

5:22–25   280
5:24   280
6–7   54
6:6   266n33
6:17   220
7   95, 101
7:14   93nk, 100
8:3–12   276
9:7–13   352
10:19   276
11–12   254
12:19   585
13:13   212
14:9   359
15:12   109
15:14–17   109
16   144
16:5–8   109
18–19   144n2
18:20–32   144
18:31–32   144
18:32   109
19   144
19:27   221n6
19:28 MT   221n6
20   144
21   219
22   253, 254, 255, 281
22:1   247na
22:2   247nb, 247nc
22:3   247nd, 247nf
22:5   248nh
22:7   248ni, 248nj
22:8   248nk
22:11   248nl
22:12   248nm, 248nn
22:13   248no
22:14   248np
22:15   248nq
22:16   248nr
22:20–26   255
22:23   249ns
22:25   249nu
22:26   249nv
22:28   249nw
22:29   270n38
22:32   249nx
22:33   250ny, 250nz
22:36   250nc
22:38   250ne
22:39   250nf
22:42   250ng, 275n45
22:43   250nh, 250ni
22:44   250nj, 250nk
22:46   251nm
22:47   251np
22:48   251nr
22:49   251ns
22:51   251nt
23:1   143nk, 592
24:14   106, 587

Index of Scripture and Other Ancient Writings

1 Kings
1:31 314
1:34 591
1:47 304
1:50 189
2:28–30 220
3:5 101
4:25 124
5:5 MT 124
7:7 88
7:26 558
8 48, 51
8:4 220
8:12 262
8:31–32 144
8:63 425
8:66 304
11:37 313
14:27 439n6
17:12 488ne
19:11 142na
21 129, 164no
22:17 348

2 Kings
3:3 483
4:1 527
6:15 391
6:17 481
8:5 427
10:29 483
10:31 483
11:12 100
18–19 182, 391
18–20 324
18:29–30 213
18:30–35 110
19:4 277
19:16 277
19:35 176
23:5 196nj
25 492

1 Chronicles
11 271
13:13–14 154
15:20 170
15:21 135, 595
16 47
16:2 304
16:4 539
16:4–5 154
16:28–29 415
16:41–42 555
17:20 494
21 425n1
22:11 85
22:13 400
24:5 229
28:18 263
28:20 173, 400
29:11 155
29:15 555, 563

2 Chronicles
5:12 555
7 47
7:11 79nc, 86
17:3–4 173
17:9 80
20 47, 48, 303, 362, 363
23:19 224
25:15 173
28:15 349
32:7 400
32:8 112
32:16 254

Ezra
3 47
4:1 109
6:16–17 425
6:21 173
9 48, 64, 368, 550
9:7 296
9:8 207, 292
9:9 173
9:13 296

Nehemiah
1 49
2:3 314
3:25 597
4 391
4:5 MT 109
4:5 454
4:11 109
5 527
5:7 148
5:14–18 586
9 64, 550, 551
9:12 350
9:13 291
9:17 173
9:19 173
9:21 348
9:31 173
10:29 229
10:30 MT 229

Esther
3:1 206–7
9 51

Job
1–2 164no, 200
1:6 415
1:10 111
1:17 237nn
1:22 556
2:1 415
2:10 556
2:13 556
3:23 111
3:24 138, 543, 544
4:13 232
5:13 82
6:11 558
7:16 559
7:17–18 158
7:18 240
7:19 563
8:15 87n16
9:1–2 564
9:13–15 136
9:28 295
9:32 88
10:3 82
10:14 295
10:14–15 564
10:15 111
11:4 103, 291
11:19 349
12:5 382
14:3 88
14:6 563
14:13 136
15:16 214
15:30 467
16:9 136
16:10 120
18:5–6 270, 545
19:4 240n5
19:5 120
19:9 120
19:11 136
19:13–14 398
20:21 164nq
21:16 82
21:17 270
21:17–19 244
21:18 86, 492
22:4 88
22:13–14 264
22:18 82
22:30 267
23:2 138, 544
23:10 240, 240n5, 382
24:8 216
25:6 329
26:11 265
27:10 520
27:18 263
28:13 37
28:28 291
29:10 332
29:20 120
30:1 333
30:12 266n35
31 146
31:5 359
31:33 456
31:38 275
32:8 448
33:5 125nb, 129
33:15 232
34:14 386
34:36 240
37:10 376
37:11 264
37:22 155
38–40 419
38:8 330
38:24 264
38:33 285
38:37 468
38:40 263
39:5 99
39:20 155
39:28 257
40:11 264
40:23 330
41:12 MT 261
41:13 MT 262
41:20 261
41:21 262
42:7–8 564
42:10 217
42:11 586

Psalms
1 21n1, 23, 24, 25, 36, 46, 57, 58n65, 80, 83, 84, 84n12, 84n13, 85, 88, 90, 91, 94, 95, 97, 103, 104, 156, 211, 219, 284, 296, 380, 387, 412, 413, 454, 469, 517, 518, 530, 581, 588, 589
1–2 109
1–35 12
1–41 591
1:1 79na, 81, 82, 85, 87, 87n16, 87n19, 89, 150, 383, 453, 589
1:1–2 129
1:1–3 81, 82
1:2 41, 80, 83, 89, 95, 97, 129, 163nj,

623

290, 327, 482, 530, 589, 600
1:2–4 87n15
1:2–6 79na
1:3 84, 85, 86, 87, 89, 276
1:4 86, 492
1:4–5 86
1:4–6 89
1:5 87, 87n19, 88, 89, 593
1:5–6 82, 89
1:6 38, 41, 87, 88, 89, 129, 589, 591, 593
1:7 88, 93nj, 93nn
1:8 196
1:8–19 88
1:10–12 93nn
1:11 93nn
1:12 93nn
2 21n1, 24, 25, 26, 36, 40, 42, 56, 57, 72, 73, 76, 90, 94, 95, 102, 104, 105, 105n28, 114, 276, 284, 412, 413, 469
2:1 39, 40, 95, 97, 120, 276, 600
2:1–2 40, 42, 96, 97, 98, 101
2:1–3 96, 97, 100
2:1–9 38, 105
2:2 39, 40, 41, 98, 129, 591
2:3 39, 40, 97, 98, 100, 102
2:3–5 39
2:4 39, 40, 99, 111, 327, 524, 596
2:4–6 96, 99, 100
2:4–12 97
2:5 39, 40, 99, 137
2:6 39, 40, 96n3, 100, 111, 112, 220, 595
2:7 39, 40, 92nh, 100
2:7 MT 120
2:7–9 96, 100
2:8 39, 40, 97, 101, 105, 598
2:8–9 104
2:9 39, 101, 113, 351
2:10 102
2:10–12 96, 101, 105–6
2:11 97, 102
2:12 95, 103, 129, 145
2:12 MT 97

3 24, 28, 36, 59, 63, 70, 95, 108
3:Heading 109, 117, 127, 284, 409
3–7 25
3–41 35
3:1 109, 110, 113, 117
3:1–2 108, 109, 113
3:2 107nb, 109, 110, 111, 113, 113n8, 117
3:2 MT 117
3:2–3 599
3:3 110n4, 111, 112, 132, 395
3:3 MT 117
3:3–4 MT 599
3:3–6 108, 109, 110, 112, 113
3:3–8 109
3:4 110n5, 111, 112, 117, 139, 327, 595
3:4 MT 132, 395
3:4–5 110n5, 112
3:4–6 110n5, 111n5, 112
3:5 108, 110n5, 112, 117
3:5 MT 117, 139, 327, 595
3:6 112, 113, 195nd, 395, 599
3:6 MT 117
3:6–7 199
3:7 108, 110n5, 112, 113, 113n9, 114, 118, 119n5, 147, 199
3:7 MT 395, 599
3:7–8 108, 112
3:7–8 MT 199
3:8 107nb, 108ni, 109, 114, 114n12, 360
3:8 MT 118, 119n5, 147, 199
3:9 MT 360
3:37 MT 454
4 24, 36, 46, 47, 65, 108
4:Heading 117, 123n16, 124, 127, 188, 284, 437, 562, 600
4:1 117, 118, 119, 121, 122, 136, 173, 179, 184, 267, 350, 375, 376, 396, 441, 442, 594, 598

4:2 92na, 111, 120, 121, 129, 132, 571, 593
4:2 MT 136, 173, 179, 184, 267, 350, 375, 376, 396, 441, 594, 598
4:2–3 120n8
4:2–5 118, 119, 122, 127, 139
4:3 MT 92na, 111, 129, 132, 571, 593
4:3 117, 120n8, 121, 184, 456
4:3–6 MT 139
4:4 121, 240, 509, 521, 596
4:4 MT 184, 456
4:4–5 120n8
4:5 120, 122
4:5 MT 521, 596
4:6 117, 117nf, 118, 121, 122, 123, 593, 594, 596
4:6–8 122
4:7 117, 117nf, 122, 123
4:7 MT 593, 594, 596
4:7–8 118, 122
4:7–9 120n8
4:8 41, 108, 112, 117, 123
4:9 MT 41, 108, 112
4:21 MT 442
5 24, 47, 59, 70, 108, 127
5:Heading 127, 190, 562
5:1 127, 128, 134nb, 554ne
5:1–2 37, 125na, 125nb, 127, 128, 128n5
5:1–3 138
5:1–6 129
5:2 107nf, 127, 128, 183, 598
5:2 MT 134nb, 554ne
5:2–3 MT 37
5:2–4 MT 138
5:2–7 128n5
5:3 127, 128, 129, 130, 132, 184, 597
5:3 MT 107nf, 183, 598
5:3–7 127, 128
5:3–9 131
5:4 41, 127, 128, 129, 267

5:4 MT 184, 597
5:4–5 129
5:4–6 128, 129, 130
5:5 129, 383, 405, 591
5:5 MT 267, 509
5:5–6 150
5:6 120, 126nl, 129, 165nt, 238, 483, 592
5:6 MT 383, 405, 591
5:6–7 MT 150
5:7 50, 129, 130, 153nc, 174, 191, 595, 599
5:7 MT 165nt, 238, 483, 592
5:8 MT 50, 153nc, 174, 191, 595, 599
5:8 130, 132, 139, 140, 350, 398, 600, 601
5:8–9 127, 130
5:8–12 128
5:9 77, 127, 130, 198
5:9 MT 139, 140, 350, 398, 600, 601
5:10 MT 77, 198
5:10 127, 131, 132, 598
5:10–12 127, 131
5:11 103, 131, 132, 510, 597
5:11 MT 598
5:11–12 126nl, 131
5:12 127, 132, 491
5:12 MT 510, 597
5:13 MT 491
5:19 MT 597
6 24, 32, 46, 47, 59, 63, 64, 108
6:Heading 135, 197, 199, 258, 335, 347, 425, 426, 428, 437, 443, 540, 550, 552, 600
6:1 99n12, 136, 540
6:1–3 135
6:1–7 140, 141
6:2 MT 99n12, 540
6:2 136, 140, 141, 425, 594
6:2–3 99, 136, 137, 425
6:3 135, 137, 141, 205, 497
6:3 MT 425, 594
6:3–4 MT 99, 425
6:4 135ne, 137, 138, 141, 592

624

Index of Scripture and Other Ancient Writings

6:4 MT 205, 497
6:4–7 135, 137
6:5 137, 138, 170, 175, 425, 428, 431, 456, 599
6:5 MT 592
6:6 138, 544, 599
6:6 MT 170, 175, 425, 428, 431, 456
6:6–7 137
6:7 139, 140, 165na, 442
6:7 MT 544
6:8 119, 139, 140, 449, 594
6:8 MT 165na, 442
6:8–9 139, 184, 259, 440
6:8–10 135, 137, 139, 140
6:9 MT 119, 449, 594
6:9 140, 431, 449, 594
6:9–10 MT 184, 259, 440
6:10 37, 134nb, 139, 140, 141
6:10 MT 431, 449, 594
6:11 MT 37
6:13 600
7 24, 28, 59
7:Heading 144, 148, 166n2, 189, 254, 380, 380n3, 399, 437, 438
7:1 103, 145, 352, 438
7:1–2 144, 145, 152
7:1–5 239n4
7:2 MT 103, 352, 438
7:2 145, 151, 331, 597
7:2–6 MT 239
7:3 145, 519
7:3 MT 331, 597
7:3–5 144, 145, 148, 152
7:4 142nd, 144, 145, 146, 222, 366na
7:4 MT 519
7:4–5 152
7:5 144, 146, 232n12, 332, 424nf
7:5 MT 222
7:6 136, 144, 146, 147, 148, 199

7:6 MT 232n12, 332, 424nf
7:6–7 147
7:6–8 380
7:6–9 144, 146
7:6–11 152
7:7 147
7:7 MT 199
7:7–9 MT 380
7:8 144, 147, 148, 377, 381, 525, 592, 595
7:9 148, 151, 192, 232n9, 380, 382, 593
7:9 MT 377, 381, 525, 592, 595
7:10 149, 151, 377, 596
7:10 MT 192, 232n9, 380, 382, 593
7:10–13 152
7:10–16 144, 148, 149, 151
7:11 149, 151, 593
7:11 MT 377, 596
7:11–16 149
7:12 143nl, 143nm, 147, 149, 151, 190n5, 515ng
7:12 MT 593
7:12–13 143nm, 152
7:13 149, 150, 179n14, 193
7:13 MT 190n5, 515ng
7:14 143nm, 144, 150, 151, 152, 180, 376, 594
7:14 MT 179n14, 193
7:15 144, 150, 151, 178
7:15 MT 180, 376, 594
7:15–16 152, 176
7:16 38, 144, 151, 376, 600
7:16–17 MT 176
7:17 MT 38, 376, 600
7:17 143nk, 144, 149, 151, 204n3, 279, 456, 597
7:18 204n3
7:18 MT 279, 597
8 24, 25, 46, 51, 71
8:Heading 154, 157, 158n16, 160, 166n2, 284, 417, 417n12

8:1 155, 157n8, 158, 159, 160, 597
8:1–2 153na, 154, 155, 159
8:2 155, 156, 157n8, 178
8:2 MT 597
8:3 158
8:3 MT 178
8:3–4 154, 158, 159
8:4 158
8:5 159, 420
8:5–6 159
8:5–8 154, 159
8:5–9 159
8:6 154nd, 159
8:6 MT 420
8:6–7 160
8:7 159
8:8 159
8:9 154, 160, 597
8:10 MT 597
8:12 261, 513
9 26n13, 35n34, 47, 71, 166, 166n2, 166n3, 169
9:Heading 170, 258
9–10 24, 25, 37, 59, 166n2, 171, 367, 391, 396, 477, 568, 601
9:1 168, 170, 448, 456
9:1–2 170, 174
9:1–4 170, 175
9:1–12 166, 167, 175
9:2 168, 170, 171
9:2 MT 448, 456
9:3 164np, 167, 168, 171, 171n9, 177, 183
9:3–4 167, 170, 171
9:4 164np, 168, 171, 173, 174, 176, 178, 180, 238n2, 592
9:4–6 167
9:5 164nq, 168, 172, 597
9:5 MT 238n2, 592
9:5–6 172, 173, 177
9:5–10 172, 175
9:6 163nd, 168, 172, 177, 183
9:6 MT 597
9:7 165ns, 165nt, 168, 172, 174, 178, 180
9:7–8 167, 172, 173
9:7–10 174
9:8 168, 173, 176, 180, 592

9:9 168, 173, 179, 180, 181, 184, 445, 595
9:9 MT 592
9:9–10 172, 173
9:10 163ne, 165nw, 167, 169, 173, 174, 176, 215, 325, 591, 597
9:10 MT 445, 595
9:11 169, 174, 178
9:11 MT 325, 591, 597
9:11–12 174
9:12 167, 169, 171, 174, 177, 199, 592, 593, 595, 597, 601
9:13 41, 169, 174n12, 175, 177, 179, 426, 591
9:13 MT 199, 592, 593, 595, 597, 601
9:13–14 166, 167
9:13–18 174
9:14 MT 41, 426, 591
9:14 168, 169, 175
9:15 168, 175, 176, 178, 439
9:15–16 167, 171, 176, 179
9:15–18 167
9:16 168, 169, 175, 176, 180
9:16 MT 439
9:17 168, 169, 176, 599
9:17–18 167
9:18 168, 169, 174, 174n12, 176, 177, 183, 199, 206n9, 595, 597, 601
9:18 MT 599
9:19 167, 168, 169, 177, 178, 180, 182, 199
9:19 MT 199, 206n9, 595, 601
9:19–20 178, 184
9:19–10:2 166, 167, 177, 179
9:20 168, 169, 177, 178, 456, 591
9:20 MT 199
9:21 MT 456, 591
10 26n13, 35n34, 166, 166nn2–3, 169, 325
10 LXX 26n13
10:1 168, 177, 178, 180, 205, 325, 445

625

10:2   162nc, 167, 168, 169, 174n12, 177, 178, 179, 180, 512, 522, 578, 593, 596, 601
10:3   167, 168, 169, 179, 183, 442, 593, 598
10:3–4   182
10:3–11   168, 179, 182
10:4   168, 169, 179, 180, 199, 213, 593
10:4–5   181
10:4–6   181
10:4–10   167
10:5   168, 169, 180
10:6   169, 179, 180, 181, 429, 592, 594, 596
10:7   77, 180, 239, 376, 483
10:7–10   180
10:8   169, 180, 181
10:8–9   181, 295
10:8–10   169, 181
10:9   169, 174n12, 181, 331, 601
10:10   168, 169, 181, 184, 543
10:11   167, 169, 181, 182, 206n9, 593, 595, 596
10:12   169, 174, 182, 199, 601
10:12–15   166, 168, 182
10:13   122, 168, 169, 180, 182, 593, 596
10:14   167, 169, 181, 182, 184, 376, 595
10:15   168, 169, 182, 593
10:16   167, 168, 169, 171, 183, 184
10:16–18   166, 168, 183
10:17   168, 169, 174n12, 183, 184, 483, 544, 596, 601
10:17–18   167, 184
10:18   41, 168, 169, 181, 183, 184
11 MT   26n13
11   27, 32, 65, 188
11:Heading   189, 191, 194, 196, 202, 204, 208, 209, 345
11–15   35

11:1   103, 107nb, 189, 189n2, 190, 194, 196, 510
11:1–2   188, 189, 194
11:2   189n2, 190, 191, 193, 291, 596
11:3   188, 190, 191, 196, 593
11:4   99, 187nb, 191, 192, 193, 595, 597
11:4–5   189
11:4–7   188, 189, 191, 194
11:5   191, 192, 193, 196, 591, 593, 600
11:6   188, 192, 193, 231
11:6–7   194
11:7   191, 193, 194, 196, 291, 593
11:12 MT   103
12   47, 57, 59, 63, 135, 140, 149, 196
12:Heading   197, 204, 207, 407, 409
12:1   200, 201
12:1–2   197, 592
12:1–4   200
12:2   197, 198, 593
12:2–3 MT   592
12:3   201
12:3 MT   593
12:3–4   197, 198
12:4   198, 199, 201
12:5   57, 123, 178, 199, 201, 406, 597
12:5–6   197, 199
12:6 MT   57, 123, 178, 405, 597
12:6   196, 200, 291
12:7   200, 201
12:7 MT   291
12:7–8   197, 200
12:8   200, 201, 206
13   59, 70, 204, 204n4
13:Heading   205, 205n5, 208, 209, 325
13:1   205, 206, 207, 593
13:1–2   204, 205, 206, 208
13:2   206, 208, 209
13:2 MT   593
13:3   182, 204ng, 207
13:3–4   204, 207, 208
13:4 MT   182
13:4   207, 208
13:5   208, 592, 600
13:5–6   204, 208

13:6   171, 209
13:6 MT   592, 600
14   27, 36, 40, 57
14:Heading   212, 409
14:1   122, 212, 214, 215, 216, 594
14:1–2   212, 215
14:1–3   77, 180, 212, 217
14:1–5   212
14:2   99, 212, 213, 214, 215, 216
14:3   214, 594
14:3–4   212, 214
14:3–5   214
14:4   210nc, 212, 214, 215, 216, 591, 594
14:4–6   212
14:5   211nd, 212, 214, 215
14:6   211nf, 212, 215, 216
14:6–7   212, 215
14:7   211nf, 212, 215, 216
15   57, 71, 90, 219
15:Heading   219, 228, 358, 359, 380
15:1   129, 219, 220, 223, 224, 395, 595
15:2   221, 223, 595, 600
15:2–3   218ne, 222
15:2–4   222, 223
15:2–5   219, 220, 223, 224
15:3   221, 222, 223, 443
15:3–5   221
15:4   218nd, 222, 223, 515nf
15:5   221, 222, 223, 228, 232, 235nc, 429, 528
16   26, 32, 32n22, 36, 65, 189, 228
16:Heading   228, 233, 234, 238, 258
16:1   228, 230, 231, 232, 238, 415
16:1–2   230
16:1–4   228
16:2   228, 229, 594, 596
16:2–4   228
16:3   226nd, 229, 229n4, 231, 233, 481, 595
16:4   227ng, 229, 229n4

16:5   193, 229, 230, 231, 238
16:5–6   228
16:5–11   230
16:6   229, 231, 232, 233
16:7   50, 230, 231, 232, 238, 407, 601
16:7–8   228
16:8   228, 232, 235nc, 238, 430
16:8–11   234
16:9   146, 227nl, 230, 232, 232n9
16:9–11   228
16:10   238, 269, 431
16:11   229, 233, 238, 593
16:17   167
17   36, 59, 238
17:Heading   238, 245, 259, 262n25, 380, 562
17:1   237, 238, 239, 244, 483, 599
17:1–2   237, 238, 240, 244, 245
17:1–5   269n27, 382n6
17:2   237, 239, 242, 380, 591, 593
17:3   192, 232, 236nd, 237, 238, 239, 239n5, 245, 380, 457n6
17:3–4   240, 241, 242
17:3–5   237, 239
17:4   237, 238, 239, 240
17:4–5   241, 242, 495
17:5   82, 223, 237, 238, 240, 570, 594
17:6   237, 238, 240, 242, 259, 438, 483
17:6–9   237, 240, 244
17:7   121n10, 237, 238, 241, 243, 592
17:7–8   598
17:8   237, 238, 241, 242, 262n25, 510, 599
17:8–9   229
17:9   237, 241, 242, 593
17:10   237, 239, 242
17:10–12   237, 242
17:11   237, 242
17:12   242, 243, 331
17:12–13   243
17:13   237, 243, 593
17:13–14   244

17:13–15   237, 243
17:14   237, 237np, 238, 243, 244, 442n10
17:15   237, 238, 243, 244, 593
17:17   428
17:18 MT   428, 456
18   28, 39n45, 42, 55, 70, 72, 74, 95, 253
18:Heading   254, 275n45, 278, 279, 280, 281, 284, 285, 286, 294, 297, 302, 303, 307, 311, 313, 318, 338, 355na, 437, 438, 451nc, 507
18:1   29n19, 253, 256
18:1–2   247ng, 252, 256, 258
18:1–6   260
18:1–34   273
18:2   247ng, 252, 256, 256n13, 257, 271, 272, 274, 275, 277, 302, 325, 439, 570, 592, 593, 595, 598, 599
18:3   251no, 252, 258, 259, 264, 266, 275, 593
18:3 MT   302, 325, 439, 570, 592, 593, 595, 598, 599
18:3–6   252, 258, 277
18:3–15   317
18:4   258, 317, 585
18:4 MT   593
18:4–5   258, 266
18:4–16 MT   317
18:4–50   258
18:5   248nh, 258, 599
18:5 MT   585
18:6   251, 252, 258, 259, 266, 274, 275, 302, 317, 326, 483, 597
18:6 MT   599
18:6–15   254
18:7   259, 261, 264, 265, 418n13
18:7 MT   302, 326, 483, 597
18:7–8   259, 261, 264, 265
18:7–14   265
18:7–15   252, 255, 259, 260, 273, 280, 307

18:8   260, 261, 262, 264
18:8 MT   418n13
18:9   261, 262, 263
18:9–11   264, 268
18:9–15   260
18:10   261, 262, 263
18:11   261, 263, 264
18:12   263, 264
18:12–13   264
18:12–14   193, 260, 262
18:12–15   264, 268
18:13   252, 261, 264, 264n30, 265, 597
18:13–14   261
18:13–15 MT   193
18:13–15   264
18:14   264, 264n30
18:14 MT   597
18:15   261, 265
18:16   252, 266, 271, 417
18:16–18   265, 267, 270
18:16–19   280
18:16–29   249nt, 252, 265, 273
18:16–48   260
18:17   266
18:17 MT   417
18:17–18   266
18:18   266
18:19   267, 330
18:19–20   265, 268, 269, 270
18:20   249nt, 267, 268, 291
18:20 MT   330
18:21   252, 268, 271, 326
18:21 MT   291
18:21–23   265, 268, 273
18:22   268, 285
18:22 MT   326
18:23   250na, 268, 269, 291
18:23 MT   285
18:24   249nt, 268, 291
18:24 MT   291
18:24–26   270
18:24–27   265, 268, 269, 270
18:25   253, 269, 291
18:25 MT   291
18:25–26   269, 269n36, 592
18:25–29   270
18:25–30   252

18:26   269, 270
18:26 MT   291
18:26–27 MT   592
18:27   252, 270, 275, 277, 593
18:28   252, 270, 326
18:28 MT   593
18:28–29   265, 270
18:29   252, 271, 274, 277, 326
18:29 MT   326
18:30   200, 252, 253, 258, 271, 272, 274, 285, 291, 377, 598, 599, 601
18:30 MT   326
18:30–31   252
18:30–34   271
18:30–48   252, 253
18:31 MT   200, 285, 291, 377, 598, 599, 601
18:31   252, 272
18:32   252, 272, 272n40, 275, 291
18:32–34   250na, 272
18:32–36   280
18:33   252, 272, 272n40, 274
18:33 MT   291
18:34   253, 272, 272n40
18:35   250nd, 258, 273, 274, 275, 302, 316, 593, 599
18:35–36   273
18:35–38   273
18:35–45   273, 276
18:36   273, 274, 382, 530
18:36 MT   302, 316, 593, 599
18:36–38   273
18:37   266, 274, 275, 352
18:37 MT   382, 530
18:37–38   273, 275, 276, 280
18:37–41   271
18:38   252, 273, 274, 302
18:38 MT   352
18:38–39   252
18:39   252, 267, 274
18:39 MT   302
18:39–40   273
18:39–41   273
18:40   266, 273, 275, 276
18:41   250nd, 273, 275, 275n45, 593

18:42   273, 275, 276
18:42 MT   593
18:42–45   273
18:43   252, 273, 276, 491
18:43–45   273, 276
18:44   276
18:44 MT   491
18:44–45   276
18:45   273, 276
18:45–46   279
18:46   37, 201, 252, 277, 407, 448, 593
18:46–48   277
18:47 MT   37, 201, 407, 448, 593
18:47   157n13, 252, 277, 278
18:47–48   277, 278
18:48 MT   157n13
18:48   252, 266, 267, 277, 278, 426, 600
18:49   278, 279, 302, 456
18:49 MT   426, 600
18:49–50   252, 253, 278
18:50   271, 279, 591, 593
18:50 MT   302, 456
18:51 MT   591, 593
19   51, 71, 83, 284, 285, 286
19:Heading   286, 294, 297, 299, 412, 417, 417n12
19:1   286, 287, 287n9, 288, 289n13, 415
19:1–4   289n14
19:1–6   285, 286, 287, 295, 298, 299
19:2   284, 285, 287, 288, 288n11, 288n12, 289, 289n13, 327
19:2 MT   415
19:2–4   286
19:2–7   282na
19:3   284, 285, 288, 288n12, 289n13
19:3 MT   327
19:3–4   286
19:4   286, 287, 288n12, 289, 289n13, 290
19:4–6   286, 287, 288
19:5   285, 287, 289, 290
19:5–6   287
19:6   284, 290

Index of Scripture and Other Ancient Writings

19:7   285, 288, 290, 292, 296, 350
19:7–8   291, 292
19:7–9   285, 290, 292, 293
19:7–10   286
19:7–11   285, 286, 290, 291, 294, 295, 298, 299
19:7–13   285, 297
19:7–14   285, 288, 299
19:8   207, 285, 290, 290n17, 292
19:8 MT   350
19:9 MT   207
19:9   285, 290, 291, 292, 293
19:10   288, 293, 561
19:10–11   290
19:11   286, 292, 294
19:11 MT   561
19:11–14   286
19:12   284, 294, 295, 296
19:12–13   283ng, 296
19:12–14   285, 286, 294, 295, 298
19:13   284, 285, 286, 294, 295, 296
19:14   285, 296
19:15   163nj
20   54n62, 57, 65, 72, 301, 302, 303
20:Heading   303, 309, 311, 313, 316, 409, 412
20:1   301, 304, 304n7, 305n8, 306, 307, 308, 327, 595, 597
20:1–4   305
20:1–5   301, 303, 304n6, 306, 308
20:2   216, 301, 302, 304, 304n7, 305n8, 307
20:2 MT   327, 595, 597
20:2–4   306
20:3 MT   216
20:3   304, 305, 306, 307
20:4   305, 306
20:5   301, 304, 304n6, 305, 306, 307, 307n14, 308, 313, 464n5, 597
20:6   111, 301, 304, 306, 307n15, 308, 313, 316, 327, 456, 591
20:6 MT   464n5, 597
20:7   50, 305, 307, 308n16, 539, 597
20:7 MT   111, 316, 327, 456, 591
20:7–9   301, 307
20:8 MT   50, 539, 597
20:8   302, 308, 308n17
20:9   301, 308, 313, 327
20:10 MT   327
20:28   383
20:29   244
21   55, 72, 303, 311
21:Heading   312, 318
21:1   311, 312, 313, 318
21:1–6   319
21:1–7   312, 315, 318
21:2   312, 313, 314, 544
21:2–5   313, 318
21:2–6   315
21:2–7   311, 312, 313, 315
21:3   313, 314, 315, 317, 594
21:3 MT   544
21:3–4   315
21:4   312, 313, 314
21:4 MT   594
21:5   111, 312, 313, 314
21:6 MT   111
21:6   312, 314, 315, 316, 318, 593
21:6–7   315, 318
21:7   312, 313, 315, 316, 430
21:7 MT   593
21:8   316
21:8 MT   430
21:8–12   311, 312, 315, 316, 318
21:8–13   312
21:9   312, 316, 317, 318
21:10   311nf, 317, 318
21:11   316, 317, 522, 578
21:11–12   318
21:12   317
21:12 MT   522, 578
21:13   50, 201, 311, 312, 318
21:14 MT   50, 201
22   44, 59, 60, 63, 69, 70, 71, 97–98, 140, 167, 323
22:Heading   324, 325, 326, 327, 340, 342, 345, 347, 352, 436, 437, 440, 447, 504, 552, 588
22:1   205, 324, 326, 327, 331, 334, 335, 351, 448, 528, 543
22:1–2   324, 327, 329, 334
22:1–5   337
22:1–11   61
22:1–18   334
22:1–21   323
22:2 MT   205, 351, 448, 528, 543
22:2   326, 327, 335
22:2–12 MT   61
22:3   327, 328, 329, 337, 595
22:3–5   323, 327, 342
22:4   327, 328, 330
22:4 MT   595
22:4–5   328, 329, 447
22:5   328, 593
22:5–6 MT   447
22:6   329, 336
22:6 MT   593
22:6–8   328, 329, 340, 342
22:7   329
22:7–8   341
22:8   329, 334, 521
22:9   321ne, 330
22:9 MT   521
22:9–10   330, 342, 442n10, 447
22:10   321ne, 325, 330
22:10–11 MT   442n10, 447
22:11   331, 332, 334, 595
22:11–18   331, 340, 342
22:12   331
22:12 MT   595
22:12–13   331
22:13   331
22:14   332
22:14–15   331, 332
22:15   331, 332, 339
22:16   331, 332, 333
22:17   331, 333
22:17–18   331
22:18   333, 341
22:19   324, 334, 336
22:19–21   335
22:19–22   333, 342
22:19–25   61
22:20   334
22:20–26 MT   61
22:21   323, 331, 334
22:22   323, 335, 336, 340, 341
22:22–26   598
22:22–31   278, 323
22:23   50, 335, 336, 339
22:23–25   335
22:23–27 MT   598
22:23–31   343
22:23–32 MT   278
22:24 MT   50
22:24   336, 337, 338, 338n30, 449, 593
22:25   328, 335, 337
22:25 MT   449, 593
22:26   335, 336, 338, 599
22:26–31   337
22:27   336, 338, 416
22:27 MT   599
22:27–31   323n1
22:28   336, 338
22:28 MT   416
22:29   332, 339
22:30   322nm, 339, 596
22:31   322no, 339, 593
22:31 MT   596
22:32 MT   593
23   39, 42, 43, 44, 65, 70, 130, 345
23:Heading   347, 353, 511
23:1   347, 350
23:1–3   346, 347, 350, 353
23:1–4   346, 347
23:1–5   352
23:2   39, 346, 348n12, 349, 350, 519
23:2–3   439, 467
23:3   347, 349, 350, 353, 597
23:4   39, 101, 346, 347, 349n16, 350, 351, 353, 559, 592
23:4–5   347
23:5   193, 344nc, 346, 347, 352, 353
23:5–6   346, 347, 352
23:6   39, 220, 346, 347, 352, 353, 592, 594
23:6 LXX   394

628

Index of Scripture and Other Ancient Writings

24   57, 71, 90
24:Heading   356, 364, 380, 412
24–26   380n1
24:1   357
24:1–2   356, 357, 358, 362
24:2   357
24:3   87n16, 219, 220, 358, 385, 595
24:3–6   356, 358, 361, 373
24:4   76, 103, 239, 267, 291, 358, 360, 368, 384, 593
24:4–5   358
24:5   359, 361
24:6   50, 358, 360, 593
24:7   361, 362, 363
24:7 MT   591
24:7–10   356, 361, 362, 595
24:8   356nf, 361, 362, 363
24:9   363
24:10   361, 363
25   37, 59, 168, 367
25:Heading   368, 370n4, 380, 381, 387, 388, 391, 398, 477
25:1   355nc, 359, 368, 377
25:1–2   367
25:1–3   368, 368n1, 370, 371
25:1–7   375
25:1–11   375
25:2   369, 380
25:2–3   376, 377, 438
25:3   369, 371, 375, 376, 596
25:4   370, 372, 374, 591
25:4–5   370, 372
25:4–7   370, 372
25:4–9   372
25:5   367, 369, 370, 371, 372, 596, 600
25:6   371, 372
25:6–7   370, 597
25:7   371, 373, 593
25:8   83, 291, 372
25:8–9   372
25:8–11   371
25:9   372, 373, 375, 376, 591
25:9–10   601
25:10   372, 373, 374, 380, 600

25:10–11   372
25:11   373, 376, 377, 380, 597
25:12   373, 374
25:12–14   373
25:13   373, 374, 594
25:14   370n5, 373, 374
25:15   139, 373, 375, 387
25:15–19   375
25:15–21   369, 375
25:16   375, 376, 380, 386, 571
25:16–22   368
25:17   367, 375, 377
25:18   373, 375, 376, 453
25:18–19   498
25:19   375, 376, 600
25:20   229
25:20–21   377
25:20–22   368n1, 376
25:21   369, 376, 377, 380, 381, 596
25:22   372, 376, 377, 386, 477n1, 598
26   59
26:Heading   381, 388, 391, 398, 403, 478
26:1   377, 380, 381, 383, 386, 387, 530, 595
26:1–2   381
26:1–11   387
26:2   143nj, 192, 381, 382
26:3   380, 382, 383, 600
26:3–5   381, 382, 384, 386
26:4   383, 384, 593
26:4–5   382, 384
26:5   383, 387, 591
26:6   384, 384n11, 386, 387
26:6–8   381, 384
26:7   107nf, 170, 384, 385
26:8   385, 391
26:9   386, 405, 592
26:9–11   381, 385, 386
26:10   386
26:11   37, 136, 377, 380, 381, 386, 387, 595, 598
26:12   231, 381, 383, 387, 391
27   40, 59

27:Heading   391, 403, 438, 568
27:1   195ne, 392, 393, 397, 439, 533, 596
27:1–2   391, 395
27:1–6   389nc, 391, 396, 399
27:2   392, 393, 395, 397
27:3   393, 400
27:3–4   405
27:3–6   391, 393
27:4   120, 220, 385n15, 391, 393, 397, 399, 597
27:4–5   353, 393, 398
27:5   391, 394, 395, 397, 426, 592
27:5–6   220
27:6   111, 395, 599
27:7   136, 396
27:7–9   397
27:7–11   398
27:7–12   391, 396, 399
27:7–14   391, 396
27:8   120, 361, 396, 397, 593
27:9   64, 397, 593
27:9–10   325
27:10   330, 397
27:11   350, 387, 391, 600, 601
27:11–12   397, 398
27:12   242, 398, 399, 495, 594, 600
27:13   244, 399, 594
27:13–14   391, 399
27:14   400, 449, 569n5, 596
28   59
28:Heading   404, 421, 437
28:1   339, 395, 404, 405, 407, 427, 570
28:1–2   404, 438
28:1–4   403
28:1–5   407
28:2   369, 404, 405, 407, 592
28:3   405, 406, 532, 594, 601
28:3–4   404, 405, 408, 409
28:4   182n17, 406, 407
28:5   37, 404, 406, 407
28:6   407, 408, 448, 449, 601

28:6–7   407
28:6–8   404
28:7   157n8, 408, 409, 456
28:7–8   408
28:8   403nf, 404, 408, 591, 600
28:9   404, 409, 598
29   30, 38, 51, 412, 413, 414
29:Heading   414, 415, 416, 417, 418n14, 421, 426
29:1   413, 415, 421
29:1–2   413, 414, 417, 420, 421
29:1–4   421
29:2   416
29:3   266, 417
29:3–4   413, 417, 418, 420
29:4   417
29:5   418, 419
29:5–6   412ne, 418
29:5–9   38, 413, 417, 418, 420
29:6   411nc, 412ne, 413, 418, 419
29:7   418, 419
29:7–8   413, 419
29:7–9   418, 419
29:8   412ne, 418, 419
29:9   413, 418, 419, 420, 597
29:9–10   413, 419, 420, 421
29:9–11   421
29:10   413, 414, 419, 420
29:11   413, 420, 421, 601
30   36, 46, 48, 55, 74, 256, 258, 339, 393, 424
30:Heading   425, 427, 437, 448, 457, 479, 569, 574, 575
30:1   424, 425, 426
30:1–2   427
30:1–3   425, 427
30:2   425, 426, 448, 592
30:2–3   424
30:3   423na, 426, 427, 431, 570, 599
30:3 MT   448, 592
30:4   424, 425, 428, 432, 456, 592
30:4 MT   570, 599
30:4–5   427, 457, 571

629

30:5   132, 424, 428, 429, 597, 599
30:5 MT   456, 592
30:5–6 MT   457, 571
30:6 MT   132, 597, 599
30:6   429, 430, 594
30:6–7   424, 429, 569
30:6–10   583
30:6–11   426
30:6–12   429
30:7   425, 430, 431, 593
30:7 MT   594
30:7–11 MT   583
30:8   430
30:8 MT   593
30:8–10   424, 430, 431
30:9   50, 233, 332, 423nb, 425, 431, 456, 558, 592, 600
30:10 MT   50, 332, 456, 558, 592, 600
30:10   430, 431, 438, 595
30:11   424, 431, 432
30:11 MT   438, 595
30:11–12   430, 431, 457
30:12   424, 432, 435, 456, 578, 592
30:12–13 MT   457
30:13 MT   435, 456, 578, 592
31   36, 59, 189, 436
31:Heading   438, 450
31:1   238, 437, 438, 439
31:1–2   439, 440
31:1–3   437
31:1–4   598
31:1–5   304, 438, 439, 440, 441, 445, 447
31:1–8   436
31:2 MT   238
31:2   395, 438, 439, 443, 483, 600
31:2–5 MT   598
31:3   349, 350, 439, 570
31:3 MT   395, 443, 483, 600
31:3–4   257, 439, 440
31:4 MT   349, 350, 570
31:4   439, 600
31:4–5 MT   257
31:4–5   439

31:5   436, 437, 439, 440, 442, 450, 598, 600
31:5 MT   600
31:5–8   439, 447, 450
31:6   437, 440, 443, 591, 593, 600
31:6 MT   598, 600
31:7   437, 441, 442, 443, 498, 591
31:7 MT   443, 591, 593, 600
31:7–8   436
31:8   387, 441
31:8 MT   498, 591
31:9 MT   387
31:9   442
31:9–10   437, 442
31:9–13   436, 437, 442, 445, 450
31:9–20   448
31:9–24   436, 437, 440
31:10   138, 332, 443, 449, 544
31:11 MT   138, 332, 544
31:11   442, 443, 444
31:11–12   442, 444
31:12   444
31:12–14   450
31:13   442, 444, 445, 479
31:14   437, 445, 600
31:14 MT   479
31:14–15   445
31:14–20   437, 445, 450
31:15   437, 445, 450
31:15 MT   600
31:15–16   445
31:16   207, 437, 446, 447, 593
31:17 MT   207, 593
31:17   437, 445, 446, 599
31:17–18   122, 445
31:18   446, 449n14, 594, 596
31:18 MT   599
31:18–19 MT   122
31:19   437, 447, 594
31:19 MT   594, 596
31:19–20   445
31:20   263, 390ne, 447, 593
31:20 MT   594
31:21 MT   263, 390ne, 593
31:21   407, 437
31:21–24   437, 447

31:22 MT   407
31:22   438, 448
31:23   449, 596
31:24   449, 600
31:24 MT   596
31:25 MT   600
32   26, 36, 55, 64
32:Heading   453, 461, 464, 469, 550, 551, 581, 582
32:1   376, 453, 454, 598
32:1–2   452ne, 453, 454, 455, 456, 457, 459, 594
32:2   439n6, 452ne, 454, 455, 459, 601
32:3   443, 455, 457, 543
32:3–4   457, 458n6
32:3–5   453, 455
32:3–7   458
32:4   327, 451nc, 455, 456
32:5   376, 451nc, 452ne, 456, 592, 593, 598, 601
32:6   266, 417, 457, 460, 592, 598
32:6–7   453, 457, 458
32:7   458, 460
32:8   453, 458, 459, 582
32:8–10   453
32:9   459
32:9–10   459
32:9–11   453, 459
32:10   459, 593
32:10–11   459
32:11   459, 460, 464
33   35n34, 36, 51, 463, 464, 473, 477, 538
33:1   50, 464, 465
33:1–3   464, 472
33:2   464, 465, 592
33:2–3   465
33:3   396, 464, 465, 599
33:4   291, 466, 467
33:4–5   466, 467, 473
33:4–7   464, 466, 468
33:5   293, 462nf, 466, 468, 591
33:5–6   481
33:6   363, 462nf, 467, 468, 473
33:6–7   473
33:7   417, 467, 509
33:8   50, 464, 468, 471

33:9   468, 469
33:9–10   468
33:9–11   469, 480
33:9–12   468, 469, 473
33:9–14   476nd
33:9–19   464
33:10   468, 469
33:10–11   82, 469
33:10–19   464
33:11   468, 469
33:12   464, 469, 594, 598
33:13   99, 470
33:13–14   470
33:13–15   469, 471
33:13–19   111, 469, 473
33:14   470
33:15   470
33:16   470, 471
33:16–17   469, 471
33:17   470, 471, 594
33:18   471, 472, 472n13, 473, 600
33:18–19   469, 471, 483
33:19   427, 471, 472, 472n13
33:20   403nc, 442, 472, 473, 595, 599
33:20–22   464, 472
33:21   472
33:22   473, 600
33:29   596
34   28, 38, 55, 168, 258, 377, 425, 477
34:Heading   477, 481, 481n5, 486, 490
34:1   231, 478, 479
34:1–2   479
34:1–3   478
34:1–6   477, 483
34:2 MT   231
34:2   478
34:3   479
34:4   479, 480, 482, 484, 599
34:4–6   479, 480
34:5   375, 477, 479
34:5 MT   599
34:6 MT   375
34:6   479, 480, 484
34:7   480, 481, 490, 492
34:7–14   480, 482, 483
34:7–22   480
34:8   469, 478, 480, 481, 482, 486, 594

Index of Scripture and Other Ancient Writings

34:8 MT   490, 492
34:9   229, 480, 481, 595
34:9 MT   469, 594
34:10 MT   229
34:10   348, 480, 481, 490, 498, 594, 595, 599
34:11 MT   348, 490, 498, 594, 599
34:11   480, 482
34:11–18   495
34:12   480, 482, 483, 594
34:12–16   483
34:13   239, 482, 483, 592
34:13 MT   594
34:14 MT   239, 592
34:14   352, 480, 483, 592, 594
34:15 MT   352, 592, 594
34:15   375, 483, 484
34:15–22   483
34:16 MT   375
34:16   483, 484, 592, 593
34:17   484, 593
34:17 MT   592, 593
34:17–18   483
34:18   439n6, 484
34:18 MT   593
34:19 MT   439n6
34:19   483, 485
34:20   483, 485
34:21   483, 485
34:22   477, 483, 485, 598
34:23 MT   598
35   45n52, 59, 481, 489
35:Heading   490, 491, 504, 509n4, 597
35:1   490, 491
35:1–3   490, 491, 494, 503
35:1–10   489, 490
35:2   195ne, 490, 491
35:2–3   491
35:3   107nb, 110, 491, 492, 494, 597
35:4   491, 492, 501, 597
35:4–6   490, 491, 493
35:4–8   490, 503
35:5   86, 490, 492
35:6   490, 492
35:7   490, 492, 493, 495, 597

35:8   377, 490, 493
35:9   493, 494, 597
35:9–10   490, 493, 495, 503
35:10   257, 494, 597
35:11   399, 495, 600
35:11–16   495, 503
35:11–18   489, 490, 493, 503
35:12   488nc, 495, 496, 597
35:12–14   495
35:13   496, 503n17, 597
35:14   496, 497
35:15   497, 555
35:15–16   497
35:16   497, 524
35:17   292, 334, 495, 497, 500, 596, 597
35:18   495, 498
35:19   498, 501, 502, 594
35:19–26   503
35:19–28   489, 490, 493, 498
35:20   376, 499, 502, 601
35:20–21   498, 499, 502
35:21   499
35:22   325, 499, 500, 562n12, 596
35:22–24   498, 499
35:23   37, 491, 500, 596
35:24   500, 501, 502
35:24–26   498
35:25   242, 501, 502, 597
35:25–26   501
35:25–27   501
35:26   501, 502, 581nd
35:27   501, 502, 601
35:27–28   498, 500, 502
35:28   328, 502, 600
36   65, 254
36:Heading   507
36:1   77, 383, 506, 513
36:1–4   505na, 506, 507, 511, 512
36:2 MT   77, 383
36:2   457n6, 508
36:3 MT   457n6
36:3   508, 509
36:3–4   512
36:4   122, 240, 508
36:5 MT   122, 240

36:5   509, 600
36:5–6   509, 510
36:5–7   510
36:5–9   506, 509
36:6   509, 510, 591
36:6 MT   600
36:7   510, 598, 599
36:7 MT   591
36:7–9   510, 511, 513, 596
36:8   510
36:8 MT   599
36:8–10 MT   596
36:9   511
36:10   377, 511
36:10–11   512
36:10–12   506, 511
36:11 MT   377
36:11   512, 596
36:12   512
36:12 MT   596
37   38, 58, 70, 90, 370n4, 517, 518
37:Heading   518, 534, 535, 538, 556
37:1   519, 521, 522, 529
37:1–2   517, 520
37:1–6   528
37:2   37, 276, 519, 523, 532
37:3   519, 520, 522, 525, 529, 594
37:3–4   517
37:4   519, 523
37:5   330, 520
37:6   520
37:7   79nc, 122, 519, 521, 523
37:7–15   521
37:8   519, 522, 529
37:8–9   133
37:9   198, 369, 515nf, 522, 523, 529, 531, 596
37:10   523, 531, 532
37:11   76, 374, 518, 522, 523, 534, 601
37.12   497, 522, 523
37:12–15   530
37:13   99, 523, 524, 531, 596
37:14   523, 524, 531, 597
37:15   524
37:16   517, 523, 525
37:16–26   525
37:17   112, 523, 525, 527
37:17–20   538

37:18   525, 532, 591, 595
37:18–19   525
37:19   525, 526, 531
37:20   157, 523, 526
37:21   523, 526, 528
37:21–22   517
37:22   198, 522, 526
37:23   527
37:24   527, 530
37:25   325, 517, 528, 529, 530, 531
37:25–26   529
37:26   527, 528
37:27   528, 529
37:27–33   528
37:28   198, 522, 528, 529, 530, 531, 532, 533, 592
37:29   522, 529
37:30   530, 538, 600
37:31   382, 530, 570
37:32   165nv, 523, 530
37:33   325, 530, 531
37:34   198, 516nl, 522, 531, 532, 596
37:34–40   531
37:35   523, 531
37:35–36   517, 532
37:36   531, 532
37:37   532, 595, 601
37:38   198, 522, 523, 532
37:39   533, 538, 600
37:40   523, 533
38   45, 46, 59, 64, 135, 538
38:Heading   539, 540, 546n13, 551, 554, 555, 576
38–39   576
38–40   584
38–41   539n3
38:1   537, 538, 539, 540, 541, 550, 554
38:1–3   136
38:2   538, 540, 554
38:2 MT   554
38:2–3   540
38:2–4 MT   136
38:2–5   538, 540, 548
38:2–8   544
38:2–10   538
38:3   538, 540, 541, 542, 543, 593, 601
38:3 MT   554
38:3–4   538, 548
38:3–5   540
38:4   538, 541, 542
38:4 MT   593, 601

631

Index of Scripture and Other Ancient Writings

38:4–5   541
38:5   538, 541, 542
38:6   37, 538, 542, 543
38:6–8   542
38:6–10   538, 542, 545
38:7 MT   37
38:7   538, 543
38:8   538, 543
38:8 MT   598
38:9   138, 538, 544, 546, 547, 548, 554, 596
38:9–10   542, 544
38:10 MT   138, 554, 596
38:10   443, 538, 544, 545
38:11 MT   443
38:11   537nb, 538, 545, 546, 554, 561
38:11–12   545, 546, 547
38:11–16   538, 545
38:11–19   538
38:11–20   538
38:12   538, 549, 600
38:12 MT   554, 561
38:13   538, 546, 554
38:13 MT   600
38:13–14   547
38:14   538, 546, 547, 554
38:14 MT   554
38:15   538, 547, 554, 596, 600
38:15 MT   554
38:15–16   547
38:16   547, 548, 581nd
38:16 MT   554, 596, 600
38:17   538, 548
38:17 MT   581nd
38:17–20   545, 548
38:18   538, 548, 549
38:19   549, 594
38:19–20   549
38:20   352, 538, 542, 549
38:20 MT   594
38:21   325, 538, 550
38:21 MT   352
38:21–22   538, 550
38:22 MT   325
38:22   538, 550, 596
38:23 MT   596
39   59
39:Heading   555, 565

39:1   554, 555, 556, 557, 560, 593
39:1–2   560
39:1–3   555
39:2   554, 555, 556, 560, 560n11, 561
39:2 MT   593
39:2–3   556
39:3   554, 555, 556, 557
39:4   554, 557, 558
39:4–7   555, 557
39:5   237nn, 554, 555, 558, 561
39:5–6   558
39:5–7   557
39:6 MT   237nn
39:6   555, 558, 559
39:7   191n7, 554, 555, 559, 565, 595, 596
39:8 MT   191n7, 595, 596
39:8   560
39:8–13   555, 557, 559
39:9   554, 560, 560n11, 561
39:10 MT   233
39:10   554, 555, 560, 563
39:11   546n13, 554, 555, 559, 560, 561, 562, 564
39:12   220, 554, 555, 561, 564, 565
39:12 MT   546n13
39:13 MT   220
39:13   555, 563
40   59, 568
40:Heading   569, 574, 578
40:1   568, 569, 592, 596
40:1–3   569, 572, 574, 575, 581
40:1–12   568, 575, 581
40:2   569, 570
40:2 MT   592, 596
40:3   37, 465, 570, 575
40:4 MT   37, 465
40:4   120, 568, 571, 571n9, 572, 594, 600
40:4–5   571
40:4–10   581
40:4–12   581
40:5 MT   120, 594, 600

40:5   568, 572, 575
40:6   568, 572, 573, 577
40:6–8   567nd, 569, 572
40:6–10   576
40:7   573, 574, 574n11
40:7–8   574
40:8   482, 567nd, 567nf, 568, 573, 574, 577
40:8–9 MT   569
40:9 MT   482
40:9   568
40:9–10   573, 574, 574n13
40:10   567ne, 568, 592, 600
40:11   568, 575, 576
40:11 MT   592, 600
40:11–12   575, 581
40:12   569, 575, 576
40:13   568, 577, 578
40:13–17   568, 574, 574n13, 575, 576
40:14   568, 577
40:14–15   577, 578
40:15   577
40:16   568, 577, 578, 578, 580na, 596, 597
40:18 MT   580na, 596, 597
40:27   217
41   23, 55, 426, 469
41:Heading   582, 588, 589
41:1   582, 583, 594, 598
41:1–2   589
41:1–3   581n1, 582, 583, 584, 588
41:2   242, 581n1, 582, 583
41:2 MT   594, 598
41:2–3   583
41:3 MT   242
41:3   581n1, 582, 583
41:3–4   426
41:4   136, 582, 584, 586, 589
41:4–5 MT   426
41:4–9   583
41:4–10   583, 588
41:5 MT   136
41:5   584
41:5–6   583, 584, 585
41:5–8   583
41:6   584, 586, 593
41:7   585

41:7 MT   593
41:7–8   585
41:8   583, 585, 588
41:9   76, 532, 585, 586
41:9–10   583
41:10 MT   532
41:10   586, 588, 589
41:11   330, 587, 587n15, 588, 589
41:11–12   587, 587n15, 589
41:12 MT   330
41:12   587n15, 588, 595
41:13   590
41:13 MT   595
42   23, 27, 59, 63
42–43   38, 41, 44, 72, 208, 347, 400, 437, 489
42–49   35
42–83   36
42:1   265
42:1–2   442
42:1–6   597
42:2 MT   265
42:2   277
42:2–3 MT   442
42:2–7 MT   597
42:3 MT   277
42:3   327
42:4 MT   327
42:5   600
42:6 MT   600
42:6–11   489
42:7–8   541
42:8   39, 327
42:8–9 MT   541
42:9 MT   39, 327
42:9   257, 325
42:10 MT   257, 325
42:11   600
42:12 MT   600
42:24   217
43   59, 489
43:1   217
43:2   325, 600
43:3   111, 220, 353, 377, 385, 596
43:4   36
43:5   600
44   59, 64, 70, 91, 166, 174, 303
44:1   287
44:2 MT   287
44:3   567nf, 577, 596
44:4 MT   567nf, 577, 596
44:5   37
44:6 MT   37

Index of Scripture and Other Ancient Writings

44:6   600
44:7 MT   600
44:8   598
44:9   362
44:9 MT   598
44:10 MT   362
44:18   570
44:19 MT   570
44:21   239
44:22 MT   239
44:23   500
44:23–24   325
44:24 MT   500
44:24–25 MT   325
44:25   442n10
44:26 MT   442n10
44:26   598
44:27 MT   598
45   57
45:2   594
45:3 MT   594
45:6   387
45:7   36
45:7 MT   387
45:8 MT   36
45:17   308
45:18 MT   308
46   38, 53, 54, 65
46:1   157n8, 170, 216, 600
46:2 MT   157n8, 216, 600
46:3   417
46:4   85, 385
46:4 MT   417
46:5 MT   85, 385
46:5   430, 597
46:6 MT   430, 597
46:7   595
46:8 MT   595
46:9   157
46:10 MT   157
46:10   201
46:11 MT   201
46:11   595
46:12 MT   595
47   51, 71, 174, 278
47:1   174, 599
47:2   144no
47:2 MT   174, 599
47:3 MT   144no
47:4   598
47:5 MT   598
47:5   599
47:6 MT   599
48   51, 72
48:1–2   220
48:2–3 MT   220
48:3–4   37
48:4–5 MT   37
48:4–7   103

48:9   597
48:10 MT   597
49   38, 58
49:1   237nn
49:2   116nb, 597
49:2 MT   237nn
49:3 MT   116nb, 597
49:4 MT   549n15
49:5   581nd
49:6 MT   581nd
49:6   598
49:7 MT   598
49:7–8   598
49:8–9 MT   598
49:14   597
49:14–15   599
49:15 MT   597
49:15   598
49:15–16 MT   599
49:16 MT   598
49:16–17   595
49:17–18 MT   595
49:29   445
50 LXX   26n13
50   35, 52, 53, 54, 56, 57, 71, 90, 305
50:2   216
50:14–15   337
51 MT   26n13
51   28, 29, 60, 64, 254
51–72   27n14, 35
51:1   442, 598
51:1–9   38
51:2   601
51:3 MT   442, 598
51:3   598
51:3–11 MT   38
51:4   77
51:4 MT   601
51:5 MT   598
51:5   601
51:6 MT   77
51:7 MT   601
51:8   543
51:9   593, 601
51:10   291
51:10 MT   543
51:11   593, 601
51:12 MT   291
51:13   268, 598
51:15 MT   268, 598
51:17   543
51:18–19   29n17
51:19 MT   543
51:19   601
51:20–21 MT   29n17
51:21 MT   601
52   28, 65, 70
52:1   598
52:3 MT   598

52:4   455
52:6 MT   455
52:6   524
52:7   600
52:7–8   600
52:8 MT   524
52:9 MT   600
52:9–10 MT   600
53   36, 57, 211, 215n9
53:1   210na
53:2 MT   210na
54   28, 32, 59, 562, 600
54:5   600
54:7   322nj
54:7 MT   600
54:9 MT   322nj
55   32n24, 59, 562
55:1   594
55:2   37
55:2 MT   594
55:3 MT   37
55:5   599
55:6 MT   599
55:8   37
55:9   37, 600
55:9 MT   37
55:10 MT   37, 600
55:10   327
55:10–11   180
55:11   165nt
55:11 MT   327
55:11–12 MT   180
55:12 MT   165nt
55:12   581nd
55:13 MT   581nd
55:14   97
55:15 MT   97
55:15   599
55:16 MT   599
55:18   598
55:19   327
55:19 MT   598
55:20   180, 532
55:20 MT   327
55:21 MT   180, 532
55:22   223, 330
55:23 MT   223, 330
56   28, 59
56–60   228
56:2   600
56:3 MT   600
56:3–4   600
56:4   466, 558
56:4–5 MT   600
56:5 MT   466, 558
56:13   596
56:14 MT   596
57   28, 38, 59, 189, 284

57:1   598, 599
57:2 MT   598, 599
57:5   156
57:6 MT   156
57:8   324
57:9   174
57:9 MT   324
57:10 MT   174
57:11   156
57:12 MT   156
58   59, 71
58:2   600
58:3   442n10
58:3 MT   600
58:4 MT   442n10
58:5   585
58:6 MT   585
59   28, 59
59:1   38, 595
59:2 MT   38, 595
59:5   364
59:6   333
59:6 MT   364
59:7 MT   333
59:8   99, 524
59:9 MT   99, 524
59:9   595, 600
59:10   322nj, 600
59:10 MT   595, 600
59:11 MT   322nj, 600
59:14   333
59:15 MT   333
59:16   595, 597, 600
59:17   595, 600
59:17 MT   595, 597, 600
59:18 MT   595, 600
60   28, 57, 59, 63, 284, 303
60:2   136
60:4   37
60:4 MT   136
60:6 MT   37
60:6   595
60:6–9   57
60:8 MT   595
60:8–11 MT   57
60:9   25, 191n7
60:10   362
60:11 MT   25, 191n7
60:12 MT   362
61   65, 562
61:1   599
61:2   277
61:2 MT   599
61:2–3   257
61:2–4   395
61:3   207, 216
61:3 MT   277
61:3–4 MT   257
61:3–5 MT   395

633

61:4 MT   207, 216
61:4   220
61:5 MT   220
62   38, 65
62:2   257, 430, 595
62:3   119, 205
62:3 MT   257, 430, 595
62:3–4   37
62:4 MT   119, 205
62:4–5 MT   37
62:5   122, 521, 595
62:6 MT   122, 521, 595
62:6   430, 595
62:7   111, 600
62:7 MT   430, 595
62:7–8   216
62:8 MT   111, 600
62:8–9 MT   216
62:8–10   600
62:9   116nb, 120, 559
62:9–10   37
62:9–11 MT   600
62:10 MT   116nb, 120, 559
62:10–11 MT   37
62:11   600
62:12 MT   600
63   28, 59, 65
63:1   325
63:2 MT   325
63:3   50
63:4 MT   50
63:4   231, 369
63:5 MT   231, 369
63:6   597, 600
63:7 MT   597, 600
63:7   598, 599
63:8 MT   598, 599
64   59
64:2   97, 374
64:3 MT   97, 374
64:4–6   37
64:5–7 MT   37
65   51, 71
65–68   36
65:1–2   337
65:2–3 MT   337
65:4   219, 220, 594, 597
65:5 MT   219, 220, 594
65:5   238, 600
65:6 MT   238, 600
65:6   596
65:7   570
65:7 MT   596
65:8 MT   570
65:9   85
65:10 MT   85
65:12   349
65:13 MT   349
66   55, 599
66:4   338
66:7   165nv, 201
66:8   174, 601
66:10   382
66:16–20   38
66:19–20   598
67   59, 338, 599
67:2   601
67:3 MT   601
67:3–5   174
67:4   387
67:4–6 MT   174
67:5 MT   387
68   36, 51, 599
68:2   332
68:3 MT   332
68:5–14   78
68:6–15 MT   78
68:10   601
68:11 MT   601
68:16   561
68:17 MT   561
68:18   77
68:19 MT   77
68:24   325
68:25 MT   325
68:29   597
68:30 MT   597
69   26, 32, 59, 66, 75, 197
69:1–2   266, 417
69:2   570, 570n7
69:2–3 MT   266, 417
69:3   138, 139, 443, 600
69:3 MT   570, 570n7
69:4   76
69:4 MT   138, 139, 443, 600
69:5   542, 549n15
69:6   369
69:6 MT   542
69:7 MT   369
69:14–15   266, 417
69:15   259
69:15–16 MT   266, 417
69:16 MT   259
69:16   375, 571
69:17 MT   375, 571
69:18   485, 598
69:19 MT   485, 598
69:20   596
69:21 MT   596
69:22–25   66
69:23–26 MT   66
69:24   99
69:25 MT   99
69:26   93ni, 352
69:27 MT   93ni, 352
69:29   595
69:30 MT   595
69:32   338
69:33 MT   338
69:33   597
69:34 MT   597
70   46, 59, 568, 575
70:5   595, 597
70:6 MT   595, 597
71   59, 189, 437
71:2   238
71:2–3   257
71:3   570
71:5   595, 600
71:6   442n10
71:8   37
71:9   325
71:11   325, 352
71:12   325
71:14   600
71:16   308
71:17–18   287
71:18   183, 325
71:19   494
71:22   595, 600
72   23, 34, 57, 65, 72, 95, 301, 303, 590
72:4   597
72:9   332
72:12   592, 597
72:13   597, 598
72:14   165nt, 600
72:14–15   304
72:15   598
72:18–19   407
72:20   238
73   23, 55, 58, 58n65, 63, 453, 517, 518
73–83   35
73:1   103, 267
73:2   570
73:3   125ne
73:11   191n7
73:13   384
73:17   597
73:23   232
73:24   232
73:25   482
73:26   231, 443
74   59, 157, 420
74:1   261
74:1–2   409
74:2   111, 220
74:3 MT   111
74:7   385
74:10   137, 179, 205
74:13   417
74:16   327
74:18   179, 212
74:18–23   601
74:22   212
74:23   157
75   65
75:4   125ne
75:5 MT   125ne
75:8   193
76   65, 72
76:4   155
76:5 MT   155
76:8   123
76:9 MT   123
77   65
77:2   327, 599
77:3 MT   327, 599
77:11   308
77:12 MT   308
77:20   350
77:21 MT   350
78   51, 70, 251
78:3–4   287
78:4   170, 175n13, 328
78:5   291
78:8   439n6
78:11   170
78:13   467
78:14   350
78:18   382
78:25   233
78:32   170
78:41   382
78:47–48   264
78:49   99
78:53   350
78:55   231
78:56   382
78:70   254
79   31n21, 59
79:1   191, 597
79:9   193
79:10   332
79:11   199
79:13   175n13
80   59, 70
80:1   263, 327
80:1–3   348
80:2 MT   263, 327
80:2–4 MT   348
80:4   137, 191n7, 205, 261
80:5 MT   137, 191n7, 205, 261
80:8   107ng
80:9 MT   107ng
80:14   111, 182
80:15 MT   111, 182
81   57, 70
81:13   268
81:14 MT   268
82   56, 57, 71

Index of Scripture and Other Ancient Writings

82:1   415, 510
82:2   137
82:2 MT   510
82:3–4   598
82:5   191
82:7   416
83   59, 98
83:2   111
83:3 MT   111
83:3   374
83:4 MT   374
84   65, 72, 469
84–88   35
84:2   277
84:3 MT   277
84:6   310nd
84:7 MT   310nd
84:8   562
84:9 MT   562
84:11   594
84:11–12   594
84:12 MT   594
84:12–13 MT   594
85   59
85:2   376, 454
85:3 MT   376, 454
86   35, 59, 238
86:2   229
86:4   359, 368
86:8   494
86:9   338
86:11   472
86:16   375
87   51
88   45, 59, 68n81, 74
88:1   544
88:2 MT   544
88:4   324, 339
88:5 MT   324, 339
88:5   448
88:6 MT   448
88:7   64
88:8 MT   64
88:14   325
88:15 MT   325
89   23, 59, 71, 72, 91, 95, 157, 174, 396, 568, 590
89:5   229
89:6 MT   229
89:6   415, 567nb
89:7   229
89:7 MT   415, 567nb
89:8 MT   229
89:8   494
89:9 MT   494
89:9–10   572
89:10–11 MT   572
89:13   318
89:14   293
89:14 MT   318

89:15 MT   293
89:15   596
89:16 MT   596
89:19   403nc
89:20 MT   403nc
89:26   100, 325
89:27 MT   100, 325
89:28   291
89:29 MT   291
89:46   64
89:47 MT   64
89:47   237nn
89:48 MT   237nn
90   23, 58, 59, 158, 238
90:5–6   519
90:7   99
90:8   544
90:13   137, 205
90:17   148, 394
91   57, 60, 65, 156, 301, 518
91:2   257
91:3   585
91:4   132, 257, 598
91:6   585
91:8   452nf
91:9   257
91:10   220
91:11   322nj
92   55, 453
92:2   327
92:3 MT   327
92:3   465
92:4   163nj
92:4 MT   465
92:12 MT   322nj
93   36, 51, 71, 157, 158
93:1   158
93:4   155, 266, 417
93:5   462na
94   59
94:3   137, 205
94:12   594
94:18   223, 387
94:22   257
95   26, 31n21, 44, 45, 48, 49, 50, 51, 56, 91, 437, 458, 459
95–98   155
95–99   36, 51
95–100   103
95:1   50
95:1–2   47, 102
95:2   50
95:3   510
95:3–5   50
95:6   47, 49, 50, 102
95:7   50
95:9   192

96   51, 70, 71, 174, 413, 415, 416, 420
96–100   468
96:1   465
96:6   157
96:7–8   415
96:10   147, 158, 420
97   51
97:1   102
97:2   262, 293
97:4   102
97:5   332
97:7   598
97:10–11   596
98   51, 278, 338
98:1   465
98:9   147
99   51, 71
99:1   121, 263, 327
99:1–3   327
99:2   216
99:3   472
99:5   426
99:8   376
99:9   220, 426
100   31n21, 44, 45, 48, 49, 50, 51, 56, 437
100:1–2   47, 102
100:2   49, 50
100:3   51
100:4   47, 48
100:5   51
101   65, 356
101:3   259, 383
101:5   295
101:6   291
101:7   383
102   59, 64, 238
102:3   443
102:4 MT   443
102:5   138
102:6 MT   138
102:15   472
102:16 MT   472
102:20   199
102:21 MT   199
102:23–24   325
102:24–25 MT   325
103   55
103:6–7   268
103:10   267
103:15   519
103:18   291
103:21   363
104   32, 51, 71, 284
104:1–9   419
104:4   156
104:5   594
104:7   265
104:18   216, 257

104:27   375
104:29   332, 386
104:29–30   439n6
104:32   261
104:35   83, 179
105   51, 70
105:3   472
105:4   120, 396, 599
105:5   338
105:11   231
105:42   466
106   23, 59, 70, 590
106:7   170
106:8   328
106:9   172
106:10   328
106:12   328
106:20   120
106:22   170
106:24   466
106:47   472
107   23, 55, 58, 70, 425
107:9   242
107:32   82, 383
108   65, 284
108:3   174
108:4 MT   174
108:4–5   156
108:5–6 MT   156
108:11   362
108:12 MT   362
109   26, 32n24, 59, 244, 484
109:3   458
109:31   232
110   26, 28, 56, 57, 72, 356
110:1   505na
110:5   232
110:7   111
111   38, 51
111:1   88, 170
111:2   251no
111:7   291
111:9   472
111:10   373, 599
112   38, 57, 469
112:1   83
112:1–3   594
113 LXX   26n13
113   51
113–14   36
113–18   36, 54, 385
113:4   156
113:7   332
114 LXX   26n13
114   51
114–15 MT   26n13
115 LXX   26n13
115   65, 245

635

115–18 36	124:6 407	142:5 231	3:1 81, 482
115:9 403nc	124:8 595	142:6 MT 231	3:3 383
115:10 403nc	125 65	143 59, 64	3:5–6 89
115:11 403nc	125:1 430	143:1 238	3:11 482
115:17 339	126 59	143:2 77, 88	3:13 81
115:18 231	126:4 265	143:7 339	3:21 482
116 MT 26n13	127 57, 81, 469	143:8 359, 368	3:26 89
116 55, 258	127:3 442n10	143:10 387	3:30 267
116:1 256	128 57, 81, 469, 594	144 59, 469	3:31–36 88
116:3 457	128:1 268	144:1 253, 407	3:33 89
116:8 387	128:5 216	144:1–2 257	3:34 83
116:13 193	129 65	144:2 599	4:1 482
117 51	129:6 519	144:3 158	4:18–19 90
118 42, 55, 72, 278, 464	129:8 108ni, 304	144:4 559	5:7 482
	130 64, 74	144:5 261, 262	5:14 88
118:7 195ne	130:3 77	144:5–6 259	5:23 542
118:13 403nc	131 32n22, 65	144:6 264	6:13 499
118:14 157n8	132 65, 71, 72	144:7 266	6:16–19 213
118:25–27 384	132:5 385	144:9 465	6:19 399
118:26 304	132:10 254	144:15 594	7:2 81, 241
118:27 207	132:11 442n10	145 38, 51	8:8 269
118:28 325	133 57	145:1–2 231	8:29 261
119 38, 46, 58, 65, 81, 251, 284, 294, 298, 518	134 51	145:2 179	8:32 81
	134:3 216	145:14 112	8:34 81
	135 51	145:15 375	9:1–2 352
119:3 268	135–36 36	145:18–19 485	9:5 586
119:4 291	135:4 469	145:21 231, 472	9:15 126nj
119:8 325	135:6 509	146 51	10:9 269
119:14 291	135:21 179, 407	146–50 36	10:10 499
119:21 295	136 55	147 26n13, 51	10:12 454
119:25 466	136:12 257	147:1 462na	10:24 479
119:25–32 40	136:18 155	147:3 426	11:1 213
119:30 232n10, 374	137 35, 59, 157, 469	147:6 308n17	11:13 454
119:35 83, 482	137:1 25	147:14–16 218ne	12:12 561
119:51 295	137:6 332	148 51, 284	12:16 454
119:57 231	137:8 251no	148:2 363	13:1 82
119:69 295	137:8–9 67, 496	148:7 510	13:25 442
119:78 295	137:9 156, 317	148:13 156	14:1 542
119:82 139	138 55, 425	149 51	14:3 542
119:85 295	138–45 35	149:1 465	14:5 399
119:119 157	138:1 170	149:4 601	14:8 542
119:120 507	138:2 597	150 23, 51, 58n65	14:12 90
119:122 295	139 43, 44, 45, 60, 65, 74, 326, 380, 510		14:17 542
119:123 139		**Proverbs**	14:18 542
119:132 375			14:24 542
119:137 291	139:8 138	1 88	14:25 399
119:140 200	139:11–12 327	1–9 80, 89, 96	14:29 542
119:143 457	139:13 442n10	1:1–7 88, 508	14:30 443
119:173 374	139:14 121n10	1:2–3 530	15:21 126nj
120 55	139:23 192	1:2–8 102	15:22 374
120–34 26, 36, 46	140 59	1:7 8, 102, 291	15:30 443
120:2–3 455	140:3 77	1:8 482	16:3 330
121 65	140:4 MT 77	1:8–19 81, 88	16:6 383
121:5 232	140:4 229	1:9–19 82n5	16:8 525
121:6 327	140:5 MT 229	1:10 83	16:16 525
122 51, 72	140:6 325	1:22 82, 561	16:19 525
123 59	140:7 MT 325	2 464	16:22 102
123:1 327, 369	141 59	2:1 482	16:23 232
123:2 375	141:8 139, 375	2:15 269	16:32 525
124 55	141:9 229	2:21–22 529	17:9 454
124:4–5 266, 417	142 28, 59, 238		17:22 332

636

18:2   83
18:20   442
19:2   593
19:3   542
19:18   359
19:29   82
20:8   88
20:22   587
21:1   84
21:20   293
23:15–16   479
23:24–25   479
24:2   97
24:4   233
24:13   293
24:19   519
24:24–25   149
25:13   292
25:21   586
26:24   206
28:4   81
28:6   269
28:7   81
28:9   81
28:13   456
28:18   269
29:13   165nt
30:5   200, 253
31:9   238n2
31:12   267

Ecclesiastes

2:18–23   559
3:7   556
5:1 MT   564
5:1–7   564
5:2   564
10:20   122
12:9–14   90, 564
12:12   7

Song of Songs

2:4   306n11
2:9   470
5:10   306n11
6:4   306
6:10   306

Isaiah

1:2   296
1:5–6   539
1:8   175, 263
1:10   81
1:15   145, 178–79
1:15–16   267
2:3   216
3:14   88
4:1   586
5:1   247ne
6:11   137
8:8   541
8:18   220
8:19   97
9:1–6 MT   104
9:2–7   104
10:5   351
10:6   99n12
11   73, 160
11:1–9   72, 104
13   67n76
13–23   96
13:13–19   67
14:13   509
14:14   213
14:16   470
14:24–27   469
17:2   349
17:13   86
17:14   244
19:24   315
24:18   261
25:5   592
25:9   569n5
26:14   87
26:16   585n10, 585n11
26:19   87, 245
28:2   264
28:10   282nb
28:13   282nb
28:15   120
28:17   120, 264, 458
29:5   86
30   308
30–31   304, 305
30:1   305
30:1–2   304
30:7   120
30:15   209
30:30   155
30:33   193
31:1   307
31:4   97
32:2   458
32:5   212
33:7–12   196
33:14–16   224
34:9   194
34:9–12   193
37:22   99
38:9–20   228
40–49   217
40–55   351, 469
40:1   351, 469
40:8   469
40:11   348, 349
40:18   567nb
40:21   261
40:22–23   103
40:28   210nc
40:28–31   449
40:29   443
40:31   369, 443
41:2   86
41:6   449
41:8–9   469
41:10   351
41:14   243, 329
42:3   271
42:21   226nd
44:1–2   469
44:7   37
44:17   325n8
44:22   457
44:28   348
45:5   124
45:6   124
45:7   406
45:18   124
46:10–11   469
47:6   469
47:8–9   496
48:1   308, 308n16
48:5   468
48:12   469
48:13   468
48:15   79nc
49:4   97, 448
49:10   349
49:15   398
49:23   369
51:1–2   150
51:9–11   158
51:10   266n34, 417
51:13   290n16
51:17–23   193
51:18   349
52   362
52:2   175
53:7   556
54:17   85
55   73, 95
55:2   520
55:3–5   73
55:6   457n6
55:7–9   469
55:11   97
56:1   440
57   196
57:15   328
58:9   118
59:3   145
59:6   145
63:8   241
64:1   262
65:1   457n6
65:23   98
66:4   479
66:11   520

Jeremiah

1:10   406
2:11   120
2:13   511
2:27   275
3:15   102
3:21   601
4:4   406
4:11–12   88
5   196
6:2   175
6:25   445
6:30   222
7   219, 224
7:29   222
8:8   81
9:9 MT   349
9:10   349
10:5–7   494
11:20   238n2
12:1   85, 88
12:14   172
12:17   172
13:25   193
14–15   57
15:3   333
15:9   137
15:19   201
16:13   527
16:19   157n8
17   84, 84n13, 85
17:5–8   84
17:5–10   586
17:8   84
17:13   511
17:14   328
18:20   503
18:22   503
20:3–4   445
20:7   503
20:10   445, 586
20:11   503
22:26   527
22:28   527
22:30   85
23   73
23:5   102
23:5–6   72
23:10   349
23:12   492, 503
23:26   137
23:31   507
24:6   406
27:2   99
29:14   457n6
30:9   27
31:10   348
31:13   432
31:28   406
31:31–34   574

31:40   172
32:39   198
36:4   153nb
36:6   153nb
36:17   153nb
36:27   153nb
38   570
38:22   586
40:7   439n6
41:10   439n6
44:18   348
46:4   98
46:5   445
46:14   98
47:6   205
49:37   99n12

Lamentations

1:4   138, 544
1:5   156
1:6   175
1:8   138, 201, 544
1:11   138, 292, 544
1:16   292
1:19   292
1:21   138, 544
1:22   544
2–4   168
2:11   156, 332
2:12   332
2:14   593
2:19   156
2:20   156
2:22   445
3:24   231
3:25   369, 569n5
3:33   89, 116nb
3:40   338
3:54   448
3:56   179
4:4   156, 332
5   464
5:15   432

Ezekiel

1–3   263
1:13–14   262
3:26   332
7:14   99n12
7:22   240
8   295
9–10   263
9:3   263n27
10:2   263n27
10:4   263n27
16:53   217
17:1–10   84
17:15   85

18:10   240
18:20   148
19:10–14   84
24:8   454
33:4–6   294
34   348
34:14–15   349
34:23–24   27
34:25–29   124
37:11   332, 448
37:24–25   27

Daniel

2:4   314
3:8   389na
6:24   389na
7   87
8:6   290n16
9   49, 64, 368
10   421
12:2   245
12:10   269

Hosea

1:9   101
2:17   230
2:19 MT   230
3:5   27
4   196
4:8   359
6   57
7   196
7:14   122n11
12:6   440
12:7 MT   440

Joel

1:19–20   349
2:16   289
2:22   349

Amos

1:1   259
1:2   349
2:4   120
2:6–7   527
4:1   331
6:10   308
7:2   87n16
7:5   87n16
7:8   240
8:2   240
9   510

Obadiah

7   586

Jonah

2   63
2:2   118
2:3   458
2:4 MT   458
2:5   458
2:6 MT   458
2:9   440
3:10   457
4:5   263

Micah

2:1   122
3:1–3   215
6:6–8   219
6:12   455
7   196
7:17   251nn

Nahum

1:6   87n16
2:7   496
2:8 MT   496

Habakkuk

1   196, 199
1:2   205
2:13   98
3   238
3:1   27
3:3   155

Zephaniah

1:16   396
2:2   86
2:3   396
3:8   99n12
3:13   349

Haggai

2   219

Zechariah

3   200
7   219
7:13   205
8:4   351
8:13   315
9:12   569n5

11:3   326
14:5   259

Malachi

2:13   199
3:20 MT   599
4:2   599

New Testament

Matthew

2:16–18   156
3:17   104
5:3–12   76
5:5   76, 518, 534
5:8   76
6:24   388
6:32–33   234
6:33   534
7:23   136n4
16:18   258
17:5   104
21:14–16   157n8
28:16–20   105

Mark

1:10   262
2:1–12   460
12:35–37   26
14:26   36
14:34   63, 137
15:24   341
15:29   341
15:34   63, 341

Luke

2:34   309
6:28   309
7:46   352
10:41–42   394
11:28   90
12:16–20   559
13:27   136n4
16:19–31   75n90
17:11–19   579
18:1–8   409
22:69   75n90
23:34   133
23:43   75n90
23:46   450
23:49   545
24:27   76

John

3:16   513
4:10   513
5   105n28
5:28–29   75
6:35   513
9:3   460, 579
10:22   51, 425
12:27   136n4
13:18   76, 586n12
15:25   76, 503
16:23   21
19:24   341
20:17   75n90

Acts

1:15–20   26
1:16   66, 77
1:20   66
2:25–31   234
2:25–32   26
2:30   77
2:33–35   26
4   26
4:24–28   26
4:25–26   104
4:25–28   72
13:32–33   72
13:33   90, 104
13:35   234

Romans

1:20   287
3:1–20   77
3:10–12   217
3:13–18   217
3:18   508
4:6–8   26
4:7–8   460
8   401
8:22   160
8:31–39   400
8:36   64
10:18   289
11:9–10   26, 66
12:14   309
13.4   281
15:9   279

1 Corinthians

4   145
4:12   309
11:29–30   460
15:27   160

2 Corinthians

3:6   299
5:19   342
6:2   75n90

Ephesians

2:5–6   75n90
4:8   77
4:26   116nc
5:18–20   21
6:18   22

Philippians

1:23   75n90

1 Thessalonians

4:13–18   75

2 Thessalonians

1:6–9   67
1:8–9   313, 318

1 Timothy

2:1–2   22

2 Timothy

3:14–17   24

Hebrews

1:5   104
2:6–8   160
2:12   341
3:7–4:10   75n90
4:7   26
5:5   104
10   578, 579n17
10:5–7   573n10
11:13   565

James

3   198
4:2   520

1 Peter

2:3   481
2:11   565
3:10–12   483
4:6   75n90

2 Peter

1:17   104

1 John

3:18–22   239

Revelation

2:26–27   104
2:26–28   73
2:27   101n17
6:9–11   67
12:5   101n17, 104
19:15   101n17, 104
20:11–15   75

Old Testament Apocrypha

1 Maccabees

2:28   190
4:52–59   425

Sirach

4:29   221n6
5:14   221n6
38:9–11   539

Babylonian Prayers

For Forgiveness

lines 19–32   34

To the Goddess Ba'u

lines 24–47   33–34

Qumran / Dead Sea Scrolls

4QpPsa

on Ps. 37   518
on Ps. 37:36   516nk

Rabbinic Writings

Mishnah

Sukkah

4.5   384

Tosefta

Berakot

32b   562n13

Babylonian Talmud

Baba Batra

14b–15a   26

Berakot

9b   90

Soperim

42a   425

Church Fathers

John Chrysostom

Commentary on the Psalms

on Ps. 6:1   99n12

Thomas Aquinas

Commentary on Psalms

on Ps. 2   21n1
on Ps. 18   297n27
on Ps. 35   509n4